# INSTITUTIONS, INNOVATION, AND INDUSTRIALIZATION

# INSTITUTIONS

ESSAYS IN ECONOMIC HISTORY AND DEVELOPMENT

# INNOVATION AND

EDITED BY AVNER GREIF, LYNNE KIESLING & JOHN V.C. NYE

# INDUSTRIALIZATION

PRINCETON UNIVERSITY PRESS

*Princeton and Oxford*

# CONTENTS

# INSTITUTIONS, INNOVATION, AND INDUSTRIALIZATION

# INTRODUCTION

The Enlightened Economist

## AVNER GREIF, LYNNE KIESLING, & JOHN V. C. NYE (EDITORS)

Few economic historians have generated new knowledge of such breadth, depth, and volume as Joel Mokyr—and he continues to do so. His contributions to economic history range far and wide, from industrialization itself (with the technological advances and institutional changes that underpin it) to its demographic consequences and the networks of natural philosophers and tinkerers who facilitated the creation of useful knowledge that undergird these processes. Joel has developed new ideas and new techniques for analyzing and interpreting historical data and has delved into areas formerly thought beyond the scope of economic history per se. His writings on innovation and the Industrial Revolution, particularly his magisterial books *The Lever of Riches* and *The Enlightened Economy*, have become touchstones for all those interested in understanding the critical issues surrounding the rise of Britain as the first industrial economy and understanding how technology came to play such an overwhelming role in the modern world.

Now that economists and other social scientists are coming to appreciate the importance of history as a laboratory for testing ideas about economic development and growth, it is worth paying tribute to a scholar who has been extraordinarily successful in keeping economic thinking about modern growth in the mainstream of economics and history. At a time when many lament the current era as one of stagnation and stasis, it has become all the more pressing to look back and see which factors have played a large role in promoting or suppressing growth and innovation.

The chapters in this volume reflect the breadth and depth of Joel's insights and influence in the original research that his work has inspired. In 2011 we organized a conference to celebrate Joel's sixty-fifth birthday and invited both Joel's current and former graduate students and his collaborators to participate. With two exceptions, the chapters collected here were presented at that conference and generated lively conversation and debate.

One exception is the chapter by Cormac Ó Gráda, who unfortunately could not attend the conference. His chapter highlights the rich demographic research on which he and Joel have collaborated to generate a deeper understanding of the health effects of industrialization. The other exception is the work by Joel himself; he has contributed an original work on the cultural underpinnings of technological progress and the intellectual and communication networks for the creation and transmission of useful knowledge in the seventeenth and eighteenth centuries.

The other chapters in the volume do not merely reflect the many topics and issues on which Joel has worked; they reflect the many ways Joel's influence has extended well beyond his scholarship. He has mentored numerous students and trained many young scholars. The bulk of the contributions in this volume are by those (such as the three editors of this volume) who had the privilege and pleasure of having Joel supervise their doctoral dissertations. Joel Mokyr is in many ways an ideal advisor—engaging and demanding, yet never seeking to impose a particular vision on his students' work. He encourages them to develop and follow through on their own ideas while providing constructive criticism or serving as a helpful sounding board for the concerns and struggles they face as they venture into scholarly research. For many years, Joel and his colleagues at Northwestern have been some of the most productive, if not the most productive, sources of full-time economic historians in the world—and Northwestern is still going strong.

A single volume can accommodate works by only some, but by no means all, of Joel's students, and the contributions are organized around three core themes associated with Joel's work: institutions, innovation, and industrialization.

## INSTITUTIONS

Part I examines the institutional foundations of well-being and their historical evolution. The chapter by Avner Greif, "Coercion and Exchange: How Did Markets Evolve?" is motivated by the observation that the modern market economy, characterized by impersonal exchange, first emerged in the West. The chapter presents a theory of market development and evaluates it based on the histories of England, China, and Japan. The analysis focuses on how distinct *coercion-constraining institutions* that secure property rights differentially interact with *contract-enforcing institutions*. Although different combinations of such institutions can support markets, only some coercion-constraining and contract-enforcing institutions (ones that enforce impersonal exchange) can be at equilibrium. In particular, the analysis highlights the relations between the internal organization of the state and legal development, and the logic behind the observation that impersonal exchange and political representation historically co-emerged.

Gergely Baics, in the chapter on "Meat Consumption in Nineteenth-Century New York: Quantity, Distribution, and Quality, or Notes on the 'Antebellum Puzzle,'" examines the regulatory function of the state and the welfare implications of the resulting combination of product offerings, their quality and quantity. The setting is the observation that welfare, as measured by the biological standard of living, deteriorated in the antebellum United States, despite rapid economic growth and increasing per capita income. The chapter substantiates that, as far as meat consumption in New York City is concerned, the decline in welfare was due to three factors: a smaller quantity of meat consumed, a lower quality of meat consumed, and increasingly unequal access to meat products due to rising social disparities. The ultimate cause of these changes is the shift in food chains from regional to national sources, and the gradual informalization and, eventually, deregulation of retail meat markets; by 1834 the city had lost control over the quality of meat, thereby hurting the poor in particular.

Mauricio Drelichman and Hans-Joachim Voth go beyond markets and states and focus on empire building. In the chapter on "Funding Empire: Risk, Diversification, and the Underwriting of Early Modern Sovereign Loans," they consider the financial underpinning of the empire of Philip II of Spain. Specifically, the issue is not who loaned to the emperor, but the sources of the funds of the Genoese banking families who gave the loans to the emperor and the risk they assumed. In particular, they examine two account books from Genoese merchant families preserved in the Doria Archive in Genoa and focused on loans related to Philip's fourth bankruptcy in 1596. The analysis establishes that the Genoese system for financing and arranging short-term loans effectively spread the risk from lending to capricious monarchs. Complete ruin due to a sovereign debt crisis was unlikely as a result of diversification of risk at the level of the final investors.

Noel D. Johnson, Mark Koyama, and John V. C. Nye examine the relations between beliefs in the supernatural and legal order. Their chapter, "Establishing a New Order: The Growth of the State and the Decline of Witch Trials in France," innovatively uses data on witch trials and taxation in twenty-one French regions between 1550 and 1700 to substantiate that the growth of the French state in the seventeenth century led to a more regular, even liberal legal order. Regions where higher taxes were collected were less likely to see witch trials. Thus, fiscal consolidation promoted a more rational law and legal standardization that extended the rule of law.

## INNOVATION

Part II focuses on innovation and the different ways that innovation contributes to economic growth. Innovation can take the form of organizational innovation, one of the hallmark features of the merger wave in British banking in the late nineteenth and early twentieth centuries. Fabio Braggion, Narly R. D. Dwarkasing, and Lyndon Moore analyze the mergers and acquisitions that took place, and how the structure of the banking industry changed over a forty-year period. Their creation and analysis of a new set of data suggest that the merger wave did not result in as much concentration as previously thought, with banking remaining more regional and less national even after consolidation. Nationally, banking became more networked, while concentration was unchanged at the county level because these networks expanded into new counties through this merger process.

Peter B. Meyer uses Joel's concept of macroinventions to explore the invention of the airplane. While he argues that we have no theory of where macroinventions come from, he finds that the sharing of information and experiments across a broad international group of experimenters characterized the process. This sharing of useful knowledge as it is generated resonates with the innovation processes Joel identified in the seventeenth and eighteenth centuries.

Innovation can also take the form of technological change, as Karine van der Beek explores in her chapter on the complementarity between new machine tool technologies and skilled labor during industrialization in Britain. She analyzes data on apprentice contracts (1710–70) to examine how workers responded to the increased demand for skilled labor during the early decades of industrialization. She finds that workers increased their skills, and that skilled machine tool labor and technological change were more complements than substitutes in this period.

Finally, innovation is an important consideration methodologically within economic history as well as historically. Rick Szostak explores some ways that economic history could grow as a research field by exploiting its openness to heterogeneous methods of analysis. He argues that the main purpose of economic history is understanding the causes and consequences of economic growth and that economic historians should engage more deliberately in comparative history that enables the drawing of generalized lessons regarding economic growth.

## INDUSTRIALIZATION

Part III brings together research that deals with issues relating to the (first) Industrial Revolution of the eighteenth century or to economic and social changes in the period of late industrialization at the end of the nineteenth century. Hoyt Bleakley, Louis Cain, and Joseph Ferrie examine and compare the fates of the two groups that supplied the bulk of the unskilled labor force that powered American development in the late nineteenth century—blacks and the Irish—by studying the fates of Civil War veterans. Native-born Irish fared about as well as non-Irish whites, while the immigrants tended to lag behind. For blacks, the more startling contrast is between those born in slave states, who performed especially poorly, versus a substantial fraction of blacks born in free states, nearly half of whom did quite well and enjoyed survival rates comparable to those of non-Irish whites.

Ralf R. Meisenzahl's piece is a contribution to the long-standing debate on Britain's supposed decline in the second half of the nineteenth century. His thesis is that the technological leadership that derived from Britain's skilled craftsmen and engineers was lost in this later period as Germany caught up and surpassed the British in terms of technical competence, mostly due to its superior systems of apprenticeship and technical training.

Carolyn Tuttle and Simone A. Wegge deal with the important question of child labor and its regulation in the nineteenth century by comparing the experiences of Belgium and Germany with those of Britain. In this comparison, the early adoption of child labor laws does not seem to have made much of a difference between those countries (such as Britain and Germany) that sought to restrain and regulate child labor versus those, such as Belgium, that thought of children's employment as a societal necessity. Changes in the law seemed to move in tandem with or even lag the general decline in child labor throughout Europe.

Joyce Burnette, using data from the Pepperell Manufacturing Company of Maine, returns to the problem of the occupational wage gap between males and females during industrialization and seeks to distinguish between differences caused by differential pay in the same or similar jobs versus differences in average wages because of differential sorting of males and females into very different occupations. In general, within-occupation differences declined substantially over the late nineteenth century and sorting between occupations tended to explain the persistence of average pay gaps.

Finally, Eric Jones concludes the section with a grand overview of the causes of the Industrial Revolution—in particular, whether that transformation was long delayed and what role changing institutions played in first hindering and then aiding in industrialization. Jones concludes in a guardedly optimistic fashion that although eighteenth-century British laws and property rights were not ideal and were often opposed to the demands of a transforming economy, there was enough flexibility in the legal system and enough adaptation to the demands of a changing market that changes in rights became possible within the existing framework. They were especially notable in permitting necessary improvements in transport and transport networks.

One thread common to all contributions to this volume, and among the participants in the conference, is deep and profound appreciation and respect for the influence Joel Mokyr has had on each one of us in our work and play, on the body of economic history knowledge, and on the practice of economic history. His energetic, enthusiastic, and original mind has contributed to economic history, and his unalloyed enthusiasm and passion for ideas and learning infect all of us who have contributed to this book.

# NEITHER FEAST NOR FAMINE

England before the Industrial Revolution

## CORMAC Ó GRÁDA

### NEITHER FEAST NOR FAMINE

In recent years, a standard-of-living debate about conditions in England during the first Industrial Revolution, to which Joel Mokyr contributed his share in the 1980s and 1990s (e.g., Mokyr and Savin 1978; Mokyr 1988; Mokyr and Ó Gráda 1988, 1989, 1996; Mokyr and Burnette 1995), has largely given way to a broader debate about living conditions before the Industrial Revolution. The broader debate links two questions. The first is about levels: how well off were the English on the eve of the Industrial Revolution compared to others at the time, and compared also to the poor of today's less developed countries? The question matters because it addresses low incomes as a potential constraint on industrialization. The second is about trends: how much richer were the English on the eve of the Industrial Revolution than, say, before or after the Black Death?

Few would dispute nowadays that wages and incomes in England circa 1800 were "high" relative to most other places at the time. Even though (according to Gregory Clark) farm laborers still spent about three-quarters of their income on food, their wages were generous "by the measure of the modern Third World" (Clark 2007a, 43; compare Maddison 1983). Answers to the second question are less straightforward. Clark employs a real wage series that implies little improvement between 1200 and 1800 to argue that productivity in medieval English agriculture must have been quite respectable. Others question whether his wage series can capture trends in living standards over time.

Not only were the English better off than others in the early modern era: they knew it. Already by the 1530s they sensed that "in France, Italy and Spain the commons without fail are more miserable and poor than they are here with us" (Slack 1988, 116). In 1676 Sir William Petty observed that "the poor of France have generally less wages than in England; and yet their victuals are generally dearer there" (Petty 1899, 294). In the following decade Gregory King offered more precision; he reckoned that England's and France's "produce of trade, arts and labour" in 1688 was £30.5 million and £52 million, respectively. That would imply that English nonproperty income per head was more than double that of France.[1] With Petty, King, and Davenant only the apparent advantage of the Dutch rankled, and that would not last (Slack 2009).

Recent estimates of English food supplies muddy the waters, however. Craig Muldrew's generous "global estimates of food production" on the eve of the Industrial Revolution are consistent with an "industrious" workforce that ate well. This finding contrasts sharply with that of Robert Fogel in *Escape from Hunger*: he interpreted his output estimates as implying that a non-negligible percentage of Englishmen and Englishwomen were too malnourished to work effectively on a regular basis. Fogel reached this striking conclusion by applying a plausible distribution of calories across the entire population to his estimates of mean consumption per head. Roderick Floud and his coauthors (who include Fogel) temper Fogel's earlier results considerably, but the implications of new estimates of food supplies per capita from Stephen Broadberry and his collaborators are as gloomy as Fogel's original numbers (Muldrew 2011, 161; Floud et al. 2011, 161; Fogel 2004, 9; Broadberry et al. 2011b).

So how well off were the English on the eve of the Industrial Revolution and before it? Was a labor force as ill fed as that implied by Broadberry et al. capable of sustaining an Industrial Revolution, or were high wages a precondition for one? These questions are the subject of the present chapter. One way of approaching such questions is through the lens of exogenous shocks, and the effectiveness of policy in combating them. This is the focus of the first section. Another is through considering how well nourished and schooled English workers were on the eve of the Industrial Revolution. These issues are the focus of the second and third sections. Throughout our focus is on issues that have interested Joel Mokyr at various points in his career.

## GREAT DEATH AND FAMINE

Famines are nearly always linked to economic backwardness. Their virtual elimination globally (in peacetime) is one of the achievements of modern economic growth. In early modern England, too, the gradual eradication of famines has been linked to economic progress (e.g., Appleby 1978; Palliser 1982; Hoyle 2010; Mokyr 2010, 195–96). But, as Mokyr made plain in his classic study of the Great Irish Famine, *Why Ireland Starved*, excess famine mortality is also a function of human agency or institutions. During the Irish famine the authorities in London placed much of the blame on Irish landlordism. But the authorities were hardly blameless themselves: indeed, Mokyr (1983, 291) insisted that "the British simply abandoned the Irish and let them perish. There

---

1    That is assuming populations of 5.5 million and 20 million. Angus Maddison (1983) implies that British GDP per head was only 37 percent higher than France's in 1700, but his figure for Great Britain includes Ireland.

is no doubt that Britain could have saved Ireland." Whether Britain could have saved all those who perished in the 1840s is contestable, but the broader point about human agency stands. Amartya Sen's "law" that famines and democracy don't mix highlights the role of institutions,[2] but even hard-line opponents of famine relief on moral hazard grounds, such as Garret Hardin, do not question the ability of government to reduce mortality in the short run. Indeed, none other than Thomas Robert Malthus ([1800] 1970, 19) credited the old poor law with reducing excess mortality during the crisis of 1799–1800:

> The system of poor laws, in general, I do most heartily condemn . . . but I am inclined to think that their operation in the present scarcity has been advantageous to the country. . . . It was calculated that there were only two-thirds of an average crop last year. Probably, even with the aid of what we imported, the deficit still remained a fifth or sixth. Supposing ten millions o people in this island; the whole of this deficiency, had things been left to their natural course, would have fallen almost exclusively on two, or perhaps three millions of the poorest inhabitants, a very considerable number of whom must in consequence have started. The operation of the parish allowances, by raising the price of provisions so high, caused the distress to be divided among five or six millions, perhaps, instead of two or three, and to be by no means unfelt even by the remainder of the population.

Consider England's two best-known famines, those of 1315–17 and 1595–97. Excess mortality during the Great Famine of 1315–17—England's worst "in recorded history" (Dyer 2002, 233)[3]—can only be guessed at, but may well have reached 10 percent of the population, or about half a million. Excess mortality in the 1590s was only a fraction of that. Comparing Wrigley and Schofield's estimate of the aggregate deaths rate in 1597 and 1598 with the average of those in 1589–96 and 1599–1606 implies an excess death rate of 10.1 per thousand. In a population of 3.9 million, that would have meant about 40,000 lives lost. By the same token the number of births "lost" was about 34,500 (derived from Wrigley and Schofield 1981, 531–32).

It is tempting to link the huge difference between excess mortality in the 1310s and the 1590s to economic progress in the interim. Higher incomes would have offered a stronger defense against any given proportional harvest shortfall. But what if the adverse weather and consequently the harvest failures of the 1310s were far, far worse than those of the 1590s? Certainly, the

---

2  The trouble is that while open government may help prevent famine, it is also less likely to prevail in environments that are vulnerable to famine. Measures of vulnerability to famine such as life expectancy at birth and GDP per head are highly correlated with measures of openness and democracy (Ó Gráda 2011, 58–59).

3  For more on the famine, see also Lucas (1930), Kershaw (1973), Jordan (1996), Childs (2005, 110–11, 120–23, 154–57).

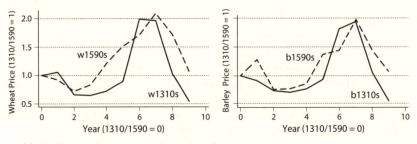

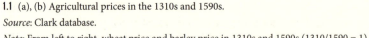

**1.1** (a), (b) Agricultural prices in the 1310s and 1590s.

*Source*: Clark database.

*Note*: From left to right, wheat price and barley price in 1310s and 1590s (1310/1590 = 1)

apocalyptic tone of some accounts of famine in the 1310s are missing from those of the 1590s; but what if that tone was more a reflection of the famine's symptoms (deaths) than its causes (poor harvests)?

Although the kind of "clear and consistent environmental signal" that Campbell (2009) and others have identified for the 1310s is lacking for the mid-1590s, there is ample impressionistic evidence for harvest shortfalls in the latter period (e.g., Dawson 1993, 391; Appleby 1978, 112–16). The severity of those shortfalls is often inferred from price movements (e.g., Walter 1985, 95–96; Hoskins 1964, 38; Appleby 1978, 112–13). Figure 1.1 compares the prices of wheat and barley during the 1310s and the 1590s, using 1310 and 1590 as base years. Surprisingly, the increases during both crises were of the same order; if

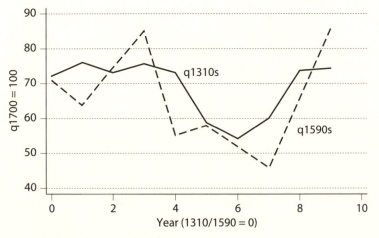

**1.2** Agricultural output in the 1310s and 1590s.

*Source*: Broadberry et al. database.

anything, prices remained high for longer in the 1590s. On the basis of price data alone the crises would seem to have been of roughly equal intensity.

Price data, however, are a fallible guide to famine intensity for a number of reasons. For one thing, the higher are incomes, the greater the harvest shortfall associated with any given proportionate price increase. Lower GDP per head in the 1310s would thus have entailed a lower proportionate harvest shortfall. On the other hand, transfers of purchasing power from the rich to the poor could have driven up grain prices in the 1590s, as Malthus (see above) claimed had happened during the near-famine of 1799–1800.

What of more direct evidence on agricultural output? The output series recently compiled by Broadberry et al. (on which more in the second section below) makes the 1590s seem worse, if anything, than the 1310s and the 1590s (see Figure 1.2). The data employed in the 1590s are fallible, however. Whereas those for the earlier famine are as recorded in manorial accounts, those for the later famine are inferred from probate inventories, using a complex formula that attempts to take account of tithe payments and the putative (rather than the actual) costs of reaping, threshing, and carting (Broadberry et al. 2011b: 2–3).

Nor are the signals from data on nutrition, income, wages, and population as clear as one would like. On the one hand, Broadberry et al. reckon that daily calorie supplies were no higher in the 1600s than in the 1300s (see Table 1.1). On the other, they put GDP per head at about one-quarter higher, and both Allen and Clark report that real wages were over one-half higher (Allen 2001; Clark 2007b).[4] Why did higher incomes not result in higher food consumption? Note too that England's population was much higher in the 1310s than in the 1590s. Broadberry et al. (2011b) imply totals of 4.7 million circa 1315 and 3.9 million circa 1595, whereas Clark (2007a, 30) reckons population was 6 million in 1316. At the very least, relative living standards should have tilted the balance against famine-related mortality in the later period.

There is less ambiguity about the role of government. King Edward II did little to relieve victims in 1315–17. Two of his actions—a partial prohibition on grain exports and the imposition of lay subsidies (taxes on moveable property such as livestock) in 1315 and 1316—were motivated by the need to keep his beleaguered northern garrisons fed, not in order to fund famine relief. The latter measure weighed heavily on poorer peasants. Two other measures—guarantees of safe conduct for merchants as a means of eliciting grain shipments from areas in relative surplus and moral suasion in the form of urging bishops

4  For a caution on the interpretation of wage data, see Hatcher (2011). Broadberry et al. (2011b) put average daily noncrisis kcal supplies at 1,983 in the 1310s and 2,082 in the 1600s, while their index of GDP per head rises from 50.17 in 1310–14 to 64.54 in 1590–94. Allen's (2001) London real wage series rises from 3.74 in 1310–14 to 5.76 in 1590 and Clark's (2007b) from 50.2 in the 1310s to 76.0 in the 1590s.

**TABLE 1.1**  Four Recent Estimates of English Calorie Consumption per Capita ca. 1300–1800

A. Muldrew (2011)

| Year | [1] Kcals | [2] Vegetal | [3] Animal | [3]/[1] (%) |
|------|-----------|-------------|------------|-------------|
| 1600 | 3,062 | 1,968 | 1,094 | 35.7 |
| 1700 | 3,579 | 2,682 | 897 | 25.1 |
| 1770 | 5,047 | 3,985 | 1,062 | 21.0 |
| 1800 | 3,977 | 3,189 | 788 | 19.8 |

B. Allen (2005)

| Year | [1] Kcals | [2] Vegetal | [3] Animal | [3]/[1] (%) |
|------|-----------|-------------|------------|-------------|
| 1300 | 1,791 | 1,502 | 289 | 16.1 |
| 1500 | 3,397 | 2,733 | 664 | 19.6 |
| 1700 | 3,255 | 2,601 | 654 | 20.1 |
| 1750 | 3,803 | 2,962 | 841 | 22.1 |
| 1800 | 2,938 | 2,248 | 690 | 23.5 |
| 1850 | 2,525 | 2,019 | 506 | 20.0 |

C. Broadberry et al. (2011)

| Year | [1] Kcals | [2] Vegetal | [3] Animal | [3]/[1] (%) |
|------|-----------|-------------|------------|-------------|
| 1275 | 2,188 | 1,771 | 417 | 19.1 |
| 1305 | 2,041 | 1,610 | 431 | 21.1 |
| 1315 | 1,983 | 1,561 | 422 | 21.3 |
| 1385 | 2,447 | 2,056 | 391 | 16.0 |
| 1425 | 2,132 | 1,702 | 430 | 20.2 |
| 1455 | 2,162 | 1,698 | 464 | 21.5 |
| 1605 | 2,082 | 1,676 | 406 | 19.5 |
| 1655 | 1,909 | 1,540 | 369 | 19.3 |
| 1705 | 2,162 | 1,752 | 410 | 19.0 |
| 1755 | 2,248 | 1,729 | 519 | 23.1 |
| 1805 | 2,165 | 1,580 | 585 | 27.0 |
| 1835 | 1,947 | 1,436 | 511 | 26.2 |
| 1845 | 2,160 | 1,652 | 514 | 23.8 |
| 1855 | 2,104 | 1,576 | 538 | 25.6 |
| 1865 | 2,471 | 1,951 | 542 | 21.9 |

**TABLE 1.1** *continued*

D. Floud et al. (2011)

| Year | [1] Kcals | [2] Vegetal | [3] Animal | [3]/[1] (%) |
|------|-----------|-------------|------------|-------------|
| 1700 | 2,229 | 1,667 | 562 | 25.2 |
| 1750 | 2,347 | 1,537 | 810 | 34.5 |
| 1800 | 2,472 | 1,740 | 732 | 29.6 |
| 1850 | 2,544 | 1,921 | 623 | 24.5 |

*Sources*: Muldrew (2011, 156); Allen (2005, 39, table 12); Broadberry et al. (pers. comm., 2011); Floud et al. (2011, 167, table 4.13).
*Note*: Floud et al.'s 1750 total adjusted for correction as suggested by Deborah Oxley.

to preach against speculators and pleading with the rich to go easy on lavish food consumption—were unlikely to achieve much. There is no evidence of public relief in the form of food or cash transfers. William Jordan has described Edward II's efforts as a combination of incompetence, procrastination, and "at times, almost criminal self-interest" (Jordan 1996, 177). Buchanan Sharp (2012) is more positive, concluding that the famine was the first to produce "evidence of official attempts at remedial actions," but also conceding the likely ineffectiveness of the measures taken.

Few would claim for the state in Edward II's day, as Michael Braddick (2000, 93) has for the early modern state, that "it was useful to all sorts of people . . . and far from having to penetrate the localities was frequently invited in." The institutional context in the later period was very different. Admittedly, it is tempting to regard the Elizabethan poor law, enacted in successive measures between the 1560s and the 1600s, as simply a response to increasing population and consequent impoverishment. But Malthusian pressures in preceding centuries had not led to public action in support of the poor. Now, for the first time, the law of the land made the better off legally liable for poor relief. Thanks to "an intellectual and above all a political achievement," the principle that the impotent poor should be entitled to "reasonable relief" financed by local parish poor rates was embodied in national legislation in 1598–1601 (Slack 1988, 113–14, 128).[5] True, the famine of 1595–97 prompted the legislation that followed. But that legislation was built on earlier experimentation at parish level, and particularly in urban parishes (Elton 1953; McIntosh 2005). It would take several more decades before it was fully effective, but it was already operational in the towns where the 1590s was a "crisis contained" due to poor relief (Clark 1985, 44).[6]

5  The provision that the able-bodied poor should be provided with work proved more troublesome to implement.

6  A revisionist literature on the old poor law awards it high marks for offering those at risk a safety net without compromising and possibly even supporting economic growth (e.g., Solar 1995).

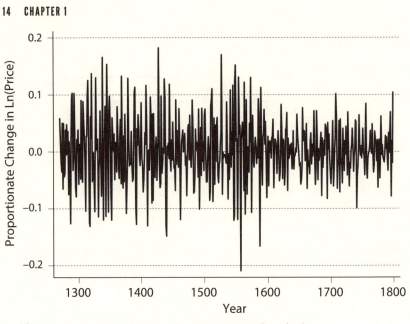

**1.3** Annual proportional wheat price changes, 1270–1700 (log values).
*Source*: http://www.nuffield.ox.ac.uk/General/Members/allen.aspx.

Despite the bold declaration by the mayor of London in 1596 that he had found "by experience the rule to be true that a free market, without anie restraint to bring & sell at what prices they can, maketh a plenty & plentie of itselve will bring down the price" (cited in Outhwaite 1981, 400; compare Power 1985; Hipkin 2008), the role of market integration in relieving famine before circa 1600 is unclear. Figure 1.3 describes the trend in year-to-year fluctuations in grain prices between 1270 and 1800. It suggests little improvement before the end of the sixteenth century, but significantly lower variation thereafter (see too Ó Gráda 2009, 151–53; Appleby 1978, 139–40, 144–45). And during the seventeenth and eighteenth centuries, as Jean Meuvret (1969) pointed out long ago, the greater oscillations in French grain prices relative to English bespoke more effective English markets, more storage and foreign trade, and higher incomes.[7]

In sum, price movements during these two famine decades are not so readily squared with harvests in the 1310s being worse than in the 1590s, since mit-

---

7  A fall in the seasonality of wheat price movements in England offers some hint of a reduction in storage costs. Using Nicholas Poynder's database of monthly prices (Poynder 1999) to compare the pre-1400 and 1540–1620 periods, I infer a drop from 9.9 percent to 2.1 percent in the average price increase between September and December and the following March to June. But this is based on only 123 observations before 1400 and 166 observations in 1540–1620, and the coefficients of variation are very high. The much smaller number of observations on oats in the database ($n=33$) yields an average seasonal price rise before 1400 of only 4.7 percent.

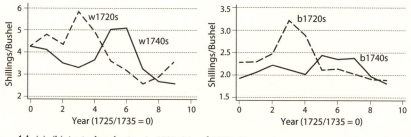

**1.4** (a), (b) Agricultural prices in 1725–34 and 1735–44.

*Source*: Clark database.

*Note*: From left to right, wheat price and barley price in 1725/1735.

igating factors, on balance, are likely to have reduced grain price increases in the interim. It is not easy to argue from price data alone that the earlier harvest failure was worse than the later. It probably was, but this remains unproven. The famine of the 1590s, England's last major famine, was less murderous in part because of institutional innovation and in part because the economy had progressed since the 1310s.

The history of English famine did not quite end there, however. Appleby (1978), Outhwaite (1981), Wrigley and Schofield (1981), Hindle (2008), and Hoyle (2010) have drawn attention to local crises during the seventeenth century, but these were all minor compared to what went before, and their severity declined over time. The late 1720s and the early 1740s were also periods of excess mortality bearing some of the hallmarks of subsistence crises. Grain prices rose, though the increases were modest relative to the 1590s (Figure 1.4). The crisis of the late 1720s resulted in an excess mortality of 0.2 million, or over 3 percent of the population; that of 1740–42 of about 80,000 deaths. Both crises led to corn imports, exceptionally for Britain in the first half of the eighteenth century (Campbell 2009; Kelly and Ó Gráda 2011, 359n29).

The first crisis followed poor harvests in 1727 and 1728, and coincided with an excess mortality that rose in each year to 1729 and remained high in 1730 and 1731. But the persistence of high mortality long after grain prices had peaked (see Figure 1.5)[8] would seem to corroborate contemporary accounts that diseases other those normally associated with famine were mainly responsible for the excess mortality.[9] Dublin-based physician John Rutty referred to horses in the west of England in November 1727 being "suddenly seized with a cough and weakness," followed by the same symptoms, sometimes accompanied by nose-bleeding, "in Dublin and remote parts of Ireland." A month later "a cough and sore throat [had] seized mankind in Dublin." Two years later

8  In the 1590s both the death rate and the price of wheat peaked in the same year (1597).
9  On famine disease, see Mokyr and Ó Gráda (2002).

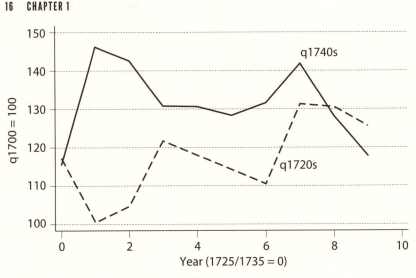

**1.5** Agricultural output in 1725–34 and 1735–44.
*Source:* Broadberry et al. database.

Rutty described an influenza-like "universal epidemic catarrh, scarce sparing any one family" which "visited London before us," and was "attended with a cough, soreness of the breast, and some pain of the head and back, and a slight fever" (Rutty 1770, 17; Creighton 1894, 342–43).

This crisis was undoubtedly compounded by the added, largely exogenous shock (or shocks) of a deadly influenza-like epidemic. Timmins (2005) reports that in Deane in Lancashire, most victims died "of agues, pluraisy, etc, tho a fever came ye first," and "in some respects ye disorder resembled ye Plague," while Gooder (1972) notes that in Warwickshire harvest failures in 1727 and 1728 were followed by a likely outbreak of influenza in late 1729. For Wrigley and Schofield (1981, 663–64n44, 681–84) the data indicate a minor subsistence crisis followed by an influenza-like epidemic, and Healey's (2008) careful study of Lancashire corroborates. Such a nosological sequence would help explain why mortality was so high and the crisis so protracted, although the prices of cereals rose only modestly (Figure 1.4).

The second crisis lasted from late 1739 to 1742. The attendant bitterly cold weather, poor harvests, and diseases are well documented (Post 1984; Dickson 1997). Deaths rose and births fell, and some of the disease symptoms described by Rutty (1770, 86–97, 99; see also Landers 1993, 278–79) recall famine fever. However, Wrigley and Schofield (1981, 669) note that there was "relatively little crisis mortality in 1740 and the first half of 1741," which "counts against the view that they were produced by the poor harvest of 1740 or, even more implausibly, by the exceptionally cold winter of 1739–40."

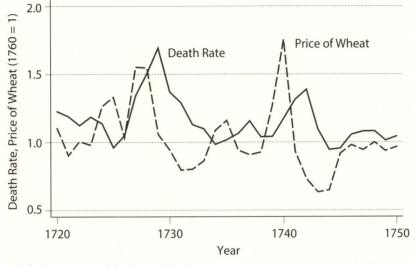

**1.6** Wheat prices and death rate, 1720–50.

In neighboring Ireland it was a very different story (Dickson 1997; Ó Gráda and Ó Muirithe 2010), but in England once again it would seem that a minor subsistence crisis was followed by a surge in largely exogenous mortality. This supposition is supported by two curious features of this crisis, the *rise* in births in 1743 in the wake of the peak in deaths in 1742, and the late timing of the peak in deaths, long after food prices had begun to fall (see Figure 1.6).[10]

The crises of the 1720s and 1740s are reminders that England's retreat from famine was slower and more hesitant that we used to think. Indeed, the first half of the eighteenth century witnessed the temporary return of a positive check absent in the data in the previous half century (Kelly and Ó Gráda 2014). At the same time, while harvest shortfalls may account for some of the excess mortality of the late 1720s and (to a much lesser extent) the early 1740s, those crises are hardly true measures of the vulnerability of the English poor to crop failures at that juncture. By the eighteenth century English wealth and English institutions were insurance enough against the Third Horseman. By then, the demographic challenge facing England was no longer to end crisis mortality but to reduce noncrisis mortality (compare Fogel 2004; Mokyr 2009, 196).

Reductions in the year-to-year variation in crop yields and falling transportation costs may also have contributed to the retreat from famine. Bruce

10    As Wrigley and Schofield (1981, 669) note, "The delay in the epidemic outbreaks until July 1741 also counts against the view that they were produced by the poor harvest of 1740 or, even more implausibly, by the exceptionally cold winter of 1739–40" (compare Post 1984, table 1).

Campbell and I have made a case for the former by comparing cereal yields derived from manorial accounts in the medieval era and yields derived from farm accounts in the eighteenth century. The implied reduction in yield variability points to an overlooked achievement on the part of English farmers and their suppliers. And, in support, there is increasing evidence for a specialist trade in seeds from the seventeenth century onward and also for an increasing range of "useful knowledge" in print about the damage caused by rain, fungi, weeds, and pests. While the efficacy of specific "remedies" remains unproven, there are signs of the kind of experimentation, adaptation, and learning by doing that Mokyr has repeatedly highlighted in other contexts (Campbell and Ó Gráda 2011, 873–74; compare Mokyr 2002; 2009, 110–11, 187; Meisenzahl and Mokyr 2012).

For a rough, tentative sense of the change in transport costs we compare estimates of the cost of carrying wheat in Essex in the late Middle Ages and in the 1760s. James Masschaele (1999) reckons that transporting wheat by cart in fourteenth-century England cost about 1.5 pence per ton-mile. It cost most, 2.3 pence per ton-mile, in Essex. Compare this to Arthur Young's claim that it cost two pounds sterling to carry ten quarters of wheat twenty-five miles in Essex in the 1760s (cited in Perren 1989, 219). Given quarters of 480 pounds, this works out at 3.5 pence per ton-mile.[11] Since the cost of living was four to five times higher in the 1760s than in the fourteenth century (Clark 2007b), a significant drop in the real cost of carriage in the interim is implied.

Alternatively, transporting wheat for ten miles would have added 4 percent to its cost in the fourteenth century (Masschaele 1999), and less than half that in the 1760s, assuming that wheat at source then cost about forty shillings per quarter (Mitchell 1971, 487). Presumably some of this modest productivity improvement was due to the exploitation of scale economies, but the replacement of medieval carts and packhorses by heavier four-wheeled wagons and better roads in the seventeenth and eighteenth centuries also played a part (Chartres 1977, 1990; Gerhold 1996; Bogart 2005; Mokyr 2009, 204–5). Both such advances and the agricultural improvements suggested above would have contributed to the reduction in year-to-year price fluctuations indicated in Figure 1.5.

## AGRICULTURAL OUTPUT

Calculating past agricultural output is an inexact science.[12] Mokyr (2009, 180) has likened it to "putting together a jigsaw puzzle with most of the pieces miss-

---

11  Factoring in savings made by back-hauling coal might reduce this by one-third (Perren 19689, 219).

12  This section borrows freely from Kelly and Ó Gráda (2013).

ing." The challenge of producing reliable or plausible estimates of agricultural output in an era when key components such as crop acreages, crop and milk yields, seed ratios, carcass weights, and losses from processing and wastage are disputed is clear. Even the most careful estimates are subject to an unknown but non-negligible margin of error. Obviously, then, estimates of agricultural output in the past must be treated with caution, as must interpretations of economic growth and well-being that lean heavily on such estimates. Yet in a discipline where the creation of newly minted data earns fewer credits than new interpretations of the past based on such data, the temptation to combine data construction and interpretation is almost irresistible. And so it is with four recent attempts at estimating output before and during the Industrial Revolution, all accompanied by four competing interpretations of economic trends (Allen 2006; Broadberry et al. 2011b; Floud et al. 2011; Muldrew 2011).

The four estimates, summarized in Table 1.1, differ strikingly in their assessments of nutritional status. Muldrew's figure for 1770 is more than double those of Broadberry et al. for both 1750 and 1800. Bob Allen reckons that calorie consumption per head was significantly higher in 1750 than in 1270, but that it decreased sharply during the Industrial Revolution, and that as a result it was no higher in the mid-nineteenth century than in 1500 (though not in 1300). Broadberry et al. tell quite a different story to that of Allen, finding remarkably little variation and no significant sustained increase in per capita consumption over the entire period between 1300 and 1850. The gap between these two estimates is very wide except at the outset; Allen's estimate of calories per diem circa 1750 is nearly two-thirds higher than that of Broadberry et al. Floud et al. come closest to Broadberry et al., but their estimates, unlike the rest, envisage a rise in calorie consumption after 1800, in which the increasing contribution of imports plays an important role.

Muldrew's assessment is by far the most optimistic of the four. His generous estimates contrast sharply with those of Robert Fogel in *Escape from Hunger and Premature Death*. Fogel interpreted his own output estimates as implying that a non-negligible percentage of Englishmen and Englishwomen were too malnourished to work effectively on a regular basis. Fogel reached this striking conclusion by applying a plausible distribution of calories across the entire population to his estimates of mean consumption per head. Roderick Floud and his coauthors (who include Fogel) temper Fogel's earlier results considerably; the former report 2,514 calories for 1750 and 2,439 calories for 1800, whereas the latter reports 2,168 and 2,237 calories, respectively. But the implications of new estimates of food supplies per capita from Stephen Broadberry and his collaborators are as gloomy as Fogel's original numbers (Floud et al. 2011, 161; Fogel 2004, 9; Broadberry et al. 2011b).[13] They reckon that per capita

13   We used Floud et al's (2011) "A" estimates (with Deborah Oxley's adjustment of their 1750 total).

daily calorie consumption fell from an already low 2,248 kilocalories in the 1750s to 2,165 kilocalories in the 1800s and 1,947 kilocalories the 1830s. They also argue that food consumption fluctuated within very narrow limits between 1200 and 1800.

The four estimates also offer contrasting perspectives on nutritional status during the eighteenth century. While Broadberry et al. envisage essentially no change in calorie consumption over the century, both Allen and Muldrew see big increases to midcentury, followed by big declines to 1800, while and Floud et al. an increases in each half century between 1700 and 1850. While Allen reckons that consumption declined over the century as a whole, Muldrew reckons that it rose. Finally, while Broadberry et al. and Floud et al., and to a lesser degree Allen, envisage an increase in the share of animal products in total calorie consumption during the eighteenth century, Muldrew implies that the opposite was the case. The estimates also disagree on conditions after 1800, with Floud et al. implying improvement in nutritional status and Allen sharp deterioration.[14]

Broadberry et al.'s estimates of calorie supplies per capita in 1755, 1805, and 1835—2,248, 2,165, and 1,947 kilocalories, respectively—are barely higher than best-guess estimates for France in the same era (Toutain 1995, 772; Grantham 1995, 774; Fogel 2004, 9). This does not tally with contemporary English popular opinion that John Bull was much better fed than Louis Baboon. More concretely, it does not readily square with the common understanding that real wages in mid- and late eighteenth-century England were roughly double those in France (Allen 2001). Broadberry et al.'s estimate is not so easily reconciled either with the considerable productivity advantage of English workers over French workers. That advantage is corroborated by the longer life expectancy of the English and their significant height advantage on the eve of the Industrial Revolution (Kelly, Mokyr, and Ó Gráda 2012).

It is somewhat troubling when far-reaching generalizations about the character and timing of English economic progress in the early modern and preindustrial eras rest on such wildly conflicting estimates of food supply. Elsewhere Kelly and Ó Gráda (2013) analyze possible reasons for differences between these estimates and propose a compromise estimate of calorie supplies circa 1750 and circa 1800. Our attempt at producing a compromise estimate of food availability focuses on the second half of the eighteenth century. Treating the estimates of Muldrew and Broadberry et al. as upper- and lower-bound estimates, respectively, of the true value, we show that there is considerable scope for narrowing the initially very wide gap between them. While Muldrew's estimates are confirmed to be overgenerous, those of Broadberry et al. require significant revision in the opposite direction. Our ecumenical estimate of calorie

14  See too Gazeley and Horrell (2013) on trends in calorie consumption during the nineteenth century.

**TABLE 1.2** Suggested Amendments to Upper- and Lower-Bound Estimates of per Capita Calorie Supplies ca. 1750–1800

| Broadberry et al. (2011) | Original | | Amended | |
|---|---|---|---|---|
| Year | 1750 | 1800 | 1750 | 1800 |
| Arable | 1,709 | 1,414 | 1,999/2,029 | 1,554/1,584 |
| Meat + dairy | 319 | 385 | 786 | 708 |
| Fish + poultry | 200 | 200 | 100 | 100 |
| Imports | 20 | 166 | 110/115 | 170/185 |
| Total | 2,248 | 2,165 | 2,995/3,030 | 2,532/2,577 |
| Animal share (%) | 23 | 27 | 33 | 38 |

| Muldrew (2011) | Original | | Amended | |
|---|---|---|---|---|
| Year | 1770 | 1800 | 1770 | 1800 |
| Arable | 3,985 | 3,189 | 2,320 | 1,959 |
| Meat + dairy | 1,020 | 746 | 786 | 708 |
| Fish + poultry | 42 | 42 | 100 | 100 |
| Imports | 0 | 0 | 110/115 | 170/185 |
| Total | 5,047 | 3,977 | 3,316/3,321 | 2,937/2,952 |
| Animal share (%) | 21 | 20 | 30 | 32 |

*Source*: Kelly and Ó Gráda (2013).

supplies has four important implications for the understanding of nutritional status and productivity on the eve of the Industrial Revolution. First, it makes room for a rise in English calorie supplies in the very long run, in line with—though not the same as—the posited rise in GDP per head.

Our compromise estimates for 1750 and 1800 are given in Table 1.2. They are comfortably higher than both Allen's 1,791 kilocalories for 1300 and Broadberry et al.'s 2,188 kilocalories for 1275. They imply an income elasticity of demand for calories of around 0.2, broadly similar to those yielded by analyses of food consumption in present-day less developed countries. Second, by allowing for an increasing margin over the basal metabolic rate that increased over time, they help explain why crisis mortality lessened over time. Third, they restore England's calorific advantage over France circa 1750 to 1800. And fourth, in the spirit of Muldrew, they allow for the presence of a more "industrious" English labor force, the productivity of which was not constrained by the lack of food before the Industrial Revolution.

## LITERACY AS HUMAN CAPITAL

Today both theoretical and applied research highlights the link between educational achievement as a measure of human capital and economic growth. There is even some evidence that educational human capital matters more in less developed economies than in more developed economies (e.g., Mankiw, Roemer, and Weil 1992; Hanushek and Kimko 2000). [15] But perhaps it was different two centuries ago? Did literacy give a fillip to England's Industrial Revolution?

The jury is still out on these questions. On the one hand, literacy rates grew impressively in pre-industrial England. The measuring rod usually used—ability to sign a marriage register—is imprecise guide to functional literacy, but it has the merits of broad coverage and of being a measure of an output rather than an input such as years of schooling. W. B. Stephens summarizes the literature to circa 1990 as follows:

It now seems likely that, despite times of stagnation and even decline, proportions of men able to sign their names in England rose from a very low level (of perhaps 10 percent) at the end of the fifteenth century to some 20 percent in the next century, 30 percent in the mid-seventeenth, and to about 45 percent by 1714. Women were almost universally unable to sign their names in 1500, and by 1600 only 10 percent could do so, the proportion rising to about 25 percent by 1714. Between 1714 and 1754 quantifiable evidence is sparse, though it has been calculated that in northern England male literacy rose from 58 percent in the 1720s to 70 percent by the 1740s, and female literacy from 26 to 32 percent.

In other words, between circa 1500 and circa 1750 England shifted from being mainly a society of illiterates to one where half of brides and grooms could at least sign a marriage register. However, England was hardly noteworthy for its literacy rates at this juncture: "more or less on a par with Belgium, slightly better than France, but worse that the Netherlands and Germany" (Mokyr 2009, 239; Reis 2005, 2002). Table 1.3 suggests that England had a comfortable edge over France circa 1700, but that its lead was narrowing in the eighteenth century.[16] Against this, a recent study of secular trends in book publishing in Europe places Britain well ahead of France in both the seventeenth and eighteenth centuries. It finds that English book consumption per head exceeded French by 179 percent in 1651–1750 and 63 percent in 1751–1800 (Buringh and van Zanden 2009).

There are indications that numeracy levels rose too. Keith Thomas (1987, 128) made the case for an increase in a classic paper, but maintained that "the change cannot be quantified." Others have employed estimates of age heaping

15   True, this result is mainly given by the inclusion of several high-growth East Asian countries, but excluding those countries still leaves a highly significant impact in the rest (Hanushek and Woessmann 2012b).

16   And this glosses over considerable regional variation within France (Houdaille 1977).

**TABLE 1.3**  Literacy in England and France, 1750–89
(Percentages Signing Marriage Register)

|         | France |    | England |    |
|---------|--------|----|---------|----|
| Decade  | M      | F  | M       | F  |
| 1740–49 | 40     | 19 |         |    |
| 1750–59 | 39     | 20 | 61      | 37 |
| 1760–69 | 44     | 23 | 62      | 37 |
| 1770–79 | 45     | 23 | 62      | 38 |
| 1780–89 | 46     | 25 | 62      | 39 |

*Sources*: Houdaile (1977, 168); Schofield (1973).

as a proxy for numeracy and, more broadly, human capital. Tine de Moor and Jan Luiten van Zanden have used age heaping "to chart and analyze the long-term development of human capital in the Low Countries during the late medieval and early modern period," while Brian A'Hearn, Joerg Baten, and Dorothee Crayen urge its use as "a measure of human capital that can yield comparable estimates across a wide range of historical contexts" (A'Hearn, Baten, and Crayen 2009; De Moor and van Zanden 2010). But this method has so far not yielded a measure of trends in numeracy in England. Moreover, it sometimes remains unclear whether the numeracy being measured was that of literate officials such as census enumerators and tax collectors or the population at large.

Still, England's failure to shine in the literacy stakes has led Mokyr (2009, 240) to reject "the notion that the Industrial Revolution depended a great deal on human capital as customarily defined." He is not alone: David Mitch (1992, 14–15, 213–14) has claimed that literacy was unlikely to have been of use to the bulk of the labor force in industrializing England, and Jaime Reis (2005, 206) argues that while literacy's "importance to the development of a differentiated, complex commercial economy needs no further rehearsal," its relevance to early industrialization remains unclear (see also Allen 2009, 226n8). Jason Long's analysis of English census data for 1851–81 is rather an outlier in that it points to significant economic returns to schooling in the mid-Victorian era (Long 2006, 1047).

Schooling's role is complicated by both its dual consumption and human capital aspects and by its dual affective and cognitive functions. In accounting for the demand for it before circa 1800 Reis (2005, 217) highlights its role in enhancing the "capacity to enjoy." Some of the consumption demand for literacy was, presumably, driven by religion; in the seventeenth and eighteenth centuries the parish clergy everywhere played a key role in running the schools and controlling the curriculum. There was scope for compromise, however, between the desire to save souls and the demand for literacy.

To what extent did clerical control constrain what people read? In England, even in the late seventeenth century religious publications hardly dominated; the British Library's catalogue of early printed books indicates that in 1670 items devoted to narrowly religious topics (i.e., prayer books, sectarian disputes, ecclesiastical history, etc.) accounted for about one-quarter of all publications; in 1680–81, when popish plots were much in the air, for 30 percent. There is some evidence of a drift toward more secular reading during the following century. *Eighteenth Century Collections Online*, for instance, indicates that the proportion of books published in England devoted to religious and philosophical subjects, more broadly defined, fell from about 38 percent of the total in the 1700s to about 21 percent in the 1790s. The decline in the share of religious publishing in eighteenth-century France was, if anything, more radical.[17] In France, there are signs too that poetry and the liberal arts ceded share to what Mokyr dubs "useful knowledge" (Furet 1965, 21; Darnton 1985, 167–83; Mokyr 2002).

As elsewhere in Europe (Houston 1988, 130–33), in England being able to read and write had strong social class, urban-rural, and gender dimensions. Schooling was costly and its cost a deterrent to the poorest (Houston 1988, 52–53). No matter, imply Ralf Meisenzahl and Joel Mokyr (2012), noting that average literacy levels in England were "surprisingly low for an industrial leader." What mattered most, they maintain, was the human capital embodied in "the top few percentiles" of those skilled mechanics and instrument makers whom they dub "tweakers-and-implementers." They propose that we focus on neither the average nor the "superstars" but on that crucial group in-between.

The strong class bias to literacy in the preindustrial era would seem to corroborate the claim that what really mattered was the literacy of the middle classes. Yet if England was an economy with significant mobility between occupations and regions,[18] the likely payoff to literacy and numeracy at one level may have increased the demand for it at another. This tallies with Hanushek and Woessmann (2012a, 299), who surmise that "achieving basic literacy for all may well be a precondition for identifying those who can reach 'rocket scientist' status. In other words, tournaments among a large pool of students with basic skills may be an efficient way to obtain a large share of high-performers." The early history of schooling in Ireland accords with this view. When industrialization and globalization began to create opportunities for prospective emigrants, both those who emigrated and those who though they might emigrate were prompted to acquire schooling (Ó Gráda 2013). In this view the endogenous spread of literacy to those who didn't emigrate or didn't join the middle class

---

17  According to Houston (2011, citing François 1982), pious books continued to dominate in southern Germany, but in nine western French towns their share of books owned at death dropped from "nearly half" ca. 1700 to less than 30 percent in 1789.

18  Mokyr (2008) follows François Crouzet (1985) in arguing that entrepreneurs came disproportionately from the "the lower middle class of small merchants and artisans."

amounts to a kind of "brain gain," albeit worth much less than the literacy of those who succeeded.

Most economic historians are prone to consider agricultural laborers and factory workers in the past as devoid of skills. Thus, Marco van Leeuwen and Ineke Maas's HISCLASS ranking of occupational skill levels, which allocates occupations to one of four categories (unskilled, low skilled, medium skilled, and highly skilled) assigns such workers to the "unskilled" category. But Joyce Burnette (2006) has shown how the agricultural wages paid to a sample of English farm workers in the 1830s and 1840s rose by an average 3 percent per year while they were in their twenties; since strength profiles were flat or declining at that stage of the life cycle, she declares that "all of the wage growth can be attributed to increases in skill" (2006, 706). Similarly, H. M. Boot (1995, 299) used data from an official inquiry into factory work in 1833 to generate an earnings-by-age profile that rose steeply to age thirty-five years or so. This outcome was generated mainly "by the process of human capital formation as factory workers in general invested in on-the-job training and skills acquisition." As a result the "average level of skill among British factory workers . . . was surprisingly high, even by modern standards." James Bessen's analysis of the skills of textile workers in Massachusetts in the 1830s and 1840s corroborates the claims of Burnette and Boot, and also points to a link between literacy and earnings, even in occupations where such a link might not have been suspected (Bessen 2000, forthcoming). But it is worth recalling here that the cognitive skills and the personality traits acquired in the classroom—the ability to remain silent and punctuality, for example—were joint products of schooling. Perhaps the link that mattered most in the textile factories was that between schooling and affective skills rather than that between schooling and literacy (Graff 2010; Bowles and Gintis 2011).

Burnette's and Boot's focus is on acquired skills, while Bessen implies that prior schooling eased the acquisition of on-the-job skills. But all three studies question our assumptions about the skills of farm and factory workers in the past. In sum, the link among schooling, literacy, human capital, and industrialization may be more complicated and indirect than we realize.

## CONCLUSION

The late Paul Bairoch liked to relate how only two scholars in the world were able to converse and write fluently about economic history in English, French, Dutch, and Hebrew: Paul Bairoch and Joel Mokyr. Bairoch greatly admired Mokyr but never convinced him of his conviction (e.g., Bairoch 1979) that living standards in England on the eve of the Industrial Revolution were only marginally higher than in the rest of the world. Though Mokyr is no believer in a lost golden age of early modern and preindustrial England, his "enlightened economy" was far from hovering close to Third World levels: it was already at a post-Malthusian stage where agricultural progress outstripped population growth. The evidence presented above tallies with Mokyr's view that in order to be "enlightened" England's economy and its people required a comfort zone above bare subsistence.

## ACKNOWLEDGMENTS

I am grateful to Bernard Harris, Richard Hoyle, Morgan Kelly, John Nye, Deb Oxley, Karl-Gunnar Persson, and Peter Solar for useful comments and information on various points.

## BIBLIOGRAPHY

A'Hearn, Brian, Joerg Baten, and Dorothee Crayen. 2009. "Quantifying Quantitative Literacy: Age Heaping and the History of Human Capital." *Journal of Economic History* 69 (3): 783–808.

Allen, Robert C. 2000. "Economic Structure and Agricultural Productivity in Europe, 1300–1800." *European Review of Economic History* 3 (1): 1–25.

———. 2001. "The Great Divergence in European Wages and Prices from the Middle Ages to the First World War." *Explorations in Economic History* 38 (4): 411–47.

———. 2006. "English and Welsh Agriculture, 1300–1850: Output, Inputs, and Income." Oxford University. http://www.helsinki.fi/iehc2006/papers3/Allen.pdf.

———. 2009. *The British Industrial Revolution in Global Perspective*. Cambridge: Cambridge University Press.

Apostolides, Alexander, Stephen Broadberry, Bruce Campbell, Mark Overton, and Bas van Leeuwen. 2008. "English Agricultural Output and Labour Productivity, 1250–1850: Some Preliminary Estimates." http://www.basvanleeuwen.net/bestanden/agriclongrun1250to1850.pdf.

Appleby, Andrew B. 1978. *Famine in Tudor and Stuart England*. Liverpool: Liverpool University Press.

Bailey, M., and S. Rigby, eds. 2012. *Town and Countryside in the Age of the Black Death: Essays in Honour of John Hatcher*. Turnhout: Brepols.

Bairoch, Paul. 1979. "Écarts internationaux des niveaux de vie avant la révolution industrielle." *Annales: Histoire, Sciences Sociales* 34 (1): 145–71.

Bessen, James. 2000. "The Skills of the Unskilled in the American Industrial Revolution." Unpublished manuscript.

———. Forthcoming. "Was Mechanization De-skilling? The Origins of Task-Biased Technical Change." *Journal of Economic History*.

Bogart, Dan. 2005. "Did Turnpike Trusts Increase Transportation Investment in Eighteenth-Century England?" *Journal of Economic History* 65 (2): 439–68.

Boot, H. M. 1995. "How Skilled Were Lancashire Cotton Factory Workers in 1833?" *Economic History Review* 48 (2): 283–303.

Boulton, Jeremy. 1996. "Wage Labour in Seventeenth-Century London." *Economic History Review* 49 (2): 268–90.

Bowles, Samuel, and Herbert Gintis. 2011. *Schooling in Capitalist America: Educational Reform and the Contradictions of Economic Life*. New ed. Chicago: Haymarket Books.

Braddick, Michael J. 2000. *State Formation in Early Modern England c. 1500–1700.* Cambridge: Cambridge University Press.

Broadberry, Stephen, Bruce Campbell, Alexander Klein, Mark Overton, and Bas van Leeuwen. 2011a. "Appendix for British Economic Growth, 1270–1870: An Output-Based Approach." http://www2.lse.ac.uk/economicHistory/pdf/Broadberry/BritishGDPappendix.pdf.

———. 2011b. "British Economic Growth, 1270–1870: An Output-Based Approach." December 18. http://www2.lse.ac.uk/economicHistory/pdf/Broadberry/BritishGDPLongRun16a.pdf.

Broadberry, Stephen, Bruce Campbell, and Bas van Leeuwen. 2011a. "Arable Acreage in England, 1270–1871." http://www2.lse.ac.uk/economicHistory/pdf/Broadberry/acreage.pdf.

———. 2011b. "When Did Britain Industrialize? Sectoral Distribution of the Labour Force and Labour Productivity in Britain, 1381–1851." http://www2.lse.ac.uk/economicHistory/pdf/Broadberry/SectoralsharesGB13c.pdf.

Buringh, Eltjo, and Jan Luiten van Zanden. 2009. "Charting the 'Rise of the West': Manuscripts and Printed Books in Europe, a Long-Term Perspective from the Sixth through Eighteenth Centuries." *Journal of Economic History* 69 (2): 410–45.

Burnette, Joyce. 2006. "How Skilled Were English Agricultural Labourers in the Early Nineteenth Century?." *Economic History Review* 59 (4): 688–716.

Campbell, Bruce M. S. 2009. "Four Famines and a Pestilence: Harvest, Price, and Wage Variations in England, 13th to 19th Centuries." In *Agrarhistoria på manga sätt; 28 studier om manniskan och jorden. Festskrift till Janken Myrdal på hans 60-årsdag,* edited by Britt Liljewall, Iréne A. Flygare, Ulrich Lange, Lars Ljunggren, and Johan Söderberg, 23–56. Stockholm: KSLAB.

Campbell, Bruce M. S., and C. Ó Gráda. 2011. "Harvest Shortfalls, Grain Prices, and Famines in Preindustrial England." *Journal of Economic History* 71 (4): 859–86.

Carter, Karen E. 2008. "Les garçons et les filles sont pêle-mêle dans l'école: gender and education in early modern France." *French Historical Studies* 31 (3): 417–43.

Chartres, John A. 1977. "Road Carrying in England in the Seventeenth Century: Myth and Reality." *Economic History Review* 30 (1): 73–94.

———. 1990. "Introduction." In *Agricultural Markets and Trade: Chapters from the Agrarian History of England and Wales, Volume IV,* edited by Joan Thirsk and John Chartres. Cambridge: Cambridge University Press.

Childs, Wendy R. 2005. *Vita Edwardi Secundi: The Life of Edward the Second.* Oxford: Oxford University Press.

Clark, Gregory. 2007a. *Farewell to Alms: A Brief Economic History of the World.* Princeton: Princeton University Press.

———. 2007b. "The Long March of History: Farm Wages, Population and Economic Growth, England 1209–1869." *Economic History Review* 60 (1): 97–135.

———. 2013. "1381 and the Malthus Delusion." *Explorations in Economic History* 50 (1): 4–15.

Clark, Gregory, Joseph Cummins, and Brock Smith. 2012. "Malthus, Wages, and Preindustrial Growth." *Journal of Economic History* 72 (2): 364–92.

Clark, Peter, ed. 1985. *The European Crisis of the 1590s: Essays in Comparative History.* London: Allen & Unwin.

Creighton, Charles. 1894. *A History of Epidemics from the Extinction of Plague to Present Time.* Cambridge: Cambridge University Press.

Crouzet, François. 1985. *The First Industrialists: The Problems of Origins.* Cambridge: Cambridge University Press.

Cummins, Neil, Morgan Kelly, and C. Ó Gráda. 2012. "Births and Deaths in London during the Plague Era." http://papers.ssrn.com/sol3/papers.cfm?abstract_id=2289094.

Darnton, Robert. 1985. *The Literary Underground of the Old Regime.* Cambridge, MA: Harvard University Press.

Dawson, Ian. 1993. *Tudor Century.* Walton-on-Thames: Nelson.

De Moor, Tine, and Jan Luiten van Zanden. 2010. "'Every Woman Counts': A Gender-Analysis of Numeracy in the Low Countries during the Early Modern Period." *Journal of Interdisciplinary History* 41 (2): 179–208.

de Vries, Jan. 2008. *The Industrious Revolution: Consumer Behaviour and the Household Economy, 1650 to the Present*. Cambridge: Cambridge University Press.

Dickson, David. 1997. *Arctic Ireland: The Extraordinary Story of the Great Frost and Forgotten Famine of 1740–41*. Belfast: White Row Press.

Dyer, Christopher. 2002. *Making a Living in the Middle Ages: The People of Britain 850–1520*. New Haven, CT: Yale University Press.

Dyos, H. J., and D. Aldcroft. 1969. *British Transport*. Leicester: Leicester University Press.

Elton, Geoffrey R. 1953. "An Early Tudor Poor Law." *Economic History Review* 6: 55–67.

Emmison, F. G. 1931. "Poor Relief Accounts of Two Rural Parishes in Bedfordshire, 1563–1598." *Economic History Review* 3 (1): 102–16.

Feather, John. 1986. "British Publishing in the Eighteenth Century: A Preliminary Subject Analysis." *Library* 8 (1): 32–46.

Floud, Roderick, Robert W. Fogel, Bernard Harris, and Sok Chul Hong. 2011. *The Changing Body: Health, Nutrition, and Human Development in the Western World since 1700*. Cambridge: Cambridge University Press.

Fogel, Robert W. 2004. *The Escape from Hunger and Premature Death 1700–2100*. Cambridge: Cambridge University Press.

François, Etienne. 1982. "Livre, confession et société urbaine en Allemagne au XVIIIe siècle: l'exemple de Spire." *Revue d'Histoire Moderne et Contemporaine* 29: 353–75.

Furet, François. 1965. "La 'librairie' du royaume de France au 18e siècle." In *Livre et société dans la France du xviiie siècle*, edited by Genevieve Bollème, Jean Ehrard, François Furet, Daniel Roche, and Jaques Roger, 1–32. Paris: Mouton.

Gazeley, Ian, and Sara Horrell. 2013. "Nutrition in the English Agricultural Labourer's Household over the Course of the Long Nineteenth Century." *Economic History Review* 66 (3): 757–84.

Gerhold, Dorian. 1996. "Productivity Change in Road Transport Before and After Turnpiking, 1690–1840." *Economic History Review* 49: 491–515.

Gooder, A. 1972. "The Population Crisis of 1727–30 in Warwickshire." *Midland History* 1 (4): 1–22.

Graff, Harvey J. 2010. "The Literacy Myth at 30." *Journal of Social History* 43 (3): 635–61.

Grantham, George W. 1995. "Food Rations in France in the Eighteenth and Early Nineteenth Centuries: A Reply." *Economic History Review* 48 (4): 774–77.

Hanushek, Eric A., and Dennis D. Kimko. 2000. "Schooling, Labor Force Quality, and the Growth of Nations." *American Economic Review* 90 (5): 1184–1208.

Hanushek, Eric A., and Ludger Woessmann. 2012a. "Do Better Schools Lead to More Growth? Cognitive Skills, Economic Outcomes, and Causation." *Journal of Economic Growth* 17: 267–321.

———. 2012b. "Schooling, Educational Achievement, and the Latin American Growth Puzzle." *Journal of Development Economics* 99: 497–512.

Hatcher, John A. 2011. "Unreal Wages: Long-Run Living Standards and the 'Golden Age' of the Fifteenth Century." In *Commercial Activity, Markets and Entrepreneurs in the Middle Ages: Essays in Honour of Richard Britnell*, edited by Ben Dodds and Christian D. Liddy, 1–24. Woodbridge: Boydell & Brewer.

Healey, Jonathan. 2008. "Socially Selective Mortality during the Population Crisis of 1727–1730: Evidence from Lancashire." *Local Population Studies* 81: 58–74.

Hindle, Steve. 2008. "Dearth and the English Revolution: The Harvest Crisis of 1647–50." *Economic History Review* 61 (s1): 64–98.

Hipkin, Stephen. 2008. "The Structure, Development, and Politics of the Kent Grain Trade, 1552–1647." *Economic History Review* 61 (1): 99–139.

Hoskins, W. G. 1964. "Harvest Fluctuations and English Economic History 1480–1619." *Agricultural History Review* 12 (1): 28–46.

Houdaille, Jacques. 1977. "Les signatures au mariage de 1740 à 1829." *Population* 32: 165–89.

Houston, Robert A. 1988. *Literacy in Early Modern Europe: Culture and Education 1500–1800.* London: Longman.

———. 2011. "Literacy." *Europäische Geschichte Online*, 1–23. http://www.ieg-ego.eu/en/threads /backgrounds/literacy/robert-a-houston-literacy.

Hoyle, R. W. 2010. "Famine as Agricultural Catastrophe: The Crisis of 1622–4 in East Lancashire." *Economic History Review* 63 (4): 974–1002.

Jordan, William Chester. 1996. *The Great Famine: Northern Europe in the Early Fourteenth Century.* Princeton: Princeton University Press.

Kelly, Morgan, and C. Ó Gráda. 2011. "The Poor Law of Old England: Resource Constraints and Demographic Regimes." *Journal of Interdisciplinary History* 41 (3): 339–66.

———. 2013. "*Numerare est errare*: Agricultural Output, Calories, and Living Standards in England Before and During the Industrial Revolution." *Journal of Economic History* 73 (4): 1132–63.

———. 2014. "Living Standards and Mortality since the Middle Ages." *Economic History Review* 67 (2): 358–81.

Kelly, Morgan, Joel Mokyr, and C. Ó Gráda. 2014. "Precocious Albion: A New Interpretation of the British Industrial Revolution." *Annual Reviews of Economics* 6: 16.1–16.27.

Kershaw, Ian. 1973. "The Great Famine and Agrarian Crisis in England 1315–1322." *Past & Present* 59: 3–50.

Landers, John. 1993. *Death and the Metropolis: Studies in the Demographic History of London 1670–1830.* Cambridge: Cambridge University Press.

Lindert, Peter H. 2000. "Three Centuries of Inequality in Britain and America." In *Handbook of Income Distribution*, vol. 1, edited by Anthony B. Atkinson and François Bourguignon, 167–216. Amsterdam: Elsevier.

Long, Jason. 2006. "The Socioeconomic Return to Primary Schooling in Victorian England." *Journal of Economic History* 66 (4): 1026–53.

Lucas, Henry S. 1930. "The Great European Famine of 1315, 1316, and 1317." *Speculum* 5 (4): 343–77.

Maddison, Angus. 1983. "A Comparison of Levels of GDP per Capita in Developed and Developing Countries, 1700–1980." *Journal of Economic History* 43 (1): 27–41.

Malthus, Thomas Robert. (1800) 1970. "Essay on the High Cost of Provisions." In *The Pamphlets of Thomas Robert Malthus*, 5–26. New York: Kelley.

Mankiw, N. Gregory, David Roemer, and David Weil. 1992. "A Contribution to the Empirics of Economic Growth." *Quarterly Journal of Economics* 107 (2): 407–37.

Masschaele, James. 1999. "Transport Costs in Medieval England." *Economic History Review* 46 (2): 266–79.

McIntosh, Marjorie. 2005. "Poverty, Charity, and Coercion in Elizabethan England." *Journal of Interdisciplinary History* 35 (3): 457–79.

Meisenzahl, Ralph R., and Joel Mokyr. 2012. "The Rate and Direction of Invention in the British Industrial Revolution: Incentives and Institutions." In *The Rate and Direction of Inventive Activity Revisited*, edited by Josh Lerner and Scott Stern, 443–79. Chicago: University of Chicago Press.

Meuvret, Jean. 1969. "Les oscillations des prix des céréales aux XVIIe et XVIIIe siècles en Angleterre et dans les pays du bassin parisien." *Revue d'Histoire moderne et contemporaine* 19: 540–54.

Mitch, David. 1992. *The Rise of Popular Literacy in Victorian England.* Philadelphia: University of Pennsylvania Press.

Mitchell, Brian R. 1971. *Abstract of British Historical Statistics.* Cambridge: Cambridge University Press.

Mokyr, Joel. 1983. *Why Ireland Starved: A Quantitative and Analytical History of the Irish Economy, 1800–1850.* London: Allen & Unwin.

———. 1988. "Is There Still Life in the Pessimist Case? Consumption during the Industrial Revolution, 1790–1850." *Journal of Economic History* 48 (1): 69–92.

———. 2002. *The Gifts of Athena: Historical Origins of the Knowledge Economy.* Princeton: Princeton University Press.

———. 2008. "Entrepreneurship and the Industrial Revolution in Britain." In *Entrepreneurs and Entrepreneurship in Economic History*, edited by William J. Baumol, David S. Landes, and Joel Mokyr, 183–210. Princeton: Princeton University Press.

———. 2010. *The Enlightened Economy.* New Haven, CT: Yale University Press.

Mokyr, Joel, and Joyce Burnette. 1995. "The Standard of Living through the Ages." In *The State of Humanity*, edited by Julian Simon, 135–47. Oxford: Blackwell.

Mokyr, J., and C. Ó Gráda. 1982. "Emigration and Poverty in Prefamine Ireland." *Explorations in Economic History* 19 (4): 360–84.

———. 1988. "Poor and Getting Poorer? Irish Living Standards before the Famine." *Economic History Review* 51 (2): 209–35.

———. 1989. "The Height of Irishmen and Englishmen in the 1770s." *Eighteenth Century Ireland* 4: 74–83.

———. 1996. "Height and Health in the United Kingdom 1815–1860: Evidence from the East India Company Army." *Explorations in Economic History* 33: 141–69.

———. 2002. "What Do People Die of during Famines? The Great Irish Famine in Comparative Perspective." *European Review of Economic History* 6 (3): 339–64.

Mokyr, J., and N. Eugene Savin. 1978. "Some Econometric Problems in the Standard of Living Controversy." *Journal of European Economic History* 7 (2–3): 499–516.

Muldrew, Craig. 2011. *Food, Energy and the Creation of Industriousness* Oxford: Oxford University Press.

Ó Gráda, C. 1983. "Across the Briny Ocean: Some Thoughts on Irish Emigration to America, 1800–1850." In *Ireland and Scotland 1600–1850*, edited by Tom Devine and David Dickson, 118–30. Edinburgh: John Donald.

———. 2009. *Famine: A Short History.* Princeton: Princeton University Press.

———. 2011. "Famines Past, Famine's Future." *Development & Change* 42 (1): 49–69.

———. 2013. "School Attendance and Literacy before the Famine: A Simple Baronial Analysis." In *Irish Primary Education in the Early Nineteenth Century: An Analysis of the First and Second Reports of the Commissioners of Irish Education Inquiry, 1825–6*, edited by Garret FitzGerald, 113–32. Dublin: Royal Irish Academy.

Ó Gráda, C., and Diarmaid Ó Muirithe. 2010. "The Irish Famine of 1740–41 in Gaelic Poetry." *Éire-Ireland* 45 (3–4): 41–62.

Outhwaite, R. B. 1981. "Dearth and Government Intervention in English Grain Markets, 1590–1700." *Economic History Review* 33: 389–406.

———. 1986. "Progress and Backwardness in English Agriculture, 1590–1700." *Economic History Review* 39 (1): 1–18.

Palliser, David M. 1982. "Tawney's Century: Brave New World or Malthusian Trap?" *Economic History Review* 35 (3): 339–53.

Perren, Richard. 1989. "Markets and Marketing." In *The Agrarian History of England and Wales, vol. VI 1750–1850*, edited by Gordon E. Mingay, 190–274. Cambridge: Cambridge University Press.

Persson, Karl-Gunnar. 2008. "The Malthusian Delusion." *European Review of Economic History* 12 (2): 165–73.

Petty, Sir William. 1899. *Economic Writings.* 2 vols. Edited by C. H. Hull. Cambridge: Cambridge University Press.

Post, John D. 1984. "Climatic Variability and the European Mortality Wave of the Early 1740s." *Journal of Interdisciplinary History* 15 (1): 1–30.

Poynder, Nicholas. 1999. "Monthly Grain Prices in England, 1270–1955." http://www.iisg.nl/hpw/poynder-england.php.

Reis, Jaime. 2005. "Economic Growth, Human Capital Formation and Consumption in Western Europe before 1800." In *Living Standards in the Past: New Perspectives on Wellbeing in Asia and Europe*, edited by Robert C Allen, Tommy Bengtsson, and Martin Dribe, 195–225. Oxford: Oxford University Press.

Ruggles, Steven. 1999. "The Limitations of English Family Reconstitution: English Population History from Family Reconstitution 1580." *Continuity & Change* 14 (1): 105–30.

Power, M J. 1985. "London and the Control of the 'Crisis' of the 1590s." *History* 70 (230): 371–85.

Rutty, John. 1770. *A Chronological History of the Weather and Seasons, and of the Prevailing Diseases in Dublin*. London: Robinson & Roberts.

Schofield, Roger. 1973. "Dimensions of Illiteracy 1750–1850." *Explorations in Economic History* 10: 437–54.

Sharp, Buchanan. 2012. "Royal Paternalism and the Moral Economy in the Reign of Edward II: The Response to the Great Famine." *Economic History Review* 66 (2): 628–47.

Slack, Paul. 1988. *Poverty and Policy in Tudor & Stuart England*. London: Longman.

———. 2009. "Material Progress and the Challenge of Affluence in Seventeenth-Century England." *Economic History Review* 62 (3): 576–603.

Solar, Peter M. 1995. "Poor Relief and English Economic Development before the Industrial Revolution." *Economic History Review* 48 (1): 1–22.

Stephens, W. B. 1990. "Literacy in England, Scotland, and Wales, 1500–1900." *History of Education Quarterly* 30 (4): 545–71.

Stolz, Yvonne, Joerg Baten, and Jaime Reis. 2013. "Portuguese Living Standards, 1720–1980, in European Comparison: Heights, Income, and Human Capital." *Economic History Review* 66 (2): 545–78.

Takats, Sean. 2011. *The Expert Cook in Enlightenment France*. Baltimore: Johns Hopkins University Press.

Thomas, Keith. 1987. "Numeracy in Early Modern England: The Prothero Lecture." *Transactions of the Royal Historical Society* 37: 103–32.

Timmins, Geoff. 2005. "Dying in Droves: History Mysteries and Parish Records." http://www.bbc.co.uk/history/trail/htd_history/evidence/hist_mysteries_and_recs_01.shtml.

Toutain, Jean-Claude. 1995. "Food Rations in France in the Eighteenth and Early Nineteenth Centuries: A Comment." *Economic History Review* 48 (4): 769–73.

Turner, Michael, John V. Beckett, and Bethanie Afton. 2001. *Farm Production in England, 1700–1914*. Oxford: Oxford University Press.

van Leeuwen, M. H. D., and I. Maas. 2011. *HISCLASS. A Historical International Social Class Scheme*. Leuven: Leuven University Press.

Walter, John. 1985. "A 'Rising of the People'? The Oxfordshire Rising of 1596." *Past & Present* 107: 90–143.

Wrigley, E. A., R. S. Davies, J. E. Oeppen, and R. S. Schofield. 1997. *English Population History from Family Reconstitution, 1580–1837*. Cambridge: Cambridge University Press.

Wrigley, E. A., and R. Schofield. 1981. *The Population History of England 1541–1871: A Reconstruction*. London: Edward Allen.

# 2

# PROGRESS, USEFUL KNOWLEDGE, AND THE ORIGINS OF THE INDUSTRIAL REVOLUTION

## JOEL MOKYR

Why and how does culture precisely matter to economic growth? The most obvious channel works through trust, loyalty, and what Tabellini calls "general morality" or public-mindedness: individuals contribute to social well-being even if narrow egotism might have suggested otherwise.[1] Suitable attitudes and beliefs about the behavior of others support markets and the production of public goods and reduce transactions and enforcement costs. Culture makes cooperation without third-party enforcement easier, and thus may be crucial to the emergence of markets, the division of labor, and the infrastructure that made them possible. In that sense the effect of culture is *indirect*: it affects institutions, either formal or informal, and "cultural beliefs" as defined by Greif (1994, 2005) play a central role in the emergence of markets and commercial development.

Writing about the cultural origins of the Industrial Revolution used to be a risky undertaking in the early days of cliometrics, when using words like "institutions" and "culture" immediately would brand the speaker as a "soft" sociologist or worse. This was particularly true for the economic history of the Industrial Revolution.[2] The revolution brought about by the work of Douglass North and Avner Greif has rehabilitated the concept of institutions, and by now it has been embraced by mainstream economists (Zak and Knack 2001; Acemoglu, Johnson, and Robinson 2005; Acemoglu and Robinson 2012). If institutions have been rehabilitated, can culture be far behind?[3]

In addition to providing the foundation for markets and exchange, culture could also affect economic activities in a *direct* fashion through determining some of the preferences and attitudes of individuals in the spirit of (among

---

1 This finding is supported in the experimental literature as surveyed, for example, in Bowles (2004, 110–19).

2 The one scholar who courageously stepped into that breach was Flinn (1966), who dedicated a short chapter to the intellectual and social origins of the Industrial Revolution.

3 Some economic historians, above all of course David Landes, have maintained all along that culture was central to economic growth (see Landes 1998, 2000). Among the most notable papers in formal theory is the influential work of Bisin and Verdier (2001). Empirical work includes the work of Tabellini (2008, 2010).

others) Max Weber and David Landes.[4] The argument relies on the assumption that preferences are to a large extent acquired through socialization and not wholly hardwired. It hardly makes any difference to the economy if individuals prefer spicy to bland food, and (perhaps) only a minor difference if they have a strong preference for alcohol. But the preference for leisure may well determine labor force participation and number of hours worked; time preference will determine the rate of capital formation (including human capital),[5] attitudes toward risk (which determined, presumably, the rate of entrepreneurial activity in the economy), and the importance that parents attached to the education of their children, either because they cared about their income or for other (e.g., religious) reasons.

In this essay, I propose a third and hitherto neglected mechanism through which culture might have affected economic outcomes, and specifically suggest a new way of thinking about the "Great Divergence" between East and West after 1700 or so. This mechanism concerns the cultural (and institutional) underpinnings of technological progress. Technological progress and invention involve certain metaphysical assumptions One component involves the relationship with the natural environment and the role of humans in the creation. As Lynn White and many others have pointed out, technology will advance faster if individuals adhere to a set of anthropocentric notions in which the universe is believed to have been created for the service of mankind. A second component is intelligibility: people are more inclined to manipulate natural forces if the universe is not believed to be beyond our comprehension, even if the entity that supposedly created it may be (Dear 2006). A third component, and the one I focus on here, is the belief in progress itself and the capability of science and technology (what I refer to as "useful knowledge") of bringing it about.

What is the connection between economic growth and a belief in progress? As I have argued in Mokyr (2009a, 33–35), sustained economic progress depended on three factors. First, that progress (of any sort, but specifically material progress driven by growing useful knowledge) was believed to be at all *possible* and that history was capable of producing an upward trend, albeit a non-monotonic one. Second that such a trend was *desirable* and that material progress and economic sophistication would improve some social welfare function, whether utilitarian or other. Third, if the first two are answered in the affirmative, such progress would not happen on its own but depended on a concrete program that would actually bring it about. This account is not quite

---

4 A recent and powerful statement of this kind of cultural change as a fount for economic success is McCloskey (2006).

5 This is one of the arguments made by Doepke and Zilibotti (2008), who refer to the concept as *patience capital* and explicitly model it as a cultural variable passed on from parents to children, using a model similar to Bisin and Verdier. In similar fashion, they model the preference for leisure as being inculcated by parents through the process of socialization.

the teleological model it may seem: the program for economic progress was put forward by a relatively small group of intellectuals, who disagreed heartily among themselves and had to fight for its implementation and in many cases used it as an excuse to advance a fairly narrow interest. The set of beliefs that emerged out of that struggle is what I have called the Industrial Enlightenment, and they shared two rather vague principles. One was that material progress could be brought about by the growth and diffusion of science and technology. The other was that economic well-being demanded the reform of social and political institutions (and they had quite divergent ideas on how to bring these about). But why did the people who held these beliefs emerge triumphant in Europe, and why not elsewhere in a similar form?

Such a victory was far from preordained and resulted from the special circumstances that prevailed in early modern Europe. While in that sense it may have been quite historically contingent, it provides a possible answer to questions about the origins of the Great Divergence. What we should focus on is the competitive market for ideas in which intellectual innovators presented their ideas and tried to persuade others of their value and validity. This market determined the success or failure of efforts in what we would call today "R&D" in increasing productivity broadly defined. In the past, arguments about the market for ideas were influenced by the somewhat tired dispute regarding historical materialism versus idealism: does culture adapt to the material needs of society determined by geography, demography, technology and so on, or is culture an independent actor that controls economic forces and thus determines performance?[6] In more recent years, a new approach has been proposed that seems more fruitful, namely cultural evolution (e.g., Boyd and Richerson 2005; Mesoudi 2011). In this approach, culture is seen as a set of beliefs and preferences that is learned rather than hardwired. The default option is always to learn from one's parents, but as additional inputs are encountered during socialization and later life, the individual may abandon the default and pick a different variant.

Cultural choices are not quite like other choices in economics, and hence the concept of a "market for ideas" does not correspond neatly to other markets. Of course, we use the idea of a "market" for other areas in which goods are not bought and sold for a price, such as the "marriage market" and the "political market." But at least in the marriage market, the opportunity cost of picking a partner is well defined in monogamous societies. In the market for ideas, the opportunity costs are less clear-cut. In some cases, of course, much like the marriage market, the choice is clear: one cannot be a Catholic and a Jew or believe in Ptolemaic and Copernican universe at the same time. But in many other cases buying into a new notion may not crowd out existing beliefs but simply be added to them. In evolutionary terms, this would be equivalent to

6 For a detailed and insightful discussion of these debates, see Jones (2006).

saying that the selection environment is not very stringent.[7] All the same, what is happening in the market for ideas is that the sellers of ideas try to persuade an audience of the merit of their views and adopt it as part of their beliefs.

The notion of *persuasion* is critical to the operation of the market for ideas. There is no precise equivalent to the concept of a price, but ideas and beliefs are accepted or rejected on the basis of their inherent quality and other environmental parameters. Such persuasion means that people abandon the default option, and are subject to what cultural evolution scholars have called *biases*. I have described these biases in detail elsewhere (Mokyr, 2014). What is meant by bias here is that cultural choices follow certain identifiable patterns that make people "choose" one cultural element over another (Richerson and Boyd 2005). Biases are a choice procedure that is somewhere halfway between the rational and informed decision making of neoclassical agents and the mindless evolutionary behavior of Dawkinsian replicators. They guide the infrequent choices made a few times over a lifetime in which people make cultural decisions, such as whether to be conservative or liberal, religious or not, and whether to become a vegetarian or a dog lover. Because there are often considerable fixed information costs in making such choices, some of the biases are determined by those costs. Thus there is a *direct bias*, in which choices are made by individuals following authorities and experts, and there is *conformity* (or frequency-dependence) *bias* in which agents simply choose what the majority of others around them choose assuming that others have acquired the information necessary. These biases then play themselves out in the market for ideas and determine which ideas survive in the struggle for survival in defined social groups.

The outcomes depend to a large extent on the parameters of the "market for ideas." The most important element of the effectiveness of a market is its competitiveness, the ease of entry, and its size, all of which are of course very much related. A critical component of the market for ideas is the ability of incumbents to defend their turf and reduce contestability by declaring some ideas as beyond debate. Concepts such as "heresy" and "apostasy" express the ability of existing ideas to erect barriers to entry and keep others from challenging the ruling conventional wisdom. Doctrinaire historical materialism would stress economic interests as the main determinant of the outcomes. More nuanced approaches would stress not only the structure of the market, but also rhetorical conventions: what counts as a valid argument, what is ad-

---

7 People might believe that there are natural regularities to which there are exceptions (such as magic). The selection criteria on any kind of cultural belief are contingent, and it is easy to envisage a climate in which the question "but is it true?" can be routinely answered by "sometimes" or "maybe" or "if God wills it." An example is the Jain belief of *syadvada*, which can be summarized to say that "the world of appearances may or may not be real, or both may and may not be real, or may be indescribable, or may be real and indescribable, or unreal and indescribable, or in the end may be real *and* unreal *and* indescribable" (Kaplan 1999, 45, emphasis added).

missible as evidence, and who is an authority. It also recognizes that there is a certain historical contingency in the outcome of academic and intellectual competition.[8]

The argument I am making below is simple: between 1500 and 1700, the market for ideas changed in dramatic ways in large parts of Europe, paving the way for the Enlightenment. The changes occurred on all three dimensions: the material interests of an urban mercantile ("capitalist") class became much more prominent; the rules of the market changed, with entry become much more free and the capability of incumbents to suppress "heresy" weakening over time; and the importance of experimental data and systematic observations coupled to more formal methods became a more accepted means of persuasion. None of those were entirely new in 1500, but their impact on the cultural evolution of Europe underwent a sea change.

What interests me here is how this phenomenon can resolve what might be thought of as the Great Puzzle of modern European economic growth. The puzzle is basically this: if we accept the recent near consensus that institutions are one of the key components of economic performance through the rise of functioning markets, the rule of law, and well-defined property rights, it is hard to explain the Industrial Revolution. After all, the Industrial Revolution marks the rise of the *technological* component of growth, what is often called Schumpeterian Growth. Institutions are the foundation of Smithian Growth: law and order, better markets, more gains from trade and specialization, more efficient allocations, possibly more investment, all of which leads to more growth. But it is difficult to see a systematic difference between Europe and Asia in this regard as late as 1700, and we know that trade within China at that time was highly developed, and that property rights (while quite different than in Europe) were no less effective. But the Industrial Revolution was not about further Smithian Growth, it was about useful knowledge and new techniques revolutionizing production and productivity. Whence this advantage?

The obvious solution would be that Europe had some kind of institution that encouraged and supported technological change at a higher rate than elsewhere, that is, the Industrial Revolution had deep intellectual and institutional origins (Mokyr 2005, 2008). One institution that seems at first blush the obvious solution to the Great Puzzle is intellectual property rights. In many parts of Europe there was some form of patent system and other forms of incentives in which society encouraged and rewarded technologically creative people who could take credit for some important innovation. Britain had a patent system since 1624, and the Netherlands had their own patent system during the golden

---

8  For a recent restatement of the orthodox materialist position, see Morris (2010, 423, 476), in which he claims that the best theorists give their age the ideas "it needed" and ask the questions that "social developments force onto them"—a rather oversimplified argument coming from a subtle and learned scholar.

age and the eighteenth century. Yet much research has shown that the patent system covered only a small proportion of all relevant inventions, and that its net effects on technological progress are in all likelihood of a second order (Mokyr 2009b). All the same, there was more to incentivizing inventors than just patents, and rewarding them by recognizing their contribution to society may have been part of the explanation of Europe's success.[9] However, the emergence of intellectual property rights (IPRs) in Europe reflects a deeper phenomenon, namely the success of a *culture of progress* in the European market for ideas. It is that phenomenon I wish to address here.

## A CULTURE OF PROGRESS

A prevalent *belief* in the possibility and desirability of progress was probably neither a necessary nor a sufficient condition for it to occur. Yet it was an important element. One interpretation of the idea of progress is that it is logically equivalent to an implied disrespect of previous generations. As Carl Becker noted in his classic work written in the early 1930s, "A Philosopher could not grasp the modern idea of progress . . . until he was willing to abandon ancestor worship, until he analyzed away his inferiority complex toward the past, and realized that his own generation was superior to any yet known" (Becker 1932, 131). Seventeenth-century Europe already shows quite a few signs of a belief in progress, starting with Bacon and Descartes themselves and their disciples. The young Blaise Pascal, for instance, deeply influenced by Descartes, saw the world of knowledge as if it was a single infinitely lived individual, "incessantly learning" (cited by Bury [1932] 1955, 68).[10]

The notion that progress was an apt description of their own age spread among the British writers of the seventeenth century, including the work of the (non-Puritan) clergyman Joseph Glanvill (1636–80), who wrote a famous book titled *Plus Ultra, or, The Progress and Advancement of Knowledge since the Days of Aristotle* (1668), in which he proudly listed area by area the advances that science had made since antiquity, much of which he ascribed to the work of the Royal Society and its members. He noted with some exuberance that "a ground of high expectation from Experimental Philosophy is given, by the happy genius of this present Age . . . and that a ground of expecting considerable

---

9 Many important innovators in Britain who, for one reason or another, were unable to make use of the patent system were rewarded by special acts of Parliament. Among them, Edward Jenner is the best known, but others include Edmund Cartwright, Samuel Crompton, and the Fourdrinier brothers who pioneered continuous paper making in Britain.

10 In later years, Pascal was converted to Jansenism, a religious creed that was far more contemplative and morally oriented and he renounced his earlier views and wrote of the "vanity of science"—a good example of how competing religious beliefs, had they prevailed, might have thwarted the progress toward more advanced science and technology.

things from Experimental Philosophy is given by those things which have been found out by illiterate tradesmen or lighted by chance" (Glanvill 1668, 104–5).[11] To be sure, not all authors of the late seventeenth and eighteenth centuries subscribed to a belief that progress was possible or even likely, and doubting Thomases such as Hobbes never quite bought into it, pining for stability more than continuous material improvement. As Israel (2010, 4) has recently put it, Enlightenment theories of progress were tempered by a sense of the dangers and challenges facing the attempts to improve society, and their optimism rested on man's ability to create wealth by inventing technologies capable of raising production.

It is the latter that the economic historian should focus on. Material progress depends on the advances made in useful knowledge. The idea of progress, as noted, is inextricably linked to the cultural issue of how one should rate the capabilities and wisdom of one's contemporary generation relative to the wisdom of previous ones. The same age that fostered a belief in progress impudently shed their excessive respect for earlier thinkers, committing to a belief that "we can do better." Such beliefs were strongly resisted, and it is not at all clear that their triumph was preordained or inevitable. Nowhere is this struggle better illustrated than by the famous "battle of the books," which erupted in much of Europe in the late seventeenth century between the "ancients" and the "moderns."[12] Were modern scholars and authors nothing but midgets standing on the shoulders of giants, or were they giants themselves? The debate was widely regarded, then as now, as a tempest in a teapot (Levine 1981, 73).[13] But it was not: it reflected a watershed in cultural evolution that had been two centuries or more in the making (Bury [1932] 1955, chap. 4; Spadafora 1990, chap. 2). Many of the "ancients" viewed modern science as a possible attack on "learning" and made a point of dismissing the efforts of moderns as futile.

11   Elsewhere (1665, 140) Glanvill noted, somewhat insolently, that "that discouraging maxim, *nil dictum quod non dictum prius* hath little room in my estimation. Except Copernicus be in the right, there hath been new under the sun . . . the last ages have shewn us what antiquity never saw." Furthermore, he believed explicitly that "the Goods of Mankind may be much increased by the Naturalist's insights into trade"—essentially an early statement of one of the central assumptions of the Industrial Enlightenment. Glanvill would, however, not be counted as "enlightened" by our standards—he staunchly defended the existence of witches and spirits and wrote a book vehemently attacking those who doubted their existence.

12   The literature on this issue is quite substantial. The classic statement remains that of R. F. Jones ([1936] 1961). For a recent assessment, see Levine (1981).

13   There seems to be a certain coyness among modern authors to admit the obvious, which is that the "moderns" had an irrefutable case in terms of useful knowledge, just as their case was unprovable and silly as far as literature and poetry are concerned. Even Nisbet (1979), after describing Georges Sorel's ludicrous characterization of the idea of progress as "a shabby piece of bourgeois trickery" based on circular reasoning, feels the need to admit that "the reasoning was certainly circular." It was not; insofar as progress in science and technology was based on a cumulative process and there was little knowledge "lost" in the course of history, moderns had access to ancient knowledge but not the reverse.

Henry Stubbe (1632–76), a pugnacious physician and political pamphleteer, dismissed the entire scientific endeavor as futile: "All that is said about the erecting of Mechanical or Sensible Philosophy of Nature is but empty talk. Human nature is not capable of such atchievements" and then accused modern authors ("virtuosi") of being ignorant of Aristotle and other classical writers (Stubbe 1670, 15). As late as 1704, the bookseller's introduction to Jonathan Swift's famous *Battle of the Books*, a satirical essay on the battle of the ancients and moderns, concluded that "we cannot learn to which side Victory fell" (Swift [1704] 1720, 211).[14] Much of the "battle of the books" of course was about taste, and an argument whether one should prefer Shakespeare to Sophocles or Milton to Virgil seems otiose today. But dismissing R. F. Jones as "Whiggish" because he felt sympathy for those who felt that there were good grounds to prefer Galileo to Archimedes or Harvey to Galen seems unproductive. One of the debaters, the linguist and biographer William Wotton (1666–1727), indeed made the crucial distinction between areas that were cumulative (such as science and technology) and those that were not (such as rhetoric and poetry). Swift's pamphlet marks the epilogue of a battle that had been fought for two centuries and won conclusively. From that point on it was beyond any question that a reference to Aristotle or any other author in the canon, from the Bible down, would not be regarded as sufficient evidence.[15]

By the early seventeenth century, leading European intellectuals were increasingly coming to terms with their break with classical science and philos-

14   One cannot help but surmising that the classic Monty Python skit "The Philosophers' World Cup" in which Greek and German philosophers compete in an absurd soccer match was inspired by a paragraph such as this: "The Moderns were in very warm debates upon the choice of their leaders, and nothing less than the fear impending from their enemies could have kept them from mutinies upon this occasion. The difference was greatest among the horse, where every private trooper pretended to the chief command, from Tasso and Milton to Dryden and Wither. The light horse were commanded by Cowley and Despreaux. There came the bowmen under their valiant leaders, Descartes, Gassendi, and Hobbes, whose strength was such that they could shoot their arrows beyond the atmosphere, never to fall down again, but turn, like that of Evander, into meteors, or, like the cannon ball, into stars. Paracelsus brought a squadron of stinkpot flingers from the snowy mountains of Rhaetia. . . . The army of the Ancients was much fewer in number, Homer led the horse, and Pindar the light horse, Euclid was chief engineer, Plato and Aristotle commanded the bowmen, Herodotus and Livy the foot, Hippocrates, the dragoons, the allies, led by Vossius and Temple, brought up the rear" (Swift [1704] 1720, 228–29).

15   The late seventeenth-century "Battle of the Books" was in fact a rearguard action that shows how strong the position of the "moderns" had become. In the words of one scholar, "To sample a few of Temple's [William Temple, one of Wotton's main opponents] opinions about ancients and moderns gives one a sense of the genteel arrogance the Enlightenment had to put up with and overcome. . . . Temple served up a pastiche of pseudo-intellectual commonplaces. The ancients had said it all; advances in learning and art were unlikely when the originals were so perfect. . . . Where now is the great music of the past when Orpheus could move the stones and tame the beasts? Where today are the ancient arts of magic? How can the fortuitous circumstances that produced such excellences of the past ever come together again in these diminished times? Did Harvey and

ophy. In the quaint terminology that he invented, Francis Bacon spoke of the "idols of the theatre," by which he meant the defective methodology inherited from Aristotle. He launched a full-fledged attack on classical wisdom (especially in his *Advancement of Learning*) and called for nothing less than to junk classical science and start afresh, using observation and experiment rather than authority. He noted, in a famous remark, that the wisdom of the Greeks was but a wisdom of boys, it can talk but not generate, it was "barren of works."[16] The English physician and physicist William Gilbert in his *De Magnete* (1600), a widely admired and pioneering work in its time, dismissed Ptolemy's astronomy as "now believed only by idiots" and proclaimed that the only avenue to truth was experiment and observation, not the authority of Greek sages (Jones [1936] 1961, 17). In the first decades of the seventeenth century this rebellion against the "ancients" was taken further.[17] Famously, Galileo wrote in his 1613 letter to Duchess Christina of Florence that "in disputes about natural phenomena, one must begin not with the authority of scriptural passages but with sensory experiences and necessary demonstrations" (cited by Reston 1994, 137). Many of the scientists and scholars who rose to prominence in the mid-seventeenth century had accepted the critical attitude toward received authority. "Whatever the schoolmen may talk," wrote one of them, "yet Aristotle's Works are not necessarily true and he himself hath by sufficient Arguments proved himself to be liable to error. . . . Learning is Increased by new Experiments and new Discoveries . . . we have the advantage of more time than they had and knowledge is the daughter of time . . . if such great scholars, who were so eminent for their Knowledge in Natural Things, might notwithstanding be grossly mistaken in such Matters as are now evident and certain, why then we have no Reason to depend on their Assertions or Authorities" (Wilkins [1640] 1708, 146–47). The paralyzing respect for the wisdom of previous generations was melting away.

Examples of how traditional learning remained impregnable even in Europe are easy to find. Perhaps no example serves us better than the history of European Jews, an ethnic group that was on average far better educated than their gentile neighbors, and among whom male literacy was close to universal (Botticini and Eckstein 2012). Although the volume and range of Jewish learning was immense and made considerable progress in many areas, it was conformist and respectful of ancient authority. Within these constraints, there was

---

Copernicus have anything new to say? Who can tell whether it is the sun or the earth that moves?" (Traugott 1994, 504–5).

16  Preface to *The Great Instauration* (reprinted in Bacon 1999, 69).

17  The best-known writers in this tradition following Bacon and Gilbert were George Hakewill (1578–1649), a Church of England clergyman who strongly denied that a process of decay caused the intellectuals of his generation to be inferior to the ancient classics, and Nathanael Carpenter (1589–1628), an influential Oxford scholar who stressed the need to test classical authorities against new evidence.

a great deal of debate and dispute, but violating them was *kfira be'eekar* and could have terrible social consequences as Spinoza found out.[18] The outcome was that despite their disproportionate number of intellectuals and learned individuals, the great scientific and technological revolutions of the seventeenth and eighteenth centuries did not draw on much learning from Jews.[19] When remarkable Jewish intellectuals such as David Ricardo and Moses Mendelssohn did play a role, they typically were alienated from their community. Even in medicine, in which Jews had specialized for centuries, their impact was rather disappointing until the nineteenth century. The great innovators of medicine before Pasteur, from Vesalius to Sydenham, from Harvey to Jenner, were not Jewish.

In Europe, this battle was won decisively by the "Moderns" and the result was the Enlightenment, in which the "Ancients" were relegated to a polite but irrelevant niche of learning. John Clarke (1687–1734), an enlightened educational reformer who advocated the teaching of mathematics and science, wrote in 1731 that "the antients were indeed but very poor Philosophers. With regard to the Knowledge of Nature the thing is too notorious to admit of any dispute at all" (Clarke 1737, 45). Similarly, Richard Helsham, who held the Erasmus Smith professorship of natural and experimental philosophy at Trinity College Dublin from 1724 to 1738, started his wildly successful textbook in natural philosophy (still taught in Dublin as late as 1849) by disrespectfully stating that "it is a matter of no small surprize to think how inconsiderable a progress the knowledge of nature had made in former ages . . . compared with the vast improvements it has received . . . of latter times. . . . Philosophers of former ages buried themselves in framing hypotheses . . . without any founda-

---

18   Even an original thinker such as Maimonides (Rambam) discussed heresy at length in his *Mishneh Torah* and judged them severely. All Jewish evildoers will still be "part of the next world." Not so those who questioned religious authority. He distinguished among three types of them: *minim* (heretics—those who question the essence of the Jewish God), *epikursim* (apostates), and those who deny the Torah (*Mishneh Torah, Sefer Mada, hilchot Teshuva* [repentance]; chap. 3). The penalty was to be that they would not become a part "of the next world," but in chapter 8 of the same it is quite clear that the biblical penalty of *karet* would be applied to anyone who seriously questioned the scriptures, which is most likely equivalent to ostracism.

19   There were a few exceptions to this rule, such as Jacob ben Immanuel (Bonet) Lates, physician to the late fifteenth-century popes and the inventor of an important instrument to measure astronomical altitudes. Apart from an elaborate numerology in which meanings were attached to words according to the values associated with their letters, it is hard to find important Jewish mathematicians before the nineteenth century. Such mathematicians did exist and helped the Portuguese navigators in computing latitude at sea. The best known of those astronomer-mathematicians was Abraham Zacuto (1452–1515), the inventor of a new and improved astrolabe to measure latitude at sea and the compiler of detailed astronomical tables for ocean navigation. See Seed (2001, 73–82).

tion in nature [and] so lame and defective as to not answer those very phae-
nomena for whose sakes they had been contrived" (Helsham 1755, 1).

It is this kind of cultural change, that explains how and why intellectual
innovation became increasingly acceptable in all fields of knowledge, from
theology to hydraulics. The more powerful minds of the age realized, much as
Pascal (in his pre-Jansenist and more progressive days) noted that it would be
unjust to show the "ancients" more respect that they themselves had shown to
those who had preceded them, a logical point entirely missed by Jewish theo-
logians (Bury [1932] 1955, 68).[20] Progress, the "moderns" (especially Glanvill)
stressed, was inevitable because the tools of research had been improved.
Galen had no microscope, Ptolemy no telescope, Archimedes no calculus.
But more than anything, knowledge was cumulative. Cumulativeness was, of
course, itself a variable that society controlled and constructed. Knowledge, it
was recognized, could be lost.[21] For that reason Bacon proposed to move the
governance of technological knowledge from the individual to the community
(i.e., the state). After all, as Keller (2012, 242) remarks, "The value of the
inventor's knowledge for society was so great that the state could not afford its
loss."

The problem with the position of the "moderns" was (and is) that progress
was not inevitable or even very likely. While the idea of progress was based on
the retention of past useful knowledge which guaranteed that there would be
more and more of it (some knowledge can be lost, but this is comparatively
rare), the conditions for its *sustained* growth (rather than fizzling out) are fairly
strong and it took the Age of Enlightenment many decades to figure them
out. Enlightenment thinkers disagreed among themselves as to precisely what
progress would consist of and how it would be brought about (Israel 2010),
but if there was one item on which all but a few retrograde Enlightenment
writers could agree, it was that progress consisted of *material* advances relying
on the growth of *useful knowledge*. In other words, science (or "experimental
philosophy") and technology ("the useful arts") were the engines of material
progress, and evidence was slowly mounting about the huge potential of these
forces to change daily material existence of humankind.

The final "triumph of the idea of progress" as Nisbet ([1994] 2008) has called
it was slow in coming, and it was only the triumph of enlightenment thinkers
committed to the idea of progress in the eighteenth century that fully explains

20   Auguste Comte noted that "the idea of continuous progress had no scientific consistency,
or public regard, till after the memorable controversy at the beginning of the last [i.e., eighteenth]
century about the general comparison of the ancients and the moderns . . . that solemn discussion
constitutes a ripe event in the history of the human mind which thus, for the first time, declared
that it had made an irreversible advance" (Comte 1856, 441).

21   One of Bacon's inspirations, the Padua law professor Guido Pancirolli, wrote a book titled
*Two Books of Things Lost and Things Found* (1599 and 1602), in which he listed the products and
techniques that ancient civilization was believed to possess and subsequently lost.

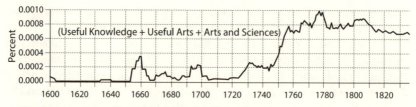

**2.1** Google n-grams of "useful knowledge" and related concepts.

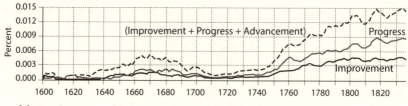

**2.2** Google n-grams of the concept of progress and related terms, 1600–1830.

the sharp turn in European history. Powerful thinkers such as Montesquieu, Hume, Smith, Diderot, and Condorcet each in their own way, had the persuasive power to convince others that indeed material progress could be brought about and the Baconian program was more than a dream.[22] This can be illustrated by showing the sharp increase in words associated with progress in the eighteenth century.

Figures 2.1 and 2.2 illustrate the timing of this triumph. It shows the Google n-grams of two key concepts of the Industrial Enlightenment. One of them is the concept of "progress" (including its related terms of "improvement" and "advancement"). The other is the central concept of "useful knowledge," which was roughly isomorphic to our modern notion of science and technology (Mokyr 2009a, 34–35).

The diagrams show, interestingly, an early flourishing of the ideas of the Industrial Enlightenment during and after the Civil War, possibly related to the rise and decline of Puritanism. The Glorious Revolution, rather than reinforcing this trend, was followed by a period of slow down. Only in the second third of the eighteenth century did these concepts once again start to grab the attention of English-language authors. It seems a bit of a stretch to argue that the onset of inventive activity after 1760 was "caused" by this, but the timing of the two phenomena is at least suggestive.

22  As Nisbet (1979) has pointed out, even Enlightenment thinkers such as Rousseau, who are widely reputed to be critical of material progress, were more objecting to the inequality and injustice that they felt accompanied material progress than to the progress itself.

## PROGRESS AND COMPETITION

What accounts for this triumph of the culture of progress? It may seem that the rise of an urban merchant and industrial class would infuse intellectual life with a more dynamic and optimistic spirit, but this tempting argument seems to fly in the face of many other highly commercialized societies (such as in India, China, and the Middle East) where which no such "progressive turn" can be detected. Pure materialistic explanations by themselves may not by themselves be persuasive here. Nor is it obvious that the Reformation changed the tone of intellectual discourse, especially because so many of the leading intellectual innovators resided in Catholic countries and some of them, such as the phenomenally versatile Athanasius Kircher (1601–80) were Jesuits. Instead, it seems that the outcome was the result of a series of debates that were played out in a marketplace for ideas in which the field was sufficiently level so that the ideas that appealed the most to intellectuals due to the kind of biases I pointed to earlier won out. Of course, it helped that Renaissance Europe was experiencing in many ways a wave of advances. Those who argued that progress was in fact part of the historical dynamic could point to a huge and growing array of facts that supported them, among them the growth of useful knowledge and technology, but also the successes that Europeans had in reaching and subjugating other parts of the world, the technological advances of the early renaissance, and the progress in areas such as painting, music, and (more controversially) literature. The causality runs not only from a belief in progress to its experience, there is clearly an important channel of reverse causality. Yet earlier successes and even the experience of progress do not guarantee that it can and will be sustained, or become the basis of a set of beliefs anchored in assumptions about improvement. Medieval Islam and Song China, despite centuries of technical and scientific advances, did not experience what happened in Europe. There were many reasons for this, and I want to focus here on one of them: differences in the market for ideas.

Success in a Schumpeterian market in which entrenched ideas are being challenged by novel ones required an even playing field, and in most societies incumbents made it very difficult for intellectual innovators to challenge the conventional wisdom. It seems rather obvious that novelty is resisted by those whose income and power are based on the status quo. It is far from obvious how and why the transformation took place in Europe. The explanation I am proposing here has nothing to do with a "Eurocentric" view about intrinsic differences and rests on a rather unique constellation of forces that emerged in Europe in the centuries before the Enlightenment, that paved the way for its eventual triumph. On the one hand, the fragmentation of polities in Europe was such that "the states system" (as E.L. Jones referred to it) ensured sufficient competition that permitted intellectual pluralism. At the same time, Europe witnessed the emergence of an institution that actively promoted and enhanced intellectual innovation, even if that was not its intention.

The institution in question was what was known as the "Republic of Letters." The importance of the Republic of Letters in the subsequent economic development of Europe has been underrated in the past even if its importance for intellectual change is well known.[23] The Republic of Letters was essentially a relatively free and open marketplace for ideas, in which intellectuals and scientists competed with one another for reputation and recognition. Like any other market, the efficiency of the market for ideas depended on its degree of competitiveness and contestability and on the capability of incumbents to block new (and possibly more capable) entrants. It was also transnational, and hence "the extent" of the market was much larger than any single political unit making it more plausible that innovators could cover the "fixed costs" of producing a new idea.

It is here that competition and free entry mattered most. The political fragmentation of Europe became a key to its intellectual development. The dark forces of reaction in the sixteenth century were no less benighted than those of the fourteenth, but it became increasingly difficult for those forces to coordinate and work together, in part because some defenders of the conventional wisdom were Protestant and others Catholic.[24] Authorities could not agree on who was a heretic, and the heretics took fully advantage of this. The unique situation in Europe, then, was that intolerance and the suppression of cultural heterodoxy, long before they fell out of fashion, could not be properly coordinated. Many innovators were able to game the political system to avoid persecution. Hostility between the European powers led to one ruler protecting the gadflies that irritated their enemies.[25] In other cases, the ability of intellectual innovators to move about the Continent to escape potential persecutors left

---

23 For exceptions, see David (2004, 2008) and Mokyr (2011–12).

24 Consider Luther's disciple Philipp Melanchthon's denunciation of Copernicus: "Some think it a distinguished achievement to construct such a crazy thing as that Prussian astronomer who moves the earth and fixes the sun. Verily, wise rulers should tame the unrestraint of men's minds" (Kesten 1945, 309). Luther himself said caustically of Copernicus, "The fool wishes to turn the entire art of Astronomy on its head" (Merton 1973, 245).

25 One of the earliest case is Bernardino Ochino (1487–1564), a highly controversial Siennese Franciscan monk and preacher, committed to free inquiry and controversy, and famous for an unusual eloquence. He managed to alienate the Catholic Church, especially attracting the hostility of the reactionary hard-line Cardinal Giovanni-Pietro Caraffa (later Pope Paul IV, 1555–59). An equal-opportunity gadfly, Ochino also alienated most protestants. He was summoned to appear before the Roman Inquisition established in 1542 (one of the first "heretics" to be so persecuted) and fled to Geneva in 1547, eventually ending up in England, whence he was driven by the ascension of the intolerant Mary Tudor. Returning to Zurich, he was again expelled and ended up in Poland (at that time a relatively tolerant nation) but was banished from it in 1564 at the instigation of the papacy and died in Moravia. Among other things he advocated divorce and was suspected of supporting polygamy (Benrath 1877, passim).

the incumbents powerless to suppress the innovations, though the causality between mobility and intellectual innovation is of course rather complex.[26] By the eighteenth century, the inability of reactionary forces to suppress innovations had become a bit of charade, and while the more outrageous *philosophes* such as Helvétius and Lamettrie still had to move about when the local authorities became disenchanted with them, they usually found welcoming hosts at other courts.

The Republic of Letters was a *virtual* institution: its operation took place primarily through publication and correspondence. It was an "invisible college" of internationally connected scholars, based on the implicit understanding that knowledge was a nonrivalrous good that was to be shared by the community so that it could be accessed where it could do the most good. It was the embodiment of a "market for ideas" in which experimentalists, philosophers, physicians, and crackpots tried to "sell" their original ideas by persuading others, and in the process acquire the main payoff, which was the recognition and respect of their peers and hopefully the patronage jobs that came with it (David 2008). The community constituted an elite group of intellectuals and scientists that exchanged and discussed new knowledge. Its operation depended heavily on the printing press and the growth of reliable postal services in Europe. But precisely because of its international character, it provided larger audiences (and more potential patrons) to intellectual innovators.

Like every market institution, the Republic of Letters set up rules and incentives that governed its daily operation. From the point of view of long-term economic impact, what mattered most for the operation of the market of ideas was its international character and free entry. At least in theory, the Republic of Letters practiced a meritocracy, in which neither social class nor nationality mattered. In practice, of course, it was limited to members of the elite, since only they had access to the education resulting from privilege. Yet clearly it could include equally the very rich and aristocratic Robert Boyle and his assistant, the parvenu Robert Hooke, as well as members of an *haute bourgeois* intelligentsia such as Christiaan Huygens and René Descartes. The Republic of Letters fancied itself an autonomous unit with its own rules and institutions and not subject to the norms and values of the rest of society, rising "above the petty concerns of state and church or so at least they claimed" (Goldgar 1995, 3). Pierre Bayle, the French Huguenot philosopher who lived in exile in Rotterdam and was one of the Republic's early focal points, wrote that "the Common-wealth of learning (Republic of Letters) is a State extremely free . . . the Empire of Truth and Reason is only acknowledged in it . . . everybody is both sovereign and under everybody's jurisdiction . . . the laws of the society

---

26  The most extreme case was without the doubt the celebrated Czech intellectual Jan Amos Comenius (Komensky), whose career was spent moving about among his native Moravia, Poland, Sweden, Hungary, London, and Amsterdam.

have done no Prejudice to the Independency of the State of Nature as [much as to] Error and Ignorance" (Bayle [1696–97] 1734, 2:389, essay on *Catius*).

Furthermore, any extant idea should be regarded as contestable. The motto "nullius in verba" (on no one's word) adopted by the Royal Society exemplifies this approach no less than Bayle's well-known restatement of the principle.[27] Many intellectuals regarding themselves as citizens of the Republic of Letters did not shy away from confrontations and sharp critiques of the masters of science.[28] Yet there was also a shared ideology, a sense of common purpose, of being part of a collaborative project of making the world a better place by jointly building a larger knowledge base through the exchange of information that allowed intellectual innovators to build on each other's work after they had verified and tested it.[29] Some of the continued emphasis on "improvement" was no doubt self-serving, even self-aggrandizing, propaganda by patronage-hungry intellectuals, yet the efforts to add to useful knowledge also counted individuals who demonstrably had no interest in patronage, such as the wealthy aristocrat Robert Boyle or the well-to-do merchant Anthonie van Leeuwenhoek.

The Republic of Letters, then, was the arena in which the battle over the idea of Progress played itself out in the closing decades of the seventeenth century. As I have shown in some detail in my *Enlightened Economy* (Mokyr 2009a), this was the foundation of what I have termed the "Industrial Enlightenment." But there was nothing self-evident or inexorable in this victory, and throughout much of early modern Europe supporters of the notion of progress had to

27  Bayle stressed that "every particular Man has the Right of the Sword and may exercise it without asking leave of those who govern . . . against Authors who are mistaken. . . . It is true, the Reputation of being a learned man which an author has acquired is sometimes diminished thereby . . . but if it be done in support of the Cause of Reason and for the interest of the Truth, no Body ought to find fault with it" (Bayle [1696–97] 1734, 389).

28  A good example is the pugnacious Dutch lens maker, astronomer, and embryologist Nicolaas Hartsoeker (1656–1725), who as a sixteen-year-old had been taught by no less a figure than Leeuwenhoek himself about microscopes, but in his later work did not hesitate to criticize and even ridicule the old man. He also attacked such pillars of science as Newton, Leibniz, and Jakob Bernoulli. Notwithstanding (and perhaps due to) his disputatious reputation, he was offered a number of patronage positions, including one by Czar Peter the Great (which he declined).

29  In the first issue of the Royal Society's *Transactions*, its secretary Henry Oldenburg (1665) wrote in the best Baconian tradition that "there is nothing more necessary for promoting the improvement of Philosophical Matters, than the communicating to such, as apply their Studies and Endeavours that way, such things as are discovered or put in practise by others. . . . To the end, that such Productions being clearly and truly communicated, desires after solid and usefull knowledge may be further entertained, ingenious Endeavours and Undertakings cherished, and those, addicted to and conversant in such matters, may be invited and encouraged to search, try, and find out new things, impart their knowledge to one another, and contribute what they can to the Grand design of improving Natural knowledge, and perfecting all Philosophical Arts, and Sciences. All for the Glory of God, the Honour and Advantage of these Kingdoms, and the Universal Good of Mankind."

struggle with the forces of reaction. Even among Enlightenment thinkers, the idea of commercial-industrial activity and the "useful arts and sciences" as the sites on which the forces of progress converged remained itself contestable—in line with the fundamental principles of the Republic of Letters. In some European countries, the debate ended in a stalemate, and the forces of progress in Europe south of the Alps and Pyrenees encountered more tenacious resistance from religious and political corners. To be sure, enlightened views about the capability of useful knowledge to power economic progress penetrated into every corner of Europe (including, for instance, Naples—see John Robertson 1997), but their impact on the economic institutions and capacity for meaningful innovation differed greatly.

It is this institution that provided the battleground in which the modern idea of progress eventually emerged victorious. Scholars have understandably differed about what kind and whose progress is involved. Nisbet ([1994] 2008), for instance, distinguishes between "progress as freedom" (which includes material progress) and "progress as power," which we might think of as the emergence of the nation-state and institutional change. More controversially, Lasch (1991), dismisses the idea of progress due to human ingenuity and the progress of arts and sciences as "vaporous tributes to the power of reason" produced by "second-rate thinkers." Instead he stresses the demand side of progress, a positive assessment of the proliferation of wants, rising expectations, newly acquired tastes and standards of personal comforts, which he attributes to Hume and Smith (Lasch 1991, 45, 52–54).[30] But the idea that stood in the very center of the progress movement was the Baconian program, which purported to increase and disseminate knowledge of nature to benefit "the useful arts." In the end, anyone purporting to understanding the Industrial Revolution needs to confront its cultural roots.

What accounts for this triumph? On the demand side, the expansion of the economies in Western Europe after 1500 gave rise to an increasingly strong contingent of *homines novi* for whom progress could not mean but economic advantage to themselves. Urban-mercantile classes naturally felt that "progress" meant—however indirectly—more commerce, more urbanization, and greater permeability of the upper classes by *arrivistes*. Yet there was more to it than economic change: the idea of progress proved consonant with Western Christianity in ways that seemed to have eluded Islam and Judaism. Judeo-Christian beliefs in millenarianism provided a sense of a historical dynamic that had an end point that was recognizably different from current reality. Medieval Europe was suffused with millenarian beliefs of history leading to a "better"

---

30  Among the minds that Lasch (1991) would have to classify as "second rate" are Descartes, Pascal, Priestley, and Condorcet.

world in which a paradise would be reinstated at the end of history.[31] At the same time, Christianity turned out to be sufficiently flexible and adaptive to accommodate strong commitments to devoutness as well as a powerful support for the "moderns" over the ancients, of experimental science over Aristotelian dogma, and of the Baconian application of useful knowledge to production and the "arts."[32]

But such emphasis on the demand side needs to take account of the supply side that depended on the correct incentives for intellectual innovators. These incentives consisted of the increased carrot of patronage and fame in the Republic of Letters, and the reduced stick of less effective resistance and threats of "heresy" accusations by fragmented and uncoordinated incumbents. Above all, it was the power of competition that governed the emergence of the idea of progress. Political units, whether nation-states, small duchies, or city-states, competed with one another for the best minds, the best artists, the best composers, and the best astrologers. Intellectuals competed with one another for reputation and the patronage associated with it. Even religions competed with one another for believers, resulting in some religious reform and improved education—as well as in some of the most destructive violence in the Continent's history.[33]

---

31   One medieval writer who tried to produce a "dynamic" vision of history of the world that led toward some kind of chiliasm was Joachim of Fiore (1135–1202), whose three-stage theory of history (each stage corresponding to one entity of the Holy Trinity) reappeared centuries later in the works of Auguste Comte and Karl Marx (Cohn 1961, 101). Whether this eschatological prophesy was a true theory of progress (as Nisbet believes) or not, it shows that within Christianity such dynamic theories were possible even if they were attacked by St. Thomas (1263) and denounced formally by the church as heretical.

32   Nisbet ([1994] 2008) points to the deep religiosity of some of the major figures of the Enlightenment, such as Priestley and Herder. This is a fortiori true for the seventeenth century. The Merton hypothesis ([1938] 2001) has argued for a strong link between the rise of Puritanism and the development of science in seventeenth-century England, and while its emphasis on England is somewhat lopsided, the link has survived much scrutiny. Puritans embraced science, in part because it simultaneously "manifested the Glory of God and enhanced the Good of Man" (Merton 1973, 232). For Puritans, as Webster ([1975] 2002, 505) has added, the ideal life was one that implied an efficient deployment of one's ability for personal advantage and public service and that the glorification of God was exercised by maximizing one's material resources. These two objectives were not separable, but complemented one another in ways that took until the end of the seventeenth century to fully work out. Deeply religious men could recognize the deep ethical implication of scientific investigation: the systematic and meticulous study of God's creation was the closest a Calvinist could get to an inscrutable deity that could not be grasped by the "cultivated intellect."

33   Lawrence Stone (1969, 81–83) has stressed the positive effect that religious competition between Anglicans and Dissenters had in England, as well as in France between Huguenots and Catholics "in the struggle for men's souls."

## CHINA, THE "NEEDHAM QUESTION," AND THE MARKET FOR IDEAS

Modern Chinese scholarship has successfully fought the notion that the West's scientific and industrial revolutions implied that China somehow "failed" and denounced it as imposing European norms on a society with very different values and norms. The famous "Needham question"—why Chinese science and technology, after first pulling ahead of Europe, were unable to keep pace with Europe's—remains, however, irrepressible (Needham 1969a, 16; Sivin 1994). A recent issue of *History of Technology* features a number of long essays dedicated to the very question.[34] One conclusion that seems acceptable to all sides in the debate is that there was nothing particularly exceptional about China; the flourishing of science and technology during the Tang and Song dynasties were followed by entrenchment and stagnation during the Ming and Qing dynasties, but there was nothing "unusual" about that retreat. Goldstone's summary statement, that it is typical for science to advance when different cultural and philosophical traditions are allowed to mix, but then for science to stagnate and even be reversed when conflict and disorder occur (Goldstone 2009, 141), is a typical example of the "revisionist" literature. What was exceptional was not what happened in China but what happened in Europe. Not only that the growth of useful knowledge did not run into some kind of barrier that stopped it in its track, but European approaches to how to acquire, vet, and disseminate it spread worldwide and eventually disrupted the equilibrium that had settled in the Middle East, in China, and elsewhere.[35]

As Kenneth Pomeranz and other members of the "California school" have suggested, as late as the middle of the eighteenth century in many dimensions China's economic institutions were not inferior to Europe's. It was commercial, monetized, educated, run by a professional bureaucracy, and able to generate and accommodate a very substantial population increase after 1680 or so without any obvious Malthusian effects. Yet some European thinkers, who may not have known much about China beyond the accounts of travelers and missionaries, sensed a difference even at that time. David Hume, for one, in his essay on the "Rise and Progress of the Arts and Sciences," made an argument similar to the one made above. He felt that political fragmentation was the main

---

34 It is worth noting that on the Needham question, O'Brien (2009, 23) can do no better than to return to the old Weberian chestnut that Confucian principles did not account for the world as a rational and explicable work of God, as if this philosophy had prevented science and technology from flourishing under the Song and as if "Confucian" did not refer to a highly diverse and often inconsistent set of principles (Bodde 1991, 344).

35 Needham cites (with some disapproval) Einstein's 1953 letter in which he says, "In my opinion one need not be astonished that the Chinese sages did not make these steps [the invention of formal logical systems and the search for causal relationships through controlled experiments]. The astonishing thing is that these discoveries were made at all" (Needham 1969a, 43).

reason behind European flourishing of useful knowledge. He was well aware of China's past achievements in science and technology and its sophisticated culture ("politeness" in eighteenth century parlance), but in his day he felt that Chinese science was making slow progress compared to Europe. The reason seemed clear to him: in China, he argued, the authority of one teacher was propagated easily from one corner of the Empire to another and "none had the courage to resist the torrent of popular opinion, and posterity was not bold enough to dispute what had been universally received by their ancestors" (Hume [1742] 1987, 122).[36]

The idea that European states and religions were in some kind of competitive market while Asia was ruled by large homogeneous empires is of course overdrawn (Goldstone 2009, 99–102). Persia, the Ottoman Empire, and the Mughals in northern India and their nemesis to the south, the Maratha Empire, competed as hard and as bloodily as Louis XIV and Frederick II in Europe, with the great battle of Panipat (north of Delhi) of 1761 being one of the most extensive and bloody clashes of the time. Religious competition, too, was comparable to Europe's with Islam divided among Sunni, Shiite, and other factions, yet competing with Hinduism in southern Asia. In China, the state, dominated by the official religion of Confucianism, suppressed Buddhism, which however flourished in southeast Asia. Within China itself, too, there were attempts to introduce a variety of heterodoxies including critiques of the ruling Neo-Confucian orthodoxy.[37]

The fact that competitive markets for ideas existed elsewhere does not mean that these markets operated in the same way they did in Europe. Competition between states is *not* like competition between firms or consumers in that there are no enforceable rules that tame and constrain the competitive process and set the parameters on what forms the competition can take. It could often resort to extreme violence or mindless trade wars and state-sponsored piracy, weakening the economy. But it could also take highly productive forms. In Europe, the competition among rulers to attract the most brilliant minds of the Continent weakened resistance to innovators, thus giving a chance to sixteenth-century intellectuals such as Luther, Paracelsus, Vesalius, and Copernicus to

36  Among the modern economic historians who have squarely blamed Chinese culture for China's falling behind Europe, most prominent is David Landes (1998, chap. 21; 2000). Most modern economic historians have taken a skeptical view of his position as "virtually unsupported assertions" (O'Brien 2009, 7) and "essentialist explanations" (Goody 2010).

37  As De Saeger (2008, 81) points out, patronage of scientists existed in China as well, they were limited to mathematics and astronomy (in part for astrological purposes). The main difference remains, however, that in China it was only at the imperial court that patronage was available, whereas in Europe many rulers competed for the best minds. This meant that in China the court controlled both the agenda and the contents of intellectual innovation, whereas in Europe they were determined as the result of a more decentralized process. As De Saeger remarks, "Patronage had an easier time escaping orthodoxy" (82).

successfully launch radical critiques of entrenched knowledge. In Asia, despite continuing warfare in many areas, there are few signs that states competed for the most prestigious scientists and artists.

In China, after its unification by the Ming in 1368, competition within the market for ideas gradually weakened and intellectual innovation was largely constrained by the limits of accepted philosophical tenets, perpetuated by the Neo-Confucian orthodoxy established by Zhu Xi in the twelfth century. If and when this orthodoxy was challenged, it was usually on the basis of alleged inconsistency with the classic teachings. The Mandarin civil service examinations, Needham insisted with some hyperbole, caused the system to "perpetuate itself through ten thousand generations" (Needham 1969b, 202). These examinations, in some opinions, remained the instrument through which the ancient texts became "an instrument of repressive conformity" (Huang 1981, 210).[38] European advances in science did filter into China through the activity of Jesuits, but apart from recalibrating their calendars, their impact was highly selective and not dramatic.[39] Had the Chinese authorities allowed other gates of entry besides Jesuits, perhaps the new approaches of Galileo and Newton might have made of an inroad. In Qing China there was a market for ideas, but barriers to entry were high, and the competition between incumbents and innovators often biased in favor of the former. This may sound odd in a land where there was no inquisition, and where there was no "index" of prohibited books. But perhaps the emergence of these institutions was a sign that in Europe the intellectual incumbents felt (justly) that they were more under threat. In China the Jesuits were allowed, but were controlled and constrained by the emperor's goodwill.

What was also missing in China was the ability of intellectuals to move to areas that were not under Chinese control. Consider the example of the

38  The effect of the imperial examination system on Chinese society has been a subject of some debate. But it is telling that in 1713 the Kangxi emperor proscribed questions dealing with natural studies in the civil examinations in an effort to keep divination and portents out of public discussion. Recent works in Qing natural studies and court translation projects on mathematical harmonics and astronomy were off-limits to examiners and examination candidates (Elman 2005, 168). For a discussion of this topic, see De Saeger (2008).

39  Deng (2009, 62) goes so far as to argue that the European influence on China's "knowledge stock" was hardly noticeable and that China "did not need European knowledge on a large scale." But Nathan Sivin has convincingly argued that China was exposed to European ideas in a heavily filtered way. He notes that "although the Jesuits' Chinese writings at first reflected conservative but open-minded current thinking, they gradually became hopelessly obsolete, out of touch with practice as well as theory. But the constraints under which they wrote, and the lack of competition from lay authors, and that the Jesuits meant that no one acknowledged or corrected crucial misstatements before the mid-nineteenth century" (Sivin [1973] 1995, 13). It is worth noting that the Jesuits did not expose China to the heliocentric view of the world until 1760. Needham (1956, 294) notes sarcastically that "one of the ironies of histories is that the Jesuits were proud of introducing to China the correct [Aristotelian] doctrine of the four elements—just half a century before Europe gave it up forever."

seventeenth-century Chinese scholar Chu Shun-Shui (1600–1682), one of the
few Chinese intellectuals who can be compared to a European intellectual in
his itinerancy. His knowledge was quite broad and extended to fields of practical knowledge such as architecture and crafts. He fled from China (he had
remained a supporter of the Ming dynasty, overthrown in 1644) first to Annam
(Vietnam) and then to Japan, where he had quite a following and eventually
became an advisor and mentor to the daimyo Mitsukuni. Chu Shun-Shui, in
Julia Ching's words, was hardly a purely abstract philosopher, but "the investigation of things referred to less to the metaphysical understanding of
principle of material forces, and more to coping with concrete situations. At the
same time, the extension of knowledge applied not only to knowledge of the
Confucian classics, but also to all that is useful in life" (Ching 1979, 217). This
may sound promising, but the fact remains that Chu's work remained unknown
in China until his rediscovery in the late nineteenth century. Having left his
homeland, he became a nonentity; this, in sharp contrast with Europe, where
reputations easily crossed boundaries.

The Chinese market for ideas rigidified in late Ming and especially in Qing
China, and became increasingly unaccommodating to intellectual innovation.
While in Europe the victory of the "moderns" relegated the classical canon to
a position in which they were admired and taught but treated with skepticism
and doubt, in China the two schools fought to a stalemate. The Neo-Confucian
annotated "four books" (*Sishu Jizhu*), written in the twelfth century by Zhu
Xi, remained as rigid a canon as the West ever had. At times, of course, it was
challenged, but contestability largely meant that Neo-Confucian doctrine
needed to be returned to the original meaning of Confucius and Mencius. The
kind of iconoclastic writers such as Ramus, Paracelsus, Gilbert, and Bacon who
completely dismissed and overthrew conventional wisdom in Europe in the
sixteenth century never took hold in China. Unlike what happened in Europe,
there was little political pluralism that "heretics" and intellectual innovators
could exploit to create a more competitive market for ideas. China grew into a
meritocracy gone awry. In a society in which public office remained "the most
important source of prestige and wealth" (Brandt, Ma, and Rawski 2014, 77),
the unassailability of these texts remained the most effective bulwark against
intellectual innovators.

How did potential intellectual innovators fare in China? An early attempt
at intellectual innovation that was more or less contemporaneous with the
European growing criticism of the "ancients" can be traced to the writings and
career of Li Zhi (1527–1602), a philosopher of heterodox inclinations, who
actually seems to have felt that one did not have to be a Confucian scholar
to be a philosopher, a truly iconoclastic position at the time (Jiang 2001, 13).
Certain views that we associate with the European radical enlightenment were
expressed by Li, including that self-interest was part of human nature and not

to be condemned, and that the pleasures of the flesh might be both virtuous and therapeutic. Huang (1981, 204) points out that Li's views were a threat to the Neo-Confucian doctrines of the dominant doctrines of Zhu Xi, and that if it were accepted that individuals could achieve the Great Unity in their own minds, much of the Confucian formal canon could be dispensed with. Such views would constitute a serious threat to the empire, "the integration of which relied to a large degree on the general acceptance of orthodox teachings by the educated elite." At least in that sense Li might be regarded as potentially as serious a threat as Martin Luther in Europe a generation or two earlier. Yet in China, the battle faced by such potential heretics was far much more uphill. Even the enfeebled late Ming Empire could coordinate the suppression of subversive ideas better than the European states.

Moreover, Li was no Galileo or Bacon. His concern was almost entirely an attempt to reconcile the undeniable private needs and desires of human beings with the obvious constraints of public morality. In any event, his heterodox views were extremely costly to him: following the publication of his heretical book *A Book to Burn*, he was arrested by the emperor's guard, jailed, and committed suicide in prison (Huang 1981, 189–221). To be sure, it is not entirely clear to what extent Li's heretical writings contributed to his fate, as opposed to his lifestyle and his pugnacious character. His career might be compared to that of his predecessor Wang Yangming (1472–1529). Wang was a successful and influential critic of Zhu Xi's thought, proposing a more idealist philosophy, and there seems to be little evidence that such criticism hurt his career as a general and administrator. For a while the more liberal approaches of Wang and his followers might have seemed to open the door to a more pluralistic approach to knowledge in China, all within the traditions of Neo-Confucianism.[40] But even in late Ming China, the authorities were able to confine innovative thinkers within the boundaries of what was permissible. Those who stepped outside those boundaries, such as Li Zhi and the populist thinker Ho Hsin-yin (1517–79), died in jail.

Another remarkable innovator in late Ming dynasty was Xu Guangqi (1562–1633). Xu's career and views in some ways mirror those of his contemporary Francis Bacon, and he shared Bacon's belief in what is known in China as *shiyong* (the practical application of knowledge in pursuit of social order).[41] His commitment to learning was motivated by the belief that it could be used to save the country, not only by military means, but also by applying science and

---

40   Needham compares Wang's views to those of such giants of western philosophy as Berkeley and Kant, but adds that "unfortunately all this, sublime as it was, could hardly be sympathetic to the development of natural science. . . . Wang could never understand the basic principle of scientific method" (Ronan and Needham 1978, 252).

41   This term is proposed by Bray and Métailié (2001, 323).

technology to make the country prosperous and powerful (Qi 2001, 361). In that regard, his beliefs are distinctly reminiscent of Bacon's, despite the obvious differences. Xu was a high-level official in the imperial administration (at the time of his death he was both deputy prime minister and minister of "rites," roughly culture and education). He was responsible for reforming the Chinese calendar based on more accurate astronomical data he learned from the Jesuits, who had access to the work of Brahe and Kepler. Remarkably, he converted to Christianity in 1603 (subsequently becoming known as "Dr. Paul") and was a close collaborator of the Jesuit missionary Father Matteo Ricci, with whom he translated Euclid's *Elements of Geometry*. Perhaps his most astonishing contribution was his monumental *Nongzheng quanshu*, an agricultural treatise published posthumously in 1639 that summarized much existing knowledge of Chinese agriculture, but also illustrated his firm belief in the importance of experimentation in augmenting knowledge in farming. The book was vast, containing seven hundred thousand Chinese characters (Bray 1984, 66). It was, by the standards of that time on any continent, full of progressive ideas. Xu reported a great deal of agricultural experimentation, at least some of which he carried out himself. He also advocated the new crops that were being introduced into China from the New World, and condemned conservative farmers reluctant to adopt new crops such as sweet potatoes because of their mistaken belief that crops will grow well only where they originated (Bray and Métailié 2001, 341). He was a practical intellect, who endorsed concrete studies (*shixue*) and perhaps serves as an indication of where Chinese intellectual innovators could have gone had they lived in a different polity (Zurndorfer 2009, 82). Yet unlike Diderot's Encyclopedia, Xu's work was not widely disseminated, and one widely traveled early Qing scholar, Lio Xanting (1648–95), complained that in ten years of searching he had not been able to find a single copy (Bray and Métailié 2001, 355).[42] No new edition appeared for two centuries. The comparison with the rapid diffusion of eighteenth-century encyclopedias in Europe is perhaps emblematic of the difference between the Chinese and European environments.

None of the late Ming writers directly challenged and refuted the basic canon of Chinese metaphysics. All the same, De Bary (1975) and Jiang (2001) are correct in noting that the various modernizing and innovative views of the world thrived in a limited way in the late Ming period.[43] What was decisive was that these tendencies could not survive what De Bary calls the Manchu

42   Bray (1984, 70) also notes that Xu's detailed program of reforming agricultural administration was never put into practice.

43   All the same, commenting on the deaths of Li Zhi and Ho Hsin-yin and a similar fate that befell another heterodox writer of his age, Tzu-po Ta-kuan (1544–1604), a contemporary noted that "if anyone behaved like a heretic, he will of course be killed. Li Zhi and Ta-kuan are good object lessons" (Kengo 1975, 60).

suppression." If it is true, as Jami (2012) and others have suggested, that the rise of the Qing dynasty was decisive to the fate of the development of science in China, it underlines the difference with Europe: there were repressive and reactionary regimes in Europe, but the high level of interstate competitiveness constrained their ability to enforce a specific orthodoxy, both because such an orthodoxy would have negative effects on their military capability and political prestige, and because it might deprive them of some of their most useful citizens. If all rulers had been rational, therefore, we would never have seen any suppression in Europe. In fact, such events did occur, the most notorious being the expulsion of Spain's Moriscos in 1609 and the revocation of the Edict of Nantes in 1685 in France. But in Europe's institutional environment, all such decisions did was to shift around *where* intellectual innovation would occur, but it could not stop it altogether.

Nothing like the open and competitive Republic of Letters emerged in China. That is not to say that Chinese intellectual life was lacking in dynamics. The Chinese attempt at Enlightenment in the seventeenth and eighteenth centuries was known as the school of *kaozheng* or "evidentiary research." In this school, abstract ideas and moral values gave way as subjects for discussion to concrete facts, documented institutions, and historical events (Elman 2001, 4). Chinese scholarship of this period was "not inherently antipathetic to scientific study or resistant to new ideas" (De Bary 1975, 205). It was based on rigorous research, demanded proof and evidence for statements, and shunned away from leaps of faith and speculation. It all sounded quite promising, but in the end these scholars were primarily interested in philology, linguistics, and historical studies "confident that these would lead to greater certainty about what the true words and intentions of China's ancient sages had been and, hence, to a better understanding of how to live in the present" (Spence 1990, 103). Equally significantly, unlike the European Enlightenment, the kaozheng movement remained of, by, and for the mandarinate, the ruling Confucian elite, which by most accounts had little interest in material progress.

The literature about the "Chinese Enlightenment" may have overstated its bias toward literary and philological topics. There was considerable interest in astronomy and mathematics, and Chinese scholars carefully examined useful knowledge that seeped in from the West. Scholars such as Mei Wending (1633–1721) carefully compared Western mathematics and astronomy to Chinese knowledge, and pointed to the advances that the West had made. Chinese scholars, however, often made an effort to try to show that this knowledge had already existed in ancient China, indicating the difficulty they had in ridding themselves of the burden of the "ancients." Mei convinced the Kangxi emperor that European learning was derivative from the Chinese and that the only source of reliable knowledge was the ancient learning of China (Elman 2005, 236). Yet Mei's rhetoric in his book *Lixue yiwen* (Doubts concerning the study of astronomy, 1693) illustrates the fundamental constraints that the accumulation and application of useful knowledge in China was subject to. First, in Mei's work the moderns are in no way superior to the ancients, and there is no progress in history; indeed "the accumulation of human knowledge is merely a token of the ancients' superior merit" (Jami 2012, 220). Second, he argued that the new astronomical knowledge such as the rotundity of the earth, while in its current version originating in Europe, had been present in China all along and thus was not foreign at all. Thus, Chinese sources invalidated in his view the claim of Westerners that they knew better (Jami 2012, 222). It was in this direction that kaozheng scholarship was increasingly applied. No such need to assert their originality seems to have been present in Europe. They borrowed useful knowledge freely from their ancestors and from foreign civilizations, acknowledging these as needed, and then went on to improve the techniques.

Unlike Europe, then, China found it difficult to shake loose from the iron grasp of the past. Mathematics, medicine, and most other forms of useful knowledge were studied and reflected on, but remained a branch of classical studies. Attempts to apply this knowledge to practical uses were taking place, and when new ideas or products appeared, the Chinese were not averse to them. But it never got to the point at which natural philosophy made material progress one of its raisons d'être. The wholesale shredding of the wisdom of earlier writers, at times quite impudently so, that was characteristic of many European writers of the sixteenth and seventeenth centuries did not catch on in China. The weight of past knowledge kept burdening and constraining original scholarship. Even Xu Guangqi massive treatise on agriculture was backward-looking: it was based for over 90 percent on citations of earlier writers (Bray and Métailié 2001, 337).[44] The work of Gu Yanwu (1613–82), one of the founding intellectuals of the kaozheng school, is revealing. Sometimes pictured as a kind of Chinese version of Arthur Young (e.g., Morris 2010, 473), Gu and his work are emblematic of the new Chinese scholarship: it was far more rigorous, and rational, and based on extensive traveling in China, where he acquired firsthand information. But it was mostly information based on philology, archaeology, and the careful analysis of early works.[45] Gu's interests were mostly historical and textual studies and politics.

A likely member of the kaozheng school to introduce a new spirit of investigation into useful knowledge may have been Fang Yizhi (1611–71). Fang published a book meaningfully titled *Small Encyclopedia of the Principles of*

44  Sivin (1975, 161) notes that "in China the new tools were used to rediscover and recast the lost mathematical astronomy of the past and thus to perpetuate traditional values rather than to replace them."

45  His magnum opus, *Ri-zhi-lu* or *Jih-chih lu* (Daily accumulation of knowledge) is a treasure of information, but is definitely stronger on Confucian classics, history, ceremony, and administration than on matters of great practical knowledge.

*Things*, which discussed potentially useful forms of propositional knowledge such as meteorology and geography. He was familiar with Western writings and quite influential in the kaozheng school of the eighteenth century. Peterson (1974, 401) has gone so far as to suggest that Fang was representative of the possibility in the seventeenth century that the realm of "things" to be investigated would center on physical objects, technology, and natural phenomena. He argued that Fang's work paralleled the secularization of science in Europe. The real question, then, becomes this: what was different about China and the West that Fang did not become a figure comparable to Bacon, and that his new ideas remained a only "possibility"?[46]

Another suggestive example of the Chinese market for ideas is the scholar and philosopher Dai Zhen (or Tai Chen, 1724–77). Dai Zhen was one of the dominant figures in the kaozheng movement, and his insistence on evidence and his mathematical capabilities would appear to make him comparable to European contemporaries. One historian described him as someone who was "a truly scientific spirit . . . whose principles hardly differed from those which in the West made possible the progress of the exact sciences" (Gernet 1982, 513). Yet by "evidence" he did not mean anything that Newton or Boyle would have been interested in—for him the focus of research was philology and phonology, exegesizing the writings of earlier generations. As such, he reinterpreted the writings of Confucius and tried to reconcile the teachings of two of Confucius's most illustrious followers, Mencius and his opponent Xunzi, and opposed the Neo-Confucian philosophy of the Song era. As such, he did criticize the writings of earlier authorities such as the Zhu Xi, but largely on the grounds that the latter had misinterpreted earlier and more authoritative sages, not on the basis of observation or experiment. The Chinese were unable to entirely liberate themselves from the shackles of their ancient classical learning.[47]

The kaozheng medical literature had its own debate of "Ancients versus Moderns," but ironically it differs from Europe's in critical dimensions: first,

---

46   Sivin (1975, 166) is far more skeptical of Fang's abilities and has compared him with European medieval scholasticism, feeling that his work was "antiquated." He points out that Fang's ideal research methodology depended on hearsay and books, not on experiment, and that "in short, the scientific revolution in seventeenth-century China was in the main a response to outmoded knowledge that gave little attention to, and consistently misrepresented, the significance of developments in the direction of modern science." Needham (1986, 137) refers to Fang as "slightly muddle-headed."

47   A telling example is the adoption of the telescope, clearly a European invention, to the study of astronomy (Huff 2011, 110–14). The telescope was introduced into China by the Jesuit missionaries, but their star catalogues were not expanded at a rate similar to that achieved by telescope-equipped European astronomers such as John Flamsteed. Huff attributes this difference to a "curiosity deficit" in China, but one cannot understand this difference without a deeper examination of the institutional and political environment in which the accumulation of useful knowledge operated.

the "ancients" were the classical writers of the Han dynasty, and the "moderns" were the writers of the Song era (still three of four centuries past); and second, the "innovative" scholars favored the earlier writers (Elman 2005, 232–36). There were no Chinese equivalents of Paracelsus and Vesalius, who threw all caution to the winds and trusted only what they (believed they) saw in the concrete evidence. Little wonder then that the verdict of historians has been that "this scientific spirit was applied almost exclusively to the investigation of the past" (Gernet 1982, 513).

What, then, explains the Needham puzzle? One tantalizing clue is a famous remark by Nathan Sivin that China has sciences but no Science (Sivin 1994, 533). In this view, China paradoxically lacked a unifying single coordinating mind, whose commanding authority imposed a set of assumptions and methods that were respected by all other agents competing in the market for ideas. In Europe, despite the political fragmentation, the market for ideas worked well enough to allow such intellectual entrepreneurs to flourish, even if they were rare and far in between. Such a "focal point" in a market for ideas, as long as it does not degenerate into an uncontestable authority figure, is a sign of a well-working market (comparable in some ways to a single price). Isaac Newton played exactly that role, as did Descartes, Galileo, Lavoisier, and a few others (Mokyr 2013). What made such entrepreneurs possible was that in Europe sacred cows were increasingly being led to the slaughterhouse. What Europe did to Aristotle, Ptolemy, and Galen, Chinese intellectuals could not do onto Confucius, Mencius, and Xunzi.

## THE MARKET FOR IDEAS AND THE INDUSTRIAL REVOLUTION

How does all this relate to economic history? The Great Puzzle cannot be resolved unless we recognize how culture affected the institutions that unleashed the avalanche of useful knowledge that eventually fueled the European Industrial Revolution. Despite the beliefs of David Landes and Max Weber, there was nothing *inherently* different about European culture that made it inevitably more innovative. An emphasis on the Judeo-Christian tradition, the legacy of classical civilization, or the heritage of feudalism (to cite just three historical differences) all make little sense. What made the difference were the unintended consequences of institutions such as the Republic of Letters and an intellectual ferment that arose as the result of historical contingencies and as the by-product of largely unrelated phenomena. Christianity, the belief in a personal God, and many other supposed metaphysical differences mattered insofar as they affected the outcomes in the market for ideas. Metaphysical beliefs may have prepared some minds for the ideas of economic progress through useful knowledge, but they might just as well have ended in a repressive and reactionary world of intellectual stagnation, in which intellectual innovators were strongly discouraged from proposing new ideas or never had a chance to enter the market for ideas.

The main novel insight that gained a large following in Enlightenment Europe, that economic and social progress could and should be attained by the accumulation of useful knowledge, was certainly not in direct contradiction with Chinese culture, and as we saw, some Ming and Qing intellectuals moved in that direction. But because the market for ideas was insufficiently competitive, innovators were insufficiently incentivized and protected, and the few radical intellectual innovators lost out. It was not until the late nineteenth century that China was sufficiently shocked by a sequence of political disasters that its institutions were dramatically revamped to change how useful knowledge was deployed.

Such a commitment to past knowledge may seem more surprising in a society such as China's, without institutionalized religion and without an organized caste of priests, rabbis, or mullahs who interpreted the sacred writings of the past. One explanation may be the huge investment of human capital in the classical writings of the past in the hope of passing the Ming civil service examination. The vast bulk of candidates failed these exams in local competitions, and large reservoirs of classically trained men were still looking for ways to extract some rents from their human capital. These people also constituted a vast audience for the books published at the time. The first three Qing emperors, who ruled for more than a century, sought to appropriate the classical legacy to "establish their dynamic prestige and political legitimacy" (Elman 2005, 238). But more generally, the often disrespectful skepticism toward the formerly sacrosanct knowledge of earlier generations that awoke in Europe when more and more beliefs of ancient authorities were questioned, tested, and found wanting by European scientists and physicians was rarely allowed to arise in China.[48]

Was there no concept of "progress" among Chinese intellectuals? In a long essay, Needham (1969c, 280) reacted to Edgar Zilsel's (1945, 325) remark that the idea of progress in useful knowledge had never occurred to Brahman, Muslim, Confucian, or Latin scholars by remarking that "he would have done better to leave Confucian scholars out of it." Needham argued that the "idea of cumulative disinterested cooperative enterprise in amassing scientific information was much more customary in medieval China than anywhere in the pre-Renaissance West."[49] Other experts have disagreed: it was pointed out

48   Even Jack Goody (2009, 238), who goes out of his way to condemn "essentialist" interpretations of Chinese history, writes that "characteristic of the cultural history of China has been a constant looking back to the Confucian classics, to 'Antiquity,' providing a continuous point of reference for both conservatives and reformers."

49   Needham adds (1969c, 277) that "no mathematician or astronomer in any Chinese century would have dreamed of denying a continual progress and improvement in the sciences they professed."

that Daoist thought felt overall that if there was a trend in history, it led from paradise to corruption; it was argued that the decline began only after early sage-kings had completed their "civilizing work" on society and that while both "cyclical" and "linear" dynamics can be found in Chinese reflections on history, the cyclical element clearly dominated (Bodde 1991, 122–33). In general, most Chinese thinkers, insofar that they recognized a trend, felt that the past was better than the present or that at worst history was a cyclical but stationary process. Strikingly, Needham's evidence for belief in progress is entirely taken from pre-Ming China, and the idea shrank and withered in China just as it was emerging triumphant in parts of Europe. Needham concedes that the effects of innovation in China were never quite as profound as in Europe and that the same innovations that dramatically altered the course of history in Europe "left Chinese society relatively unmoved" (Needham 1969c, 284).[50]

The modern idea of progress was largely a European invention, and despite some precursors, clearly emerged triumphant only in the eighteenth century. It was (and still is) seriously contested in Europe, and there is no a priori reason for it to have triumphed ineluctably. The outcomes in market for ideas eventually changed the institutions in which intellectual innovation functioned. In early modern Europe stronger incentives for such innovators emerged, from intellectual property rights to a variety of rewards and patronage positions. The economic significance of the victory of the idea of progress for the Industrial Enlightenment and the subsequent economic development of Europe is hard to quantify, but seems undeniable. After all, it was one thing to formulate a theory of progress; it was quite another to devise a detailed program of institutional change that would actually bring it about. The result was that in the eighteenth century, especially after 1760, Western Europe entered a regime of accelerated innovation that ended up changing the world.

The Industrial Revolution had many complex causes (Mokyr 1998), but at its foundation was a cultural belief in progress of a particular kind. Progress was to be achieved not by the perfection of morals or the attainment of freedom or even by the reform of political institutions (though these mattered as well), but above all by mastery over nature and the ensuing technological improvements. That such progress was possible and how it was to be achieved were decided in the market for ideas, and studying that market is an important task for economic history.

---

50 Compare this with the more recent statement of Frederic Mote (1999, 966): "Self-renovating change was constant and gradual, no sudden and disruptive and always justified by reference to past models. . . . [China] presents the fascinating enigma of archaism serving the cause of renovating change."

## ACKNOWLEDGMENTS

The helpful comments of Avner Greif, Lynne Kiesling, John Nye, and Nicolas Ziebarth on an earlier version are acknowledged.

## BIBLIOGRAPHY

Acemoglu, Daron, Simon Johnson, and James Robinson. 2005. "Institutions as a Fundamental Cause of Economic Growth." In *Handbook of Economic Growth*, edited by Philippe Aghion and Steven Durlauf, 385–465. Amsterdam: Elsevier.

Acemoglu, Daron, and James Robinson. 2006. "De Facto Political Power and Institutional Persistence." *American Economic Review* 96 (2): 325–30.

———. 2012. *Why Nations Fail: The Origins of Power, Prosperity, and Poverty*. New York: Crown.

Bacon, Francis. 1999. *Selected Philosophical Works*. Edited by Rose-Mary Sargent. Indianapolis: Hackett.

Bayle, Pierre. (1696–97). 1734. *The Dictionary Historical and Critical of Mr Peter Bayle. The Second Edition, Carefully Collated . . . by Mr Des Maizeaux, Fellow of the Royal Society*. London: J.J. and P. Knapton.

Becker, Carl L. 1932. *The Heavenly City of the Eighteenth-Century Philosophers*. New Haven, CT: Yale University Press.

Benrath, Karl. 1877. *Bernardino Ochino, of Siena*. New York: Robert Carter.

Bisin, Alberto, and Thierry Verdier. 2001. "The Economics of Cultural Transmission and the Dynamics of Preferences." *Journal of Economic Theory* 97: 298–319.

Bodde, Derk. 1991. *Chinese Thought, Society, and Science*. Honolulu: University of Hawaii Press.

Botticini, Maristella, and Zvi Eckstein. 2012. *The Chosen Few: How Education Shaped Jewish History 70–1492*. Princeton: Princeton University Press.

Bowles, Samuel. 2004. *Microeconomics: Behavior, Institutions, and Evolution*. Princeton: Princeton University Press.

Boyd, Robert, and Peter J. Richerson. 2005. *The Origins and Evolution of Cultures*. Oxford: Oxford University Press.

Brandt, Loren, Debin Ma, and Thomas G. Rawski. 2014. "From Divergence to Convergence: Reevaluating the History behind China's Economic Boom." *Journal of Economic Literature* 52 (1): 45–123.

Bray, Francesca. 1984. *Agriculture. Science and Civilization in China*, vol. 6, pt. 2, edited by Joseph Needham. Cambridge: Cambridge University Press.

Bray, Francesca, and George Métailié. 2001. "Who Was the Author of the Nongzhen Quanshu?" In *Statecraft and Intellectual Renewal in Late Ming China: The Cross-Cultural Synthesis of Xu Guangqi (1562–1633)*, edited by Catherine Jami, Peter Engelfriet, and Gregory Blue, 322–59. Leiden: Brill.

Bury, J. B. (1932) 1955. *The Idea of Progress: An Inquiry into Its Growth and Origin*. New York: Dover.

Ching, Julia. 1979. "The Practical Learning of Chu Shun-Shui, 1600–1682." In *Principle and Practicality: Essays in Neo-Confucianism and Practical Learning*, edited by W. Theodore De Bary and Irene Bloom, 189–229. New York: Columbia University Press.

Clarke, John. 1737. *An Essay upon Study*. 2nd ed. London: A. Bettesworth and C. Hitch.

Cohn, Norman. 1961. *The Pursuit of the Millennium*. New York: Harper Torchbooks.

Comte, Auguste. 1856. *Social Physics from the Positive Philosophy*. New York: Calvin Blanchard.

David, Paul A. 2004. "Patronage, Reputation, and Common Agency Contracting in the Scientific Revolution." Manuscript, Stanford University.

———. 2008. "The Historical Origins of 'Open Science': An Essay on Patronage, Reputation and Common Agency Contracting in the Scientific Revolution." *Capitalism and Society* 3 (2): 1–103.

Dear, Peter. 2006. *The Intelligibility of Nature: How Science Makes Sense of the World*. Chicago: University of Chicago Press.

De Bary, W. Theodore. 1975. "Neo-Confucian Cultivation and the Seventeenth-Century 'Enlightenment.'" In *The Unfolding of Neo-Confucianism*, edited by W. Theodore De Bary, 141–206. New York: Columbia University Press.

Deng, Kent. 2009. "Movers and Shakers of Knowledge in China during the Ming-Qing Period." *History of Technology* 29: 57–79.

De Saeger, David. 2008. "The Imperial Examinations and Epistemological Obstacles." *Philosophica* 82: 55–85.

Doepke, Matthias, and Fabrizio Zilibotti. 2008. "Occupational Choice and the Spirit of Capitalism." *Quarterly Journal of Economics* 123 (2): 747–93.

Elman, Benjamin. 2001. *From Philosophy to Philology: Intellectual and Social Aspects of Change in Late Imperial China*. 2nd ed. Los Angeles: UCLA Asia-Pacific Institute.

———. 2005. *On Their Own Terms: Science in China, 1550–1900*. Cambridge, MA: Harvard University Press.

Flinn, Michael W. 1966. *Origins of the Industrial Revolution*. London: Longmans.

Gernet, Jacques. 1982. *A History of Chinese Civilization*. Cambridge: Cambridge University Press.

Glanvill, Joseph. 1665. *Scepsis Scientifica, or, Confest Ignorance, the Way to Science*. London: Printed by E. Cotes for Henry Eversden.

———. 1668. *Plus Ultra; or, The Progress and Advancement of Knowledge since the Days of Aristotle*. . . . London: Printed for James Collins.

Goldgar, Anne. 1995. *Impolite Learning: Conduct and Community in the Republic of Letters, 1680–1750*. New Haven, CT: Yale University Press.

Goldstone, Jack. 2009. *Why Europe? The Rise of the West in World History, 1500–1850*. Boston: McGraw-Hill.

Goody, Jack. 2009. *Renaissances: The One or the Many?* Cambridge: Cambridge University Press.

———. 2010. *The Eurasian Miracle*. Cambridge: Polity.

Greif, Avner. 1994. "Cultural Beliefs and the Organization of Society: A Historical and Theoretical Reflection on Collectivist and Individualist Societies." *Journal of Political Economy* 102 (5): 912–50.

———. 2005. *Institutions and the Path to the Modern Economy: Lessons from Medieval Trade*. Cambridge: Cambridge University Press.

Headley, John M. 1997. *Tommaso Campanella and the Transformation of the World*. Princeton: Princeton University Press.

Helsham, Richard. 1755. *A Course of Lectures in Natural Philosophy*. London: J. Nourse at the Lamb.

Huang, Ray. 1981. *1587: A Year of No Significance*. New Haven, CT: Yale University Press.

Huff, Toby. 2011. *Intellectual Curiosity and the Scientific Revolution*. Cambridge: Cambridge University Press.

Hume, David. (1742) 1985. "Of the Rise and Progress of the Arts and Sciences." In *Essays: Moral, Political and Literary*, edited by Eugene F. Miller, 112–38. Indianapolis: Liberty Fund.

Israel, Jonathan. 2010. *A Revolution of the Mind*. Princeton: Princeton University Press.

Jami, Catherine. 2012. *The Emperor's New Mathematics: Western Learning and Imperial Authority during the Kangxi Reign (1662–1722)*. Oxford: Oxford University Press.

Jiang, Jin. 2001. "Heresy and Persecution in Late Ming Society: Reinterpreting the Case of Li Zhi." *Late Imperial China* 22 (2): 1–34.

Jones, Eric L. 2006. *Cultures Merging: A Historical and Economic Critique of Culture*. Princeton: Princeton University Press.

Jones, Richard Foster. (1936) 1961. *Ancients and Moderns: A Study in the Rise of the Scientific Movement in 17th Century England*. 2nd ed. St. Louis: Washington University Press.

Kaplan, Robert. 1999. *The Nothing That Is*. Oxford: Oxford University Press.

Keller, Vera. 2012. "Accounting for Invention: Guido Pancirolli's Lost and Found Things and Desiderata." *Journal of the History of Ideas* 73 (2): 223–45.

Kengo, Araki. 1975. "Confucianism and Buddhism in the Late Ming." In *The Unfolding of Neo-Confucianism*, edited by W. Theodore De Bary, 39–66. New York: Columbia University Press.

Kesten, Hermann. 1945. *Copernicus and His World*. New York: Roy.

Landes, David S. 1998. *The Wealth and Poverty of Nations*. New York: Norton.

———. 2000. "Culture Makes Almost All the Difference." In *Culture Matters: How Values Shape Human Progress*, edited by Lawrence E. Harrison and Samuel P. Huntington, 1–13. New York: Basic Books.

Lasch, Christopher. 1991. *The True and Only Heaven: Progress and Its Critics*. New York: Norton.

Levine, Joseph M. 1981. "Ancients and Moderns Reconsidered." *Eighteenth Century Studies* 15 (1): 72–89.

Maimonides (Rabbi Moshe ben Maimon). *Mishneh Torah*. http://www.chabad.org/library/article_cdo/aid/911896/jewish/Teshuvah-Chapter-Three.htm.

McCloskey, Deirdre. 2006. *The Bourgeois Virtues: Ethics for an Age of Commerce*. Chicago: University of Chicago Press.

Merton, Robert K. (1938) 2001. *Science, Technology, and Society in Seventeenth-Century England*. New York: Howard Fertig Press.

———. 1973. *The Sociology of Science*. Chicago: University of Chicago Press.

Mesoudi, Alex. 2011. *Cultural Evolution*. Chicago: University of Chicago Press.

Mokyr, Joel. 1998. "Editor's Introduction: The New Economic History and the Industrial Revolution." In *The British Industrial Revolution: An Economic Perspective*, edited by Joel Mokyr, 1–127. Boulder, CO: Westview.

———. 2005. "The Intellectual Origins of Modern Economic Growth." *Journal of Economic History* 65 (2): 285–351.

———. 2008. "The Institutional Origins of the Industrial Revolution." In *Institutions and Economic Performance*, edited by Elhanan Helpman, 64–119. Cambridge, MA: Harvard University Press.

———. 2009a. *The Enlightened Economy*. New Haven, CT: Yale University Press.

———. 2009b. "Intellectual Property Rights, the Industrial Revolution, and the Beginnings of Modern Economic Growth." *American Economic Review* 99 (2): 349–55.

———. 2011–12. "The Commons of Knowledge: A Historical Perspective." In *The Wealth and Well-Being of Nations*, vol. 4, edited by Emily Chamlee-Wright, 29–44. Beloit: Beloit College Press.

———. 2014. "Culture, Institutions, and Modern Growth." In *Economic Institutions, Rights, Growth, and Sustainability: The Legacy of Douglass North*, edited by Itai Sened, 151–91. Cambridge: Cambridge University Press.

Morris, Ian. 2010. *Why the West Rules—For Now*. New York: Farrar, Strauss and Giroux.

Mote, Frederick W. 1999. *Imperial China, 900–1800*. Cambridge, MA: Harvard University Press.

Needham, Joseph. 1969a. "Poverties and Triumphs of the Chinese Scientific Tradition." In *The Grand Titration*, 14–54. Toronto: Toronto University Press.

———. 1969b. "Science and Society in East and West." In *The Grand Titration*, 190–217. Toronto: Toronto University Press.

———. 1969c. "Time and Eastern Man." In *The Grand Titration*, 218–98. Toronto: Toronto University Press.

———. 1986. "Chemicals and Chemical Technology." In *Science and Civilization in China*, vol. 5, pt. 7, edited by Joseph Needham. Cambridge: Cambridge University Press.

———. 2004. "Science and Chinese Society, pt. 2: General Conclusions and Reflections." In *Science and Civilization in China*, vol. 7, edited by Girdwood Robinson. Cambridge: Cambridge University Press.

Nisbet, Robert. 1979. "The Idea of Progress: A Bibliographical Essay." *Literature of Liberty* 2 (1). http://oll.libertyfund.org/?option=com_content&task=view&id=165&Itemid=259.

———. (1994) 2008. *History of the Idea of Progress.* 2nd ed. New Brunswick, NJ: Transaction.

O'Brien, Patrick. 2009. "The Needham Question Updated: A Historiographical Survey and Elaboration." *History of Technology* 29: 7–28.

Oldenburg, Henry. 1665. "The Introduction." *Philosophical Transactions of the Royal Society* 1. http://www.gutenberg.org/files/28758/28758-h/28758-h.htm.

Peterson, Willard. 1974. "Fang-I-Chih: Western Learning and the 'Investigation of Things.'" In *The Unfolding of Neo-Confucianism*, edited by W. Theodore De Bary, 369–411. New York: Columbia University Press.

Qi, Han. 2001. "Astronomy, Chinese and Western: The Influence of Xu Guangqi's views in the Early and Mid-Qing." In *Statecraft and Intellectual Renewal in Late Ming China: The Cross-Cultural Synthesis of Xu Guangqi (1562-1633)*, edited by Catherine Jami, Peter Engelfriet, and Gregory Blue, 360–79. Leiden: Brill.

Reston, James. 1994. *Galileo: A Life.* New York: HarperCollins.

Robertson, John. 1997. "The Enlightenment above National Context: Political Economy in Eighteenth-Century Scotland and Naples." *Historical Journal* 40 (3): 667–97.

Ronan, Colin A., and Joseph Needham. 1978. *The Shorter Science and Civilisation in China.* Vol. 1. Cambridge: Cambridge University Press.

Seed, Patricia. 2001. "Jewish Scientists and the Origin of Modern Navigation." In *Jews & the Expansion of Europe to the West, 1450-1800*, edited by Paolo Bernardini and Norman Fiering, 73–85. New York: Berghahn Books.

Sivin, Nathan. (1973) 1995. "Copernicus in China, or Good Intentions Gone Astray." *Studia Copernicana, Colloquia Copernicana* 2 (6): 63–122. Reprinted in Sivin, *Science in Ancient China. Researches and Reflections.* Aldershot: Variorum. http://ccat.sas.upenn.edu/~nsivin/cop.pdf.

———. 1975. "Wang Hsi-shan." In *Dictionary of Scientific Biography*, vol. 14, edited by Charles Coulston Gillispie, 159–68. New York: Scribner.

———. 1994. "Why the Scientific Revolution Did Not Take Place in China—or Didn't It?" In *Transformation and Tradition in the Sciences*, edited by Everett Mendelsohn, 531–54. Cambridge: Cambridge University Press. Reprinted in Sivin, *Science in Ancient China. Researches and Reflections.* Aldershot: Variorum. http://ccat.sas.upenn.edu/~nsivin/cop.pdf.

Spadafora, David. 1990. *The Idea of Progress in Eighteenth-Century Britain.* New Haven, CT: Yale University Press.

Spence, Jonathan. 1990. *The Search for Modern China.* New York: Norton.

Stone, Lawrence. 1969. "Literacy and Education in England 1640-1900." *Past & Present*, no. 42: 69–139.

Stubbe, Henry. 1670. *Campanella Revived or an Enquiry into the History of the Royal Society.* London.

Swift, Jonathan. (1704) 1720. *A Full and True Account of the Battle Fought Last Friday between the Ancient and the Modern Books in Saint James's Library.* In *Miscellaneous Works, Comical & Diverting . . . I. The Tale of a Tub; with the Fragment, & the Battel of the Books.* London: Order of the Society de Propagando.

Tabellini, Guido. 2008. "Institutions and Culture (Presidential Address)." *Journal of the European Economic Association* 6 (2–3): 255–94.

———. 2010. "Culture and Institutions: Economic Development in the Regions of Europe." *Journal of the European Economic Association* 8 (4): 677–716.

Traugott, John. 1994. "Review of Joseph Levine, *The Battle of the Books: History and Literature in the Augustan Age*." *Modern Philology* 91 (4): 501–8.

Webster, Charles. (1975) 2002. *The Great Instauration: Science, Medicine and Reform, 1626-1660.* 2nd ed. Bern: Peter Lang.

Wilkins, John. (1640) 1708. "The Discovery of a New World." In *The Mathematical and Philosophical Works of the Right Reverend, Late Lord Bishop of Chester*. London: J. Nicholson.

Zak, Paul J., and Stephen Knack. 2001. "Trust and Growth." *Economic Journal* 111 (470): 295–321.

Zilsel, Edgar. 1945. "The Genesis of the Concept of Scientific Progress." *Journal of the History of Ideas* 6 (3): 325–49.

Zurndorfer, Harriet T. 2009. "China and Science on the Eve of the 'Great Divergence' 1600–1800: A Review of Recent Revisionist Scholarship." *History of Technology* 29: 81–101.

## PART I

# INSTITUTIONS

# COERCION AND EXCHANGE

How Did Markets Evolve?

## AVNER GREIF

Surprisingly little is known about why institutions gradually evolved to support a larger set of exchange relations in some economies and not others. This limits the ability to address questions central to economic history and economic development. Why did the modern market economy, characterized by impersonal exchange and formal institutions, first emerge in the West? Why did similar developments not transpire in, for example, China or the Muslim world, whose markets had initially been more developed than Europe's? Identifying the institutional determinants of distinct trajectories of market development is important to understanding why some economies are rich and others are poor and what factors limit development.

The literature has identified two conditions necessary for market economy: the security of property rights and contract enforceability.[1] The analysis of insecurity focused on the conditions under which confiscatory taxation is limited by an expected economic or political retribution by the economic agents. The analysis of contract enforceability focused on analyzing various contract-enforcement institutions and their interrelations. Central to this analysis is the distinction between private-order contract enforcement institutions (such as reputation-based institutions) that do not rely on the coercive power of the state and public-order contract-enforcement institutions (such as the legal system) that do. This rich literature provides little insight regarding the mechanisms underpinning the dynamic of market development.[2] It does not explain why the scope of exchange has increased in some market economies more than in others.

This chapter argues that the compatibility between institutions that secure property rights and the institutions that enforce contracts determine market evolution.[3] Specifically, *coercion-constraining institutions* (CCIs) determine the

---

1 Greif (2006) provides a recent survey of this literature.

2 North and Weingast (1989) argued that political institutions limiting rulers' discretions foster financial markets. Greif (1994) argued that individualism and collectivism determine demand for legal contract enforcement. Fafchamps (2004) presents a model of market expansion caused by scale economies.

3 This chapter builds on Greif (2005).

cost and benefit of using coercive power to abuse property rights.[4] Various combinations of CCIs and contract-enforcement institutions can support markets. Yet, CCIs differentially enable market expansion based on the introduction of public-order, contract-enforcement institutions that underpin the rise of the modern market economy. In particular, CCIs under which property rights are secured based on the state's limited administrative capacity to abuse rights are incompatible with public-order contract enforcement. This incompatibility reflects that public order fosters the capacity of the state to abuse rights. Introducing such public-order contract enforcement institutions—improving the capacity to use force to capture property—therefore undermines the security of property rights and causes markets to contact. The efficiency gains from introducing public-order institutions and the incentives to introducing and using them depend on the prevailing private-order institutions, which, in turn, are determined by more fundamental cultural and social factors.

Considering the relations among CCIs, the security of property, and contract-enforcement institutions generates predictions regarding the "organization of the society," including legal development, social structure, administrative capacity, military organization, and political representation.[5] The analysis is therefore testable and its predictions are indeed confirmed in an initial analysis of premodern England, China, and Japan.

This chapter proceeds as follows. The first section presents how CCIs secure property rights. The second section presents why contract-enforcement institutions determine the extent of the market and the role of public-order institutions in the modern markets. The third section argues that CCIs determine whether public-order contract-enforcement institutions can be introduced without undermining the market while private-order institutions determine whether they will be used if introduced. The fourth section presents the impact of CCIs on political development. The fifth section demonstrates the relevance of the theory by considering the histories of England, China, and Japan. The sixth section concludes.

## COERCION-CONSTRAINING INSTITUTIONS AND SECURED PROPERTY RIGHTS

A necessary condition for welfare-enhancing markets is the protection of property rights from those with coercive power. It is common to assert that markets require a state with a monopoly over coercive power and constitutional rules

---

4  For analyses of CCIs, see Greif (1998, 2005, 2006), Bates (2001), and Bates, Greif, and Singh (2002).

5  On the study of the state as an organization, see, for example, Tilly (1990) and Greif (1998, 2006, 2008).

limiting abuse of power (North and Weingast 1989). Yet, it is useful to consider deeper institutional determinants of the security of rights because markets require only that those who have coercive power are better off respecting, rather than abusing, rights. Accordingly, this section focuses on CCIs that influence the use of coercion in a society. To simplify the discussion, I ignore insecurity due to crime and predation by external actors and focus on constraining the coercive power of a "ruler" (warlord, duke, elite, president, etc.). Specifically, I consider the implications of a credible threat by the economic agents to impose economic, coercive, and administrative sanctions on the ruler. When the agents have such "powers," they can secure themselves some rights. Specifically, they can deter the ruler from abusing any rights worth to him less than the sanctions the agents can impose on him following an abuse. The origin and self-enforceability of various CCIs are briefly discussed at the end of the section. For simplicity of exposition, power is discussed as a discrete variable although in reality it is continuous.

Economic power (or "mobility") can secure property rights from predation by a ruler when the economic agents can credibly commit to retaliate, following an expropriation, by taking an economic action costly to the ruler. If the cost to the ruler is sufficiently high, he is deterred from expropriation. Merchants, for example, can flee with their assets once expropriation begins and craftsmen can respond by increasing the consumption of leisure or reducing the quality of their products. These responses are costly to a ruler who taxes commerce and production (e.g., Olson 1993; Greif, Milgrom, and Weingast 1994). If the ruler's gain from abusing some bundle of rights is less than the penalty the economic agents can impose on him, these rights are secured.

Coercive power in a society is *centralized* (or "monopolized") when the ruler's military capacity is sufficiently large to render futile a violent response by the economic agents following an abuse. The Soviet Union under Stalin is an example of a polity with a centralized coercive power. Coercive power is *dispersed* when there are social units such as tribes or autonomous cities with independent coercive power. Dispersed coercive power is *uncoordinated* when there is no ruler, or other means to coordinate the armed units to enforce some rule of conduct among them. Some tribal societies provide examples of such situations. Coercive power is dispersed and *coordinated* when there is a ruler, potentially with some independent military might, who can effectively coordinate—within the boundaries of his legitimate authority—the armed social units. In particular, the ruler can coordinate the military forces mustered by others to enforce some rules of conduct among them. The feudal system is a classical example.

The distribution of coercive power determines whose rights are secured and to what extent. When coercive power is centralized, rights are not secured, based on countervailing coercive power, from expropriation by the state. When coercive power is dispersed and uncoordinated, those with military power have secured rights. This security, however, is likely to be fragile as one's rights depend on random factors influencing relative coercive power.

When coercive power is dispersed but coordinated, security of those with coercive power is fostered if the ruler coordinates retaliation against any unit that used its military might against another.[6] A ruler might find coordinating retaliation optimal for him if it maintains the balance of power that supports his rule. For similar reasons, a ruler might find it optimal to protect the rights of agents without coercive power. Protecting rights in general is beneficial to the ruler if protection prevents those with coercive power from becoming stronger and challenge him. For similar reasons, ironically, the more stable the equilibria among the powerful, the less secured the property rights of those without coercive power. Abusing their property rights is less likely to undermine the equilibrium among the powerful.

Whether coercive power is centralized or dispersed, its perpetuation requires it to be an equilibrium outcome. The distribution of coercive power should be such that each social unit with coercive power is able to protect the economic and other rights required to maintain its coercive power (see Greif 1998, 2006 and Bates, Greif, and Singh 2002 for formal models). Table 3.1 summarizes the discussion of the distribution of coercive power and the security of property rights.

In addition to economic and coercive powers, CCIs can be based on administrative power (Greif 2008). Rulers have limited physical capacity to implement policy choices, including abuses implying that they have to rely on "administrators" for implementation. Administrators are individuals and organizations such as armies, tax farmers, feudal lords, bureaucracies, self-governed provinces and cities, and clans that have the capacity to implement policies. Administrative capacity, control, and the administrators' preferences, in turn, influence the costs and benefits of pursuing various policies to the ruler. In particular, administrative structure determines the cost and benefit, to the ruler, from respecting or abusing various rights.

A ruler's commitment to respect rights is fostered by having a *minimal administration*. Creating an effective administration requires time and other resources implying that having no effective administration to govern a particular

---

6 An example of such a ruler who coordinated armed social units is provided by a twelfth-century source describing the creation of the Kievan Empire in the ninth century. The local Slavic tribes drove the Scandinavian Varangians who subjected them "back beyond the sea, refused to pay them tribute, and set out to govern themselves. But there was no law among them, and tribe rose against tribe. Discord thus ensued among them, and they began to fight each other. They said to themselves, 'Let us seek a prince who may rule over us, and judge us according to custom.' Thus they went overseas to the Varangians, . . . [and told them that], 'our land is great and rich, but there is no order in it. Come reign as princes, rule over us.' Three brothers, with their kinfolk, volunteered" (*The Primary Chronicle*, cited in Zenkovsky 1974, 50).

**TABLE 3.1**  Coercive Power and the Security of Property Rights

Coercive power is . . .

|  | Centralized | Dispersed and uncoordinated | Dispersed and coordinated |
|---|---|---|---|
| Characteristics | Monopolization of coercive power | Coercive power is also held by uncoordinated social units | Coercive power is also held by coordinated social units |
| Property rights | Least secured | Better secured | Best secured |
| Examples | Soviet Union | Tribal societies | Feudal system |

economic sphere reduces the ruler's benefit from abusing rights in that sphere. A tax collection administration can be used to arbitrarily confiscate wealth, and it has the internal organization required to ensure that a high portion of the gain will reach the ruler. In the absence of such an administration, an army can be sent to capture wealth. Yet, an army organized to fight a war rather than capture wealth is likely to be less effective than a dedicated tax administration. To illustrate the role of administrative capacity in abusing rights, consider Mexico after the Revolution. Mexico's constitution called for nationalizing Mexico's oil fields, and its army could have been used to impose this decision on the multinational oil companies that operated the fields. Yet, Mexico did not expropriate the oil fields for a long time because it did not have the administrative capacity to manage them.

*Delegation* of administrative services also influences the cost and benefit of abusing rights. Delegation is a situation in which the state allows someone to make the investment in human or physical capital required to performing some administrative services.[7] If this investment is costly to expropriate and expensive and time consuming to replace, the delegates gain some power vis-à-vis the ruler. When the ruler depends, for example, on one's service to sustain his court or maintain the army, the withdrawal of this service is costly to the ruler. If the threat to withdraw services is credible, delegation enhances commitment to respect the rights of the delegates. Such threats seem to have secured the rights of the sixteenth-century Genoese financiers of the mighty Hapsburg kings.[8] These financiers had a comparative advantage in the administrative capacity of paying the royal army in Flanders.

---

7  Farming administrative posts differs from delegation. Farmers are a close substitute while delegates are monopolies.

8  The famous bankruptcies of the Spanish kings were indeed periods of debt reorganization rather than abuse of rights per se (Conklin 1998; Drelichman and Voth 2014).

An extreme form of delegation is *self-governance* or autonomy. A social unit (e.g., tribe, city, ethnic group) has self-governance when the state is absent (it has no administration to govern the unit) and the unit has its own administration. Similar to the situation in the tribal areas in contemporary Pakistan, the self-governed units can literally be a "state" within a state with its own army, taxation, and judicial system. A self-governed unit can respond to abuse both by withdrawing administrative services and using its administrative capacity against the state. Thus, self-governance both reduces the benefit and increases the cost of abusing the rights of those with autonomy. Indeed, the Hapsburg kings' army was in Flanders to subdue the autonomous cities and provinces that revolted in response to what they considered to be abuse of their economic and religious rights. Table 3.2 summarizes the discussion of the relations between administrative structure and security of rights.

The capacity of property owners to respond to abuses by those with coercive power depends on their economic power (mobility) and coercive capacity, the administrative structure, and their roles in it. In particular, agents who can move elsewhere, agents with coercive power, and agents providing administrative service to the ruler can respond to abuses in a manner costly to him. A credible threat to respond to an abuse by inflicting sufficiently high costs secures rights. The ruler is deterred from abusing any right whose holder can sufficiently reduce the gains from doing so.

Table 3.3 provides some examples of the distributions of coercive power and administrative structures that prevailed in various historical states. It illustrates that these features are observable (the bolded cases are examined in the fifth section in more detail).

The table, and the preceding discussion, does not examine the self-enforceability and origin of various CCIs. Although an extensive discussion of

**TABLE 3.2**  Administrative Power and Security of Property Rights

| | Administrative power is . . . | | |
|---|---|---|---|
| Implications | Minimal (absent state) | Delegated | Provided by autonomous units (self-governance) |
| Benefit and cost of abusing rights | Low benefit | High cost | Low benefit and high cost |
| The scope of secured rights | Encompassing everyone | Only to the delegates | Only to the autonomous units |
| Examples | Post-Revolution Mexico | Pre-Revolution France | Flanders to 1568 |

**TABLE 3.3** Historical Examples: CCIs, Markets, and Public-Order CEIs

| Coercive power | Administration type | | |
|---|---|---|---|
| | Minimal | Delegation | Autonomy |
| Centralized | **China** under the Qing[a] | Bourbon France | Hapsburg Spain |
| Dispersed | Armed caravans | | |
| Coordinated | Tokugawa **Japan**, European feudalism | Early Ottoman | **England**, early modern |

*Note*: a. China had minimal administration specifically in the commercial sector.

these issues is beyond the scope of this chapter, a few comments are in order (see Greif 2008 for a longer discussion). In the case of economic power, the self-enforceability of CCIs ultimately reflects that some property rights cannot be effectively captured using coercive power. In the case of coercive and administrative powers, self-enforceability is due to the distributional consequences of these powers. The powerful can protect their rights to the resources required to maintain their power.

Different CCIs can be an equilibrium outcome, and which one will prevail depends on initial condition, evolution, and intentional design. These factors influence selection over alternative CCIs. The distribution of military and administrative powers at the early stages of a state's formation can be beyond the ruler's control. The Ottomans who conquered the area from Syria to Egypt in 1516–17, for example, were unable to militarily subdue the nomad bedouins and had to pay them off (Etkes 2008). Protection money enabled the bedouins to maintain their independent military power. Similarly, the elected kings of Poland-Lithuania had smaller armies than many of their nobles. In facing external threats, the kings were coordinators of their nobles' military contingencies. This distribution of power was self-enforcing because rulers did not have the military might required to raise the resources needed to unilaterally change it.

But rulers might also stand to gain from creating CCIs that enable them to better respect property rights. When the Bourbons came to power (1589), the Crown auctioned short-term leases to bidders who were weak because they were perfect substitutes ex-ante and ex-post. However, the Crown's expenses grew faster than its revenues and the budgetary pressure led the Crown to expost renegotiate leases and renege on its contractual obligations. Once the farmers realized this, they reduced their bids and the budgetary crisis worsened. In response, Colbert, France's finance minister, created a strong administrator, the Company of General Farms, in the second half of the seventeenth century. The company became the sole collector of indirect taxes and thus could more credibly threaten to halt collections if the Crown reneged on its obligations. The Crown's enhanced commitment increased revenues and resolved the budgetary crisis (Balla and Johnson 2006).

CCIs that secure the rights of sufficiently many economic agents are necessary for markets to prevail. This security, and thus the market, is not a free lunch, however. Its price can be a suboptimal organization of the economy, the military, and the administration. In any case, the scope of exchange among those whose rights are secured is determined by the prevailing contract-enforcement institutions. These institutions are examined next.

## CONTRACT-ENFORCEMENT INSTITUTIONS DETERMINE THE EXTENT OF THE MARKET

The set of exchange relations that those with secure property rights will enter into is determined by the contract-enforcement institutions (CEIs) they rely upon. Exchange transactions are inherently sequential, as some time elapses between the *quid* and the *quo*, and this sequentiality implies an opportunity to renege. One will therefore not enter into an otherwise profitable exchange relationship unless one believes ex-ante (when making the decision to exchange) that one's partner will fulfill his contractual obligation ex-post (when that partner can gain from reneging).[9]

CEIs mitigate the above *fundamental problem of exchange* by linking past conduct with future payoffs (Greif 2000). An effective CEI renders breaching a contract unrewarding by sufficiently reducing the future payoffs of one who breached. If it is *ex-ante* known that one's best response *ex-post* is to fulfill one's contractual obligations, one can commit to be honest and others can trust one. CEIs can be based on diverse mechanisms such as family loyalty, economic and social reputation, legal sanctions, and supernatural beliefs.

The effectiveness of a particular CEI in enabling commitment in a particular transaction depends on the attributes of that transaction and the broader context. An impartial court, for example, might be able to support impersonal, nonrepeat exchange among strangers when conduct can be legally verified. In the same situation, an intracommunity, reputation-based CEI cannot support impersonal exchange with nonmembers. Unlike the legal system, however, this private-order institution might be able to support intracommunity exchange relations even when conduct cannot be legally verified. CEIs generally complement each other and exchange often relies on several CEIs. A modern firm typ-

---

9 See, e.g., Williamson (1985), Greif (1989, 1997, 2000), Aoki (2001), and Dixit (2004).

ically commits to its workers, suppliers, and consumers based on its reputation in these markets, legal contracts, and allocations of property rights.[10]

All market economies—in the past and present—have "private-order" CEIs. Such institutions evolve based on economic, social, and coercive sanctions imposed by economic agents. The introduction of "public-order" institutions based on the coercive power of the state can support additional exchange and particularly impersonal exchange, the hallmark of the modern economy. Public-order CEIs support impersonal exchange directly by enforcing contracts among strangers and indirectly through "hybrid" institutions. Hybrid institutions have public-order and private-order components which together enable them to support exchange that cannot be supported by either type of CEIs alone. Laws and regulations combined with reputation considerations provide the institutional foundation for large-scale impersonal exchange using credit cards (e.g., Greif 2006).

The evolution of markets is therefore being determined by the dynamics of their underpinning CEIs. In particular, markets expand when public-order CEIs mitigate the fundamental problem of exchange. Markets expand—more people exchange in more products in more situations—as more CEIs are being used.

## PUBLIC-ORDER INSTITUTIONS, COERCION, AND MARKETS DEVELOPMENT

Markets expand when additional, complementary CEIs are introduced. Complementing private-order with public-order CEIs enables the modern market to expand beyond what had been previously possible. This section presents why distinct CCIs differentially enable introducing without reducing the security of property rights, public-order CEIs, why some cultures create more demand than others for public-order CEIs, and why, when this demand is low, socially efficient public-order CEIs might nevertheless fail to foster market expansion.

To illustrate why public-order CEIs can undermine markets, consider, for example, the creation of a legal system with the capacity to enforce contracts. Creating a legal system amounts to creating the organizational and physical infrastructure required for capturing individuals and subjecting them to monetary and other penalties. This infrastructure can be used to either protect or abuse rights. More generally, creating public-order CEIs requires to make credible the threat of capturing wealth and inflicting other punishments. In the absence of countervailing forces, creating effective public-order institutions

---

10   As I elaborated elsewhere (Greif 2005, 2006), CEIs can also substitute for and even undermine each another. Broadly speaking, however, complementarity dominates.

therefore reduces the security of property rights and potentially undermine the market.[11]

Whether a public-order CEI would actually undermine the property rights of the economic agents depends on the nature and effectiveness of the CCIs protecting their rights. In particular, if abuse is prevented only by a minimal administration, introducing a public-order CEI will undermine property rights and the market. Minimal administration secures rights based on the low benefit to the ruler from predation in the absence of effective administration. Creating an effective public-order CEIs increases administrative capacity and therefore the benefit from predation. Markets cannot expand based on public-order institutions when rights are secured only by a limited administrative capacity to capture wealth.

For similar reasons, if coercive power is centralized and mobility is low, public-order CEIs are more likely to undermine the security of property rights and markets. Public-order CEIs undermine security the least when economic mobility is high, the economic agents have self-governance, and they provide the ruler with valuable administrative services. In other words, CCIs public-order institutions can be established without reducing the security of property rights when the economic agents can better credibly commit to impose heavier economic, administrative, and coercive penalties on the ruler. The more effective the CCIs are in securing the economic agents' rights, the more likely public-order CEIs are to expand markets. Table 3.4 summarizes this discussion.

Introducing public-order CEIs that do not undermine security nevertheless can fail to expand markets when the private-order institutions are efficient. Public-order institutions, particularly for impersonal exchange, exhibit network externalities. The value, for a market participant, of exchanging through an impersonal market increases as the number of other participants increases. As more people exchange through the market, search costs decline and the informational quality of price signals improves. The private return from using public-order CEIs increases as more agents use them. This implies that their viability requires that a sufficient number of individuals switch to using the public-order institutions once they are introduced. The number of individuals who would switch, in turn, depends on the efficiency of the private-order CEIs. Fewer individuals would find it optimal to switch when public-order CEIs are initially introduced when private-order CEIs are more efficient. Efficient private-order CEIs make it more likely that public-order institutions will fail establishing themselves even when impersonal exchange is socially beneficial (Greif 1994; Kranton 1996).

11 Insecurity due to public-order institutions can be user-specific. The one who uses the legal system to resolve a commercial dispute facilitates expropriating property or extorting payments from himself or herself.

**TABLE 3.4**  CCIs and Market Expansion

| Coercive power | Centralized | Dispersed and uncoordinated | Dispersed and coordinated |
|---|---|---|---|
| Administrative power | Minimal | Delegated | Autonomy |
| Economic power | Immobile | Some mobility | Mobile |

*Note:* Deterrence increases from left to right.

The efficiency of private-order CEIs varies across societies because of their interrelations with social and cultural factors. Ceteris paribus, initial social structures and cultural features influence which private-order CEIs will prevail. Social structures provide networks for information transmission while cultural beliefs and behavioral norms coordinate expectations and provide a shared understanding of the meaning of various actions.[12]

Whether a society is more "collectivist" (or "communalist") or more "individualist" (Ball 2001; Triandis 1990) is an important sociocultural feature determining the efficiency of its private-order institutions (Greif 1994, 1996, 2006). In collectivist societies, social structures that are based on innate characteristics such as kinship, place of birth, or religion (e.g., lineage, tribes, or religious sects) are prominent. These societies tend to be "segregated": each individual interacts socially and economically mainly with members of his or her group, and their members feel involved in the lives of other members of their group. Private-order CEIs in a collectivist society are therefore more likely to be based on intragroup's economic and social sanctions. In more individualist societies, the individual and family, rather than larger, innate social structures, are prominent and individuals expect that others will interfere relatively little in their affairs. Individualistic societies tend to be more "integrated": economic transactions will be conducted among people from different groups. Their private-order CEIs tend to be based on bilateral economic and social sanctions among individuals and business networks.

These sociocultural features are likely to lead to distinct private-order institutions that tend to perpetuate these features (Greif 1994, 2006).[13] A collectivist society's private-order CEIs are relatively effective in disciplining its members without public-order institutions. The ability of each social group to punish its members reduces the relative cost of intragroup economic exchange, while the

---

12  For works indicating the importance of social and cultural factors, see Granovetter (1985), Greif (1994, 1996, 2006), Clay (1997a, 1997b), McMillan and Woodruff (2000), Moriguchi (2003), Stulz and Williamson (2003), Biggs, Raturi, and Srivastava (2002), Fafchamps (2004), and Olds and Liu (2000).

13  Initial sociocultural features are not destiny. They perpetuate only as long as they and the institutions perpetuating them are equilibria.

thinness of intergroup exchange reduces the benefits to each individual from leaving his or her group and pursuing exchange outside. The private benefit to an economic agent from relying on the public order is therefore relatively low. An individualistic society's private-order CEIs are relatively ineffective in disciplining its members without public-order institutions. Higher mobility, for example, limits the ability to impose punishment (Greif 1994). The private benefit to an economic agent from relying on public-order CEIs is therefore relatively large.

Because private-order institutions in a collectivist society are relatively more efficient in the absence of public-order CEIs, investing in public order may not be socially beneficial. Moreover, even if introducing public-order CEIs is socially beneficial, using public-order CEIs may not be individually rational. The effectiveness of private enforcement implies that the private benefit from switching to use the public order is too low given that most other agents do not use them. Rulers who recognize that either of these situations prevails would not make the sunk investment required to create public-order institutions. After all, creating public-order CEIs institutions requires an up-front sunk investment in, for example, physical infrastructure and human capital, and requires inducing beliefs in the institution's effectiveness. This investment exhibits increasing return; the more people who use the system, the higher the return on the investment.

Public-order CEIs can potentially expand markets but can also undermine them by reducing the security of property rights. In particular, CCIs based on minimal administration are incompatible with public-order CEIs. More generally, the more effective the CCIs are in protecting rights, the less likely the public order is to actually reduce security and undermine the market. In addition, the more (less) effective the private order, the lower (higher) the "demand" for public order and the more (less) they will be used if created. The private order, in turn, is likely to be more effective under collectivism than under individualism. Finally, the introduction of public-order CEIs will not transpire unless the "ruler" who can create them has the motivation and resources to do so.

## THE POLITICAL IMPLICATIONS OF COERCION-CONSTRAINING INSTITUTIONS

CCIs under which public-order CEIs expand markets also motivate rulers to create political assemblies in which those whose power constrain the ruler have political voice and influence. Political assemblies in nondemocratic, premodern states are an enigma because they foster coordination against the ruler. Aristotle, for one, noted that tyrants "don't allow [even] associations for social and cultural activities or anything of that kind; these are the breeding grounds of independence and self-confidence, two things which tyrants must guard against"

(Politics 5.11).[14] Yet, representative bodies have been common in a variety of political systems, ranging from monarchies (e.g., the English Great Council) to constitutional monarchies (e.g., the English Parliament) and tribal societies (e.g., the Afghani Loya Jirga). Why did rulers allow political assemblies although such bodies facilitated organizing opposition to the ruler?

When a ruler can be penalized, given the prevailing CCIs, for deviating from the expected pattern of behavior, he also stands to gain from representative bodies. If a constrained ruler takes an action—raises an army or changes the administrative structure—that is considered a deviation and he will be penalized. Representative assemblies composed of those whose economic, coercive, or administrative power constrains the ruler are a means to coordinate on acceptable actions and avoid unnecessary conflicts. Representative assemblies are therefore more likely to be established when the ruler and those who constrain him can gain from bargaining.

We have no models of bargaining in the context of various CCIs. It is intuitive, however, that providing the ruler with additional resources risks shifting the balance of power. Those who constrain the ruler and therefore are in a position to authorize this transfer will seek to safeguard their position. They will demand various concessions—such as freedom from taxes, administrative control, military resources, legal rights, the right to supervise or authorize various actions—to increase their ability to constrain the ruler ex-post.

Ironically, representative assemblies also facilitate the abuse of property rights. They provide those whose powers limit each other freedom of actions with a means to coordinate abusing the rights for those who do not have such power. Conversely, if the economic and coercive power of groups represented in the assembly no longer constrains the ruler's actions, these groups will become, at most, a rubber stamp.

## HISTORICAL MARKETS—CHINA, ENGLAND, AND JAPAN

The above conjecture about the relations between CCIs, CEIs, and political development is testable. It specifies relations among observable variables such as military organizations, administrative structures, CEIs, market expansion, and political assemblies. It predicts, for example, that markets can prevail even in an autocratic society in which the ruler has a monopoly over coercive power and the traders' threat of taking their trade elsewhere is not credible. The traders' property rights can nevertheless be secured by limited administrative capacity in the commercial sector. The market can even be rather efficient and well integrated

---

14 Myerson (2008) argues that political representation is established by rulers when they can gain from the implied better ability to coordinate actions against them.

if the society is a collectivist one. The introduction of public-order CEIs, however, is likely to undermine, rather than promote, the market. As discussed below, the historical experience of China confirms this prediction.

Another prediction is that markets would be relatively inefficient in individualistic societies in the absence of public-order CEIs. Such societies are more likely to introduce public-order CEIs and the market would subsequently expand if the economic agents' power constrain the ruler. In this case, the ruler will consent to a political assembly that includes the economic agents. As discussed below, the historical experience of England confirms this prediction. That these and other predictions are confirmed by a tentative analysis of the histories of England, China, and Japan suggests the merit of further evaluating the analysis in a larger sample.

## China

Chinese markets, during the late imperial period, were as integrated as Europe's (Shiue and Keller 2007). The efficiency and scale of these markets challenge the conventional view that a limited government is necessary for markets. Furthermore, the military organization of the empire implies little scope for merchants to protect their rights based on coercive power. Military power was centralized, and those who served in the army were recruited from social groups uninvolved in commerce. Higham and Graff (2002, 12) noted that military leaders and civil officers were recruited from different social groups. Moreover, "from the eight century onward, a long-service, mercenary soldiery distinct from the farming population tended to predominate" and "an important role was played by specialized units recruited from among non-Han peoples" (10). In short, the organization of the Chinese state was such that CCIs based on merchants' coercive power did not protect their property rights.[15]

Merchants' economic power similarly seems to have been limited because the political, social, and legal context rendered noncredible a threat by the merchants to take their trade elsewhere in response to an abuse. Politically, the large geographical extent of the empire increased the cost of emigration. Socially, the Chinese society was clan-based. Clans provided many services to their members including protection, education, and welfare assistance in case of need. Ancestors worshiping was culturally important and centered around the clan's cemetery. Finally, one's extended family or clan were generally held liable for one's crimes and had legal and customary authority over their members. These political, social, and legal settings increased the cost of emigration.

The conjecture that coercive and administrative powers did not constrain the emperors gains further support from the observation that political assemblies were not created in China. As noted above, this is expected when property

---

15   The number and localization of peasants, however, render them militarily stronger.

rights are secured by a minimal administration rather than by the coercive and administrative powers of the economic agents. Furthermore, China's organizational history is consistent with the conjecture that social units with coercive and administrative powers did not constrain the Chinese emperors. Economic corporations were not legal entities, and guilds, although known, were few and relatively weak until the late nineteenth century when the state delegated various functions to them in response to the fiscal pressure.

Integrated, large-scale markets, as we saw, can prevail even when neither countervailing coercive nor economic power constrains the state. The security required for the market can be provided by limited administrative capacity in the commercial sector. This is more likely to be the case in a collectivist society. In any case, if security is provided by limited administrative capacity, public-order CEIs will be relatively unimportant, society is likely to be collectivists, private-order institutions will be prominent, and political assemblies will not be created. If public-order institutions are introduced, they will either undermine the market or not be used. The evidence confirms these predictions.

The Chinese state did *not* create the administrative structure required for effective predation on the commercial sector and, generally interfered much less than the European states in the operation of the market (e.g., Pomeranz 2000). Minimal administration was not due to an inability to create an effective administration. China had had an effective administration for taxing land and providing public goods, such as security, defense, famine relief, commercial infrastructure, and the distribution of better agricultural knowledge (e.g., Pomeranz 2000). The administration, although centralized, was thin and was not aimed at taxing property other than land. Beneath the roughly 1350 county-level magistrates "were several towns and hundreds of villages and a population ranging from several tens of thousands to hundreds of thousands" (Wong 1997, 108). Taxation was indeed imposed on the agrarian sector, and land tax was the main source of state revenue (e.g., Szonyi 2002, 58). Commerce, in general, was taxed less in China than in Europe.[16] This light taxation seems to have been intended to foster exchange (Wong 1997, 134).

Similarly, if limited administration secured merchants' property rights, the state could not have committed to repay loans taken from merchants. Indeed, the Chinese state, prior to 1850, did not borrow from the merchants (Wong 1997, 132–33), consistent with the conjecture that merchants' economic or coercive power did not constrain the rulers. In Europe such loans were common during the same period. More generally, an unconstrained ruler will increase taxes at his discretion rather than through consent. Indeed, in China tax increases took the form of "contributions" ( *juan*) that were not negotiated upon

---

16 Consistent with the analysis, rich merchants with state monopolies (e.g., in salt) were heavily taxed. In total, tax on commerce amounted to less than a quarter of total revenues (Wong 1997, 132–33).

but declared and imposed by the authorities. The riots that higher taxes some-times led to were subdued by force.

Consistent with the insight that public-order CEIs and CCIs based on lim-ited administration are incompatible, there was little provision of and reliance on public-order CEIs in commercial disputes. The authorities invested little in commerce-related legal infrastructure and discouraged legal adjudication of commercial disputes. There was no commercial code of law prior to the early twentieth century and the magistrates were subject to heavy penalties if they made mistakes in adjudication. Magistrates were motivated to seek compro-mises rather than legal rulings. Legal uncertainty in commercial disputes was probably high. The Chinese proverb "of ten reasons by which a magistrate may decide a case, nine are unknown to the public" (Bodde 1963, 376) is suggestive.

The lack of public-order CEIs is consistent with the Confucian ideology that disputes in general should be resolved informally, without resorting to the court of law. Administrating justice was one among the many responsibilities of the magistrates who were not trained in law and relied on secretaries with some training. "It is indicative of the Chinese attitude toward law that this secretary did not himself belong to the formal administrative system. He was merely a personal employee of the magistrate, who paid his salary out of his own private purse. Hence the secretary was not permitted to try cases himself or even to be present at the trials" (Bodde 1963, 376). It is therefore notable that public-order CEIs were created to resolve disputes in noncommercial matters. Since at least the Zhou dynasty (1122–256 BC) there was legal enforcement of contracts, par-ticularly those regarding tax-related assets such as land (e.g., Zelin 2004).

Private-order CEIs supported commerce. "In China, the absence of formal justice, at least on commercial and civil matters, spawned a plethora of informal rules in the form of family bylaws, lineage rules and guild regulations which, enforced through a collective mechanism, alleviated the pervasive information and commitment problems to effectuate the commercial expansion in Ming and Qing China. . . . Merchant groups and commercial guilds have long been a dominant form of commercial organization throughout Chinese history. His-torians often identify at least ten distinctive native-place merchant groups in China" (Ma 2004, 267).[17]

Consistent with the assertion that private-order CEIs are relatively more effective in collectivist societies, premodern China seems to have had a col-lectivist culture. As already noticed, China was a clan-based society and such societies tend to be more collectivist. Indeed, even contemporary China is rel-atively collectivist although the communist regime labored to dismantle the clans and the associated culture. Contemporary China ranked as the fifty-ninth

---

17 Historically "the Chinese society consiste[d] of networks of people whose actions are oriented by normative social relationships" (Hamilton 1994, 199). Nakamura (2004) argues that reliance on the law was more widespread than is generally recognized.

most collectivist country (out of seventy-nine). China's score is 20, out of 100, and the United States scores the highest, 91.[18]

The Chinese merchant groups seem to have recognized that protection from a predatory administration is crucial for their prosperity. They disproportionally invested in education and were successful in passing the examinations required to gain administrative positions (Ma 2004).

Moreover, as the economy grew and the demand for expanding the scope of exchange increased, these groups did not respond by approaching the state to provide public-order institutions. Arguably, this would have undermined their property rights. Instead, lineage-based or territorial-based mercantile groups responded by altering their economic organizations. These grew larger and were often based on contractual relationships, had centralized bureaucracies, and drew on outsiders' resources and talents (e.g., Herrmann-Pillath 1999).

The Qing's responses to the military and economic conflict with the West during the nineteenth century reveals the difficulties in introducing public-order institutions when property rights are secured by a limited administrative capacity. The conflict required additional revenues, and the emperors authorized taxing goods in transit. Increasing the capacity to abuse rights without creating a countervailing economic or coercive power, however, was costly. Corruption prevailed and trade suffered (Yang Li 2002; Goetzmann and Koll 2005). The state resorted to expanding the role of guilds, delegating to them such functions as commercial tax collection and provision of local public goods. Top-down industrialization and monopolistic guilds, however, hindered industrialization and commerce (Goetzmann and Koll 2005; Ma 2004).

Similarly, if the property rights required for the market were secured by a limited administration, introducing public-order CEIs should have undermined the market. This was indeed the case when commercial legal code was introduced in the early twentieth century. The legislation had three objectives: to strengthen the central government, to end the extraterritorial legal right of Western nationals, and to promote economic growth.[19] The first two objectives were achieved, but not the latter. The assumption that formal law would become an "essential vehicle for private Chinese economic development, . . . prove[d] quite mistaken" (Kirby 1995, 44). In the absence of countervailing CCIs, however, a legal system provided a conduit to abusing property rights as noted in a Chinese proverb "win your lawsuit and lose your money" (Bodde 1963, 376).[20]

---

18  See http://w.ww.clearlycultural.com/geert-hofstede-cultural-dimensions/individualism/ (accessed October 12, 2008).

19  Western powers argued that in the absence of formal law, Chinese authorities should not have legal authority over their nationals in China. Introducing a commercial law was a means to deflect this argument

20  I am unable to date this proverb.

The above evidence suggests that security of merchants' property in late medieval China was based on a limited administrative capacity to abuse rights. Limited administrative capacity reduced the ruler's gain from abusing rights. The collectivist—clan-based—Chinese society of that period produced private-order contract enforcement institutions that supported a vibrant market economy. The relative absence of the state from the commercial sphere in late imperial China that hindered development (Herrmann-Pillath 1999). Consistent with the claim that this absence was a means to committing to the security of rights, when the authorities introduced public-order CEIs, the market suffered.

## England

England's market economy was arguably not a match for China's circa 1,000 CE. By the late nineteenth century, however, it was a symbol of the emerging modern market economy in which private-order and public-order CEIs prevailed and impersonal exchange was common. England's CCIs confirm the conjecture that such market expansion predicates on having a ruler constrained by an effective combination of the economic, coercive, and administrative powers of the economic agents. Strong feudal lords, autonomous cities, corporations such as the Bank of England, a ruler without a standing army, and a Parliament that approved taxation and coordinated political actions were the manifestations of these CCIs.

Initially, William the Conqueror and his immediate successors were constrained by the coercive power of the great lords, usually referred to as the Barons. The military weakness of the Crown is reflected in the Magna Carta (1215), in which the king agreed not to have a standing army, not to recruit mercenaries, and not to tax without consent by the Great Council. That Council, in which the nobles were represented, reflected the prevailing CCIs: a balance of military power between the Crown and the Barons.

In the context of the conflict between the Crown and the lords, particularly during the thirteenth century, numerous English cities got charters recognizing their rights to self-governance. By the end of the thirteenth century, there were about five hundred such autonomous, self-governed towns (boroughs) that became an integral part of the kingdom's administration. They collected taxes, administrated justice, and mustered military units. These towns' economic, administrative, and military powers rendered them important in constraining the Crown.

That these towns became part of England's CCIs is well reflected in the events surrounding the transformation of the Great Council into a Parliament in which the towns were represented. In 1265 King Henry III dissolved the Great Council and levied unapproved taxes. Consistent with the claim that a CCI based on the Barons' military power prevailed, Earl Simon de Montfort organized a revolt. During the conflict, de Montfort attempted to summon a

"Parliament" to which he invited, in addition to the nobles and the clergy, also representatives from the towns and counties.

Although de Montfort was eventually defeated, this episode reflects the increasing importance of the counties and towns in national conflicts. Recognizing that they were part of the CCIs he was facing, King Edward I summoned the so-called model parliament (1295), which for the first time included representatives from the commercial, urban sector. It was during this parliament that the Crown issued a charter seceding the right of approving new taxes to the parliament. In 1297 Edward I confirmed the Magna Carta, asserting that it should be observed as common law, and declared that on no account were aids and taxes to be taken without the common assent of the whole kingdom and for the common benefit.

Yet, only the rights of those with a countervailing powers were respected and during that period the Crown abused, for example, the rights of Italians traders. At the same time, kings with conditional coercive power constrained the autonomous cities to compete with each other economically, but not militarily. CCIs that constrain the power of the state based on the administrative and military power of the commercial sector enable effective provision of public-order CEIs. Indeed, the latter half of the thirteenth century was a period of reform and expansion of English law and the legal system. Edward I is known as the "lawyer-king" (Hogue 1996, 69), and his legislation directly influenced the extent of the markets.

For example, before the thirteenth century, the Community Responsibility System (CRS) enabled some impersonal exchange characterized by separation between the *quid* and the *quo* (Greif 2006). English towns were motivated to punish their members who cheated members of other towns by the threat of losing their collective reputation. The CRS began to decline, however, due to the commercial expansion and the growth in the size, number, and economic and social heterogeneity of towns. Given the economic, military, and administrative power of the towns, it was possible to replace the CRS with a public-order CEI without undermining the market.[21] Furthermore, because England was an individualistic society (e.g., Morris 1972; Macfarlane 1978), these public-order CEIs were demanded and used.

The development of the Common Law courts and their increasing administrative importance further constrained the Crown. Their administrative power enabled them to protect their jurisdiction independence, and by the fifteenth century this fostered the provision of public-order CEIs. This situation is well illustrated in the first known court case in England regarding negotiable credit

---

21 This, however, was not the case in other parts of Europe. In Germany, for example, CCIs that balanced the central authority and local lords were no longer an equilibrium due to the Investiture Controversy. Although the CRS declined, a suitable alternative was not provided (Greif 2006; Volckart 2004).

instruments (1436). The London mayor's court at Guildhall had customary rights in cases involving merchants, but one of the parties approached the King's Bench to transfer the case to its jurisdiction. The mayor of London, however, refused to consent to the Bench's demand, arguing that "according to the Law Merchant and the ancient liberties and free customs of the city itself... the mayor . . . have the power and use of hearing" such cases (Munro 1990, 74.) The king withdrew his demand and negotiated credit instruments became legal. By the sixteenth and seventeenth centuries such public-order CEIs enabled the expansion of credit and bonds beyond that possible based on reputation alone (Muldrew 1998).

Subsequent events further reduced the power of the Barons and increased the administrative power of the commercial sector. The War of the Roses (1455–85) decimated the ranks of the great lords making the Crown more dependent on the administrative capacity and other resources of its autonomous towns and the local unpaid Justices of Peace. The Crown confiscated the church's large land holding in the sixteenth century in the context of establishing the Church of England, but its coercive power was sufficiently constrained at this point that it was unable to use this resource to undermine the existing CCIs. On the contrary, the increasing financial needs of the Crown due to the Military Revolution compelled it to sell this land to the gentry, thereby further strengthening them. The greater efficiency in which the gentry utilized the land probably further constrained abuse by the larger implied loss of value (Rajan and Zingales 2003). The flow of wealth from the emerging Atlantic trade may have had a similar impact (Acemoglu, Johnson, and Robinson 2005).

The Civil War of the seventeenth century was another step in this process of institutional evolution. The war made it evident that the Crown neither had the independent military ability nor the administrative capacity required to rule without the consent of the economic elite. During and after the Glorious Revolution (1688) the new balance of power was tested and formalized. New rules coordinated on appropriate behavior by the Crown and new organizations altered administrative power. Among these rules and organizations were the Bill of Rights, a better separation between the judiciary and the executive, and the Bank of England (North and Weingast 1989). That the Glorious Revolution formalized a de facto prior situation accounts for the puzzling observation that the historical evidence does not indicate that the Glorious Revolution altered the security of property rights.[22]

Indeed, once the Parliament gained supremacy, it was not in the business of protecting property rights per se. Its policy reflected the interests of those who controlled it, namely, the landed, commercial, and financial elites. The subsequent history is thus marked by gross abuses of property rights through the large increase in taxation, monopolies, parliamentary enclosures of the open

---

22  See, e.g., O'Brien (2001), Quinn (2001), Sussman and Yafeh (2000), and Harris (2004).

fields, and colonial expansion (Harris 2004).[23] Yet, a state controlled by its landed, commercial, and financial elites and later empowered by the Industrial Revolution was a boon for the extension of markets. The evolution of the modern market reached its zenith.

## Japan

The economic and political history of Tokugawa Japan (1603–1868) is particularly interesting here because it highlights that even if CCIs secure property rights based on coercive power and autonomy, the interests of the people constraining the ruler impact outcomes. More specifically, a CCI constitutes an equilibria that endogenously determine economic and other policy interests. The Japanese CCIs were based on a balance of military power, and this balance was kept by a policy of seclusion from the rest of the world and prohibiting the elite from engaging in economic activities.

During the Tokugawa period, the shogun was a de jure a ruler who was above the law. De facto, however, his military power was constrained by that of the other great lords (*daimyo*). Unlike the English Barons, however, the Japanese lords were not economic agents but a military elite. They had taxation rights but not user rights over their domains and were prohibited from any economic activities.[24] Cities were not autonomous but ruled by centrally appointed governors backed by a military contingency. The daimyo had no direct (official) interest in establishing public-order CEIs to promote trade.

Consistent with the argument that assemblies are established in response to the need to adjust rights, there was no political assembly in Japan. Japan did not face external military threat and its policy of restricting international trade—the seclusion—further maintained stability and reduced the need to adjust rights. Similar to China, limited administrative capacity of the state and the need to maintain balance of economic resources among the lords secured merchants' property rights. There was little in terms of administrative structure to collect sales or income tax from merchants. Merchants' rights were therefore generally secured although they sometimes were subjected to levies, forced

23 For economic analyses of the great English trading companies that were monopolies, see Irwin (1988), Carlos and Nicholas (1996), and Carlos (1992).

24 The interests of the clans that circumvented this ban diverged over time, and they played an important role in the Meiji Restoration. Indeed, the pivotal clan in the success of the revolution was the Satsuma clan. This clan opposed the Tokugawa during the civil wars but did not participate in the final decisive battle. Its relatively large army remained intact. The shogunate did not confront this army, which was located in the Satsuma's large domain in the relatively remote and difficult to access southern island of Kyushu. The Satsuma remained powerful and gained special privileges such as a partial exemption from having to reside in Edo. This and their trading with Korea and China, partially in defiance of the seclusion, enabled them to increase their wealth and power. When they joined the anti-shogunate forces in 1868 they tilted the balance of power against it.

loans, and even in rare cases, confiscation of their property. Consistent with our analysis, public-order CEIs were not introduced and the merchants acquired some economic power only when increasing urbanization and population rendered the regime weary of social unrest due to volatility in food prices. Gradually, the shogunate allowed food merchants to organize themselves (Okazaki 2005). The Meiji Restoration (1868) radically changed Japanese institutions, but its analysis is beyond the scope of this chapter.

## CONCLUDING COMMENTS

A market can be supported by various combinations of CCIs that secure property rights and CEIs that mitigate the fundamental problem of exchange. Different institutional configurations, however, support distinct sets of exchange relations and cause different trajectories of market development. In particular, CCIs that rely on limited administrative capacity are incompatible with public-order enforcement institutions. Public-order enforcement institutions, after all, require administrative capacity to capture wealth. Exchange has to rely on private-order CEIs and market expansion is correspondingly limited. Yet, the efficiency gains of introducing public-order institutions depends on the prevailing (private-order) CEIs. The more the private-order is efficient (as is more likely to be the case in collectivist societies), the lower is the efficiency gain from public order, if it could have been introduced. At the same time, it is also more likely that socially beneficial public-order institutions would not be utilized if introduced.

Another institutional combination is one in which coercive power is sufficiently constrained by countervailing economic, coercive, and administrative powers that contract enforcement can be provided by public-order CEIs. The less efficient the private order (as is more likely to be the case in individualistic societies), the higher the efficiency gains from public-order institutions.

Different institutional combinations also have distinct distributional implications. By determining the set of exchange relations, distinct institutional combinations also impact the distribution of gains from exchange. Private-order CEIs build on personal relations and therefore imply unequal access to the market. Public-order institutions, in contrast, can impartially provide equal access to enforcement and exchange.

Indeed, institutional foundations and dynamics of markets in premodern China, England and Japan are consistent with this analysis. In particular, because coercive power in England was constrained by countervailing economic, coercive, and administrative powers, public-order CEIs could be effectively introduced. In contrast, coercive power in China was constrained by limited administrative capacity in the commercial sector. If introduced, public-order

CEIs would have therefore undermined the security of property rights. Market expansion based on public-order was thus limited.

Specifically, market participants in England were organized in self-governed social structures such as towns and guilds. Their independent coercive power and the value of their administrative services effectively constrained other actors from abusing their property rights.

Public-order institutions that undermine the security of property rights were established without actually reducing the security of property rights. Given the prevailing individualism, relying on public-order institutions contributed to market expansion once the growing economy strained the capacity of its private-order institutions.

In late imperial China, markets were based on another set of market-supporting institutions. Although merchants had no coercive or administrative powers to constrain the state, their property rights were secured by a limited administration. Limited administrative capacity in the commercial sector reduced the benefit, to the emperors, from attempting to capture mercantile wealth. Contract enforcement was provided by private-order institutions that were highly effective in a collectivist, clan-based society. Whether the Chinese system would have effectively adapted to foster more impersonal exchange in the long run is an experiment that history does not provide. Western expansion forced changes in China's administration, policies and politics that altered the course of its institutional development.

Be that as it may, this chapter highlights that the institutional foundations of markets are deeper than legal rules and apparatus articulating property rights and enforcing contracts. A society's market-supporting institutions are an integral part of its organization. Their details and implications depend on the ways that the state implements its policies and on the prevailing sociocultural features. It may well be the case that some of the difficulties in creating market economies in developing countries is due to creating public-order institutions in the absence of appropriate CCIs. More generally, given the West's historical experience and these societies' political, social, and cultural characteristics, contemporary Western legal institutions may not be the optimal ones to adopt.

## ACKNOWLEDGMENTS

The writing of this chapter was supported by the Canadian Institute for Advanced Research (CIFAR). An earlier version of this chapter was presented in a Research Symposium on Property Rights Economics and Innovation organized by the Searle Center on Law, Regulation, and Economic Growth, Northwestern University.

## BIBLIOGRAPHY

Acemoglu, Daron, Simon Johnson, and James Robinson. 2005. "The Rise of Europe: Atlantic Trade, Institutional Change and Economic Growth." *American Economic Review*, 95: 546–79.

Aoki, Masahiko. 2001. *Toward a Comparative Institutional Analysis*. Cambridge, MA: MIT Press.

Ball, R. 2001. "Individualism, Collectivism, and Economic Development." *Annals of the American Academy of Political and Social Science* 573: 57–84.

Balla, Eliana, and Noel Johnson. 2006. "Institutional Change in the Long-Run: The Ottoman Empire and France during the Early-Modern Period." Manuscript, California State University, Long Beach.

Bates, Robert. 2001. *Prosperity and Violence: The Political Economy of Development*. New York: Norton.

Bates, Robert, Avner Greif, and Smita Singh. 2002. "Organizing Violence." *Journal of Conflict Resolution* 46 (5): 599–628.

Biggs, T., M. Raturi, and P. Srivastava. 2002. "Ethnic Networks and Access to Credit: Evidence from the Manufacturing Sector in Kenya." *Journal of Economic Behavior and Organization* 49 (4): 473–86.

Bodde, Derk. 1963. "Basic Concepts of Chinese Law: The Genesis and Evolution of Legal Thought in Traditional China." *Proceedings of the American Philosophical Society* 107 (5): 375–98.

Carlos, M. Ann. 1992. "Principal-Agent Problems in Early Chartered Companies: A Tale of Two Firms." *American Economic Review* 82 (2): 140–45.

Carlos, M. Ann, and Stephen Nicholas. 1996. "Theory and History: Seventeenth Century Joint-Stock Chartered Trading Companies." *Journal of Economic History* 56: 916–24.

Clay, Karen. 1997a. "Trade, Institutions, and Credit." *Explorations in Economic History* 34 (4): 495–52.

Clay, Karen. 1997b. "Trade without Law: Self-Enforcing Institutions in Mexican California." *Journal of Law, Economics, & Organization* 13 (1): 202–31.

Conklin, James. 1998. "The Theory of Sovereign Debt and Spain under Philip II." *Journal of Political Economy* 106 (3): 483–513.

Dixit, Avinash, K. 2004. *Lawlessness and Economics: Alternative Modes of Governance*. Princeton: Princeton University Press.

Drelichman, Mauricio and Hans-Joachim Voth. 2014. *Lending to the Borrower from Hell: Debt, Taxes, and Default in the Age of Philip II*. Princeton. Princeton University Press.

Etkes, Haggay. 2008. "Legalized Protection Payments, Taxation and Economic Growth: Evidence from Ottoman Gaza (ca. 1519–1582)." Manuscript, Hebrew University.

Fafchamps, Marcel. 2004. *Market Institutions in Sub-Saharan Africa*. Cambridge, MA: MIT Press.

Goetzmann, William N., and Elisabeth Koll. 2005. "The History of Corporate Ownership in China." In Randall K. Morck (ed.), *A History of Corporate Governance around the World: Family Business Groups to Professional Managers*. NBER Publication.

Granovetter, Mark S. 1985. "Economic Action, Social Structure, and Embeddedness." *American Journal of Sociology* 91 (3): 481–510.

Greif, Avner. 1989. "Reputation and Coalitions in Medieval Trade: Evidence on the Maghribi Traders." *Journal of Economic History* 49: 857–82.

———. 1994. "Cultural Beliefs and the Organization of Society: A Historical and Theoretical Reflection on Collectivist and Individualist Societies." *Journal of Political Economy* 102 (5): 912–50.

———. 1996. "On the Inter-relations and Economic Implications of Economic, Social, Political, and Normative Factors: Reflections from Two Late Medieval Societies." In *Frontiers of the New Institutional Economics*, edited by John N. Drobak and John Nye, 57–94. New York: Academic Press.

————. 1997. "Contracting, Enforcement, and Efficiency: Economics beyond the Law." In *Annual World Bank Conference on Development Economics*, edited by Michael Bruno and Boris Pleskovic, 239–66. Washington, DC: World Bank.

————. 1998. "Self-Enforcing Political Systems and Economic Growth: Late Medieval Genoa." In *Analytic Narratives*, coauthored by Robert H. Bates, Avner Greif, Margaret Levi, Jean-Laurent Rosenthal, and Barry R. Weingast, 23–63. Princeton: Princeton University Press.

————. 2000. "The Fundamental Problem of Exchange: A Research Agenda in Historical Institutional Analysis." *European Review of Economic History* 4 (3): 251–84.

————. 2005. "Commitment, Coercion, and Markets: The Nature and Dynamics of Institutions Supporting Exchange." In *The Handbook for New Institutional Economics*, edited by Claude Menard and Mary M. Shirley, 727–86. Norwell, MA: Kluwer.

————. 2006. *Institutions and the Path to the Modern Economy: Lessons from Medieval Trade*. Cambridge: Cambridge University Press.

————. 2008. "Toward Political Economy of Implementation: The Impact of Administrative Power on Institutional and Economic Developments." In *Institutions and Growth*, edited by Elhanan Helpman, 17–63. Cambridge, MA: Harvard University Press.

Greif, Avner, Paul R. Milgrom, and Barry R. Weingast. 1994. "Coordination, Commitment and Enforcement: The Case of the Merchant Gild." *Journal of Political Economy* 102 (4): 745–76.

Hamilton, Gary G. 1994. "Civilizations and the Organization of Economies." In *The Handbook of Economic Sociology*, edited by N. Smelser and R. Swedberg, 184–205. Princeton: Princeton University Press.

Harris, Ron. 2004. "Government and the Economy, 1688–1850." In *Cambridge Economic History of Britain*, vol. 1, edited by R. Floud and P. Johnson, 204–37. Cambridge: Cambridge University Press.

Herrmann-Pillath, Carsten. 1999. "On the Importance of Studying Late Qing Economics and Social History for the Analysis of Contemporary China, or: Protecting Sinology Against Social Science." Duisburg Working Papers in East Asian Studies 3.

Higham, Robin, and David A. Graff. 2002. "Introduction." In *A Military History of China*, edited by David A. Graff and Robin Higham, 1–18. Cambridge, MA: Westview.

Hogue, Arthur R. 1996. *Origins of the Common Law*. Indianapolis: Liberty Press.

Irwin, Douglas A. 1988. "Welfare Effects of British Free Trade: Debate and Evidence from the 1840s." *Journal of Political Economy* 96: 1142–64.

Kirby, William C. 1995. "China Unincorporated: Company Law and Business Enterprise in Twentieth-Century China." *Journal of Asian Studies* 54 (1): 43–63.

Kranton, Rachel E. 1996. "Reciprocal Exchange: A Self-Sustaining System." *American Economic Review* 86 (4): 830–51.

Ma, Dubin. 2004. "Growth, Institutions and Knowledge: A Review and Reflection on the Historiography of 18th–20th Century China." *Australian Economic History Review* 44 (3): 259–77.

Macfarlane, Alan. 1978. *The Origins of English Individualism*. Oxford: Basil Blackwell.

McMillan, John, and Christopher Woodruff. 2000. "Private Order under Dysfunctional Public Order." *Michigan Law Review* 98: 101–38.

Moriguchi, Chiaki. 2003. "Implicit Contracts, the Great Depression, and Institutional Change: A Comparative Analysis of U.S. and Japanese Employment Relations, 1920–1940." *Journal of Economic History* 63: 1–41.

Morris, Colin. 1972. *The Discovery of the Individual 1050–1200*. London: S.P.C.K. for the Church Historical Society.

Muldrew, Craig. 1998. *The Economy of Obligation*. London: Macmillan.

Munro, John H. 1990. *The International Law Merchant and the Evolution of Negotiable Credit in Late-Medieval England and the Low Countries*. Edited by Banchi Pubblici, Banchi Privati, e Monti di Piet nell'Europa Preindustriale, and Dino Puncuh. Genoa: Societ Ligure de Storia Patria.

Myerson, Roger B. 2008. "The Autocrat's Credibility Problem and Foundations of the Constitutional State." *American Political Science Review* 102 (1): 125–39.

Nakamura, Shigeo. 2004. "Law, State and Society in China: Was Traditional Chinese Law a Mere 'Model'? Part Two." *International Journal of Asian Studies* 1 (2): 297–322.

North, Douglass C., and Barry R. Weingast. 1989. "Constitutions and Commitment: Evolution of Institutions Governing Public Choice." *Journal of Economic History* 49: 803–32.

O'Brien, Patrick K. 2001. "Fiscal Exceptionalism: Great Britain and Its European Rivals—From Civil War to Triumph at Trafalgar and Waterloo." Working paper 65/01, Department of Economic History, London School of Economics.

Okazaki, Tetsuji. 2005. "The Role of the Merchant Coalition in Pre-modern Japanese Economic Development: A Historical Institutional Analysis." *Explorations in Economic History* 42 (2): 184–201.

Olds, K. B., and R. H. Liu. 2000. "Economic Cooperation in 19th-Century Taiwan: Religion and Informal Enforcement." *Journal of Institutional and Theoretical Economics* 156 (2): 404–30.

Olson, Mancur. 1993. "Dictatorship, Democracy, and Development." *American Political Science Review* 87 (3): 567–76.

Pomeranz, Kenneth. 2000. *The Great Divergence: China, Europe and the Making of the Modern World Economy.* Princeton, NJ: Princeton University Press.

Quinn, Stephen. 2001. "The Glorious Revolution's Effect on British Private Finance: A Microhistory, 1680–1705." *Journal of Economic History* 61 (3): 593–615.

Rajan, Raghuram G., and Luigi Zingales. 2003. *Saving Capitalism from the Capitalists.* New York: Random House.

Shiue, Carol H., and Wolfgang Keller. 2007. "Markets in China and Europe on the Eve of the Industrial Revolution." *American Economic Review* 97 (4): 1189–1216.

Stulz, R., and R. Williamson. 2003. "Culture, Openness, and Finance." *Journal of Financial Economics* 70 (3): 313–49.

Sussman, Nathan, and Yishay Yafeh. 2000. "Institutions, Reforms, and Country Risk: Lessons from Japanese Government Debt in the Meiji Period." *Journal of Economic History* 60 (2): 442–67.

Szonyi, Michael. 2002. *Practicing Kinship. Lineage and Descent in Late Imperial China.* Stanford: Stanford University Press.

Tilly, Charles. 1990. *Coercion, Capital, and European States, AD 990–1992.* Cambridge, MA: Blackwell.

Triandis, Harry C. 1990. "Cross-Cultural Studies of Individualism and Collectivism." In *Nebraska Symposium on Motivation,* edited by J. Berman, 41–133. Lincoln: University of Nebraska Press.

Volckart, Oliver. 2004. "The economics of feuding in late medieval Germany." *Explorations in Economic History,* 41,(3). pp. 282–299.

Williamson, Oliver E. 1985. *The Economic Institutions of Capitalism.* New York: Free Press.

Wong, R. Bin. 1997. *China Transformed. Historical Change and the Limits of European Experience.* Ithaca, NY: Cornell University Press.

Yang Li, Mu. 2002. "Essays on Public Finance and Economic Development in a Historical Institutional Perspective." PhD dissertation, Stanford University.

Zelin, Madeleine. 2004. "Managing Multiple Ownership at the Zigong Salt Yard." In *Contract and Property in Early Modern China,* edited by Madeleine Zelin, Johnathan Ocko, and Robert Gardella, 230–68. Stanford, CA: Stanford University Press.

Zenkovsky, Serge, ed. 1974. *Medieval Russia's Epics, Chronicles, and Tales.* New York: Plume.

# 4

# MEAT CONSUMPTION IN
# NINETEENTH-CENTURY NEW YORK

Quantity, Distribution, and Quality, or
Notes on the "Antebellum Puzzle"

## GERGELY BAICS

## THE "ANTEBELLUM PUZZLE"

Anthropometric history has opened an intriguing new chapter in the standard of living debate. The term "antebellum puzzle" refers to the three decades prior to the Civil War characterized by the perplexing combination of rapid economic growth and growing per capita income on the one hand, and deteriorating biological standard of living, in particular declining physical stature and rising mortality, on the other.[1]

Scholars have proposed two lines of explanation for declining body heights: deteriorating diets and worsening disease environments. The nutritional thesis asserts that the amount of protein consumed in infancy, childhood, and adolescence has a positive impact on adult physical stature.[2] John Komlos set the direction of the debate by making the case for declining meat consumption. He concluded that "after 1839, average calorie and protein intake declined and did not reach its earlier level again until the 1870s."[3] Later, Komlos included

---

1 Declining physical stature for cohorts born from about 1830 to 1860 was first noted among white Union Army recruits, and has later been found for several other samples, including West Point cadets, free blacks in Maryland and Virginia, Georgia convicts, and Ohio National Guardsmen. Further research confirmed that the phenomenon was not confined to the United States, but body heights declined in the United Kingdom, Sweden, the Habsburg Monarchy, and Bavaria in the mid- to late eighteenth century, while the American cycle in the mid-nineteenth century also had its European counterparts, affecting among other countries Britain and the Netherlands (Komlos 1998; Komlos 2012; Haines 2004; Floud et al. 2011).

2 Insofar as adult body height is positively related to meat consumption levels at infancy, childhood, and adolescence, it can serve as a useful proxy for studying living standards. Recent research also corroborates that assuming an ideal body mass, taller people tend to have more robust immune systems (Fogel 2004; Floud et al. 2011).

3 Komlos's reasoning was that since agricultural labor force grew relatively slowly, while productivity gains in agriculture remained limited, the availability of food supplies lagged behind growing demand, which was largely a result of rapid population growth and urbanization. Per

other factors into this explanation (Komlos 1998, 783–93). He argued that the recession of 1837–43 negatively impacted household food budgets. He also stressed that rising income inequality must have disproportionately decreased meat consumption for lower income groups. Moreover, he emphasized that city dwellers, a rapidly rising share of the population, paid a premium for having to import food from growing distances.[4] For data, Komlos relied on production figures from the federal censuses, which left the period prior to 1839 unaccounted for.[5] Michael Haines turned to the New York State census, which contains production figures from 1825.[6] His data confirm Komlos's thesis, suggesting declining meat consumption already between 1825 and 1835. But questions of chronology remain: When did the decline begin? Was it part of a longer trend, or did the shift occur in the 1830s from a previously higher equilibrium?

Haines also reoriented the discussion to address both nutrition and mortality. Using new data, Haines, Craig, and Weiss found that a county's urbanization rate and its access to transportation networks resulted in higher mortality for residents.[7] Looking at physical stature, they turned to the data on white Union Army recruits. They found that both the quantity and the variety of the food supply mattered. Growing up in a county with a net surplus of protein increased adult body height, whereas greater agricultural specialization, that is less diversified local diet, had a slightly negative impact. Above all, the data provide strong evidence for the importance of deteriorating disease environments. Spending infancy and childhood in a county with higher death rates resulted in lower adult body height, and so did growing up in a more urbanized county

---

capita food output declined, while rising relative food prices also pushed consumers to substitute carbohydrates for meat (Komlos 1987, 908–19, 919).

4  Until the invention of refrigerated railroad cars and ships, transportation technology was not up to the task to ensure the shipment of fresh meat and milk over long distances at sufficiently low prices to offset this trend.

5  There are methodological concerns with this approach, including the reliability of early census figures, the problem of using production data for studying consumption, and the problem of converting animal counts into pounds, calories, and proteins. This latter issue triggered a lively debate between John Komlos (1996) and Robert Gallman (1996).

6  When calculating per capita selected livestock, milk, and milk products, Haines excluded New York City, as it imported all of its food supplies, and much of it from out of state. It is also unclear what percentage of the livestock was consumed locally or exported to cities. Haines's figures therefore do not refer to actual consumption rates, but instead suggest relative consumption (Haines 1998, 5, table 3).

7  Their data did not bear out any relationship between falling per capita nutrition and higher mortality rates. However, a small but positive relationship was found between regional specialization in agricultural production and mortality. The logic behind this was that commercial farming resulted in more specialized, that is, less diversified, regional agricultural production, which in turn contributed to the deteriorating composition of local diets. Access to regional transportation networks increased county-level crude death rates by about four per thousand, while a ten-percentage-point increase in the share of a county's urban population increased mortality by about 1.3 to 1.4 deaths per thousand (Haines, Craig, and Weiss 2000, 11–14; 2003, 396–98).

or in a county with better transportation.[8] The antebellum puzzle, the authors conclude, "resulted from a complex set of factors, including urbanization, increased population mobility, worsening mortality conditions, greater contact via improved transport infrastructure, and deteriorating nutrition" (Haines, Craig, and Weiss 2003, 409).[9]

Placing emphasis on the disease environment puts a premium on urbanization in explaining the phenomenon. That population concentration adversely affected life expectancy until public health reforms reversed this trend from the latter half of the nineteenth century is well established in the literature (Szreter 1997; Szreter and Mooney 1998; Cain and Hong 2009; Floud et al. 2011, 320–29). But a closer look at cities provides more to think about the nutritional thesis. Cities by definition rely on the countryside to sustain residents. When the overall meat supply falls, city dwellers are also affected, probably more than those living in rural areas. The reverse is also true: if there is plenty of livestock available, city dwellers tend to eat better. The problem with either logic is that urban provisioning is a mediated process, whereby adequate supply is a necessary but insufficient condition. It is not enough to transport the livestock into the city, but it also matters that a range of market intermediaries function properly so that the animals are slaughtered, processed, and retailed to customers. Even if there was sufficient supply, a poorly managed infrastructure could fail to ensure the proper provisioning of residents.

A closer look at the meat markets and the butchering trade in America's first metropolis allows for a better understanding of the process by which livestock landed on the consumer's plate as meat. In particular, three issues are examined: quantity, distribution, and quality of the meat supply.[10] Declining quantity has been the focus of the biological standard of living debate. First, I compare new meat consumption estimates for New York City before 1820 to Komlos's figures for the following decades, as well as exploit data on wholesale meat prices to study more precisely the decline of meat consumption in the antebellum period. Second, shifting the focus from supply conditions to the city's market intermediaries, new data on public markets are integrated into

8 An individual who spent infancy and early childhood in a county that produced a net surplus of protein one standard deviation (70 grams) above the mean would have ended up one- to two-tenths of an inch taller. Growing up in a county with eight per thousand deaths more than the average resulted in adult body heights of 0.11 to 0.13 inches lower. Spending infancy and early childhood in a county with good access to transportation reduced adult body heights by about a quarter of an inch, while for every ten-percentage-point increase in the urban share of a county's population, adult body height would have been one-tenth of an inch lower. Finally, farmers tended to be taller than laborers, offering further evidence of the negative impact of urbanization (Haines, Craig, and Weiss 2000, 11–14; 2003, 404–7).

9 Rising per capita income "was partly purchased at a price of some deterioration of the biological standard of living" (Haines, Craig, and Weiss 2003, 409).

10 This study builds on my earlier article, which examines New York City's public market system of provisioning in the preceding period of the Early Republic (Baics 2013).

GIS mapping to show that from around the 1830s, just as New York became an immigrant metropolis, characterized by rising income disparities and intensifying residential segregation, retail food markets spatially segmented, contributing to greater inequalities in residents' access to food. The chapter concludes with an analysis of the more neglected subject of quality. I argue that at a time when Gotham's food chains shifted from regional to national sources, the gradual informalization and eventual deregulation of retail meat markets in 1843 resulted in the city's complete loss of oversight of the quality of fresh provisions. Consequently, the quality of meat generally declined, which disproportionately affected the city's poorer residents.[11]

Overall, this chapter makes the case not only that antebellum urban dwellers consumed less meat than their parents' generation, like other scholars have argued, but also that their supply was less wholesome, while its distribution segmented along the modern city's deepening class divisions of space. Declining quantity, unequal access, and worsening quality were related mechanisms by which urban residents' nutritional standards came under pressure.

## WEAKENING SUPPLY CONDITIONS

The first step is to estimate how much per capita meat consumption declined in New York in the antebellum period. For this, my own per capita meat consumption estimates for New York City for 1790–1818, 1836–38, and 1842 are compared to decadal figures generated by Komlos for the United States, starting in 1839.[12] There are two difficulties with the comparison. First, Komlos's

11   Komlos also underlines that urbanization required food to be transported across larger distances, while commercialization increasingly separated the producer from the consumer. This, in turn, could cause greater concerns over the quality of fresh food supplies, especially fresh meat and milk. Yet to arrive at even suggestive answers about quality one has to move below the national level. This chapter addresses both the quantity and quality of the urban meat supplies through an urban historical case-study (Komlos 1996, 210–11; 1998, 790).

12   For a detailed discussion of how meat consumption rates were estimated for the period between 1790 and 1818, see Baics (2013, 645–49, table 1). For sources on slaughter rates: Common Council Microfilm Database, New York City Municipal Archives (CCMD): Market Committee (1816) 59:1416, Market Committee (1818) 66:1535, Market Committee: Stalls & Licenses (July–December 1818) 66:1537, Market Committee (1819) 72:1595; De Voe (1970, 234–35, 351, 411). For sources on market fees (excise taxes): New York Common Council (1917); Matteson (1930). To estimate meat consumption in 1836–38, the Market Committee's 1839 report gives annual counts for beef cattle. For 1842, the Comptroller provides estimates for the number of cattle and the total number of small livestock slaughtered in the city. To distribute "small livestock" into the relevant categories of veal, lamb and mutton, and pork, I used the 1818 ratios for the same animals. For sources: New York Board of Aldermen (1840, vol. 6, doc. 31, 374–75); New York Board of Aldermen (1843, vol. 9, doc. 46, 412). Finally, to estimate the city's population, all available census figures were used, assuming a constant rate of population growth between the two closest known observations (Rosenwaike 1972, 18, 36).

figures refer to the entire country, whereas mines are limited to the nation's first metropolis. Second, Komlos relies on production figures derived from the federal censuses, whereas my data measure the urban supply of meat based on slaughter rates and excise taxes. Unfortunately, the census does not allow for extending the chronology backward, nor do excise taxes and slaughter rates reach beyond 1842. In lack of better data, the two series are combined in Table 4.1 to establish a baseline from which to compare the widely noted decline of per capita meat consumption.

The table points to three conclusions regarding urban meat consumption in America during the first half of the nineteenth century. First, after the Revolution per capita yearly meat consumption reached a very high equilibrium. Between 1795 and 1816, the average New Yorker consumed about 160 pounds of fresh red meat,[13] more than half of which came from beef, an amount that measures up to the highest recorded figures in the twentieth century, according to data compiled by Roger Horowitz.[14] One should note that this figure leaves out a substantial portion of the meat supply, especially pork, for it does not include processed or preserved meats, such as ham, sausage, lard, bacon, and salted pork or beef, nor does it include poultry, fowl, and game. Clearly, on the evidence of their butcher's meat consumption, Early Republican city dwellers sustained a highly carnivorous diet.

Second, meat consumption declined significantly during the recession of 1837–43. Unfortunately, the data are patchy after 1818, yet it is possible to generate estimates for the city's beef supply for at least some of the recession years. Accordingly, per capita beef consumption in New York fell from an estimated 88.2 pounds in 1836 to 62.4 pounds by 1838. In 1842, at the tail end of the recession, it still was only 69.9 pounds, about 20 to 25 percent below the Early Republican rates. When comparing consumption estimates for all fresh red meat, the decline is even sharper.

The third point concerns the period after the recession: did meat consumption recover, or did it shift to a lower equilibrium? Lacking further data for New York, the analysis turns to Komlos's figures.[15] Accordingly, in 1839, estimated per capita beef production in America was 79 pounds, and the same for mutton

13  This average excludes the war year of 1813, when meat consumption was exceptionally low, and 1818, when there is good evidence that slaughter rates may have been slightly undercounted.

14  Horowitz cites more precise urban meat consumption figures for the twentieth century. In 1909, per capita meat consumption was 136.1 pounds for lower-, 163.7 pounds for middle-, and 201.6 pounds for higher-income families. In 1942, as a result of the Great Depression, respective meat consumption rates fell to 107.5, 143.6, and 166.1 pounds. Yet by 1965, they reached record levels: 205.2, 219.4, and 230.2 pounds for the same groups. The corresponding per capita beef consumption rates were 81.5 (1909), 69.4 (1942), and a staggering 104.7 pounds (1965) (Horowitz 2006, 11–17).

15  Alternatively, more recent per capita meat production estimates by Floud et al. (2011, 310, table 6.4) present very similar results, with the exception of mutton. For pork: 130.25 (1840), 116.91 (1850), and 106.93 (1860) pounds; for beef and veal: 78.70 (1840), 71.09 (1850), and 73.07 (1860) pounds; and for mutton: 1.17 (1840), 1.42 (1850), and 1.82 (1860) pounds. The 1840 figure of

**TABLE 4.1** Per Capita Meat Supply (Pounds), in New York City and the United States, 1790–1859

| Year | Fresh butcher's meat (NYC) | | | | | Production (USA) | | | | Consumption (USA) |
|------|------|------|--------|------|-------|------|--------|------|-------|-------|
| | Beef | Veal | Mutton | Pork | Total | Beef | Mutton | Pork | Total | Total |
| 1790 | 76.5 | 16.3 | 28.3 | 11.2 | 132.3 | | | | | |
| 1795 | 96.3 | 20.5 | 35.7 | 14.1 | 166.5 | | | | | |
| 1800 | 89.5 | 19.0 | 33.1 | 13.1 | 154.7 | | | | | |
| 1805 | 93.2 | 19.8 | 34.5 | 13.6 | 161.2 | | | | | |
| 1813 | 76.1 | 16.2 | 28.2 | 11.1 | 131.6 | | | | | |
| 1816 | 92.1 | 19.6 | 34.1 | 13.5 | 159.3 | | | | | |
| 1818 | 85.9 | 16.9 | 28.6 | 10.7 | 142.0 | | | | | |
| 1836 | 88.2 | | | | | | | | | |
| 1837 | 69.9 | | | | | | | | | |
| 1838 | 62.4 | | | | | | | | | |
| 1839 | | | | | | 79 | 18 | 142 | 239 | 213 |
| 1842 | 69.9 | 12.3 | 20.9 | 7.8 | 111.0 | | | | | |
| 1849 | | | | | | 72 | 14 | 121 | 207 | 194 |
| 1859 | | | | | | 73 | 11 | 99 | 183 | 181 |

*Sources:* Figures for the United States: Komlos (1987, 913, table 9); for NYC: Baics (2013, table 1), note 12.

was 18 pounds. These figures compare reasonably well with my 1838 and 1842 New York City estimates, especially if allowing for some wastage between farm production and urban processing. Continuing to the next decades, Komlos's 1849 and 1859 figures for beef and mutton indicate that after the recession, meat consumption shifted to lower levels. Importantly, he found the same declining trend for pork—unfortunately, no comparable data are available for New York—pushing his total per capita meat consumption estimates down from 213 pounds in 1839 to 181 pounds in 1859. This decline was further exacerbated by the Civil War, and continued even after.[16] Moreover, data compiled by Haines based on the New York State census confirm a trend decline in the production of cattle, hog, and sheep, starting already before 1835.[17] Overall, insofar as Komlos's and my series are comparable, Early Republican citizens seem to have consumed about 25 percent more beef—and about twice as much mutton—as those living in the antebellum era. In short, the fragmentary evidence suggests a notable decline in meat consumption between the two periods.

The role of the recession, however, needs to be scrutinized more closely. In Komlos's view, "the decline in heights of the second half of the 1830s may very well have been caused, or at least exacerbated, by the recession of 1837" (Komlos 1998, 788). Indeed, the New York City figures between 1836 and 1842 leave little space for doubt that households responded to the recession by forsaking a substantial portion, about 20 to 30 percent, of their meat consumption.[18] At the same time, evidence from Komlos and Haines that after the recession meat consumption settled at a lower equilibrium, despite that the American economy expanded for nearly two decades, suggests a long-term shift in the supply curve, instead of weakening demand, as the main reason behind deteriorating diets. The primacy of deteriorating supply conditions is further confirmed by Haines's finding that meat production in New York State contracted already before the recession.

---

78.7 pounds for beef and veal also compares well with my 1842 figure of 69.9 pounds, especially if considering that mine does not include the estimated 12.3 pounds of veal in that year.

16   His estimates for beef, pork, and mutton production and overall meat consumption after the Civil War are as follows: for beef, 56 (1869) and 64 (1879) pounds; for pork, 61 (1869) and 88 (1879) pounds; for mutton, 12 (1869) and 11 (1879) pounds; and for overall meat consumption, 130 (1869) and 161 pounds (1879). (Komlos 1987, 913).

17   According to Haines (1998, 27, table 3), per capita production of hog, cattle, and sheep in New York State (excluding the population of New York City) already declined between 1825 and 1835. The figures between 1821 and 1840 are as follows: 0.973 cattle and 1.719 sheep in 1821; 1.013 hog, 1.045 cattle, and 2.414 sheep in 1825; 0.815 hog, 0.989 cattle, and 2.235 sheep in 1835; 0.898 hog, 0.903 cattle, and 2.419 sheep in 1840. This decline continued until after the Civil War.

18   Better data for the twentieth century confirm that a severe economic depression could undermine urban meat consumption; see note 14 regarding the effect of the Great Depression on urban diets.

What do prices say about the meat supply of New York City over the first half of the long nineteenth century, and especially during the antebellum decades between 1830 and 1860? Figure 4.1 compares wholesale prices for beef and pork in New York, and for "all meats and meat products" and "industrial commodities" in Philadelphia between 1796 and 1859.[19] The comparison with industrial commodities prices serves to trace relative prices, in effect changes in the terms of trade between agricultural meat imports and urban industrial exports.

The price data outline three distinct periods, punctuated by two episodes of crisis. From the 1790s until the early 1810s, wholesale meat prices, while highly volatile, did not undergo any trend rise or decline, and the relative price of meat to industrial goods remained unchanged. The War of 1812, however, sent wholesale meat prices to unprecedented heights, especially in the conflict years of 1814 and 1815. Only by the end of the decade did meat prices stabilize again. Industrial commodities prices charted the same course, albeit the cycle began and ended a few years earlier. The second period lasted through the 1820s and early 1830s, and was characterized by very stable meat prices, and similarly stable, albeit slightly decreasing industrial prices. The relative price of meat to industrial goods therefore showed a modest rise in this period. Stability ended by the mid-1830s, when meat prices rose sharply, reaching a plateau in the first years of the recession of 1837–43. Soon after, meat prices fell to stabilize by the early 1840s at slightly lower rates compared to the 1820s. Meanwhile industrial commodities prices remained largely unchanged, and hence the relative price of meat rose sharply from 1835 until about 1840. The third period began in the late 1840s and lasted until the Civil War. It was characterized by gradually and persistently rising meat prices, and stable industrial prices.

The price series substantiate the earlier conclusions in three important ways. First, they underline that Early Republican urban meat consumption, proven to be remarkably high, was sustained by unchanging relative meat prices. The War of 1812 disrupted this equilibrium, but in the 1820s, it appears, meat consumption returned to the prewar rates. Second, rising meat prices from 1835 suggest that the recession did not trigger but rather exacerbated a declining trend in urban meat consumption, driven chiefly by deteriorating supply conditions. This view was echoed by market officials in New York, who when addressing in December 1839 the causes of the "late high prices of beef," blamed "the scarcity of the supply" (New York Board of Aldermen 1840, vol. 6, doc. 31, 374). This is not to overlook the role of the recession: rather, urban meat con-

---

19  Prices refer to barreled (= 200 pounds) beef and pork, but it is unlikely that fresh meat prices followed different trends. For Philadelphia prices for all "meats and meat products" are used, for they are more comprehensive, and strongly correlate with beef ("r" = .9) and pork ("r" = .97) prices. In addition, the comprehensive industrial commodities index is used, which strongly correlates ("r" = .93) with the prices of textile fabrics (Bezanson, Gray, and Hussey 1936, 1:392, 394, 2:9, 171; Cole and International Scientific Committee on Price History 1938).

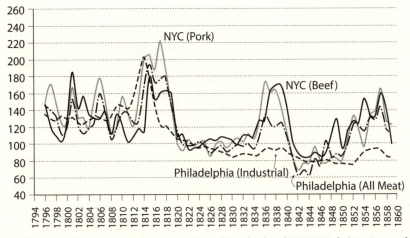

**4.1** Wholesale price indexes (base years 1821–25): Beef and pork in New York City, meat products, and industrial commodities in Philadelphia, 1796–1859.

*Sources*: Bezanson, Gray, and Hussey (1936, 1:392, 394, 2:9, 171); Cole and International Scientific Committee on Price History (1938).

sumption was squeezed both from supply and demand. By the mid-1830s, urban appetite for meat, for the first time, was outgrowing the availability of supplies, which resulted in rising meat prices. Soon after, however, the recession cut deeply into urban household incomes, pushing demand for meat down, which resulted in the fall of meat prices in the early 1840s.

Importantly, and this is the third point, even as demand recovered, supply—as documented by the evidence of rising meat prices—continued to lag behind until after the Civil War. This is additional evidence that antebellum urban meat consumption moved to a lower equilibrium compared to the Early Republic mainly as a result of a long-term shift in the supply curve. Indeed, between 1840 and 1860, the United States experienced its first period of accelerated urbanization, which pushed New York City's population above 800,000 and Philadelphia's close to 600,000. Even as new transportation technologies enabled cities to tap into vast new hinterlands for resources, growing demand for meat in America's booming cities still outpaced the availability of supplies.[20]

---

20 In essence, this was the argument presented by Komlos, which recently was reaffirmed by Floud et al., who concluded: "The general trend of food production prior to the Civil War was not favorable. Rapid population growth by urbanization and immigration had fettered food supplies per capita for major foodstuffs, though their gross levels were increasing" (Komlos 1987, 920; Floud et al. 2011, 316, 332).

Bringing the two sets of documentation together, two conclusions can be drawn about Gotham's meat supply in the antebellum era. First, confirming what Komlos and other scholars have argued, meat consumption declined considerably from the early to the mid-nineteenth century. It is also true that the decline followed a period of historically high rates of meat consumption. Considering that New Yorkers ate about 160 pounds of fresh red meat per capita in the Early Republic, an estimated 20 to 25 percent decline, while certainly substantial, may have not been all that dramatic. Indeed, one could argue that early American city dwellers had an excessive appetite for meat, in particular beef. From this viewpoint, the actual health effects of the antebellum decline may have not been unambiguously negative. Second, the evidence suggests that the recession of 1837–43 did not trigger but rather exacerbated an already unfolding declining trend in urban meat consumption, which was driven chiefly by deteriorating supply conditions. As a result of accelerated urbanization, urban demand for meat began to outgrow the availability of supplies, even as canals and railroads linked cities to ever expanding hinterlands. The recession resulted in a temporary setback of urban demand. However, the driving force behind falling meat consumption was a long-term shift in the supply curve, already evident by the mid-1830s.

## FROM PUBLIC TO PRIVATE RETAIL MEAT MARKETS

Thus far the analysis was limited to the supply of meat reaching New York City. The materials presented have said nothing about its distribution, in particular, how declining meat consumption affected different social strata of residents. Yet in a rapidly expanding metropolis, increasingly stratified by income and immigrant status, unequal access to plentiful and wholesome provisions was an important constraint determining households' nutritional standards. Since the question escapes any direct documentation, the chapter's second section pursues an indirect approach, probing Gotham's changing infrastructure and geography of food retailing.

In colonial and Early Republican New York, as in other major American cities, the retail trade of fresh red meat was restricted to licensed butchers, working out of municipally owned and managed public markets.[21] The underlying rationale of this central clause of the market laws was to enforce fair business practices and basic standards of food quality, by bringing the retail

---

21  Relevant legislation in New York dates back to the 1670s, and until deregulation in 1843, the Common Council repeatedly affirmed this crucial clause of the market laws. For example, the 1793 market laws stated that "no Person other than a licensed Butcher, shall cut up in any of the said public Markets or in any Street in this City, any Beef, Pork, Veal, Mutton or Lamb, or expose the same for sale, by the Joint or in Pieces, under the Penalty of Ten Shillings" (New York 1793, 7; Beal 1998, 314–15).

end of the provisioning chain under the watchful eye of the city government. In fact, by limiting the sale of fresh butcher's meat, such a key component of the American urban diet, into a handful of privileged locations, city officials artificially agglomerated the sale of all fresh food into the public marketplaces. For New Yorkers and residents across urban America, this meant that in their daily routine to provision their households, the neighborhood market served as the primary source of all fresh food supplies, including meat, fish and shellfish, milk and dairy products, vegetables and fruits. The municipal market system defined the political economy, geography, and daily experience of food shopping in American cities from the colonial era to the mid-nineteenth century.[22] In New York, only after two centuries, in 1843, did the city's legislative body, the Common Council, deregulate the retail food markets.[23]

Given the market laws' restrictions, studying the geography of food provisioning in early nineteenth-century New York City requires a spatial analysis of the municipal market system. The first step is to examine the extent to which the city's food retail infrastructure expanded at a sufficient rate to keep up with urbanization. Until 1843, this had to be limited to the public markets, and consequently it depended on the decision of city officials to erect new facilities in rapidly urbanizing northern neighborhoods, while also enlarging existing market buildings in more densely inhabited central areas. In order to capture both processes, the best way to measure the development of the public market system is to track the number of market stalls. Figure 4.2 presents the total number of butcher stalls in New York, and how many residents on average they supplied between 1800 and 1860.[24] For 1845, 1847, and 1850, it also plots the number of private meat shops, by then legally operating in the city, and the number of residents for each retail outlets, butcher stalls, and meat shops combined. One criticism of this method could be that the ratio of residents per stall needs not

22   For a discussion about urban provisioning in early New York, and the public market system more specifically, see Beal (1998); Tangires (2003, esp. 3–94); Horowitz, Pilcher, and Watts (2004); and Lobel (2014, 11–38).

23   On the causes and process of deregulation, see Tangires (2003, 71–94) and Horowitz (2008, 167–77).

24   I computed the number of butcher stalls for each year between 1800 and 1860 using Thomas F. De Voe's published books and manuscripts and the Common Council's published and archival records. Sources give stall counts and/or butcher lists for specific years only. For the missing years, I made informed estimates based on De Voe's histories of the individual marketplaces. Sources by De Voe: De Voe (1970); Thomas F. De Voe, *Manuscript Records*, New-York Historical Society, Manuscript Division [NYHS-MD]: "Ground Plans of the Public Markets in New York City, 1694–1866," "List of Butchers in N.Y.C. with Some Biographical Notes, 1656–1844," "New York City Markets Collection, ca. 1817–ca. 1878," 1–2. Council records: New York Common Council (1917); Matteson (1930). Additionally, from the New York City Municipal Archives, the Market Committee files in CCMD (1670–1831) and the City Clerk Filed Papers [CCFP] after 1831 were consulted: CCMD: Market Committee (1818) 66:1535; CCFP: "Returns of Different Markets, 1847, 1848, 1855, 1867." Further sources: New York (1809). For the number of meat shops, see Beal (1998, 346, 354) and Horowitz (2006, 25).

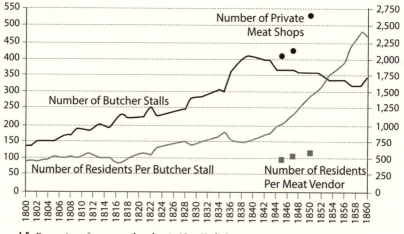

**4.2** Expansion of meat retail outlets in New York City, 1800–1860.
*Sources*: See note 24 for a detailed list of sources.

to be a constant, for butchers could expand the volume of their business. However, two structural constraints limited the extent to which this was possible. On the one hand, the lack of cheap mass transit limited the retail butcher's clientele to customers living within walking distance.[25] And on the other, the lack of modern refrigeration technologies required butchers to prepare only about as much meat as they expected to sell on any given day.

Figure 4.2 outlines three distinct periods in the spatial development of Gotham's food retail industry between 1800 and 1860. In the first one, which lasted through the 1810s, the City Council assumed a leading role in food provisioning and invested sufficient resources into the public market system. Even as the city's population quadrupled, the number of customers supplied by an average butcher remained close to 500. The market laws may have restricted open entry to trade. Still, city officials consistently expanded the market infrastructure to accommodate additional butchers to serve a growing population. In the second period, from the 1820s until 1843, the Council was more reluctant to expand the market system, and so the number of consumers per stall rose from about 500 to 750. To meet growing demand, butchers increased their volume of trade within the margins possible. At the same time, as anecdotal evidence confirms, unlicensed retailers also stepped in, occupying the economic niches left open by the official system. By the 1830s, the informal economy's share

25  Moreover, lacking reliable refrigeration, customers conducted three to four marketing trips per week. Accordingly, the local marketplace should not have been farther than about a ten- to fifteen-minute walk from one's home.

may have reached 20 to 25 percent of the city's retail meat trade.[26] In the third period, between 1843 and 1860, the Council no longer invested in the public market system, while deregulation allowed private meat shops to proliferate. Consequently, the number of consumers per outlet, even as city officials closed two marketplaces, returned to the early nineteenth-century level of 500. This confirms the earlier point about the limitation of the retail butcher's volume of trade, while at the same time suggests that many of these newly registered businesses belonged to butchers who had already sold meat informally before 1843.[27]

Interestingly, changes in supply conditions and the city's provisioning infrastructure followed similar chronologies. From the late eighteenth to the early nineteenth century, when New Yorkers could draw on abundant and affordable meat supplies, the city government also heavily invested in the expansion of the municipal market system. By the 1830s, just as supplies were becoming stretched and relative meat prices were increasing, the Council's waning commitment to the market system resulted in the proliferation of unlicensed vendors. Finally, from the mid-1840s to the 1850s, when supply conditions further deteriorated, and meat prices rose again, the Council officially abandoned its traditional responsibility of maintaining and monitoring retail food markets. As a consequence, meat markets further fragmented, and by the mid-nineteenth century market butchers, meat shop owners, grocers, as well as unlicensed street vendors served customers. The landscape of provisioning clearly shifted from the public to the private domain. And while the exact chronology may have differed from one city to another, the general trend across mid-nineteenth-century urban America was a similar shift to increasingly deregulated and fragmented retail food markets.

## GROWING INEQUALITIES IN ACCESS TO FOOD SUPPLIES

Fragmentation is, of course, a spatial concept, and thus a better understanding of the process requires an analysis of the geography of New York's food retail infrastructure. Importantly, in a booming metropolis, whose population increased from 120,000 to 800,000 between 1820 and 1860, and where

---

26  Assuming that the ratio of 491 consumers (the average of 1800–1820) per butcher stall persisted, the share of the informal economy would be as high as 37 percent of the city's retail meat trade in the 1830s. However, this is an exaggerated figure, for it ignores the margin by which licensed market butchers were able to increase their daily turnover. It is more reasonable to suggest that the informal economy in the 1830s represented about 20 to 25 percent of the city's retail meat business.

27  In reality, retail outlets in the mid-nineteenth century, on average, served more than five hundred consumers because many of the butchers at Washington and Fulton Markets increasingly focused on wholesale business.

population densities constantly shifted, the optimal allocation of food retail outlets was also a moving target. So how well did the public market system perform in distributing meat and other fresh food supplies to residents? To address this question, a series of GIS maps are presented (see Figure 4.3) drawing on a range of public market data from the City Council records. The maps examine first how closely the spatial allocation of the market system corresponded to shifting population densities, and second whether or not residential segregation based on income or ethnicity determined unequal access to food retail outlets.[28]

The first three GIS maps (Maps 1–3) study the relative volume of trade of the public markets in relation to ward-level population densities. The size of the circles represents the amount of excise taxes (1818) or butcher rents and fees (1835, 1855) the marketplaces generated. The maps show that whereas in 1818 a strong association existed between ward-level population densities and the relative hierarchy of the public markets, over the second quarter of the century, this relationship weakened, while by the mid-nineteenth century there was no correspondence at all between the two variables. Put differently, in the early nineteenth century, public markets played a positive role in sustaining urban

28  The maps document the changing internal hierarchy of the public market system between 1818 and 1855. For each map, the size of the circle represents the marketplace's relative importance within the public market system. Four kinds of indicators are used: for 1818, I use excise taxes; for 1835, 1845, and 1855, butcher rents and/or market fees (daily fees collected from all other vendors, including fishmongers, farmers, and hucksters); and for 1828 and 1850, the average annual rents butchers paid for their stalls. For 1818, the sources are: CCMD: Market Committee (1818) 66:1535, Market Committee: Stalls & Licenses (July–Dec. 1818) 66:1537; De Voe (1970, 235). For 1828: De Voe, *Manuscript Records* [NYHS-MD]: "Ground Plans of the Public Markets in New York City, 1694–1866." For 1835, 1845, 1850, and 1855: New York (1836, 62–63; 1846, 67–70; 1851, 36–39; 1856b, 48–53). The market hierarchy maps are overlaid on ward-level population density maps, taking into account the city's changing ward boundaries in the period. For ward-level population data and other socioeconomic indicators, I used the federal and New York State censuses. For sources: Rosenwaike (1972, 36); U.S. Census Office (1821, 62; 1832, 50–51); New York, Secretary's Office (1836, 1846); U.S. Census Office (1853, 102); New York, Secretary's Office (1857). For projecting catchment areas, I used an 1849 petition on behalf of the butcher Thomas F. De Voe of Jefferson Market to locate the residences of eighty-seven of his customers. First, I projected circles at one or two standard distances from the center of these locations, comprising 70 percent or 95 percent of the addresses. Second, I used Jefferson Market to project catchment areas for all the other markets based on two methods. First, I assumed that larger markets drew customers from larger distances, yet within their catchment areas, they generated the same density of exchanges. Second, I assumed the reverse: that all markets relied on an equally large territory, yet larger markets generated more trade within their area. The reality was somewhere in between. Here I present catchment areas for 1845 and 1855, using the first assumption. For the source, see De Voe, *Manuscript Records* [NYHS-MD]: "New York City Markets Collection, ca. 1817–ca. 1878," 1. Finally, for sources of Map 6, listing market law violations in 1841, and the locations of new meat shops in 1843–44: CCFP: "Violations of Market Laws, Nov.–Dec. 1841," Markets (1843); "Applicants for Butcher's License for Meat Shops," Markets (1844). For a more detailed spatial analysis, see Baics (2009, 141–85, 250–67, esp. 162–72).

growth by distributing food supplies to residents. By the 1830s, however, due to the Council's waning commitment to expand the market system, Gotham began to outgrow its traditional food retail infrastructure. The spatial misallocation of the market facilities, in turn, opened up economic niches to informal vendors. Retail fragmentation was further accelerated by the Council's decision to deregulate the meat markets in 1843.

Looking more closely at the maps, two distinctive spatial patterns—one running from south to north and another from west to east—also emerged in this period. By the mid-nineteenth century, north of Fourteenth Street, residents had no public markets to rely on, and therefore had to procure daily provisions entirely from groceries, meat shops, or unlicensed vendors. In the city's central and southern districts, the transition was subtler, as residents continued to have access to public markets, while they could also turn to a range of licensed and informal vendors outside of the public market system. Unlike the south to north pattern, which was the outcome of the City's reluctance to open new marketplaces after 1836, the west to east pattern reflected changes in customer preferences. By the 1840s and especially 1850s, the relative volume of trade of the public markets decreased from west to east, but this did not reflect ward-level population densities. On the contrary, food markets were smallest and generated the least amount of revenues in precisely those areas that were the most densely populated.

Taking the analysis one step further, Maps 4 and 5 compare the average stall rents butchers paid to do business at their individual marketplaces. They show that whereas in 1828 this indirect measure of the real estate value of vending space reflected the centrality of a public market's location as well as the surrounding area's residential density, by the mid-nineteenth century a clear west to east divide emerged, whereby public markets located in the less densely populated western wards commanded higher rents than those in the more densely populated eastern wards. Evidently, butchers working at Jefferson, Clinton, and Centre Markets were willing to invest two or three times as much capital into their businesses as their fellow tradesmen at Union, Essex, and Governeur Markets.[29] The significant spatial mismatch between rents and population size seeks explanation, for one would expect that a larger pool of customers would generate greater business turnover and thus higher profits for the butchers.

There are two possible ways to account for this discrepancy. On the supply side, market butchers serving eastern neighborhoods may have faced greater competition from licensed meat shops and/or informal food purveyors. On the

29  Washington and Fulton Markets were the only exception to the west to east pattern, which reflects their orientation to wholesale functions by this period. Even Catharine Market, once one of the city's largest and best, declined from the 1830s in terms of both its volume of trade and the rental value of its stalls, clear evidence that much of its business was captured by nearby stores and unlicensed vendors.

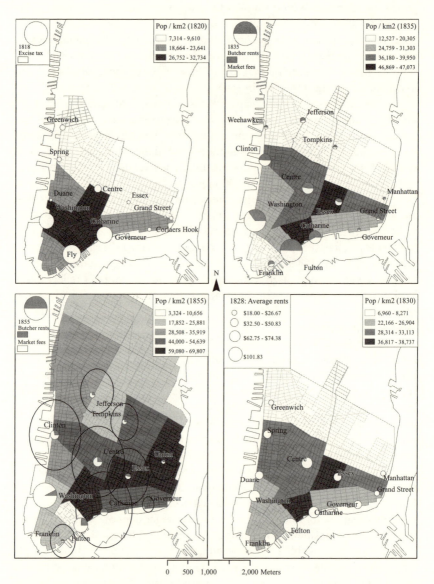

**4.3** Map 1: The public market system, 1818.

**4.3** Map 2: The public market system, 1835.

**4.3** Map 3: The public market system, 1855.

**4.3** Map 4: Rental value of market space, 1828.

For all maps 1–10 see note 28 for a detailed list of sources and a description of the methods.

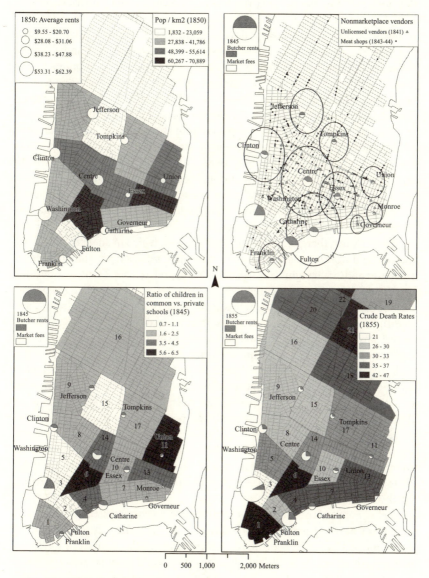

**4.3**  Map 5: Rental value of market space, 1850.

**4.3**  Map 6: Nonmarketplace vendors, 1841 & 1845.

**4.3**  Map 7: Sociospatial relations– schooling, 1845.

**4.3**  Map 8: Sociospatial relations– crude death rates, 1855.

demand side, it is possible that residents of the city's eastern districts, as a result of lower incomes or cultural preferences, purchased lesser amounts and/ or lower quality cuts of meat. Addressing the first hypothesis, Map 6 locates the addresses of fifty-nine cases of market law violations in 1841 and 273 meat shops, which had just opened in the city in 1843–44. The map points to two spatial patterns. First, if Centre Market represents the east-west divide, over 60 percent of documented informal meat sales occurred in the eastern wards. Second, and more important, in the eastern wards, both informal vendors and meat shops succeeded in directly penetrating the projected catchment areas of the nearby public markets, whereas in the western wards they were more confined to the spaces falling in between. Evidently, market butchers in the eastern wards faced greater competition from nonmarket vendors. This must have been because residents in these areas generated relatively more demand for the smaller quantity and lower quality sales, which were the trademark of street vendors, grocers, and even meat shop owners.

The key story, therefore, is differential demand, which in an increasingly immigrant and working-class metropolis must have reflected growing income inequalities and/or changing ethnic and cultural preferences. Komlos underlines that rising disparities of income, which characterized the antebellum period, disproportionately affected the nutritional status of lower income groups, and thus the decline in physical stature was observable above all with lower income Americans.[30] Accordingly, the last part of the analysis explores how social class and immigrant status corresponded to differential access to food.

Meat consumption differed with income in two principal ways. First, better-off New Yorkers could afford to eat more meat. It is also true that in New York even the poorest ate an impressive amount, despite that per capita consumption declined from the mid-1830s. Second, and perhaps more important, wealthier residents ate what were considered better quality cuts of meat. In general, wealthier New Yorkers preferred boneless, tender, and more flavorful cuts, which they usually ate as roasts or steaks, whereas poorer residents depended on tougher, leaner, bonier pieces served mostly in stews and soups (Horowitz 2006, 22–24).

A closer analysis of sociospatial relations offers a more systematic approach. Historians have argued that in the second quarter of the nineteenth century, social inequalities increased in New York, while at the same time rapid urban growth was complemented by intensifying residential segregation based on class and ethnicity (Pessen 1971, 1019–27; Stansell 1987; Blackmar 1989; Wilentz 1984; Stott 1990; Scherzer 1992). The question is what role segregation played in differential access to food supplies. Addressing this issue, Maps 7 to 10 examine how the hierarchy of the marketplaces, in particular their declining

---

30  See Komlos (1998, 783–85) and Komlos (2012, 51–54). This is also suggested by Haines, Craig, and Weiss (2003, 383–84, 409) and Haines (2004, 254).

scale from west to east, corresponded to ward-level social indicators from the 1845 and 1855 New York State censuses.

Lacking income data, the first map uses the ratio of children attending public versus private schools in 1845 as a proxy for the class composition of the wards.[31] The literature suggests a strong association between working-class status and public instead of private schooling, and a further advantage of this measure is that it reflects disposable income.[32] Looking at Map 7, one finds consistently increasing reliance on public schooling moving from west to east. The highest ratios were in the far eastern wards 11 and 13, and in the central-eastern wards 4, 6, and 14. In addition, wards 7 and 17, also on the city's eastern side, had relatively high ratios. In contrast, ward 15, corresponding to the Greenwich Village, the city's wealthiest area, had the lowest rate of public schooling.

Map 8 looks more directly at the biological standard of living, by charting ward-level crude death rates in 1855. It documents generally increasing mortality from west to east. Excluding ward 1, the commercial business district, where few people resided, and ward 21, a yet thinly populated urbanizing northern area, the city's most unhealthy district was ward 6, east of Broadway in the center, where the notorious and overcrowded Five Points slum was located. The second tier of high mortality rates was confined to the central-eastern wards of 4, 7 and 13, the northeastern ward 18, and the northwestern ward 20. The third tier included wards 11 and 17 also on the east, ward 14 in the center, and ward 5 on the southwest. Wards 5 and 20 were, in fact, the only western districts with relatively high mortality. All the other western wards (8, 9, 15, and 16) belonged to the city's healthier areas.

Shifting focus to immigrant status, Maps 9 and 10 examine the share of Irish- and German-born residents in each ward in 1855. Representing 28 percent of the city's population, the Irish lived all over New York, but especially in overcrowded and unhealthy tenement districts, located in the central and southeastern wards 4, 6, 7, and 14 and in the northeastern wards 18, 19, and 21.[33] The Germans, who constituted 16 percent of the city's population, concentrated in around Klein Deutschland, a densely populated tenement area at the intersection of the eastern wards 10, 11, 13, and 17. Combining the two groups, it is evident that the distribution of immigrants followed the much familiar west to east pattern. In general, east of Broadway and the Bowery and south of Fourteenth Street were the city's most densely populated immigrant

31  Using other measures, for example, the share of mechanics as a working-class and that of attorneys as a more middle-class occupation across the wards, produces very similar results (Baics 2009, 256–60).

32  By the 1840s, private schools requiring tuition usually served the wealthy, whereas working-class families sent their children to common schools. Middle-class families were more divided on their choice (Kaestle 1973, 75–111, esp. 85–100; 1983, 116–18).

33  While the percentage of the Irish-born was among the highest in wards 1 and 2, by the 1840s these southern areas had very small populations.

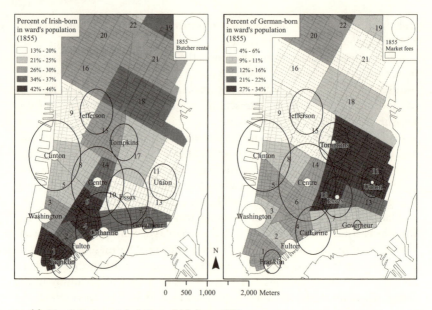

**4.3**  Map 9: Sociospatial relations– Irish-born, 1855.

**4.3**  Map 10: Sociospatial relations– German-born, 1855.

neighborhoods. In contrast, the most native-born wards (8, 9, and 15) were all located on the west. Not surprisingly, these were also the city's healthiest and wealthiest districts.

That east of Broadway—and further north, east of the Bowery—the city's wards were more working-class and immigrant in character is hardly a new finding (Stott 1990, 191–211; Scherzer 1992). But comparing these more widely noted residential patterns to the spatial distribution of food retailers allows for new interpretations concerning a much understudied aspect of the standard of living: household provisioning. Unfortunately, the analysis has to be limited to south of Fourteenth Street, as communities north of this line were left without convenient access to public markets, and no comparable data are yet available to study nonmarket retailers.

Two conclusions can be drawn from the sociospatial analysis. First, the west to east decline of the public market system strongly reflected Gotham's increasingly demarcated class relations of space. Residents living in working-class eastern wards had to be satisfied with smaller and lower quality food markets. This was most pronounced in wards 10, 11, 13, and 17, a vast area of densely packed working-class districts, which were left systematically underserved by this municipal infrastructure. Given the inadequate market facilities, local residents chiefly relied on groceries, meat shops, and street vendors. The same pattern, albeit to a lesser extent, applied to the southeastern wards of 4, 6, and 7.

Residents here still had access to Catharine, tiny Governeur, and marginally to Essex and Centre Markets. Yet by the 1840s, with the exception of Centre, they became insufficient to supply these crowded working-class wards. At the other end of the spectrum were the western wards of 8, 9, and 15. These middle-class districts had access to larger and better quality public markets: Clinton and Centre in the inner, and Jefferson and Tompkins in the outer ring. In particular, ward 15, the city's wealthiest area, was conveniently situated between the two most expensive outer ring retail markets, Jefferson and Tompkins.

The second conclusion concerns ethnic status. Wards 10, 11, 13, and 17, the area with the least access to public markets, composed the German settlement of Klein Deutschland. As Robert Ernst points out, Germans engaged in the butchering trade more than any other ethnic group. Capitalizing on their Old World skills as food purveyors, and serving a traditionally meat-eating clientele, German butchers operated meat shops across the city, and especially in their neighborhood.[34] Residents of Klein Deutschland may have been left without adequate public markets. Yet many of the local meat shops, groceries, and street vendors were run by their fellow countrymen. The Irish faced a far more difficult situation. The northeastern wards 18, 19, and 21 were left without public markets, while the southeastern wards 4, 6, and 7 had access to food markets, but these were insufficient to supply the teeming populations. Local residents largely depended on meat shops, groceries, and street vendors, but unlike the Germans, they could count less on shared ethnicity with food purveyors, while they were also less skilled in buying and handling meat products.[35] In stark contrast to this situation, residents in the more native-born western wards 8, 9, and 15 continued to purchase meat at larger and better quality public markets from craftsman butchers, most of whom were also native-born. Of course, meat shops and groceries also served these areas.[36] Differences in the daily routines of provisioning were a matter of degree in a city where even the most native-born ward was one-third immigrant. Still, living in ward 15 and being supplied with fresh meats from De Voe's neatly kept stall at the high-end Jefferson Market was a profoundly different condition of food provisioning than shopping at the dilapidated Catharine Market or at the corner groceries, meat shops, and street peddlers of the Irish ward 4.

34  According to Ernst, by 1846, about half of New York City butchers were immigrants, mostly of German but also of Irish and English origin. By 1855, two-thirds of the foreign-born butchers were German. An ethnic divide likely persisted between market and shop butchers. In fact, market laws protected native-born butchers from the competition of newcomers. Deregulation in 1843 opened the floodgates of immigrants entering the trade, and Germans seized the opportunity (Ernst 1949, 87, 214–17; Horowitz, Pilcher, and Watts 2004, 1073).

35  By the 1850s, corner groceries had already passed from Irish to German hands, and the Irish did not enter the butchering trade at any comparable rate. As food retailers, they engaged in marginal trades as fish and oyster dealers, hucksters, fruit and produce vendors, or street peddlers (Ernst 1949, 87, 214–17).

36  Groceries were relatively evenly distributed across the city (Baics 2009, 174–75).

To conclude, by the mid-nineteenth century, residential location determined New Yorkers' options of food retailers. This represented a profound shift
compared to the early nineteenth-century geography, whereby all residents depended on a select number of municipal marketplaces for their fresh meat and
other provisions.[37] During the antebellum decades, the public market system
fragmented into a variety of formal and informal retail arrangements, including
meat shops, groceries, and unlicensed vendors, which gradually mapped onto
Gotham's emerging ethnic and class divisions of space. The new free-market
geography responded to urban expansion with spatial dispersion, and accom-
modated intensifying residential segregation with the segmentation of retail
food markets. Of course, these spatial patterns only complemented the more
obvious source of inequality in access to food: that poorer residents had less
disposable income, and therefore could afford to purchase lesser quantity and/
or lower quality meats and other fresh provisions.

## DETERIORATING QUALITY

This last point leads to the problem of food quality. The literature is more hesitant to address this issue, probably because unlike quantity, the subject defies
any systematic way of measurement. In what follows, I pursue an institutional
approach, asking how informalization, deregulation, and the resulting spatial
fragmentation of market intermediaries affected the quality of meat and other
fresh food supplies. A good starting point is the Common Council, which in the
turn of the 1830s and 1840s endlessly debated the question of deregulation.
The Market Committee was strongly in favor of maintaining and bolstering
the public market system. In response to complaints about the "market monopoly of meat" by some, or its violations by others, its report from December
1839 clearly stated that the underlying purpose of the market laws was to promote the "public health" of citizens (New York Board of Aldermen 1840, vol. 6,
doc. 31, 363–77, 375).

> The various and important duties which are now performed by the Super-
> intendents and the Deputy Clerks of the Markets, in guarding the pub-
> lic health, by examining as to the wholesomeness of provisions; whether
> stale, or blown, plaited, raised or stuffed, measly or affected by disease;
> and whether proper cleanliness is observed; and as to other important Po-
> lice regulations, as to weights, measures, &c., if the business of vending
> meats, &c., is not confined to the Public Markets, become entirely vain and
> nugatory. . . . The health of our city is a matter of the highest consideration;

37  For more discussion of the food distribution system of Early Republican New York, see
Baics (2013, 651–54).

and the cleanliness, upon which it mainly depends, and which now characterizes our Public Markets, cannot possibly be preserved, if the business of dealing in all kinds of meats be diffused throughout the city.

Portraying the public market system as one of the city's central pillars of public health was a common line of reasoning.[38] Even the Council's Select Committee, charged with an unbiased study of the subject, arrived at the same conclusions in March 1840. "It is unnecessary to enter into a full discussion of the effect of an unregulated pursuit of the business of butchers upon the public health and convenience." Only if police regulations were fully carried out, "slaughter houses be removed entirely out of the populated parts of the city," as well as "all meats offered for sale undergo a proper supervision, as in other large cities in Europe," they added, could the market laws be abolished without harmful consequences for public health (New York Board of Aldermen 1840, vol. 6, doc. 55, 567–68). Despite such warnings, when deregulation was passed in January 1843, no such cautionary measures were taken.[39]

That debates about the market laws were articulated in the discourse of public health should be no surprise. By the late 1830s, the sanitary movement had gained enough ground to push public health into the forefront of a wide range of urban reforms (Duffy 1990; Melosi 2008). Yet market laws in American cities had reflected the same awareness for generations. In fact, as I argued elsewhere, the public market system had traditionally instituted five mechanisms of quality control of the city's food supplies.[40]

To summarize, city governments directly attended to public health issues. The Common Council set market hours from sunrise to midday, prohibited the sale of highly perishable foodstuffs in certain seasons, and entrusted market officials with extensive authority to monitor that the provisions offered for sale were wholesome, and that marketplaces were kept clean (Tangires 2003, 3–25, esp. 15–17; Duffy 1968, 50–52, 83–86, 222–27, 420–39). Second, by agglomerating hundreds of competing and complementary vendors into a handful of locations, the public market system fostered competition under government oversight. At the same time, the public market carried all varieties of fresh food, hence allowing customers to shop for quality and price. Third, market vendors used formal and informal means to suppress violations such as shirking or the

38   In their petition of February 1840, for example, the butchers accused the critics of the market laws with trying "to break down every barrier, and destroy every guard that the law has erected for the preservation of peace, health and morality" (New York Board of Aldermen 1840, vol. 6, doc. 55, 565–73, 572).

39   In fact, the revised ordinances extended the same sanitary regulations to shop butchers that applied to market butchers, and entrusted the superintendent of markets, the alderman, assistant alderman, street inspector, and health warden of each ward to enforce them (New York Board of Aldermen 1843, vol. 9, doc. 31, 257–62).

40   On the public market system's five mechanisms of quality control, see Baics (2013, 655–57).

sale of unwholesome food.[41] Above all, the butchers, who sold meat every day by their stalls, had a strong interest in safeguarding the general character and reputation of their marketplace.[42] The butcher's trade also had two features that promoted quality. Butchers were organized as a traditional trading craft, with a rigorous apprenticeship system to acquire their highly specialized skills.[43] They were granted a retail privilege in exchange of their public responsibility to handle a highly perishable and essential food product. Accordingly, obtaining a stall required formal petitioning to the Council, endorsed by other butchers and customers.[44] Moreover, butchers and customers conducted hundreds of face-to-face transactions, and personal trust between the two parties ensured that the meat offered for sale was reliable.[45]

By integrating five institutional mechanisms of quality control—government oversight, consumer choice, peer pressure, skilled craftsmanship, and direct sustained relations between vendors and customers—the public market system played a central role in sustaining food quality. The question is how it compared to alternatives. Certainly, informal retailing had a negative effect. First, even if unlicensed vendors, selling meat and other fresh foodstuffs on the streets, from their homes, or at shops, faced occasional fines from inspectors, on a regular basis, if they avoided being caught, their goods could be as poor quality as customers tolerated. Second, with the exception of those meat shop butchers who entered unlicensed retailing because they could not obtain a market stall, informal vendors were relatively less skilled in slaughtering and preparing fresh meat for consumers. Third, lacking membership in a tightly knit urban craft meant that nonmarket butchers faced less peer pressure from fellow tradesmen. Individual butchers working outside of the market system may have worried about their business reputation, but they did not have to uphold the standing of their craft. Fourth, the ongoing direct relationship between buyer and seller was less structured in the case of unlicensed vending. Informal trade, especially street vending, was by definition an unstable endeavor both

41  The market laws institutionalized peer pressure. If a butcher was suspected of selling unwholesome meat, the deputy clerk had to consult with two other butchers to make their judgment (New York 1812, 157). On conflicts with "shirk butchers," see Beal (1998, 317–20).

42  New York butchers were associated with a specific market stall from 1735 (New York Board of Aldermen 1854, vol. 21, book 1, doc. 41, 680–85; De Voe 1970, 130–31).

43  Butchery was one of the last traditional trading crafts in American cities (Wilentz 1984, 55, 137–39, 262, 270, 315–16; Tangires 2003, 61–68, 71–94).

44  For example, De Voe's 1849 petition to the Common Council was signed by 107 regular customers. De Voe, *Manuscript Records* (NYHS-MD): "New York City Markets Collection, ca. 1817–ca. 1878," 1.

45  A lasting merchant-client relation was sustained by two structural constraints: the spatial stability of the butcher's trade and residents' frequent shopping trips. On the butcher's side, market stalls were in short supply, and hence a butcher, who was granted a vending space, had the incentive to hold on to his stall. On the consumer side, the lack of modern refrigeration required households to make three to four marketing trips each week.

spatially and temporally. Of course, a shop butcher or a grocer, even if unlicensed, needed a stable clientele as well (Beal 1998, 394–413). But the reputation of the market butcher was further bolstered by the sanction of the city and other butchers. In general, informal retail required sales to be kept in disguise, which meant that the buyer had to trust more blindly the seller.

The legalization of meat shops in 1843, in theory, did away with some of the concerns that derived from the clandestine nature of informal food retail. Still, problems remained. Meat shop butchers and grocers, who sold fresh meat, did not have to undergo the same long years of apprenticeship as did market butchers. As these businesses mushroomed, while the Council lacked the manpower to monitor their transactions, they easily avoided the oversight of city officials and other butchers. Besides, even after deregulation, the boundary line between official and unofficial meat shops remained porous. Surveying the city's meat shops in 1847, the police found 426 of them dispersed across urban space, yet according to the superintendent of markets, only 178 held valid licenses and paid fees (Beal 1998, 354–55). Four years into liberalization, meat shops continued to escape government oversight. It appears that the Select Committee's warning from 1840 was right on target: in absence of sufficiently extended police power, deregulation would create a landscape of uncertainty, whereby a handful of municipal marketplaces were replaced by hundreds of dispersed and unmonitored sites.

Unregulated retail, however, was only part of the problem. Public health experts also worried about the unmonitored and decentralized practice of slaughtering. According to reports from 1850, besides the city's 11 public markets and 531 private meat shops, no fewer than 206 private slaughterhouses, many of them located in densely populated districts, generated hundreds of thousands of animal carcasses (Horowitz 2006, 25; 2008, 170). The decentralization of slaughter, which intensified during the early nineteenth century, caused grave nuisances to residents, as live animals were driven across the streets, while the removal of animal waste and meat byproducts posed insurmountable sanitary challenges.[46]

More important, deregulation left the city without any institutional capacity to inspect the quality of its meat supplies. This was the case because in New York, the deregulation of retail meat markets was not compensated by increased regulation higher up in the provisioning chain, in particular at slaughterhouses and/or a central wholesale market. Paris—even if with interludes—and Mexico City went through similar processes of deregulation decades earlier (Horowitz, Pilcher, and Watts 2004, 1067–74). Yet in Paris, in 1810, Napoleon I ended the practice of slaughtering within the city boundaries, and ordered that five public abattoirs be built in the city's outskirts, which opened eight years later

---

46  For a detailed analysis of the history and spatial organization of slaughtering in early nineteenth-century New York, see Day (2008, esp. 180–90) and Horowitz (2008, 169–71).

(Horowitz, Pilcher, and Watts 2004, 1074–75; Lee 2008, 50–62). The point is that the free market may have been the appropriate way to organize the daily exchanges between vendors and customers, but only insofar as the meat offered for sale was thoroughly inspected at abattoirs and/or a central market.

What is puzzling about New York is that city officials were fully aware of the issue, yet failed to act. In the 1840s and 1850s, public health experts in vain called for replacing Gotham's hundreds of private slaughterhouses with municipal abattoirs to be located north of Fortieth Street along the two rivers. The first to raise the subject was City Inspector John H. Griscom in his 1842 annual report (New York 1843, 181–84). Three years later, City Inspector Cornelius B. Archer expanded on Griscom's points, and advocated the adoption of the Parisian model of abattoirs, demanding that "all animals slaughtered at these places, should be subjected to rigorous inspection, condemning all that are unsound, and that no meat should be offered for sale in our market that had not been inspected and approved of" (New York 1846, 172–83, 181). Report after report, city inspectors expressed the same concerns: if after 1850 they devoted fewer pages to this subject, it must have reflected their frustration with having to repeat the same arguments at no avail.

All in all, by the mid-1850s, city inspectors became increasingly alarmed about unwholesome provisions. According to George W. Morton, while the sale of diseased meat disproportionately affected the poor, "to whom cheapness of price is an irresistible inducement" (New York 1857, 203–4), unsound provisions were sold not only by hucksters and peddlers, but also at markets and in basements across the city.[47] The institutional analysis presented here strongly suggests that informalization and deregulation at the retail level, coupled with the lack of investment in higher-order provisioning infrastructures, resulted in New York's complete loss of oversight of its entire provisioning chain from slaughtering to processing and retailing. This in turn must have had a negative impact on the quality of meat and other fresh food supplies. According to Horowitz, after deregulation "consumers may have found obtaining meat more convenient" in terms of the distances they had to walk, but their meat was "almost certainly not as wholesome" (Horowitz, Pilcher, and Watts 2004, 1073). The same assessment could be said about the entire range of fresh provisions. And even as the actual public health effects of deregulation may be impossible to measure, it is safe to conclude that New Yorkers must have paid a price in their biological well-being for relinquishing all their institutional capacity to inspect the quality of their food supplies.

Importantly, the adverse health effects of uninspected food supplies and unregulated market intermediaries were not distributed equally among citizens.

---

47 Diseased meat "is sold in our markets by the quantity, and is extensively retailed in basements throughout the city. On Saturday nights our avenues and minor streets are traversed with wagons and hand carts laden with it" (New York 1856a, 190–91).

From the consumers' viewpoint, the gradual shift of provisioning from the public to the private domain meant that households were left to their own devices to monitor quality. They could no longer count on the external authority of municipal officials or the internal mechanisms of the public market system to assist them in their choices. The problem was that consumers did not have equal access to information or resources to privately enforce quality. By definition, asymmetrical information characterized every food retail transaction, because the seller always knew more about the merchandise than the customer. And whereas better-off residents could protect themselves by choosing the most reliable food vendors, for poorer households prices severely constrained their pool of retailers, and thus the quality of their food supplies. In fact, by instituting basic standards of quality across all food retail transactions, the public market system protected above all the city's poorer residents from purchasing substandard provisions. On the contrary, unregulated and spatially segmented retail food markets contributed to increasing inequalities in access to healthy food supplies across households and neighborhoods of different socioeconomic status.

## CONCLUSIONS

This chapter offers a series of new conclusions about meat consumption in antebellum New York City. And while the limitations of a case study are obvious, looking at America's first metropolis offers new insights about urban living standards in general and the antebellum puzzle in particular. By comparing meat consumption estimates from Early Republican New York to the antebellum United States, this study indicates a 20 to 25 percent decline in per capita meat consumption between the two periods. It is also true that the Early Republican figure of 160 pounds of fresh red meat per capita represented a historically high level: compared to this base, the antebellum decline, while certainly significant, may not have been all that negative for the health of citizens. Additional price data substantiate Komlos's claim that the decline was related to the recession of 1837–43. This chapter suggests that the recession did not trigger but rather exacerbated an unfolding declining trend in meat consumption, which was driven by a long-term shift in the supply curve, already evident by the mid-1830s. Overall, this chapter provides further evidence that it was an insufficiently expanding supply, falling behind rapidly growing demand, that kept urban meat consumption at relatively lower levels in the antebellum period.

The urban angle also brings the vital issue of food quality into focus. Indirect evidence strongly suggests that Gotham's shift to increasingly informal and unregulated retail food markets adversely affected the overall quality of the city's meat and other fresh food supplies. Importantly, the process of deregulation explored in the case of New York was paralleled by similar developments in other major American cities. Suggestively, the general trend toward unregulated food markets coincided with rising urban mortality rates and declining physical stature across the nation. Establishing direct causal relations is beyond the reach of historical evidence. Still, it is reasonable to suggest that New Yorkers, and residents of other major cities experiencing similar transitions must have paid a price in their biological well-being for giving up all institutional capacity to monitor the quality of their fresh food supplies. The failure of city governments to offset deregulation at the retail level by investing in modern institutions of quality control at the levels of slaughtering and wholesale presents one important piece of evidence in explaining how changing food systems adversely affected the nutritional standards of American urban dwellers in the antebellum period.

Moreover, the spatial analysis documents the ways in which intensifying residential segregation based on income and ethnicity became intricately tied to the city's increasingly segmented and unequal landscape of household provisioning. By the mid-nineteenth century, American cities acquired clearly defined social geographies. The crucial point about segregation was that residential location increasingly determined unequal access to life's most basic resources, including shelter, sanitary infrastructures, and wholesome provisions. New York was at the forefront of nineteenth-century urbanization, and the city's residents experienced staggering inequalities in many aspects of their living standards. While housing and sanitation may have attracted the most attention from scholars, this chapter calls attention to another fundamental layer of spatial inequality in the urban environment: access to healthy food options.

New York City, of course, is only one case, and it is easy to see how it may not be representative. Further case studies are needed to arrive at more definitive conclusions about antebellum urban food consumption not only with regard to quantity, but also concerning the less studied aspects of quality and inequality. Such a renewed and comprehensive approach to how American cities managed their infrastructure of provisioning in response to rapid urban growth would have the added benefit of providing joint pieces of the antebellum puzzle in support of both lines of explanation: the nutritional thesis and the focus on urbanization and disease environments.

## ACKNOWLEDGMENTS

I would like to thank Joel Mokyr and Josef Barton at Northwestern University, and David F. Weiman at Barnard College for their helpful comments with this chapter.

## BIBLIOGRAPHY

Baics, Gergely. 2009. "Feeding Gotham: A Social History of Urban Provisioning, 1780–1860." PhD dissertation, Northwestern University.

———. 2013. "Is Access to Food a Public Good? Meat Provisioning in Early New York City, 1790–1820." *Journal of Urban History* 39 (4): 643–68.

Beal, Thomas D. 1998. "Selling Gotham: The Retail Trade in New York City from the Public Market to Alexander T. Stewart's Marble Palace, 1625–1860." PhD dissertation, State University of New York at Stony Brook.

Bezanson, Anne, Robert D. Gray, and Miriam Hussey. 1936. *Wholesale Prices in Philadelphia, 1784–1861*. Philadelphia: University of Pennsylvania Press.

Blackmar, Elizabeth. 1989. *Manhattan for Rent, 1785–1850*. Ithaca, NY: Cornell University Press.

Cain, Louis, and Sok Chul Hong. 2009. "Survival in 19th Century Cities: The Larger the City, the Smaller Your Chances." *Explorations in Economic History* 46 (4): 450–63.

City Clerk Filed Papers, New York City Municipal Archives [CCFP].

Cole, Arthur H. 1938. *Wholesale Commodity Prices in the United States, 1700–1861. Statistical Supplement: Actual Wholesale Prices of Various Commodities*. Cambridge, MA: Harvard University Press.

Common Council Microfilm Database, New York City Municipal Archives [CCMD].

Day, Jared N. 2008. "Butchers, Tanners, and Tallow Chandlers: The Geography of Slaughtering in Early-Nineteenth-Century New York City." In *Meat, Modernity, and the Rise of the Slaughterhouse*, edited by Paula Y. Lee, 178–97. Durham: University of New Hampshire Press.

De Voe, Thomas F. 1970. *The Market Book: A History of the Public Markets of the City of New York*. New York: A. M. Kelley.

De Voe, Thomas F. *Manuscript Records*. New-York Historical Society, Manuscript Division [NYHS-MD].

Duffy, John. 1968. *A History of Public Health in New York City, 1625–1866*. New York: Russell Sage Foundation.

———. 1990. *The Sanitarians: A History of American Public Health*. Urbana: University of Illinois Press.

Ernst, Robert. 1949. *Immigrant Life in New York City, 1825–1863*. New York: King's Crown Press.

Floud, Roderick, Robert W. Fogel, Bernard Harris, and Sok Chul Hong. 2011. *The Changing Body: Health, Nutrition, and Human Development in the Western World since 1700*. Cambridge: Cambridge University Press.

Fogel, Robert W. 2004. *The Escape from Hunger and Premature Death, 1700–2100. Europe, America, and the Third World*. Cambridge: Cambridge University Press.

Gallman, Robert E. 1996. "Dietary Change in Antebellum America." *Journal of Economic History* 56 (1): 193–201.

Haines, Michael R. 1998. "Health, Height, Nutrition, and Mortality: Evidence on the "Antebellum Puzzle" from Union Army Recruits in the Middle of the Nineteenth Century." NBER Historical Working Paper Series 107.

———. 2001. "The Urban Mortality Transition in the United States, 1800–1940." NBER Historical Working Paper Series 134.

———. 2004. "Growing Incomes, Shrinking People—Can Economic Development Be Hazardous to Your Health? Historical Evidence for the United States, England, and the Netherlands in the Nineteenth Century." *Social Science History* 28 (2): 249–70.

Haines, Michael R., Lee A. Craig, and Thomas Weiss. 2000. "Development, Health, Nutrition, and Mortality: The Case of the 'Antebellum Puzzle' in the United States." NBER Historical Working Paper Series 130.

———. 2003. "The Short and the Dead: Nutrition, Mortality, and the "Antebellum Puzzle" in the United States." *Journal of Economic History* 63 (2): 382–413.

Horowitz, Roger. 2006. *Putting Meat on the American Table: Taste, Technology, Transformation*. Baltimore: Johns Hopkins University Press.

———. 2008. "The Politics of Meat Shopping in Antebellum New York City." In *Meat, Modernity, and the Rise of the Slaughterhouse*, edited by Paula Y. Lee, 167–77. Durham: University of New Hampshire Press.

Horowitz, Roger, Jeffrey M. Pilcher, and Sydney Watts. 2004. "Meat for the Multitudes: Market Culture in Paris, New York City, and Mexico City over the Long Nineteenth Century." *American Historical Review* 109 (4): 1055–83.

Kaestle, Carl F. 1973. *The Evolution of an Urban School System: New York City, 1750–1850*. Cambridge, MA: Harvard University Press.

———. 1983. *Pillars of the Republic: Common Schools and American Society, 1780–1860*. New York: Hill and Wang.

Komlos, John. 1987. "The Height and Weight of West Point Cadets: Dietary Change in Antebellum America." *Journal of Economic History* 47 (4): 897–927.

———. 1996. "Anomalies in Economic History: Toward a Resolution of the "Antebellum Puzzle."" *Journal of Economic History* 56 (1): 202–14.

———. 1998. "Shrinking in a Growing Economy? The Mystery of Physical Stature during the Industrial Revolution." *Journal of Economic History* 58 (3): 779–802.

———. 2012. "A Three-Decade "Kuhnian" History of the Antebellum Puzzle: Explaining the Shrinking of the US Population at the Onset of Modern Economic Growth." Munich Discussion Paper No. 2012-10. http://ssrn.com/abstract=2021060.

Lee, Paula Y. 2008. "Siting the Slaughterhouse: From Shed to Factory." In *Meat, Modernity, and the Rise of the Slaughterhouse*, edited by Paula Y. Lee, 46–70. Durham: University of New Hampshire Press.

Lobel, Cindy R. 2014. *Urban Appetites: Food and Culture in Nineteenth Century New York*. Chicago: University of Chicago Press.

Matteson, David M. 1930. *Minutes of the Common Council of the City of New York, 1784–1831: Analytical Index*. New York: M. B. Brown.

Melosi, Martin. 2008. *The Sanitary City: Environmental Services in Urban America from Colonial Times to the Present*. Pittsburgh: University of Pittsburgh Press.

New York (N.Y.). 1793. *Laws and Ordinances, Ordained and Established by the Mayor, Aldermen and Commonalty of the City of New-York*. New-York: Hugh Gaine.

———. 1809. *List of the Constables, Marshals, Butchers, Cartmen, and Porters, for the City and County of New-York, in the Mayoralty of De Witt Clinton, esq*. New-York: H.C. Southwick.

———. 1812. *Laws and Ordinances, Ordained and Established by the Mayor, Aldermen and Commonalty of the City of New-York*. New-York: Pelsue and Gould.

———. 1836. *Annual Report of the Comptroller, with the Accounts of the Corporation of the City of New-York, for the Year Ending with the Thirty-First Day of December, 1835. Also, the Account Current of the Commissioners of the Sinking Fund, for the Same Period*. New-York: Childs and DeVoe.

———. 1843. *Annual Report of the Internments in the City and County of New-York for the Year 1842*. New-York: James Van Norden.

———. 1846. *Annual Report of the City Inspector of the City of New-York for the Year 1845*. New York.

———. 1846. *Annual Statement of the Funds of the Corporation of the City of New-York, for the Year Ending December 31, 1845, Including Accounts of Its Revenues and Expenditures in Detail, and of the Receipts and Investments of the Commissioners of the Sinking Fund, during the Same Period*. New-York: L. L. O'Sullivan.

———. 1851. *Comptroller's Annual Report of the Revenues and Expenditures of the City of New York, for the Year 1850: Including an Account of the Receipts and Investments of the Commissioners of the Sinking Fund during the Same Period*. New York: McSpedon & Baker.

——. 1856a. *Annual Report of the City Inspector of the City of New York for the Year Ending December 31, 1855*. New York: McSpedon & Baker.

——. 1856b. *Annual Report of the Comptroller of the City of New York, of the Receipts and Expenditures of the Corporation, for the Year 1855*. New York: McSpedon & Baker.

——. 1857. *Annual Report of the City Inspector, of the City of New York, for the Year 1856*. New York: Charles W. Baker.

New York (N.Y.). Board of Aldermen. 1840. *Documents of the Board of Aldermen of the City of New York*. Vol. 6. New York: Bryant & Boggs.

——. 1843. *Documents of the Board of Aldermen of the City of New York*. Vol. 9. New York: Charles King.

——. 1854. *Documents of the Board of Aldermen of the City of New York*. Vol. 21. New York: McSpedon & Baker.

New York (N.Y.). Common Council. 1917. *Minutes of the Common Council of the City of New York, 1784–1831*. New York: M. B. Brown.

New York (State). Secretary's Office. 1836. *Census of the State of New York for 1835; Containing an Enumeration of the Inhabitants of the State, with Other Statistical Information*. Albany: Croswell, Van Benthuysen & Burt.

——. 1846. *Census of the State of New York for 1845. Containing an Enumeration of the Inhabitants of the State, with Other Statistical Information*. Albany: Carroll & Cook.

——. 1857. *Census of the State of New York for 1855. Prepared from the Original Returns*. Albany: C. Von Benthuysen.

Pessen, Edward. 1971. "The Egalitarian Myth and the American Social Reality: Wealth, Mobility, and Equality in the "Era of the Common Man." *American Historical Review* 76 (4): 989–1034.

Rosenwaike, Ira. 1972. *Population History of New York City*. Syracuse, NY: Syracuse University Press.

Scherzer, Kenneth A. 1992. *The Unbounded Community: Neighborhood Life and Social Structure in New York City, 1830–1875*. Durham, NC: Duke University Press.

Stansell, Christine. 1987. *City of Women: Sex and Class in New York, 1789–1860*. Urbana: University of Illinois Press.

Stott, Richard B. 1990. *Workers in the Metropolis: Class, Ethnicity, and Youth in Antebellum New York City*. Ithaca, NY: Cornell University Press.

Szreter, Simon. 1997. "Economic Growth, Disruption, Deprivation, Disease, and Death: On the Importance of the Politics of Public Health for Development." *Population and Development Review* 23 (4): 693–728.

Szreter, Simon, and Graham Mooney. 1998. "Urbanization, Mortality, and the Standard of Living Debate: New Estimates of the Expectation of Life at Birth in Nineteenth-Century British Cities." *Economic History Review* 51 (1): 84–112.

Tangires, Helen. 2003. *Public Markets and Civic Culture in Nineteenth-Century America*. Baltimore: Johns Hopkins University Press.

U.S. Census Office. 1821. *Census for 1820. Published by Authority of an Act of Congress, under the Direction of the Secretary of State*. Washington, DC: Gales & Seaton.

——. 1832. *Fifth Census; or, Enumeration of the Inhabitants of the United States, 1830. To Which Is Prefixed, a Schedule of the Whole Number of Persons within the Several Districts of the United States, Taken According to the Acts of 1790, 1800, 1810, 1820*. Washington, DC: Duff Green.

——. 1853. *The Seventh Census of the United States: 1850*. Washington, DC: Robert Armstrong.

Wilentz, Sean. 1984. *Chants Democratic: New York City and the Rise of the American Working Class, 1788–1850*. New York: Oxford University Press.

# 5

# FUNDING EMPIRE

Risk, Diversification, and the Underwriting of
Early Modern Sovereign Loans

## MAURICIO DRELICHMAN AND HANS-JOACHIM VOTH

At the dawn of sovereign lending, the relationship between princes and their
bankers was crucial. Edward III's failure to repay his debts bankrupted the Flor-
entine families of the Peruzzi and the Bardi. The Medici Bank's many woes in
the late fifteenth century were precipitated by ill-fated loans to the Lancastrian
side in the Wars of the Roses.[1] Charles V famously bribed the electors of the
Holy Roman Empire with a loan from Jacob Fugger the Rich, who also refused
to cash the bills of exchange supplied by Charles's main competitor.[2]

A large literature has focused on the effects of sovereign defaults on the
prominent international bankers who risked their wealth (and sometimes their
lives) on a monarch's whim or good fortune. Most of this literature is written
as if loans were extended directly by wealthy financiers, writing large checks to
sovereigns at their discretion.[3] In actual fact, bankers would seldom offer a loan
using only their own capital. Rather, much as modern banks do, they would tap
a variety of financing sources, including demand deposits and the sale of shares
in the sovereign lending ventures. These arrangements enabled them to supply
much larger loans than their own resources could allow, while at the same time
limiting their exposure and spreading the risk among their customers and eq-
uity partners.

In this chapter, we reconstruct the chain of financing of two large sovereign
loans to Philip II of Spain. Using archival documents from both the king's
treasury and Genoese banking families, we document the terms that international bankers negotiated with the king in Madrid, and then trace some of the
ultimate risk bearers to a partnership of merchants back in Genoa. Since the
two loans were caught in Philip's fourth bankruptcy in 1596, we are also able
to explore how the losses were apportioned, and what the impact of the

---

1  See De Roover (1966), still the classic account on the Medici Bank.

2  See Parker (1999, 121).

3  For some classic examples, see Carande (1987), De Roover (1966), Braudel (1966), and
Reinhart and Rogoff (2009). Notable exceptions are De Maddalena and Kellenbenz (1986) and
Neri (1989).

default on the balance sheets of each participant was. The Genoese system for financing and arranging short-term loans effectively spread the risk of lending to capricious monarchs. Complete ruin as a result of a sovereign debt crisis was unlikely because of diversification of risk at the level of the final investors. This would even have been true in scenarios that are worse than the ones that actually transpired.

In previous work, we examined international loans to Philip II. We obtained each of the 435 short-term debt contracts signed between the king and his bankers from 1566 to 1598 from the Archive of Simancas. We then constructed a database capturing every single clause in the contracts, and reconstructed the agreed cash flows. Based on these data, we concluded that Castile's fiscal position was sustainable throughout Philip's reign, and that the defaults that fell within our period of analysis were temporary liquidity crises (Drelichman and Voth 2010). We also explored the incentives that governed the relationship between the king and his lenders, finding that repayment was enforced through a network of lenders. This network—a private-order institution, in the parlance of Greif (2006)—wielded considerable market power. In good times, the king serviced his loans; after each default, he came back to the negotiating table as soon as his fiscal position allowed (Drelichman and Voth 2011a). Lending to the king was profitable—the average short-dated loan generated returns that were higher than the opportunity cost of funds (Drelichman and Voth 2011b). Much of the lending involved contingent clauses. These allowed the king and the bankers to effectively share the risk of adverse fiscal events (Drelichman and Voth, forthcoming).

In this chapter, we move from the profitability of individual loans brokered by international bankers to the profitability of lending to the king of Spain for the final investor. We investigate the chain of financial intermediation that linked the king to investors small and large throughout Europe, who ultimately bore the risks. To do so, we rely on two account books from Genoese merchant families preserved in the Doria Archive of Genoa.[4] They document the purchase of participations in two large loans to Philip II, and the subsequent performance of these investments during the 1596 default. For the individuals in question, these loans constituted a small part of highly diversified portfolios. In consequence, the bankruptcies had only a minimal impact on the overall performance of the partnerships. International bankers were successful in effectively spreading the large risks of lending to the Spanish crown. Multiple layers of financial intermediation parceled out the many loans that underwrote Spanish power, and a large number of investors benefitted from the high returns available from lending.

---

4  One of these books was discussed by Felloni (1978), while the other one is not mentioned in the literature. Prior to our work, however, it was not possible to link these documents to the specific loans to Philip II, or to compare their relative performance.

We proceed as follows. The second section provides a short historical primer on Castilian debt instruments and on debt crises. The third section gives a detailed description of two loan contracts between the king and international bankers. The fourth section shows how the bankers then spread their risk, selling shares in the loans to downstream investors in Genoa. The fifth section analyzes the impact of the 1596 default on all the parties involved, and the sixth and final section concludes.

## HISTORICAL BACKGROUND

### Castilian Debt Instruments

Philip II relied mostly on two types of debt instruments: long-term bonds backed by stable sources of revenue (*juros*) and short-term unsecured bank loans (*asientos*). Juros were either perpetual or lifetime bonds. Their issuance was subject to a limit set by the Cortes, the representative assembly of the cities of Castile. The Cortes designated the revenue streams that could be used as collateral. This limit was kept well below the fiscal capacity of the state, which made juros very safe investments. Their interest rates exhibited a slow secular decline throughout the sixteenth century; during the reign of Philip II, most juros yielded between 5 percent and 7.14 percent. The bonds were transferrable with permission from the Crown, which charged a fee for it.[5]

Juros were the cheapest source of funds for the Crown, and at any given time they constituted between 75 percent and 90 percent of total royal debt.[6] They nonetheless suffered from some important drawbacks. Finding investors with sufficiently deep pockets and long horizons on short notice could be problematic, as the Crown did not have a financial network of its own. As the sixteenth century progressed, the domestic capital market became more and more saturated with the bonds, forcing the king to place them abroad through intermediaries. More important, once the debt ceiling was reached, the king had to seek permission from the Cortes to increase it. This inevitably led to protracted negotiations and costly concessions. Finally, highly volatile revenues such as the remittances of American treasure could not be used to back perpetual bonds.

When issuing juros to satisfy financing needs was not practical, the Crown turned to asientos. First introduced during the reign of Charles V, these short-term unsecured loans were underwritten by Spanish and international

---

5 The study of juros is notoriously difficult, as the relevant archival sources are vast, disorganized, and uncatalogued. The most complete study to date is Toboso Sánchez (1987). See also Torres López and Pérez-Prendes (1963).

6 See Drelichman and Voth (2010).

financiers.[7] Their amounts, maturities, interest rates, and other terms and conditions varied enormously. Among the 435 contracts in our database, some are as large as 25 percent of yearly Crown revenue, while others are underwritten for seemingly trivial amounts. A large proportion of asientos were used to supply the battlefield needs of the Spanish armies throughout Europe, and hence they involved transfer services and foreign exchange operations. Short-term loans also served to supply the needs of the court in Madrid, and to pay for special projects like the building of the palace-monastery of El Escorial. Repayment was promised from every available revenue source, from the silver fleets to the sales taxes of various cities. The returns of asientos were sometimes enhanced by granting the bankers favorable treatment in other financial operations.[8]

*Crises*

Philip II suspended payments on short-term debt four different times during his reign. The first two episodes, in 1557 and 1560, affected debts granted by the Fugger and Welser families to Charles V. They were settled with the transfer of Crown assets, including the lucrative masterships of the military orders and the mercury mines at Almadén.[9] Philip's own short-term borrowing began in earnest in the mid-1560s, relying mainly on a network of Genoese banking families. In Drelichman and Voth (2011a) we showed how this network created the incentives for the king to consistently repay his debts, combining market power with a cheat-the-cheater mechanism. The two further bankruptcies, in 1575 and 1596, happened in the wake of unusually adverse events—expensive military defeats and very low silver remittances. Because their triggers were outside the king's control and independently verifiable, these defaults were considered excusable, and bankers did not impose penalties on Castile once the situation was resolved (Grossman and Van Huyck 1988; Drelichman and Voth, forthcoming).[10]

We have elsewhere shown that Castile's defaults under Philip II were the result of temporary—if serious—liquidity crises, and that the long-run fiscal situation was sustainable throughout (Drelichman and Voth 2010). Consistent with this, the king suspended payments on his short-term unsecured debt,

7   The most complete account on the asientos of Charles V is Carande (1987).

8   For example, bankers could be allowed to export bullion in excess of the amount needed to fulfill their commitments, hence allowing them to profit from arbitrage across different markets. Another common concession was the ability to swap low-yield juros for high-yield ones.

9   A detailed account of the 1557 suspension and the period running up to the 1560 one can be found in Rodríguez-Salgado (1988).

10   The 1575 default was preceded by a large increase in military expenditure and an unexpected revenue shortfall due to unusually poor treasure fleets. The 1596 default was similarly triggered by increase expenditures following British and French attacks.

while continuing to service the juros that were backed by stable revenues. The defaults, therefore, never affected more than 25 percent of outstanding debt (the 1575 ratio), and in the case of 1596 happened on barely 10 percent of total liabilities. Settlements were negotiated very quickly, even by modern-day standards. The 1575 bankruptcy was resolved in two years, and the 1596 one in less than twelve months. All lenders were treated equally and capital losses were moderate.[11] Lending resumed immediately, and the terms and conditions of the new loans were statistically indistinguishable from those prevailing before the suspensions (Drelichman and Voth, forthcoming).

The 1575 bankruptcy is perhaps the most studied event in Castilian financial history.[12] It affected nearly two years' worth of revenue, and put the Genoese lending system to the test. In some accounts, the default is even held directly responsible for Castile's military setbacks in the Netherlands.[13] The pressing need to find short-term resources triggered a feverish round of political bargaining between the king and the Cortes, which concluded with the first major tax increase of Philip's reign.[14] In the end, the large military expenditures that helped trigger the default waned as Castile reduced the intensity of its warfare, while silver remittances returned to their previous volume. The reversal of the liquidity shocks, together with the capital reductions and the tax increases, provided the king with ample fiscal breathing room that would last for almost a decade.

The payment stop of 1596 was much less dramatic. According to Castillo (1972), the suspension decree was hastily promulgated in the mistaken belief that the Crown would have to make disbursements in excess of fourteen million ducats in the very near term.[15] The date of the suspension, November 29, 1596, was just days before payments for over two million ducats came due. As was common practice, royal accountants conducted a full audit of outstanding debts after the decree; to their surprise, they found that the estimates were overblown by a factor of two, and that outstanding asientos amounted to only seven million ducats.[16] This represented about two-thirds of annual revenue,

11    The 1575 bankruptcy concluded with an average capital loss of 38 percent for lenders; the 1596 one saw a haircut of 20 percent. The Argentine default of 2001 inflicted losses on the order of 80 percent.

12    See, among many others, Lovett (1980, 1982), De Carlos Morales (2008), and the online appendix to Drelichman and Voth (2010).

13    Conklin (1998) argues that the bankers' refusal to transfer funds to Flanders was a punishment mechanism that resulted in the mutiny of Spanish troops and the subsequent sack of Antwerp. In Drelichman and Voth (2011a) we present detailed historical and archival evidence contradicting this view.

14    For a detailed description of the negotiations and outcome of the Cortes of 1576, see Jago (1985).

15    Sanz Ayán (2004) also echoes this view.

16    Early modern states had a very incomplete picture of the state of their finances at any given time. Accounting methods were not conducive to the construction of consolidated budgets

an easily manageable sum for the royal treasury, especially after the arrival of the very rich fleet of 1596. As a result, the Cortes were not asked for further tax increases, and a settlement was reached in short order. Most of the capital was repaid in good quality juros, with the only haircut resulting from an interest rate reduction on a portion of the outstanding bonds. Bankers accepted a capital loss of 20 percent, and lending resumed.[17]

## TWO ASIENTOS FROM 1596

In this section we turn our attention to two contracts jointly underwritten by Agustín Spinola and Nicolás De Negro in February and July 1596.[18] Spinola and De Negro were members of two prominent Genoese banking families. The Spinola were the largest lenders to Philip II, supplying over sixteen million ducats between 1566 and 1600. They accounted for over 20 percent of total short-term borrowing over the period.[19] While the scale of lending by the De Negro was more modest, amounting to some 770,000 ducats in total, they were also among the leading business families in Genoa.[20] Agustín and Nicolás—to whom, in accordance with the loan documents, we refer by their Spanish names—lived permanently in Madrid, and were in charge of managing the financial operations their families entered into with the king. This included negotiating new loans, arranging the disbursements promised in Madrid, and issuing the necessary letters of exchange to authorize disbursements abroad. They were also responsible for collecting the repayments, which required skill at navigating the royal bureaucracy, and trustworthy agents in the many places were treasurers in charge of different royal revenue streams were stationed. Finally, the bankers had to obtain the necessary permits to remit the proceeds

---

and financial statements. The only comprehensive descriptions of the fiscal situation of sixteenth-century Castile based entirely on primary data are provided by the audits ordered after the bankruptcies.

17 The actual loss might have even been lower. As the final details of the settlement were negotiated, the consortium of bankers agreed to transfer 600,000 écus to Flanders in exchange for what amounted to an annualized yield of 89 percent. This extremely high rate could have been offered only in compensation for something else—possibly accepting the 20 percent haircut on outstanding loans (Archivo General de Simancas, Contadurías Generales, Legajo 93).

18 These contracts are located at the Archivo General de Simancas, Contadurías Generales, Legajo 92.

19 In Drelichman and Voth (2011a), we document and discuss the concentration of lending to Philip II and the role of the Spinola family.

20 We report cumulative sums actually disbursed by the Spinola and De Negro families, rather than contracted ones. For example, in the second contract we discuss in this section, Spinola and De Negro agreed to lend over one million ducats, but disbursed only 127,000 before the payment stop of 1596 put a premature end to the contract. We use the latter amount in our calculations. The complete methodology used in obtaining these figures is discussed in Drelichman and Voth (2011b).

back to their families in Italy or wherever else they were needed, and had to ensure that the bullion was delivered to a port of exit and shipped safely.

The first asiento was concluded on February 24, 1596. Spinola and De Negro first agreed to deliver 90,000 écus in Milan. Half of the amount was due immediately, and payable upon presentation of the letters of exchange by the royal officials. The other half would be disbursed in three equal payments in the months of April, May, and June. In addition, the bankers promised to deliver 112,500 ducats in Madrid, in six equal payments. The first two payments had already been made on January 1 and February 1, 1596; the remaining four installments were to be paid once a month.[21] The contract valued the Italian écus at 404 maravedíes each, which represented a 1 percent premium over their gold content of just under 400 maravedíes (1.067 ducats). The combined principal of the contract therefore amounted to 209,460 ducats.

The king promised to repay the capital using the proceeds of the tres gracias from the years 1597 and 1598, as well as those from the ordinary and extraordinary servicios.[22] The contract stipulated that the proceeds of these taxes would be disbursed to bankers in six installments, starting in July 1598, and every four months thereafter. The interest rate would be 1 percent per month, not compounding; each capital repayment would also be accompanied by the accrued interest on that part of the capital only. The first installment would also include an extra two months of interest. As additional compensation, the bankers were allowed to swap juros worth up to 485 ducats for other bonds of their choice. This allowed them to purchase nonperforming bonds at bargain prices in the open market, exchange them at the treasury for choice securities, and net a profit that could not have been much less than the face value of the juros.[23]

The contract also included a number of additional provisions. First, the bankers were allowed to export bullion for the entire amount of the principal. Although 112,500 ducats were to be delivered in Castile, the bankers would be raising the necessary funds outside the kingdom, and would hence need to export the repayments to meet their own liabilities. The bankers were also given permission to export an additional 60,000 ducats to Portugal. These

21 It was not unusual for disbursements and payments to predate the actual signing of an asiento. The contracts carried the date on which they were signed by the king. Bankers and royal officials, however, might have come to an agreement weeks or months earlier, and several of the promised cash flows might have already happened by the time the documents were formally signed.

22 The tres gracias were three income streams (cruzada, subsidio, and excusado) that the Church collected on behalf of the Crown, and forwarded to the royal treasury. The servicios were direct taxes approved by the Cortes.

23 Since this transaction would have taken place in March 1596, the bankers would have collected the entire yearly interest of the new juro in November 1596, although they would have held it for only nine months. This would have increased the present value of the operation from 485 to 502 ducats. The small amount of this transaction suggests that the bankers already had a nonperforming juro worth exactly 485 ducats in hand, and took advantage of this asiento to get rid of it.

export licenses were valuable, as they allowed their holders to arbitrage between different currency markets. Bankers could sell them to other businessmen. If a license went unused, the treasury would on occasion buy it back.

Spinola and De Negro were also given the option of collecting their repayments from alternative income streams. In particular, they were allowed to choose to be repaid from the fleets of 1596 and 1597. This would likely have allowed them to start collecting a few months earlier, at the cost of forfeiting the extra 2 percent on the first installment. Alternatively, the bankers could request that repayment be made in the form of lifetime juros. This would have allowed them to receive payment almost immediately, but at a higher cost.[24] The contract also allowed bankers to opt for perpetual juros, but they would have to wait until the originally promised repayment dates to collect them. This last option would be valuable only if, for some reason, the original income streams from where the repayments were promised failed to perform. Finally, the contract allowed the bankers the use of one or two royal galleys to transport bullion to Italy.

Table 5.1 shows the agreed cash flows from the asiento of February 24. All the disbursements occur in the first six months of the contract and, with the exception of the small profit from the juro operation, no repayments are promised until July 1598, a full thirty months after the beginning of the contract. In laying out the cash flows, we abstract from the several options that the bankers could exercise, such as choosing different repayment streams or converting part of their credits into juros. Most of these would have resulted in some small variation to the profitability of the contract. The actual sign and magnitude of the change depended on the conditions of the debt and money markets at the time, which are unobservable to us. In order to produce a conservative estimate of rate of return, we also omit the profit from the license to export bullion to Portugal.[25]

Had the contract been honored as originally signed, the bankers would have realized a yearly rate of return of 10.4 percent.[26] If they chose to exercise some of the built-in options—for example, requesting payment from the fleets while

---

24   For accounting purposes, juros were valued as perpetual streams. Lifetime bonds, however, stopped performing at the death of their holders, and hence had a lower present value than perpetuities.

25   This would have likely yielded between 1 and 2 percent of the 60,000 ducats under license, and hence perhaps enhanced the overall profitability of the contract in the order of 0.2 percent to 0.4 percent per year, depending on the timing and actual yield of the transaction. Since the actual return depended on the relative conditions of the Spanish and Portuguese money markets, which we do not observe, we refrain from including this additional profit in our calculations.

26   We calculate the profitability of asientos using the modified internal rate of return (MIRR), with a finance rate of 5 percent and a reinvestment rate of 7.14 percent. For a detailed discussion of the properties of the MIRR and a justification of our choice of parameters, see Drelichman and Voth (2011b).

**TABLE 5.1** Agreed Cash Flows from the Asiento of February 24, 1596

| Month | Disbursement | Repayment | Net cash flow | Description |
|-------|--------------|-----------|---------------|-------------|
| Jan-96 | 18,750 | | −18,750 | First Madrid disbursement (presigning) |
| Feb-96 | 18,750 | | −18,750 | Second Madrid disbursement (presigning) |
| Mar-96 | 66,688 | 502 | −66,186 | Third Madrid disbursement; first Milan disbursement; profit from the juro operation |
| Apr-96 | 34,729 | | −34,729 | Fourth Madrid disbursement; second Milan disbursement |
| May-96 | 34,729 | | −34,729 | Fifth Madrid disbursement; third Milan disbursement |
| Jun-96 | 34,729 | | −34,729 | Sixth Madrid disbursement, fourth Milan disbursement |
| Jul-98 | | 46,081 | 46,081 | First repayment plus interest (including the one-time payment of two months of additional interest) |
| Nov-98 | | 46,779 | 46,779 | Second repayment plus interest |
| Mar-99 | | 48,176 | 48,176 | Third repayment plus interest |
| Jul-99 | | 49,572 | 49,572 | Fourth repayment plus interest |
| Nov-99 | | 50,969 | 50,969 | Fifth repayment plus interest |
| Mar-00 | | 52,365 | 52,365 | Sixth repayment plus interest |

forfeiting the extra months of interest—the returns could have climbed to 11.7 percent per year. The bankruptcy decree of November 1596 came once the bankers had disbursed the entire principal, but had not yet received a single repayment. In terms of timing, this is the worst scenario that bankers could find themselves in. The settlement of 1597 gave the bankers juros worth 80 percent of the outstanding debt. The promised returns evaporated. Evaluated at its terminal date of March 1600, considering the capital loss and adding the yield of the juros, the operation netted a loss of 1.08 percent per year.[27]

The second asiento was signed on July 26, 1596. This was a much larger contract. Spinola and De Negro agreed to deliver one million écus of fifty-seven plaques in Flanders in fourteen payments. The first thirteen payments were to amount to 65,000 écus each, and the fourteenth would have consisted of the remaining 155,000 écus. The disbursements were to start on September 1, 1596, and continue at a monthly frequency. For accounting purposes, the Flemish écus were being valued at 1.088 ducats each, although their theoretical gold content amounted to only 0.977 ducats. The contract thus provided for a potential profit of 10.5 percent in the exchange operation alone, although the actual profit would have depended on the market value of the Flemish écus.

The king agreed to repay a total of 1,088,267 ducats of principal, which represented 1,000,245 écus at the agreed conversion rate.[28] As with the February contract, interest would be added to each installment at the time of repayment. Because of the size of the loan, the king had to tap several revenue sources to repay it. Thus, he promised the bankers the following:

1. 75,133 ducats from the royal direct and indirect taxes corresponding to the year 1595, and payable by the end of 1596.
2. 75,133 ducats in taxes owed by the city of Seville, and charged on the goods brought by the fleet, also payable by the end of 1596.
3. 75,000 ducats from the proceeds of the goods of Cardinal Don Gaspar de Quiroga.[29]
4. 466,667 ducats from the fleet expected between September and November 1596.

27 Because the MIRR incorporates the opportunity cost of funds, its value depends on the terminal date of the contract. We use the terminal date originally specified in the contract to calculate the losses sustained in the restructurings. The reason is that the bankers expected to have their funds tied up until that time, and would have made their original investment decisions based on that terminal date. This also ensures comparability between the expected and actual rates of return.

28 The additional 245 écus are a rounding error due to the specific unit of account used.

29 Don Gaspar de Quiroga y Vela was a towering figure in the Spanish ecclesiastical hierarchy. He held its two most coveted posts, those of inquisitor general and archbishop of Toledo. He enjoyed large rents and possessions, many of which reverted to the Crown upon his death in November 1594. This contract shows that the Crown did not transfer them entirely to the new archbishop, but chose to use part of them to satisfy its financial obligations.

5. 263,000 ducats from the proceeds of the tres gracias and the servicios, in three installments beginning in July 1598 and continuing every four months.
6. 133,333 ducats from payable in the same fashion as the previous clause, but in 1599.

The yearly interest rate applied to each payment was 12 percent (simple, not compounding), calculated from July 1596. Payments from the *tres gracias* received an extra month of interest, while payments from the servicios received an extra two months of interests, and an additional two months for not otherwise specified "costs." The bankers were given broad authority to collect their payments from alternative revenue streams; however, they could convert only up to one hundred thousand ducats of repayments into juros, and another hundred thousand ducats from the 1596 payments into silver from the Indies. The king also provided galleys for the transportation of the bullion. Table 5.2 shows the agreed cash flows from the asiento of July 26.

This asiento is very different from the one signed on February 24. A large proportion of the repayments are stipulated early in the life of the contract—in November and December 1596. In fact, if those two repayments had actually taken place, the bankers would have had a cash surplus until September 1597. There are only two periods when the bankers would have found themselves in the red: September and October 1596, and between October 1597 and March 1599. In effect, this contract can be thought of as consisting of three components:

1. A relatively small loan of 127,000 ducats disbursed in September and October 1596, and repaid in November 1596.
2. A large transfer to Flanders, for which the king prepays in November and December 1596 (with an additional disbursement in July 1597), and which the bankers actually carry out between November 1596 and August 1597.[30]
3. A loan of some 215,000 ducats in September and October 1597.

It is not possible to separate the compensation for each of the three components, as they are not identified in the contract itself. The profit is nonetheless all back-loaded, as the bankers swing decisively into surplus with the last six repayments. The options built into the contract only allowed the bankers to switch the source of the repayments; since they did not affect their timing or amount, this would not have affected the rate of return. Had the contract been honored as agreed, the annualized rate of return would have been 17.6 percent.

---

30 This contract illustrates how both parties to the contract bore risks. The bankers were cash flow positive for ten months, as they gradually transferred to Flanders the large sum the king had given them upfront. Had Spinola and De Negro gone bankrupt, the king would have lost money.

**TABLE 5.2** Agreed Cash Flows from the Asiento of July 26, 1596

| Month | Disbursement | Repayment | Net cash flow | Description |
|---|---|---|---|---|
| Sep-96 | 63,488 | | -63,488 | Monthly disbursement of 65,000 ecús, valued at their gold content of 0.977 ducats |
| Oct-96 | 63,488 | | -63,488 | Monthly disbursement |
| Nov-96 | 63,488 | 485,333 | 421,845 | Monthly disbursement; repayment from the fleet (clause 4) plus four months' interest |
| Dec-96 | 63,488 | 236,530 | 173,042 | Monthly disbursement; repayments from clauses 1 to 3 plus 5 months' interest |
| Jan-97 | 63,488 | | -63,488 | Monthly disbursement |
| Feb-97 | 63,488 | | -63,488 | Monthly disbursement |
| Mar-97 | 63,488 | | -63,488 | Monthly disbursement |
| Apr-97 | 63,488 | | -63,488 | Monthly disbursement |
| May-97 | 63,488 | | -63,488 | Monthly disbursement |
| Jun-97 | 63,488 | | -63,488 | Monthly disbursement |
| Jul-97 | 63,488 | 99,940 | 36,452 | Monthly disbursement; first installment from clause 5, plus interest |
| Aug-97 | 63,488 | | -63,488 | Monthly disbursement |
| Sep-97 | 63,488 | | -63,488 | Monthly disbursement |
| Oct-97 | 151,395 | | -151,395 | Final disbursement of 155,000 ecús |
| Nov-97 | | 103,447 | 103,447 | Second installment from clause 5, plus interest |
| Mar-98 | | 106,953 | 106,953 | Third installment from clause 5, plus interest |
| Jul-98 | | 56,000 | 56,000 | First installment from clause 6, plus interest |
| Nov-98 | | 57,778 | 57,778 | Second installment from clause 6, plus interest |
| Mar-99 | | 59,556 | 59,556 | Third installment from clause 6, plus interest |

This contract mirrored a number of other loans, which called for large repayments in the months of November and December 1596. Indeed, it is quite likely that the time of the payment stop was dictated by this fact.[31] As the next section illustrates, the bankers managed to collect part of the first payment prior to the November 1596 suspension, and recovered 80 percent of the remaining amount in 1597. When evaluated at the terminal date of March 1599, the operation resulted in an annualized loss of 4.82 percent.

## PARCELING OUT THE RISK

Families like the Spinola regularly entered into asientos worth hundreds of thousands of ducats. Even if they had had the financial wherewithal to remain liquid whenever the king declared a payment stop, lending such enormous amounts to a single borrower may not have been a good business strategy. In Drelichman and Voth (2011b), we calculated the excess return from asiento lending. After losses from the bankruptcies and after the opportunity cost of funds, it amounted to 3.16 percent. While such a return compared favorably to other available financial instruments, and even to some commercial ventures, it came with the considerable risk of extended periods during which loans were not serviced. The solution adopted by international bankers was to sell shares in their asiento ventures in exchange for a fee. This allowed them to spread the risk involved among other investors while fine-tuning their own exposure. Parceling out the risk was so central to the asiento system that most large contracts gave bankers a few months of lead time before the main disbursement. This allowed them to tap the European payment fairs for the needed funds.[32] In some cases, the king even advanced "working capital" to the bankers, providing them with a sum of money that could be used to round up prospective investors.[33]

While the original contracts preserved at the Archive of Simancas identify only the main underwriters, it is possible to find shares of Spanish asientos in the account books of merchant families based in Genoa. One such book is the *libro mastro* of a society formed by the brothers Lazzaro and Benedetto Pichenotti, and Gio Girolamo Di Negro, preserved in the Archivio Doria at the

31  The king had received net inflows for 3.1 million ducats between January and October 1596. In November and December, he was expected to have net outflows of 1.5 million ducats. The payment stop, declared just before the end of November, froze these disbursements.

32  For insights into the workings of the Italian payment fairs, see Pezzolo and Tattara (2008) and Marsilio (2008).

33  For example, on July 1, 1572, the king entered into a contract with Pablo de Grimaldo for 800,000 ducats, to be delivered in October 1573. The agreed repayment structure shows that the king was to make the first repayment of 125,000 ducats in July 1573, three months before the banker made his initial disbursement. This practice was not uncommon in large contracts, particularly those involving international transfers.

University of Genoa.[34] The Pichenotti belonged to a well-known merchant family, which nonetheless never lent directly to the king of Spain. Gio Girolamo Di Negro was a member of the De Negro family that participated in the asientos, although his name is never found in the contracts themselves.[35]

The Pichenotti–Di Negro society purchased shares in both the asientos described in the previous section. They contributed 5,265 ducats and 4,500 écus to the one concluded on February 24, and 30,000 écus to the one signed on July 26. Half of the capital was supplied by the Pichenotti brothers, and the other half by Di Negro. The society would make the disbursements and collect repayments under the same conditions that the Spanish bankers had stipulated with the king. The intermediation fee payable to the Spanish bankers was 1 percent.

The suspension decree was published on November 29, 1596. At that point Spinola and De Negro had not yet collected any repayments from the February 24 asiento. They nonetheless forwarded 12,200 ducats to the Genoese society on account of a partial repayment of their share in the July 26 contract. This indicates that the king had already made a partial repayment himself, even though none was expected before the end of November. The most likely reason for this is that the fleet must have arrived a month earlier than expected, hence allowing the bankers to collect the 466,667 ducats that had been promised from that source before the payment stop.[36]

The default froze all further cash flows on the Pichenotti–Di Negro participation. The situation began to thaw with the settlement of November 1597, in which the bank debt was converted into juros. Two-thirds of the debt was repaid in 7.14 percent bonds, which largely traded at par. The remaining third was repaid through a bond swap, reducing the interest rate on juros acquired or already held by the bankers, and entailing a net loss of 20 percent of the original capital of the outstanding asientos. The Spanish bankers collected the bonds corresponding to the settlement, calculated the share of principal and interest corresponding to the Genoese society, deducted their fees and collection and conveyance expenses, and forwarded the remainder to Genoa using the same mix of assets they had received from the king. Paying creditors in this fashion was known as the provision of *la misma moneda*—literally, "the same currency." Since bankers received bonds in the settlements, requiring them to pay their creditors back in cash would have created serious liquidity problems for them.

---

34   Archivio Doria, Inventario Doria 193. This book was first identified by Felloni (1978). Our description closely follows his account.

35   When referring to bankers based in Genoa, we use the Italian spelling of their names.

36   The asientos at Simancas allow us to observe only the promised cash flows, not the actual ones. The Pichenotti–Di Negro account book thus provides a rare window into what actually transpired after the contracts had been signed. This example makes it clear that deviations from the letter of the contracts did not always harm the bankers—the early arrival of the fleet meant that they collected a portion of their debts earlier than expected, hence mitigating the impact of the bankruptcy.

The arrangement of *la misma moneda* allowed international lenders to forward the bonds downstream to the smaller investors that had supplied them with capital. This applied regardless of whether investors had purchased specific shares in an asiento, or just made a demand deposit with the banking house.[37]

The accounts of the Pichenotti–Di Negro society were finalized and closed in 1600. By that point, with no more credits outstanding, they had received a total of 38,741 ducats net of costs, in cash and bonds of different characteristics. This represented a loss of 8.4 percent of their original capital.[38] Because the loss was spread over several years, however, the annualized rate of return was substantially less negative. While we do not observe the actual dates of every cash flow for the Genoese venture, we can exploit the fact that its investment was structured to mimic the Spanish asientos, whose cash flows we do know. After adding the 1 percent intermediation fee, Pichenotti and Di Negro obtained an annualized return of –1.32 percent for their share in the February 24 contract, and –5.19 percent for their participation in the July 26 one.[39] Their overall (weighted) annualized return was thus –4.27 percent.

## THE IMPACT OF NEGATIVE SHOCKS ON GENOESE TRADING FAMILIES

The true test of any risk-sharing system comes in bad times. The rhetoric during the bankruptcies was harsh enough. Bankers complained loudly to the king about how poorly he rewarded their loyalty.[40] Contemporary business commentators bemoaned the plight of the widows and orphans of Genoa.[41] Scholars such as Fernand Braudel assumed that the suspension decrees were

37  See Neri (1989) for an overview of the impact of the provision of la misma moneda on Genoese firms and individuals.

38  In the Pichenotti–Di Negro account book, the écus are valued at the exchange rate agreed to between the king and the Madrid bankers, rather than at their metallic content. This suggests that the Madrid bankers did not pass through the profits obtained in the exchange operation.

39  To obtain conservative estimates, we assume the intermediation fee was front-loaded.

40  On December 22, 1575, Lorenzo Spinola wrote to the king, complaining that he had been enormously harmed by the suspension decree and reminding him of the many services and favors he had provided over the years. He then asks the king to make good on his promises because "the word of a king is a law" ("pues la una ley es la palbra de v.m. y me la dio de que esto se haria assi conmigo por mis muchos servicios y los que tengo de hazer"). Instituto Valencia de Don Juan, Envío 22, Caja 33, TB 144.

41  Writing in 1638, Venetian merchant Giovanni Domenico Peri described the effects of the 1627 bankruptcy as follows: "Oltre la rovina degli Assentisti, hanosi questi ritirato a dietro molti, che gli soccorevano di rivelantissime partite, e fra gli uni, e gli altri, sono restate esterminate molte ricche famiglie, e molte Vedove, e pupilli insiememente ridotti a miserabile povertà" (In addition to the ruin of the bankers, several other financiers who provided them with funds exited the business. Between ones and the others, many rich families were exterminated, and many widows and orphans were at the same time reduced to miserable poverty) (Peri 1672).

catastrophic events, periodically forcing a good portion of Europe's financial elite into personal ruin.[42]

In Drelichman and Voth (2011b), we showed that asiento lending was profitable on average over the long run, and for almost all participants. While the bankruptcies caused short-term losses on specific contracts, these were more than offset by high profits during normal times. Our result applied to the families that kept representatives in Madrid and dealt directly with the king. It is nonetheless possible that the bankruptcies had a stronger impact on those smaller financiers that supplied the international bankers with capital. We now explore this issue in more detail using a second document preserved in the Doria Archive of Genoa.

Gio Girolamo Di Negro—who partnered with the Pichenotti brothers to invest in the two ill-fated asientos described in the third section—also kept his own master account books, as was customary. These *libri mastri* detailed all the assets, liabilities, and profits or losses for the relevant period. The book covering the period between April 1596 and October 1598 is preserved in the Doria Archive, allowing us a window into the impact of the November 1596 default.[43] At the end of the period, in October 1598, Di Negro had not yet received the settlement payments corresponding to his participation in the asientos.[44] He recorded his participation in the society with the Pichenotti brothers as an asset worth 7,500 Genoese lire, and he also had another 1,116 lire invested in a different asiento.[45] The final balance sheet shows that Di Negro had total assets worth 96,252 Genoese lire. He turned a profit of 6,025 lire. Since these were earned over a period of thirty months, the annual profit was 2.4 percent. Di Negro was not doing particularly well by the standards of the time. Investing in long-term bonds would have netted him 7 percent or more, with little risk (but also less of a chance to receive the principal back anytime soon, or without a discount).[46] However, his poor performance overall must have stemmed overwhelmingly from his commercial ventures, which represented over 90 percent of his port-

42  Braudel alludes to the negative effects of the Spanish bankruptcies in several passages throughout *The Mediterranean*, writing, for example, "every time the state declared itself bankrupt, bringing contracts to a violent end, there were always some actors who lost, fell through a trapdoor, or tiptoed away towards the wings" (Braudel 1966, 362–63).

43  Archivio Doria, Inventario Doria 192.

44  This is consistent with the society's book, which records the final settlement in 1600.

45  This contract is identified as the *assiento del millione*, a common name given to contracts for a million ducats or écus. Since there were four different asientos for that amount open at the time of the 1596 suspension, it is not possible to identify the exact one Di Negro had invested in.

46  While Gio Girolamo Di Negro did not report any juros among his assets, most businessmen kept a diversified portfolio that included Spanish bonds backed by various income streams. For example, his relative Ambrogio Di Negro in 1560 had juros backed by the taxes on silk in Granada, by the internal customs of Seville, by the sales taxes of Carmona, by the royal taxes on wool, and by the yearly payments that the king received from the shepherds' guild (Ambrogio Di Negro, Libro Mastro, Archivio Doria 342).

folio. More important, he was in no danger of financial ruin as a result of Castile's default. Had Philip II completely repudiated his debts, Di Negro would have lost less than 9 percent of his assets. Over the period covered in the account book, this would have translated into annualized excess losses of 3.5 percent. This result is consistent with our findings for the top-level bankers, and yields a powerful insight into the strength of the overall system. While the defaults of Philip II caused substantial losses, no link in the chain of financial intermediation was exposed to catastrophic risk when they occurred.

## CONCLUSION

When does the repackaging and reshuffling of risk work? There are many reasons today to question the benefits of securitization. As the financial crisis of 2008 to 2010 made clear, new securities consisting of repackaged mortgages failed to provide risk diversification. Losses in a small corner of the financial system soon threatened to overwhelm it in its entirety. We go back to the sixteenth century to look at a successful example of how financial intermediation can "work," by offering a combination of attractive returns and relatively modest risk. In part, it did so by passing on some of the exposure from bankers to final investors.

Short-term lending to the Spanish Crown involved relatively large loans, underwritten by a handful of powerful financiers. The concentrated structure of lending facilitated coordination between bankers, and allowed them to put pressure on the Crown to settle on generous terms in times of crisis. To avoid the risk implied by a few bankers making very large loans, these were often parceled out into smaller packets, and sold on to private investors (for a fee).

We examine the performance of two such investments during Philip II's fourth and final default, in 1596. The Pichenotti–Di Negro partnership bought participations in two short-term loans to the king, underwritten by Agustín Spinola and Nicolás De Negro. They were affected by the payment stop. We carefully reconstruct the profitability of these two investments, and interpret them in the context of the investors' portfolio overall. The original underwriters achieved a full risk transfer—they owed the partnership only the respective proportion of the money that they received from the king. We find that losses were modest overall, and that these investments did not constitute a large fraction of the partners' wealth. While a sudden payment stop was not a small matter for investors, there was no domino effect—no wave of defaults as one creditor after another sees a large share of his assets disappear or turn illiquid.

By effectively selling "shares" in loans made to the king of Spain, Genoese bankers could achieve a dual objective. They continued to monopolize access to the short-term lending market. This was necessary for lending to be sustainable (Drelichman and Voth 2011a), and it cannot have been bad for profitability.

At the same time, selling parts of the loans reduced the principal lender's risk. In this way, securitization was remarkably successful: it provided funds to the Spanish monarchy at the height of its powers, and the system weathered the effect of temporary negative shocks such as the 1596 bankruptcy.

## ACKNOWLEDGMENTS

We are indebted to Andrea Zannini for help in accessing and interpreting the documents at the Archivio Doria di Genova. Funding from SSHRCC, the UBC Hampton Fund, and the Spanish Ministry of Education is gratefully acknowledged.

## BIBLIOGRAPHY

Braudel, Fernand. 1966. *The Mediterranean and the Mediterranean World in the Age of Philip II.* 2nd rev. ed. Glasgow: William Colins.

Carande, Ramón. 1987. *Carlos V y sus banqueros.* Barcelona: Crítica.

Castillo, Alvaro. 1972. " 'Decretos' et 'Medios Generales' dans le système financier de la Castille. La crise de 1596." In *Melanges en l'honneur de Fernand Braudel,* vol. 1, 137–44. Toulouse: Privat Éditeur.

Conklin, James. 1998. "The Theory of Sovereign Debt and Spain under Philip II." *Journal of Political Economy* 106 (3): 483–513.

De Carlos Morales, Carlos Javier. 2008. *Felipe II: El Imperio en Bancarrota.* Madrid: Dilema.

De Maddalena, Aldo, and Hermann Kellenbenz. 1986. *La repubblica internazionale del denaro tra XV e XVII secolo.* Bologna: Il Mulino.

De Roover, Raymond A. 1966. *The Rise and Decline of the Medici Bank: 1397–1494.* New York: Norton.

Drelichman, Mauricio, and Hans-Joachim Voth. 2010. "The Sustainable Debts of Philip II: A Reconstruction of Castile's Fiscal Position, 1566–1596." *Journal of Economic History* 70 (4): 813–42.

———. 2011a. "Lending to the Borrower from Hell: Debt and Default in the Age of Philip II." *Economic Journal* 121: 1205–27.

———. 2011b. "Serial Defaults, Serial Profits: Returns to Sovereign Lending in Habsburg Spain, 1566–1600." *Explorations in Economic History* 48 (1): 1–19.

———. forthcoming. "Risk Sharing with the Monarch: Excusable Defaults and Contingent Debt in the Age of Philip II, 1556–1598." *Cliometrica.*

Felloni, Giuseppe. 1978. "Asientos, juros y ferias de cambio desde el observatorio genovés (1541–1675)." In *Dinero y Crédito (siglos XVI al XIX). Actas del Primer Coloquio Internacional de Historia Económica.* Madrid.

Greif, Avner. 2006. *Institutions and the Path to the Modern Economy: Lessons from Medieval Trade.* Cambridge: Cambridge University Press.

Grossman, Herschel I., and John B. Van Huyck. 1988. "Sovereign Debt as a Contingent Claim: Excusable Default, Repudiation, and Reputation." *American Economic Review* 78: 1088–97.

Jago, Charles. 1985. "Philip II and the Cortes of Castile: The Case of the Cortes of 1576." *Past and Present* 109: 22–43.

Lovett, A. W. 1980. "The Castilian Bankruptcy of 1575." *Historical Journal* 23: 899–911.

———. 1982. "The General Settlement of 1577: An Aspect of Spanish Finance in the Early Modern Period." *Historical Journal* 25 (1): 1–22.

Marsilio, Claudio. 2008. *Dove il denaro fa denaro. Gli operatori finanziari genovesi nelle fiere di cambio del XVII secolo.* Novi Ligure: Città del Silenzio.

Neri, Enrica. 1989. *Uomini d'affari e di governo tra Genova e Madrid.* Milan: Vita e Pensiero—Pubblicazioni dell'Università Cattolica.

Parker, Geoffrey. 1999. "The Political World of Charles V." In *Charles V and His Time, 1500–1559,* edited by Hugo Soly, 113–225. Antwerp: Mercatorfonds.

Peri, Giovanni Dominco. 1672. *Il Negotiante.* Venice.

Pezzolo, Luciano, and Giuseppe Tattara. 2008. "'Una fiera senza luogo.' Was Bisenzone an International Capital Market in Sixteenth-Century Italy?" *Journal of Economic History* 68 (4): 1098–1122.

Reinhart, Carmen M., and Kenneth Rogoff. 2009. *This Time Is Different: Eight Centuries of Financial Folly.* Princeton: Princeton University Press.

Rodríguez-Salgado, M. J. 1988. *The Changing Face of Empire. Charles V, Philip II and Habsburg Authority, 1551–1559.* Cambridge: Cambridge University Press.

Sanz Ayán, Carmen. 2004. *Estado, monarquía y finanzas. Estudios de historia financiera en tiempos de los Austrias.* Madrid: Centro de estudios políticos y constitucionales.

Toboso Sánchez, Pilar. 1987. *La deuda pública castellana durante el Antiguo Régimen (juros) y su liquidación en el siglo XIX.* Madrid: Instituto de Estudios Fiscales.

Torres López, Manuel, and J. M. Pérez-Prendes. 1963. *Los Juros (aportación documental para una historia de la deuda pública en España).* Madrid: Fábrica de Moneda y Timbre.

# 6

# ESTABLISHING A NEW ORDER

The Growth of the State and the Decline of Witch Trials in France

## NOEL D. JOHNSON, MARK KOYAMA, AND JOHN V. C. NYE

The safety of the people requireth further from him or them that have the sovereign power, that justice be equally administered to all degrees of people, that is, that as well the rich and mighty as poor and obscure persons may be righted of the injuries done them, so as the great may have no greater hope of impunity when they do violence, dishonor, or any injury to the meaner sort than when one of these does the like to one of them.

—THOMAS HOBBES, *LEVIATHAN*

The central problem of political economy can be described as the Smith versus Hobbes problem. The central message of classical economics is that voluntary exchange is mutually beneficial, and hence that trade and commerce with diverse partners increase specialization, productivity, and the gains from trade. But if the implications of Smithian economics are that enlarging the scope and scale of market transactions is good, why was large-scale integrated trade so slow to emerge and generally unstable? The answer to this puzzle is to be found in Hobbes. Hobbes argued that the threat of violence in the absence of the state was sufficient to inhibit trade and guarantee widespread poverty. Because classical economists, after Smith, presupposed the existence of an institutional framework capable of enforcing voluntary exchange, they largely avoided the problem of violence and human conflict. But in the absence of a secure political order, usually enforced from without, trade is more easily encouraged in smaller groups that are more homogeneous, more conservative, and more isolated than would be expected in a stable wealth-maximizing world.

The modern debate about the proper limits of the state has tended to focus on the emergence of the state and has paid little attention to the conflict between a large, national state government and more autarkic and independent local authorities. Throughout the preindustrial period, local authorities limited the reach of Leviathan. On the one hand, this helped to preserve some measure of cultural and social autonomy. On the other hand, the power of local authorities typically rested on rental streams that relied on restricting trade and limiting market integration and effectively left regions as semiautarkic zones facing high transactions costs (Epstein 2000).

The two most powerful states in early modern Europe, Britain and France, developed centralized institutions that promoted national markets, broke down regional barriers, and pushed through reforms that enhanced market integration and competition. This was largely the unintended consequence of urban or parliamentary elites attempting to increase their own authority and status by undermining barriers and restrictions. Rural elites were bribed to defect and abandon centuries old laws that limited integration. Although the process of eliminating entrenched local elites typically led to rent seeking by new centralized elites, as this chapter will argue, shifting tax and legal authority away from local jurisdictions also had beneficial economic and social side effects.

Recent research highlights the ways in which local arrangements were overridden in early modern Britain and France, sometimes through Coasian bargains and sometimes as a power grab on the part of elites who saw their efforts at regulation as contributing both to a more efficiently run government and to increasing the rents that would flow into their pockets (Mokyr and Nye 2007; Lamoreaux 2011; Bogart and Richardson 2012; Franck, Johnson, and Nye 2014). Thus, a purely ideological reading of history might treat high tariffs on wine and spirits in Britain as inconsistent with parliamentary initiatives to promote better land use and more effective private bargaining to allow improved transport and increased drainage. From an ideological perspective, the two seem greatly at odds. But once one recognizes that this was part of a movement by central elites to displace provincial elites, the two can be seen as consistent (Nye 2007). Likewise, the creation of the centralized tax monopsony known as the Company of General Farms in seventeenth-century France appears a move toward less integrated markets and greater inefficiency. However, in practice, it allowed for a group of urban elites centered around Paris to impose their authority on the rest of the country and in the process harmonized the collection of indirect taxes (Johnson 2006; Balla and Johnson 2009; Johnson and Koyama 2014a).

State action did not always result in an improvement on preexisting local arrangements. However, the relevant comparison was rarely between free markets and state control or between open competition and governmental rent seeking, but between different levels of state power, that is, between rent seeking that was decentralized and conducted at a local level and rent seeking that occurred at the level of the central government. In many parts of Europe the feudal system remained partly intact and powerful aristocrats or their vassals controlled production through a decentralized political hierarchy (Root 1987). Elsewhere economic activity was regulated by local cities or guilds. This system was decentralized but was not open or competitive (see, e.g., Ogilvie 2011).[1] Thus the struggle over control of the political order was partially determined by

---

1 By "open" here we mean something akin to "open access order" as opposed to a "limited access order" in the same sense that North, Wallis, and Weingast (2009) use the terms.

whose rules—those of the Crown or those of local authorities—would prevail and to what extent these rules would be universal in application.

Of course in some cases, the state was less liberal than were local political authorities.[2] But what is interesting about early modern Europe is the extent to which much of the centralization of authority that accompanied the expansion of the tax state was tied to the liberalization of trade and the creation of less particularistic and more universal laws. This was sometimes a byproduct of new ideas and ideologies, as Mokyr (2002, 2009) has argued concerning the Enlightenment, and as McCloskey (2010) argues with respect to the rise of bourgeois values. In this chapter, however, we focus on how simply increasing the scale of the administrative and fiscal apparatus of the state drove improvements in rule of law at the local level and resulted in a decline in witchcraft trials, independent of changing ideology. To establish our argument we draw on data that is analyzed in more detail in Johnson and Koyama (2014b). The improvements we identify were driven by an attempt of the state to lower the costs of collecting taxes. Local authorities also cared about revenues, *but* to the extent that inefficiencies were driven by regional externalities, the rules imposed by the monarchy often represented an improvement since they internalized these external costs. In this respect the transition from a feudal domain state to a centralized tax state inadvertently helped to establish the necessary preconditions for modern economic growth.

## FISCAL AND LEGAL CAPACITY

Our chapter contributes to a growing literature in political science and economics that emphasizes the importance of state capacity in explaining comparative economic performance.[3] This literature stresses the twin significance of fiscal capacity and legal capacity. The former enables states to raise tax revenues relatively efficiently, whereas the latter refers to the ability of a state to enforce contracts.

It has long been known that the British state levied comparatively high taxes in the eighteenth century (Mathias and O'Brien 1976). John Brewer stressed the transformation that the British state underwent between the Civil War and the Treaty of Utrecht, a transformation "which put muscle on the bond of the British body politic, increasing its endurance, strength and reach" (Brewer 1988, xvii). More recently Bogart and Richardson (2012) have argued that the power of the British Parliament to overrule and reorganize property rights played an important role in improving the efficiency of the economy in the period leading

---

2  Cf. Fukuyama (2011) for an extended discussion of the destruction of local elites for the benefit of national authority in early China.

3  See the essays collected in Evans, Rueschemeyer, and Skocpol (1985) and Tilly (1990).

up to the Industrial Revolution. These historical findings have influenced other fields within economics. Timothy Besley and Torsten Persson (2011), for example, have developed a model in which prior investments in both fiscal and legal capacity constrain a state's ability to raise revenue or regulate markets. As such, they argue that legal capacity and fiscal capacity are strategic complements that develop in tandem.

This chapter examines the relationship between fiscal and legal capacity by studying seventeenth-century France. France poses an interesting counterpoint to Britain. Early modern states lacked both fiscal and legal capacity and, from a modern perspective, appear fragmented and weak (Dincecco 2009). Britain was the exception: a precociously centralized state. The strength of the British state stemmed from the unity of the English elite as a political class, which, in turn, rested on the early legal and fiscal centralization in the Middle Ages. By the early modern period the English elite was small and, though membership was still based on the ownership of land, it was metropolitan-based and its members shared a common set of assumptions and beliefs. Such a coherent and centralized elite enabled the eighteenth-century British state to function effectively, despite high levels of corruption and rent seeking (Root 1991; Mokyr and Nye 2007).

Compared to England, France was not centralized early, but rather remained a "mosaic state" in many respects until the Revolution (Hoffman 1994). It was made up of "morsels" and "shreds" of provinces, towns, and semi-independent kingdoms (Goubert 1969). No national equivalent of the English Parliament emerged. J. Russell Major observed that during the Middle Ages the French monarch had to make concessions to local interests in order to survive: "They had encouraged the codification of local customs instead of trying to create a common law. They had accepted the growth of provincial loyalties. . . . In short, at the very time when they appeared to be creating a unified kingdom by driving the English out, they were permitting the formation of centrifugal forces that threatened to keep the nation forever divided" (Major 1994, 57). This feudal inheritance shaped the distinctive path France took toward modernity and sustained economic growth.

Because of this very different history, the French monarchy could not follow the British path of state formation and economic development in the seventeenth and eighteenth centuries. Nevertheless, France did undergo an important process of centralization prior to the French Revolution and thus provides an alternative laboratory for studying the transition from a feudal to a modern state.[4] Ancien régime France was relatively successful in overcoming many of the limitations that it inherited from the Middle Ages, as attested to by the

---

4 The modernity of ancien régime France is the subject of much historical debate (see Parker 1996, 6–27 for a survey). Steven Pincus writes in this context about the ideology and practice of "Catholic modernity" (Pincus 2009).

ability of post-Revolutionary France to achieve its own path to modern economic growth in the nineteenth century. Alexis de Tocqueville commented on this phenomenon, noting that in "the eighteenth century the government was already . . . very centralized, very powerful and extremely active" and that there were "many traits of modern France in the France of the old regime" (Tocqueville 1998, 84). When did the old regime acquire these modern traits, and what does the history of their acquisition teach us about legal capacity, fiscal capacity, and rule of law more generally?

## THE COSTS OF FRAGMENTATION

Fiscal fragmentation impeded economic growth in medieval and early modern Europe (Epstein 2000). Merchant guilds regulated and restricted commerce and trade (Ogilvie 2011). Overlapping jurisdictions, internal tariffs, and different weights and measures prevented European economies from fully realizing Smithian gains from trade.[5] The north and south of the country had different systems of regulation and administration. To get between Rouen and Nantes one paid thirty different tolls—each one providing an opportunity for a local official to overcharge by as much as 300 or 400 percent (Heckscher 1955, 84–85).[6] Before the seventeenth century, despite significant effort, the Crown had met with little success overcoming local barriers to trade or centralizing other institutions. As Heckscher says, "The endeavors of the French monarchy to end the disorder were almost as old as the monarchy itself" (Heckscher 1955, 81).

One reason for this lack of success was that fiscal centralization was all but impossible so long as the monarchy was legally fragmented. The law remained in the hands of provincial *parlements* and the local nobility (Beik 1985). This inhibited the ability of the king or his ministers to regulate at a national level and resolve economy-wide coordination problems. Legal fragmentation impeded the provision of local public goods (such as irrigation projects) as high transactions costs created holdup problems and ensured that Coasian bargains could not be made (Rosenthal 1992; Hoffman 1996). Property rights were often contested, and the resulting litigation was often interminable and costly as local coalitions blocked reforms. France lacked a meta-institution like the English Parliament that was able to reorganize property rights in an efficient manner.

5 Shiue and Keller (2007) and Bateman (2011) have shown that Continental European markets remained highly fragmented during the early modern period. Koyama (2010) argues that the prohibition on usury continued to distort capital markets into the early modern period. Grafe (2012) examines how local authorities at the city level impeded market integration in early modern Spain. Dincecco (2010) finds that the major Continental European economies remained divided into semiautarkic regions throughout the seventeenth and eighteenth centuries.

6 Johnson (2006a) discusses how the fragmented system of collecting indirect taxes contributed to high marginal tax rates and corruption.

The authority of the king remained weak in many parts of the country where the provincial nobility still reigned as semi-independent rulers. Even in those areas where the authority of the king was strong, local families dominated the regional parlements and elections, and they used the courts in order to maintain their privileges (Beik 1985, 81). Because the state remained underdeveloped, the king relied upon local elites to raise taxes like the *taille* and *aides*. France was divided between the *pays d'état* and the *pays d'élection*. The pays d'élections constituted the original territories of the kingdom and were, more or less, centered around Paris. The pays d'états, by contrast, were later additions. In pays d'état, like Brittany or Burgundy, the provincial nobility retained discretion over the allocation of the tax burden and they resisted increases in direct taxation because they sought to extract taxes from the peasantry themselves (Collins 1995, 20–21).

Local fragmentation and decentralization diverted revenue streams and rents into the hands of local political supporters and thereby helped to ensure domestic peace (Major 1962, 1964, 1994). However, as many scholars have pointed out this practice of centralized rent sharing became increasingly costly in an age of intensified military competition because it limited the amount of revenue that reached the state (see Gennaioli and Voth 2013). Beginning in the 1620s during the reign of Louis XIII (1610–43), and then gaining momentum after France's entry into the Thirty Years' War in 1635, there was a systematic effort made by the monarchy to restrict the influence of the traditional nobility who had originally gained prominence through their ability to fight (*noblesse d'épée*) with newer elites drawn from the *noblesse de robe* who gained their status through their ability to provide administrative services to the state. The noblesse de robe were lawyers rather than soldiers, and while they certainly were not above rent seeking, they did so through the political institutions of the monarchy rather than through local institutions. And as Mancur Olson famously argued, centralized rent seeking was less costly than decentralized rent seeking (Olson 1982).

Louis XIII's advisor, Cardinal Richelieu, while himself the son of an older noble family who had originally sought a military career, came to exemplify this new breed of elite. Acting under Richelieu's advice, Louis called an Assembly of Notables in 1626–27 with the express purpose of obtaining support for the king's desire to suppress the Protestant Huguenot movements.[7] The Assembly issued a critique of local elites (grandees and provincial governors), which enabled Richelieu to seize control of the military away from the old nobility. The members of the Assembly complained about the disastrous fiscal situation

---

7 As Collins (1988, 45) explains, this move resonated with the gradual abandonment of witch trials as the state encroached on localities since Louis objected to Huguenots, not so much because he did not want Protestants worshipping in his lands, but because the Huguenots themselves were intolerant of Catholic worshippers.

of the government and recognized the need to increase tax revenues. Most important, the Assembly confirmed Richelieu's view that the judicial and fiscal administrative apparatus was too fragmented to be of great use (Collins 1988, 47). This last issue was addressed immediately following the Assembly by a rewriting and consolidating all administrative law in France under a set of rules known as the Code Michau.

The efforts of Richelieu to centralize fiscal and legal authority were only partially successful (see Moote 1971). And in subsequent years, the French state was stretched thin by the Thirty Years' War and the civil war known as the Fronde. But, after 1660, Louis IV's (1643–1715) finance minister Jean-Baptiste Colbert was able to lay the foundations of a new "absolutist" state.[8] A system of centralized rent seeking was consolidated, a "welfare state for the privileged," that aimed at weaning the nobility away from the more costly local rent-seeking arrangements (Kwass 1998, 301). The nobility were obliged to stay at Versailles, but the government patronage with which they were rewarded was more than sufficient to compensate them for the rents they lost by no longer being able to supervise and tax the local economy (Root 1991). A new set of Paris-based administrators known as *intendants* were imposed on top of the provincial elite, and sent out into the provinces to supervise tax collection and the administration of the local elections. Drawn from a new elite, quite separate from the provincial nobility, the intendants enabled the state to enforce its new laws (Moote 1971; Hurt 2002).[9] The number of royal officials increased from 4,041 in 1515 to at least 46,047 in 1665, an expansion that one historian describes as "staggering" (Kwass 2000, 29). The intendants overwhelmingly came from the noblesse de robe and were commissioned employees of the Crown who could be sacked at will (Collins 1988, 54). Their self-interest was aligned with the central government, and not the provinces. This resulted in a top-heavy and inefficient state, but, as we will show below, it was in many ways an improvement on the uncoordinated and fragmented local institutions that preceded it.

As we have already seen with regard to issuance of the Code Michau, legal reforms were a vital part of the process of building fiscal capacity. From the point of view of Louis XIV's finance minister, Colbert, "judicial reform dovetailed perfectly with the financial reforms he promoted. . . . If justice could be dispensed swiftly and inexpensively, all segments of the population would have more funds at their disposal to develop the economy and to place in the service of the monarchy" (Hamscher 1976, 157). Colbert commissioned an enquiry into the administration of justice in 1665. This report attributed the

8 Of course this success was relative. The "absolutist" state of Louis XIV remained constrained in many respects. See Beik (1985), Collins (1988), and Hurt (2002).

9 Colbert instructed the intendants to look for any lapses by parlements or other law courts concerning such disputed taxes as the stamped paper or the consignation des amendes. His successors continued the surveillance, so that the parlements were never again free of some watchful eye (Hurt, 2002, 58).

inefficiencies and corruption of the existing system to the existence of multiple overlapping jurisdictions: "There were simply too many jurisdictions" and too many venal judicial offices; together these resulted "in perennial jurisdictional conflicts among the courts and in great expense to litigants who faced a vast judicial hierarchy if they were entitled to appeal a decision from a lower court" (Hamscher 1976, 160).

There is ample qualitative evidence that fiscal consolidation and legal reform accompanied one another. For example, the activity of the local, seigniorial courts declined in this period as the royal courts became more prominent (Collins 1995, 147–48). However, identifying consistent measures to follow this process presents a challenge. Since tax records survive, the fiscal capacity of the centralized state can be measured with some level of accuracy. However, legal centralization is much more difficult to quantify. This is particularly true if we are interested in the kinds of rules that governed everyday economic activities (as opposed, for example, to changes in rules that affected the terms on which the monarch could borrow). Was the French monarchy able to overcome vested local interests and achieve a measure of legal centralization and, if so, when? Furthermore, were fiscal and legal capacity correlated across time and space? If so, why? We investigate these questions using panel data on direct tax receipts from the taille to proxy for fiscal capacity and data on the prosecution of witchcraft trials. We argue that legal centralization led to fewer trials of suspected witches. Hence, in the context of seventeenth-century France, witch trials can be used as an indirect proxy for increased legal capacity.[10]

## THE EUROPEAN WITCH HUNT

The history of European witch trials offers unique insight into how the process of legal centralization and state building curtailed the discretionary authority of local elites. Alfred Soman described witch trials as a measure of the weakness of a state (Soman 1989, 17). Certainly, the witch hunts were at their most intense in the small, fragmented states of Central Europe. While a small number of individual witch trials occurred across Europe, the governments of the major European states were comparatively reluctant to sanction large-scale trials. Witch panics took place in weakly governed states or during periods when the grasp of central government was weak. The worst episodes of witch killings occurred in fragmented states: the Jura region, the Basque country, Scotland, and southwestern Germany.[11]

Why was this the case? At first glance the history of the witch trials is puzzling. They were not a product of medieval superstition; rather they peaked in

---

10  The material that follows draws heavily on Johnson and Koyama (2014b).

11  See Monter (1971, 1976, 1997), Midelfort (1972), Behringer (1997).

the early modern period and overlapped with the Scientific Revolution and the early Enlightenment. From a long-run perspective, the relationship between state building and witch hunting was clearly non-monotonic. While belief in witchcraft was almost universal in preindustrial Europe, formal trials of witches began only once the secular legal system began to take an interest in the superstitions and complaints of the peasant population.

Witchcraft beliefs were more or less universal across Europe in the early modern period, but the existence of these beliefs was not sufficient reason for trials of witches to take place. Magistrates and judges had to believe in harmful magic, witches' Sabbaths, the possibility of a covenant with the Devil, and nocturnal flying (see Cohn 1975). The printing and distribution of treatises on witchcraft such as the *Malleus Maleficarum* played a key role in creating a common notion of what witchcraft was.

Witchcraft, however, was almost impossible to prosecute under standard legal procedures because it was very difficult to find physical evidence that an act of sorcery or bad magic (*maleficium*) had been committed. Standard legal procedures limited the use of torture.[12] However, if these standards were upheld few witches would ever be convicted. In the opinion of many magistrates many acts of witchcraft could be proven only through a confession, and given the paucity of physical evidence, torture was seen as the only way in which a confession could be obtained. For this reason, witchcraft was treated as unique type of crime—a *crimen exceptum*—and in many jurisdictions local judges employed laxer and less stringent standards of evidence and the freer use of torture to obtain a confession. These departures were often justified with reference to works of demonologists or in response to witch trials conducted in neighboring regions.

Where individual judges had the discretionary authority to license torture or allow suspects to be swum, or searched for the marks of the devil, trials of individual witches could quickly become mass witch hunts or panics as suspects were induced to incriminate their relatives and neighbors. Such trials required local legal authorities to have a free hand in interpreting evidence and in employing torture. If a local judge or magistrate or group of judges or magistrates became convinced of the existence of a large number of witches covens, they might begin a process that could lead to dozens or even hundreds of individuals

---

12 Contemporaries were aware of the incentive suspects had to incriminate themselves under interrogation (Langbein [1976] 2006, 9). In England it was the responsibility of the jury to ascertain the truth so torture was employed only in exceptional circumstances and with Parliament's permission. In Germany the use of torture was directed by the Lex Carolina of 1532, which stipulated that evidence obtained through torture had to be independently corroborated if it was to be used. In witch trials these guidelines were routinely flouted. See Roper (2004, 46), Levack (2006, 82–88), and Langbein ([1976] 2006, 5).

being tried. Once begun, large-scale trials were hard to control.[13] Mass trials and panics drew in individuals who would not normally be suspected of witchcraft and, because respectable citizens often ended up executed, ended by discrediting the whole process of the trials themselves.

The apparent relationship between political centralization and the decline of witch killings is an established historical finding, but there is no consensus as to why this was the case. A number of different explanations have been proposed. Perhaps these were regions where the hold of Christianity was weakest, as Chaunu (1969) suggested. Levack offered two reasons: First, "local authorities who presided over witch trials were far more likely than their central superiors to develop an intense and immediate fear of witchcraft," while central courts were "less likely to be affected by the hysterical mood that often engulfed towns and villages when witch-hunts occurred." Second, "central judges were generally more committed to the proper operation of the judicial system and more willing therefore to afford accused witches whatever procedural safeguards the law might allow them" (Levack 2006, 97).

## INFORMATION CASCADES AND THE SPREAD OF WITCH TRIALS

A theoretical mechanism that is consistent with Levack's explanations, but also adds insight into why there were significant differences in the attitudes of local and central authorities with regard to witchcraft prosecutions, comes from the theory of information cascades. An information cascade occurs in a sequential game when it is optimal for an agent to follow the behavior of those who have moved before him or her regardless of the information available to him or her specifically (Bikhchandani, Hirshleifer, and Welch 1992). In the case of witchcraft the concept of an information cascade can explain why a judge in one region might find it optimal to convict a witch (or allow a witch suspect to be tortured into producing a confession) simply because the number of convictions in nearby regions has increased the perceived threat.

Suppose local courts attached an a priori probability to the possibility that witches exist and pose a large threat to society. Based on this probability or belief, the courts determined what kind of evidence could be accepted in court and what forms of interrogation or torture could be used. If the danger posed by witches was truly great, then this could justify departing from the legal proscriptions concerning what kind of information can be elicited from a suspect during interrogations. Hence the higher this probability the more witches that would be executed by the local court.

---

13 The largest witch hunts, involving more than 250 executions within a relatively short space of time, took place in Trier, Lorraine, Würzburg, Bamberg, Baden, Cologne, Mainz, Pays de Vaud, and the Basque region.

This probability was affected by exogenous shocks (periods of unusually bad weather, for example, as in Oster 2004). However it was also influenced by trials in other nearby regions. If a witches' coven was discovered elsewhere, this raised the probability that there might be a similar such coven here undetected. Thus the decisions of one local court imposed an externality on other courts. If this externality was large enough then it could generate an information cascade in which judges passed sentences independently of local circumstances or the evidence before them. A mechanism like this could explain the witch panics that gripped parts of Germany between 1560 and 1660. However, even if this externality was not so large as to generate a pure information cascade, it still might be large enough to make larger-scale witch trials far more likely in regions where there were many independent courts, each with their own discretionary authority, than they would be under a centralized legal system that would be able to internalize it. This was the case in early modern France, as we discuss below.

There is plenty of evidence that is consistent with this simple framework. The majority of trials took place in response to popular outbreaks of fear about witchcraft (Monter 2002, 19). Belief in the threat posed by witches received apparent confirmation from the trials themselves. As we noted, it was difficult to prove or disprove the crime of witchcraft except by obtaining a confession. This lent the process of investigating witchcraft a degree of circularity: "By extracting confessions, usually under torture, to the activities that he believed the witch had engaged in, the inquisitor received confirmation of his suspicions, and thus the beliefs acquire validity" (Levack 2006, 53). Trials therefore increased overall belief in the existence of a witch threat. Tales of black magic, midnight Sabbaths, and satanic pacts grew in the telling and the fear these tales aroused could spread from village to village and town to town in a fashion that resembled a contagious illness.[14] Unusual weather or bad harvests were often trigger factors, but trials in which the charges were publically read aloud and distributed by pamphlets were the propagation mechanism (Behringer 1995). "The news of witch-hunts and executions in other parts of a country could easily fan popular and elite fears and create a mood that was conducive to witch-hunting in a village or town. It was because of such communications that many hunts spread from village to village, even when confessing witches did not implicate accomplices outside their communities or when witch-hunters did not move from place to place" (Levack 2006, 178–79). It was the contagious and self-confirming nature of the witch panics that posed a danger to public order and accounts for why witch hunting was so much more prevalent in the politically fragmented parts of Central Europe than it was in Western Europe.

---

14  "Probably the most common source of an atmosphere that was conducive to witch-hunting was the public discussion of witchcraft itself" (Levack 1996, 178–79).

This argument suggests that witch hunting was fiercer in legally fragmented jurisdictions because local authorities did not take into account the effects that their decisions would have on the overall level of witchcraft belief in nearby regions. In taking action to try a witch suspect, they quelled local fears, but they also lent credence to the view that malevolent witchcraft was widespread. Trials begat further trials because they increased both the perceived likelihood that witches truly existed; and they increased the threat posed by witchcraft in general, thereby justifying harsher and more severe punishment.

For this reason, Robin Briggs, remarked that "no well-organized major state in Europe was prepared to tolerate genuine witch-hunting for very long" (Briggs 1996, 190–91). Furthermore, witch trials were often accompanied by the, unauthorized and presumably largely unrecorded, lynching of suspected witches (Larner 1984; Soman 1989; Monter 2007). It was not so much that magistrates or judges were skeptical about the possibility of witchcraft; on the contrary, they believed in it. But public order and interests of state were the priority. The Inquisition in Spain was comparatively skeptical of witchcraft accusations, particularly from 1610 onward (Henningsen 1980). James I was the author of *Daemonologie*, and in the 1591 he conducted a large-scale trial in which dozens were executed, but by 1597 he was worried about panic-based persecutions and curbed the power of local lords to try witches (Larner 1984, 17–18).[15]

After 1600, the rulers of Europe's stronger states engaged in a project of centralization that involved imposing uniform economic and legal institutions across their territories. In regions where legal standards were strictly adhered to, witch trials never became witch panics. Local English courts tried a very small number of witches each year. And, with the exception of East Anglian trials, inspired by Matthew Hopkins during the Civil War, England did not experience large-scale witch hunts in which dozens or hundreds of suspects were tried and executed in a single year (Macfarlane 1970; Gaskill 2005). Wary of inciting fear of witchcraft, central governments internalized the externalities generated by witch trials. But politically fragmented lands, where local authorities were free from central oversight, were overwhelmingly more likely to see large-scale witch hunts. In the Holy Roman Empire, for example, the legal autonomy of small principalities and bishoprics resulted in large-scale witch panics. Witch trials were an indirect measure of legal centralization. Therefore we would expect centralized states to prosecute fewer witches (all else equal) and the process of state centralization and fiscal consolidation to result in a decline in the number of witch trials.

---

15 This account provides evidence in favor of our simplified model of witch trials. Certainly the trials of 1591 greatly increased fear of witchcraft in Scotland so that "the witch doctrine had by this time taken an almost complete hold of the clergy, gentry and legal profession of Scotland. This in turn encouraged already existing village belief, and allowed villagers and townsmen complete license in their accusations" (Larner 1984, 17–18).

## EMPIRICAL ANALYSIS: FISCAL CENTRALIZATION AND THE DECLINE OF WITCH TRIALS

Monter commented that the "rapid collapse of witch-hunting in the second half of the seventeenth century is as difficult to explain as its general acceptance until then" (Monter 1976, 37). Can our theory explain the demise of the witchcraft trials? Is there any evidence that as the centralized fiscal state imposed itself on outlying regions, witchcraft trials became less likely? We test this proposition using a unique data set on witchcraft trials across twenty-one regions of France between 1550 and 1700.[16] We combine the data on trials with data on direct tax revenues from the taille during the same period.

### The Data

The French fiscal system during the sixteenth and seventeenth centuries was highly complex. Nonetheless, receipts were generally separated into two categories, ordinary revenues and extraordinary revenues.[17] Extraordinary revenues were particularly important during times of war and could come from temporary surtaxes or loans (sometimes forced) from the wealthy. Ordinary revenues could be further broken down into local taxes like the *octrois*, which were collected by cities (Franck, Johnson, and Nye 2014), indirect taxes, which were usually collected through tax farms (Johnson 2006; Johnson and Koyama 2014a), and finally direct taxes, the most important of which during this period were the tailles. Before 1661, the tailles typically represented approximately two-thirds of the ordinary revenues of the Crown. This value dropped to about one-third after 1661. The reason for the decline was not because receipts through the taille decreased (as will be shown in detail below), but rather because of the even more dramatic increase in the value of the tax farms after the Fronde (Johnson 2006; Balla and Johnson 2009).

We focus on the tailles as a measure of fiscal capacity for several reasons. First, the tax base for each of the individual tailles was known as a *généralité*, and these were fairly stable from about the early sixteenth century until the Revolution. This is in contrast to the indirect taxes collected through the tax farms, which, by their very nature, were constantly being consolidated and reorganized. The second attractive feature of the taille data is that in the eighteenth century Jean-Roland Malet published the details of the royal budgets from the entire seventeenth century down to the généralité level (Bonney 1991). This is in stark contrast to other years in which the only extant tax records are the

---

16   The trial data come from a compilation made by Marc Carlson at the University of Tulsa. They are available for download at http://www.personal.utulsa.edu/~marc-carlson/witchtrial /france.html. The trials are given for specific cities, villages, or, in some cases, regions in France. We then recoded the data to correspond to the appropriate généralité in the seventeenth century.

17   The classic overview of financial records during the ancien régime is Guéry (1978).

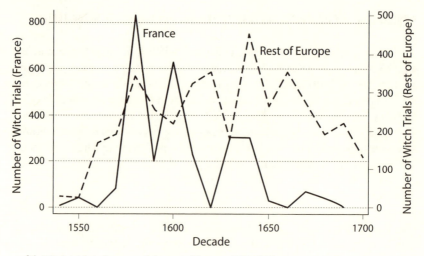

**6.1** Witch trials in France and the rest of Europe, 1540–1700.

accounts *abrègés*, which only contain nationally aggregated data. We can exploit the taille data from the seventeenth century to make inferences about changes in fiscal capacity across regions in addition to through time. This is a significant improvement on other work on French finances, which rarely exploits the within-country variation in taxes.

Figure 6.1 shows the overall numbers of witch trials between 1500 and 1720 in France (solid line) compared to the rest of Europe (dotted line).[18] Several facts are immediately apparent from the figure. First, witchcraft prosecutions started around 1550 across all of Europe. Second, while the overall number of trials in France was lower in total than in the rest of Europe (2,804 versus 4,435), French regions were very active in persecuting witches between 1550 and the middle of the seventeenth century.[19] Finally, and most important, French trials ended rather abruptly between 1635 and 1660 (marked by vertical lines), whereas in the rest of Europe, there was no such slowdown. Something unique to France apparently happened in the middle of the seventeenth century that was correlated with a decline in witchcraft persecutions.

What seems to have been going on at the same time that trials became less likely in France is that the fiscal capacity of the centralized state was expanding

18  The data for France are from the panel constructed by the authors and described below. The data on the "Rest of Europe" come from Oster (2004) and include the numbers of trials in the Bishopric of Basel, Essex, Estonia, Finland, Geneva, the Home Circuit (England), Hungary, Neuchatel, and Scotland.

19  We should note that one very important omitted region in Europe is the German States, where some of the most severe witch hunts occurred during the period (see Midelfort 1972). The total number of witchcraft trials was probably around sixty thousand.

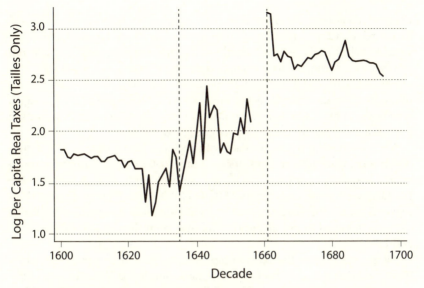

**6.2**  Log real per capita tax revenues in France, 1600–1700.

*Note*: For each region, the per capita fiscal capacity measure is constructed as net direct tax revenue (taille revenue) divided by estimated population in 1700. This is then multiplied by the silver content of the livre tournois to convert to real values. The value on the y-axis is equal to the average of the logged fiscal capacity measures for all twenty-one regions in each year.

dramatically. Figure 6.2 illustrates this by showing the per capita receipts from the tailles between 1600 and 1700.[20] Between 1635 and 1660 (vertical bars) tax revenues per capita increased by more than one log point (about 170 percent). This evidence of a positive correlation between aggregate tax receipts and the aggregate number of witch trials in France is suggestive, but it would be better if we could exploit the regional variation in taxes and trials over time in order to test two propositions: (1) At a given moment in time, were trials more likely to occur in regions with lower fiscal capacity? (2) Within a given region, as tax revenues per capita increased over time, did this correlate with a lower likelihood of a trial?

To this end, we create a panel spanning the years 1550 to 1700 for witchcraft trials across twenty-one regions in France.[21] One problem with analyzing the data on trials is that they are highly skewed. Five or six regions account for most of the raw numbers of trials, even though over half of the regions in France

20  We use généralité-level taille receipt data from Malet. We use population data from around 1700 contained in Dupâquier (1988) to create per capita values. We then converted these numbers into real values using data on the silver content (in grams) of the livre tournois provided by Wailly (1857). The final numbers, then, are the log of taille receipts per capita in terms of grams of silver.

21  The procedures used to construct the panel are available in a data appendix upon request.

experienced at least one trial between 1550 and 1700. Since we are interested in the relationship between trials and fiscal capacity we begin by creating a variable called "trials," which is equal to 0 if a region experienced no witch craft prosecutions during the period and is equal to 1 if at least one witch was prosecuted. Aside from eliminating outliers and allowing for a more robust analysis of the data, the rationale for doing this is inspired by the words of Montaigne, who wrote in his *Essais* that "it is putting a very high price on one's conjecture to roast a man alive for them" (Montaigne [1580] 1993).

We combine the witchcraft data with regional tax receipts by the central government (the tailles receipts) for the years 1600 to 1700. Since there are no region-level data on tax receipts for the period 1550 to 1599, we average the tax data over three periods (1550–1610, 1611–50, 1660–1700) and assume that regional tax receipts between 1600 and 1610 are good proxies for the relative share (as opposed to overall level) of receipts from the regions between 1550 and 1599.[22]

Figure 6.3 depicts the relationship between real taxes per capita across French regions and the likelihood that the region has at least one witch trial during the period. Dark bars represent fiscal capacity in regions with no witch trials. Lighter bars represent regions with at least one trial. The numbers in the bars ($n$) represent the number of regions with and without witch trials. Numbers in parentheses indicate the total number of trials recorded. Figure 6.3 provides support for our hypothesis that as the fiscal capacity of the central state increased, rule of law also improved. Regions with high amounts of fiscal capacity were also unlikely to prosecute individuals for witchcraft. Furthermore, while fiscal capacity in witchcraft regions failed to increase throughout the 150-year period, the number of regions engaging in witchcraft prosecutions declined. Between 1550 and 1610, twelve out of twenty-one regions had trials. Between 1611 and 1650 this declined to seven out of twenty-one, and after the dramatic increase in fiscal capacity illustrated in Figure 6.2, only three out of twenty-one regions had trials. Importantly, Figure 6.3 also shows that, on average, tax collections across witchcraft regions were constant. By contrast, fiscal capacity in regions without trials either increased or stayed the same over all periods. This implies that regions that abandoned trials were doing so at the same time as their tax capacity was increasing.[23]

22  This assumption is bolstered by the extant data we do have on aggregate tax receipts from 1497 to 1597 provided by Guéry (1978). In 1552 "net revenues" (comparable to our unadjusted tailles data) were 8,548,000 livres tournois. This compares to the average amount of receipts in 1600 of 9.4 million livres tournois. Thus, the identifying assumption we're relying on is that the *distribution* of fiscal capacity from 1600 to 1610 was roughly similar to what it was between 1550 and 1599.

23  Johnson and Koyama (2014b) provide more formal econometric analysis. They show that this relationship is robust to the inclusion of region fixed effects and time dummies and controls of urbanization and access to trade routes.

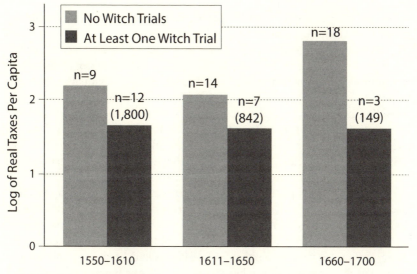

**6.3**  Fiscal capacity and witch trials across French regions, 1550–1700.

*Note*: For each region, the per capita fiscal capacity measure is constructed as net direct tax revenue (taille revenue) divided by estimated population in 1700. This is then multiplied by the silver content of the livre tournois to convert to real values. The value on the y-axis is equal to the average of the logged fiscal capacity measures for the regions in each category during each period. In each bar, (n) is equal to the number of regions in each category (witch trial = 0 or witch trial = 1). Values in parentheses indicate the number of trials across all witch trial regions during that period.

## DID INCREASES IN FISCAL CAPACITY CAUSE THE DECLINE OF WITCH TRIALS?

We have argued that the process of fiscal centralization played a causal role in increasing the ability of the central state to intervene and overrule local courts, thereby bringing the age of witch trials to an end. The first additional piece of historical evidence supporting our argument comes from the accounts contained in the secondary literature concerning the amount of corruption, nepotism, and inefficiency that characterized the local courts.

The costs of legal fragmentation were evident in the administration of justice. France did not possess a single criminal code and the concept of equality before the law was "unknown" (Heckscher 1955, 168).[24] The absence of a common criminal code placed discretion in the hands of local elites who staffed the courts and who used this power to extract rents (Beik 1985). Nepotism

---

24  "One man might be punished for a business practice which the next would carry on with impunity. This would sometimes happen illegally by corruption and personal favoritism, but even within the framework of the law, individual exceptions to any prescription whatever were frequently granted through personal influence" (Heckscher 1955, 168).

was common, corruption was widespread, and standards were lax.[25] Legal fragmentation meant that the administration of justice was highly uneven across France. Judges had great latitude in deciding what constituted a crime and its appropriate punishment. Local courts had a tremendous amount of discretionary authority. Even in ordinary criminal cases "many individuals withered in prison for months before their cases were heard, and upon the decision of the presiding magistrate prisoners were denied counsel and subjected to torture" (Hamscher 1976, 161–62). Reporting directly to Colbert, Nicholas Potier de Novion described the conduct of local judicial officials as "worse than one can imagine" as "all the cases that have been brought before us have been poorly prepared and judged" (quoted in Hamscher 1976, 168–69).

These local courts often used unorthodox methods to try and convict suspected witches. While the Parlement of Paris was comparatively reluctant to reduce legal standards in order to convict witches, regional courts adhered to much laxer standards. In the witch panic of the late sixteenth century the Parlement of Paris discovered that "village judges in the region of Champagne-Ardennes were relying far too heavily on the dubious practice of 'swimming' suspects on the slightest evidence" (Soman 1989, 6). "In 1609 the Parlement of Bordeaux condemned to death a young man, a Protestant of Nerca, on his simple confession, without witnesses" (Lea 1957, 1296–97). This is consistent with the mechanism we outlined in the second section of this chapter and suggests that causation ran from increased fiscal capacity to increased legal capacity to fewer witchcraft trials. Regional courts tried many more witches than did the courts closer to the capital, and as the fiscal power of the state increased, the trials were brought to a gradual end.

The second piece of evidence that supports our interpretation of the relationship between fiscal capacity and witch trials comes from the number and composition of laws (edicts) promulgated by the monarchy. These edicts were compiled by François-André Isambert and his collaborators between 1820 and 1833.

Figure 6.4 shows the raw counts of the number of edicts registered by the monarchy between 1550 and 1679. Legislative activity was not uniform throughout the 130-year period. There were large spikes of activity during the years spanning 1550 to 1583. This was followed by a relatively quiescent period from about 1590 to 1630. Then, between 1630 and 1680, the Crown became legislatively active again.

One interpretation of the pattern in the data on royal edicts is that causality ran from fiscal to legal capacity and that increased legal capacity led to

---

25 "When judges were extensively interrelated through birth and marriage, they were frequently called upon to decide cases involving the friends of their ever-expanding family circles. This in turn generated a flood of appeals and the time-consuming and expensive process of evoking cases from one court to another" (Hamscher, 1976, 159–60).

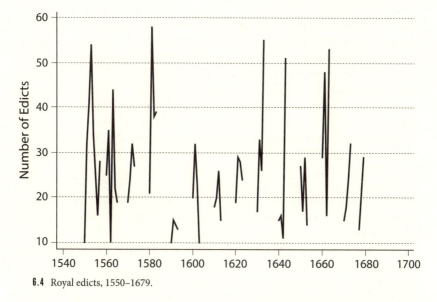

**6.4** Royal edicts, 1550–1679.

the decline in witch trials. In the period of early legislative activity in Figure 6.4 witchcraft trials were taking off in France, as shown in Figure 6.1. In other words, despite the fact that the central monarchy was attempting to impose its legal opinion on the rest of France during the sixteenth century, local judges in fiscally weak regions were exercising their independent authority and prosecuting men and women as sorcerers and witches. By contrast, the second period of high legislative activity, which starts after 1630 or so, corresponds to precisely the time when the fiscal state was expanding (cf. Figure 6.2) and witch trials were on the decline. If witch trials really do serve as a proxy for the weakness of the central state's legal apparatus, then this is suggestive evidence that laws on their own were not enough. It took laws in combination with the institutional capacity to collect revenues in order to get a true deepening of legal capacity across the regions of France.

We identify nine consistent categories into which the edicts fall. Those categories are (1) exemptions, gifts, creation of noble titles, pardons, and other venal acts; (2) regulations concerning health; (3) laws concerning the money supply; (4) laws concerning the military and international affairs; (5) laws confirming previous laws (actes de jussion); (6) laws that increase fiscal capacity; (7) laws that increase legal capacity; (8) laws that suppress former offices and privileges; and (9) uncategorized.

Categories 2, 3, 6, 7, and 8 are plausibly associated with increases in state capacity. This is confirmed by reading what the edicts say. In 1576, for example, under "laws which increase legal capacity," there is an edict "portant défenses à tous Juges d'expedier sous leurs noms, ou autrement, aucunes Lettres de celles qui doivent estre expediées dans les Chancelleries des Parlements, ou des Presidiaux" (Isambert, Decrusy, and Taillandier 1820–33, 14:195). This is an explicit injunction designed to limit the authority of judges to act outside the authority of the more centralized Parlements. Similarly, also in 1576 there is an edict that creates an office for the presidency of the Parlement of Dijon. With regard to fiscal capacity, there is an edict that creates an office of "Treasurer of France" and "General of Finances" in each of the généralités of Lyon, Orleans, an Limoges. Directly below this is a "reglement general pour les Finances dans le ressort du Parlement de Bourdeux" (Isambert, Decrusy, and Taillandier 1820–33, 14:197).

In 1664 there are also edicts that increase the legal capacity of the central state, like one requiring the election of *Echevins* (municipal magistrates) in Rouen (Isambert, Decrusy, and Taillandier 1820–33, 18:525). There is another rule addressed to the tax court responsible for disputes concerning the "Aides" (sales taxes collected by the General Farms) which explicitly instructs those enforcing penalties not confiscate "beds, clothing, bread, or horses or cattle serving as field labor." Another overrides the law concerning marriage and inheritance in "Lyon, Lyonnois, Masconnois, and Beaujollois." With regards to taxation there is a law *reducing* taxes in coastal towns and establishing entrepôts funded by the state. There is another that hypothecates revenue from the Royal General Farms toward payments on debt issued by the Hôtel de Ville. Another issues a "reglement general" for the tailles in Normandy (Isambert, Decrusy, and Taillandier 1820–33, 14:522–25).

Figure 6.5 presents two pie charts showing the proportions of the different kinds of edicts being issued in 1576 ($n = 48$) and 1664 ($n = 37$). In general, the proportion of laws issued in the categories most easily associated with an increase in central authority (categories 2, 3, 6, and 7) looks about the same between the two dates. The only significant difference is that a lot more privileges were being suppressed in 1664 than in the earlier period (category 8). So, for example, in 1664 there is an edict revoking letters granting noble status since 1614. The fact that this law was registered in the Cour des Aides, a tax court, implies that its purpose was likely to reduce the number of local elites who were exempt from taxation. A similar edict does the same thing, but specifically for Normandy. Another edict suppresses offices created for "waters and forests" since 1635. Two edicts reduce the number of ancillary officers in regional Parlements (Isambert, Decrusy, and Taillandier 1820–33, 14:522–24). The suppression of offices is consistent with the historical narrative outlined above in which, for the purposes of increasing fiscal capacity, After the 1630s, the French state made a deliberate attempt to weaken the provincial nobility in favor of those elites whose interests aligned with the centralized tax state (e.g., intendants). Revoking noble status using edicts is just one method for doing this that is particularly well preserved in the historical record.

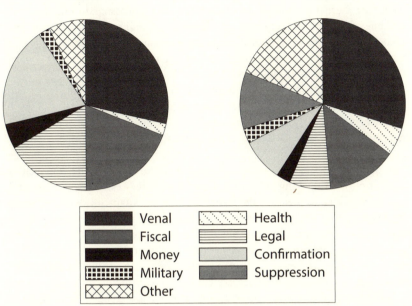

**6.5**  Composition of edicts issued by the monarchy, 1576 and 1664.

Further data collection is no doubt necessary. Nonetheless, based on the data for 1576 and 1664, it appears that increasing state capacity not only involved issuing laws but also required the creation of institutions that could enforce these laws, like the intendancies. Similarly, the increased prevalence of edicts suppressing privileges of local elites and older noblesse d'épée in the 1664 data was part of the process of substituting a new set of institutions, managed by a Paris-based elite, for the existing local arrangements. The development of this enforcement capability seems to coincide with both the increase in fiscal capacity of the middle of the seventeenth century and the decline in witch trials.

## DISCUSSION AND CONCLUSION

This chapter has used witchcraft trials to trace some of the consequences of the expansion of the fiscal state in early modern France. Our findings should be interpreted in relation to two separate literatures: (1) the recent literature on state capacity in political science, political economy, and development economics, and (2) the recent work by historians reevaluating the role played by mercantilist policies in the early modern period. The main claim underlying much

recent work in political science, political economy, and development economics is that there is a strong link between the ability of a state to raise large tax
revenues from a broad segment of the economy and good governance. In a
related vein, recent work by historians and economic historians has suggested
a more positive interpretation of state-building efforts by mercantilist governments in the early modern period (Ormrod 2003; O'Brien 2011).

The main implications of the argument of this chapter are consistent with
both of these claims. It is important to stress, however, that the increased size of
the fiscal state in early modern France did not bring direct benefits to the ordinary population. Increased fiscal capacity does not necessarily imply increased
provision of public goods. And, indeed, in ancien régime France, tax revenues
were generally spent on warfare or diverted to the elite and the conspicuous
consumption of the king at Versailles. Revisionist reassessments of mercantilism tend to fall into precisely the error identified by Adam Smith of identifying
the visible power of the state with the welfare of the population. Real incomes
stagnated or fell during the seventeenth century. Collins notes that it was the
peasants who paid five or six *livres* a year in taxes who were now unable to save
or invest (Collins 1988, 207). This increased their vulnerability to agricultural
crises, which continued to occur, particularly in wartime.

However, in the long run there do appear to have been benefits for ordinary
Frenchmen and Frenchwomen from this process of state building and administrative centralization. John Komlos (2003) has shown that after the agricultural
crises at the end of the seventeenth century, the welfare of French peasants, as
measured by their heights, entered a sustained period of improvement. One
way in which this apparently paradoxical outcome—an increase in the size of
a predatory state combined with a gradual improvement in the welfare of the
ordinary citizen—can be resolved is to note that the increases in fiscal capacity
were accompanied by a more standardized and centralized legal system. Higher
taxes are generally bad, but better laws are good. For France, the benefits of the
improvements in legal capacity of the seventeenth century may have influenced
events in the eighteenth century through several channels.

First, increased legal capacity lowered the transaction costs faced by centralized elites in organizing and thereby enable them to credibly constrain
the Crown. The Company of General Farms, which was composed of forty
or so noblesse d'robe, obtained monopsony control of all indirect taxes between 1661 and 1681 (approximately two-thirds of ordinary receipts). Johnson
(2006a, 2006b; Johnson and Koyama 2014a) outlines how these tax farmers
constrained the Crown by threatening to withhold loans if he reneged on his
agreements with them. In order to do this, they had to solve a collective action
problem that stemmed from the powerful incentives facing each individual tax
collector to deviate from this punishment strategy and offer a loan to the king.
Legal innovations enabled tax farmers to separate ownership from control in
the administration of the tax farms. This was important and allowed tax farm-

ers to amass the necessary amount of capital required to credibly sanction in the king in the event of a default (Balla and Johnson 2009).

Second, the imposition of legal standardization in early modern France was associated with the recognition of rights for minority groups including Protestants and Jews (Johnson and Koyama, 2013; Anderson, Johnson, and Koyama 2013). The granting of legal rights to Protestants was disastrously reversed by Louis XIV with the revocation of the Edict of Nantes in 1685. However, the right of Jews to practice their religion in France, first tacitly recognized by Richelieu in the 1620s when he refused to allow the prosecution of Portuguese Conversos for practicing Judaism, became codified by 1722 (Israel 1985, 96–97). In this respect, legal standardization helped pave the way for religious toleration, even though that toleration remained fragile in a country ruled by an absolute monarch.

The final respect in which increased legal capacity during the seventeenth century set France on the path of modern growth was that it may have directly affected the social identity of Frenchmen and Frenchwomen.[26] Sociologists distinguish between ascriptive and meritocratic social systems. Ascriptive systems define a person's social identity in terms of roles assigned at birth (e.g., race, caste, place of origin, etc.). Meritocratic systems, on the other hand, allow status to be earned. Recent research suggests that when individuals are primed on their ascriptive social identity, they are less responsive to economic incentives, regardless of their status in the ascriptive regime.[27] Rigid, status-bound social systems can therefore inhibit economic and entrepreneurial activity both directly and indirectly.

The legal changes we have discussed in this article homogenized the law. The Code Michau outlined the procedures for collecting taxes and conducting court cases in *all* regions of France and had to be written in a general enough way to apply everywhere. In a similar fashion, the intendants did not owe loyalty to ancestry or local custom, they owed it to Versailles. Johnson (2014) shows that in places where the absolute monarchy was better able to impose its fiscal and legal institutions, affiliation with national, as opposed to local, identity was stronger in 1789. While few would associate the "ancien régime" with the word "equality," the weight of the evidence is that there were many margins on which the legal and fiscal institutions developed by the French tax state were more

---

26   Mokyr (2008) places considerable emphasis on the importance of social norms in generating an environment conducive to economic growth and innovation in eighteenth-century England.

27   For example, in a recent study, Hoff and Pandey (2014) used randomized lab experiments to show that children from northern India who were primed on caste (ascriptive identity) responded less to economic incentives than those in a control group. Importantly, this finding held for all castes, not just dalits. As a social identity, the caste system is not just highly inequitable; it may also be incompatible with economic incentives.

equitable (less ascriptive) than the local institutions being displaced (family, village, church, etc.). Witchcraft trials are just an extreme, and for that reason observable, example of this tendency.

In the elusive quest for the sources of modern economic growth, a recent literature argues that it was spurred by changes in the way people *thought* well before the steam engines were invented and the factories organized (Mokyr 2002, 2009). Another line of reasoning has argued that institutional innovations that created secure property rights in the seventeenth century acted as the catalyst for what would come (North and Weingast 1989). We see our research as consistent with both points of view. Formal institutions did matter. However, we place particular emphasis on the importance of legal standardization and the growth of state capacity. In France, fiscal and legal centralization had profound effects, not just on the Crown's ability to access credit, but also on the rest of the population, including those who faced accusations of witchcraft. By providing a broader, more open-minded identity for all Frenchmen and Frenchwomen to call upon, the fiscal and legal revolutions of the seventeenth century may have laid the foundations for modern economic growth.

## BIBLIOGRAPHY

Allison, P. D., and R. P. Waterman. 2002. "Fixed-Effects Negative Binomial Regression Models." *Sociological Methodology* 32 (1): 247–65.

Anderson, R. W., N. D. Johnson, and M. Koyama. 2013. "Jewish Persecutions and Weather Shocks." GMU Working Paper in Economics No. 13-06.

Balla, E., and N. D. Johnson. 2009. "Fiscal Crisis and Institutional Change in the Ottoman Empire and France." *Journal of Economic History* 69 (3): 809–45.

Bateman, V. N. 2011. "The Evolution of Markets in Early Modern Europe, 1350–1800: A Study of Wheat Prices." *Economic History Review* 64 (2): 447–71.

Behringer, W. 1995. "Weather, Hunger and Fear: Origins of the European Witch Hunts in Climate, Society and Mentality." *German History* 13 (1): 1–27.

———. 1997. *Witchcraft Persecutions in Bavaria*. Translated by J. C. Grayson and David Lederer. Cambridge: Cambridge University Press.

Beik, W. 1985. *Absolutism and Society in Seventeenth-Century France*. Cambridge: Cambridge University Press.

Besley, T., and T. Persson. 2011. *Pillars of Prosperity*. Princeton: Princeton University Press.

Bien, D. D. 1988. "Les offices, les corps, et le crédit d'état: l'utilisation des privilèges sous l'ancien régime." *Annales ESC* 43 (2): 379–404.

Bikhchandani, S., D. Hirshleifer, and I. Welch. 1992. "A Theory of Fads, Fashion, Custom, and Cultural Change as Informational Cascades." *Journal of Political Economy* 100 (5): 992–1026.

Blanchard, G. 1687. *Table Chronologique, Contenant un Recueil en Abrègé des Ordonnances, Edits, Declarations, et Lettres Patentes des Rois de France qui Concernent la Justive, la Police, et les Finances*. Paris: Charles de Servcy.

Bogart, D., and G. Richardson. 2012. "Property Rights and Parliament in Industrializing Britain." *Journal of Law & Economics* 54 (2): 241–74.

Bonney, R. 1991. "Jean-Roland Malet: Historian of the Finance of the French Monarchy." *French History* 5 (2): 180–233.

Brewer, J. 1988. *The Sinews of Power*. Cambridge, MA: Harvard University Press.

Briggs, R. 1996. *Witches and Neighbours*. London: Penguin.

Chaunu, P. 1969. "Sur la fin des sorciers au xviie siècle." *Annales. Histoire, Sciences Sociales* 24 (4): 895–911.

Cohn, N. 1975. *Europe's Inner Demons*. London: Pimlico.

Collins, J. B. 1988. *Fiscal Limits of Absolutism*. Berkeley: University of California Press.

———. 1995. *The State in Early Modern France*. Cambridge: Cambridge University Press.

Dincecco, M. 2009. "Fiscal Centralization, Limited Government, and Public Revenues in Europe, 1650–1913." *Journal of Economic History* 69 (1): 48–103.

———. 2010. "Fragmented Authority from Ancien Régime to Modernity: A Quantitative Analysis." *Journal of Institutional Economics* 6 (3): 305–28.

Dupâquier, J. 1988. *Histoire de la population Francaise*. Vol. 4. Paris: PUF.

Epstein, S. R. 2000. *Freedom and Growth: The Rise of States and Markets in Europe, 1300–1700*. London: Routledge.

Evans, P., D. Rueschemeyer, and T. Skocpol, eds. 1985. *Bringing the State Back In*. Cambridge: Cambridge University Press.

Franck, R., N. D. Johnson, and J. V. C. Nye. 2014. "From Internal Taxes to National Regulation: Evidence from a French Wine Tax Reform at the Turn of the Twentieth Century." *Explorations in Economic History* 51: 77–93.

Fukuyama, F. 2011. *The Origins of Political Order*. London: Profile Books.

Gaskill, M. 2005. *Witchfinders: A Seventeenth-Century English Tragedy*. London: John Murray.

Gennaioli, N., and H. J. Voth. 2013. "State Capacity and Military Conflict." Manuscript.

Goubert, P. 1969. *L'Ancien Regime*. Paris: Armand Colin.

Grafe, R. 2012. *Distant Tyranny: Markets, Power, and Backwardness in Spain, 1650–1800*. Princeton Economic History of the Western World. Princeton: Princeton University Press.

Greif, A. 2006. *Institutions and the Path to the Modern Economy*. Cambridge: Cambridge University Press.

Guéry, A. 1978. "Les finances de la monarchie française sous l'ancien régime." *Annales E.S.C.* 33: 216–39.

Hamscher, A. N. 1976. *The Parlement of Paris after the Fronde, 1653–1673*. Pittsburgh: University of Pittsburgh Press.

Hausman, J. A., B. H. Hall, and Z. Griliches. 1984. "Econometric Models for Count Data with an Application to the Patents-R&D Relationship." NBER Technical Working Papers 0017, National Bureau of Economic Research.

Heckscher, E. F. 1955. *Mercantilism*. Vol. 1. Translated by E. F. Soderlund. London: George Allen & Unwin.

Henningsen, G. 1980. *The Witches' Advocate*. Reno: University of Nevada Press.

Hoff, K., and P. Pandey. 2014. "Making Up People—The Effect of Identity on Performance in a Modernizing Society." *Journal of Development Economics* 106: 118–31.

Hoffman, P. 1994. "Early Modern France, 1450–1700." In *Fiscal Crises, Liberty, and Representative Government, 1450–1789*, edited by P. Hoffman and K. Norberg, 226–52. Stanford: Stanford University Press.

———. 1996. *Growth in a Traditional Society*. Princeton: Princeton University Press.

Hurt, J. J. 2002. *Louis XIV and the Parlements: The Assertion of Royal Authority*. Manchester: Manchester University Press.

Isambert, François-André, Alfred Jourdan Decrusy, and Alphonse-Honoré Taillandier. 1820–33. *Recueil général des anciennes lois françaises, depuis l'an 420 jusqu'à la Révolution de 1789, contenant la notice des principaux monumens des Mérovingiens, des Carlovingiens et des Capétiens, et le texte des ordonnances, édits, déclarations, lettres patentes, règlemens de la troisième race, qui ne sont pas abrogés, ou qui peuvent servir, soit à l'interprétation, soit à l'histoire du droit public et privé . . . , par MM. Jourdan, Decrusy, Isambert. . . .* 29 vols. Paris: Belin-Leprieur, Plon.s

Israel, Jonathan. 1985. *European Jewry in the Age of Mercantilism, 1550–1750*. Oxford: Oxford University Press.

Johnson, N. D. 2006a. "Banking on the King: The Evolution of the Royal Revenue Farms in Old Regime France." *Journal of Economic History* 66 (4): 963–91.

———. 2006b. "The Cost of Credibility: The Company of General Farms and Fiscal Stagnation in Eighteenth Century France." *Essays in Economic and Business History* 24 (4): 963–91.

———. 2014. "Taxes, National Identity, and Nation Building: Evidence from France." Working paper.

Johnson, N. D., and M. Koyama. 2013. "Legal Centralization and the Birth of the Secular State." *Journal of Comparative Economics* 41: 959–78.

———. 2014a. "Tax Farming and the Origins of State Capacity in England and France." *Explorations in Economic History* 51 (1): 1–20.

———. 2014b. "Taxes, Lawyers, and the Decline of Witchcraft." *Journal of Law and Economics* 57: 1.

Komlos, J. 2003. "An Anthropometric History of Early-Modern France." *European Economic Review* 7: 159–89.

Koyama, M. 2010. "Evading the 'Taint of Usury': The Usury Prohibition as a Barrier to Entry." *Explorations in Economic History* 47 (4): 420–42.

Kwass, M. 1998. "A Kingdom of Taxpayers: State Formation, Privilege, and Political Culture in Eighteenth-Century France." *Journal of Modern History* 70 (2): 295–339.

———. 2000. *Privilege and the Politics of Taxation in Eighteenth-Century France: Liberté, Égalité, Fiscalité*. Cambridge: Cambridge University Press.

Lamoreaux, Naomi R. 2011. "The Mystery of Property Rights: A U.S. Perspective." *Journal of Economic History* 71 (2): 275–306.

Langbein, J. H. (1976) 2006. *Torture and the Law of Proof*. Chicago: University of Chicago Press.

Larner, C. 1984. *Witchcraft and Religion: The Politics of Popular Belief*. Edited by A. Macfarlane. Oxford: Basil Blackwell.

Lea, H. C. 1957. *Material toward a History of Witchcraft*. London: Thomas Yoseloff.

Levack, B. P. 1996. "State-Building and Witch Hunting in Early Modern Europe." In *Witchcraft in Early Modern Europe*, edited by J. Barry, M. Hester, G. Roberts, 96–118. Cambridge: Cambridge University Press,

———. 2006. *The Witch-Hunt in Early Modern Europe*. 3rd ed. Harlow: Pearson.

———. 2008. *Witch-Hunting in Scotland*. London: Routledge.

Macfarlane, A. 1970. *Witchcraft in Tudor and Stuart England*. London: Routledge & Kegan Paul.

Major, J. R. 1962. "The French Renaissance Monarchy as Seen through the Estates General." *Studies in the Renaissance* 9: 113–25.

———. 1964. "The Crown and the Aristocracy in Renaissance France." *American Historical Review* 69 (3): 631–45.

———. 1994. *From Renaissance Monarchy to Absolute Monarchy: French Kings, Nobles & Estates*. Baltimore: Johns Hopkins University Press.

Mandrou, R. 1968. *Magistrats et sorciers en France au XVII siècle: une analyse de psychologie historique*. Paris: Plon.

Mathias, P., and P. K. O'Brien. 1976. "Taxation in Britain and France, 1715–1810: A Comparison of the Social and Economic Incidence of Taxes Collected for the Central Governments." *Journal of European Economic History* 5: 601–50.

McCloskey, D. N. 2010. *Bourgeois Dignity: Why Economics Can't Explain the Modern World*. Chicago: University of Chicago Press.

Midelfort, E. 1972. *Witch Hunting in Southwestern Germany*. Stanford: Stanford University Press.

Mokyr, J. 2002. *The Gift of Athena: Historical Origins of the Knowledge Economy*. Princeton: Princeton University Press.

———. 2006. "Mercantilism, the Enlightenment, and the Industrial Revolution." In *International Trade, and Economic History*, edited by R. Findlay, R. G. H. Henriksson, H. Lindgren, and M. Lundahl, 269–305. Cambridge, MA: MIT Press.

——. 2008. "The Institutional Origins of the Industrial Revolution." In *Institutions and Economic Performance*, edited by E. Helpman, 64–120. Cambridge, MA: Harvard University Press.

——. 2009. *The Enlightened Economy*. New Haven, CT: Yale University Press.

Mokyr, J., and J. V. C. Nye. 2007. "Distribution Coalitions, the Industrial Revolution, and the Origins of Economics Growth in Britain." *Southern Economic Journal* 74 (1): 50–70.

Montaigne, M. D. (1580) 1993. "Of Cripples." Translated by M. A. Screech. In *Michel de Montaigne: The Complete Essays*, 1169. London: Penguin.

Monter, E. W. 1971. "Witchcraft in Geneva, 1537–1662." *Journal of Modern History* 43 (2): 180–204.

——. 1976. *Witchcraft in France and Switzerland*. Ithaca, NY: Cornell University Press.

——. 1997. "Toads and Eucharists: The Male Witches of Normandy, 1564–1660." *French Historical Studies* 20 (4): 563–95.

——. 2002. "Witch Trials in Continental Europe, 1560–1660." In *Witchcraft and Magic in Europe, the Period of the Witch Trials*, edited by B. Ankarloo, S. Clark, and E. W. Monter, 3–52. London: Athlone Press.

——. 2007. *A Bewitched Dutchy: Lorraine and Its Dukes, 1477–1736*. Geneva: Librairie Droz S.A.

Moote, A. L. 1971. *The Revolt of the Judges*. Princeton: Princeton University Press.

Muchembled, R. 1985. *Popular Culture and Elite Culture in France, 1480–1750*. Translated by Lydia Cochrane. Baton Rouge: Louisiana State University Press.

Munro, J. H. 2001. " 'The New Institutional Economics' and the Changing Fortunes of Fairs in Medieval and Early Modern Europe: The Textile Trades, Warfare, and Transaction Costs." *Vierteljahrschrift für Sozial- und Wirtschaftsgeschichte* 88 (1): 1–47.

North, D. C., J. J. Wallis, and B. R. Weingast. 2009. *Violence and Social Orders: A Conceptual Framework for Interpreting Recorded Human History*. Cambridge: Cambridge University Press.

North, D. C., and B. Weingast. 1989. "Constitutions and Commitment: The Evolution of Institutions Governing Public Choice in Seventeenth Century England." *Journal of Economic History* 49: 803–32.

Nye, J. V. C. 2007. *War, Wine, and Taxes: The Political Economy of Anglo-French Trade, 1689–1900*. Princeton: Princeton University Press.

O'Brien, P. K. 2011. "The Nature and Historical Evolution of an Exceptional Fiscal State and Its Possible Significance for the Precocious Commercialization and Industrialization of the British Economy from Cromwell to Nelson." *Economic History Review* 64 (2): 408–46.

Ogilvie, S. 2011. *Institutions and European Trade: Merchant Guilds, 1000–1800*. Cambridge: Cambridge University Press.

Olson, M. 1982. *The Rise and Decline of Nations: Economic Growth, Stagflation, and Social Rigidities*. New Haven, CT: Yale University Press.

Ormrod, D. 2003. *The Rise of Commercial Empires: England and the Netherlands in the Age of Mercantilism, 1650–1770*. Cambridge: Cambridge University Press.

Oster, E. 2004. "Witchcraft, Weather and Economic Growth in Renaissance Europe." *Journal of Economic Perspectives* 18 (1): 215–28.

Parker, D. 1996. *Class and State in Ancien Regime France: The Road to Modernity*. London: Routledge.

Pincus, S. 2009. *1688 The First Modern Revolution*. New Haven, CT: Yale University Press.

Root, H. L. 1987. *Peasants and King in Burgundy: Agrarian Foundations of French Absolutism*. Berkeley: University of California Press.

——. 1991. "The Redistributive Role of Government: Economic Regulation in Old Régime France and England." *Comparative Studies in Society and History* 33 (2): 338–69.

Roper, L. 2004. *Witch Craze*. New Haven, CT: Yale University Press.

Rosenthal, J.-L. 1992. *The Fruits of Revolution*. Cambridge: Cambridge University Press.

Ross, L., and R. Nisbett. 1991. *The Person and the Situation: Perspectives of Social Psychology*. New York: McGraw-Hill.

Shiue, C. H., and W. Keller. 2007. "Markets in China and Europe on the Eve of the Industrial Revolution." *American Economic Review* 97 (4): 1189–1216.

Soman, A. 1978. "The Parlement of Paris and the Great Witch Hunt (1565–1640)." *Sixteenth Century Journal* 9 (2): 31–44.

———. 1989. "Decriminalizing Witchcraft: Does the French Experience Furnish a European Model?" *Criminal Justice History* 10: 1–22.

Swidler, A. 1986. "Culture in Action: Symbols and Strategies." *American Sociological Review* 51: 273–86.

Tilly, C. 1985. "Warmaking and Statemaking as Organized Crime." In *Bringing the State Back In*, edited by P. Evans, D. Rueschemeyer, and T. Skocpol, 169–92. Cambridge: Cambridge University Press.

———. 1990. *Coercion, Capital, and European States, AD 990–1990.* Oxford: Blackwell.

Tocqueville, A. D. 1998. *The Old Regime and the Revolution.* Vol. 1. Chicago: University of Chicago Press.

Wailly, N. D. 1857. "Mémoire sur les variations de la livre tournois, depuis le règne de saint louis jusqu'à l'établissement de la monnaie decimate." *Mémoires de l'Academie des Inscriptions et Belles-Lettre* 21 (11): 398–401.

# PART II

# INNOVATION

# INCREASING MARKET CONCENTRATION IN BRITISH BANKING, 1885 TO 1925

## FABIO BRAGGION, NARLY R.D. DWARKASING, AND LYNDON MOORE

The late nineteenth and early twentieth centuries witnessed a rapid expansion of financial intermediation in England and Wales. From around 2,400 bank branches spread across these regions in 1885, banks aggressively expanded their branch networks. Banks would often start and then expand the branch network around the head office location (see Collins 1988, 77). By 1925 almost 9,000 branches operated in the same area. At the same time as banking was being pushed into smaller and smaller towns (and into the suburbs of the growing cities) a consolidation movement was taking place as London-based banks took over their provincial rivals.

Innovation and technological changes had an influence on the merger wave. The spread of financial and general journalism, the improvement of accounting techniques, and the birth of trade protection societies provided broader access to information on creditworthiness. Easier communication by rail brought the provinces closer to London (see Crafts and Mulatu 2006), and the development of telegraph and telephone lines offered an easy way to have branches to stay in contact with their headquarters (see Hannah 2008, 49–50). More mobile bank clients meant more demand for bank services in multiple localities. In addition, as the Second Industrial Revolution technologies led to larger and larger firm sizes, with concomitant large supplier networks, a large bank with multiple branches meant lower banking costs for the customer (see Hannah 2008). The period also coincided with a growth in the nationwide spread of firms in such areas as retailing (see Godley 2003). The rise of economies of scale in the British economy generally led to pressure for British banks to expand, either organically or by merger (see Collins 1988). Collins (1988, 78) attributes some of the expansion of the banking sector to "general improvements in communication," although banks were very slow to take up new communication technologies. As late as the 1890s most banks had only a single telegraph line (to their head office) and some not even that. By the early 1920s there had been little advance in the utilization of communication technologies; only the largest branches in the big cities had telegraph connections, and generally only the head office had (multiple) telephone connections.

In addition to technological innovations there arose the development of new commercial facilities and managerial practices. The bigger banks introduced new services for their clients, especially in the large cities. They would offer safe deposit services and remittance facilities, provide financial advice, act as trustees and executors, and provide foreign exchange (see Collins 1988, 260). The growth of the large bank was accompanied by the transfer of professional, rule-based procedures from head office to the branches. Pre-1914 banking, even industrial banking, was "a matter of personal relations between bank and client" (Capie and Collins 1999, 42). After the provincial banks were taken over they were often forced to follow head-office "circulars" or newly developed staff regulations. This increased professionalization (or bureaucratization) after a merger did not necessarily imply a loss of autonomy to the head office, since in most cases those at the head office were wise enough to leave some discretionary power in the hands of local managers. The premerger directors (or partners in the case of a private bank) were often retained as "local directors," a practice that continued until the late twentieth century.

Although bank concentration at the national level (i.e., treating England and Wales as a single market) increased more than sixfold, from a Herfindahl-Hirschman Index (HHI) of 0.022 in 1885 to 0.155 in 1925, the change at the county level was far more muted, indicating a rise of just 15 percent. If we treat each county as a separate market, calculate county-specific concentration measures, and then take an equally weighted average across counties, the national HHI increases from 0.248 to just 0.285. The explanation for this seeming anomaly is quite simple. If there were (say) four different provincial banks operating a branch network in a particular county in 1885, then there would be (roughly) four banks operating branch networks in the same county in 1925. The difference is that by 1925 the banks operating those networks would be national banks, based in London, whereas forty years earlier they had usually been local banks.

This work provides a detailed account of the evolution of banking concentration at a local level. We present Herfindahl indexes of banking concentration for each English and Welsh county every year between 1885 and 1925. To the best of our knowledge, this is the first analysis that constructs and discusses historical series of banking concentration at a subnational level. These data are important as they may serve as the basis for an analysis of the evolution of lending and deposit taking behavior or other aspects of the British banking system. The notion of local competition in banking is extremely important, and it has been shown to have implications for banks lending behavior (Degryse and Ongena 2005; Park and Pennacchi 2009). Our work provides a useful tool to tackle these issues in a historical context. Furthermore, by looking at three banks that survived over the period 1885 to 1925, we map the evolution of their branching network over time, thereby gaining more insight into the geographical expansion of these banks. We find that concentration at the national level increased largely over time, whereas concentration at the county level remained roughly stable as national banks did open branches in areas where they did not operate previously. This indicates that if banking still was regional, concentration should not have been an issue for competition policy as we find that on a regional level the HHI remains fairly unchanged and stable over time.

The banking merger wave started during the 1860s, and picked up pace toward the end of the nineteenth century (see Collins 1988, 78). This process continued the movement of financial resources from the counties to London. Capie and Rodrik-Bali (1982) find that in 1880 the largest ten banks in England and Wales controlled 36.2 percent of the banking system's deposits. By 1920 this had risen to 96.6 percent (see their table I). The largest banks (Barclays, Lloyds, Midland, National Provincial, and Westminster) controlled four-fifths of English and Welsh bank deposits.

Grossman (1999) explains that toward the end of the nineteenth century apprehension in the U.K. marketplace grew about the effects of limited bank competition. Bankers were naturally aware of the effects their mergers would have on the banking system. For example, Grossman (1999) reports that an official of the London, City, and Midland Bank (following a meeting with a representative of the Yorkshire Banking Company) stated that "our bank combined with his would command the best business and destroy active competition." Collins (1988) and Griffiths (1973) both accuse the English banks of operating an effective cartel, or a bankers' trust, with collusion on interest rate spreads as the culmination of the merger process. Collins states that all banks set rates so that current accounts received no interest, and term deposits 1.5 percent less than Bank Rate from 1886 onward. However, the U.K. Treasury report (1918) that investigated the merger movement in British banking concluded, "there is at present no idea of a Money Trust." A Federal Reserve report (1930) on U.K. banking echoed the conclusions of Treasury and stated that "the consensus of responsible opinion appears to be that effective competition for deposits and commercial loans has not been lessened as a result of the concentration movement."

In this article we focus on the banking system of England and Wales. Scottish and Irish banks are excluded for two reasons. First, they were subject to different banking laws, and, second, they operated in geographically distinct markets.[1] Only English and Welsh banks operated branch networks within England and Wales, although many Irish, Scottish, and foreign banks maintained a single office in the financial hub of London. Similarly, English and

---

1 For example, Scottish banks were allowed to issue their own notes within Scotland under the Bank Notes (Scotland) Act, 1854. Ireland had its own bank, the Bank of Ireland, that performed many central bank functions.

Welsh banks did not operate branches abroad (with the exception of a handful of branches just north of the Scottish border). Capie and Rodrik-Bali (1982, 280) also divide U.K. banks along the same lines as we do, since "the Irish and Scottish banking systems [are] quite different."

This chapter brings two innovations to the study of the British banking system. For the first time it is possible to measure banking concentration at the county level. The second is that the welfare effects of increased concentration, at the national level, need to be tempered by the consideration of the relevant market for banking services. If banking did retain its predominantly local character after the merger wave finished by 1919, then the merger wave was far more benign for consumers. National banks, with convenient branch structures and less arbitrary lending policies, had replaced the small local institutions, and perhaps the (modest) decline in concentration at the local level was worth it.

## BANK CONSOLIDATION

U.K. banks were allowed to incorporate with unlimited liability by the Banking Copartnership Act of 1826, as long as they were not located within sixty-five miles of London.[2] An act of Parliament in 1857 permitted banks to become limited liability concerns, under certain conditions, which relatively few banks chose to do (see Turner 2009). Following the failure of the City of Glasgow Bank, the Companies Act of 1879 required banks to be independently audited and eased the rules on limited liability (which banks quickly took advantage of; see Turner 2009).

Capie and Rodrik-Bali (1982) find that in 1870 a total of 387 banks were operating in the United Kingdom. During the end of the nineteenth century and up until just after World War I, the British banking industry experienced considerable growth in mergers and acquisitions activity. Between 1870 and 1921, 264 bank mergers occurred (or "amalgamations," as contemporaries referred to them). By 1920, only 75 banks were left in the United Kingdom (the majority of which were in Scotland and Ireland), and only 20 were English or Welsh public (also known as "joint-stock") banks (see Capie and Rodrik-Bali 1982 and the *Economist's Banking Supplement*).

The merger wave was mostly characterized by London banks taking over provincial banks. During the nineteenth century takeovers were usually undertaken to expand the acquiring bank's network. The acquiring bank would often take over a smaller bank located in a geographically separate, but nearby, region of England and Wales. In the twentieth century the banks that were taken over were more likely to operate in the same geographical area as the bidder. The

---

2   The geographical restriction of sixty-five miles was removed in 1833.

**TABLE 7.1**  British Bank Deposit Concentration, 1870–1920: Sum of the Largest Banks' Deposits Divided by the Sum of All Banks' Deposits

|      | Top 10 banks | | Top 5 banks | |
|------|------|---------------|------|---------------|
|      | U.K. | England/Wales | U.K. | England/Wales |
| 1880 | 32.5 | 36.2 | 20.6 | 26.4 |
| 1890 | 32.0 | 38.0 | 21.0 | 26.5 |
| 1900 | 41.0 | 46.3 | 25.5 | 31.0 |
| 1910 | 56.0 | 64.7 | 35.5 | 43.0 |
| 1920 | 73.7 | 96.6 | 65.5 | 80.0 |

culmination of this process was the emergence of the "Big Five" banks in Britain by 1918: Barclays, Lloyds, Midland, National Provincial, and Westminster.

Table 7.1 shows that in 1880 the top ten banks in the United Kingdom (in terms of deposit collection) had a share of about 32 percent of the total deposits: this figure grew to 74 percent by 1920. Even more astonishing was the increasing concentration when we examine only England and Wales: in 1880 the top ten banks controlled about 36 percent of deposits; this figure increased to 96.6 percent by 1920. The results are similar if we measure concentration as a proportion of deposits controlled by the top 5 banks: in the United Kingdom this figure increased from 20.6 percent in 1880 to 65.5 percent in 1920, and in England and Wales from 26 percent to 80 percent. By 1920 the British banking system looked much like those in countries that today have a high degree of concentration, such as Belgium or the Netherlands.

## DATA

We create a new data set on bank concentration by collecting annual data on the branch networks of all English and Welsh banks from 1885 to 1925. Branch data were retrieved from *London Banks and Kindred Companies*, the *Banker's Magazine*, and the *Banking Almanac*. These periodicals list the headquarters and the physical location of all branches of the bank. If there was only one branch in a town, the town's name was recorded. If there were multiple branches in a town, a street or other identifying notation was used for each branch. We do not distinguish among *branches* (full-service locations with a manager, located either in a city or a country town), *sub-branches* (a separate physical location that shared a manager with a branch), and country *agencies* (which often opened only several days per week). We place each branch into one of the fifty-four historic counties of England and Wales, using the Association of British Counties' *Gazetteer of British Place Names*.[3]

We obtain population, by county, from the U.K. censuses in 1881, 1891, 1901, 1911, and 1921. From the census data we estimate annual county populations by linear interpolation between census dates.

## MARKET CONCENTRATION

In 1885 there were 243 banks operating at least one branch in England and 23 operating at least one branch in Wales (see Table 7.2). In all, 251 banks were operating in either England or Wales or both. There were 2,417 branches open for business in 1885 across the country, a number that increased to 3,531 in 1895, 5,127 in 1905, 6,708 in 1915, and 8,858 by 1925. There were seven to ten times as many branches in England as there were in Wales, although on a per capita basis Wales was better catered to by the banking system.[4] By 1925, when the merger wave had finished, there were just 22 banks (20 of which were joint stock) that operated in England, and of these 8 operated in Wales

We measure the degree of market concentration in a county in a given year with a *County HHI*. The index uses the number of banks present in a county, and the number of branches each bank has, to measure concentration. In general a higher index number indicates a more concentrated market and ceteris paribus a less competitive environment. The index is constructed by summing the squared market shares for each bank, where market share is defined as the number of branches of a certain bank in a county divided by the total number of branches in that county. County HHI in county $c$ is defined as

$$
\text{HHI}_c = \sum_{i=1}^{N^c} \left( \frac{\text{branches}_{i,c}}{\sum_{i=1}^{N^c} \text{branches}_{i,c}} \right)^2
$$

where $Nc$ is the number of banks that operate in county $c$, and branches $i,c$ are the number of branches that bank $i$ operates in county $c$. For example, if there were three banks that each operated one branch in county $c$ then County HHI would be equal to

3  See http://www.gazetteer.co.uk/.

4  Given that Wales was predominantly rural, and many of the branches were in fact country agencies that operated only several days per week, our measure probably overstates the better branch coverage in Wales.

$$\left[\frac{1}{3}\right]^2 + \left[\frac{1}{3}\right]^2 + \left[\frac{1}{3}\right]^2 = \frac{1}{3}$$

We calculate county-level HHI annually. With the county-year observations of concentration we divide England and Wales into five areas: London, Urban England,[5] Rural England, Urban Wales (Glamorgan and Monmouthshire), and Rural Wales. In Table 7.3 we present the total number of branches present in these five regions, and the average (equally weighted) County HHI for those five regions. Finally, we take an equally weighted average of all of the County HHIs to create the average for England and Wales.

London was the least concentrated market in 1885, with an index value of 0.091, less than half that of the other regions. At the start of the period there were many small, private banks that operated one or a handful of branches in the capital. However, as the merger wave proceeded almost all of these were swallowed up, as indeed were many of the smaller London joint-stock banks, so that by 1925 concentration in London, at 0.227, was only just below the levels recorded in Urban England (which had the second lowest level of concentration). Over forty years there was a 150 percent rise in market concentration in London, far below the more modest rises in the other regions. In Urban England concentration rose by 27.8 percent, in Rural England by 31 percent, and in Urban Wales by 40.2 percent. Rural Wales actually witnessed a fall in market concentration (of 9.8 percent), despite the disappearance of all Welsh-based banks due to takeovers by English rivals.

The final column of Table 7.3 shows the national HHI measure. National HHI is constructed by treating England and Wales as a single market and summing the squared market shares, where the market share is calculated over the entire area of England and Wales. National HHI increases from 0.022 to 0.155, a 610 percent rise, over the entire period. Our result is broadly consistent with that of Grossman (1999), who uses market capitalization to construct his concentration measure. By using bank branches we are able to include the effect of disappearing private banks (that cannot be accounted for in his measure), and we find that concentration roughly triples between 1885 and 1914, whereas he finds that it increases by approximately 50 percent. Capie and Rodrik-Bali (1982, table 4) find results very similar to ours for England and Wales, with their HHI (based on bank deposits) showing that concentration increased by 512.5 percent between 1880 and 1920.

---

5  Urban is defined as all counties that had more than five hundred thousand inhabitants in the 1881 census. The urban counties are Cheshire, Devon (Plymouth), Durham, Essex, Gloucestershire (Bristol), Hampshire (Southampton and Portsmouth), Kent, Lancashire (Liverpool and Manchester), Staffordshire (Stoke-on-Trent), Warwickshire (Birmingham), and Yorkshire (Leeds, Bradford, Sheffield).

**TABLE 7.2** Banks, Branches, and Population

| Year | England | | | | Wales | | | | England and Wales | | | |
|---|---|---|---|---|---|---|---|---|---|---|---|---|
| | Banks | Branches | Pop. (m) | Pop./branches | Banks | Branches | Pop. (m) | Pop./branches | Banks | Branches | Pop. (m) | Pop./branches |
| 1885 | 243 | 2,201 | 25.54 | 11,606 | 23 | 216 | 1.64 | 7,597 | 251 | 2,417 | 27.18 | 11,247 |
| 1886 | 251 | 2,294 | 25.83 | 11,260 | 22 | 218 | 1.66 | 7,631 | 259 | 2,512 | 27.49 | 10,945 |
| 1887 | 252 | 2,343 | 26.12 | 11,147 | 22 | 220 | 1.69 | 7,664 | 259 | 2,563 | 27.80 | 10,848 |
| 1888 | 251 | 2,392 | 26.40 | 11,039 | 22 | 220 | 1.71 | 7,767 | 258 | 2,612 | 28.11 | 10,763 |
| 1889 | 248 | 2,477 | 26.69 | 10,775 | 22 | 225 | 1.73 | 7,694 | 255 | 2,702 | 28.42 | 10,519 |
| 1890 | 240 | 2,646 | 26.98 | 10,196 | 23 | 263 | 1.75 | 6,669 | 247 | 2,909 | 28.73 | 9,877 |
| 1891 | 237 | 2,782 | 27.26 | 9,800 | 21 | 278 | 1.78 | 6,390 | 242 | 3,060 | 29.04 | 9,490 |
| 1892 | 231 | 2,930 | 27.59 | 9,415 | 21 | 316 | 1.80 | 5,696 | 236 | 3,246 | 29.39 | 9,053 |
| 1893 | 223 | 3,008 | 27.91 | 9,278 | 19 | 324 | 1.82 | 5,629 | 227 | 3,332 | 29.73 | 8,923 |
| 1894 | 215 | 3,119 | 28.23 | 9,051 | 19 | 331 | 1.85 | 5,581 | 219 | 3,450 | 30.08 | 8,718 |
| 1895 | 209 | 3,187 | 28.55 | 8,959 | 18 | 344 | 1.87 | 5,439 | 212 | 3,531 | 30.42 | 8,616 |
| 1896 | 206 | 3,289 | 28.87 | 8,779 | 18 | 353 | 1.89 | 5,367 | 209 | 3,642 | 30.77 | 8,448 |
| 1897 | 185 | 3,447 | 29.20 | 8,470 | 18 | 353 | 1.92 | 5,434 | 188 | 3,800 | 31.11 | 8,188 |
| 1898 | 176 | 3,615 | 29.52 | 8,165 | 16 | 359 | 1.94 | 5,409 | 179 | 3,974 | 31.46 | 7,916 |
| 1899 | 172 | 3,815 | 29.84 | 7,822 | 15 | 371 | 1.97 | 5,298 | 174 | 4,186 | 31.81 | 7,598 |
| 1900 | 167 | 4,033 | 30.16 | 7,479 | 15 | 378 | 1.99 | 5,263 | 169 | 4,411 | 32.15 | 7,289 |
| 1901 | 152 | 4,161 | 30.48 | 7,326 | 16 | 391 | 2.01 | 5,148 | 154 | 4,552 | 32.50 | 7,139 |
| 1902 | 146 | 4,300 | 30.80 | 7,163 | 16 | 400 | 2.05 | 5,134 | 148 | 4,700 | 32.86 | 6,990 |
| 1903 | 129 | 4,449 | 31.12 | 6,995 | 16 | 419 | 2.09 | 4,999 | 131 | 4,868 | 33.21 | 6,823 |

**TABLE 7.2** *continued*

| | | | | | | | | | | | | |
|---|---|---|---|---|---|---|---|---|---|---|---|---|
| 1904 | 121 | 4,598 | 31.44 | 6,837 | 16 | 432 | 2.14 | 4,943 | 123 | 5,030 | 33.57 | 6,674 |
| 1905 | 99 | 4,685 | 31.75 | 6,778 | 17 | 442 | 2.18 | 4,923 | 101 | 5,127 | 33.93 | 6,618 |
| 1906 | 95 | 4,767 | 32.07 | 6,728 | 17 | 442 | 2.22 | 5,016 | 97 | 5,209 | 34.29 | 6,583 |
| 1907 | 89 | 4,859 | 32.39 | 6,666 | 16 | 452 | 2.26 | 4,995 | 91 | 5,311 | 34.65 | 6,524 |
| 1908 | 84 | 4,985 | 32.71 | 6,561 | 16 | 464 | 2.30 | 4,954 | 86 | 5,449 | 35.01 | 6,424 |
| 1909 | 83 | 5,099 | 33.02 | 6,477 | 17 | 484 | 2.34 | 4,833 | 85 | 5,583 | 35.36 | 6,334 |
| 1910 | 71 | 5,269 | 33.34 | 6,328 | 14 | 537 | 2.38 | 4,432 | 71 | 5,806 | 35.72 | 6,153 |
| 1911 | 68 | 5,328 | 33.66 | 6,317 | 13 | 559 | 2.42 | 4,331 | 69 | 5,887 | 36.08 | 6,129 |
| 1912 | 66 | 5,501 | 33.81 | 6,146 | 13 | 592 | 2.44 | 4,129 | 67 | 6,093 | 36.25 | 5,950 |
| 1913 | 63 | 5,629 | 33.96 | 6,032 | 13 | 653 | 2.47 | 3,780 | 64 | 6,282 | 36.42 | 5,798 |
| 1914 | 60 | 5,756 | 34.11 | 5,925 | 13 | 772 | 2.49 | 3,227 | 61 | 6,528 | 36.60 | 5,606 |
| 1915 | 53 | 5,925 | 34.25 | 5,781 | 13 | 783 | 2.52 | 3,212 | 54 | 6,708 | 36.77 | 5,481 |
| 1916 | 52 | 5,998 | 34.40 | 5,736 | 12 | 779 | 2.54 | 3,259 | 53 | 6,777 | 36.94 | 5,451 |
| 1917 | 49 | 5,964 | 34.55 | 5,793 | 11 | 756 | 2.56 | 3,389 | 50 | 6,720 | 37.11 | 5,523 |
| 1918 | 49 | 5,918 | 34.70 | 5,863 | 11 | 746 | 2.59 | 3,466 | 50 | 6,664 | 37.29 | 5,595 |
| 1919 | 37 | 6,326 | 34.85 | 5,509 | 9 | 851 | 2.61 | 3,066 | 38 | 7,177 | 37.46 | 5,219 |
| 1920 | 30 | 6,641 | 35.00 | 5,270 | 8 | 922 | 2.63 | 2,856 | 30 | 7,563 | 37.63 | 4,976 |
| 1921 | 26 | 6,905 | 35.15 | 5,090 | 8 | 975 | 2.66 | 2,725 | 26 | 7,880 | 37.80 | 4,797 |
| 1922 | 24 | 7,349 | 35.29 | 4,803 | 7 | 1,009 | 2.68 | 2,656 | 24 | 8,358 | 37.97 | 4,544 |
| 1923 | 24 | 7,456 | 35.44 | 4,754 | 8 | 1,021 | 2.70 | 2,648 | 24 | 8,477 | 38.15 | 4,500 |
| 1924 | 22 | 7,624 | 35.59 | 4,668 | 8 | 1,041 | 2.73 | 2,620 | 22 | 8,665 | 38.32 | 4,422 |
| 1925 | 22 | 7,797 | 35.74 | 4,584 | 8 | 1,061 | 2.75 | 2,593 | 22 | 8,858 | 38.49 | 4,345 |

**TABLE 7.3** Bank Concentration by Region

| Year | London Branches | London HHI | Urban England Branches | Urban England Avg. HHI | Rural England Branches | Rural England Avg. HHI | Urban Wales Branches | Urban Wales Avg. HHI | Rural Wales Branches | Rural Wales Avg. HHI | England and Wales Branches | England and Wales Avg. HHI | England and Wales National HHI |
|---|---|---|---|---|---|---|---|---|---|---|---|---|---|
| 1885 | 220 | 0.091 | 1,064 | 0.183 | 903 | 0.217 | 83 | 0.191 | 133 | 0.376 | 2,417 | 0.248 | 0.022 |
| 1886 | 245 | 0.089 | 1,116 | 0.180 | 919 | 0.221 | 82 | 0.200 | 136 | 0.370 | 2,512 | 0.248 | 0.021 |
| 1887 | 258 | 0.087 | 1,141 | 0.173 | 930 | 0.218 | 83 | 0.202 | 137 | 0.369 | 2,563 | 0.245 | 0.021 |
| 1888 | 271 | 0.091 | 1,169 | 0.173 | 938 | 0.218 | 83 | 0.202 | 137 | 0.369 | 2,612 | 0.245 | 0.021 |
| 1889 | 275 | 0.091 | 1,235 | 0.169 | 953 | 0.219 | 88 | 0.202 | 137 | 0.369 | 2,702 | 0.244 | 0.020 |
| 1890 | 297 | 0.094 | 1,328 | 0.177 | 1,007 | 0.219 | 116 | 0.179 | 147 | 0.346 | 2,909 | 0.240 | 0.020 |
| 1891 | 330 | 0.108 | 1,380 | 0.176 | 1,058 | 0.218 | 131 | 0.151 | 147 | 0.366 | 3,060 | 0.243 | 0.021 |
| 1892 | 348 | 0.105 | 1,455 | 0.172 | 1,113 | 0.215 | 142 | 0.157 | 174 | 0.317 | 3,246 | 0.230 | 0.021 |
| 1893 | 352 | 0.110 | 1,508 | 0.171 | 1,134 | 0.215 | 145 | 0.170 | 179 | 0.320 | 3,332 | 0.231 | 0.022 |
| 1894 | 362 | 0.109 | 1,583 | 0.166 | 1,160 | 0.220 | 152 | 0.172 | 179 | 0.333 | 3,450 | 0.236 | 0.022 |
| 1895 | 371 | 0.110 | 1,602 | 0.167 | 1,200 | 0.214 | 160 | 0.180 | 184 | 0.327 | 3,531 | 0.232 | 0.022 |
| 1896 | 380 | 0.107 | 1,683 | 0.167 | 1,210 | 0.215 | 164 | 0.183 | 189 | 0.327 | 3,642 | 0.233 | 0.023 |
| 1897 | 407 | 0.116 | 1,762 | 0.183 | 1,260 | 0.233 | 162 | 0.185 | 191 | 0.324 | 3,800 | 0.242 | 0.026 |
| 1898 | 435 | 0.108 | 1,832 | 0.187 | 1,328 | 0.237 | 160 | 0.192 | 199 | 0.326 | 3,974 | 0.246 | 0.028 |
| 1899 | 483 | 0.109 | 1,925 | 0.185 | 1,387 | 0.234 | 163 | 0.190 | 208 | 0.326 | 4,186 | 0.244 | 0.029 |
| 1900 | 518 | 0.108 | 2,046 | 0.182 | 1,449 | 0.232 | 165 | 0.190 | 213 | 0.320 | 4,411 | 0.241 | 0.030 |
| 1901 | 538 | 0.109 | 2,120 | 0.183 | 1,480 | 0.232 | 172 | 0.183 | 219 | 0.321 | 4,552 | 0.241 | 0.032 |
| 1902 | 564 | 0.107 | 2,188 | 0.178 | 1,523 | 0.232 | 175 | 0.183 | 225 | 0.317 | 4,700 | 0.238 | 0.033 |
| 1903 | 586 | 0.107 | 2,259 | 0.178 | 1,579 | 0.239 | 189 | 0.191 | 230 | 0.318 | 4,868 | 0.242 | 0.037 |

**TABLE 7.3** *continued*

| | | | | | | | | | | | | | |
|---|---|---|---|---|---|---|---|---|---|---|---|---|---|
| 1904 | 610 | 0.108 | 2,333 | 0.178 | 1,629 | 0.238 | 195 | 0.190 | 237 | 0.313 | 5,030 | 0.240 | 0.040 |
| 1905 | 614 | 0.106 | 2,393 | 0.181 | 1,650 | 0.243 | 200 | 0.184 | 242 | 0.311 | 5,127 | 0.242 | 0.042 |
| 1906 | 622 | 0.108 | 2,421 | 0.179 | 1,696 | 0.246 | 200 | 0.184 | 242 | 0.310 | 5,209 | 0.243 | 0.042 |
| 1907 | 631 | 0.108 | 2,474 | 0.182 | 1,726 | 0.249 | 207 | 0.190 | 245 | 0.312 | 5,311 | 0.246 | 0.047 |
| 1908 | 641 | 0.108 | 2,548 | 0.179 | 1,768 | 0.248 | 213 | 0.192 | 251 | 0.312 | 5,449 | 0.245 | 0.048 |
| 1909 | 659 | 0.106 | 2,601 | 0.181 | 1,811 | 0.249 | 228 | 0.192 | 256 | 0.304 | 5,583 | 0.244 | 0.049 |
| 1910 | 671 | 0.118 | 2,712 | 0.177 | 1,858 | 0.250 | 267 | 0.198 | 270 | 0.314 | 5,806 | 0.246 | 0.055 |
| 1911 | 672 | 0.119 | 2,739 | 0.178 | 1,889 | 0.250 | 276 | 0.203 | 283 | 0.312 | 5,887 | 0.246 | 0.056 |
| 1912 | 684 | 0.120 | 2,841 | 0.178 | 1,948 | 0.253 | 300 | 0.200 | 292 | 0.315 | 6,093 | 0.248 | 0.058 |
| 1913 | 704 | 0.119 | 2,893 | 0.176 | 2,004 | 0.252 | 323 | 0.197 | 330 | 0.308 | 6,282 | 0.245 | 0.059 |
| 1914 | 721 | 0.119 | 2,951 | 0.176 | 2,056 | 0.253 | 372 | 0.200 | 400 | 0.311 | 6,528 | 0.247 | 0.062 |
| 1915 | 727 | 0.120 | 3,055 | 0.197 | 2,115 | 0.256 | 360 | 0.219 | 423 | 0.365 | 6,708 | 0.265 | 0.076 |
| 1916 | 728 | 0.120 | 3,107 | 0.194 | 2,134 | 0.257 | 358 | 0.221 | 421 | 0.360 | 6,777 | 0.262 | 0.077 |
| 1917 | 731 | 0.120 | 3,100 | 0.191 | 2,104 | 0.257 | 352 | 0.223 | 404 | 0.352 | 6,720 | 0.261 | 0.082 |
| 1918 | 732 | 0.120 | 3,079 | 0.191 | 2,078 | 0.258 | 346 | 0.225 | 400 | 0.350 | 6,664 | 0.261 | 0.082 |
| 1919 | 752 | 0.245 | 3,337 | 0.256 | 2,209 | 0.315 | 389 | 0.274 | 462 | 0.355 | 7,177 | 0.311 | 0.147 |
| 1920 | 789 | 0.235 | 3,520 | 0.251 | 2,304 | 0.313 | 417 | 0.273 | 505 | 0.351 | 7,563 | 0.306 | 0.148 |
| 1921 | 809 | 0.236 | 3,669 | 0.248 | 2,397 | 0.301 | 439 | 0.268 | 536 | 0.350 | 7,880 | 0.299 | 0.153 |
| 1922 | 892 | 0.228 | 3,866 | 0.243 | 2,561 | 0.292 | 452 | 0.269 | 557 | 0.343 | 8,358 | 0.292 | 0.154 |
| 1923 | 925 | 0.228 | 3,909 | 0.239 | 2,591 | 0.288 | 456 | 0.269 | 565 | 0.344 | 8,477 | 0.289 | 0.155 |
| 1924 | 946 | 0.228 | 4,017 | 0.237 | 2,629 | 0.287 | 465 | 0.267 | 576 | 0.339 | 8,665 | 0.286 | 0.154 |
| 1925 | 977 | 0.227 | 4,114 | 0.234 | 2,674 | 0.285 | 470 | 0.267 | 591 | 0.339 | 8,858 | 0.285 | 0.155 |

We then investigate what was happening at the local level, something that has been neglected by previous authors. We average, across counties, the county-level HHIs; the average shows an increase from 0.248 to 0.285 (a 15 percent rise). This far more modest increase can be explained by two countervailing forces. The merger movement acted to increase concentration, by reducing the number of English and Welsh banks that *could have* operated a branch in a particular town or city. However, the large, national banks acted to expand their branch networks during this era and actually *did* open branches in towns where they had not been present forty years previously. Powell (1915, 453) gives an example of this second force: "In April, 1914, the new Midland Bank, upon learning that Lloyds Bank had extended its activities into a new section of the country through a merger, arranged within twenty-four hours to open new branches in the same area." The Federal Reserve report (1930, 70) studies concentration in twenty randomly selected towns in England and Wales and concludes that "in practically every case where the number of offices is five or less, each office represents a different bank. Each town on the list, with one exception, is served by two or more banks."

Although the financial statements of banks do not divulge the physical location of either borrowers or lenders, both were generally located close to the banks. Gilbart (1873, 215) stated, "It is bad policy to take the accounts of parties residing at distance, as their transactions do not come under the notice of the banker; and the fact of their passing by the banks in the neighbourhood to go elsewhere, is one that should excite suspicion." Cottrell (1979) reports that even by 1840 proximity mattered; a distant location was a sufficient reason to turn down an application for a loan. Newton (2010, 41), in discussing banking in the mid-nineteenth century, says, "In the case of English joint-stock banks, there were few instances of credits being extended to customers located beyond a bank's parochial hinterland. For example, 91 percent of credit extended by the Sheffield Union Bank between 1843 and 1846 went to customers residing or working in the town of Sheffield."

The difference between the national and the county-based indices is large and may change our interpretation of this period of financial consolidation in England and Wales. If banking were thought to have been already a national market in 1885, then this dramatic increase in market concentration is clearly worrisome from the perspective of bank clients and society at large. However, if banking was primarily a local affair, which the literature indicates was the case, then the county-based measure is more accurate and a conclusion of a moderate increase in concentration is warranted. Moreover, most of the increase in concentration comes during the period 1914 to 1919, during which time the mega-mergers that culminated in the Big Five were concluded. Griffiths (1973) claims that the government during the war accepted increased concentration arguments that came from the larger banks. They argued that the British banking system needed increased concentration to facilitate postwar reconstruction, compete successfully against the large German banks, and retain London as an international financial center.

## CONCENTRATION AT THE COUNTY LEVEL

The 15 percent increase in (county) average HHI aggregates many different experiences across counties, and even breaking England and Wales up into rural and urban regions obscures much of the variation at the local level. For example, despite the roughly 30 percent rise in concentration in England (outside of London) there were several counties in which concentration fell by more than 10 percent, namely, Cheshire, Hampshire, Kent, Somerset, Westmorland, and Wiltshire (see Table 7.4).

For example, in 1885 Cheshire was mainly served by provincial banks, based in Manchester: Manchester and Liverpool District Banking, Manchester and County Bank, and Union Bank of Manchester, as well as the London-based Parr's. Despite the takeover of Parr's by London, County, and Westminster in 1918 and Union Bank of Manchester by Barclay's in 1919, other London banks had expanded northward to offer more competition in the Manchester and Liverpool hinterland. Lloyds, Williams Deacon's, the Midland, and National Provincial had all developed branch networks in Cheshire by 1925. The overall effect was to decrease concentration in the county by 20 percent over the forty-year period.

The drop in Kent was even greater, almost 37 percent over the years from 1885 to 1925. At the start, Kent was dominated by London and County Banking, who operated twenty-nine of the fifty-four branches in the county. The National Provincial Bank was the only other to offer any kind of a branch network in the county, with five branches. Small, private partnerships provided some competition, although the number of locations served was small. Beeching and Co. had four branches, while Cobb and Co. and Hammond and Co. had three apiece. The remaining branches were operated by private banks, with some London-based joint-stock companies operating one or two branches in the area. In 1925 London and County (then in the form of Westminster Bank) maintained an important presence, with 70 of the 281 branches. However, the nation's other large banks had moved in to provide substantially greater competition: Barclays with forty-seven, Lloyds with sixty-nine, the Midland with thirty-two, the National Provincial with forty-two, and even the Bank of Liverpool with twenty-one outlets (mostly in the London metropolitan area). At that stage all the private banks had disappeared.

Naturally, to offset this decreased concentration in some counties there was dramatically increased concentration in others. Concentration more than doubled in Cambridgeshire, Cornwall, Devon, Oxfordshire, Suffolk, and York-shire. Yorkshire displayed the most dramatic rise in concentration, more than

TABLE 7.4 Bank Concentration by County—England

| | 1885 | | 1895 | | 1905 | | 1915 | | 1925 | |
|---|---|---|---|---|---|---|---|---|---|---|
| | Branches | HHI | Branches | HHI | Branches | HHI | Branches | HHI | Branches | HHI |
| Bedfordshire | 11 | 0.256 | 15 | 0.209 | 19 | 0.280 | 22 | 0.298 | 27 | 0.262 |
| Berkshire | 19 | 0.197 | 23 | 0.153 | 34 | 0.138 | 44 | 0.183 | 55 | 0.251 |
| Buckinghamshire | 21 | 0.134 | 32 | 0.115 | 43 | 0.167 | 56 | 0.170 | 67 | 0.228 |
| Cambridgeshire | 23 | 0.146 | 27 | 0.139 | 20 | 0.275 | 24 | 0.330 | 41 | 0.312 |
| Cheshire | 55 | 0.161 | 82 | 0.117 | 131 | 0.121 | 174 | 0.126 | 281 | 0.129 |
| Cornwall | 39 | 0.147 | 97 | 0.209 | 104 | 0.267 | 120 | 0.285 | 171 | 0.307 |
| Cumberland | 43 | 0.224 | 54 | 0.178 | 68 | 0.165 | 79 | 0.213 | 133 | 0.251 |
| Derbyshire | 42 | 0.119 | 73 | 0.182 | 110 | 0.181 | 134 | 0.194 | 154 | 0.184 |
| Devon | 97 | 0.143 | 153 | 0.153 | 185 | 0.165 | 216 | 0.237 | 302 | 0.338 |
| Dorset | 34 | 0.225 | 35 | 0.228 | 38 | 0.312 | 50 | 0.343 | 59 | 0.300 |
| Durham | 49 | 0.213 | 71 | 0.182 | 139 | 0.208 | 193 | 0.210 | 255 | 0.228 |
| Essex | 38 | 0.270 | 55 | 0.230 | 95 | 0.307 | 133 | 0.262 | 171 | 0.357 |
| Gloucestershire | 73 | 0.174 | 93 | 0.174 | 126 | 0.165 | 158 | 0.204 | 186 | 0.263 |
| Hampshire | 53 | 0.280 | 75 | 0.210 | 133 | 0.231 | 195 | 0.244 | 272 | 0.251 |
| Herefordshire | 16 | 0.156 | 18 | 0.185 | 20 | 0.190 | 21 | 0.202 | 27 | 0.262 |
| Hertfordshire | 27 | 0.166 | 29 | 0.149 | 40 | 0.306 | 67 | 0.270 | 90 | 0.288 |
| Huntingdonshire | 10 | 0.280 | 10 | 0.280 | 11 | 0.322 | 13 | 0.325 | 15 | 0.280 |
| Kent | 55 | 0.302 | 77 | 0.208 | 129 | 0.167 | 187 | 0.169 | 281 | 0.191 |
| Lancashire | 284 | 0.067 | 444 | 0.069 | 632 | 0.091 | 780 | 0.113 | 1,050 | 0.120 |

**TABLE 7.4** *continued*

| Leicestershire | 22 | 0.240 | 32 | 0.186 | 61 | 0.205 | 72 | 0.205 | 99 | 0.250 |
|---|---|---|---|---|---|---|---|---|---|---|
| Lincolnshire | 68 | 0.143 | 79 | 0.166 | 103 | 0.163 | 149 | 0.171 | 183 | 0.243 |
| Middlesex | 220 | 0.091 | 371 | 0.110 | 614 | 0.106 | 727 | 0.120 | 977 | 0.227 |
| Norfolk | 42 | 0.280 | 65 | 0.280 | 80 | 0.378 | 91 | 0.384 | 120 | 0.384 |
| Northamptonshire | 31 | 0.145 | 43 | 0.204 | 54 | 0.182 | 65 | 0.188 | 82 | 0.227 |
| Northumberland | 54 | 0.160 | 65 | 0.190 | 127 | 0.182 | 148 | 0.211 | 181 | 0.231 |
| Nottinghamshire | 37 | 0.194 | 49 | 0.161 | 84 | 0.152 | 109 | 0.172 | 113 | 0.224 |
| Oxfordshire | 23 | 0.108 | 27 | 0.095 | 33 | 0.118 | 38 | 0.133 | 47 | 0.298 |
| Rutland | 4 | 0.500 | 4 | 0.500 | 4 | 0.500 | 3 | 0.556 | 3 | 0.556 |
| Shropshire | 35 | 0.133 | 45 | 0.202 | 59 | 0.167 | 76 | 0.188 | 97 | 0.218 |
| Somerset | 82 | 0.327 | 98 | 0.282 | 112 | 0.224 | 148 | 0.237 | 170 | 0.288 |
| Staffordshire | 69 | 0.171 | 89 | 0.181 | 122 | 0.191 | 140 | 0.198 | 205 | 0.189 |
| Suffolk | 48 | 0.152 | 59 | 0.154 | 70 | 0.352 | 93 | 0.347 | 109 | 0.371 |
| Surrey | 23 | 0.263 | 38 | 0.211 | 90 | 0.181 | 161 | 0.153 | 215 | 0.256 |
| Sussex | 44 | 0.277 | 61 | 0.216 | 115 | 0.219 | 165 | 0.205 | 216 | 0.279 |
| Warwickshire | 51 | 0.177 | 77 | 0.256 | 119 | 0.234 | 136 | 0.280 | 206 | 0.282 |
| Westmorland | 22 | 0.339 | 26 | 0.314 | 37 | 0.344 | 34 | 0.327 | 43 | 0.298 |
| Wiltshire | 42 | 0.392 | 45 | 0.383 | 57 | 0.387 | 66 | 0.363 | 76 | 0.335 |
| Worcestershire | 41 | 0.166 | 51 | 0.211 | 57 | 0.205 | 67 | 0.264 | 81 | 0.305 |
| Yorkshire | 240 | 0.055 | 386 | 0.059 | 582 | 0.110 | 743 | 0.123 | 905 | 0.224 |

quadrupling from 0.055 in 1885 to 0.224 in 1925. In 1885 no fewer than forty-five different banks operated branches in the three ridings of Yorkshire, mostly provincial outfits, with many private banks among them. The National Provincial Bank was the only London-based one that offered a substantial presence in the region. By 1925 the vast majority of these provincial banks had been purchased by the national branch operators. The major players in Yorkshire at the end of the period were the Bank of Liverpool, Barclays, Lancashire and Yorkshire Bank, Lloyds, Westminster, Midland, and the National Provincial.

In Cornwall, where concentration rose by 110 percent over forty years, the situation was somewhat different. In 1885 there were several important players in the Cornish banking market: the joint-stock banks of Capital and Counties, Cornish Banking, Devon and Cornwall Banking, and Western Counties, as well as two smaller private banking firms, Batten, Carne and Carne, and Dingley and Co. By 1925 all of the private banks had gone, but only four of the Big Five were present in the market: Barclays, Lloyds, National Provincial, and the Midland in a modest way. The Westminster Bank had not moved into the local market, and of the second-tier banks that remained the Bank of Liverpool operated a single branch in St. Hilary.

The experience in Cambridgeshire mirrored aspects of both Cornwall and Yorkshire. As in Yorkshire, only National Provincial was present in 1885 of the London-based banks. In a similar fashion to Cornwall there was a strong private banking presence, with Fordham, Gibson and Co., Foster and Co., Gurney, Birkbeck, Barclay and Buxton, and John Mortlock and Co. serving the area. Forty years later the private banks had all disappeared (Gurney, Birkbeck, Barclay and Buxton being one of the twenty founding banks of Barclays in 1896), and despite the proximity to London, as in Cornwall, neither the Westminster Bank nor the second-tier banks had a presence in 1925.

The situation in Wales was more homogenous than that of England. There was a moderate rise in concentration in the urban counties of Monmouthshire and Glamorgan, as well as in Carmarthenshire, Montgomeryshire, and Radnorshire (see Table 7.5). In all other counties, market concentration fell. The principal explanation for this is that Wales, outside the Cardiff and Swansea region, was not well served by the large banks in the late nineteenth century. Only the National Provincial and the North and South Wales banks had much of a network in the rural areas. By 1925 Barclays, Lloyds, and the Midland banks had all moved into the Welsh countryside in a serious manner. Again, the Westminster Bank was conspicuous by its absence.

The situation in Glamorgan, where both Cardiff and Swansea are found, was different. At the start of the period the county was well served by the London-based banks of National Provincial and London and Provincial. In addition, the provincial joint-stock banks of Bristol and West of England, Glamorganshire Banking Co., National Bank of Wales, and South Wales Union Bank were all present. By 1925 the provincial banks had all been acquired by London-based

**TABLE 7.5** Bank Concentration by County—Wales

| | 1885 | | 1895 | | 1905 | | 1915 | | 1925 | |
|---|---|---|---|---|---|---|---|---|---|---|
| | Branches | HHI | Branches | HHI | Branches | HHI | Branches | HHI | Branches | HHI |
| Anglesey | 10 | 0.420 | 13 | 0.325 | 15 | 0.289 | 25 | 0.389 | 35 | 0.295 |
| Brecknockshire | 9 | 0.284 | 13 | 0.231 | 18 | 0.228 | 33 | 0.197 | 41 | 0.256 |
| Caernarfonshire | 23 | 0.342 | 32 | 0.287 | 36 | 0.255 | 49 | 0.424 | 85 | 0.292 |
| Cardiganshire | 10 | 0.320 | 12 | 0.250 | 23 | 0.244 | 41 | 0.291 | 58 | 0.276 |
| Carmarthenshire | 9 | 0.210 | 15 | 0.200 | 29 | 0.165 | 69 | 0.249 | 100 | 0.261 |
| Denbighshire | 12 | 0.333 | 17 | 0.294 | 25 | 0.286 | 36 | 0.279 | 48 | 0.240 |
| Flintshire | 9 | 0.432 | 15 | 0.333 | 17 | 0.315 | 25 | 0.312 | 42 | 0.273 |
| Glamorgan | 56 | 0.204 | 124 | 0.191 | 156 | 0.201 | 261 | 0.231 | 342 | 0.268 |
| Gwynedd | 1 | 1.000 | 1 | 1.000 | 1 | 1.000 | 1 | 1.000 | 1 | 1.000 |
| Merioneth | 10 | 0.440 | 14 | 0.327 | 15 | 0.307 | 32 | 0.410 | 43 | 0.328 |
| Monmouthshire | 27 | 0.177 | 36 | 0.168 | 44 | 0.166 | 99 | 0.206 | 128 | 0.266 |
| Montgomeryshire | 13 | 0.231 | 14 | 0.265 | 16 | 0.227 | 34 | 0.292 | 43 | 0.319 |
| Pembrokeshire | 18 | 0.315 | 28 | 0.230 | 33 | 0.219 | 60 | 0.249 | 71 | 0.265 |
| Radnorshire | 9 | 0.185 | 10 | 0.180 | 14 | 0.194 | 18 | 0.284 | 24 | 0.267 |

ones and Glamorgan was dominated by Barclays, Lloyds, Midland, and National Provincial. The Westminster bank operated only two branches in Cardiff, and one in Swansea. As a result market concentration rose by 31.3 percent.

## BRANCH NETWORKS

The rapid expansion of branch networks over England and Wales raises some interesting questions. Where did banks expand? Why did they expand? And how did they expand?

An investigation of why banks expanded is beyond the scope of this chapter, although Collins (1988) attributes much of the expansion to network effects and economies of scale. Instead we focus on where banks expanded by examining the case studies of three banks that survived from 1885 until 1925 without being swallowed by larger banks. Part of the answer of how banks expanded can be linked to the merger movement, but this is far from a complete answer. Clearly, some of the expansion (at the individual bank level) was driven by mergers. However, at the aggregate level roughly 6,600 new establishments opened their doors over a forty-year period. We select three of these banks: Lloyds, Bank of Liverpool, and London, City, and Midland (later Midland Bank) and plot the evolution of their branch networks.

The Bank of Liverpool merged with nine other banks over this forty-year period, and expansion through merger was their main strategy. From 1885, when they had 10 branches (8 of which were in Lancashire), they had expanded to 375 branches in 1925, almost all spread across the North of England with a small cluster in suburban London that came from their merger with Martin's Bank (16 branches) in 1918. The Bank of Liverpool started their expansion locally, by buying up the Liverpool Commercial in 1889, then Wakefield, Crewdson (21 branches) in 1893. They then moved into the Northeast of England when they obtained Craven Bank (40 branches) in 1906 and Halifax Commercial in 1919 (55 branches), both of which served the West Yorkshire market. The acquisition of North-Eastern Banking (102 branches) was effected in 1914, which was centered on Northumberland and Durham, and in the same year they swallowed up their small, local rival, the Palatine Bank, which served the Lancashire market. By the end of the period we analyze the Bank of Liverpool was the largest of the non–Big Five banks. Although their branch network was only slightly larger than that of Manchester and Liverpool Bank, their balance sheet was almost 20 percent bigger.

Lloyds began in 1885 headquartered jointly in Birmingham and London, but with most of their fifty-six branches located in Birmingham and the surrounding counties. They then began expanding rapidly, often by merging with private, county banks. Expansion in the first ten years was mainly in the area surrounding Birmingham (via the acquisition of Birmingham Joint Stock and Worcester City and County Banking) and into South Wales (via Wilkins and Co. in 1890 and Bristol and West of England in 1892). They continued to expand in Wales and the West of England from 1896 to 1905 with both acquisitions (Williams and Co. and County of Gloucester, both in 1897) and natural expansion. A small foray into the Liverpool market occurred at this time with the purchase of the Liverpool Union Bank in 1900.

The third decade of our study (1906–15) saw Lloyds continue to expand in its traditional stronghold of Wales and the Southwest, with the acquisitions of Devon and Cornwall Banking in 1906 and Wilts and Dorset in 1914. It was only very late in the period that Lloyds became a truly national bank with locations in the East, Southeast, and North of England. Lloyds participated in one mega-merger, with Capital and Counties, in 1918 to acquire their extensive rural network of 473 branches; this permitted entry to the East, Southeast, and London areas. They followed this up by merging with West Yorkshire (36 branches) in 1919 to expand in the North of England. By 1925 they had 1,662 branches in every county except Gwynedd in Wales and were one of the Big Five banks. Stovel and Savage (2005) argue that by 1930 the branch network of Lloyds had largely stabilized. They show that most of the branches that Lloyds opened directly were located in familiar areas to the bank: Birmingham, London, and South Wales. Expansion in the rest of the country was mostly achieved by merger activity.

London, City, and Midland began as the Birmingham and Midland Bank in 1885. At this time they had a network of just fourteen branches, mostly in the region around Manchester and Liverpool, with four branches in the Birmingham area. Following a merger with Central Bank of London in 1891, which possessed eleven branches in the capital, the bank restyled itself the London and Midland Bank. At this time the bank was expanding into nearby territory by a process of mergers. They took over Coventry Union to expand near their headquarters in Birmingham, then Manchester Joint Stock, Exchange and Discount, and Leeds and County to consolidate and then enlarge eastward the northern network that had been centered on the Mersey River. They also forayed into the Welsh market, with twelve greenfield openings in South Wales in 1893.

The second ten-year period (1896–1905) saw the bank focus on its core areas: Birmingham, Lancashire, the West Riding of Yorkshire, and London. Expansion in the vicinity of Birmingham area was a mix of greenfield openings and takeovers of smaller rivals: City of Birmingham (1899) and Leicestershire Banking Co. (1900). Following a merger with City Bank in 1898, the name was again changed, this time to London, City, and Midland. The expansion in the North was mainly driven by merger activity with Carlisle City and District (1896), North-Western (1897), Huddersfield (1897), Yorkshire Banking (1901), and Sheffield Union (1901), all falling to the rapidly growing upstart. The third decade saw a renewed focus on Wales, with most of the activity happening here with the acquisition of the North and South Wales Bank in 1908, then the mega-merger with Metropolitan of England and Wales in 1914, which had 171 branches, primarily in Wales. West Yorkshire continued to remain a region of interest with takeovers of Bradford Banking Co. in 1910, and then Sheffield and Hallamshire Bank in 1913.

The final duration, 1916 to 1925, saw just one amalgamation, with the London Joint Stock Bank in 1918. Despite being London-based, London Joint Stock's network of 309 branches included many in the unexploited (as far as the London, City, and Midland was concerned) northern counties of Cumberland, Durham, Northumberland, and Yorkshire's North Riding. The Midland's branch network in the Southwest and Southeast was not strong even as late as 1925, mainly due to the failure to acquire a rival with a strong presence in that area. Most of the expansion there occurred after World War I, and was mainly due to the openings of new branches. In total the Midland acquired twenty-six banks over the forty years, including mega-mergers with the Metropolitan and then London Joint Stock in 1918. The final merger managed to increase the number of branches in London by over 50 percent.

From the geographical expansion of banks' branch networks, it can be clearly seen that over time banks tended to operate branches further and further away from their initial operating area in terms of physical distance. This could be related to innovations and technological changes such as the development of telegraph and telephone lines. Often it was the case that expanding in an area further away from the initial geographical location was done via a takeover of an existing bank. The innovative part of such a takeover strategy, where expansion was mostly based upon absorbing existing branches rather than opening new offices, lies in the fact that a national banking sector was created with a few large players on one hand, but on the other hand the value and reputation effects of the existing relationships could be preserved. In most cases the taken over bank's directors or partners were retained as "local directors," and more than 80 percent of branch managers were kept in their positions after the merger was complete.

## CONCLUSION

There was a general increase in bank concentration in England and Wales during the period 1885 to 1925. The extent to which this affected borrowers and lenders depends on how we view the structure of the banking market. To consider England and Wales as a single market for bank services would lead one to conclude that concentration increased substantially, with a Herfindahl-Hirschman Index based on bank branches rising from 0.022 to 0.155. However, if one were to assume that competition was primarily local, and that counties were the relevant markets, then calculating an average HHI across counties would show an increase in concentration only from 0.248 to 0.285.

This period encompasses the great merger wave in British banking. Although the overall effect was to increase market concentration, there was substantial heterogeneity at the county level. As the banks that grew to become the Big Five expanded their networks, by both amalgamations and opening new branches, they brought new banking services to parts of the country that had previously been served by small, often private, banks. The effect of this was to dramatically increase concentration in a few counties, and slightly ameliorate concentration in others.

Finally we document, by examining the rise of three banks that survived until 1925, how banks tended to expand geographically. Banks in 1885 were often concentrated in one or two geographic areas. As time progressed they tended to expand into geographically distinct, but proximate, regions. As such, there remained a lot of persistence to bank networks. A bank that began in a strong position in a certain local market tended to remain strong in that market for decades. It was very difficult to capture a great deal of market share by opening de novo branches in a new part of the country; by far the easiest way to expand rapidly in a new market was to merge with a bank that had a strong local presence.

## BIBLIOGRAPHY

Ackrill, Margaret, and Leslie Hannah. 2001. *Barclays: The Business of Banking 1690–1996.* Cambridge: Cambridge University Press.

Capie, Forrest, and Michael Collins. 1999. "Banks, Industry and Finance, 1880–1914." *Business History* 41 (1): 37–62.

Capie, Forrest, and Ghila Rodrik-Bali. 1982. "Concentration in British Banking, 1870–1920." *Business History* 24: 280–92.

Collins, Michael. 1988. *Money and Banking in the U.K.: A History.* Beckenham: Croon Helm.

Cottrell, Philip. 1979. *Industrial Finance: 1830–1914.* London: Metheum.

Crafts, Nicholas, and Abay Mulatu. 2006. "How Did the Location of Industry Respond to Falling Transport Costs in Britain before World War I?" *Journal of Economic History* 66 (3): 575–607.

Degryse, H., and S. Ongena. 2005. "Distance, Lending Relationships, and Competition." *Journal of Finance* 60 (1): 231–66.

Federal Reserve Committee on Branch, Group, and Chain Banking. 1930. *Branch Banking in England.* Washington, DC: Federal Reserve Board of Governors.

Gilbart, J. W. 1873. *Principles and Practice of Banking.* London: George Bell and Sons.

Godley, Andrew. 2003. "Foreign Multinationals and Innovation in British Retailing: 1850–1962." *Business History* 45 (1): 80–100.

Griffiths, Brian. 1973. "The Development of Restrictive Practices in the U.K. Monetary System." *Manchester School* 41 (1): 3–18.

Grossman, Richard. 1999. "Rearranging Deck Chairs on the Titanic: English Banking Concentration and Efficiency, 1870–1914." *European Review of Economic History* 3: 323–49.

Hannah, Leslie. 2008. "Logistics, Market Size, and Giant Plants in the Early Twentieth Century: A Global View." *Journal of Economic History* 68 (1): 46–79.

Lee, C. H. 1979. *British Regional Employment Statistics, 1841–1971.* Cambridge: Cambridge University Press.

Newton, Lucy. 2010. "The Birth of Joint-Stock Banking: England and New England Compared." *Business History Review* 84: 27–52.

Park, K., and G. Pennacchi. 2009. "Harming Depositors and Helping Borrowers: The Disparate Impact of Bank Consolidation." *Review of Financial Studies* 22 (1): 1–40.

Powell, Ellis. 1915. *The Evolution of the Money Market 1385–1915: An Historical and Analytical Study of the Rise and Development of Finance as a Centralised, Co-ordinated Force.* London: Financial News.

Report of the Treasury Committee on Bank Amalgamations. 1918. Cd. 9052, Parliamentary Papers 1918, VI, 333–39.

Stovell, Katherine, and Mike Savage. 2005. "Mergers and Mobility: Organizational Growth and the Origins of Career Migration at Lloyds Bank." *American Journal of Sociology* 111 (4): 1080–1121.

Turner, John. 2009. "Wider Share Ownership? Investors in English and Welsh Bank Shares in the Nineteenth Century." *Economic History Review* 62 (s1): 167–92.

# THE CATAPULT OF RICHES

The Airplane as a Creative Macroinvention

## PETER B. MEYER

Technical progress usually comes from small changes to existing technologies. New computers for example are better than old computers insofar as their components are smaller and faster, they can run new software, and they connect to new devices. These improvements are driven by product-focused profit-oriented research and development, which is partly predictable. People remember the earlier generations of devices, and by asking people who know the subject one can often trace back many years of the process of imitation and improvement that brought the latest generation of devices into being. This is normal technological change, analogous to Kuhn's characterization of normal science. The technical innovations and improvements are *microinventions*, in the language of Mokyr (1990).

If one traces back far enough, one often finds a version of a technology for which the preceding generation, or variant, is not clearly identified. There was a first known vaccine, for smallpox, and no clear precedent for it. There was a first balloon that lifted into the air. These gaps, or larger steps, are called *macroinventions*. As defined by Mokyr (1990), these are novel epistemic steps that are complementary to a wave of microinventions that follow. By the broader definition in Meisenzahl and Mokyr (2011), they are economically influential.

The invention of the airplane was such a macroinvention by several of the overlapping definitions. The aircraft the Wright brothers developed in 1903–5 had radical novelty insofar as (1) they functioned, technically, in an unprecedented way to lift persons into the air and could be controlled and directed in a different and better way than balloons, gliders, or projectiles could; (2) a wave of technical improvements and applications followed quickly; and (3) a new industry with hundreds of start-up firms existed by 1911.

This case exemplifies the recurrent phenomenon of *open-source innovation* in which technological progress depends on the use of information that is not secret and not proprietary in practice (Meyer 2013). In the airplane's case, open-source information sharing generated waves of preparatory microinventions that *preceded* the key successful macroinvention.

Vast documentation and historical research are available on the developers of early airplane technology and their precursors. A *Bibliography of Aeronautics*

(Brockett 1910) lists more than thirteen thousand publications related to aircraft up to 1909, principally from France, Britain, Germany, and the United States. In these same countries, hundreds of patents were filed for aircraft in the nineteenth century, and hundreds of airplane-manufacturing establishments started before the First World War. From various sources we have data on such publications, patents, clubs, and firms. These databases are works in progress, from which some conclusions are now possible.

Early twentieth-century inventors of working airplanes knew a lot about the prior efforts. The Wright brothers, for example, read key works by Otto Lilienthal, Samuel Langley, and Octave Chanute. Chanute's 1894 survey book on the developing field of aerial navigation, *Progress in Flying Machines*, defined the field for many. We can trace the networks of innovators who produced this information and transmitted it. Detailed documentation is available on the publications, patents, exhibitions, conferences, clubs, and letters related to aeronautics and early aviation, and I am collecting and organizing databases of this information.

The data are useful to consider a research issue framed in Mokyr (1990): where do macroinventions come from? Some macroinventions were made quickly, by focused research and development in hierarchical organizations—for example, the atom bomb, and the rocket to the Moon. These have focused narratives. The airplane case is at a different extreme. Hundreds of literate people communicated about aeronautics for deades in writing. Thousands of publications, patents, and letters remain from that time, and dozens of books tell detailed narratives of how progress was made across the industrial countries, and they largely agree on matters of fact. So for the airplane case, there is a broad spectrum of fine-grained data and statistics on decentralized networks of technologists who made a macroinvention.

In the case of the airplane, substantial experimental and scientific effort occurred, and can be identified before the macroinvention worked. The participants are motivated by their own frank interest in the subject, and appear generally not to have expected to profit from it. They shared experimental information and designs frequently. I have called this pattern "open-source innovation" (Meyer 2013). If we make the assumption that they are interested in the problem intrinsically, not in external payoffs, and are not in competition, a model can be fashioned in which self-motivated agents—"tinkerers"—generate flows of innovation and perhaps ultimately a macroinvention. In economics language, they generate a *supply* of inventions, which may or may not match a market demand. This addresses the question partially: when tinkerers can or do form networks of shared information to address a possible invention, the invention is more likely to occur, and their intellectual descendants are more likely to eventually form such an industry.

I have argued elsewhere (Meyer 2013) that this sharing of information by aircraft experimenters has parallels to open-source software development. These attributes characterize open-source innovation:

- Contributors were autonomous, often with distinct visions, projects, and specializations
- Contributors were drawn to the activity because of the appeal and potential of the technology, not because of connections or similarities to the other participants
- Contributors routinely shared inventions and discoveries without explicit exchanges or payoffs
- Some contributors found intellectual property institutions detrimental to inventive progress
- Organizers, writers, and evangelists had roles beyond technical experimentation

Similar dynamics have occurred in other cases. Creative experimenters and hobbyists have advanced other technologies, in the computers, software, and online fields, for example, to the point that entrepreneurs could start businesses on the basis of open new technology. The open-source innovation dynamic sometimes outperforms the research and development mode in which the researchers are hierarchically authorized, funded, equipped, and motivated by explicit rewards. Open-source innovation seems to outperform best in fields where technological uncertainty is greatest.

This chapter offers a general economic model of open-source innovation, in which the ambitions of the experimenters—"tinkerers"—are the force driving technological change. Their technological creativity is not realistically sufficient if they were to work alone, but the network links the participants together into webs of knowledge and communities of practice. The catapult of this chapter's title refers both to flight itself—and in fact some early aircraft were launched that way—and to these flexible webs of people and knowledge from which the new craft metaphorically sprang. Analogous communities of practice have supported other inventions to help them launch. The model here relates the enlightened minds described in Mokyr (2009) to the technological creativity described in Mokyr (1990) and thus leads to the knowledge economies of Mokyr (2002).

It is useful to begin by first illustrating the technological creativity of these individuals. They are the atoms of creativity in the model; a society has institutions that more or less efficiently tolerate and benefit from such individuals.

## THEMES OF AERIAL NAVIGATION EXPERIMENTS

Modern airplanes trace back to British scientific experimenter George Cayley's designs of fixed-winged aircraft around 1800. Cayley's attention was drawn to flying by the recent invention of balloons and the first helicopter designs (Gibbs-Smith 1962). This fixed-wing idea was an important and necessary departure from the more natural and recognizable mechanisms of birds, balloons, and rockets. Its success was slow, however, and thousands of experiments came between the idea and its practical application.

Significant innovators in the succeeding century came from a variety of backgrounds and locations. They include Alphonse Penaud and Louis Mouillard of France, Lawrence Hargrave of Australia, Americans Samuel Langley and Octave Chanute, and Otto Lilienthal of Germany. Below we lay out some of the technological dimensions they and others explored over the course of the century after Cayley's first publication. The larger point is to illustrate the great diversity of experimentation that came about without organized and directed research and development; and that much of this diversity was necessary to the eventual success.[1]

**FLAPPING WINGS** The experimenters came to the topic of aircraft with a dream of flying like a bird. Cayley returned to the idea of propulsion by flapping wings again and again in his five decades of experimentation, and even after 1890 Hargrave and others did too. But aircraft with mechanical or human-powered flapping wings ("ornithopters"), though intuitively appealing, were flimsy, underpowered, and difficult to construct. Humans can power flapping wings, and did so in some of Cayley's experiments, but humans cannot provide enough power to keep themselves aloft in this way. Propellers would turn out to be more efficient and practical.

**BALLOONS AND DIRIGIBLES** Hot-air and hydrogen balloons had carried people since the 1780s. They improved throughout the nineteenth century. Powered steerable balloons (dirigibles), often with elongated shapes and skeleton frames, were developed. Still, balloons could not be made to move in quick controlled ways. Alberto Santos-Dumont was one of the few who made both piloted dirigibles and then airplanes. There were a variety of attempts to make compound craft with both a gas bag and wings.

**RIGID FIXED WINGS** Fixed wings with an upturned front edge can provide lift while speed is provided some other way. This was Cayley's central insight and a subject of many of his experiments. Cayley worked out, with partially correct logic, that an airplane can fly more stably if its wingtips are higher than the place where the wings attach to the fuselage.[2] Among the widely known later experiments of the nineteenth century was Louis Mouillard's effort to make wings of wood designed like birds' wings that he wore, then leaped from hills. Jean-Marie Le Bris created a large bird shape in wood and sat inside as it rested on a cart, pulled by a galloping horse, until the wooden bird lifted off. Mouil-

---

1   Most of the characterizations of these experimenters referred to in the list are in Gibbs-Smith's (1966) masterful and concise *Invention of the Aeroplane*.

2   In modern language, the wings have a positive dihedral angle.

lard and Le Bris were not too seriously injured and were widely cited within the world of aerial navigation. At the end of the nineteenth century, Hiram Maxim demonstrated that with enough power, even entirely flat wings would be enough to launch an experimental flying machine. The overall theme is that the designs that turned out to work drew from soaring birds and kites, leading to gliders and then to powered gliders.

**TAIL** Cayley already had horizontal and vertical control surfaces—rudders—in his early designs. Alphonse Penaud extended this with experiments on small models powered by rubber bands. He showed that for the nose of the aircraft to stay lifted high enough the tail should have a lower angle with respect to the oncoming airflow than the wings do. This "Penaud tail" design feature was necessary for longitudinal stability and equilibrium in flight and was widely studied and imitated.

**STACKED WINGS** Since large wooden wings were structurally weak, Cayley put one wing on top of the other to achieve more lift on a smaller craft.[3] This idea was explored with many variations. Hargrave in particular studied box kites and showed that they were able to remain stable in the air, and that the rigid box gave strength to the structure without much weight. Imitations of this led to the biplane configuration of many early airplanes.

**CAMBERED WINGS** Cayley worked out that a wing should not be flat but rather rise from the front edge then curve down to be lowest at the posterior edge. A wing with this shape is said to be "cambered." The optimal shape differs depending on the speed and angle of the oncoming air flow. There were many experiments to determine why and how. A curved shape of this kind generates a partial vacuum above the wing and therefore lift, and also pushes air down at the posterior of the wing to generate further lift. These principles did not become entirely clear during the nineteenth century and good mathematical models of the magnitude were not available until after the first airplanes were working.

**WING ASPECT RATIO** Cayley and some successors made wings approximately square, which is a poor shape to achieve lift. More optimally for lift, the wingspan should be much longer than the width of the wing. Many shapes were explored, and the result was convincingly known only after wind tunnels were used in the 1870s. Progress required both propositional and prescriptive information, and both scientific and technological information (Mokyr 2009, 41–42).

---

3   Gibbs-Smith (1962, 113–14) discusses this invention, described by Cayley in an 1843 publication.

**ENGINES** Experimenters tried to fly models and gliders with steam engine power, despite the weight and the danger. John Stringfellow made tiny, precise award-winning engines for airplane models. Cayley sought another way, and made what may have been the earliest working hot-air engine, and gunpowder engines too. Samuel Langley, believing that a powerful engine was necessary to power a strong stable craft, invested tens of thousands of dollars in an advanced internal combustion engine.

**PROPELLERS** Most propellers for aircraft were designed like "water screws" used on ships, which were designed to push water backward. A critical insight waited until the Wrights found it in 1902—that an aircraft's propeller should be cambered, like a wing, so that it generates "lift" in the forward direction.

**PILOTING AND CONTROL** With enough power, anything would fly. How could a pilot control the craft? Otto Lilienthal was the first to make gliders that he could fly for many minutes at a time, to learn the skill of being in the air and controlling the craft to some extent. After him, Octave Chanute and the Wrights followed this practice.

There are economic principles underlying such basic research. Here "production" includes experiments, voyages, publication, patents, letters—both doing and talking—about scientific and technological information that the participants think is related to the subject of aerial navigation. One of the crucial inputs is the experimenter's own enthusiasm to understand the ideas, locate the resources, and perform experiments.[4]

## THE OBJECTIVES OF EXPERIMENTERS

The experimenters did not often state their objectives clearly, but one can make inferences based on what they wrote. Most found bird flight absorbing and imagined flying themselves. The experimenters had a thorough prior belief in natural laws and that it was possible to make devices that depended on these laws. They allowed themselves to explore what it would mean to fly like a bird, to begin with, and to contrast soaring wings to flapping ones. The problem of how to make this work, if it ever could, was absorbing. These are said to be *intrinsic* objectives. Another recurring theme was the thought that the world would be a better place with flying machines—travel would be easier and contract between people would bring about peace. These are *social* or *altruistic* objectives.

Experimenters may think they can get external, or *extrinsic*, prizes. Several hoped to play a role in a great invention, either for pride or for fame or—I think principally—for the respect of others. More pecuniary career rewards

---

4 The phenomenon is associated with other new technologies too, illustrated in Meyer (2003).

were not obvious—it was widely thought that the search to make a flying machine was a hopeless effort, or that it might work but be useless, and in any case was certainly dangerous. One might suppose that they wished to manufacture a new kind of device and sell it, but I see few plausible references to this idea in the period under consideration. Given all the effort and little observed success, aircraft production was not a likely avenue of success; the technological uncertainty was extreme, more so than in other cases of invention that I have studied.

Ballooning, a parallel business, was mainly an expensive leisure activity with few practical applications. I am convinced that few of the important experimenters ever expected to deliver an aircraft product line. One cannot prove that, but few of them ever did even once it was technically possible. Otto Lilienthal, having invented a new kind of hang glider in his experimentation, attempted to sell them as sports equipment but may have sold only ten.[5] The Wright brothers appear, from their quotes and actions, not to have expected to become financially successful in their first years of experimentation:

- "I am an enthusiast . . . as to the construction of a flying machine. I wish to avail myself of all that is already known and then if possible add my mite to help on the future worker who will attain final success." (Wilbur Wright, 1899 letter)
- "Our experiments have been conducted entirely at our own expense. At the beginning we had no thought of recovering what we were expending, which was not great." (Orville Wright 1953, 87)

If their motivations were intrinsic, their actions seem rational. Thus it is plausible to describe the experimenters as having intrinsic or altruistic motivation. These particular ones had also various resources that were useful to make progress in a technologically uncertain situation.[6] In the model to follow, we shall assume that intrinsically motivated experimenters exist.

## CLUBS AND NETWORKING

Existing clubs on ballooning incorporated discussions on *aerial navigation*, which often meant a focus on fixed-wing, heavier-than-air designs for *flying machines*. New clubs with this navigation orientation also appeared. At least a

---

5  Bernd Lukasch, director of the Otto-Lilienthal Museum in Anklam, Germany, told me this in a 2011 conversation. The buyers were generally aerial navigation experimenters who did not focus on it as a sport.

6  Economists do not regularly refer to a standard model of such characters, with a shorthand for their utility functions, environments, and constraints. Partial models are in Harhoff, Henkel, and von Hippel (2003), Polanski (2007), von Hippel (2006), Gambardella and Hall (2006), and Meyer (2007).

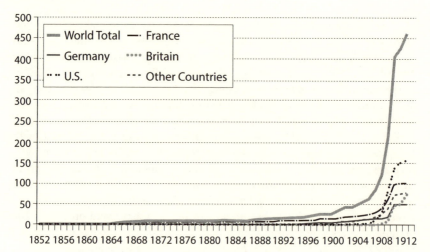

**8.1** Aeronautics-related clubs and societies.

*Source*: Author's list, based on many sources.

*Note*: These are counts of the clubs that have ever been founded. The figure does not account for any exits, which are rare. Many clubs are first seen in a 1910 directory, which partly accounts for the spike then.

dozen such societies were founded in the nineteenth century, sometimes with hundreds of members. Important ones included the Aeronautical Society of Great Britain and the Aéro Club de France. Several of these societies produced regular journals. Membership fluctuated, but overall interest grew over time as is evidenced by a growing number of clubs with some attachment to aerial navigation. The clubs and their members developed connections over time. Figure 8.1, showing club data gathered by over the course of years, describes the population of the relevant clubs and societies.[7] The Wright's first successful controlled powered flight was at the end of 1903. By that time there were more than forty clubs with an attachment to aerial navigation and flying machines.

The number continued to grow after the airplane's definite arrival. By 1914 tens of thousands of people had joined some kind of aeronautical society, and millions had seen an airplane fly (Meyer 2013). Most of the new clubs were locally oriented, and referred in their names to a city or region as well as a technology.

A particular organizer named Octave Chanute was a central figure. Having retired in Chicago after becoming wealthy as a railroad engineer and manager, he focused for years entirely on flying machines. He organized a conference at the Chicago World's Fair in 1893 on aerial navigation, and was in contact by letter with every experimenter he could find. He summarized the state of the art

---

7  The data are discussed further in Meyer (2014).

in an 1894 book with the optimistic title *Progress in Flying Machines*. By surveying the flying machine activity broadly, Chanute served as a social connector
or moderator who identified key persons and technologies and incorporated
them into his thinking. Chanute's speeches and writings were "noteworthy
for fostering a spirit of cooperation and encouraging a free exchange of ideas
among the world's leading aeronautical experimenters" (Stoff 1997, iv),[8] which
he believed would make success possible. The individuals cited most often in
*Progress in Flying Machines* are mentioned above in the section on the major
technological themes. Almost all had substantial numbers of publications and
most had patents (Meyer 2013).

## PUBLICATION AND PATENT DATA

The Smithsonian Institution in Washington, D.C., had been an early participant and publisher of works on aeronautics, and when experimenter Samuel
Langley became the Smithsonian's director, he brought his collection of publications there. The Smithsonian developed a large library on aeronautics and an
associated bibliography, systematically including references to works that were
not in its own collection. Smithsonian librarian Paul Brockett published a series
of books of aeronautical bibliography. The first lists more than thirteen thousand publications related to aeronautics before 1910, including many that were
not at the Smithsonian. It has been scanned and put online at archive.org by
Cornell University and the University of Michigan. After cleaning up the elec-
tronically scanned text, we have for most of these publications a title, authors,
year of publication, journal of publication, language of the text, and country of
publication. Excluding entries for which these data are not complete, we have a
database that can track the evolution of this technical literature.

The rough data at this early stage, seen in Figure 8.2, show a substantial
and sharply growing literature in the 1880s and 1890s before the airplane was
a proven technology. French and English were the most common languages
in this literature, followed by German. The literature in German grew more
quickly over time than the other languages. I do not have a specific explanation
for these comparative rates, though it could be associated with an expanding
technical education system in Germany. With further extensions and refine-
ments to the data it will be possible to study this question quantitatively.

The bibliography includes few patents per se. From a variety of sources, colleagues and I have collected thousands of early aeronautical and ballooning
patents. These data cover on the order of half the relevant patents for the period
up to 1910, and are not consistently coded for technology topic yet. Sources
identifying a patent as relevant to ballooning or aeronautics are numerous and

---

8  I have argued that analogous open-minded moderators played a similar role in the 1970s
microcomputer revolution and in open-source software networks (Meyer 2003, 2013).

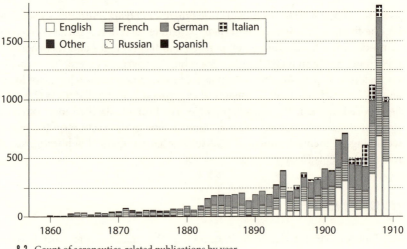

**8.2**  Count of aeronautics-related publications by year.

*Source*: Brockett's *Bibliography of Aeronautics* (1910).

*Note*: For 1909 only half a year is included in the original data.

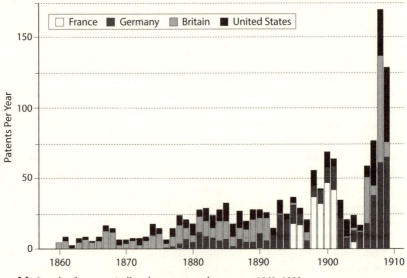

**8.3**  Sample of aeronautically-relevant patents by country, 1860–1909.

*Source*: National patent bureaus and contemporary publications.

eclectic, and include some ex post facto classifications by the patent agencies. For examining the patents themselves, we have used Google Patents and espacenet.com. For source information and the latest data, please contact the author. The data are large, though not complete. Figure 8.3 displays the sample of aviation-related patents by country between 1860 and 1909.

The point here is that the patent counts are rising just as publications did. In principle, patents are intellectual property claims, but aeronautical patents seemed to have had no traction in this way until 1906; I do not know of any fixed-wing aircraft patent until then that was licensed or otherwise earned any revenue. This environment changed after the Wrights' main patent was granted in 1906. The U.S. courts interpreted their patent broadly, and the Wrights enforced it vigorously.

Yearly patent counts related to aeronautics rise immediately in 1907 and afterward, because the basic technological uncertainty had been resolved; specialists then knew that airplanes could work and believed there would be a market for new related inventions.

## THE WRIGHT BROTHERS AND THE MACROINVENTION

Wilbur and Orville Wright were technically proficient mechanics who ran a bicycle shop and in 1899 took a specific interest in fixed-wing aircraft.[9] Wilbur wrote to the Smithsonian Institution for information and received a list of relevant publications. The Wrights followed these leads, and began a long correspondence with Chanute. Nearly complete records of these letters exist (McFarland 1953).

The Wrights began their research with a kite designed like Chanute's glider of 1896,[10] which they studied at length. Over the next years they made larger, heavier, stronger kites and gliders with similar basic designs made of canvas stretched over wood frames. During this time they participated in the open-source, collectively inventive process as other experimenters had done. They discussed technical issues and previous work with Chanute frequently. At Chanute's invitation, Wilbur gave a public speech to the Western Society of Engineers, and the Wrights published two journal papers in 1901, one of which has been characterized as an important contribution to the understanding of aeronautics (Anderson 2004, 110–11). They hosted visitors to their experimental flights, helped to test other people's wings and aircraft, and took advice from others (Crouch 2002, 249–53).

The Wrights had a control system that was better than anyone else's, and it enabled them to get more experience in the air than others had done. It came about from a creative insight. The story is told that Orville held a cardboard box for an inner tube in his hands, and twisted the box. It occurred to him, then, that a glider wing could be twisted the same way. A wing need not be soft like a balloon, or hard like a wooden board; it might twist. This was a useful, creative

---

9   This section draws from Jakab (1990), Crouch (2002), and Meyer (2013).

10   Wilbur's first letter to Chanute in 1900 said so: "The apparatus I intend to employ . . . is very similar to the 'double-deck' machine with which the experiments of yourself and Mr. Herring were conducted in 1896–7."

insight: the wing of a glider, a "hard" thing, might twist at its tip to impart a small change in direction to the craft. This could be implemented with bicycle wires attached from the wingtips to give some control to the pilot. The pilot would then have direct and specific control of the craft and make rapid adjustments analogous to those a bicyclist would make. Described this way the insight is a three-dimensional technical vision, of a kind that can be diagrammed on paper. It arrived as a tacit insight, however, insofar that the Wrights had experience in the air and had therefore ways to think about and process the issue that were different from the insights of those working on paper alone (Jakab 1990, 51–57). They later extended this idea (when its first implementation was unstable) and wired the wingtips to the rudder and elevator at the tail of the plane in a way that made the aircraft more stable as it turned. This package of design elements made up their major patent claim.

In 1902 the Wrights made a wind tunnel that was unusually precise for its time, and this enabled them to make efficiently shaped wings, and then, having been absorbed for months in the study of wings, they had the striking insight that a propeller should be shaped like a wing so that it develops a partial vacuum ahead of itself and pulls the aircraft forward. In 1903 they added an engine once they felt the other elements were finished, and December of that year they flew several short controlled flights on the beach at Kitty Hawk, North Carolina.

These internal moments of creativity are associated with substantial preparation. The Wrights had used a design platform of kites or gliders whose designs they had chosen and partly inherited. They had extensive experience working with these craft, and with other people on them. The technological creativity of an economy depends on social constructions of the diffuse network kind. A technologically creative society is not only one with technically competent persons (as illustrated by Meisenzahl and Mokyr 2011) but also one with networks of people who construct support systems for imagining technical futures. I submit that the kinds of technically creative insights that break through technological uncertainty would be more rare for societies under social repression.

Was the Wright airplane a macroinvention? I think it fits the defining elements well.[11] Like other macroinventions, the airplane did not appear in response to microeconomic incentives; it arose in the context of particular individuals and their genius and luck; and it required vast subsequent improvements to work properly and a sympathetic environment to succeed technically and economically. It did not have a large or even positive economic effect at first; application was difficult. Most centrally it was a device that represented a clear break from previous practice or technique, except for the practices of aerial navigation experimenters that led to it.

11　I draw these from Mokyr (1990, 13–14, 291–98).

## INDUSTRIAL COMPETITION BEGINS

Successes came from the open literature; the macroinvention resulted from microinventions and copies of earlier designs.[12] The Wrights became more secretive as they believed they were near to making the first functioning, controllable, fixed-wing airplane (Crouch 2002).

The Wrights filed for a patent on their control system—the wiring of the wingtips to the tail and to a control lever—in 1903. After much back and forth with the U.S. Patent and Trademark Office, they were awarded their patent in 1906. Octave Chanute had encouraged the Wrights to file for a patent but was discouraged that they then enforced it vigorously with lawsuits, and the Wrights became unpopular with many American aviators.

A new airplane industry began. In 1907 there was a sharp increase in the number of patent filings and of other publications. A wave of new firms appeared starting in 1908, in several industrial countries. From 1908 through 1911 there were large public exhibitions of airplane flights, and some of these exhibitions were very profitable. No single source creates a database of these companies; the author and assistants have collected entries from Gunston (1993, 2005), Bell (2002), and other sources. Figure 8.4 summarizes entry into the airplane industry.

The founders, investors, and aircraft designers of these new firms were from a different mold. Almost none of them were creative experimenters before 1900. The list of hundreds of nineteenth-century experimenters, authors, theorists, and patentees overlaps little with the list of founders, designers, and funders of the new companies in 1908 and afterward. Most strikingly, it seems that not one of the major contributors to the information stream in the 1890s was a central figure in the infant industry of 1910.

This sharp turn in the history of technology and industry results from the combination of both (1) great technological uncertainty and open-source/tinkering behavior before the transition and (2) the need for capital-intensive manufacturing and R&D in the new industry. The geographically widespread start to the industry, unmoored from the original inventors, tells us that the key knowledge was widely available, not in fact coming from one invention or one place.

Rapid growth followed. Revenues in the early years came from the military and from exhibition ticket sales as millions of people wanted to see the new aircraft. Only later were there significant revenues from passenger service, mail delivery, freight, or private buyers. Starting in 1910 there were substantial patent battles, and industrial competition of a conventional kind began.

---

12  This section draws from Meyer (2013).

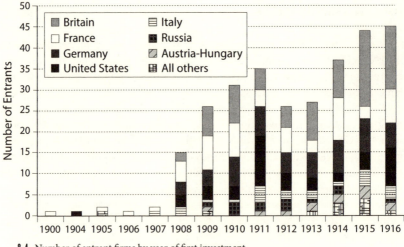

**8.4** Number of entrant firms by year of first investment.

*Sources*: Gunston (1993, 2005); Smithsonian directory.

## MODELING THE DEVELOPMENT OF A MACROINVENTION

To an extent, then, the invention of the first airplanes—a macroinvention—was based largely on open-source information and networks of colleagues. How can we model a period of open hobbyist tinkerers and the transition into a new industry? The phenomenon overlaps with *open science* (David 1998), with *user innovation* (von Hippel 2006), and with *collective invention* (Allen 1983); but the dramatic result of a new capability of control in the air and the resulting appearance of a novel industry is an essential new element not characterized by the models or framings above.

This process matches a model of open-source technology development in which the participants care greatly about the advance of the technology itself or some other ideal, and are not mainly competing. It is helpful to assume also that the technology is not yet understood well enough for it to be clear how to generate profits from it. This assumption (a strong version of "technological uncertainty"[13]) is necessary to explain why existing firms do not directly seize the opportunity with their own research and development. If no market is established and the technical problems are too hard or unclear, existing profit-oriented firms would shy away from them. Under such conditions scientists or hobbyists will rationally share information and engage in specialization,

---

13 For similar characterizations of technological uncertainty, see Tushman and Anderson (1986), Dosi (1988), and Rosenberg (1996).

standardization of designs and terminology, evangelism, and editing and moderation of joint journals, clubs, and interaction.

Some experimenters, such as Chanute, devoted energy to surveying and documenting the work of the others, apart from his own experiments. We can explain why a tinkerer would do this in terms of his or her opportunities. If tinkering is rewarding because of the progress it generates, then maybe actively recruiting others to join the network brings faster progress, and is the preferred option. Thus we do not need to think of the experimenter and the author or speaker as having different interests; these are differentiated behaviors but are designed to meet the same objective. If we assume that information travels quickly among the interested participants, we can ignore the exact shape or linkages within the network.

Some experimenters, such as Hargrave, decided not to patent anything, that is, not to impose any claim of intellectual property. If there is no market of consumers, only other tinkerers, then restrictions on the flow of information between them is socially inefficient. A particular productive tinkerer may benefit, but the mechanism gets in the way of progress. Hargrave's choice was intended to help get quickly to the technological goal.

An experimenter who never joins into such a network or withdraws too soon may pour resources into a direction that other experimenters have demonstrated is a dead end. By being in the network, one has the exploration tree pruned by other experimenters. Chanute explicitly stated that such time saving was a motive for publishing his book.

We can think of all these tinkerers as working on a technology the future of which is shrouded behind a veil of technological uncertainty. The tinkerer may have an insight about what is behind the veil, and envision an implementable form of the technology, then choose to leave the network, stop giving and receiving information, and start directed research and development to make a product. Thus an industry can start, and this tinkerer leaves the network of open-technology sharing. The network can continue if others keep it going. A private company might share private knowledge without payment, for several reasons discussed in the collective invention literature.[14] However, that

---

14 Collective invention is defined and discussed in Allen (1983), Nuvolari (2001, 2004), and Meyer (2003). Know-how trading (von Hippel 1987) is similar. Among the reasons a company would do this are the following: (1) better public technology may raise the value of assets owned by the innovator, as in Allen (1983); (2) the innovating firm garners favorable publicity by making its successes known; (3) an organization conserves on the costs or effort to keep its privately developed information secret (which would be hard if, say, many employees move between employers); (4) publications in an open environment give employers a useful way to judge the contributions, skills, or certifications of a specialized employee; (5) to establish desirable engineering standards even if it requires upgrading a competitor's technology (network effects of features can justify this, per Meyer, 2003); (6) the firms follow different paths of research and they expect future innovations to depend on advances made outside their own firm, as in Nuvolari (2001, 2004) and Bessen and Maskin (2009).

literature does not describe the behavior of networks of individuals operating outside organizations.

## MODEL OF CREATIVE TINKERERS WHO PRODUCE A MACROINVENTION

With simple and extreme assumptions we can model self-motivated tinkerers of the kind who could conceivably invent an airplane or another macroinvention. Their progress toward internal or altruistic goals can be represented in their utility functions. This specification is drawn from Meyer (2007), which spells out the algebra more completely.

Define a *tinkerer* to be a person with a unique project, activity, or technology A. The notation A stands for an aircraft or anything related to it—a glider, a model airplane, an experiment on wings, or even a membership in a balloon club. The tinkerer enjoys A and may imagine that future honors and profits could derive from it. At present, there are no honors or profits, and future honors or profits are unlikely and uncertain. Assume A does not depreciate, and it has little market value, far less than what it is worth to the tinkerer.

The tinkerer receives a flow of positive utility from the existence or discussion of A. Let the tinkerer be risk-neutral, and value alternative choices according to the net present value of expected utility at time $t = 0$ in this equation,

$$U = \sum_{t=0}^{\infty} \beta^t a_t \tag{1}$$

where $a_t$ is a positive scalar utility expected from A in each discrete time period $t$, and $\beta$ is a discount factor between zero and one applied to utility anticipated in future periods. Each future $a_t$ equals a fixed known $a_0$ unless A changes or circumstances change.

The tinkerer can choose to "tinker with" or "experiment on" A in some way that will raise his or her future benefits $a_t$. Tinkering is an investment, costing one unit of utility in the present period for the effort, expenses, and the opportunity cost of time spent. The agent believes that tinkering will raise his or her future utility by $p$ units each time period in the future. The notation $p$ stands for a rate of progress, which is subjectively experienced by the agent. For simplicity assume $p$ is fixed and positive and that the tinkerer's forecast is correct. We normalize the tinkerer's outside option to have period utility of zero.

A tinkerer chooses to tinker if the expected utility benefits exceed the costs, which can be calculated based on the assumptions above. The gross utility benefits from one effort to tinker have a value of $p$ in each subsequent period. The gross payoffs to tinkering in the present period can be compressed into a single fraction, by a standard series summation formula:

$$p\beta + p\beta^2 + p\beta^3 + \ldots = \frac{p\beta}{1-\beta}$$

The investment required to receive this payoff was one utility unit at time zero.

So, the net payoff to tinkering in period zero is $\frac{p\beta}{1-\beta} - 1$. The benefits exceed

this cost if $p > \frac{1-\beta}{\beta}$. An example makes this clearer: for a tinkerer who per-

ceives $\beta = .95$ and $p = .07$, tinkering is worth the effort. These parameter values are useful for illustration but are not drawn from any specific example.

The optimal choice about whether to tinker is not a function of the level of $a_t$ at the time of the choice, unless it is so negative that the tinkerer should

optimally abandon the project, which is not the case of interest. So if $p > \frac{1-\beta}{\beta}$,

the agent will tinker in every period, and each $a_{t+1} = a_t + p$. Call an agent who meets these conditions a *classic tinkerer* on project A. For a classic tinkerer, the period utility value in each future time period will be $a_t = a_0 + pt$ and the investment's utility cost each period will be 1. The net expected utility ($EU$) payoff stream can be expressed in parameters which were known at time zero, as follows:

$$EU_{t=0} = \sum_{t=0}^{\infty} \beta^t (a_t - 1) = \sum_{t=0}^{\infty} \beta^t (a_0 + pt - 1) = \frac{a_0}{1-\beta} - \frac{1}{1-\beta} + p\sum_{t=0}^{\infty} \beta^t t$$

The last summation term can be put into closed form by simplifying its time series sums:

$$\sum_{t=0}^{\infty} \beta^t t = \beta + 2\beta^2 + 3\beta^3 + \ldots = (\beta + \beta^2 + \beta^3 + \ldots) + (\beta^2 + \beta^3 + \beta^4 + \ldots)$$

$$+ (\beta^3 + \beta^4 + \beta^5 + \ldots) = \frac{\beta}{1-\beta} + \beta\frac{\beta}{1-\beta} + \beta^2\frac{\beta}{1-\beta} + \ldots = \frac{\beta}{1-\beta}$$

$$(1 + \beta + \beta^2 + \ldots) = \frac{\beta}{1-\beta}\left(\frac{1}{1-\beta}\right) = \frac{\beta}{(1-\beta)^2}$$

Substituting that back into the expected utility equation, the present value of utility at time 0 is:

$$EU_{t=0} = \frac{a_0}{1-\beta} - \frac{1}{1-\beta} + \frac{p\beta}{(1-\beta)^2} \tag{2}$$

Thus, simple assumptions about $p$ (the payoff of progress to this tinkerer) and $\beta$ (his or her discount factor)—parameters that could characterize his fanatical obsession with a technical vision that others do not recognize–quickly lead to conclusions about his payoffs and behavior in common language. The first term of equation 2 is the present value of the expected utility from possessing $A$ in its original state. The second term has the present value of the costs of endless tinkering. The third term has the present value of the benefits of endless tinkering.

Again using parameters $p = .95$ and $\beta = .07$, the second and third terms add up to 6.6. So, for these parameters, endless tinkering raises the tinkerer's present value utility by 6.6 times the cost of a one-time investment. *This self-motivated tinkerer is a perpetual innovation machine, of the kind who could make a macroinvention.*

## TINKERERS WOULD BE WILLING TO SHARE

Suppose there are two tinkerers with identical utility functions working on similar projects $A_1$ and $A_2$, and that their experimental findings and innovations could be useful to one another. Let each one believe that the other has no way to profit from the project using the existing technology or any likely foreseeable technology. Let the subjective rate of progress of the first player be $p_1$, and the subjective rate of progress of player 2 be $p_2$. Let fraction $f$, between zero and one, of player 2's innovations be useful to player 1's project, and the same fraction of player 1's innovations are useful to player 2. Because there are costs to interacting with others, let $f$ be an inflow net of any costs. (So for some pairs of tinkerers, $f$ could be negative, but in the cases of interest, $f$ is positive.)

Suppose the two tinkerers have the option of making a costless, verifiable, enforceable agreement to share a well-defined set of the functional design changes in $A_1$ and $A_2$ and their experimentally discovered effects. This agreement forms a *network* for future information. At any time, either partner can depart from the network, and then does not learn about the subsequent innovations of the other and ceases to share his or her own.

The agreement does not require sharing everything the experimenters know or learn. They do not meld minds, memories, or objectives. For example, a tinkerer may discover or learn descriptive, propositional, or scientific knowledge which is not embodied in $A$, and an open-source agreement does not require sharing that.

If player 1 thinks player 2 will tinker and produce *any* positive flow of innovations, he or she is made better off by joining the sharing institution. It pays off when he or she receives any useful information from player 2. Player 2's subjectively determined rate of progress must have met the criterion $p_2 > \dfrac{1-\beta}{\beta}$ since he or she is a tinkerer, but the rate of innovations useful to player 1 might be small.

If player 1 expects both players to join, tinker, and share forever, his or her expected utility is

$$EU_{t=0} = \frac{a_0}{1-\beta} - \frac{1}{1-\beta} + \frac{p_1\beta}{(1-\beta)^2} + \frac{fp_2\beta}{(1-\beta)^2} \tag{3}$$

The new fourth term has the benefits player 1 receives from the flow of information coming from player 2. This addition to the expression in equation 2 tells us that the tinkerer prefers to join the network than to work alone. Thus *the classic tinkerer assumptions generate an individually rational model of groups conducting open-source technology development.* This is the central claim of this model.

## TINKERERS WOULD BE WILLING TO STANDARDIZE AND SPECIALIZE

The fraction $f$ of the usefulness of the findings and inventions made by player 2 are usable to player 1, but perhaps the players can coordinate to improve this communication flow. This models the choice to adopt an design or engineering standard from an external source.

Suppose for a cost $c_s$ player 1 can adjust some arbitrary elements of his project $A_1$ to look more like $A_2$, and that this would raise the fraction of player 2's innovations which applied directly to his own project to $f_2$, where $f_2 > f$. If tinkerer one pays this cost, his or her expected utility is

$$EU_{t=0} = \frac{a_0}{1-\beta} - \frac{1}{1-\beta} + \frac{p_1\beta}{(1-\beta)^2} - c_s + \frac{f_2p_2\beta}{(1-\beta)^2} \tag{4}$$

Comparing this to equation 3, a player would find it optimal to pay the standardization cost if: $\frac{\beta p_2(f_2 - f)}{(1-\beta)^2} > c_s$.

So in the model, a tinkerer benefits more from adopting a standard if, holding other things constant: (1) the other tinkerers are producing a large flow of innovations $p_2$; (2) the cost of standardizing $c_s$ is small; and (3) the gain in the fraction of useful innovations from the others that become useful $(f_2 - f)$ is large. These are intuitively sensible, and the model formalizes them.

The same formal argument can explain why experimenters develop and try to standardize on their technical language for describing their new technologies. This can reduce communication costs and also clarify thinking. For example, Wilbur Wright published a journal article (Wright [1901] 2000) asking other experimenters to cease using "angle of incidence" to mean the angle between a wing (or other airfoil) and the ground. The better definition, he argued, was the angle between the airfoil and the flow of air coming at it; the angle with respect to the ground was not relevant. This request was an effort both to improve the thinking processes of other experimenters and to lower frictional losses in communication. In a more important example, Lawrence Hargrave's experiments showed that a box-shaped kite was more stable than a single flat kite was in a gust of wind. This specialist contribution helped glider flyers standardize on a biplane (two-wing) design for gliders.

The standardization trade-off expressed in equation 4 explains partly why tinkerers would agree to publish their findings. The fewer unnecessary differences between experiments there are, the lower the future communication and adoption costs will be. A tinkerer may also take steps to make the device easier to learn or easier to use, which is a parallel pathway to delivering faster progress or the inflow of information.

These trade-offs are important in the software context where a project can "fork"—split over time into incompatible versions—if the contributors do not agree to standardize. In the history of UNIX there was a painful fork, and programmers can refer to this history to convince others to pay some price in effort to reunify a project on which people work independently. In this model, they are willing to pay some price to maintain the economies of scale of the project.

Standardization and specialization are intrinsic to technological and scientific development; they are a natural result of exchanging information, and *in this setting they can be explained without reference to competition or market exchanges*. It is useful and necessary here to escape Adam Smith's proposition that specialization is bounded by the extent of the market, because scientists and inventors do it without market-priced exchanges.

The network is itself a technology—a social or search technology for tinkerers to get possible valuable information that they do not obtain by their own experiments. Other aspects of the environment affect $f$ also. If for example the tinkerers can upgrade from sending letters (which arrive slowly and some of which did not arrive at all) to email communication, $f$ would rise, whereas if the email system became clogged with unhelpful spam, $f$ would fall. Meyer (2007) discusses further examples of those like Chanute who manage the network itself, recruit new members, introduce them to one another, and moderate publications, all of which can be modeled as efforts to raise progress and information flows represented here by $p$ and $f$.

## ENTREPRENEURIAL EXITS

When they believed they were about to invent the airplane, the Wrights withdrew somewhat from their interpersonal network. They shared less. The model can incorporate the possibility that a tinkerer (or an entrepreneur who persuades the tinkerer) decides dynamically, as the Wrights did, to take activity A private. Even anticipating that possibility, the parameters may be such that a tinkerer might participate in a network while recognizing that he may later have an insight into how to implement something from activity A that could be provided to customers profitably, and then want to exit. Meyer (2007) shows this, and a relevant implication here is that tinkerers may optimally work together, even anticipating that one of them may want to break away when he or she suddenly sees an outside option to (perhaps) get rich. They are driven by subjective goals early in the process, and by market goals, perhaps, in a later phase.

## TINKERERS MAY PURPOSEFULLY AVOID INTELLECTUAL PROPERTY

In the real-world episodes discussed some tinkerers preferred to avoid formal intellectual property institutions. Examples include pioneering aircraft experimenter Lawrence Hargrave and programmer Richard Stallman. This behavior can be rationalized in this model. Effort devoted to establishing intellectual property rights in a presently unprofitable technology may not seem worth it to them, compared to the benefits of pushing it forward to become better and perhaps profitable.

Suppose in the model that each tinkerer could charge for the flow of his or her own innovations that were used by others, and that there were small administrative costs to this. Many, probably most, tinkerers would find this to be net unprofitable. Social costs would exceed social benefits, so the establishment of this intellectual property institution would not have been Pareto optimal. This outcome could change if an entrepreneur developed a version of the technology that was profitable, because then there would be an inflow of external revenue.

This logic rationalizes why tinkerer types such as Hargrave and Chanute preferred to keep the information flow open, not secret, and generally unprotected by intellectual property institutions. The Wrights may also have held that view but changed their behavior in late 1902 to become protective because they had started to think they could manufacture airplanes for sale.

## CONCLUSIONS

When the airplane appeared as a macroinvention, it already had an extensive and well-documented prehistory. A growing international scientific and technical literature was oriented toward the vision of a flying machine that could navigate through the air. Experimenters on the subject were generally motivated intrinsically, and within both the history and the model we can see why they shared information and built common institutions given the technological uncertainty they faced and the enthusiasm they shared. The sudden appearance of the new industry in many industrial countries at once shows that the main knowledge needed to make an airplane was widely held, not the private province of particular researchers.

The tinkerers' network model is relevant to the airplane case, and to other cases of invention when certain kinds of evidence are present:

- Individuals communicate novel technical findings and designs to one another without explicit rewards.
- Experimenters do not all have extrinsic motivation, for example because they are working on something that has no obvious price or does not fit into an existing, standard product market when they enter the field.
- Some participants specialize in managing or expanding the network.
- The activity evolves over time, in response to events that participants interpret as *progress*, such as discoveries or inventions. For example, when Hargrave reported results from his box kite experiments, other aeronautical experimenters learned and adapted to the findings. They responded to and interpreted discoveries about natural law; they did not just imitate.

In such a situation the model predicts that participants would specialize in aspects of the technology, and standardize on some tools, as opportunities permit. It suggests that the latent predictions about the future form or importance of the technology are diverse and uncertain in the sense of Dosi (1988) and Rosenberg (1996). It predicts that members who do not expect to sell a related product will avoid imposing intellectual property constraints on the system. And it predicts this kind of ferment could lead to participants jumping out into entrepreneurial opportunities, whose value is hard to predict. Thus these behaviors can lead to a macroinvention.

## ACKNOWLEDGMENTS

The author thanks Ceceile Kay Richter, Leo Zimmermann, John Russell Herbert, and Adam Hyland for valuable research assistance. For valuable advice the author thanks Joel Mokyr, Lynne Kiesling, Tomonori Ishikawa, Leo Sveikauskas, Simine Short, Richard Meyer, and participants at the joyful Mokyr festschrift conference. The author is a research economist at the U.S. Bureau of Labor Statistics. Views expressed in the chapter are those of the author and do not represent the Bureau. The current work draws from the data and the line of thought in Meyer (2013, 2014).

# BIBLIOGRAPHY

Ackroyd, J. A. D. 2011. "Sir George Cayley: The Invention of the Aeroplane near Scarborough at the Time of Trafalgar." *Journal of Aeronautical History* 2011/6: 130–81.

Allen, Robert C. 1983. "Collective Invention." *Journal of Economic Behavior and Organization* 4: 1–24.

Anderson, John D. 2004. *Inventing Flight*. Baltimore: Johns Hopkins University Press.

Bell, Dana, ed. 2002. *The Smithsonian National Air and Space Museum Directory of Airplanes: Their Designers and Manufacturers*. Mechanicsburg, PA: Stackpole Books.

Bessen, James, and Eric Maskin. 2009. "Sequential Innovation, Patents, and Imitation." *RAND Journal of Economics* 40 (4): 611–35.

Brewer, Griffith, and Patrick Y. Alexander. (1893) 1965. *Aëronautics*. Amsterdam: Boekhandel en Antiquariaat, B. M. Israel N.V.

Brockett, Paul. 1910. *Bibliography of Aeronautics*. Washington, DC: Smithsonian Institution.

Chadeau, Emmanuel. 1987. *De Blériot à Dassault: Histoire de l'industrie aéronautique en France, 1900–1950*. Paris: Fayard.

Chanute, Octave. (1894) 1997. *Progress in Flying Machines*. New York: American Engineer and Railroad Journal.

Crouch, Tom D. 2002. *A Dream of Wings: Americans and the Airplane, 1875–1905*. 2nd ed. New York: Norton.

David, Paul A. 1998. "Common Agency Contracting and the Emergence of 'Open Science' Institutions." *American Economic Review* 88 (2): 15–22.

Dosi, Giovanni. 1988. "Sources, Procedures, and Microeconomic Effects of Innovation." *Journal of Economic Literature* 26 (3): 1120–71.

Gambardella, Alfonso, and Bronwyn H. Hall. 2006. "Proprietary versus Public Domain Licensing of Software and Research Products." *Research Policy* 35 (6): 875–92.

Gibbs-Smith, Charles. 1962. *Sir George Cayley's Aeronautics, 1796–1855*. London: HMSO.

———. 1966. *The Invention of the Aeroplane, 1799–1909*. London: Faber & Faber.

Gunston, Bill. 1993. *World Encyclopedia of Aircraft Manufacturers*. 1st ed. Annapolis, MD: Naval Institute Press.

———. 2005. *World Encyclopedia of Aircraft Manufacturers: From the Pioneers to the Present Day*. 2nd ed. Stroud: Sutton.

Harhoff, Dietmar, Joachim Henkel, and Eric von Hippel. 2003. "Profiting from Voluntary Information Spillovers: How Users Benefit from Freely Revealing Their Innovations." *Research Policy* 32 (10): 1753–69.

Inkster, Ian. 1991. *Science and Technology in History*. New Brunswick, NJ: Rutgers University Press.

Jakab, Peter L. 1990. *Visions of a Flying Machine*. Washington, DC: Smithsonian Institution.

Jakab, Peter L., and Rick Young. 2000. *The Published Writings of Wilbur and Orville Wright*. Washington, DC: Smithsonian Institution.

Lakhani, Karim R., and Bob Wolf. 2005. "Why Hackers Do What They Do: Understanding Motivation and Effort in Free/Open Source Software Projects." In *Perspectives on Free and Open Source Software*, edited by J. Feller, B. Fitzgerald, S. Hissam, and K. R. Lakhani. Cambridge, MA: MIT Press.

Langley, Samuel Pierpont. 1902. *Experiments in Aerodynamics*. 2nd ed. Washington, DC: Smithsonian Institution.

Levy, Stephen. 2001. *Hackers: Heroes of the Computer Revolution*. New York: Penguin.

McFarland, Marvin W., ed. 1953. *The Papers of Wilbur and Orville Wright*. Vols. 1–2. New York: McGraw-Hill.

Meisenzahl, Ralf R., and Joel Mokyr. 2011. "The Rate and Direction of Invention in the British Industrial Revolution: Incentives and Institutions." NBER Working Paper 16993.

Meyer, Peter B. 2003. "Episodes of Collective Invention." U.S. Bureau of Labor Statistics Working Paper WP-368.

———. 2007. "Network of Tinkerers: A Model of Open-Source Innovation." U.S. Bureau of Labor Statistics Working Paper 413.

———. 2013. "The Airplane as an Open Source Invention." *Revue économique* 64 (1): 115–32.

———. 2014. "An Inventive Commons: Shared Sources of the Airplane and Its Industry." In *Governing Knowledge Commons*, edited by Brett M. Frischmann, Michael J. Madison, and Katherine J. Strandburg. Oxford: Oxford University Press.

Mokyr, Joel. 1990. *The Lever of Riches: Technological Creativity and Economic Progress*. Oxford: Oxford University Press.

———. 1993. "Editor's Introduction." In *The British Industrial Revolution: An Economic Perspective*, edited by Joel Mokyr, 1–131. Boulder, CO: Westview.

———. 2002. *The Gifts of Athena: Historical Origins of the Knowledge Economy*. Princeton: Princeton University Press.

———. 2009. *The Enlightened Economy: An Economic History of Britain, 1700–1850*. New Haven, CT: Yale University Press.

Nuvolari, Alessandro. 2001. "Open Source Software Development: Some Historical Perspectives." ECIS working paper.

———. 2004. "Collective Invention during the British Industrial Revolution: The Case of the Cornish Pumping Engine." *Cambridge Journal of Economics* 28: 347–63.

Penrose, Harald. (1988) 2000. *An Ancient Air*. London: Wrens Park Publishing.

Polanski, Arnold. 2007. "Is the General Public Licence a Rational Choice?" *Journal of Industrial Economics* 55 (4): 691–714.

Rosenberg, Nathan. 1996. "Uncertainty and Technological Change." In *Mosaic of Economic Growth*, edited by Ralph Landau, Timothy Taylor, and Gavin Wright, 334–53. Stanford: Stanford University Press.

Stoff, Joshua. 1997. "Introduction." In *Progress in Flying Machines*, iii–vii. Mineola, NY: Dover.

Tise, Larry E. 2009. *Conquering the Sky*. New York: Palgrave Macmillan.

Tushman, Michael L., and Philip Anderson. 1986. "Technological Discontinuities and Organizational Environments." *Administrative Science Quarterly* 31: 439–65.

von Hippel, Eric. 1987. "Cooperation between Rivals: Informal Know-How Trading." *Research Policy* 16: 291–302.

———. 2006. *Democratizing Innovation*. Cambridge, MA: MIT Press.

Wright, Orville, with Fred C. Kelly and Alan Weissman. 1953. *How We Invented the Airplane: An Illustrated History*. New York: Dover.

Wright, Wilbur. (1901) 2000. "Angle of Incidence." In *The Published Papers of Orville and Wilbur Wright*, edited by Peter L. Jakab and Rick Young, 109–12. Washington, DC: Smithsonian Institution.

# ENGLAND'S EIGHTEENTH-CENTURY DEMAND FOR HIGH-QUALITY WORKMANSHIP

Evidence from Apprenticeship, 1710–1770

## KARINE VAN DER BEEK

The notion that technological changes and investment in human capital are positively correlated has been empirically validated in the modern context, mainly in the case of computer-based technologies. Such a correlation has not been demonstrated in the case of the Industrial Revolution. In his seminal book *The Enlightened Economy*, Joel Mokyr (2009, 112) argued that "in Britain the high quality of workmanship available to support innovation, local and imported, helped create the Industrial Revolution." By these, Mokyr refers to "the top 3–5 percent of the labor force in terms of skills: engineers, mechanics, millwrights, chemists, clock- and instrument makers, skilled carpenters and metal workers, wheelwrights, and similar workmen" (Meisenzahl and Mokyr 2012, 447). This article provides empirical evidence from a variety of sources supporting Mokyr's claim. It uses wage books from textile mills, labor contracts from Bolton and Watt's engine shop, advertisements in newspapers, as well as the stamp tax registers on apprenticeship contracts, and shows that indeed the innovations and technological changes that were taking place in eighteenth-century England increased the demand for these high-quality mechanical workmen and that their numbers were rising throughout the period as a result. It also shows that the most relevant occupation within this group was the wright, a workman who "erects and installs, in place of use, machinery and other mechanical equipment" (Van Leeuwen, Maas, and Miles 2002).

These findings are consistent with the assumption made in many models of economic growth, of a positive relationship between technological change and human capital. It supports the view that acceleration in technological progress increases the demand for skilled workers (i.e., skilled-biased technical change).[1] This hypothesis could thus far not be empirically tested in the context of the eighteenth-century Industrial Revolution in England, due to the scarce and scattered evidence from this period. This chapter uses

---

1  A more systematic examination of the existence of skilled-biased technological change in eighteenth-century England is available in Feldman and van der Beek (2014).

different primary sources to identify the response of the labor markets to the technological changes in eighteenth-century England. Mainly, it uses for the first time an exceptional and comprehensive set of evidence that allows a serious examination of questions relating to developments and changes in the composition of skilled labor in England during the first phases of its Industrial Revolution. It uses stamp tax records of the duty that was raised on apprenticeship contracts all over England in 1710, covering the period 1710 to 1770. The advantages of this data set are not only that it is very large (a sample of 50,200 entries) and systematic, but also that it provides direct annual information on skill formation, both in terms of quantities and prices. Data on individual apprentices and masters include the occupation and location of the master, as well as the payment he received from the apprentice's parents. I use this information to examine the response of the human capital markets in eighteenth-century England to the technological changes by looking at changes in the composition of occupations that apprentices chose throughout the century. I find that technological changes did have an effect on the skill formation and composition, with a growing number of children being apprenticed to high-quality workmen.

## THE DEMAND FOR HIGH-QUALITY WORKMEN—DIFFERENT SOURCES

Technological changes and the adoption of machinery in cotton mills obviously had an important effect on the demand for skilled mechanical workers. Their skills were required in order to maintain and fix the machinery in the newly created cotton mills, as described by S. D. Chapman (1972, 54): "The mill owners' problem can only be understood by examining the recruitment of skilled workers (machine builders, millwrights and mule spinners) separately from that of the unskilled machine minders who formed the majority of labour force in Arkwright-type mills. The fundamental difficulty in obtaining skilled men was simply the consequence of the rapid growth of the cotton industry, which made artisans with relevant skills very much at a premium. Local newspaper advertisements, memoirs, private correspondence and high wage rates all bear testimony to the acute shortage of craftsmen whose skills could be applied to textile machine building or to the installation of water wheels and transmission systems." The wage books of some of the earliest mechanized cotton mills support Chapman's observations, including Strutt, Need and Arkwright at Cromford, Derbyshire (erected 1771), Strutt's later mill in Belper, Derbyshire (1778), and Greg's Quarry Bank Mill in Styal, Cheshire (1784).[2] These wage books, which list their employees by the different rooms in which they worked, contain a remarkable number of workmen enlisted as a separate category. For example, in Greg's Quarry Bank Mill wage book craftsmen such as clock makers, smiths, joiners,

2  Manchester Central Library, C5/1/15/1, March 1790.

and turners are listed in December 12, 1789, under the category "Sundrys," which consists of about 14 percent of the 230 employees (see Figure 9.A.1).

The rising need for machine maintenance, however, was not the only reason for the increasing demand for skilled mechanical workers. Eighteenth-century technological changes had another critical effect on economic development besides their effect on textile manufacturing. According to Musson and Robinson (1960, 209–10), focusing on the sources of engineering, "The tremendous growth of the Lancashire cotton industry, from about 1770 onward, based on the mechanical inventions of Hargreaves, Arkwright, Crompton, and Cartwright, powered by water wheels and steam engines, gave rise to an equally rapid development of mechanical engineering. Lancashire soon came to manufacture not only cotton, but also cotton machinery, steam engines, boilers, machine tools, and, later on, railway locomotives, iron bridges, gasworks plant, and a vast range of other engineering product." The rise in machine manufacturing required skilled mechanical labor as well, and it therefore contributed to the increased demand for these workmen who were already required in the cotton mills. Musson and Robinson present a large number of eighteenth-century contemporary job advertisements (1770–1800) from the *Manchester Mercury*, illustrating this phenomenon and allowing the identification of the type of occupations that were in demand in the growing machinery sector. For example, according to the advertisements that are presented in Figure 9.1, Mr. Stopford from Manchester, who describes himself as "inventor of the spinning machine," was looking for "three or four journeymen carpenters" for his workshop in 1785. In 1789, Peter Whitaker from Manchester, a "cotton and worsted machine-maker," was looking to employ an iron turner, and more of this type of advertisements can easily be found in the newspaper.[3]

As for engine production, only a few men were employed in this industry in the 1770s, and therefore the data used in this chapter do not capture its demand. Nevertheless, the following evidence suggests that the engine industry required the same type of skills as machinery, with a bias toward smiths, filers, and founders. At Boulton and Watt's Soho Manufactory, for example, the workforce gradually grew as the workshops expanded and the engine business increased, and the construction of Soho Foundry from 1795 marked a major increase in the workforce.[4] An examination of the Foundry's Articles of Agreement (1796–1800) demonstrates the skills that were in demand in this industry toward the end of the century.[5] The majority of the men employed were metalworkers of some description—smiths, forgers, founders, filers, turners, and fitters. Carpenters, bricklayers, furnace men, and laborers were also employed.

---

3  Manchester Central Library Microfilm—MFMM1-N.

4  Boulton and Watt's partnership was formed in 1775 to exploit Watt's patent and had a monopoly on steam engine construction.

5  The agreements are conserved in the Birmingham City Archives under reference code GB 143 BCA MS3147/8.

**9.1** Examples of job advertisements from the *Manchester Mercury* (top, March 10, 1785; bottom, February 24, 1789).

In addition to the workforce at Soho, Boulton and Watt also employed traveling field engineers or "engine erectors" to attend the customers' premises, erect the engine, and if necessary train someone to work the engine. In the first few years of the business, they tended to hire local engineers on an ad hoc basis, but by the late 1790s the firm had a network of erectors based not just at Soho but also in Cornwall, London, Manchester, and Newcastle upon Tyne. The following correspondence between Boulton and Watt, and Peter Ewart, an engine erector in Manchester, illustrates again the trouble of finding and employing skilled mechanical workers in Lancashire by the end of the century. Ewart reported that it was almost impossible to get good millwrights, turners, and filers and that "the very few general good filers and turners that are here, are all engaged for a term of years in the different Cotton Mills. . . . There is not a hand that is good for anything can be had here for less than 17 or 18 Shill. pr. week" (Musson and Robinson 1960, 220).

## THE DEMAND FOR HIGH-QUALITY WORKMEN—THE STAMP TAX REGISTERS

The main source that is used in this study is the payment register of the Board of Stamps of the moneys received in payment of the duty on apprentices' contracts.

As children grew up and reached their early and midteens, many left their homes for schools, apprenticeships, and domestic and agricultural service. The formal structure of early modern apprenticeship can be traced back to the Middle Ages in the practices of guilds and cities. It was applied nationwide in 1563 in the Statute of Artificers until its repeal in 1814. While some details were negotiable, the core of English apprenticeship contracts was fixed by law. Unlike pauper apprenticeship, classic apprenticeship, involved a written contract (*indenture*), bounding master and apprentice for a prespecified period, usually of seven years, during which the master undertook to teach the apprentice and introduce him to the modus operandi of his trade, as well as provide him with board and lodging and safeguard his moral welfare.[6] The apprentice, on his side, took an oath "duly and truly to serve," and a *premium*, or cash payment, was commonly paid to the master. Children were usually fourteen when indentured; however, this age varied with the specific requirements.[7] For example,

6  Pauper apprenticeship involved children who could not be cared for by their own family because they had no parents or came from a poor family. These children were a problem to the poor law administrators, as they frequently lacked any means of support and were too young to earn their own living. The Poor Law Act of 1597 gave Overseers of the Poor and Churchwardens the power to set these children to work, and so a large number of pauper children were put out as apprentices by parish officers.

7  According to Wallis, Webb, and Minns (2009), the age of apprenticeship in early modern London apprentices in London was bound around the age of 16 in the sixteenth century, and this age declined throughout the eighteenth century, reaching 15.5 by 1810.

in trades requiring physical strength (e.g., tanner, baker, butcher, bricklayer, blacksmith) or greater maturity (e.g., milliners, mantua makers, or hairdressers), older boys, aged fifteen or sixteen, were more useful. Occupations that indentured substantial numbers of children younger than fourteen, such as nailing and other small-metal trades, framework knitting, ribbon weaving, and shoemaking, were mostly low-skilled and labor-intensive (Lane 1996, 12–13).[8] Interestingly, it seems that many apprentices did not complete their terms of indenture, and late arrival and early departure from the master's household were widespread. According to Wallis (2008), neither masters nor apprentices risked significant loss from such early termination due to the value of apprentices' unskilled labor in the first years of their term, and the patterns of presence and absence reflect the external opportunities available to apprentices.

Until 1710, there was no centralized record of apprentices. In 1710 a stamp duty payment on private indentures of apprenticeship was raised and the records of the duty paid were kept by the Inland Revenue.[9] The tax was at the rate of 6 pence to the pound (2.5 percent) on agreements of £50 or less, plus one shilling (5 percent) for every pound above that sum. In modern terms, if we take an average tuition of £20 and the 1750 labor value of a pound in 2010, which is about $2,700, this represents a tax payment of about $1,350. The payment of the tax was entered on the reverse of the indenture, which was void without this payment. It is important to note, however, that masters did not have to pay stamp duty on the indentures of pauper apprentices, taken on at the common or public charity. It was also ruled that the Statute of Apprentices did not apply to *modern* trades, which did not exist when the law was passed in the sixteenth century. This element does not bias my results in any significant manner since the sums that were raised by the overseers of the poor were just high enough to attract masters to take children, so that paupers were not preferred to other children in any way (Lane 1996). Second, paupers were sent in large numbers to housewifery, husbandry, and large-scale industry, which are low-skilled occupations (Lane 1996).

Besides the masters who did not have to pay stamp duty, using information from tax record also raises the issue of tax evasion, which may be problematic, mainly if it varies over time and across occupations. It would, however, be reasonable to assume that, if at all, evasion would bias our results on the prosperous occupations (mainly in services and sales), where status and large amounts were involved, rather than on the manufacturing occupations, which comprise more than 70 percent of the observations and for which tuitions were relatively low (£10–20).

---

8  For the specific requirements of the different trades, see also Humphries (2011) and Justman and van der Beek (2014).

9  The manuscripts are conserved at the National Archives, Kew, under series IR 1.

Furthermore, the premiums reported in the stamp tax registers have been compared to those registered in the company (guild) books by Minns and Wallis (2013), and no evidence that masters reported lower premiums for tax purposes was found.

The stamp tax registers were originally organized in seventy-two volumes, which are available in a microfilm format at the National Archives, Kew, in London. The volumes consist of city or town registers, October 1711 to January 1811, with daily entries of the indentures upon which duty was paid in London; country registers, May 1710 to September 1808 with entries, made in London, of the indentures upon which duty had been paid to district collectors and which were then sent in condensed batches to be stamped. An index of these records was compiled by the Society of Genealogists at the beginning of the twentieth century, covering the period 1710 to 1774.[10] In addition to the sums received, the index records the date of the contract, the name, location, and trade of the master, and the name and location of the apprentice.

## THE STAMP TAX DATA SET

The analysis that is presented in this chapter is based on a stratified random sample of 50,200 entries out of about 300,000 entries in the index of the stamp tax records, registering the duty payment on apprenticeship premiums, covering the period 1710 to 1774 (14.3 percent). The sample was constructed so as to keep the proportion of observations of apprentices' surnames beginning with the same letter. For example, apprentices' surnames beginning with the letter "B" compose 11 percent of the entries in the index. This proportion was kept in the sample.

Each observation in the database represents an apprenticeship contract and contains information about the year of the contract, the trade and location of the master, and the premium paid by the apprenticeship. After omitting entries from years prior to 1710 and later than 1770, which could be misrepresentative of the year, I am left with about forty-eight thousand observations. Interestingly, as can be observed in Figure 9.2, the distribution of entries over the period is not smooth and contains some serious drops in the number of entries. This is mainly true for the years 1726 to 1740 and, with more moderate drops, for the years 1745 to 1751. These drops can most probably be explained by exogenous shocks of small pox outbreaks that caused high mortality, mainly among young children.[11] Wrigley and Schofield (1981, 162) place this sharp rise in

10   The indexes for the years 1710 to 1774 are kept with the apprenticeship books at the National Archives, Kew, under series IR 1. They are also available online at Origins Network, a family history website.
11   I am grateful to Joel Mokyr for pointing out demography as a possible of explanation.

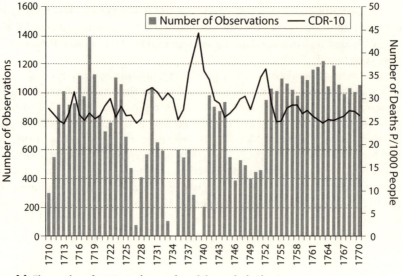

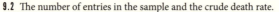

**9.2** The number of entries in the sample and the crude death rate.

*Sources*: Number of entries from the stamp tax registers. Crude death rates from Wrigley and Schofield (1981, table A3.3).

deaths precisely in the years that show a drop in the number of entries: "Their (the deaths') upsurge in the early eighteenth century owes much to some years exceptionally high mortality in the 1720s and early 1740s, and it is noteworthy that around 1750 the number of deaths sinks back to a level not much higher than had obtained in the last quarter of the seventeenth century." Figure 9.2 illustrates both the annual number of entries in the sample, where every entry represents an apprenticeship contract, and the crude death rate (CDR), which represents the number of deaths in England per one thousand people. The CDR is presented with a lag of ten years in order to examine the actual effect of the deaths ten years later, when children could potentially become apprentices. The figure shows that indeed periods of high mortality were followed by a decline in the number of children that had been bound to masters.

Masters' trades have been classified into occupational groups, using two alternative methods. The first uses the occupational information system HISCO (Historical International Classification of Occupations), a system that offers information on occupations in the past, for example occupational titles from countries and languages around the world and descriptions of the content of the work, images, and mainly; it allows coding occupational titles into a classification system that containing 76 major occupational groups and 296 minor groups, as well as groups of social class (HISCLASS) (Van Leeuwen, Maas, and Miles 2002). The second method uses occupational groups from relevant literature, mainly the ones in Williamson (1982). This classification has the advantage of being more convenient for the purpose of presentation and comparison, as well as containing occupational groups that are of interest for the purpose of this analysis, for example, skilled in building trades, skilled in shipbuilding, textile trades, machine and instrument makers, and so on. An elaborated list of the occupational groups and the occupations they include can be found in Feldman and van der Beek (2014; Table A.1).

## FRAMEWORK OF ANALYSIS

The two variables of interest in this analysis are the annual number of new apprentices and the average tuition paid, in each occupation. These variables can be viewed as proxies for changes in the demand for skills and their supply in the labor markets.

Thus, as depicted in Figure 9.3, assuming that the number of skilled workmen is inelastic, an exogenous increase in the relative demand for skilled workmen (or for a group of workers with specific skills) from $D_0^{LS}$ to $D_1^{LS}$ raises the relative wages of these workers from $W_0^S$ to $W_1^S$ in the short run, moving us from an equilibrium, such as in point A, to point B in the skilled labor market. These higher wages increase the present values of the stream of incomes viewed by potential workers and as a result increase the demand for acquiring the relevant occupations from $D^A(W_0^S)$ to $D^A(W_1^S)$, moving us to an equilibrium in point B in the apprenticeship market. Note that at this point tuitions will increase, depending on the elasticity of supply of the apprenticeship

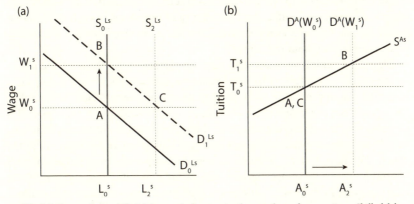

**9.3** (a) Demand for skilled labor and changes in the number of apprentices: Skilled labor market.

**9.3** (b) Demand for skilled labor and changes in the number of apprentices: Apprenticeship market.

institution, and the number of apprentices in the relevant occupations increases from $A_0^S$ in the initial period to $A_2^S$, the number of workers required to satisfy the higher demand for skilled workmen. Once these apprentices join the labor force, we reach the long-run equilibrium in the skilled labor market (point C), in which the supply of skilled workers reaches $S_2^{LS}$, the number of skilled workmen increases to $L_2^S$, and the wages move back to $W_0^S$.

Note that the span of the short run, in which a skill premium exists, depends on the elasticity of supply in the market for apprentices. If the apprenticeship institution in eighteenth-century England was efficient, as claimed by recent economic historians, we might not be able to observe rising wages and tuitions, yet, as Figure 9.3 clearly demonstrates, we will still observe an increase in the number of apprentices.[12] This explains why I concentrate in this article on changes in the composition of occupations to which they were bound, as a proxy to the changes in the demand for these occupations in the labor markets.

## THE SHARE OF HIGH-QUALITY WORKMEN

The largest share of apprentices in eighteenth-century England was bound to masters in the manufacturing trades. The share of such apprentices composes almost 80 percent of the observations, rising from 76.8 percent in the 1710s to 82.2 percent in the 1760s (see Table 9.1). The following two sectors are the service sector (barbers, shopkeepers, doctors, attorneys, bankers, etc.) and the sales sector (including different type of merchants, sellers, and shop owners), each composing about 10 percent of the observations. The administration and agricultural trades come last, composing less than 1 percent.

Apart from a rise in the agricultural trades, which cannot be statistically supported given the small annual number of observations in each year, manufacturing was the only sector in which the share of skilled labor was continuously rising throughout the century.

Figure 9.4 depicts an index that has been calculated to measure the changes in the share of apprentices in each economic sector, indicating a rising share of skilled (i.e. apprenticed) labor in manufacturing. Nevertheless, this relative increase in the share of skilled labor in manufacturing is not definite, and it depends on the representativeness of the tax registers in all the sectors. That is, it is not clear to what extent the changes in the share of tax registers in the elite occupations (mainly in trade and services) represent the changes in share of apprentices in these occupations, due to the possibility that the magnitude of tax evasion in these occupations changed over time. Yet changes in composition within the manufacturing sector, which is believed to be representative over time, are informative in the sense that they do represent changes in the

---

12  See Humphries (2003, 2011), Justman and van der Beek (2014), as well as Mokyr (2009).

**TABLE 9.1** Occupations, Number of Observations and Average Tuitions in the Sample

| Economic sector | | 1710–20 | 1721–30 | 1731–40 | 1741–50 | 1751–60 | 1761–70 |
|---|---|---|---|---|---|---|---|
| Administration | No. of obs. | 101 | 52 | 17 | 27 | 68 | 70 |
| | Share in % | 1.1 | 0.8 | 0.5 | 0.4 | 0.7 | 0.7 |
| Agriculture | No. of obs. | 28 | 20 | 8 | 25 | 44 | 40 |
| | Share in % | 0.3 | 0.3 | 0.2 | 0.4 | 0.5 | 0.4 |
| Manufacturing | No. of obs. | 7,106 | 5,209 | 2,662 | 4,971 | 7,778 | 8,803 |
| | Share in % | 76.8 | 76.9 | 75.1 | 77.5 | 81.2 | 82.2 |
| Sales | No. of obs. | 1,140 | 679 | 318 | 491 | 829 | 944 |
| | Share in % | 12.3 | 10.0 | 9.0 | 7.7 | 8.6 | 8.8 |
| Services | No. of obs. | 875 | 811 | 538 | 900 | 865 | 856 |
| | Share in % | 9.5 | 12.0 | 15.2 | 14.0 | 9.0 | 8.0 |
| Whole sample | No. of obs. | 9,250 | 6,771 | 3,543 | 6,414 | 9,584 | 10,713 |

*Source*: Stamp tax registers: the National Archives, Kew, under Series IR 1.

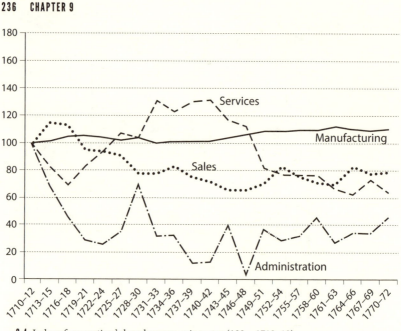

**9.4** Index of apprentices' share by economic sector (100 = 1710–12).
*Source:* Stamp tax registers.

real economy. To explore this question I decomposed the manufacturing sector in the first stage into two groups, mechanical and nonmechanical occupations, to test whether more parents wished their children to obtain a mechanical occupation in a period of technological change. Mechanical occupations include, for example, carpenters, joiners, coopers, turners, coach makers, smiths, braziers, wheelwrights, and shipbuilders. Nonmechanical occupations include masons, tillers, weavers, tailors, bakers, dyers, and painters.

As shown in Figure 9.5, the mechanical occupations, which accounted for 40 percent of the apprentices in manufacturing at the beginning of the period, accounted for 50 percent by the late 1730s and on, an increase of about one-third. Interestingly, this substantial rise in demand for mechanical occupations toward the middle of the eighteenth century was not characteristic of all the mechanical occupations. It was in fact the occupations of the high-quality workmen identified by Mokyr as critical to Britain's industrial precocity that seem to have been in growing demand. Figures 9.6a and 9.6b show that indeed the share of the group of occupations classified here as "Engineers, Machine and Instrument Makers" was rising significantly during this period.

The share of this group, which contains many of the occupations specified by Mokyr (wheelwrights, millwrights, spectacle makers, instrument maker, plough wrights, pump makers, stocking frame makers, etc.) increased not only relative to the share of apprentices in the nonmechanical occupations (textile, leather processing and others), but also relative to the share of other mechanical occupations. The nonmechanical share remained practically unchanged, while the other mechanical shares were increasing, but not by as much as the share of the high-quality mechanical occupations.

Studies that advance the idea that human capital did not play any role in the process of the Industrial Revolution base their claims, among other studies, on Clark's work (2005, 2007). In these studies Clark shows that the relative wages of skilled artisans to those of unskilled day laborers in the building trades did not change significantly during the eighteenth century, implying that there was no increase in the relative demand for skilled workers as a result of the technological changes. These studies may, nevertheless, be misleading. First, as discussed in the previous sections, the skill premium is a short-run phenomenon, which depends on the responsiveness of the supply of skilled workers. Thus, the skill premium may remain constant even in the presence of an increase in demand for skilled workers relative to that for unskilled workers. Another important reservation regarding Clark's argument was raised by Mokyr and Voth (2010), who questioned the relevancy of the wage series, which is based mainly on evidence from southern England and consists of wages of workmen in the building trades (Mokyr and Voth 2010, 25). Figure 9.7 shows that the demand for building trades—as a group—was not affected by the Industrial Revolution, while the demand for those specialized in machine manufacturing was strongly affected by it.

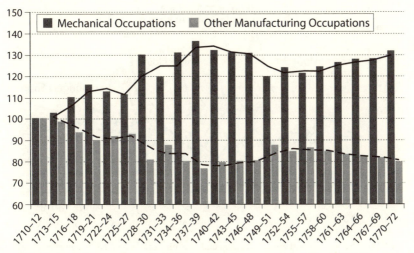

**9.5** Mechanical versus nonmechanical manufacturing occupations (100 = 1710–12).
*Source*: Stamp tax registers.

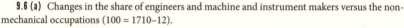

**9.6 (a)** Changes in the share of engineers and machine and instrument makers versus the non-mechanical occupations (100 = 1710–12).

*Source:* Stamp tax registers.

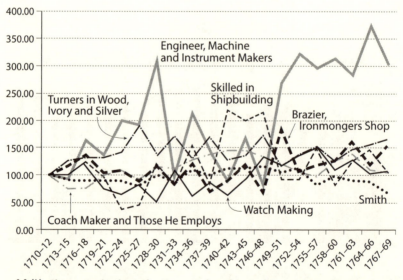

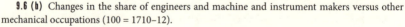

**9.6 (b)** Changes in the share of engineers and machine and instrument makers versus other mechanical occupations (100 = 1710–12).

*Source:* Stamp tax registers.

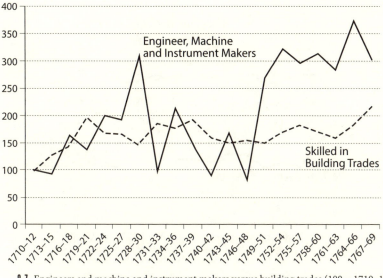

**9.7** Engineers and machine and instrument makers versus building trades (100 = 1710–12). *Source*: Stamp tax registers.

To ensure that I am identifying the right type of occupation, I decompose the occupational groups and look into the changes in share of specific occupations that were relevant to mechanization. For example, Wrights account for about 90 percent of the group "Engineers, Machine and Instrument Makers" (e.g., millwrights, wheelwrights, plough wrights) as well as the occupational group "Skilled in Shipbuilding." Carpenters and joiners, which are relevant mechanical occupations, are contained in "Skilled in Building trades," and smiths can also be find in other groups, including "Armorers."

Decomposing the groups and looking into the specific occupations indicates that indeed there was an increasing demand for wrights throughout the eighteenth century; however, Figure 9.8 shows that a shock in the demand for carpenters, joiners, and turners also occurred in the first half of the century, but the demand for clock makers does show an increase in the half of the century; however this change only brings us back to the share of apprentices in clock making in the beginning of the century. The demand for those specialized in metal, however, stays stable all through the period, as expected.

Thus, the findings in this chapter are consistent with Mokyr's view of the relevancy of specific skills to the Industrial Revolution, showing that indeed the occupations that were most significantly affected by the mechanization and technological changes of the Industrial Revolution in its first stages were wrights, carpenters, joiners, and turners.

Wrights, which were commonly millwrights or wheelwrights, as the ones illustrated in Figure 9.9, were in fact already identified by Musson and Robinson

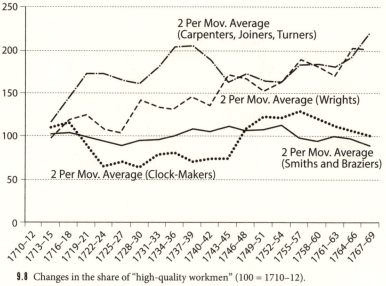

**9.8** Changes in the share of "high-quality workmen" (100 = 1710–12).
*Source*: Stamp tax registers.

(1960, 210–11) as the most relevant class of workmen to machine manufacturing, far before the eighteenth century. Their claim was that machines existed before the Industrial Revolution and were constructed by specialized wood and metal workmen, but that millwrights were of particular importance in this business. In their words,

> Power-driven machinery was not a new thing in the eighteenth century. There had long been wind, water, and horse mills for grinding corn, fulling cloth, working blast furnaces, hammers, and rollers in iron works, and

**9.9** Millwrights repairing a mill.
*Source*: Pyne (1806).

driving drainage engines in mines or fenland districts. There had long been specialized metal workers: ironfounders, brassfounders, blacksmiths and whitesmiths, locksmiths, clockmakers, instrument makers, etc. There must also have been specialization in the making of such primitive textile machines as spinning wheels, hand looms, and knitting frames. . . . Almost anyone, in fact, who was used to working in wood or metal might be employed to make machinery or set up millwork. . . . At a fairly early date, however, a special class of millwrights emerged, who were of particular importance in setting up the early mills and factories, and from whom sprang many of the early engineers.

What do we know about this class of workmen? The eighteenth-century millwright was described by W. Fairbairn (himself originally a millwright) as "a kind of jack-of-all-trades, who could with equal facility work at the lathe, the anvil, or the carpenter's bench. . . . He could handle the axe, the hammer, and the plane with equal skill and precision; he could turn, bore, or forge" (quoted in Musson and Robinson 1960, 211). They fall into the HISCO category "Machinery Erector and Installer" and are defined as follows: "erects and installs, in place of use, machinery and other mechanical equipment" (Van Leeuwen, Maas, and Miles 2002). As to their education, it is interesting to note that according to Musson and Robinson (1960, 211) millwrights generally had a good knowledge of arithmetic, geometry, and theoretical as well as practical mechanics: "It appears, in fact: that these millwright-engineers were not-as is often suggested-rough, empirical, illiterate workmen, but had usually acquired somehow a fairly good education or training."

## CONCLUSIONS

This article uses various historical sources of evidence to challenge the common view among scholars that technological changes were skill substituting in eighteenth-century England. Despite the scarce and scattered evidence for this period, it demonstrates through wage books from textile mills, labor contracts from Bolton and Watt's engine shop, advertisements in newspapers, as well as a comprehensive set of data on apprenticeship contracts that mechanical workmen were in high demand during the second half of the eighteenth century. They were employed both in the new textile mills and in the rising machinery sector. The exceptional and comprehensive set of evidence from the stamp tax registries enabled us to observe the distribution of skills that young people in England acquired since the beginning of the century and to trace their response to the great changes that were taking place throughout the century up to 1770. We show that the early technological changes of the eighteenth century were complementary to mechanical skills, mainly to those skills relevant to machine production and maintenance, including carpenters, joiners, joiners, braziers, clock makers, and, mainly, wrights. This finding is consistent with Meisenzahl and Mokyr's (2012, 446) argument that the high-quality workmanship that helped create the Industrial Revolution was able to "follow the blueprint with a high level of accuracy, carry out the instructions embodied in the technique, and to have the ability to install, operate, adapt, and repair the machinery and equipment under a variety of circumstances."

## APPENDIX

**9.A.1** Craftsmen's wages in Greg's Quarry Bank Mill, December 12, 1789.

*Source*: Greg's Quarry Bank Mill wages book, Manchester Central Library (C5/1/15/1).

## ACKNOWLEDGMENTS

I gratefully acknowledge the financial support from the Israel Science Foundation (Grant No. 1097/11).

## BIBLIOGRAPHY

Chapman, S. D. 1972. *The Cotton Industry in the Industrial Revolution*. London: Macmillan.

Clark, Gregory. 2005. "The Condition of the Working-Class in England, 1209–2004." *Journal of Political Economy* 113 (6): 1307–40.

———. 2007. *A Farewell to Alms: A Brief Economic History of the World*. Princeton: Princeton University Press.

Feldman, Naomi, and Karine van der Beek. 2014. "Skill Choice and Skill Complementarity in Eighteenth Century England: 1710–1770." SSRN Working Paper Series No. 2417894.

Goldin, Claudia, and Larry Katz. 1998. "The Origins of Technology-Skill Complementarity." *Quarterly Journal of Economics* 113: 693–732.

Humphries, Jane. 2003. "English Apprenticeship: A Neglected Factor in the First Industrial Revolution." In *The Economic Future in Historical Perspective*, edited by David A. Paul and Mark Thomas, 73–102. Oxford: Oxford University Press.

———. 2011. *Childhood and Child Labour in the British Industrial Revolution*. Cambridge: Cambridge University Press.

Justman, Moshe, and Karine van der Beek. 2014. *"Market Forces Shaping Human Capital in Eighteenth Century London" Economic History Review*. Forthcoming.

Lane, Joan. 1996. *Apprenticeship in England, 1600–1914*. London: UCL Press.

Meisenzahl, Ralf R., and Joel Mokyr. 2012. "The Rate and Direction of Invention in the British Industrial Revolution: Incentives and Institutions." In *The Rate and Direction of Inventive Activity Revisited*, edited by Josh Lerner and Scott Stern, 443–79. Chicago: University of Chicago Press.

Minns, Chris, and Patrick Wallis. 2013. "The Price of Human Capital in a Pre-industrial Economy: Premiums and Apprenticeship Contracts in 18th Century England." *Explorations in Economic History* 50: 335–50.

Mokyr, Joel. 2009. *The Enlightened Economy: An Economic History of Britain, 1700–1850*. London: Penguin.

Mokyr, Joel, and Joachim Voth. 2010. "Understanding Growth in Europe, 1700–1870: Theory and Evidence." In *An Economic History of Modern Europe, vol. 1, 1700–1870*, edited by Stephen Broadberry and Kevin O'Rourke, 7–42. Cambridge: Cambridge University Press.

Musson, Albert, and Eric Robinson. 1960. "The Origins of Engineering in Lancashire." *Journal of Economic History* 20: 209–33.

Pyne, H. 1806. *Microcosm or a Picturesque Delineation of the Arts, Agriculture and Manufactures of Great Britain*. London.

Van Leeuwen, Marco H. D., Ineke Maas, and Andrew Miles. 2002. *HISCO: Historical International Standard Classification of Occupations*. Leuven: Leuven University Press.

Wallis, Patrick. 2008. "Apprenticeship and Training in Premodern England." *Journal of Economic History* 68: 832–61.

Wallis, Patrick, Cliff Webb, and Chris Minns. 2009. "Leaving Home and Entering Service: The Age of Apprenticeship in Early Modern London." *Continuity and Change* 25: 377–404.

Williamson, Jeffrey G. 1982. "The Structure of Pay in Britain, 1710–1911." *Research in Economic History* 7: 1–54.

Wrigley, E. A., and R. S. Schofield. 1981. *The Population History of England 1541–1871: A Reconstruction*. London: Edward Arnold.

# 10

# A GROWTH AGENDA FOR ECONOMIC HISTORY

## RICK SZOSTAK

The thoughts I will share in this chapter regarding the future of economic history have their roots in my experience over a quarter century ago as a graduate student supervised by Joel Mokyr. Joel was the most open-minded of supervisors. Indeed we joked as I wrote my dissertation that I never followed his advice. Of course this was not true at all; those who read my dissertation or the book that grew out of it (Szostak 1991) characteristically spoke of how Joel's influence shone through. But Joel was one who respected his students' ideas, and encouraged them to follow their own instincts in matters of choice of guiding question or theory or method. Joel had a very broad view of the field of economic history. He insisted (rather pointedly) only on clarity of analysis. And perhaps most of all Joel was a teacher and a supervisor who infused his students with an enthusiasm for economic history. The way forward that I chart here reflects that enthusiasm and that open-mindedness. What better way to celebrate Joel than to encourage a more prosperous and influential economic history?

Joel has often stressed the importance of innovation in human societies. And he has carefully analyzed how ideas become accepted within epistemic communities. This chapter will suggest some innovations that could be readily adopted within the community of economic historians but with far-reaching consequences.

In our interactions Joel was agnostic about how much could be learned from economic history. I have always suspected that we could learn a great deal. This instinct was borne out most clearly for me when I wrote the book, *The Causes of Economic Growth: Interdisciplinary Perspectives* (Szostak 2009). In that book I surveyed what scholars across several disciplines had to say about the causes of economic growth, and used techniques of interdisciplinary analysis to integrate their insights (one of these techniques, mapping, is discussed below; others include redefining key concepts, adjusting theoretical assumption to alleviate conflicts, extending theories to embrace additional variables, and replacing false dichotomies with continua; see Szostak 2012a). Economic history—which I treated as a distinct discipline—proved to have more to contribute to answering the question than any other scholarly field. (I do not think that this was because an economic historian was the author—though it would have been hard for an outsider to identify the key lessons generated by our field, since these are not collected in one or even a handful of places.) This should hardly be a surprise: economic growth is a very complex process that can best be understood by detailed examination of the past. Yet one would have to search very hard to find economic historians willing to trumpet our claim as the main source of wisdom—or even as a critical source of wisdom—into the causes of economic growth.

Some of that hesitation may be rooted in the understanding that history never repeats itself. But while complex events or processes are never repeated in their entirety, particular cause-effect relationships are repeated all the time. Since almost all variables that human scientists investigate interact with almost all others (Szostak 2003), the sort of generalizations that can be drawn from history are often highly context-dependent: A influences B in manner X, but only if C and D are in place and F is absent. Only very careful historical analysis can identify such generalizations. And they will be subject to the problem of induction: we may find that novel cases (whether novel cases from the past, or future experiences) suggest further clarifications. Nevertheless, messy and imperfect historical generalizations can be a very useful input into public policy. They are certainly better than no generalizations.

Some economic historians may also shy away from emphasizing the study of growth due to a justifiable fear that growth—especially in our day—may do more harm than good, at least in the developed world.[1] Several arguments could be made in this respect (see Szostak 2009, chap. 1; 2012b). Growth is still critical to lift billions out of poverty (as it did in the past that we study). A type of growth in which we collectively took the benefits of increased productivity in terms of increased leisure rather than more stuff (or a type of growth that fostered the right sort of technological innovation) could be compatible with both a healthier environment and more benign cultural attitudes. That is, we could hope for a kind of growth that is "decoupled" from negative environmental (and cultural) effects.[2] If we wish to work toward such an outcome, we need to understand both the causes and consequences of (different kinds of) economic growth.

A greater barrier to our collective self-recognition of the role that we do and should play within the academy is our guiding methodology. Detailed historical case studies of particular events or processes are our strength.[3] Yet the disadvantage—happily a surmountable disadvantage—is that the case study approach tempts us away from the critical task of historical comparison. And

1  I thank Brooks Kaiser for raising this point with me after my presentation at the conference.

2  I thank John Van Breda for introducing me to the term "decoupling," which has often been used of late in the field of sustainability studies.

3  More precisely it is our combined use of different methods (including models and regressions) in the comparative examination of different times and places that is our strength. Methodological issues are addressed in the next section of the chapter.

without comparison there can be no generalizations. And generalizations are essential if we are to contribute to wider scholarly discourse, or even just impress other economists of the value of our field.

There are exceptions of course. Joel Mokyr's *Lever of Riches* (1991) is perhaps the most notable of these. In that book Joel tries to identify factors that influence the rate of technological innovation by comparing across three comparisons: classical Europe versus Middle Ages Europe, Europe versus Asia, and Industrial Revolution England versus the rest of Europe. Scholars of institutional change have likewise attempted to identify commonalities across historical experiences of institutional change. If not for these and other exceptions, I would hardly have been able to draw so heavily on economic history in my book on the causes of economic growth. I can only imagine that this collective contribution would have been much greater if these exceptions were the rule.

Of course, informed comparisons must be grounded in thoughtful analyses of cases. But the link between case study and generalization is a two-way street. Case studies will be better if—while maintaining a critical eye toward the idiosyncrasies of any situation—they are *explicitly* grounded in an understanding of how particular cause-effect relationships seem to have worked in other times and places. And case studies can often, though not always, be comparative themselves. One of the many pieces of Joel's advice I did take while writing my dissertation on the British Industrial Revolution was to compare the experience of Britain explicitly with that of France. That comparison served both to clarify and to strengthen my arguments.

We have already identified two of my recommendations for the field. These deserve to be stated clearly:

1. Economic history should recognize that its main purpose is the study of the causes (and consequences) of economic growth. This need not be its sole purpose: we can draw lessons from history about questions of importance to macro- and micro-theory as well. Economic historians who do not directly study growth processes should in no way be deterred from their inquiries. But note that macro- and micro-insights also indirectly inform our understanding of growth, since business cycles are inextricably linked to growth processes, and the economist instinct that economic efficiency is a good thing for growth is likely true much of the time. We can claim that we are the main contributor (or at least a critical contributor) to scholarly understanding of economic growth. (I will provide below even more powerful arguments for the centrality of economic history to the study of growth.)
2. We should be more explicitly comparative, and more willing to draw contextualized generalizations from our work. Note that it is hard to imagine how such precise generalizations can emerge in any other way than through the careful comparison of diverse historical cases.

A third recommendation flows fairly automatically from the second:

3. Our textbooks and our courses should reflect these efforts to compare and generalize. Imagine if the textbooks and courses in industrial organization all focused on particular sectors or countries. What would other economists think of that field? To be sure, one of the greatest tests of the combined body of scholarly theory is how well it allows us to understand particular historical experiences of economic growth. And thus (explicitly comparative) courses and books focused on particular times and places will always be important. And they should be supplemented by courses and books that explicitly pursue the generalizations of the field. I teach a course (at the sophomore or second-year level) called Technology, Institutions, and Economic Growth. It is more than just an economic history course, but it is mostly economic history, and draws many students into my senior courses in Canadian or European economic history (in both of which I stress the lessons we can draw about economic growth more generally). Notably, my macro colleagues insist that only I teach the course on growth; they do not want to teach a course about growth unless students have the prerequisites for a course that is entirely about formal models. I suspect that economic historians in most other economics departments could also make such a course their own.

The next two sections of this chapter both justify and extend these recommendations. The next section examines the nature of economic growth, and argues that only (an explicitly comparative) economic history can draw together insights from other scholarly fields in order to generate a coherent understanding of the economic growth process. The succeeding section looks at the methodological lessons that can be drawn from economic history for other economists and social scientists. The (lengthy) section after that then provides a number of suggested avenues for economic history research that flow from the recommendations made in the first three sections of the chapter. A brief final section concludes.

## THE NATURE OF ECONOMIC GROWTH

In my dissertation and first book (Szostak 1991), I produced a flowchart (see Figure 10.1) that showed the various ways that the improvements in transport infrastructure that occurred in eighteenth-century Britain influenced each of the three key characteristics of the Industrial Revolution: regional specialization, the emergence of the factory, and the increase in the rate of technological innovation. At the time, Joel Mokyr pointed out acerbically that economic historians were more accustomed to seeing such arguments in the form of a mathematical model. I did not see how anyone could do justice to the variety of

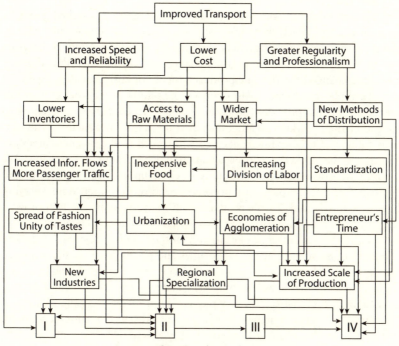

Stages of Technological Innovation

**10.1** Transport improvements and the Industrial Revolution.
*Source*: Szostak (1991, p. 29).

complex dynamic processes captured in the flowchart within the confines of a mathematical model. And I liked the flowchart, and kept it in the dissertation and book despite Joel's misgivings. But I have not published another one since.

One drawback of my flowchart approach is that it leaves the mistaken impression that every arrow is of equal importance. If I could rewrite that book I would stress a couple of key causal chains, and perhaps indicate these visually through the use of fatter arrows. The causal chain most naturally and frequently associated with my book involves market expansion and division of labor.[4] But my favorite argument was more novel and likely more powerful: transport improvements induced changes in methods of distribution; this change in turn rewarded product standardization; and this in turn required/encouraged both gathering workers in one place and mechanization. With the emergence of a national network of turnpike roads in mid-eighteenth-century Britain, entrepreneurs changed the way they distributed goods, a phenomenon that is well documented. Rather than leading packhorse trains around to fairs and markets,

4   Eric Jones invoked this argument in his presentation at the conference.

they sent out salesmen with samples and/or catalogues, dispatched goods by common carrier (which there was only now a national network of), and received payment by post or carrier. This transformation is dated to the years 1740 to 1770. But critically one could change the way one distributed goods only if one changed the way one produced them, for customers buying on the basis of sample or catalogue insist upon a more standardized product than cottage industry could provide. Thus entrepreneurs faced a powerful incentive to first gather their workers together and then mechanize production. The timing is right, and the argument fits well with much of the business literature that stresses the marketing concerns that often drive production decisions. We as economic historians are often guilty of overemphasizing production, and too easily forget that typical entrepreneurs spend most of their time worrying about how to sell stuff. Textile producers did not just produce cotton or wool but struggled to produce particular textile products *that they could sell.*

Though I sketched this line of causation for the British Industrial Revolution, it deserves to be pursued across other times and places. Many of the problems with agency that Avner Greif (and others) has examined for many countries and eras involve difficulties in ascertaining the quality (taken here to mean any characteristic of a good that is not easily measured but might affect the willingness of distant consumers to purchase it) of a good at a distance. If entrepreneurs are producing/selling nonstandardized goods, they effectively face two choices: selling face-to-face or operating through an agent. The option of sales at a distance to strangers is not available to them. The production of a standardized good allows a much easier, more direct, quicker (important for fashion goods in particular) and lower cost method of distribution. The quantitative dimensions of this transformation deserve to be measured. In the preturnpike, prerailway era, shipping goods by land long distances was expensive, and the nature of water transport has always favored the consignment of large volumes of goods. There was thus limited scope for direct sales at a distance to consumers or small retailers. With decent roads and then railways the world changed. Economic historians have always appreciated that mass production presupposes a mass market. But we have not fully appreciated that the particular sort of mass production that we most often wish to understand (production of standardized goods, usually in centralized workplaces) responds to a particular sort of mass market in which dispersed consumers and retailers expect to receive a highly standardized product. The savings in distribution costs may have been as impressive as the savings in production costs; moreover they came first and both encouraged and allowed the latter. When economic historians marvel at the size of some pre-factory putting out firms, they should explicitly appreciate that these were producing a nonstandardized output for a market that was reached through face-to-face sales and/or large consignments to distant agents. The emergence of the factory and increased mechanization of production are inextricably intertwined with the increased advantages of producing standardized output.

For present purposes, the point I want to make is that the flowchart approach need not give the mistaken impression that each arrow is of the same importance. Graphically, different arrow widths could be used to indicate hypothesized importance. I could thus have signaled the critical importance of the causal chain outlined above, while still noting that there were still several other ways that transport improvements fostered the Industrial Revolution (including the simple fact that innovators and industrialists were able to—and did—visit each other, and thus share insights regarding machines and processes not easily communicated by written word). And if we as a field became more accustomed to thinking in terms of flowcharts, then these would be interpreted more accurately.

As I look back on my career, the fact that I have not published another flowchart is particularly odd, for I have often urged others to draw such diagrams. In my ongoing research on how to perform interdisciplinary research, I have argued that only by mapping the various causal relationships identified by different authors can we be sure when they are talking about the same thing or different things. In Szostak (2003), I identified a lengthy list of the main phenomena of study in the social sciences and humanities, and discussed how these could serve as the nodes in a giant map of how the social world works. But I did not attempt to draw even a part of that complex map. And my book on growth talked at length about the complex interactions involved in generating growth, but did not try to diagram these (though I have asked my students to take a stab at this on their final exams).

While my original flowchart was designed to show the effects of transport improvements, it could be broadened to illustrate other causal arguments. Joel's arguments concerning the Enlightenment (Mokyr 2010) could, for example, be added: Enlightenment attitudes could have influenced not just technological innovation but the spread of information more generally. And various other nodes and arrows could be imagined. The point to stress here is that in our debate regarding the Industrial Revolution we are in fact discussing the relative importance of different nodes and arrows on such a flowchart. And we might just do a much better job of this if we recognized that this is what we were doing.

This point becomes much clearer if we pull back from discussing one particular time and place, and instead think about the process of economic growth itself. Figure 10.2 represents the study of economic growth, or in other words what economic history is primarily about. And, yes, it also represents the second flowchart I have drawn in my academic career, almost thirty years after I set the first one down on paper. And I am much better placed now than then to argue for the importance of flowcharts in general and this one in particular. (And the software for producing these is much better now too.)

Even this messy flowchart simplifies the complexity of economic history (for reasons of space and presentation) in many ways:

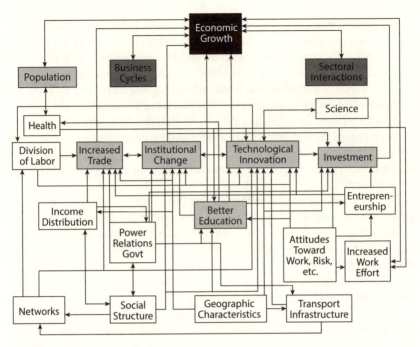

**10.2** Economic history.

*Source*: Based on the analysis in Szostak (2009).

- More arrows could be added (such as feedbacks from growth).
- More complicated interactions than the simple arrows drawn in Figure 10.2 are common: growth often requires new technology to be embodied in new equipment.
- More boxes could and should be added: human psychology perhaps, social capital probably not (Szostak 2009 argues that this is best treated as trust plus networks).
- Most boxes deserve to be multiplied: different cultural attitudes or institutions or types of education have different (causes and) effects, process innovation has quite different effects from product innovation, and microinventions from macroinventions; gender discrimination operates differently from ethnic discrimination, and so on.
- Path-dependent processes (may) operate within several key boxes.

So the real flowchart that defines our field is much messier than that in Figure 10.2.

Let us start with a few observations regarding Figure 10.2:

- Some economic historian has discussed (and argued for the importance of) each node and arrow on the diagram.

- Some scholar in some other field has likewise studied each node and arrow on the flowchart (see Szostak 2009 for justification of these two points).
- At least at the present state of understanding, it is not possible to capture all of these relationships adequately within a formal mathematical model. It may never be possible. Whatever one's opinion of the future possibilities of mathematical models, it makes sense to draw flowcharts now. These may or not set the stage for better mathematical models.
- Modeling exercises tend to assume that there is one way that economic growth occurs. But Figure 10.2 suggests that economic growth might just be driven by quite different forces in different times and places. Given the number of different causes, who can doubt that institutional change may be the dominant force sometimes but technological innovation be central in others? If so, then the sort of contextual generalization that is possible will not be accurately captured in the sort of mathematical model that is commonly applied. The flexibility of the flowchart approach is thus advisable.
- The subject matter of economic history is incredibly complex. What we do is discuss the relative importance in different situations of a wide array of phenomena and causal processes.

From these observations, further recommendations for the practice of economic history follow:

4. We must face up explicitly to the complexity of our subject matter. And the most straightforward way of doing so is to place a flowchart such as Figure 10.2 into our consciousness by placing it up front in our textbooks, and letting our students (and ourselves) know that what we do is strive to understand which causal relationships are most important under which circumstances and how precisely they operate.
5. Doing so is perhaps the best antidote to the siren song of monocausality. Joel Mokyr warned his students of the dangers of oversimplification. Yet we are all often guilty of providing a simple explanation of complex processes. If the economic growth process is a complex interaction of multiple causal forces (most/all of which are found to be of some importance sometimes), then is it not likely that major changes in the speed or direction of economic growth will reflect more than one change in causal factors? Monocausality exerts its fatal attraction upon us only because we do not see ourselves as trying to put various explanations together. But how on earth can we hope to understand economic growth within any time and place, much less more generally, if we do not try to pull the pieces together?
6. We should thus carefully place our arguments for the importance of a particular causal chain in a particular time and place within a broader understanding that there are always multiple causal chains of importance at work.
7. Economic history, as an explicitly interdisciplinary enterprise that has examined every relationship in Figure 10.2, is best placed to serve as the nodal

point for scholarly study of economic growth. That is, we can and should interact with all scholars studying particular causal links and strive to develop the best possible understanding of each node and arrow (and any emergent properties that can only be understood at the level of the system as a whole). If economic history is not going to assume this role, who will? (My discussion of methodology in the next section will provide further support for this point.) We have the capacity (and should have the will) to communicate with economists, historians (including business historians), geographers, sociologists, anthropologists, and others. The title of our field signals an interdisciplinary orientation. We should embrace this interdisciplinary identity.

8. Economic historians have known since at least the time of Gerschenkron that growth processes are historically contingent; we need to actively reflect that fact in our methodology. We are not pursuing the sort of noncontingent generalization that can be captured well in a growth model. We are pursuing more context-specific sorts of generalization.

Note that the flowchart itself serves several purposes. It changes the gestalt of economic historians, such that they see that they are working on parts of a more complex puzzle. It serves as an organizing device, so that we can place each economic historian's insights (plus those emanating from other fields) into their proper place. This in turn means that economic historians focused upon quite different nodes and arrows can nevertheless readily appreciate their shared purpose.

## THE METHODOLOGY OF ECONOMIC HISTORY

The perceived failure of economists to predict adequately or to cope with the most recent recession has encouraged much-needed self-reflection within the discipline.[5] Of course, this self-examination may well subside until the next time that the profession appears largely clueless in the face of some economic transition. Nevertheless, this moment of introspection within economics may be a good time for economic historians to extol the virtues of our methodology. This we can do only if we are self-conscious of our approach.

Why has economic history been so successful as a field in understanding the causes of economic growth? One part of the answer is that among economists, only we have been willing to follow complex historical processes across lengthy periods of time. One can hope to understand processes of gradual change only by doing so. Yet this alone can hardly explain our success. And since our

---

5 Many/most of the critiques of the discipline that are current today were foreshadowed in Szostak (1999).

success is measured against the contribution of other social science disciplines, it makes sense to turn for the answer to one of the best books ever written on social science methodology.

James B. Rule's *Theory versus Progress in Social Science* (1997) made a simple but telling point. He worried that social scientists focus on testing theories rather than explaining social processes. One problem with the former approach was that once a theory went out of vogue the research devoted to testing it became practically worthless. Given the tendency of at least microeconomists to cling to the same theory, this has been a less obvious problem in economics than in other disciplines. A second problem was that scholars thus looked only at phenomena or data implicated by their favored theory. This problem, one could argue, has been clearly evident in economics, *but much less so in economic history.* The perceived failure of economists to predict the most recent recession as well as the simplistic advice given to transition economies can both be attributed in large part to a failure to appreciate the role played by complicated financial regulations (and a bureaucracy capable of enforcing them). Since economic historians look at a wider array of information—and in particular the messy details of institutional form and enforcement—we can reasonably claim that we are much less likely to overlook such things.

Of course, scholarship is always grounded in theories. But Rule's point was about the emphasis a scholarly field places on theory versus explanation. Does a field prioritize the testing of theory, and look for nice data sets with which to do so? Or does it focus on explaining particular events and processes, and thus look for (or create) the best (set of) theory(ies) to explain that event or process? Economics as a discipline can be placed fairly firmly in the former camp (though there are of course exceptions). Economic history at its best falls firmly in the second camp: we focus on explaining particular events or processes (and then can draw generalizations from these). It is arguably unique among fields in economics in doing so (though some development economists pursue an explanation-focused strategy as well). I mentioned above that economic history can provide the best possible test of scholarly theory as a whole. But it can do so only by focusing on explanation and then asking whether there is some combination of extant theories that allow us to comprehend history. If the answer is negative, the explanation approach then calls for the development of new theories. Faced with the failure of theory to explain events, a theory-focused approach instead seeks either to modify the theory (as little as possible) or to ignore or mischaracterize the events that refuse to accord with theory. This analysis leads to two additional recommendations:

9. Economic historians need to communicate to economists and other social scientists the core message that a focus on explanation is indeed superior to a focus on theory testing. It is that very focus on explanation that has guided us to examine the details of technological innovation and institutional

change, and every other node and arrow in Figure 10.2. It is that focus on explanation that allows us to make context-rich generalizations, where the theory testers might simply ignore variables outside their theory.

10. Moreover, that focus on explanation encourages a host of other valuable methodological practices. Most obviously it encourages us to draw upon a wider range of theories: economic historians often apply evolutionary theory in particular. And the explanation approach encourages us to alter and combine theories. Likewise, it guides us to employ a wide range of scholarly methods. And this flexibility with respect to theory and method makes us inherently interdisciplinary.[6] Last but not least, our focus on explanation guides our editors and referees to ask "Does this paper tell us something new about the course of history?" rather than "Does this paper utilize the latest wrinkle in theory or method?," at least to a greater extent than elsewhere in economics. I have expanded on the value of these methodological practices elsewhere (Szostak 2006).

Some conference participants were troubled by these last two recommendations. They favored an "excel at their own game" approach to fellow economists: we can impress them only by employing their favored methodology excellently. To be sure, economists do reify their methodology and even in the present state of supposed self-reflection look askance at other disciplines where scholars might actually find it useful to talk to their subjects or read what they have written. But the glib answer is "We have tried that for fifty years; it is time for Plan B." Since the Cliometric Revolution, economic historians have produced many remarkable applications of the latest models and econometric techniques. This has not caused (especially second-tier) economics departments to increase their demand for economic historians.

A more powerful answer comes from reflecting on the nature of economic history. If we appreciate that some of the best insights in economic history come from books like *Lever of Riches* or the work of institutional economic historians in detailing the course of particular institutional changes, then we simply cannot do our field justice while maintaining that only models and regressions are valuable. I extol the explanation versus theory-testing distinction in large part because it provides a convenient way of saying that models and regressions are important, but neither necessary nor sufficient for quality economic history. What sort of field practices a broad methodology internally but is wary of advertising this fact externally? We cannot do our field justice unless we celebrate all of its accomplishments.

Why do we practice a broad methodology internally? Given that we are not entirely enthused about doing so, it must seem that we have in fact placed our

---

6 It is no fluke, I think, that two of the three editors of the most recent book on how to perform interdisciplinary research are economic historians (Repko, Newell, and Szostak 2012).

desire to explain above our desire not just to test theory but also to advertise our math skills. We should be proud of this fact. We should be proud that we have chosen explanation, that we have been seduced by the complexity and importance of the questions we address rather than by the siren song of methodological orthodoxy (though we have at times come close to crashing on the rocks of orthodoxy). We should be especially proud of this given that we rely on the sirens for our jobs and raises. It is time to remove the wax from our ears and sing our own song of explanation and flexibility.

Szostak (2004) detailed how all disciplines choose a mutually reinforcing set of theory, method, and subject matter. The rational choice theory that underpins neoclassical economics is perfectly suited to mathematical modeling and statistical analysis. Evolutionary theories (and other theories that economic historians might draw upon) are much less amenable to these methods. Appreciating an evolutionary process is difficult without carefully identifying mutations, transmission mechanisms, and selection environments. If in our search for explanation we draw upon theories beyond rational choice, we will not be able to test their applicability adequately through models and regressions alone. The same argument applies to types of data: if we find it useful to consult evidence that is hard to quantify (such as the details of a particular technological or institutional innovation), we will not be able to fully appreciate or advertise its importance if we cling to modeling and statistical analysis exclusively.

In sum, we simply cannot do our field justice—either internally or externally—if we accept the narrow methodological preferences of other economists.

I will devote the rest of this section to discussing what happens when our research questions overlap those of other economists (notably growth theorists and macroeconomists). Such areas of overlap provide the most obvious opportunity for us to advertise the virtues of an emphasis on explanation. Sadly, we generally succumb to the temptation of theory testing in such areas of overlap. I hope that I can thus encourage a more self-consciously explanation-focused approach as befits the grand tradition of our field.

One example of overlap is unified growth theory (Galor 2005). The essence of these models is threshold effects such that a slowly changing causal variable suddenly exerts a huge impact on another variable when a particular threshold is reached. These models are an undoubted boon to the theoretically inclined, for they allow us to explain *any* major transformation in history in terms of *any* gradual change in *any* variable. As the discussion of monocausality above suggests, there likely burns within the hearts of all economic historians a desire to explain their favorite event or process in terms of their favorite small change. If we were mere theorists, we could each happily employ unified growth theory and declare victory. But an explanation-focused field must appreciate that the theory here is the easy part. The very fact that the theory allows any transformation to be attributed to any gradual change (for the wonder of unified growth theory is that amazing things happen when a threshold is achieved) cries out for the production of evidence for any posited application of the theory. Let me be clear: I am not saying that unified growth theory is wrong; indeed I long suspected that it might be correct with respect to population density long before it was formalized. My point is that in refereeing a paper applying unified growth theory, the theory itself should be of scant interest. The referee should focus on whether there is evidence for the posited threshold effect, a careful description of how the threshold effect works in practice, and most important clear evidence that the posited transformation occurred wherever the (carefully defined) threshold was reached (or a convincing explanation provided for exceptions, along the lines of the context-rich generalizations urged earlier). In other words, the focus of the referee should be almost entirely on whether a sound comparative case study has been performed. And thus our celebration of unified growth theory should be muted at best: it is a tool as likely to lead us into error as into understanding, and one that provides only the first small step in any effort to understand particular growth processes.[7]

Some economic historians may wish to explain their favorite event or process in terms of some small one-time change (as opposed to a gradual change). Unified growth theory cannot help them. But there is still hope, for expectation-based explanations of the Great Depression (e.g., Temin 1989) perform this feat. Decades of mathematical modeling have failed to produce a model that can generate anything near the severity of the Great Depression within the confines of any/all macroeconomic theories. But what if we imagine that smallish changes (say a slight cut in money supply, or slightly increased tensions within the gold standard) made people feel pessimistic *despite the fact that no macroeconomic model suggests that these should have had much impact.* Then of course we can explain anything.

As with unified growth theory, it is critical that we appreciate that the "sudden mood swing theory of history" can potentially explain almost anything. People felt good, so we got the Industrial Revolution. People felt bad, so we got the French Revolution. (And we might publish our musings in both economic history and psychology.) If we accept the theory without question, we need never worry about oomph again. As with unified growth theory, though, we should appreciate that positing sudden mood swings is just the first small step. Theory-focused macroeconomists may celebrate the miraculous solution of their modeling woes. But explanation-focused economic historians must ask for evidence of the mood swing itself, its causes, and its effects. And there of course there is a problem, for conventional wisdom is not entirely misguided in its belief that the Great Depression was *a surprise.* Just as the business elite aboard the *Titanic* did not predict the iceberg, businesspeople steamed into the Depression voicing little fear. Moreover, to the extent that businesspeople were

---

7 I am reminded as I write this of a rather vivid memory of J. R. T. Hughes expostulating in class upon the value of empiricism over theorizing.

worried in the 1920s, they were worried about industry-specific challenges of saturated markets and lack of product innovation, not monetary policy (and even bankers in the 1930s may have been more worried about industry-specific problems than monetary policy when they refused loans). Again, I am not saying that the sudden mood swing theory is necessarily wrong, just that a self-consciously explanation-focused field of economic history would demand hard evidence for any posited mood swing.

The only application to economics of Rule's distinction between explanation-driven and theory-driven approaches of which I am aware is Szostak (2005). That paper identified ten turning points in the historiography of the Great Depression; at each point economists decided to focus on testing theory rather than explaining the Great Depression. That is, at each point there were potential answers to the questions that were troubling theorists that lay outside of the variables they stressed; these were in each case simply ignored. In particular, macroeconomists have simply ignored the highly unusual technological trajectory of the interwar period.

As noted above, economic historians study particular sectors (and their technological and institutional trajectories) in detail in the eighteenth and nineteenth centuries. But when we study the interwar period we almost exclusively apply macroeconomic theory. Yet students of technology know these things:

- That three of the most important process innovations of the modern world—assembly lines, continuous processing, and electrification—were adopted primarily during the interwar period. That is, this was when the steep part of the S-shaped diffusion curve occurred for all three. Worse yet, the investment required to introduce these largely occurred in the 1920s but productivity continued to increase through the 1930s as managerial challenges associated with the new technologies were addressed.
- That there was hardly any new product innovation between 1925 and 1934 (the electric refrigerator of 1931 being the big exception; notably hundreds of thousands were produced and sold in the depth of the Depression).
- That it is entirely plausible that the medium-term effect of process innovation is (usually) to reduce employment, and of product innovation to increase it. These effects may be masked much of the time as product innovations absorb workers shed because of process innovations.
- The imbalance between product and process innovation observed in the interwar period appears to be historically unique.[8]

---

8  Each of these points is addressed at length in Szostak (1995). In particular, models generating the medium-term effects of product versus process innovation are reviewed.

I submit that a more self-consciously explanation-focused field of economic history would have explored these stylized facts in as much detail as we probe the effects of technological innovation in earlier time periods. And I would note that the field of economic history can more obviously make a unique contribution to understanding the Great Depression through exploring its technological roots rather than its macroeconomic aspects.

The question of the causes of the Great Depression is quite simply *not just* a question in macroeconomic theory. *It is a question in economic history.* It thus deserves to be treated in precisely the same way we approach other questions in economic history (when theorists are not looking over our shoulder). To be sure a minority of economic historians have indeed studied technological aspects of the Great Depression.[9] But there is no critical mass, and thus such works can easily drown in a sea of macroeconomic theorizing. Ironically this is a shame even for macroeconomists, for their angst at being unable to explain the Depression with any (combination of) standard macroeconomic models might be reduced if they came to accept that some part of the Depression experience reflected causal forces outside the usual purview of macroeconomic theory. But it is an even greater shame for economic history, for adding insight to one of the most vexed questions in economics would advertise the value not just of our field but of our explanation-based approach.

Let me close this section with a final recommendation:

11. Economic historians can more/only convincingly communicate our message of the advantages of a focus on explanation if we as a field are more self-conscious in our dedication to that approach. When we interact with others we need to extol the value of our approach rather than default to theirs.

## PARTICULAR AVENUES FOR ECONOMIC HISTORY RESEARCH

This lengthy section outlines several lines of research that flow from the recommendations made in preceding sections. There is no pretense of exhaustiveness in this list. Yet it illustrates the types of research that economic historians should pursue. Given the arguments for theoretical and methodological flexibility above, the subsections below focus more on the questions we should be asking than the ways of answering these, though some suggestions of the latter type are made.

---

9  I thank Charlie Calomiris for raising this point.

## Different Paths to Growth

Growth accounting exercises, both in their earlier time-series guise and their more recent cross-section guise, are grounded in an implicit assumption that there is some central tendency in economic growth processes: that there is one way in which growth is supposed to occur. As noted above, the same is true of growth modeling efforts. The work is valuable but the assumption is dangerous. Easterly (2002) discusses how this assumption led the World Bank into decades of misguided policies (as when the bank's leaders calculated the "necessary" investment needed to achieve particular growth targets and then poured that amount into countries ill prepared to invest it). Economic historians have long appreciated that growth occurs in different ways in different times and places. There are differences across and within "generations" of industrializers, and within countries over time. In all three of these types of comparison, the obvious questions to ask involve the relative role of technological innovation, investment in physical capital, education, infrastructure, institutional innovation (especially financial institutions and property rights institutions), and structural change (the relation between agriculture, industry—and perhaps different industries, and services).

Economic historians were justified in rejecting the simplifications of Rostow's theory of stages of economic growth. His list of necessary preconditions was too easily shown to be anything but necessary (though some minimal level of infrastructure and institutions is likely necessary everywhere). This does not mean that each of these preconditions does not generally exert a positive influence—though more at some times than others. Nor does it mean that there might not be a limited set of possible combinations of these that are jointly necessary for growth.[10] Notably, economists have recently adopted the idea of "social capability" first put forward by Simon Kuznets but popularized by Moses Abramowitz (the economic historian) as an explanation of why some poor countries fail to catch up (converge). Economic historians could usefully flesh out what social capability might mean.

The task is daunting to be sure. But it is important, and clearly lies within the domain of economic history. If we do not take on the task it will not be done. And if it is not done, naïve generalizations will likely continue to exert an undue influence on both academic and policy discussions. While daunting, the task is finite: a handful each of different types of comparison, and of key variables to look for. A meta-analysis of the existing body of country studies would provide us with an overview of the present state of knowledge, and guide further research that would refine these comparisons.

---

10  The patterns of development identified for the early postwar era by Chenery and Syrquin (1975) and applied to the nineteenth century by Crafts (1984) are relevant here.

*Interactions among Variables*

Sachs (2005) and others have recently revived "big push" theories of economic growth. These theories rest on a different sort of attack on the growth accounting assumption noted above: that the supposedly independent variables in such regressions in fact interact in important ways. The problem the World Bank faced in simplistically applying the coefficient on investment from growth accounting exercises was precisely the fact that the relationship between investment and growth depends on the level of infrastructure, technology, and institutional development in the country. Big push theories suggest that growth occurs fastest when synergistic advances of different types occur together.

This insight renders the daunting task of the preceding section even more challenging. It is important not just to identify the relative importance of these various causal factors but to evaluate how they interact. The meta-analysis suggested above would still be valuable, but would be even more so if attention were paid to interactions. And this takes us back to the flowchart in Figure 10.2: we need to understand each causal relationship on that diagram.[11]

*Catching the Wave*

Might the success of some countries be related to the dominant technologies of the day? While resources are clearly not essential for economic growth, they can exert a positive influence on growth. And thus the relative rise of some countries with little coal but lots of hydroelectric power potential in the late nineteenth century may not be coincidence. If this is true for resources, it may also be true for institutions. Economic historians could usefully investigate the degree to which particular countries are successful in particular epochs because they are for some reason well suited to particular technological trajectories.

Gerschenkron had hypothesized that follower nations catch up in existing industries with existing technology. In the Second Industrial Revolution, though, Germany and the United States each excelled in new industries. Chandler and Hikino (1997) have suggested that existing firms have dominated more recent technological developments (they ignore information technology here it seems), and thus it has been harder for follower nations to catch up in new technologies. Economic historians could usefully clarify whether "catching the wave" is a more viable path to economic growth during some epochs than others.

11 Confusion will reign if studies of these diverse causal links are not organized. The flowchart in Figure 10.2 can be supplemented as necessary by reference to a common map of the scholarly enterprise. Szostak (2003) derived a hierarchical classification of the phenomena of interest to human scientists (the classification of cultural phenomena reproduced in Figure 10.2 constitutes one part of this) and showed how the diverse links associated with cultural change could best be appreciated in the context of this map.

## Creative Destruction

Nick Crafts has appreciated that one key insight of economic history involves the importance of creative destruction in the growth process (in Snowdon 2002). But we can still say relatively little about the precise nature of the sectoral interactions involved in growth. That is, we know that growth historically has been closely associated with structural change (and thus that policy makers need to appreciate that growth involves losers as well as winners), but we know relatively little about how sectoral interactions might *generate* growth.[12] The growth accounting exercises of Denison and others in the 1980s had suggested that shifts in sectoral composition of output were an important source of economic growth (they stressed the movement of resources toward high productivity sectors), but this insight has been little heeded by growth theorists.

Economic historians rarely use the phrase "leading sectors." Again, it was soon shown that Rostow had exaggerated the importance of these in the examples he provided. But in studying particular countries at particular times, economic historians have tended to emphasize the role of a handful of sectors. This attitude accords well with the outlook of the modern business press, which tends to the view that future economic prosperity hinges on the success of biotechnology or microelectronics. And of course many versions of endogenous growth theory emphasize technological spillovers from one sector to another.[13]

Social savings calculations capture some of the static effects of particular innovations but inevitably miss more dynamic effects: technological spillovers, investments that would not otherwise have been undertaken (in the case of transport improvements, the much greater interaction between entrepreneurs and innovators that resulted, and the opportunities created by a national market),[14] and so on. A more nuanced appreciation of cross-sectoral interactions is both desirable and possible. It may well be that the positive spillovers from some sectors to others play a major role in the growth process.

---

12  I focus in this section on sectoral interactions, but note here that economic historians could usefully integrate the generally distinct literatures on cross-sectoral and cross-firm interactions.

13  Szostak (1991) argued that the existence of a capital goods sector in Britain (especially in textiles) greatly stimulated innovation. Recent regressions by DeLong and Summers suggest a positive correlation between having a capital goods sector and growth. Yet many development economists are wary of devoting resources to creating such a sector in poor countries.

14  Ville (1990) argued that in the case of transport social savings calculations suffered not only from their static nature but also ignored the benefits of increased speed, regularity, and reliability of service, and moreover assumed demand to be homogenous. Nick Crafts has recently—including in his address to the 2007 ENEH conference—urged economic historians to examine the agglomerative economies suggested by the new economic geography, and thus to examine dynamic interactions missed by social savings calculations.

What of negative linkages? The idea of creative destruction suggests that the rise of some sectors causes the decline of others.[15] While this causal link often occurs, sectoral decline may occur for other reasons such as changes in tastes or access to raw materials. If sectoral decline is defined in terms of the proportion of the labor-force employed, then labor-saving process innovation is often the source of "decline." Szostak (1995) argued that the Great Depression largely reflected the shedding of labor in many sectors for this reason (due to assembly lines, continuous processing, and electrification) at a time when there were very few sectors with growth potential (due primarily to the almost complete absence of new product innovation in the decade after 1925). As noted above, economic historians in studying the eighteenth and nineteenth centuries tend to stress developments in a few key sectors—but for the interwar period sectoral analysis is abandoned in favor of applications of macroeconomic theory. If in fact aggregate growth *results from* (at least in part) the existence of more growing sectors than declining sectors, our approach to the eighteenth and nineteenth centuries has been appropriate (if undertheorized, and with too little attention to which if any sectors were declining), but our approach to the interwar period incomplete.

Product innovation usually encourages sectoral expansion, while process innovation usually encourages sectoral decline (in terms of employment; the results depend on elasticities of demand and substitution). A rough balance most of the time between these two types of innovation may obscure the importance of the relative size of growing and declining sectors in determining aggregate economic performance.[16] But it could well be that small differences in this balance generate much of the observed differences in aggregate growth rates across time and place.

Why are periods of rapid growth associated with low unemployment? Process innovation generates increases in productivity, but job losses. Product innovation does not necessarily enhance productivity but creates jobs. What we commonly call economic growth must thus at least usually involve both types of innovation. If only process, per capita incomes do not rise because of increased unemployment. If only product, we may observe employment stability but productivity slowdown

---

15 The obvious case is where a new industry produces a good that substitutes for the output of an older industry. But a more benign case is where labor proves more willing to leave declining industries when there are jobs available in growth sectors. It is thus possible that some of the growth attributed to investment (or education) in growth accounting reflects the fact that sectoral shifts are thus facilitated.

16 And may simultaneously provide us with an exaggerated confidence that the equilibrating mechanisms posited by macroeconomic theory work faster than our experience of the 1930s or even 1970s or 2000s suggests that they do. Of course, over the longer term, these equilibrating mechanisms will ensure some balance between growing and declining sectors—but this eventual steady state may be characterized by little aggregate growth or a great deal of aggregate growth.

The discussion above can be usefully phrased in a different way: Is growth primarily a macroeconomic or microeconomic process? If the former, then balanced budgets and appropriate interest rates are the key to success (and the miserable performance of African countries pursuing these policies for decades a deep mystery). More likely, growth is not something that happens magically at the level of entire economies: it is simply measured at that level. If so, then economic growth is the aggregated result of a host of entrepreneurial and innovative decisions. These will, to be sure, be powerfully influenced by expectations regarding macroeconomic performance. But entrepreneurs and innovators are primarily concerned with a particular industry (or two), and they will collectively generate growth if they see many opportunities at the sectoral level.

One hypothesis worth investigating is whether aggregate growth rates are positively correlated with variance in sectoral growth rates. If it turned out that a positive correlation was observed, this would provide empirical support for the idea that growth to a significant extent results from the existence of several (but never all) rapidly growing sectors. Of course, the existence of aggregate growth may dampen the pressures on some sectors to decline and thus weaken the correlation between growth and variance. Careful empirical analysis should distinguish between the two types of causal effect.

## Business Cycles and Growth

Growth theory has until recently been taught as one topic in advanced undergraduate courses in macroeconomics. (Happily textbooks now exist, such as Weil [2005], that facilitate the teaching of courses about growth itself, and as early as the second year—but these texts tend to be very weak in the very areas where economic history is strong. I use Szostak [2009] as my text.) This treatment implies that growth is somehow a result of business cycles (or perhaps macroeconomic policies; see above). But would we have (severe) business cycles in a static world? Business cycles, it must seem, are in large part a reflection of (the uncertainties associated with) economic growth and the structural change we have seen to be associated with this. Macroeconomists are only in the earliest stages of reorienting their field so that growth rather than cycles is seen as primary.

Economic historians might have progressed further in detailing the precise relationship between cycles and growth. Unfortunately, economic historians have tended to borrow macroeconomic theory uncritically rather than strive to place this in a longer run context. Robert Solow (among others) has recently called for a theory of the medium term—he notes that economic history is characterized by alternating periods of a decade or more in which growth is either fast or sluggish/negative (in Snowdon 2002). Such periods are longer than standard business cycles but short relative to the scope of growth theories (which tend to focus on some steady state completely absent from the historical record). Business cycles tend to be more severe during the latter type of era than the former.

Solow also noted that economists are unlikely to understand the relationship between growth and fluctuations if different theories are used to explain each. Economic historians have in other areas not just borrowed but developed theories of their own, and should not be shy of developing theories that capture the interaction between growth and cycles.

I have already outlined my own "theory of the medium term" in the previous section (and note that some macroeconomists have in recent years begun to explore the possibility of explaining business cycles in terms of sectoral interactions). I would stress here that the understanding of the medium term, and the influence of medium term performance on business cycles, is a subject admirably suited to economic history analysis, but one that has only recently been addressed in much depth in the economic history literature.

This is not to suggest that standard macroeconomic analysis has no place in economic history. Indeed I have long suspected that monetary authorities have been overzealous in their inflation targets in recent decades, especially in Canada. Economic historians could useful explore the costs in terms of growth of raising interest rates (or the benefits of stabilization policies in reducing uncertainty). The work of Greg Clark and others suggests that permanently higher interest rates deter investment, but it is less clear what the effects of intermittently high rates are. Will investment foregone in one year be taken up when rates fall?. If so, is there still a cumulative cost because the multiplier effect and learning by doing set in later? Economic historians can also explore the important question of whether sectoral adjustments to reflect different rates of productivity growth are indeed easier to achieve with positive rates of inflation (because workers accept real wage cuts more readily than nominal wage cuts).

A third possible causal relationship is also worthy of exploration. Both business cycles and growth may reflect technological innovation. Unfortunately, the link between technology and cycles is generally associated with real business cycle models, and the myriad shortcomings of RBC models have discouraged this type of investigation. A more nuanced and realistic exploration of this link is possible by appreciating that both investment and consumption decisions are influenced by the development of new products.

### Technological Innovation

Szostak (2006) and (2009) celebrates the contributions of economic historians to scholarly understanding of the causes and effects of technological innovation. I suggest here what seem to be particularly promising avenues for future research:

- Endogenous growth models have their uses, but economic historians have an important role to play in outlining the noneconomic influences on innovation: most obviously of the previous path of innovation itself but also political, social, and cultural influences.[17]
- The idea of general purpose technologies has been championed by Lipsey, Carlaw, and Bekar (2005) and others. The idea bears some strong similarity to Joel Mokyr's long-standing stress on "macroinventions." Economic historians can usefully investigate to what extent the causes of such innovations are different from the causes of other more incremental innovations.[18] They can also better than anyone else trace the myriad effects of GPTs through time. Notably, the extant literature on GPTs makes little reference to the distinction between product and process innovation, despite the quite different effects these have. Economic historians can usefully explore differences in both the causes and effects of product versus process innovation.
- George Grantham has recently celebrated the work of Abbott Payson Usher.[19] I would recommend the continued use of Usher's four-stage process of innovation: recognizing the problem, setting the stage, the act of insight, and critical revision. This simple model accords well with the latest thinking in the history of science where it is appreciated that an intuitive act of insight is always preceded by lengthy preparation and succeeded by careful analysis. Different causal forces affect the first, second, and fourth stages of this process (see Figure 10.1). Failure to appreciate this fact must blunt any efforts to achieve generalizations as to why some countries innovate more than others. (In particular, countries or organizations that are poor at critical revision may see their ideas stolen.) While the "invention/innovation" distinction is often overdrawn in the literature, Usher's process

17 Notably, Sherer has argued that companies increase research expenditures when they think a discovery is imminent. Correlations between research spending and innovation may thus reflect reverse causation. The ongoing research of Mokyr regarding the connection between the Enlightenment and the Industrial Revolution is an example of research on the link between culture and innovation.

18 Hage and Meeus (2006) argue that the sociological/management theory of innovation is simple: radical innovation in particular requires a diversity of perspectives, integration of these, and a high-risk strategy by group leaders (without any one of these, incremental innovation is more likely). Networks are critical. The interdisciplinary orientation associated by Hage and Meeus with radical innovation is noteworthy.

19 In a "classic" review archived on eh.net. Usher argued that innovation is of necessity a "historical" event. Indeed he saw a/the special role for economic history in the explanation of the emergence of (technological and institutional) novelty. Innovation cannot be predicted in advance, but can be explained after the fact in terms of the information that was combined in the mind of the innovator and the innovator's incentives to innovate. Particular innovations, that is, must be explained in terms of an analytical historical narrative.

might be extended to include later stages (developing prototypes, testing in the market/factory, and so on).

### Institutional Change

As with technology, economic history has much to be proud of with respect to scholarly understanding of the causes and effects of institutional change. Growth theorists, though, have noted that the developed world is characterized by a fairly wide range of institutional structures. That is, there appear to be more than one way to enforce contracts, provide financial intermediation, and make credible commitments of nonexpropriation. The danger is that this casual empiricism blunts the insight of economic history that institutions matter very much. The antidote is to delineate more carefully

- The key *functions* served by institutions. Financial institutions serve a variety of functions. Even "property rights" has several key elements, and moreover must be appreciated as a means to the end of efficiency in resource use rather than an end in itself.[20]
- The range of institutions observed to perform these functions (with attention to whether some perform these better than others). Rodrik (2005, 989) urges a "search and discovery" approach to institutional reform in less developed countries, in which attempts to achieve general goals (such as property rights or macroeconomic stability) that suit a particular country are tried and carefully evaluated. If economic historians could delineate the range of feasible institutions, such a search would be less prone to error.
- How the importance of these functions varies across time and place. Jones (2006, 131) applauds the argument recently made by Lindert that in the earliest stages of economic development European countries needed to focus on property rights but later they needed to develop systems of education. This transition is important, for governments move from playing a primarily permissive role in economic growth to playing a positive role. While Jones (2010) also appreciates the role of earlier transport improvements, it seems that Lindert neglects the earlier importance of transport infrastructure, and thus a positive role for governments much earlier in the development process.[21] The point to stress here is that the meta-analysis suggested

---

20 Norrie and Szostak (2005) show how the "Admiral system," by which scarce Newfoundland shoreline was allocated to seasonal fishermen in terms of order of arrival, led to superior resource utilization compared to private property. The change to private property was inextricably tied to year-round residence in Newfoundland, and made economic sense only in that context.

21 Transportation is another area of developed government expenditure with a huge influence on economic growth. Despite its similarity in both respects to education, transportation has received much less attention in the literature. Notably, both education and transport share some of

above should ideally be performed with respect to a wide range of institutional functions.

- How institutions evolve. The debate regarding the nature of institutional evolution is more heated than it need be. Of course there are forces at work that encourage the development of "better" institutions from the standpoint of economic efficiency, but these are not the only forces at work, and thus optimality is far from guaranteed (particularly if the environment evolves rapidly). And of course humans have limited foresight,[22] and recognize that institutions operate within a web of other institutions and cultural elements that we imperfectly understand, and thus tend to make incremental path-dependent decisions, but we also have the capacity to recognize some mistakes (especially if others have followed a better path) and correct these. Rationality is surely at work (sometimes altruistically, sometimes selfishly), but both imperfect foresight and the difficulty of transforming culture intentionally (and the success of institutions generally depends on cultural support) limit rationality's impact.

- Institutional quality. Kohli (2004), a political scientist, argues that the key difference in developmental prospects is between countries that can manage/enforce *any* institutions well, and countries that can manage/enforce *no* economic institutions well. Economic historians should play close attention to how effective enforcement mechanisms are. Such a strategy accords well with the emphasis on "institutional quality" when economists attempt to include institutional variables in growth regressions.[23]

## Culture

Culture has received a fair bit of attention from economic historians of late. Landes (1998) hails its importance while Jones (2006) suggests that cultural evolution is more a result than cause of economic transformation. Greif (2006) argues that cultural elements are a necessary complement to successful

---

the challenges of measurement associated with technological and institutional innovation (since each road and school has unique impacts).

22  Norrie and Szostak (2005) introduce the concept of an "intermediate institution," put in place by those in power to serve their needs but which sets in train a process of institutional change that they did not foresee and would not have deliberately encouraged. Similar, less formal arguments have often been made with respect to the decline of feudalism.

23  The results of such empirical efforts have been ambiguous for a variety of reasons: the very difficulty of measuring quality, but also ambiguous definitions of institutions (which economic historians could clarify), a tendency to stress political rather than economic institutions (economic historians could clarify how the former primarily exert indirect effects on growth via the latter), the different theoretical arguments applied by different economists (case studies can be invaluable in clarifying theories regarding the role of institutions in growth), and the tendency to conflate quite different institutional effects in one indicator (again case study research can be invaluable in isolating particular causal linkages). See Aron (2000).

institutions, but urges economic historians to assume the existence of rather than analyze separately these "unobservable" elements. Yet while cultural elements are less tangible than formal institutions, they are hardly unobservable. And thus the debate between Landes and Jones can be subjected to careful empirical analysis.

The first step is to deal with terminology. "Culture" is perhaps the vaguest term in all of human science. Notoriously, thousands of different definitions exist in the literature. Yet in practice culture can be disaggregated (or "unpacked" in the terminology of realist philosophy) into a hundred or so fairly well-defined attitudes or behaviors. The frustratingly elliptical arguments of many scholars of culture can generally be understood upon close reading to engage only a few of these at a time (see Szostak 2003). A detailed list of key cultural elements is developed and explained in detail in Szostak (2003).

Many of these cultural elements will be of limited interest to the economic historian. But those elements that are—openness to outsiders, trust, family versus community, and so on—are generally subject to some sort of measurement: by surveys or interviews or textual analysis.[24] And thus we can move past the literature rightly condemned by Jones and Greif that tends to assume (tautologically) that economies that fail to prosper must be characterized by unsupportive attitudes or behaviors. We can investigate connections between cultural elements and institutions or innovation or investment or other more precise components of the economic growth process.[25] Jones is undoubtedly correct that cultures evolve, but a reasonable hypothesis would seem to be that cultural elements, like institutions (and likely even more so since they are less subject to purposeful manipulation) do not immediately evolve to some sort of optimum from the perspective of economic efficiency.[26] It is also likely

24  Notably, when economists include "institutional" indicators in growth equations, they generally rely on survey information because of the importance of issues of institutional quality (see Aron 2000).

25  Guiso, Spienza, and Zingales (2006) note that economists have until recently paid much less attention to culture than have other social scientists. One popular approach is to look at whether membership in particular ethnic or religious group affects economic outcomes. Such memberships are easily measured and are also largely inherited. Both internationally and within countries, ethnic and religious differences do generate different economic outcomes (though within countries, studies of immigrants suggest that these will lessen over time). Moreover these differences are correlated with different values and beliefs (trust, social mobility, fairness, hard work, fertility, thrift) in both regressions and experiments. Guiso, Spienza, and Zingales admit that such studies can only be suggestive of links between such values and economic growth, and these links are hard to establish statistically. Comparative case studies focused directly on links between culture and growth seem thus to be desirable.

26  Blim (2005) devotes several pages to detailing differences in institutions (especially industrial organization and the role of government) across modern economies (including poor economies), and then shows that these both reflect and support value differences. He argues that causation is important in both directions, but does not explore the effects on economic performance (he instead

that–again as with institutions—some cultural beliefs change more slowly than others).[27]

## Other Possibilities

As noted at the outset, this section does not pretend to be exhaustive. It has listed a very wide array of potential research avenues in economic history, but there are surely others. Issues of trade, networks, social structure, education, demography, and infrastructure have received less attention than they deserved in the foregoing. Various geographical arguments—about country size, latitude, and access to (internal and) foreign markets—can likewise be usefully explored by economic historians in more detail, but were not addressed above. The issue of public versus private provision of services, and goods, and indeed the role of government more generally (corruption, importance of government as a growth sector itself) has been addressed only tangentially.

## CONCLUDING REMARKS

The main arguments of this chapter are to be found in the numbered recommendations in the first three sections of the essay. Together these constitute a case for a stronger, more assertive field that is more self-conscious about its purpose and its methodology.

The rest of the chapter outlined a set of more precise research avenues that exemplify these recommendations. Much of the above research agenda requires primarily more careful efforts at classifying: stating causal arguments clearly, identifying the range of possible outcomes, and carefully documenting under what circumstances each occurs. The complementarity between classification and comparative research should be apparent. In other cases, more theorizing is called for. Economic history has produced very useful and robust generalizations in the past; this chapter has striven to encourage even more in future. When theorizing, economic historians have more often than economists explicitly compared different theoretical possibilities rather than just arguing for one theory in isolation; explicit comparison is just good scientific practice and should form the basis of all theorizing by economic historians.

---

suggests on 315 that values completely incompatible with capitalism will have been weeded out everywhere by now).

27   Reflecting on the East Asian experience, Jones (2006, 259) provides a valuable methodological warning: cultural arguments must be justified by comparisons across many cases. It is too easy to compare a couple of economies, identify differences in culture, and argue that these were the source of differences in economic performance. Only by comparing many economies can one overcome spurious correlations.

And yes this essay's title is a play on words, for it is through contributing to collective scholarly understanding of economic growth that the field of economic history itself is most likely to grow in size and importance within the academy. And that is a legacy worthy of Joel Mokyr.

## ACKNOWLEDGMENTS

I thank Simone Wegge for making several very useful comments on this chapter. I thank Brooks Kaiser, Charlie Calomiris, Margalit Mokyr, and participants at the conference for Joel Mokyr, Evanston, June 2011, for many useful suggestions. I thank Lynne Kiesling both for organizing an excellent conference and for much appreciated editorial comments. The second half of the chapter benefitted from comments received at the European Historical Economics Society conference in Lund, Sweden, June 2007, and the Canadian Economics Association conference, Vancouver, June 2008. I thank Angie Redish in particular.

## BIBLIOGRAPHY

Aron, Janine. 2000. "Growth and Institutions: A Review of the Evidence." *World Bank Research Observer* 15 (1): 99–135.

Blim, Michael. 2005. "Culture and Economy." In *A Handbook of Economic Anthropology*, edited by James G. Carrier, 306–22. Cheltenham: Edward Elgar.

Chandler, Alfred P., and Takashi Hikino. 1997. "The Large Industrial Enterprise and the Dynamics of Economic Growth." In *Big Business and the Wealth of Nations*, edited by Alfred Chandler, Franco Amatori, and Takashi Hikino, 24–60. Cambridge: Cambridge University Press.

Chenery, Hollis, and Moises Syrquin. 1975. *Patterns of Development 1950-1970*. Oxford: Oxford University Press.

Crafts, N. F. R. 1977. "Industrial Revolution in England and France, Some Thoughts on the Question, 'Why England First?'" *Economic History Review* 30: 429–41.

———. 1984. "Patterns of Development in Nineteenth Century Europe." *Oxford Economic Papers* 36: 438–58.

Easterly, William. 2002. *The Elusive Quest for Growth: Economist's Adventures and Misadventures in the Tropics*. Cambridge, MA: MIT Press.

Galor, Oded. 2005. "From Stagnation to Growth: Unified Growth Theory." In *Handbook of Economic Growth*, edited by Phillippe Aghion and Steven N. Durlauf, 171–293. Amsterdam: Elsevier North-Holland.

Greif, Avner. 2006. *Institutions and the Path to the Modern Economy: Lessons from Medieval Trade*. Cambridge: Cambridge University Press.

Guiso, Luigi, Paola Spienza, and Luigi Zingales. 2006. "Does Culture Affect Economic Outcomes?" *Journal of Economic Perspectives* 20 (2): 23–48.

Hage, Jerald, and Marius T. H. Meeus. 2006. "Conclusion." In *Innovation, Science, and Institutional Change: A Research Handbook*, edited by Hage, Jerald, and Marius T. H. Meeus, 545–59. Oxford: Oxford University Press.

Jones, Eric L. 2006. *Cultures Merging: A Historical and Economic Critique of Culture*. Princeton: Princeton University Press.

———. 2010. *Locating the Industrial Revolution*. London: World Scientific Press.

Kohli, Atul. 2004. *State Directed Development: Political Power and Industrialization in the Global Periphery*. Cambridge: Cambridge University Press.

Landes, David. 1998. *The Wealth and Poverty of Nations*. New York: Norton.

Lipsey, Richard G., Kenneth I. Carlaw, and Clifford T. Bekar. 2005. *Economic Transformations: General Purpose Technologies and Long Term Economic Growth*. Oxford: Oxford University Press.

Mokyr, Joel. 1991. *The Lever of Riches*. Oxford: Oxford University Press.

———. 2002. *The Gifts of Athena: Historical Origins of the Knowledge Economy*. Princeton: Princeton University Press.

———. 2010. *The Enlightened Economy: An Economic History of Britain 1700–1850*. New Haven, CT: Yale University Press.

Norrie, Kenneth, and Rick Szostak. 2005. "Allocating Property Rights Over Shoreline: Institutional Change in the Newfoundland Inshore Fishery." *Newfoundland Studies* 20 (2): 27–56.

Repko, Allen F., William H. Newell, and Rick Szostak, eds. 2012. *Case Studies of Interdisciplinary Research*. Thousand Oaks, CA: Sage.

Rodrik, Dani. 2005. "Growth Strategies." In *Handbook of Economic Growth*, edited by Phillippe Aghion and Steven N. Durlauf, 967–1014. Amsterdam: Elsevier North-Holland.

Rule, James B. 1997. *Theory versus Progress in Social Science*. New York: Cambridge University Press.

Sachs, Jeffrey. 2005. *The End of Poverty: How We Can Make It Happen in Our Lifetime*. New York: Penguin.

Snowdon, Brian. 2002. *Conversations on Growth, Stability, and Trade: A Historical Perspective*. Cheltenham: Edward Elgar.

Swedberg, Richard, and Mark Granovetter. 2001. "Introduction to the Second Edition." In *The Sociology of Economic Life*, edited by Mark Granovetter and Richard Swedberg, 1–28. Boulder CO: Westview.

Szostak, Rick. 1991. *The Role of Transportation in the Industrial Revolution*. Montreal: McGill-Queen's University Press.

———. 1995. *Technological Innovation and the Great Depression*. Boulder, CO: Westview.

———. 1999. *Econ-Art: Divorcing Art from Science in Modern Economics*. London: Pluto.

———. 2003. *A Schema for Unifying Human Science: Interdisciplinary Perspectives on Culture*. Selinsgrove, PA: Susquehanna University Press.

———. 2004. *Classifying Science: Phenomena, Data, Theory, Method, Practice*. Dordrecht: Springer.

———. 2005. "The Historiography of the Great Depression." *Journal of Economic Methodology* 12 (1): 35–61.

———. 2006. "Economic History as It Is and Should Be: Toward an Open, Honest, Methodologically Flexible, Theoretically Diverse, Interdisciplinary Exploration of the Causes and Consequences of Economic Growth." *Journal of Socio-Economics* 35 (4): 727–50.

———. 2009. *The Causes of Economic Growth: Interdisciplinary Perspectives*. Berlin: Springer.

———. 2012a. "The Interdisciplinary Research Process." In *Case Studies of Interdisciplinary Research*, edited by Allen F. Repko, William H. Newell, and Rick Szostak, 3–19. Thousand Oaks, CA: Sage.

———. 2012b. *Restoring Human Progress*. Reading, UK: Cranmore.

Temin, Peter. 1989. *Lessons from the Great Depression*. Cambridge MA: MIT Press.

Ville, Simon. 1990. *Transport and the Development of the European Economy 1750–1918*. New York: St. Martin's Press.

Weil, David N. 2005. *Economic Growth*. New York: Addison-Wesley.

# PART III

# THE INDUSTRIAL REVOLUTION

# AMIDST POVERTY AND PREJUDICE

Black and Irish Civil War Veterans

## HOYT BLEAKLEY, LOUIS CAIN, AND JOSEPH FERRIE

With razor-sharp sarcasm, satirist Tom Lehrer's lyrics to "National Brother-hood Week" reminded his listeners that prejudice and discrimination were well-established phenomena: ("To hate all but the right folks is an old estab-lished rule"). In the early 1960s, one could still find signs reading "Colored Entrance" throughout the American South. It was widely believed that signs reading "No Irish Need Apply" were equally ubiquitous in northern cities at the turn of the twentieth century. Although historian Richard Jensen has ar-gued persuasively that this was largely a myth, the sentiment was real.[1] The main concern was their Catholicism, but the Irish also provoked fear among Americans because of their use of violence. Irish men often worked at job sites that were controlled through the force of Irish gangs; Irish women were often domestics. As famine wracked their homeland, the Irish migrated en masse to the United States. Despite the fears, there was no attempt to exclude them.

At different times in U.S. history, these two groups, the Irish and the blacks, supplied the unskilled labor on which a rapid rate of industrialization de-pended. For the latter half of the nineteenth century, it was the Irish immigrants. By the early years of the twentieth century, with the reduction of immigration from Europe, the "Great Migration" of blacks northward maintained needed labor supplies. In cities such as Lowell, Massachusetts, the first transition was dramatic.[2] Of the labor force, 90 percent was reported to be native-born in 1849, many of them of Irish ancestry. Six years later, only 35 percent were native-born; the balance was immigrants, largely from Ireland. This contributed to the "deskilling" of the labor force (whereby unskilled workers gradually replaced skilled craftsmen as capital substituted for labor) and to the rise of the Know Nothing Party (which was particularly strong in deskilled areas).

As industrialization preceded apace, scholars such as Oscar Handlin, who studied the Irish in Boston, found they were at the bottom of the occupational hierarchy (Handlin 1977, 70). Other scholars note that the Irish and free blacks

---

1 Jensen (2002). A song with the title "No Irish Need Apply" was published in London in 1862.
2 See Ferrie (1999, 161).

lived in the same neighborhoods and intermarried in the antebellum period.[3] Like the blacks, the Irish were often unskilled, innumerate, and subjected to discrimination. Notes Joel Mokyr,

> The Irish in Handlin's Boston were excluded from more desirable profes-
> sions not only by the prejudice and suspicion of others, but because of their
> lack of capital and training. Even the blacks, most similar to the Irish in
> occupational experience, did better than they did. . . . Even in peddling food
> and groceries to their own kinsmen the Irish seem to have done poorly in the
> USA in contrast to Britain . . . , which is fully consistent with our finding that
> the percentage of overseas emigrants in commercial occupations was very
> low and that they were, on the whole, not very numerate. (Mokyr 1983, 254)

After the Civil War, as industrialization firmly took hold, the Irish and the blacks were still near the bottom of the socioeconomic hierarchy, but there were some changes. The movement of southern blacks northward, albeit not in the magnitudes of the Great Migration, was still large enough to cause a deterioration in the relative position of northern blacks. The arrival of other Roman Catholic immigrants from Southeast Europe, many without the ability to speak English, led to an increase in the relative position of the Irish. Withal, this is still the period when prejudice against the Irish is characterized by the idea that "No Irish Need Apply."

This study examines a wide range of health and economic outcomes in a sample of Irish- and African American Civil War veterans in the second half of the nineteenth century. We find evidence of disparities between Irish and blacks and others in such variables as occupation and wealth, morbidity and mortality. The information in our data is from a variety of circumstances across the span of an individual's life, and we use that to attempt to explain whether the disparities in mortality are related to disparities in life experiences.

Our data were collected under the auspices of Robert Fogel's Early Indicators of Later Work Levels, Disease, and Death project at the University of Chicago's Booth School of Business.[4] The Early Indicators life-cycle health histories of Union Army veterans contained in the databases of the Center for Population Economics (CPE) provide insight into how well these two groups did relative to other veterans in the postbellum period. The Union Army Data Set (UA) consists of the military, pension, census, and lifetime medical records of white men from twenty-five northern states who served as infantrymen in 331 companies in the Union Army during the Civil War. The U.S. Colored Troops (USCT)

---

3  This is reported for New York in Bayor and Meagher (1996) and for Boston in Horton and Horton (1979).

4  The data set has been shown to be representative of white northern men who served in the Civil War and, more generally, of white northern men who became adults during the 1860s (Fogel and Costa 1997).

data set consists of identical records of black men who served as infantrymen in fifty-two companies of the Union Army during the war.[5]

For present purposes, the sample was limited to veterans who did not desert, who survived the war, and for whom an age at death is available. White officers were excluded from the USCT data. Whites in the UA database, both Irish and non-Irish, were divided into those born in the U.S. (native-born) and elsewhere (foreign-born). Blacks have been subdivided into those born in free states and those born in slave states (as those states were considered in 1837).[6] Table 11.1 contains the counts of veterans in each of the three groups (plus two subgroups for each group) and in the total that led to our final sample of 19,951 veterans used in the analyses that follow. For expository purposes, the four columns expressing subtractions from the initial total are expressed as percentages of the initial sample size.

Table 11.1 highlights several differences among the groups and subgroups. The foreign-born whites were much more likely to desert than the native-born; the two subgroups of Irish were less likely to desert than the respective subgroup of non-Irish. The native-born Irish had a rate similar to USCT born in a free state, while USCT born in slave states had the lowest rate of desertion. However, the slave-born USCT were 50 percent more likely to die in service than native-born non-Irish; the native-born Irish having a remarkably low rate. Finally, the database is much less likely to have an age of death for foreign-born non-Irish and blacks, whether freeborn or slave-born.

Using the individuals in the "final sample" in Table 11.1, we want to look at how mobile they were—where did they live before and after the war? In addition to their geographic mobility, we want to look at their occupational mobility; not all of them were at the bottom of the hierarchy. How many succeeded and where? We then will compare their health status by looking at the incidence of disease and their cause of death. Finally, we will look at survival rates of the various groups and calculate hazard ratios. First, however, we must discuss how we determine who is Irish—and how we can enlarge the sample.

## WHO IS IRISH?

The UA data include 1,817 individuals whom we know were born in Ireland or whose parents were born in Ireland. There are many more people with Irish surnames in the database. Some of these are third-generation (or more) Irish, for we know that neither they nor their parents were born in Ireland. Unfortunately, complete information is not available on veteran's birthplaces, much less their parents' birthplaces, and there are many individuals for whom

---

5 The work reported in this essay comes from a pilot study; the CPE is currently enlarging both databases. See UAData.org.

6 We also subtracted those who died after the Civil War ended while still in the army.

**TABLE 11.1** Sample Counts

| Group[a] | Initial sample | Deserted (%) | Officer (%)[b] | Died in service (%)[c] | No age at death (%) | Final sample |
|---|---|---|---|---|---|---|
| Non-Irish UA | 33,767 | 15.40 | 0.56 | 15.30 | 30.40 | 16,748 |
| Native-born | 24,480 | 12.10 | 0.69 | 15.70 | 23.10 | 13,704 |
| Foreign-born | 7,987 | 24.50 | 0.20 | 11.60 | 50.70 | 2,715 |
| USCT | 6,155 | 8.60 | 3.90 | 23.30 | 39.50 | 2,094 |
| Born in slave state | 5,049 | 8.80 | 0.16 | 24.40 | 37.80 | 1,869 |
| Born in free state | 636 | 9.30 | 22.80 | 12.90 | 39.50 | 179 |
| Irish[d] | 1,817 | 15.80 | 0.33 | 7.30 | 23.30 | 1,110 |
| Native-born | 469 | 9.40 | 0.43 | 0.60 | 5.80 | 395 |
| Foreign-born | 1,339 | 18.10 | 0.30 | 9.70 | 29.40 | 710 |
| Total | 41,725 | 14.40 | 1.04 | 16.10 | 31.40 | 19,951 |

*Notes*: a. Recruits' (and their parents') places of birth were determined using information found in their pension, military service, and census records. The non-Irish UA sample is divided into two subgroups: *native-born* and *foreign-born*. The former includes all recruits born in any of the present-day United States. The latter includes recruits with a birthplace outside of the United States. *Irish* is defined as any recruit born in Ireland or with at least one parent born in Ireland. This group is also divided into native-born and foreign-born groups, but the latter category includes only recruits born in Ireland. Finally, the USCT sample is divided into two groups: those born in slave states and those born in free states (as defined in 1837).

b. We dropped any recruit who ever became an officer from the black sample and only those recruits who started as officers from the Irish and non-Irish UA samples.

c. Includes all recruits who died during the war or while still enlisted in the service. For example, black troops who enlisted in 1863 (with a three-year contract) and died fighting in frontier battles or during the march home in 1866 were excluded from our final sample.

d. Subgroup totals do not equal the sum of parts because birthplace was not available for all recruits.

information is lacking to establish what generation American they are or whether they belong to a particular ethnic group.

Since some information required for our analyses involves linkage to U.S. censuses, and since roughly two-thirds of the names in the UA database could not be linked conclusively to the 1860 census, the 1,110 individuals contained in the final sample constitutes too small a number to address some of our questions. Thus, to augment the sample, we turned to the Integrated Public Use Microdata Series (IPUMS) One Percent Sample of the 1850, 1860, and 1870 censuses. We searched for surnames where at least twenty-five people had that surname and 80 percent or more of them were born in Ireland. The first restriction was to have sufficient numbers to suggest the name was not the result of a single family; the second, to make sure they were largely Irish. This generated a list of 201 surnames. In several cases, different spellings of names that would be pronounced the same were captured by this rule (e.g., Cain-Kane, Conner-Connor-O'Connor, Kelley-Kelly, O'Neal-O'Neil). As a result, we chose not to augment the list with additional homonyms (e.g., Kain or O'Neill) that did not satisfy the two restrictions. This approach added a total of 502 veterans to the 1,110 originally identified, to give us a total sample of 1,612 individuals.

The consequences of this definition were explored by examining several demographic statistics for the resulting sample against those of alternative rules of defining an Irish surname using the IPUMS sample. For example, a more restrictive definition might require that there be at least fifty people with a given surname; a less restrictive definition, ten people. All three cases assume that 80 percent or more of them were born in Ireland. Table 11.2 reports the results. Changing the rule for determining whether someone is Irish leads to minor changes in the summary statistics: the less restrictive the rule, the greater the percentage of rural veterans that are included. They are only slightly taller and are less long-lived, which means lower survival rates. Table 11.2 supports the decision to define Irish in this manner, but alternative definitions need to be explored.[7] Changes in the rule for determining whether someone is Irish lead to only small changes in these summary statistics.[8]

In Table 11.3, we use the variables reported in Table 11.2 to compare the different groups and subgroups. Height is correlated with both economic well-being and health. For non-Irish whites, the average native-born veteran was just under five feet eight inches tall, with the average foreign-born veteran approximately an inch shorter. The average native-born Irish white was

7 The 1841 Irish census was consulted, but many of the most common names found in that census are not ethnically Irish (e.g., Smith). See UAData.org.

8 Defining Irish in this manner means that it is possible that some with Irish surnames can be found in the USCT both because some slaves took the surnames of their former masters and because USCT companies included some white sergeants and other noncommissioned officers. These numbers are thought to be quite small, and we have not attempted for the purpose of this chapter to attempt to identify and remove them.

**TABLE 11.2**  Comparison of Alternative Rules for Irish Surname

| Measure | More restrictive | Our sample | Less restrictive |
|---|---|---|---|
| N | 1,437 | 1,612 | 1,848 |
| Height (inches) | 67.42 | 67.46 | 67.52 |
| Age at death | 69.04 | 68.61 | 68.56 |
| % rural at enlistment | 60.03 | 61.44 | 62.8 |
| Survival rate (1865–1900) | 72.37 | 70.86 | 70.35 |

the same height as the average non-Irish white (combining the native- and foreign-born), but the foreign-born Irish were two-thirds of an inch shorter than their native-born counterparts. The colored troops born in a free state were a half inch shorter than the average Irish troops (again combining the native- and foreign-born), while the slave-born USCT were a third of an inch shorter than their freeborn counterparts. Thus, there is a 1.3-inch difference in the average height of the tallest and shortest subgroup. It is no surprise that this measure suggests the health trajectory of slave-born blacks was poorer than that of native-born whites.

With respect to age at death, the non-Irish lived to an average age of 69.1 years, with the Irish living about six months less. The native-born Irish lived a bit longer than the native-born non-Irish, and they proved to be the longest lived of the subgroups. The foreign-born non-Irish lived six months shorter than the native-born non-Irish, but ten months longer than the foreign-born Irish did. The foreign-born Irish, in turn, lived about twenty months longer than the freeborn USCT. The shortest-lived of any group was the slave-born USCT, who lived to an average age of only 65.3 years, more than 4 years less than the native-born Irish.

The pattern in the survival rates of whites reflects the pattern in the average year of birth. The native-born non-Irish and Irish are younger than the foreign-born and a larger percentage of them are alive in 1900. The native-born Irish are about a year and four months younger, while the foreign-born Irish are about three years younger than the native-born non-Irish. USCT who were born in free states were roughly a half year younger than the native-born non-Irish, but their survival rates were several percentage points lower than what might have been predicted from the white experience. The USCT born in slave states were born, on average, at the same time as the native-born non-Irish, but the survival rate among those who survived the war was even lower than that of those born in free states.

The final column reports the percentage that were recorded as living in a rural area when they enlisted. Urban areas were defined as places where 2,500 or more individuals lived, so many of the "urbanites" are from quite small places.

**TABLE 11.3** Comparison of Various Groups and Subgroups

| Group | Sample size | Height (inches) at enlistment | Age at death | Average birth year | Survival rate (1866–1900) | % rural at enlistment |
|---|---|---|---|---|---|---|
| Non-Irish UA | 16,245 | 67.80 | 69.10 | 1837.37 | 69.31 | 76.15 |
| Native-born | 13,325 | 67.97 | 69.34 | 1837.95 | 71.57 | 79.27 |
| Foreign-born | 2,604 | 66.83 | 68.80 | 1834.73 | 60.83 | 60.26 |
| USCT | 2,094 | 66.71 | 65.29 | 1837.88 | 61.22 | 72.45 |
| Born in Free State | 179 | 66.97 | 66.25 | 1838.49 | 64.25 | 41.57 |
| Born in Slave State | 1,869 | 66.67 | 65.32 | 1837.88 | 61.69 | 75.47 |
| Irish | 1,612 | 67.47 | 68.60 | 1837.05 | 70.84 | 61.48 |
| Native-born | 773 | 67.81 | 69.50 | 1839.31 | 77.62 | 70.05 |
| Foreign-born | 821 | 67.13 | 67.94 | 1834.93 | 64.80 | 53.11 |

The freeborn blacks are the most urbanized by far, with a majority of them living in such places. The native-born non-Irish are the most rural, with almost 80 percent of them reported as such; slave-born blacks are next, at about 75 percent. The native-born non-Irish and Irish are more rural than their foreign-born counterparts, with a thin majority of the foreign-born Irish classified as rural.

## GEOGRAPHIC MOBILITY

There are two types of mobility to be investigated: geographic and occupational. Geographic mobility of the two ethnic groups can be seen in the following figures. First, consider the Irish. In Figure 11.1, we consider only those born in the United States. Of these, 52.7 percent were born in the Northeast, with another 38.3 percent born in the Midwest. By way of contrast, about 47.7 percent of the native-born non-Irish Union Army veterans were born in the Northeast, with 41.1 percent born in the Midwest. In Figure 11.2, we see where the Irish enlisted for the war, and the same distribution is present, with the percentages for the non-Irish whites at roughly 32.7 percent in the Northeast and 58.6 percent in the Midwest.

The growth of Detroit and Chicago is evident. At enlistment, we can divide the Irish into those who were born in the United States and those who were born in Ireland. The native-born Irish have already begun to migrate; only 36.3 percent of them remain in the Northeast, but 57.8 percent of the foreign-born enlist there. Of the native-born, 55.2 percent are now in the Midwest, as compared to 35.0 percent of the foreign-born.

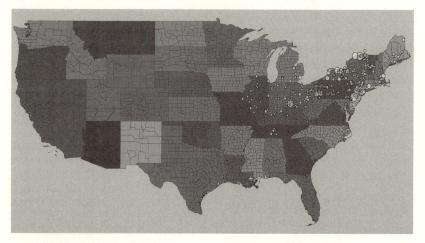

11.1  Irish birthplaces in the United States.

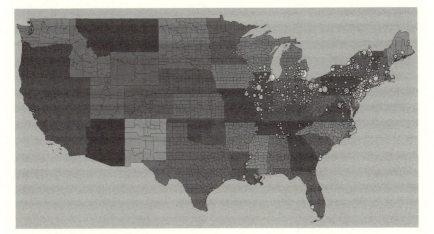

**11.2**  Irish enlistment locations.

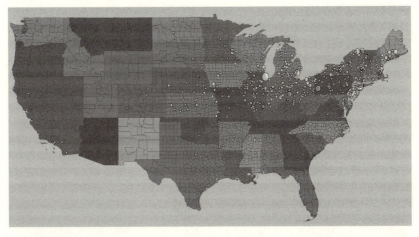

**11.3**  Irish locations 1890.

By 1890, as Figure 11.3 depicts, the percentages for the two regions have reversed for all Irishmen (35.6 percent Northeast vs. 54.0 percent Midwest). By this time, the foreign-born also have begun to migrate west, as the North-east was home to only 26.2 percent of the native-born and 44.9 percent of the foreign-born. The Midwest was home to 63.4 percent of the native-born and 44.6 percent of the foreign-born. The non-Irish exhibited a similar pattern as the native-born Irish.

Figures 11.4 to 11.6 provide the same information for blacks. Of the USCT, 88.5 percent were born in the South, with 5.2 percent born in the Northeast and

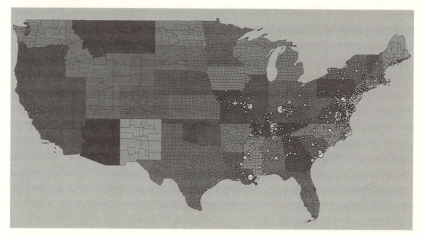

**11.4** Black birthplaces.

6.3 percent born in the Midwest. Of the native freeborn, 61.5 percent were born in the Northeast with 8.0 percent in the Midwest, and 30.5 percent in the South (as defined by the census as opposed to the Confederacy). Perhaps a tenth of those categorized as freeborn were born outside the country. Of the slave-born, 93.9 percent were born in the South, with the balance in border states. The birthplaces of USCT are shown in Figure 11.4.

The places of enlistment are roughly similar to birthplaces, with 80.1 percent in the South, but the balance is roughly evenly split between the Northeast and Midwest. For the freeborn, 66.1 percent enlisted in the Northeast, 7.1 percent

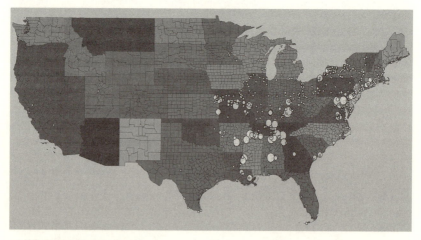

**11.5** Black enlistment locations.

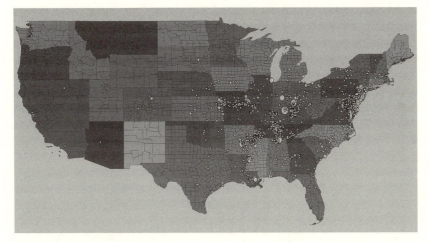

**11.6**  Black locations 1890.

in the Midwest, and the balance, 26.8 percent, in the South. For the slave-born, 85.0 percent enlisted in the South, with 4.9 percent in the Northeast (particularly the Middle Atlantic) and 10.0 percent in the Midwest (particularly the West North Central). The places of enlistment are in Figure 11.5.

In 1890, 70.4 percent of the USCT are still in the South. This includes 21.8 percent of the freeborn and 74.5 percent of the slave-born. The largest share of the former are in the Middle Atlantic, while the largest share of the latter are in the East South Central region. Of the USCT, 7.7 percent are in the Northeast. That area is home to 50.0 percent of the freeborn veterans, the vast majority of whom live in the Middle Atlantic region, but only 4.1 percent of the slave-born live in the industrializing Northeast. The Midwest has become home to 20.7 percent of the USCT, with 24.4 percent of the freeborn and 20.4 percent of the slave-born residing there. Of those living in the Midwest, the East North Central was home to 21.8 percent of the freeborn, while the West North Central was home to 12.7 percent of the slave-born. The result is in Figure 11.6.

Overall, the USCT were far less mobile than the native-born Irish and the non-Irish UA veterans. The problems faced by the slave-born are well known; nevertheless some of them are beginning to move north and west by 1890. The freeborn are slightly more mobile than the slave-born, but they too are less mobile than whites.

## OCCUPATIONAL MOBILITY

The second type of mobility to be considered is occupational mobility. We have adopted a six-way occupational distribution: high- and low-skill white-collar,

**TABLE 11.4** Occupational Distribution of UA, USCT, and Irish in 1863

| | Non-Irish UA | | | USCT | | | Irish | | |
|---|---|---|---|---|---|---|---|---|---|
| | Total | Native | Foreign | Total | Free | Slave | Total | Native | Foreign |
| N | 9,279 | 7,752 | 1,296 | 772 | 82 | 683 | 960 | 428 | 516 |
| High white-collar | 2.92 | 3.06 | 2.39 | 0.39 | 0 | 0.29 | 1.35 | 2.1 | 0.78 |
| Low white-collar | 2.14 | 2.08 | 2.47 | 0.13 | 0 | 0.15 | 2.5 | 2.8 | 2.33 |
| Farmer | 54.22 | 56.51 | 39.43 | 50.78 | 21.95 | 54.32 | 41.15 | 52.8 | 30.62 |
| High (skilled) blue-collar | 19.69 | 18.46 | 26.39 | 3.76 | 7.32 | 3.37 | 21.15 | 19.63 | 22.87 |
| Low (semiskilled) blue-collar | 6.81 | 6.36 | 9.88 | 5.96 | 10.98 | 5.27 | 10.31 | 7.48 | 12.79 |
| Unskilled | 13 | 12.18 | 19.06 | 38.08 | 58.54 | 35.72 | 22.29 | 13.08 | 30.04 |
| Unclassified | 1.22 | 1.35 | 0.39 | 0.91 | 1.22 | 0.88 | 1.25 | 2.1 | 0.58 |

**TABLE 11.5** Irish Census, Ship Registers, and Enlistment (Percentages)

| N | | 1841 Census | 1820–44 Ship reg. | 1863 Enlistment |
|---|---|---|---|---|
| 6 | High white-collar | 2.54 | 2.15 | 0.78 |
| 5 | Low white-collar | 2.37 | 2.39 | 2.33 |
| 4 | Farmers | 20.69 | 18.91 | 30.62 |
| 3 | High (skilled) blue-collar | 6.76 | 8.85 | 22.87 |
| 2 | Low (semiskilled) blue-collar | 10.85 | 17.89 | 12.79 |
| 1 | Unskilled | 55.35 | 49.80 | 30.04 |
| 0 | Unclassified | 1.45 | 0.00 | 0.58 |

farmer, high (skilled) and low (semiskilled) blue-collar, unskilled, with the balance being unclassified. We have two snapshots of these populations. The first is from the enlistment records, while the latter is from the 1890 census. The former is reported in Table 11.4; the latter, Table 11.6.

The similarities between the native-born and foreign-born Irish and non-Irish are immediately apparent. The foreign-born are much less likely to be farmers and much more likely to be unskilled, often industrial, workers. There are relatively fewer of them in the high white-collar positions, and relatively more in blue-collar positions. The slave-born are overwhelmingly either farmers or unskilled. The same is true of those born in free states, but the proportions of the two are reversed. They are more likely to be semiskilled than any group other than the foreign-born Irish. On the other hand, they are completely missing from white-collar occupations.[9]

It seems natural to inquire if this occupational distribution is consistent with other readily available information. These results are consistent with those in a sample assembled by Glatthaar for his study of the USCT, the census data assembled by Horton and Horton for their study of free blacks in Boston before the Civil War, and a sample assembled by Curry of free urban blacks in the antebellum period (Glatthaar 1990; Horton and Horton 1979; Curry 1981). In particular, Joel Mokyr calculated a fourteen-way distribution for both the 1841 Irish census and for the records of Irish migrants arriving in New York City in the years before the famine of 1848. We have compressed his fourteen categories into our six. Table 11.5 compares those results with the foreign-born Irish from Table 11.4.[10]

9 One would expect only a small number in these cells; the zeros are likely the result of a small sample size.

10 The tabulations of the 1841 Irish census and the 1840s ship registers in New York are based on Mokyr (1983, 248–49, tables 8.7 and 8.8).

**TABLE 11.6** Occupational Distribution of UA, USCT, and Irish in 1890

| | Non-Irish UA | | | USCT | | | Irish | | |
|---|---|---|---|---|---|---|---|---|---|
| | Total | Native | Foreign | Total | Free | Slave | Total | Native | Foreign |
| N | 11,652 | 9,764 | 1,697 | 1,573 | 135 | 1,414 | 1,165 | 586 | 566 |
| 6 High white-collar | 6.45 | 6.76 | 4.83 | 2.29 | 5.93 | 1.91 | 4.64 | 5.12 | 4.24 |
| 5 Low white-collar | 4.65 | 4.73 | 4.42 | 0.45 | 0.00 | 0.42 | 5.06 | 6.14 | 4.06 |
| 4 Farmer | 45.14 | 46.30 | 37.95 | 27.78 | 8.89 | 29.77 | 34.85 | 39.76 | 28.98 |
| 3 High (skilled) blue-collar | 18.03 | 17.27 | 22.16 | 4.70 | 2.22 | 4.95 | 19.48 | 20.48 | 18.55 |
| 2 Low (semiskilled) blue-collar | 8.69 | 8.46 | 10.19 | 7.88 | 13.33 | 7.43 | 13.13 | 10.75 | 15.90 |
| 1 Unskilled | 15.62 | 15.00 | 19.56 | 55.37 | 67.41 | 54.10 | 21.63 | 16.38 | 27.21 |
| 0 Unclassified | 1.42 | 1.47 | 0.88 | 1.53 | 2.22 | 1.41 | 1.20 | 1.37 | 1.06 |

It is likely the data from the 1840s and earlier reflect an older generation than that from the 1860s. Overall, white-collar workers are roughly the same total percentage in all three columns. The fact the percentage in high white-collar occupations is smaller in 1863 could be due to those that might have been in that group being officers or buying their way out of the service. The percentage of Irish-born enlistees who were farmers is somewhat higher than the percentage in the 1841 census and ship registers.[11] There is rough consistency between the census and ship registers as to the percentage of high blue-collar workers, but this increases dramatically in the enlistment records. And while the percentage unskilled is higher in the ship registers than the 1841 census, it is much lower in the enlistment records. While many of the enlistee's fathers may have reported being unskilled, the enlistees themselves learned a skill in the family's new country and worked either on farms or in high blue-collar occupations. There does not appear to be much movement toward the higher-earning part of the distribution from the 1840s to the 1860s.

Three decades later, the percentage breakdown from the 1890 census for the non-Irish and Irish in Table 11.6 shows increasing numbers of white-collar workers and a decline in the number of farmers, as one would expect during this period of industrialization. The percentage of high white-collar jobs has increased more for the native-born than the foreign-born, and more for the non-Irish than the Irish. The Irish have seen more or less equal advancement for low white-collar jobs. Otherwise, the distributions are quite similar. The difference between the native-born and foreign-born Irish has narrowed, but much larger percentages of the foreign-born are still being reported either as in semiskilled blue-collar jobs or as unskilled.

The movement off the farm is evident for the USCT as well, with respect to both the freeborn and the slave-born. As a result, more than half of them were considered unskilled in 1890, more than double the percentage of any other category. Also of note is the relative exclusion of blacks from high blue-collar occupations. It is somewhat surprising that almost 6 percent of the freeborn are now considered to be white-collar, but this is only eight people. One possible explanation for this result is that veterans of USCT regiments formed by free northern blacks were eligible for federal government jobs following the war. Clearly, a larger sample is required.

## WEALTH

The 1870 census reported wealth under two headings, Real Estate and Personal Estate. If the amount was less than one hundred dollars, it was not reported. As

---

11   The percentage of farmers in the ship registers for the 1840s (1840–48) is roughly half that in the 1841 census. This was likely to have changed once the famine struck.

Table 11.7 indicates, over 90 percent of veterans fall into this category. After all, on average, they were in their early thirties when the census was taken. Nevertheless, making allowance for the small sample size, there are some curious results.

Using the non-Irish Union Army as the comparison group, 93.0 percent report less than one hundred dollars of personal wealth and 94.8 percent report less than a hundred of real estate wealth. The percentage of the native-born Irish reporting less than one hundred dollars of personal wealth is one-half a percentage point higher, but that for the foreign-born Irish is 5 percentage points higher. A similar result is obtained for real estate wealth. There are no Irish who have accumulated personal estate worth more than five thousand dollars. In the one-hundred- to five-thousand-dollar categories there are over 3.25 times more native-born than foreign-born who report personal estate; for real estate, the relevant ratio is just over 2.25. We do not know how long any of these foreign-born veterans resided in the United States, but it appears that time in the country is correlated to wealth.

The more curious results are those of the USCT. Admittedly, the sample is small. The percentage of blacks reporting personal estate greater than one hundred dollars is larger than any of the white groups, and the percentages are higher for slave- than freeborn blacks. More research needs to be done to determine whether this result remains if the sample size is increased. Successful whites might have paid others to fight in their place, while successful blacks felt a war against slavery was their fight, even if they fought it as privates. Successful whites might have become officers, but blacks were prohibited from holding such ranks.

A similar, albeit less dramatic pattern appears with respect to real estate wealth. The freeborn USCT veterans are much more likely to report real estate, although none report real estate wealth more than five thousand dollars. This may be less curious in that the USCT came from, and returned to, rural areas. Also, by this time, former slaves were beginning to acquire land. Was land ownership somehow tied to improved health?[12] That is a question for further research.

One disappointing feature of our data is that a similar snapshot of wealth holding is unavailable at a later date for these veterans. What we can observe later in their lives is the distribution between homeowners and renters. Table 11.8 reports the division for 1900, when they were, on average, in their early sixties, and each group was experiencing some mortality.

Table 11.8 is consistent with what might be expected. The group with the highest percentage of owners was the non-Irish whites, with the Irish about 4 percentage points below, but considerably above the percentages for blacks.

---

12  Information on landholding by free urban blacks in the antebellum period can be found in Curry (1981), while W. E. B. Du Bois (1899) has information concerning Philadelphia.

**TABLE 11.7** Distribution of Personal and Real Estate Wealth in 1870

| Personal estate | N | % < $100 | $100 < % ≤ $1,000 | $1,000 < % ≤ $5,000 | $5,000 < % ≤ $10,000 | % > $10,000 |
|---|---|---|---|---|---|---|
| Non-Irish UA | 13,164 | 93.01 | 5.83 | 1.07 | 0.07 | 0.02 |
| Native | 11,364 | 93.02 | 5.83 | 1.05 | 0.08 | 0.02 |
| Foreign | 1,573 | 94.47 | 4.64 | 0.89 | 0.00 | 0.00 |
| USCT | 1,819 | 89.61 | 10.17 | 0.16 | 0.05 | 0.00 |
| Free | 159 | 91.82 | 8.18 | 0.00 | 0.00 | 0.00 |
| Slave | 1,630 | 89.45 | 10.31 | 0.18 | 0.06 | 0.00 |
| Irish | 1,398 | 95.78 | 3.65 | 0.57 | 0.00 | 0.00 |
| Native | 685 | 93.58 | 5.40 | 1.02 | 0.00 | 0.00 |
| Foreign | 702 | 98.01 | 1.85 | 0.14 | 0.00 | 0.00 |
| | | | | | | |
| Real estate | | | | | | |
| Non-Irish UA | 13,164 | 94.83 | 1.98 | 2.86 | 0.27 | 0.07 |
| Native | 11,364 | 94.91 | 1.98 | 2.78 | 0.25 | 0.08 |
| Foreign | 1,573 | 95.49 | 1.40 | 2.80 | 0.32 | 0.00 |
| USCT | 1,819 | 95.38 | 3.96 | 0.66 | 0.00 | 0.00 |
| Free | 159 | 91.82 | 5.66 | 2.52 | 0.00 | 0.00 |
| Slave | 1,630 | 95.77 | 3.74 | 0.49 | 0.00 | 0.00 |
| Irish | 1,398 | 95.85 | 2.00 | 2.00 | 0.07 | 0.07 |
| Native | 685 | 94.16 | 3.21 | 2.48 | 0.00 | 0.15 |
| Foreign | 702 | 97.58 | 0.85 | 1.42 | 0.14 | 0.00 |

**TABLE 11.8**  Owners versus Renters in 1900

|              | N     | Owner | Renter |
|--------------|-------|-------|--------|
| Non-Irish UA | 7,998 | 72.53 | 27.47  |
| Native       | 6,931 | 72.13 | 27.87  |
| Foreign      | 981   | 75.03 | 24.97  |
|              |       |       |        |
| USCT         | 924   | 42.21 | 57.79  |
| Free         | 72    | 50.00 | 50.00  |
| Slave        | 840   | 41.55 | 58.45  |
|              |       |       |        |
| Irish UA     | 778   | 68.77 | 31.23  |
| Native       | 449   | 68.60 | 31.40  |
| Foreign      | 323   | 68.42 | 31.58  |

The freeborn veterans of the USCT are almost 20 percentage points below the Irish, and they are evenly divided between owners and renters. Slave-born veterans are much more likely to rent than own, the opposite pattern of the whites. The wealth data suggest some black individuals did relatively well. How well and why they chose to join the USCT remain to be determined.

## RATED CONDITIONS AND CAUSE OF DEATH

U.S. Pension Bureau surgeons were instructed to rate veterans with respect to twenty different conditions that are listed in the left column of Table 11.9. The percentage of veterans in each group who were ever diagnosed with each condition is reported in the table.[13]

Overall, the white troops, non-Irish and Irish, are very similar. There are some differences between the foreign- and native-born Irish, but they too are very similar on the whole. With respect to the conditions where at least 10 percent of the population has been rated, the Irish are never more than, say, 20 percent different from the non-Irish, and often much closer. There are only a

---

13  These data are subject to several biases. Veterans who got on the pension rolls early (before 1890) as a result of an injury are less likely to have a chronic condition listed, as are veterans who got on the pension rolls for reaching age sixty-five under the 1907 law. Most blacks were placed on the rolls as a result of the 1890 law (they had a chronic condition) or the 1907 age law. Whites are more likely to be on because of the General Law (war-related disability) before 1890. This may lead to a different set of conditions being given and an underestimation among blacks if more are receiving a pension as a result of their age. A detailed analysis of black-white differentials based on these data can be found in Costa, Helmchen, and Wilson (2007).

**TABLE 11.9** Percentage of Recruits Rated for Condition

| Condition | Non-Irish UA | | | USCT | | | Irish | | |
|---|---|---|---|---|---|---|---|---|---|
| | Total | Native | Foreign | Total | Free | Slave | Total | Native | Foreign |
| N | 13,514 | 11,168 | 2,104 | 1,623 | 135 | 1,461 | 1,368 | 665 | 688 |
| Rheumatism | 53.71 | 53.99 | 52.66 | 64.08 | 69.63 | 64.20 | 52.41 | 53.83 | 51.45 |
| Cardiovascular | 45.29 | 46.79 | 37.83 | 37.58 | 40.74 | 37.58 | 44.37 | 49.02 | 39.68 |
| Injury | 32.09 | 32.06 | 31.94 | 32.84 | 38.52 | 32.24 | 39.25 | 34.74 | 43.75 |
| Hemorrhoid | 26.67 | 28.23 | 19.01 | 17.07 | 20.00 | 16.77 | 23.32 | 29.92 | 16.72 |
| Respiratory | 27.30 | 28.18 | 23.38 | 18.24 | 26.67 | 17.66 | 25.15 | 26.92 | 23.11 |
| General | 21.10 | 21.19 | 21.15 | 28.59 | 27.41 | 28.88 | 22.44 | 20.90 | 23.98 |
| Diarrhea | 22.21 | 23.43 | 15.92 | 5.73 | 11.85 | 5.07 | 18.13 | 24.36 | 12.06 |
| Eye | 18.48 | 18.30 | 19.58 | 25.57 | 26.67 | 25.39 | 18.13 | 17.74 | 18.17 |
| Hernia | 15.84 | 15.55 | 17.54 | 13.19 | 11.11 | 13.35 | 15.20 | 14.74 | 15.99 |
| Ear | 14.94 | 14.66 | 16.54 | 7.02 | 2.22 | 7.46 | 12.50 | 12.33 | 12.79 |
| Gastrointestinal | 13.79 | 14.45 | 10.93 | 6.47 | 12.59 | 5.95 | 13.74 | 18.20 | 9.74 |
| Nervous system | 13.13 | 13.49 | 11.45 | 7.02 | 5.93 | 7.26 | 11.26 | 11.58 | 10.90 |
| Genitourinary | 11.40 | 11.90 | 8.98 | 9.00 | 12.59 | 8.49 | 9.36 | 10.98 | 7.99 |
| Varicose veins | 7.30 | 6.82 | 9.70 | 3.51 | 5.93 | 3.29 | 8.11 | 5.71 | 10.47 |
| Liver | 6.73 | 7.05 | 5.42 | 2.40 | 4.44 | 2.26 | 5.77 | 7.52 | 4.07 |
| Infectious disease | 5.51 | 5.58 | 4.90 | 2.28 | 1.48 | 2.40 | 6.07 | 4.81 | 7.27 |
| Neoplasm | 1.53 | 1.54 | 1.52 | 2.46 | 0.74 | 2.67 | 1.17 | 0.90 | 1.45 |
| Spleen | 0.67 | 0.72 | 0.48 | 0.25 | 0.74 | 0.21 | 0.95 | 0.45 | 1.45 |
| Endocrine | 0.63 | 0.70 | 0.29 | 0.31 | 0.74 | 0.27 | 0.58 | 0.60 | 0.58 |
| Gallbladder | 0.02 | 0.02 | 0.05 | 0.00 | 0.00 | 0.00 | 0.07 | 0.15 | 0.00 |

*Note:* Subgroup totals do not equal the sum of parts because birthplace was not available for all recruits.

few differences between the two subgroups of Irishmen. The native-born were twice as likely to be rated with chronic diarrhea than the foreign-born, 84 percent more likely to be rated with a gastrointestinal condition, and 76 percent more likely to be rated with hemorrhoids. Why this should be true requires further research.

With respect to the blacks, the percentages are generally less than either of the two white groups with a few exceptions. The blacks were about a fifth more likely to be rated with rheumatism and a third more likely to be rated with an eye condition or a poor general condition than the whites. The blacks were less likely to be rated with a cardiovascular condition than native-born whites, non-Irish or Irish. This is the opposite of contemporary data, which show blacks much more likely to have cardiovascular disease than whites.[14] Both cardiovascular conditions and rheumatism received a gradation with the rating (the higher the rating, the higher the pension). Other things equal, whether blacks received a reduced rating for rheumatism while whites received an inflated rating for cardiovascular (and the likelihood of a higher pension) needs to be studied. With the exception of general appearance and hernia, for each condition for which at least 10 percent of freeborn blacks were rated, slave-born blacks were less likely to receive a rating. With the exception of rheumatism, an eye condition, or a poor general appearance, blacks were about two-thirds as likely as whites to receive a rating. When this is broken down between freeborn and slave-born, the average percentage for the residual conditions for each group divided by the average percentage for the non-Irish whites become 80 percent and 66 percent, respectively. The lack of ratings for black veterans might suggest blacks were healthier, but it is more likely explained by discrimination.[15]

The information on death by cause (see Table 11.10) raises questions similar to those from the ratings data. A cardiovascular condition is the leading cause of death in each group and subgroup, accounting for over 30 percent of deaths in whites and freeborn blacks. Curiously, slave-born blacks have a greater than 6-percentage-point lower incidence of a cardiovascular condition being reported as the cause of death than any white subgroup and over 4-percentage-point lower incidence than freeborn blacks. Since it was most unlikely that the surgeon completing the report for the Pension Bureau was the same person as the doctor signing the death certificate, there is unlikely to be a direct relationship here. However, the fact a veteran received a rating (and a pension) for a particular condition may have influenced what was listed as the cause of death. This requires additional research.

---

14  See, for example, Barr (2008), Hogue, Hargraves, and Collins (2000), or Nakamura (1999).

15  The percentage distributions for the subcategories of cardiovascular reveal three major differences between white and black: impaired circulation, palpitations, and, especially, cyanosis. Because cyanosis is identified by a bluish skin color, it is much harder to discover on darker-pigmented skins. However, this explains less than half the difference between white and black.

**TABLE 11.10** Cause of Death

| Condition | Non-Irish UA | | | USCT | | | Irish | | |
|---|---|---|---|---|---|---|---|---|---|
| | Total | Native | Foreign | Total | Free | Slave | Total | Native | Foreign |
| N | 8,917 | 7,306 | 1,438 | 1,060 | 100 | 938 | 893 | 427 | 456 |
| Cardiovascular | 33.12 | 33.59 | 31.78 | 26.13 | 30.00 | 25.69 | 31.58 | 32.32 | 31.36 |
| Respiratory | 12.68 | 12.54 | 13.00 | 16.32 | 10.00 | 17.16 | 14.45 | 13.58 | 14.91 |
| Infectious disease | 10.72 | 10.62 | 10.78 | 15.19 | 17.00 | 14.93 | 11.42 | 9.84 | 12.72 |
| Genitourinary | 9.44 | 9.57 | 8.90 | 11.13 | 10.00 | 11.30 | 10.41 | 12.41 | 8.77 |
| Nervous system | 5.51 | 5.56 | 5.29 | 4.72 | 5.00 | 4.58 | 4.93 | 5.15 | 4.82 |
| General appearance | 5.46 | 5.37 | 6.05 | 8.02 | 7.00 | 8.21 | 4.14 | 4.22 | 3.95 |
| Gastrointestinal | 5.44 | 5.39 | 5.84 | 3.40 | 1.00 | 3.73 | 3.92 | 3.75 | 3.73 |
| Neoplasm | 4.97 | 4.78 | 6.12 | 1.70 | 4.00 | 1.49 | 4.93 | 4.92 | 4.82 |
| Injury | 4.07 | 3.91 | 4.52 | 4.81 | 8.00 | 4.48 | 5.94 | 5.15 | 6.80 |
| Diarrhea | 3.50 | 3.71 | 2.09 | 3.40 | 2.00 | 3.30 | 4.14 | 4.68 | 3.73 |
| Other | 2.00 | 1.97 | 2.09 | 1.60 | 2.00 | 1.60 | 2.24 | 2.11 | 2.41 |
| Rheumatism | 1.14 | 1.04 | 1.60 | 2.08 | 3.00 | 2.03 | 0.78 | 0.70 | 0.88 |
| Endocrine | 1.10 | 1.16 | 0.70 | 0.85 | 1.00 | 0.85 | 0.67 | 0.94 | 0.44 |
| Suicide | 0.64 | 0.57 | 1.04 | 0.19 | 0.00 | 0.21 | 0.45 | 0.23 | 0.66 |
| Liver | 0.12 | 0.12 | 0.14 | 0.38 | 0.00 | 0.32 | 0.00 | 0.00 | 0.00 |
| Ear | 0.04 | 0.05 | 0.00 | 0.00 | 0.00 | 0.00 | 0.00 | 0.00 | 0.00 |
| Spleen | 0.02 | 0.03 | 0.00 | 0.00 | 0.00 | 0.00 | 0.00 | 0.00 | 0.00 |
| Eye | 0.02 | 0.01 | 0.07 | 0.09 | 0.00 | 0.11 | 0.00 | 0.00 | 0.00 |

*Note:* Subgroup totals do not equal the sum of parts because birthplace was not available for all recruits.

Respiratory conditions and infectious diseases were the second and third most common death causes for non-Irish whites. This was true for the Irish as well, but genitourinary conditions were a close fourth for the combined group. For the native-born Irish, genitourinary conditions were more common than infectious diseases. For freeborn blacks, infectious diseases were the second most common cause with an incidence 50 percent above either of the white groups. Infectious diseases were also a more common cause for slave-born blacks, but they ranked behind respiratory disease. Slave-born blacks had the largest incidence of respiratory disease; freeborn blacks, the lowest. The reasons for that require more research.

Given the lower incidence of cardiovascular causes among blacks, other causes will assume greater importance. Relative to the non-Irish, blacks were more likely to die from any of the next three ranked conditions: respiratory conditions, infectious diseases, and genitourinary conditions. The incidence of rheumatism and general appearance as a death cause are also higher, but the percentages are low. Freeborn blacks were also more likely to die of injuries. On the other hand, blacks were much less likely than the white groups to be reported dying of neoplasms. Given that many of these are likely to have been skin cancers, this isn't surprising.

Like the blacks, the Irish have greater incidences of respiratory conditions, infectious diseases, and genitourinary conditions. The former two are more prominent in the foreign-born Irish; the latter, in the native-born Irish. To the extent that respiratory conditions and infectious diseases are a reflection of people living in dense and less affluent conditions, it may help explain the higher incidence among these groups. It may also explain the lower incidence of cardiovascular disease, but it cannot explain the entire difference. Much more work is required to understand the patterns in these two tables, especially the smaller percentage of blacks reported as dying from cardiovascular conditions.

## SURVIVAL RATES

Death information exists for many of the veterans in the various groups, and this permits the construction of survival curves for each subgroup. It is important to keep in mind that these are not survival curves for the male cohort born circa 1840; these are the survival curves of groups of men healthy enough to be inducted into the Union Army and lucky enough to survive the insults of battle and disease during the war. Since most of the information about death places is found in the pension records, they are biased by those veterans who survived until 1890. Before that date, when the law creating a service pension was passed, disability pensions were awarded to those who were severely injured and impaired during the Civil War. Roughly half the veterans in the panel were not eligible for a pension initially, and may not have been able to apply under the service pension law, especially if they died before 1890. Since many veterans did not enter the pension system until after 1890, the sample found in the death records is more representative of those veterans who survived until then.

The USCT have the worst experience, with the difference between that group and the others widening. Although survival curves for the subgroups are not reported here, the reason for this is associated with the slave-born USCT. The freeborn have survival rates 6 to 8 percent higher the slave-born until they reach their early eighties. A similar pattern is true among the Irish, among whom the native-born have higher rates than the foreign-born until about the same age (early eighties). The freeborn USCT and foreign-born non-Irish have the highest survival rates at young ages. Their survival begins to fall below the native-born non-Irish in their late fifties. What is evident in both versions of the figure is that the experience of the U.S.-born non-Irish whites is typically at or near the best. More detail can be found in calculation of hazard ratios.

Figure 11.7a depicts survival curves by year (1865 = 1) for the three major groups. The Irish seem to have more or less the same experience as the non-Irish until about 1908, then their survival falls quickly. This is about when you would expect the great difference in average birth years to have its effect; 1904 is

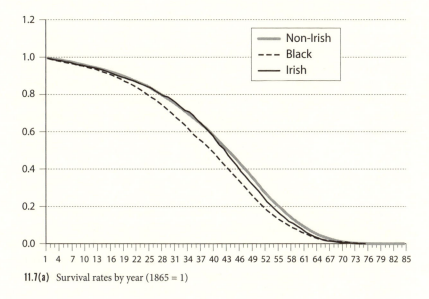

**11.7(a)** Survival rates by year (1865 = 1)

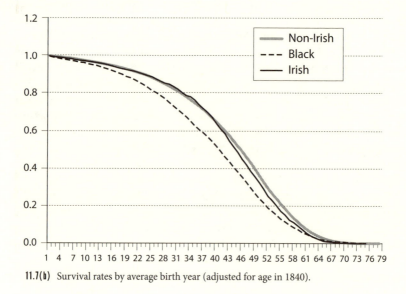

**11.7(b)** Survival rates by average birth year (adjusted for age in 1840).

the year the average foreign-born Irish veteran turned seventy. The USCT, who are approximately the same age as the others, have lower survival rates.

In Figure 11b, the curves in Figure 11.7a have been adjusted so that the horizontal axis is age as opposed to year. We shifted the Irish and black groups to the right or the left, so, on average, they match the average age of the non-Irish, who again serve as our comparison group. Given that the average non-Irishman was twenty-nine in 1866 and the average member of the USCT did not become twenty-nine until 1867, those curves have been shifted by one year to the left. The result is Figure 11.7b.

## HAZARD RATIOS

We calculated hazard ratios using a pooled logistic regression model for the discrete time hazards in the surgeons' certificates.[16] The results are in Table 11.11. We adopted 1890 as the baseline; the regressions are defined to include only those veterans who were alive in 1890, whether they received a pension before that year or not. This additional limitation is necessary given that a significant portion of our "final sample" was not eligible for a pension until the reforms of 1890, and we do not necessarily know which of them died before 1890. In these

---

16 There are well-defined problems that emerge when this specification is used with a fixed population. Each group has a survivor rate of one at the start, and they each have a rate of zero by some year.

regressions, the dependent variable is a time-dependent indicator for having died in a particular year during or after 1890. Controls include age in 1840 (the hazard ratio increases at approximately 10 percent for each additional year a veteran lived) and a cubic time trend. Coefficients with a $p$ value less than 10 percent are highlighted.

Regression I includes only an indicator for which population group a veteran belonged. The omitted group is the native-born non-Irish whites; foreign-born non-Irish whites are included as a separate group and have a ratio a little less than 10 percent higher. Slave-born blacks had a higher ratio (1.246) than freeborn blacks (1.197). That for foreign-born Irish, the first generation in the United States, was 1.219, slightly less than that for slave-born blacks. Finally, the other native-born Irish had a hazard ratio roughly 8 percent higher than native-born non-Irish. As more and more control variables are added to this basic regression, the ratio that retains $p$ values of 10 percent or less (those in bold) are the slave-born blacks. It remains high in every specification.

Regression II adds a set of controls for place. Urban (large) indicates a place larger than fifty thousand in the 1860 census; urban (small) indicates a place larger than ten thousand but less than fifty thousand; and foreign is outside the United States. The omitted group is a rural place. The places reflect three distinct time points in veterans' lives: where they were born, where they enlisted, and where they died. The urban mortality penalty is immediately evident in that the urban coefficients are generally greater than one, and urban (large) is typically greater than urban (small).[17] Furthermore, even as additional controls are added, these results persist. Consistent with the findings of Cain and Hong (2009), a foreign birthplace is as hazardous as a large American city, but there are too few veterans with foreign death places to be able to say they were in any manner different than the others.

A series of controls reflecting the person's life around the time of enlistment is added in regression III. The first is a set of occupational variables reflective of those reported in Table 11.6. The omitted group is the unskilled. High-skilled blue-collar workers had a lower hazard than any of the other occupational groups. The hazard ratios for high-skilled white-collar workers ranked second best. An early enlistment year increased one's hazard as did being wounded during the war. Being tall, being sick during the war, surviving life in POW camps, and beginning one's service as a private did little to one's hazard. That said, an increase of one inch in height increased one's hazard by a little over 1 percent. This is somewhat surprising and needs further investigation.

The final set of controls added in regression IV reflect conditions with which a veteran could be rated as part of the Union Army pension program. Everything else equal, the highest hazards were for a poor general appearance or varicose veins. Why this should be true is unclear. Why a gastrointestinal condition

---

17  See Cain and Hong (2009) for a discussion of the urban mortality penalty in a study using similar data.

**TABLE 11.11**  Hazard Ratio Regressions

| | Odds Ratio | | | |
| --- | --- | --- | --- | --- |
| | I | II | III | IV |
| **Group** | | | | |
| UA (foreign) | 1.089** | 1.184 | 1.14 | 1.134 |
| Black (free) | 1.197 | 1.169 | 1.112 | 1.108 |
| Black (slave) | 1.246*** | 1.102† | 1.168* | 1.193** |
| Irish (native) | 1.082* | 1.082 | 1.06 | 1.053 |
| Irish (foreign) | 1.219*** | 1.279* | 1.241 | 1.209 |
| **Birthplace** | | | | |
| Urban (large) | | 1.145* | 1.137† | 1.129† |
| Urban (large) | | 1.106† | 1.089 | 1.134* |
| Urban (small) | | 1.031 | 1.081 | 1.096 |
| **Enlistment** | | | | |
| Urban (large) | | 1.125** | 1.037 | 1.026 |
| Urban (small) | | 1.008 | 0.999 | 0.978 |
| **Death place** | | | | |
| Urban (large) | | 1.500*** | 1.486*** | 1.437*** |
| Urban (small) | | 1.167*** | 1.144** | 1.128* |
| Foreign | | 1.106 | 0.945 | 1.017 |
| **Occupation** | | | | |
| Unclassified | | | 1.15 | 1.123 |
| Unskilled | | | omitted | omitted |
| Low blue-collar | | | 1.071 | 1.081 |
| Farmer | | | 0.957 | 0.964 |
| High blue-collar | | | 0.822*** | 0.826*** |
| Low white-collar | | | 0.938 | 0.945 |
| High white-collar | | | 0.862* | 0.876† |
| **Enlistment** | | | | |
| 1860 | | | 0.936 | 0.93 |
| 1861 | | | 1.074† | 1.076† |
| 1862 | | | 1.089* | 1.092* |
| 1863 | | | 0.977 | 0.965 |
| 1864 | | | (omitted) | (omitted) |

**TABLE 11.11** *continued*

| | Odds Ratio | | | |
|---|---|---|---|---|
| | I | II | III | IV |
| Height | | | 1.012* | 1.011† |
| Illness | | | 0.993 | 0.99 |
| Wound | | | 1.026 | 1.023 |
| POW | | | 1.055 | 1.06 |
| Initial rank: | | | 0.962 | 0.958 |
| | | | | |
| Rated for: | | | | |
| Cardiovascular | | | | 0.93 |
| Diarrhea | | | | 0.967 |
| Ear | | | | 1.830*** |
| Endocrine | | | | (omitted) |
| Eyes | | | | 0.817 |
| Gastrointestinal | | | | 0.795** |
| General appearance | | | | 2.122* |
| Genitourinary | | | | 0.941 |
| Hernia | | | | 1.276 |
| Infectious disease | | | | 1.212 |
| Injuries | | | | 1.169* |
| Liver | | | | 0.839 |
| Spleen | | | | (omitted) |
| Gallbladder | | | | (omitted) |
| Neoplasm | | | | (omitted) |
| Nervous system | | | | 1.393 |
| Hemorrhoids | | | | 1.178 |
| Respiratory | | | | 1.28 |
| Rheumatism | | | | 1.02 |
| Varicose veins | | | | 2.191* |
| | | | | |
| Age 1840 | 1.093*** | 1.108*** | 1.108*** | 1.107*** |
| $t$ | 2.059*** | 1.716*** | 1.709*** | 1.763*** |
| $t_2$ | 0.987*** | 0.991*** | 0.991*** | 0.991*** |
| $t_3$ | 1.000*** | 1.000*** | 1.000*** | 1.000*** |
| N | 773,017 | 362,032 | 329,845 | 362,032 |
| Pseudo-$r^2$ | .2419 | .2509 | .2537 | .2551 |

*Note:* †$p < .10$. *$p < .05$. **$p < .01$. ***$p < .001$.

was, on average, protective is also unclear. Ear (deafness) and wounds were the other two conditions with $p$ values less than 10 percent. Fogel et al. (2013) suggest there was little difference between those rated for wounds who were wounded during the war (hence eligible for a pension before 1890) and those rated for wounds who were not wounded during the war.

With all these controls in place, foreign-born non-Irish whites had a hazard ratio 13 percent higher than U.S.-born non-Irish whites. Freeborn blacks had a hazard ratio roughly 10 percent higher and slave-born blacks had a hazard ratio roughly 20 percent higher than U.S.-born non-Irish whites. First-generation Irish had a hazard ratio 20 percent higher, while the native-born with Irish surnames were but 5 percent higher than their non-Irish counterparts. Most of these differences are not statistically different from zero. Nonetheless, the suspicion is that early life conditions in the southern United States and Ireland were substantially different than those in the northern United States. Understanding such differences is necessary if one wants to understand the health outcomes of these two ethnic groups.

## CONCLUSION

Joel Mokyr opined that blacks in Boston may well have done better than the Irish in the years before the Civil War. The results of this investigation suggest that well may be true if the comparison is between blacks born in the North and Irish migrants. For both groups, the bottom half of the occupational distribution was largely unskilled. Nevertheless, the proportion of freeborn blacks in high (but not low) white-collar occupations in 1890 was larger than foreign-born Irish, but this is based on an extremely small sample. On the other hand, unskilled Irish initially provided the unskilled labor for the burgeoning industrial firms of New England, whereas blacks were generally excluded until the twentieth century. For this cohort of USCT veterans, their unskilled labor was likely to take quite a different form.

Our evidence suggests that the native-born Irish were very much like their non-Irish white counterparts. They moved west at about the same time; they had similar survival rates and not very different hazard ratios. There is, however, a suggestion that the benefits they received did not rise as quickly as for the non-Irish. There is clear evidence that their foreign-born brethren lagged behind. The foreign-born began their western migration a bit later, and smaller proportions migrated when they did leave the familiar confines of the East Coast. Some became farmers, but, of those obtaining other skills, they were more likely to move into blue-collar occupations tied to industry. Their survival pattern was slightly different, and their hazard ratios a bit higher. Whatever disparities and prejudice faced the native-born Irish, it was seemingly worse for the foreign-born.

The blacks born in slave states, some of whom may have actually been free blacks, had the hardest path to trod. They were largely unskilled and overwhelmingly penniless. The generation who joined the USCT did show some northward movement, but it was cautious at best. When they became eligible for the pension, they were almost 10 percentage points less likely to be rated with a cardiovascular condition, than whites, and, while rheumatism is a relatively rare cause of death, it is at least twice as likely to appear for black veterans. A cardiovascular condition is the most common cause of death, but slave-born blacks are less likely to have that listed on the death certificates as whites and freeborn blacks. Why this should be true is unclear; was it part of a pattern of differential diagnosis that led to slave-born blacks receiving lower pensions than others? They were scarred by their experiences before the war, and their prospects after the war were little improved.

The blacks born in free states, however, are a revelation. While roughly half the group are little different than their southern brethren, the other half contains people who seemingly did quite well. Much more research needs to go into discovering how they moved into high white-collar positions, and why, despite what must have been family origins in slavery, their generation has survival rates and hazard ratios similar to non-Irish whites. There is no evidence, with so few of them in the North, they were accepted as "right folks" (in Tom Lehrer's terminology). There is evidence they suffered increasing discrimination when the Great Migration brought the slave-born blacks north. It could be that, since discrimination forbade blacks from being officers in the USCT, we simply do not have their white counterparts in these databases.

In short, the statistical evidence does not reveal disparate outcomes for all blacks and Irish, but there is evidence of inferior outcomes for slave-born blacks and foreign-born Irish. For the freeborn blacks and native-born Irish, for whom the historical tradition suggests discrimination and prejudice, the statistical evidence only hints at such problems. More digging is required to learn how real they were.

## ACKNOWLEDGMENTS

We are grateful to Alex Orsini for his help with the data, to Carlos Villarreal for his help with the maps, and to Dr. Lauren Cain for her help with epidemiological methods. We thank Joey Burton, Tim Classen, Dora Costa, Sok Chul Hong, and the participants at the Northwestern Conference in Honor of Joel Mokyr and the University of Chicago Workshop on the Economics and Biodemography of Aging for their comments. This research was supported in part by NIH program project P01AG10120, "Early Indicators of Later Work Levels, Disease and Death."

## BIBLIOGRAPHY

Barr, Donald A. 2008. *Health Disparities in the United States: Social Class, Race, Ethnicity, and Health*. Baltimore: Johns Hopkins University Press.

Bayor, Ronald H., and Timothy J. Meagher. 2005. *The New York Irish*. Baltimore: Johns Hopkins University Press.

Cain, Louis, and Sok Chul Hong. 2009. "Survival in 19th Century Cities: The Larger the City, the Smaller Your Chances." *Explorations in Economic History* 46 (4): 450–63.

Costa, Dora L., Lorens A. Helmchen, and Sven Wilson. 2007. "Race, Infection, and Arteriosclerosis in the Past." *Proceedings of the National Academy of Sciences* 104 (33): 13219–24.

Curry, Leonard P. 1981. *The Free Black in Urban America, 1800–1850*. Chicago: University of Chicago Press.

Du Bois, W. E. B. 1899. *The Philadelphia Negro: A Social Study*. Philadelphia: University of Pennsylvania.

Ferrie, Joseph P. 1999. *Yankeys Now: Immigrants in the Antebellum U.S., 1840–1860*. New York: Oxford University Press.

Fogel, Robert, Louis Cain, Joseph Burton, and Brian Bettenhausen. 2013. "Was What Ail'd Ya' What Kill'd Ya'?." *Economics & Human Biology* 11: 269–80.

Fogel, Robert W., and Dora L. Costa. 1997. "A Theory of Technophysio Evolution, with Some Implications for Forecasting Population, Health Care Costs, and Pension Costs." *Demography* 34 (1): 49–66.

Glatthaar, Joseph T. 1990. *Forged in Battle: The Civil War Alliance of Black Soldiers and White Officers*. New York: Free Press.

Handlin, Oscar. 1977. *Boston's Immigrants*. New York: Athenaeum.

Hogue, Carol J. R., Martha A. Hargraves, and Karen Scott Collins, eds. 2000. *Minority Health in America: Findings and Policy Implications from the Commonwealth Fund Minority Health Survey*. Baltimore: Johns Hopkins University Press.

Horton, James Oliver, and Lois E. Horton. 1979. *Black Bostonians: Family Life and Community Struggle in the Antebellum North*. New York: Holmes and Meier.

Jensen, Richard. 2002. "'No Irish Need Apply': A Myth of Victimization." *Journal of Social History* 36 (2): 405–29.

Mokyr, Joel. 1983. *Why Ireland Starved*. London: George Allen & Unwin.

Nakamura, Raymond M. 1999. *Health in America: A Multicultural Perspective*. Boston: Allyn & Bacon.

# HOW BRITAIN LOST ITS COMPETITIVE EDGE

Competence in the Second Industrial Revolution

## RALF R. MEISENZAHL

In the "classical" Industrial Revolution of the late eighteenth century, Britain was the technological leader as evidenced by myriad inventions and their applications in all sectors.[1] Meisenzahl and Mokyr (2012) argue that British technological leadership stemmed from Britain's comparative advantage in competence. That is, British craftsmen and engineers possessed the training and natural dexterity to carry out the "instructions" contained in the new recipes and blueprints that inventors wrote, building the parts on a routine basis with very low degrees of tolerance and still being able to fill in the blanks when the instructions were inevitably incomplete. While several macroinventions in the classical Industrial Revolution were of British origin, the British advantage was primarily in adjusting, tweaking, and implementing innovations. In other words, the British leadership was driven by skilled craftsmen and engineers, the top 3 to 5 percent of the skill distribution. These men were the products of the British apprenticeship system (Humphries 2003; Mokyr 2009; Meisenzahl and Mokyr 2012). British engineers swarmed over the Continent to sell, implement, and maintain the new technologies.[2] Despite these advantages, British technological leadership declined during the Second Industrial Revolution in the second half of the nineteenth century.

The British decline during the Second Industrial Revolution has been subject to extensive research, which yielded many different answers. For instance, Landes (1969) sees an "entrepreneurial failure," Roderick and Stephens (1978) argue that education lagged behind, Lazonick (1990) and Sanderson (1999a) fault the British apprenticeship system, and Elbaum and Lazonick (1984, 1986) see a general failure of British institutions and blamed entrepreneurs for not

---

1 For an overview and summary of inventions, see Mokyr (2009).

2 The vast majority of the technology used in Prussia at the end of the first Industrial Revolution was imported from Britain, either by traders traveling to Britain, buying machines like steam engines, obtaining information through industrial espionage, or employing British craftsmen. For instance, the puddling process implementation in Germany, first by Christian Remy (1783–1861) and then by Friedrich Harkort (1793–1880), required English and Belgian workers (Kleinschmidt 2007). Harkort, recognizing that the shortage of skilled workers in Germany was a crucial bottleneck, immediately started training German workers.

tackling institutional shortcomings. Others, for instance, McCloskey and Sandberg (1971) and McCloskey (1973), have argued that entrepreneurs did not fail, in the sense that they view institutions as exogenous constraints.[3]

This chapter investigates how and why Britain lost its comparative advantage in competence in the late nineteenth century. Landes (1969) already saw an enormous gap in educational achievements in relation to industry. Many studies document Germany's catch-up by looking at university and higher education and its relation to industry research.[4] However, the competence Meisenzahl and Mokyr (2012) allude to is not taught at universities.[5] New ideas and their successful implementation required the support of competent industry workers who helped to debug, tweak, and commercialize these new ideas. By studying the origins of and developments in skill formation and their political economy in Germany and Britain, this chapter sheds light on which British and German institutions generated the competence of the respective workforces, and thereby on why Britain was unable to maintain its advantage in competence through the Second Industrial Revolution.

To complement and support the university-trained scientists, industry workers needed to understand the underlying science, too. The British apprenticeship system was not able to supply this type of industry worker.[6] While training in Britain's master–apprentice relationship was useful to pass on tacit knowledge, it lacked training in scientific methods and systematic research needed to debug and improve inventions in industry. The market solution was the Mechanics' Institutes, which, despite the need for more formal education, never lived up to their founders' expectations (Wrigley 1982, 1986). Technical education was widely debated in Britain, and various commissions examined the industry needs. But the state intervened only after Britain had already fallen behind. Even then, the Science and Art Department encouraged only education that applied to all industries, while local manufactures and livery companies pushed specialized instruction catering to local needs.

---

3  Dintenfass (1999) and Kirby (1992) provide a complete overview of the arguments.

4  The classic case is the chemical industry; see Marsch (2000). The importance of higher education is also emphasized in Roderick and Stephens (1978). Lee (1997) rejects the idea that education made a difference by pointing to the contribution of Scottish universities in the Industrial Revolution.

5  To be clear, university education played its role. Although most inventions in the classical Industrial Revolution had little or no scientific base, scientific methods played a more prominent role in the inventive activity in the Second Industrial Revolution, as exemplified by advances in chemicals, electricity, and engines (Mokyr 1999).

6  Elbaum (1989) argues that the British apprenticeship persisted because of its efficiency advantages and customs that favored training certification for entry into skilled jobs. Yet Lazonick (1990) argues that the persistence of the apprenticeship system was part of the British decline. The efficiency advantages gave way to an inefficient labor aristocracy that flourished under the British apprenticeship system. Sanderson (1999a) also argues that the British failed to develop an effective apprenticeship system.

So what was done differently on the Continent? In Prussia, Frederick II, influenced by the Protestant preacher Johann Hecker (1707–68), issued a degree in 1763 that is seen as the beginning of compulsory schooling. But schools were a municipal affair that did not receive federal money, and enforcement was weak. Nevertheless, Protestants, eager to increase the population's ability to read the Bible, pushed education, and literacy in Prussia was comparatively high in the early nineteenth century. In addition, defeated by Napoleon, Prussian conservatives and progressives sought to modernize the state. Education was a common ground, although each side had very different reasons. With Britain undefeated and being the technological leader in the early nineteenth century, British politicians had little reason to overcome their religious differences, which, together with British liberalism, stalled many attempts of government intervention in education.

But did education reform matter? Mitch (2004) points out that the average level of education of the laboring class in Britain hardly made a difference to the outcome. Yet a recent study by Becker, Hornung, and Woessmann (2011) finds that basic education significantly accelerated nontextile industrialization in Prussia. This finding is consistent with the literature on technology diffusion. For instance, Nelson and Phelps (1966) argue that educational attainment becomes more important as technology progresses and that education is likely to facilitate technology adaption, which may be particularly important for technological followers. In a similar vein, Benhabib and Spiegel (1994, 2005), Barro and Sala-i-Martin (1995), and Vandenbussche, Aghion, and Meghir (2006) show that the level of educational attainment matters for development and for technology adaptation.

In what follows, I argue that, different from the British apprenticeship system, Prussian and later German education and vocational training institutions both provided their economies with competent industry workers who were not only able to adapt to new technology to support the university-trained research elite but also highly inventive themselves. Myriad educational institutions, which hitherto have received little attention by the literature on skill formation (for instance in Thelen 2004), facilitated technology adaption and thereby transformed mere literacy into actual productivity.[7]

---

7 Perhaps the best example for literacy aiding the inventive process and leading to an increase in productivity is the British locomotive engineer and inventor George Stephenson. Illiterate at the age of eighteen, he paid a tutor to teach him to read so that he could finally inform himself about the Watt engine that he had heard so much about (Smiles 1879). But the argument here is not solely about literacy. An additional secondary school education can be seen as reaching a higher level of education attainment that increases the ability to adapt to new technologies. It is worthwhile to note that, in his discussion of education and skill of the British labor force for the period 1700–1860, Mitch (2004) does not discuss secondary or continuation schools, even though he acknowledges that science-based technical change in the second half of the nineteenth century increased the importance of formal education.

I identify five components of the German success in producing competent workers in the Second Industrial Revolution. First, *Realschulen*—schools that emphasize teaching sciences rather than Latin and Greek—were established across the country, replacing Latin and Greek with science classes and preparing students for theoretical and practical training. Second, a complex system of continuation and trade schools developed on a regional level without federal intervention. Third, Prussia founded the *Gewerbeinstitut*—a higher education institution that mainly educated high-level administrators in Berlin—and later regional but federal government-sponsored *Provinzial-Gewerbeschule*, which would send their highest-skilled students to Berlin. These Provinzial-Gewerbeschule also served to foster local economic growth. Fourth, Prussia and other German states offered strong incentives for continued education by introducing school certificates and skill certification as early as 1814. Prussia offered additional perks, such as highly salaried government positions and the shortening of the military service for Gewerbeinstitut graduates. Fifth, guilds were preserved in *Innungen* and enlisted in quality control, as they were responsible for certification of skills. Hence, skill control was in the hands of the employers.

These factors enabled Germany to, as the Smail (1914, 5) report on trade and technical education in France and Germany to the London County Council puts it, "[build] up a great industrial nation partly by the thorough training of the leaders as experts, partly by the training of the middle-grade workers, such as draftsmen and foreman, as thoroughly accurate and careful managers, and partly by the training of all grades of workmen and mechanics as skilled craftsmen and good citizens."

## EDUCATION AND SKILL FORMATION IN GERMANY

### The School System

It is useful to understand how the Prussian school system evolved. Literacy itself may not increase the ability to adapt or tweak new technology, but it facilities further studies. Hence, before describing secondary-education institutions and continuation schools that taught science, I start with basic education.

Although Prussia legally established compulsory schooling in 1763, it wasn't until 1808 that education was elevated to a significant municipal goal and service. The school system underwent a radical reform in 1810, focusing on a balanced education that fostered personal development.[8] With the recent defeat that the

---

8  Wilhelm von Humboldt (1767–1835) was a main figure in the process. He also was briefly in charge of the Prussian school system before he became special envoy to Vienna. However, the reform built upon the ideas of Julius Eberhard von Massow, a Prussian minister for state and

German states and Prussia had suffered from Napoleon in mind, reformers of every political color agreed on one point: Education can contribute to the modernization of the state, and as such, education and the political system are intertwined. Of course, the respective reasons differed. Conservatives argued that (limited) education would improve the health of military draftees and their loyalty to the state, while for others education was the ultima ratio to fighting poverty. All the same, reformers were seeking to educate students for a new (post-Napoleonic) society. In that society, the nation itself was supposed to be the overarching leitmotif, purging the old, hierarchical structure. As a result, a key assumption in the reform process was that learning and understanding math did not depend on class. In other words, the reformers intended to break the link between education and a specific job that was predetermined by class and therefore by birth (Jeismann 1969).[9]

By 1816, 54.1 percent of German children attended elementary or middle school. While enrollment rates were high in the western provinces, the eastern provinces, with few exceptions, exhibited low enrollment rates. Between 1820 and 1835, school construction boomed, but school attendance increased rapidly in part because enforcement of compulsory school attendance became more effective. Schools issued graduation certificates, which often were needed for communion or confirmation. Local authorities fined parents if students missed school, and pastors scolded parents whose children missed school during mass.

By 1846, 78 percent of children went to school, in 1864, 85 percent, and in 1871, 86.3 percent. The eastern provinces contained by far the larger share of the illiterate population. The high illiteracy rate indicates an extreme lack of human capital in the eastern providence as these regions already lagged in school enrollment in 1816 (Becker, Hornung, and Woesmann 2011).

Table 12.1 shows that federal expenses for elementary education covered only a small fraction of the total expenses—less than 5 percent in 1861 and 1871. Municipalities and school tuition covered more than 95 percent. Municipalities bore, on average, 76 percent of the burden of financing elementary schools. Tuition covered about 19 percent of the cost (Königliches Statistisches Bureau 1888). The school expenditure's share of total municipal spending rose throughout the nineteenth century.[10]

---

justice, who had already criticized the strong focus on Latin and the lack of math in schools. He started working on school reform in 1798 (Jeismann 1987).

9  The assumption that class and "ability" were unrelated is in sharp contrast to the hypothesis put forward in Clark (2008). The reformer assumed that (genetic) heritage did not matter for ability and for economic outcomes.

10  For instance, the share of school expenditures rose from 3.6 percent (1814) to 22.4 percent (1900) in Coesfeld (Hilgert 1910), from 6.9 percent (1810) to 16.0 percent (1900) in Halle an der Saale (Allendorf 1904), and from 0.2 percent (1800) to 26.3 percent (1900) in Osnabrück (Sunder 1904).

**TABLE 12.1** Elementary Schools and School Financing in Prussia

| Year | Number of schools | Number of teachers (including assistants) | Number of students | Schooling expenses per student (mark) | Percentage of cost covered by federal funds |
|------|------|------|------|------|------|
| 1821 | 20,440 | 21,220 | 1,427,045 | — | — |
| 1831 | 21,786 | 24,719 | 1,917,934 | — | — |
| 1840 | 22,323 | 28,507 | 2,224,239 | — | — |
| 1849 | 24,201 | 32,865 | 2,453,062 | — | — |
| 1861 | 25,156 | 34,925 | 2,778,208 | 10.37 | 4.47 |
| 1871 | 33,120 | 52,059 | 3,900,655 | 14.27 | 4.86 |
| 1886 | 33,919 | 65,718 | 4,471,000 | 24.10 | 12.16 |

*Source:* Königliches Statistisches Bureau (1888).

However, the considerable differences across Prussian provinces persisted. For instance, municipalities in Posen covered 88 percent of elementary schooling expenses, while tuition covered only 4 percent in 1871. By contrast, municipalities in Brandenburg covered 64 percent of elementary schooling expenses, while tuition covered 31 percent in the same year. Similarly, the expenditure per elementary student varied from 8.06 mark in the district of Oppeln to 19.23 mark in the district of Stralsund in 1871. Public school quality mirrored expenditures. In 1882 in the district of Oppeln, only 29 percent of all school-aged children in a public elementary school were educated in "normal-sized" classes—that is, up to 80 students per class in schools with a single class and up to 70 students in schools with two or more classes. At the same time in the district of Stralsund, 86 percent of school-aged children in a public elementary school were educated in normal-sized classes.[11]

Thus far, I have described the evolution of only basic education. However, basic education in itself may not matter as much for technology adaption, but it is the prerequisite for secondary education and, as I will show later, continuation schools. Building on the basic education, students could enroll in secondary schools. Two (main) types of secondary schools existed: the *Gymnasium* and the *Realschule*. The key difference between these schools was the projected future occupation of the student. While the Gymnasium, with a curriculum emphasizing Greek and Latin, was seen as preparation for university, the Realschule developed in response to a need for practically trained students.

11  The expenditure in Berlin was 59.50 mark per student, and about 93 percent of all school-aged children were educated in normal-sized classes; see Königliches Statistisches Bureau (1888).

Johann Hecker, who founded the first Realschule in 1747, recognized the importance of teaching science.[12] The name of this Berlin-based institution, Ökonomisch–mathematische Realschule (economics–math Realschule), in itself is telling. Students learned more science, less Greek and Latin, and were asked to intern in companies. The explicit goal was practical education and preparation for a business career. The demand for this new type of school grew rapidly (Schiersmann 1979).[13] It is worthwhile to note that the Realschulen taught English instead of Greek. While some Realschulen still included some Latin in the curriculum (Realschulen 1. Ordnung), others (Realschulen 2. Ordnung) dropped Latin in favor of even more math and science.

The curriculum for a Prussian gymnasium in 1837 listed 134 out of a total of 316 semester hours of Latin and Greek compared with 70 semester hours of math and science over ten years. The Realschule 1. Ordnung taught only 60 semester hours of Latin but 100 semester hours of math and science and 11 semester hours of English in 1859. The Realschule 2. Ordnung dropped Latin and increased the course load in math and science to 117 semester hours. The course load in German and French was also increased (Friederich 1987). Magnus (1888, 39) notes that "drawing [in German real-schools] is always taught well, and the schools generally contain good chemical laboratories, as well as collections of physical apparatus and museums. From the children of these schools the ranks of foreman are largely recruited. They receive no special trade instruction, but the general training is so arranged as to qualify them for higher posts in industrial works." By 1859, 43,047 students went to one of the 159 Gymnasien (24 per 10,000 population) and 20,853 students went to one of the 68 Realschulen (12 per 10,000 population). These numbers increased rapidly to 56,360 students in 180 Gymnasien (27 per 10,000 population) and 29,666 students in 102 Realschulen (15 per 10,000 population) in 1867. By 1885, the numbers had further increased to 93,602 students in 298 Gymnasien (34 per 10,000 population) and 57,939 students in 270 Realschulen (20 per 10,000 population) in the Prussian parts of Germany. These numbers exclude the new provinces of Hannover, Hessen-Nassau, and Schleswig-Holstein in 1867 (Königliches Statistisches Bureau 1888).

The Prussian reforms also addressed student examinations and teacher training. By 1812 the final examination in the Gymnasium (Abitur) was

---

12  Hecker, who had studied theology, was a preacher in Berlin, where he became increasingly involved with general education. His goal was to provide education to young men not qualified for university to ensure a successful career in firms, trade companies, and manufactures (Schindler 1969). He also was instrumental in convincing Frederick the Great of the need for compulsory education.

13  Similarly, the earliest educational institutions addressing skill formation were private sector solutions. Merchants founded the first commercial schools, most prominent the Handelsschule, a merchant school, in Hamburg 1771.

harmonized and mandatory; however, the law was enforced only from 1834 onward. Teaching instruction and certification emerged in private settings, such as the *Seminar für Lehrer* (teacher seminar) founded by Hecker in 1748, which was the predecessor to the Prussian *Lehrerseminar*. In 1820 about 20,000 teachers were employed in Prussians schools. The teacher seminars educated 1,500 teachers in 1825 (Königliches Statistisches Bureau 1888). The number of teachers in schools drastically increased to 30,000 (of which 5,000 taught in secondary schools) by 1837 and to about 52,000 in 1870.[14] The reform of 1810 introduced a university examination for teachers in secondary schools to ensure quality standards. The standards were rather high so that about 100 new teachers were accredited for secondary schools every year (Tenorth 1987).

General education had two goals: (1) to form well-behaved, religious individuals and (2) to stimulate interest in further (self-)education (Friedrich 1987). Some authors have argued that the first point, imprinting social norms, contributed to the rise of factories, but clearly all employers would benefit from a sober, punctual, and reliable workforce.[15] The focus of this chapter is the second point, though both points reinforce each other. Basic education facilitated continuing education and specialization, which in turn increased the technological and commercial competence of the workforce. The following sections therefore examine institutions that, by building upon general education, provided valuable training for jobs.

### Continuation Schools

The institutions that provided further education for workers, apprentices, and journeymen, who often did not receive a secondary education, were continuation schools. In Prussia many of these schools were established already in the eighteenth century with little differentiation. In the nineteenth century, however, they exhibited a wide variety not only in names (Construction Trades School, Crafts Continuation School, Continuation School, Art School, Sunday School, Sunday Trade School) but also in the classes offered. The differences in the continuation school curricula reflected the fact that the schools were financed on a local level and therefore how regional demand for certain skills

14 The implied teacher-to-student ratio is 1:18 in Prussia in 1837, which is already lower than the ratio in Austria in 1850 (1:20).

15 Stone (1969) discusses the arguments that were made in England in support of more elementary education. Contemporaries expected that more schooling would lead to sobriety, to lower crime rates, and, in general, to breaking the "habits of the working class." Consequently, Sunday schools expanded and attendance rose with the rise of the factory, even though the British institution tended to emphasize religious contents.

drove the education offered.[16] Most of the continuation schools in bigger cities taught accounting, technology, and mechanics and had their students copying models. Rural schools also focused on increasing literacy and, in some cases, offered religious studies.

Perhaps the best example of how local conditions affected the curriculum of a continuation school is the continuation school in Essen (founded 1861). Financed by the city and the steelmaking company Krupp, the school offered classes in math, engineering, and physics as well as financial mathematics and accounting. The classes, which met Sundays between eight and eleven in the morning, were taught by teachers of the Realschule and engineers. Roughly one-third of the students were employees at Krupp. In contrast, the continuation school in Rheydt (today a borough of Mönchengladbach) offered classes in German, business correspondence, accounting, arithmetic, geometry, and drawing. Most of the clientele were apprentices in carpentry and metalworking, who could attend for free, and journeymen, who had to pay a small tuition. By 1877, 213 schools with 21,272 students existed in Germany (Harney 1987).

König (2006) notes that by 1880 the supply for university trained engineers was much lower than demand. Yet firms viewed continuation school graduates as acceptable substitutes for university-trained engineers. In fact, many managers preferred engineers with practical training, so that even university-trained engineers—such as Emil Rathenau (1838–1915), who later founded the Allgemeine Elektrizitätsgesellschaft (AEG), and Friedrich von Hefner-Alteneck (1845–1904), who became chief engineer at Siemens—had to start at low-level, hands-on positions. However, these examples are not meant to imply that practical training trumps theory. On the contrary, practical training and scientific instruction were seen as highly complementary. For instance, taking some classes at continuation schools was often required to become a foreman (Wrigley 1986).

By 1902, 203,250 pupils attended one of the 1,684 (mostly public) continuation schools, the vast majority as part of their apprenticeship (Beringer 1906). In general, these schools, even the commercial ones, offered classes in math, physics, chemistry, and studies of materials (Howard 1907). Thus German employers could draw on a large pool of workers who understood the production process and thereby increase the chances of further improvement in production. Similarly, managers and sales representatives who understood at least the basic science of the product aided the rise of large corporations.

16 In Prussia, continuation schools received federal subsides only from 1870 on. In Saxony, the state already supported Sunday schools in the first half of the nineteenth century. Forty-two Sunday schools, which taught German, math, geometry, and drawing, received a total subsidy of 3,120 thaler from the Saxon government in 1839. In addition, the Saxon government offered free technical drawing classes in four local schools to cover local industry needs (mostly in the textile industry).

*Gewerbeschulen*

Successful students of secondary schools and of continuation schools had a unique opportunity in Prussia: they could attend *Gewerbeschulen*—a new type of higher education with more practical training than students received at universities but still with considerable science coursework.

At first the Prussian state was involved in higher education only to educate civil servants and engineers in the Berliner Bergakademie (founded 1770) for mining and the Bauakademie (founded 1790) for construction and civil engineering. Beginning in 1821, the state increased its involvement beyond civil servant education. In addition to establishing the Berliner Gewerbeinstituts, the state also founded a system of regional schools (*Provizial-Gewerbeschulen*).[17] These schools, which students could attend only after obtaining a general education, offered classes in math, science, and engineering. Hence their students joined the technical elite. Their best students received stipends and were offered the possibility to study at the Berliner Gewerbeinstitut.[18] The Prussia ministry of trade pushed this new system of guided career paths (Harney 1987).

The Gewerbeinstitut and its regional cousins were a success exemplified by the fact that most founding members of the Verein der deutschen Ingenieure (Society of German Engineers, founded 1856) graduated from the Gewerbeinstitut (König 2006). The Gewerbeschulen were popular because they allowed for social mobility.[19] Not only did the graduates do well on the job market—for instance, they successfully competed for high-salary government jobs—but their military service was also shortened by two years to one year at the officer rank, a benefit previously reserved for nobility. This crucial incentive was also recognized as such by the British educationalist Sir Philip Magnus (1842–1933).[20]

But the Provinzial-Gewerbeschulen, which were also financed by the Prussian state, were intended not only to supply Berlin with the most skilled stu-

17  The Gewerbeinstitute, the Berliner Bergakademie, and the Berliner Bauakademie merged; the university is today known as the Technische Universität Berlin and still focuses on engineering and sciences.

18  Jacobi (1842) notes that the Gewerbeinstitut issued its own textbooks on math, architecture, construction, mechanics, and chemistry. The textbook on industrial chemistry by Ernst Ludwig Schubarth was immediately translated into French.

19  Examples for this social mobility are Johann Friedrich August Borsig (1804–54), a locomotive builder and industrialist whose father was a craftsman, Carl Hoppe (1812–98), a steam engine and locomotive builder whose father was a local priest, and Louis Schwartzkopff (1825–92), a machine manufacturer whose father was an innkeeper and wood dealer (Kaelble 1972).

20  Magnus wrote one of the first comprehensive studies on industrial education. See Magnus (1888).

dents but also to foster regional economic growth.[21] The state planned one school in each of the twenty-five administrative districts. By 1849, twenty-one local Provinzial-Gewerbeschulen were established, but they differed in size, curriculum, and institutional setup. The schools in Posen, Frankfurt/Oder, and Erfurt were evening and Sunday schools. Six schools (Königsberg, Gumbinnen, Danzig, Graudenz, Potsdam, and Oppeln) had one (daytime) class, eight schools (Stettin, Stralsund, Halberstadt, Naumburg, Bielefeld, Hagen, Cologne, and Müster) had two classes, and the Liegnitz school had three classes. Three schools (Elberfeld, Aachen, and Trier) were connected to the local Realschule.[22]

The Prussian state financed the Provinzial-Gewerbeschulen, and most students obtained stipends to attend them. Jacobi (1842) reports that the Gewerbeinstitut in Berlin received about 8,300 *thaler* annually and each of the twenty Provinzial-Gewerbeschulen received between 500 and 1,200 thaler annually from the Prussian ministry for interior affairs. The money was in part spent on teaching materials in English and French as well as laboratory equipment for physics and chemistry lectures. The Provinzial-Gewerbeschulen also received support from the respective cities or municipalities. For instance, cities usually offered public buildings for rent-free use or paid for the construction of new buildings. In about thirty cities, either local authorities or local societies established local Gewerbeschulen for the advancement of industriousness. These schools, mostly continuation schools, will be discussed later.

To attend a Provinzial-Gewerbeschule, students were required to either have received an elementary education, gone through apprenticeship, and taken classes at a continuation school or have finished at least eight years of schooling. Upon completion, students were required to work for one year before entering the three-year program at the Berliner Gewerbeinstituts. Most graduates, however, went to work in local industries or administrations. Students who completed the Gymnasium could also apply to the Gewerbeinstituts after one year of work experience.[23]

Since no complete record of attendance at Provinzial-Gewerbeschulen exists, several snapshots of enrollment have to suffice. In 1849, 587 students enrolled in twenty Gewerbeschulen; for another two, Cologne and Trier, the number of students is unknown.[24] In 1854, 780 were enrolled in twenty-two

21  The Prussian state issued permissions for some crafts, which had to be bought before opening shop. State officials acknowledged that if the state was paid for those permissions, the state should also provide free education for these crafts. See Jacobi (1842).

22  For a complete description, see Schiersmann (1979).

23  These were the two opinions between 1850 and 1870. In some cases preparation classes were required. Before 1850 the requirements were less strict. After 1870 the requirements were refined. Schiersmann (1979) provides a complete description of the changes.

24  The districts Breslau, Bromberg, Koblenz, Köslin, and Madgeburg had no Provinzial-Gewerbeschule (Jacobi 1842). The "Königliche Provincial-Gewerbeschule" in Krefeld was founded

Provinzial-Gewerbeschulen. At that time, three schools (Stralsund, Liegnitz, and Hagen) also offered preparation classes.

What did these institutions teach? Table 12.2 summarizes the curricula of Provinzial-Gewerbeschulen in the Rhineland and Westphalia. The education concentrated on drafting and design, which often included math and copying blueprints. While the actual courses syllabi are not preserved, a list of textbooks for these institutions is provided by Jacobi (1842). Seven books are concerned with algebra and geometry, two on mechanical engineering, two on construction, and one on technical chemistry. Not all were sold to the public. Since only a few of them are still available, two examples will have to suffice. The first one is Schubarth's book on technical chemistry. This book first introduces chemical processes and experiment methods before it describes the properties of various elements, as well as respective acids and alloys and detailed instructions on how to produce them (Schubarth 1835). The second example is Brix's book on statics and its technical application. This book develops general mathematical proofs before discussing the application to levers, screws, and power transmission in simple machines (Brix 1831).

Table 12.2 also shows considerable differences in the curricula of the Rhineland and Westphalian schools. Three schools were in cities, Aachen, Cologne, and Düsseldorf, in close proximity to places that accounted for the vast majority of steam engines employed in production in 1836 (Adelmann 1967). Hence, it is not surprising that the Provinzial-Gewerbeschule in Cologne, at the center of the region, focused on physics and mechanics.[25] It is worth noting that some schools offered optional classes in French and English. Schiersmann (1979) documents that between 1834 and 1840 about 85 percent of all students at the Münster Provinzial-Gewerbeschule attended French classes and roughly 20 percent choose additional English classes. She attributes this strong interest in languages to a lack of a continuation school that typically offered these classes in this region. The type of classes offered indicates a vivid interest in continuing education beyond the technical aspect. The Provinzial-Gewerbeschulen were later transformed into full-time schools catering to the local labor market where the focus was again on math and sciences (Harney 1987).

In addition to the Gewerbeschulen, Prussia copied some of the French higher education institutions for engineering in the late eighteenth and early nineteenth centuries. The Prussian state founded academies for the military and civil servants (which are today *Technische Universitäten*).[26] However, mining

---

in 1851. The focus was on math and science. As such, it was equipped with a modern chemistry laboratory.

25  Aachen already had a local continuation school, founded in 1818. The school also taught engineering and science (Harney 1987).

26  Olesko (2009) argues that the Prussian territorial expansion crucially shaped the technical education of engineers as the Northern European Plain presented various challenges in civil engineering.

**TABLE 12.2** Curricula of Provinzial-Gewerbeschulen (Hours per Week)

| Topic | Münster (1829) | Elberfeld (1826) | Hagen (1824) | Trier (1831) | Cologne (1839) First | Second | Aachen (1824) | Bielefeld (1831) |
|---|---|---|---|---|---|---|---|---|
| Drafting and design | 12 | 20 | 12 | 20 | 14 | 14 | X[a] | X |
| Math | 6 | 8 | 6 | 8 | 16 | 8 | X | X |
| Physics | 4 | 2 | 2 | 2 | 6 | 12 | — | X |
| Chemistry | — | 4 | 2 | — | — | — | X | X |
| Natural history | — | 2 | — | — | — | — | — | — |
| Architecture | — | — | — | — | — | — | X | — |
| Mechanics | — | — | — | — | — | 6 | — | — |
| German | — | — | 2 | — | 2 | — | — | — |
| Penmanship | — | 2 | — | — | — | — | — | X |
| Total | 22 | 38 | 24 | 30 | 38 | 40 | ? | ? |

*Source:* Schiersmann (1979, 95).
*Note:* a. Actual number of hours unknown.

academies and the Gewerbeschulen were new institutions in the international comparison. For instance, France established its version of the Gewerbeschulen only in 1857. Lundgreen (1987) notes that the Gewerbeschulen educated applied engineers for the metal industries who successfully competed with the academically trained engineers. Of course, these institutions taught complementary skills. For instance, the flight pioneer Otto Lilienthal (1848–96) first attended the Gewerbeschule in Potsdam before studying at the Gewerbeakademie in Charlottenburg (Schulz 1985).

The establishment of Gewerbeschulen in Saxony mirrored the Prussia blueprint. The main institution was the Technical School in Dresden. More than half of the school library's 2,800 books were on science and technology (124 on construction, 204 on math and machines, 210 on geography and statistics, 436 on physics and chemistry, and 731 on technology). Drawing classes could use more than 2,500 design samples and blueprints. The school also owned various machines, including an American power loom, an English dandy loom, and an Austrian Jacquard machine, and ninety-three models of steam engines and other machinery. The schools in Chemnitz, Zittau, and Plauen were modeled after the Dresden school. Together, the schools had about 250 students in 1839.[27]

The Gewerbeinstitut and its regional cousins fostered the accumulation of technical and commercial skills. Despite a relative low number of students, the Gewerbeschulen contributed to industrialization because regional factors were taken into account in the curricula. These institutions also increased social mobility by allowing mostly lower-middle-class students to rise through the ranks (Harney 1987).[28]

In sum, Prussian and German states exhibited a large number of school types that allow individual and regional specialization to flourish. Workers who had received only basic education had the opportunity to learn about science and the scientific method in myriad continuation schools. For the best and brightest, the state established Gewerbeschule, with a focus on applied science. The complex system provided the education necessary to foster technical com-

27　The budget for the Technical School in Dresden increased from 5,000 thaler in 1834 to 6,100 thaler in 1840. Different from the Prussian signature school and the Provinzial-Gewerbeschulen, students in Saxony had to pay a tuition that depended on their courses. The three regional schools' budgets were substantially smaller (between 1,500 and 1,850 thaler). At least three additional Gewerbeschulen existed in German states in 1838. The school in Stuttgart offered various classes, totaling fifty-seven hours of technical instruction, fifty-two hours of math, thirty hours of science, twenty-nine hours of foreign languages, twenty-four hours of drawing, and twelve hours of humanities per week. The Gewerbeschulen in Nürnberg and Karlsruhe had similar scopes (Jacobi 1842).

28　The students of the Gewerbeschulen appreciated the value of continuing education. For instance, the industrialist Carl Hoppe (1812–98), an alumnus of the Gewerbeinstitut, was known for teaching his employees and ensuring that apprentices received superb instruction (Arnold 1972).

petence of the workforce. Of course, this system is effective only when used properly. As the next section will show, the apprenticeship system made heavy use of the educational institution by requiring apprentices to attend continuation schools.

## APPRENTICESHIP AND SKILL CERTIFICATION

Over the course of the nineteenth century, continuation schools not only targeted apprentices and journeymen as audience but also became part of the apprenticeship system. Skill certification and formal education were thought to be remedies for declining standards in the education of apprentices. Kurhessen introduced examinations at the end of apprenticeships to certify skills as early as 1814 (Stratmann 1987). In particular, Kurhessen's law (para. 313) required that an apprentice presented the transcript of a continuation school, here specifically a *Handwerksschule* (trade school), at yearly examinations, which were conducted by his master and another guild master. If attendance was incomplete and grades insufficient, the apprenticeship was to be extended by up to six months, while good grades could be rewarded with a shorter apprenticeship (Klauhold 1855).[29] Hence, much of skill certification and quality control were delegated to Innungen, which took schools achievements into account.[30] This organization of certification left craft masters, who typically were the employers, in control. Of course, skill certification by an outside organization—in the case of Kurhessen, the presence of another guild master—not only guaranteed a minimum knowledge base but also made skills easily verifiable for potential new employers and transferable between firms.

Prussia introduced free enterprise as part of the Stein-Hardenberg reforms. This reform meant that craft restrictions did not apply to factories, allowing the industrial sector to take off while leaving the old structure virtually unchanged (Biernacki 1995). The restrictions on the number of apprentices were also removed. Consequently, in 1845 when Prussia dissolved craft guilds, which were seen as tools of an absolutist regime, it preserved the guild structure in Innungen, serving mainly as employer organizations with mandatory membership.[31]

Four years later, in 1849, Prussia abandoned its liberal labor market policies, which had viewed vocational training as a contract between master and apprentice and, therefore, as part of the regular labor market.[32] Thus, Prussia

29  Interestingly, this paragraph also included a nondiscrimination rule. Masters could not reject a candidate on the basis of birth, class, or religion.

30  This division of labor between the state as rule writer and employer organizations as implementer remained unchanged; see Schriewer (1986).

31  For an overview of legislation affecting Innungen, see Beringer (1906).

32  For instance, the length of apprenticeship was set to three years, which still is the length of the average apprenticeship in Germany today.

followed the Kurhessen example and required a minimum knowledge at the end of the apprenticeship for many professions. To ensure quality standards, the German states issued handbooks for each profession. The Prussian Industrial Code of 1869 then set up the legal structure for apprenticeship throughout the German Reich (Stratmann 1982, 1987).

As described above, apprenticeship requirements started to include formal education. Continuation schools, mostly built upon private initiative and then supported by the authorities, already targeted apprentices and journeymen by offering classes related to all trades (Frommberger and Reinisch 2002).[33] In other cases, Innungen opened their own schools, as in the case of Tilsit, in which four continuation schools were owned by different Innungen in 1859 (Ministerium der geistlichen 1859). By 1902, 291 of 1,093 continuation schools with a focus on crafts were owned by Innungen. These schools also offered classes for master and shop owners, such as accounting (Beringer 1906). The Imperial Law of Industry in 1891 explicitly allowed municipalities to pass by-laws that made attendance to continuation schools compulsory, and the Handicrafts Law of 1897 made continuation school attendance for up to nine hours a week mandatory, with German employers being fined if an apprentice missed class.[34]

## COMPETENCE IN THE GERMAN AUTOMOBILE INDUSTRY

How did this variety of educational institutions described above matter? Consider the emerging automobile industry. How were the German inventors and mechanics in this industry educated? First, let's examine three of the German pioneers, who exhibited their automobile at the first Internationale Automobil-Austellung in 1897: Carl Benz (1844–1929), Gottlieb Daimler (1834–1900), and Friedrich Lutzmann (1859–1930).

Benz went to Karlsruher Lyzeum, a gymnasium with a focus on science. He continued studying at the Polytechnischen Schule in Karlsruhe for four years before he became a millwright, first in a locomotive factory, then in a vehicle factory. Prior to constructing cars, Benz worked in bridge construction (Bröcker 1955). Before starting an apprenticeship as a gunsmith, Daimler attended a Realschule. Upon the completion of the apprenticeship, he had the chance to study at the Königliche Landesgewerbeschule. After having briefly worked in a locomotive factory, he went to the Polytechnischen Schule in Stuttgart (Schildberger 1957). Lutzmann attended the local Bürgerschule before

---

33  For later developments on the school level, see Bennett (1937).

34  For a detailed description of classes offered at compulsory continuation schools in various German cities, see Smail (1914).

going to the gymnasium. He apprenticed as a building fitter and toolmaker. During his mandatory years on the road as a journeyman, Lutzmann worked in shops in Leipzig, Apolda, and Koblenz (Riedel 1999). Again, the certification at the end of the apprenticeship required not only continuation school attendance but also a sound theoretical knowledge, as school grades had to be sufficient. Thus, all three exemplify the mix of practical and theoretical training that was crucial to the German catch-up with Britain.

The German automobile industry was not driven by three men only. There were, of course, the engine designers Nikolaus Otto (1832–91) and Rudolf Diesel (1858–1913). Otto had attended a Realschule and completed an apprenticeship in commerce.[35] Diesel went to Augsburg at the age of twelve to attend first the Gewerbeschule and then an industry school. Later he studied mechanical engineering at the Technischen Hochschule München (Diesel 1957).[36] One of Diesel's assistants at Maschinenfabrik Augsburg-Nürnberg (MAN), Franz Lang (1873–1956), who had apprenticed as locksmith, was granted some 170 motor-related patents (Seherr-Thoß 1982).

Three other well-known car designers and manufacturers, Wilhelm Maybach (1846–1929), August Horch (1868–1951), and Ferdinand Porsche (1875–1951), were also products of the German continuation school system. Maybach, whose parents died early, was first instructed in drawing and design at his guardian's office, who recognized his talents. Maybach also took evening classes at the local Realschule and the local continuation school (Seherr-Thoß 1990). Horch, who worked for Benz before eventually founding AutoUnion—the present-day Audi—was apprenticed as a smith. After his years on the road as a journeyman, which took him to Austria, Hungary, Serbia, and Bulgaria, he attended the Technikum Mittweida, an engineering school in Saxony (Herrmann 1972). Porsche apprenticed as a tinsmith, attended a mandatory continuation school, and took a class in electrical engineering at Staatsgewerbeschule in Reichenberg (Parr 2001).

Less well-known car manufacturers and designers, such as Franz Komnick (1857–1938), whose truck won the Leningrad–Tiflis reliability rally in 1924, and Joseph Vollmer (1871–1955), who designed tanks in World War I and later worked for Skoda, also apprenticed before taking evening classes (Komnick) or attending the Technikum Mittweida (Vollmer).[37]

The list above is clearly only the tip of the iceberg, but these men are instructive examples of the significance of the German system of continuation schools

35   While Otto had the ideas and some skill, he relied on Michael Zons and Franz Reuleaux in this research and innovation process (Seherr-Thoß 1998).

36   The Technische Hochschule München, founded in 1868, was renamed Technical University in 1877 but was granted the right to award doctorates only in 1901.

37   See Zincke (2001) and Seherr-Thoß (1979).

and formal training required during apprenticeships. The argument here is one of continuity. Revealing how the first and second layer of engineers and inventors in Germany were educated sheds light on the importance of continuation schools and formal training outside of universities as a whole. Almost all of the car manufacturers and motor designers listed above completed an apprenticeship, which usually required additional formal education. Most of them were already exposed to science in school and later took additional classes in engineering in the continuation school system.[38] Thus, it is fair to say that the mix of practical and theoretical training offered by the complex system of continuing education was a crucial component of Germany's fast economic development in the Second Industrial Revolution.

## COMPARISON TO EDUCATION AND SKILL FORMATION IN GREAT BRITAIN

### The School System

Literacy rates in Britain lagged behind those in the Northern European countries in the early nineteenth century. This was partly the result of the British liberalism that opposed compulsory schooling and preferred market solution, though most of the liberal philosophers were sympathetic to the idea of compulsory education with centralized tests. Adam Smith, for instance, recognized the importance of education but did not advocate state involvement. John Stuart Mill feared a dominant role of the state in education even though he himself, his father James Mill, and Jeremy Bentham acknowledged that public schooling may be necessary to achieve equal opportunities for all, but their preference was to make education not schooling compulsory (Deissinger 1994).[39] Roderick and Stephens (1978) conclude that up to the end of the nineteenth century, government intervention in education was actually fought, since compulsory schooling would infringe personal freedom. However, they find that elementary education grew rapidly between 1800 and 1840 without government intervention.

---

38 Of course institutions also started to specialize. König (2009) points out that as some institutions, mostly the *Polytechnikschulen* that later became technical universities, focused on theory while others remained practically oriented. The latter are today known as Fachhochschulen (or universities of applied sciences, as they are most recently granted the right to award doctorates in some circumstances). For a detailed description of the development of technical universities, see Manegold (1970).

39 Compulsory education, however, lacked enforcement. The Health and Morals of Apprentices Act of 1802, which was pushed by the textile manufacturer Sir Robert Peel the Elder (1750–1830), mandated that pauper apprentices had to be taught elementary-school-level material. Without any enforcement mechanism, the act had basically no effect.

The rapid growth in elementary education is reflected in the number of schools. The 1851 Census of Great Britain, Education, England, and Wales lists 44,836 all-day schools, two-thirds of them private. Of the 15,411 public schools, more than 10,000 were supported by religious bodies, and only 610 were financed by general or local taxation. The Society for the Diffusion of Useful Knowledge attacked religious societies for not teaching anything useful, but the 1831 campaign for secular state education fell flat. In addition, the Newcastle Commission pruned the respective syllabus to bare essentials, which meant that teacher training for teaching the poor was rudimentary at best (Goldstrom 1972).

The first state intervention was proposed in 1833 by Lord Althorp, whose bill granted twenty thousand pounds to aid private subscription for the erection of school houses. However, it was only an interim measure, and most of the money went to large cities. Since Parliament was unable to pass any bill on education because of religious controversy between Anglicans and Nonconformists, mainly about the separation of church and state, a special department of the Privy Council—the Committee of the Privy Council on Education—was established to supervise the grants in 1839. The Privy Council Committee on Trade also secured the first government grant for the establishment of a school of design—the first school teaching art as applied to commerce and industry—in 1836 with more schools to be supported from 1841 onward (Morton 1997). The British continuation schools in general, mostly evening schools, were recognized in 1851 with government grants to compensate for the lack of daytime schools. However, this policy meant that most British continuation schools were confined to elementary instruction. After the 1851 Great Exhibition, government support for secondary schools was revisited, and from 1854 on the British government began supporting these schools, particularly those with technical education (Kruger 1986).

Only after falling behind economically did education reforms in Britain take shape. In the 1860s, the campaign for state education (for instance, by the British National Education League [founded in 1869] led by Joseph Chamberlain) had gained momentum. The first major intervention that allowed schooling to be compulsory but not entirely subsidized was the Elementary Education Act of 1870 (Foster Act), which gave local authorities the option to pass bylaws making schooling compulsory and to establish rate-aided elementary schools where there were not enough voluntary schools.[40] In 1880, all areas were required to have these bylaws (West 1991).[41] Nonconformists objected, as state funds supported schools sponsored by religious bodies, mostly the Anglican

---

40  Sanderson (1999b) claims that most of the school system deficiencies were dealt with after 1870 and Britain's catch-up was fast in terms of education. Dintenfass (1992), however, still sees a misallocation in funds.

41  For a description of local schools and their shortcomings, see Tiffen (1935).

Church (Auspos 1980). The 1902 Education Act (Balfour Act) then modernized the supervision of schools, which included some government control over voluntary schools including the mostly Anglican church schools by giving them funding. Nonconformists, the Liberal Party, and the Labor Movement opposed the act. Sectarian fights about church influence in schooling, which also raised the question of separation of state and church, had put their stamp on the history of government intervention in British education. Galor and Moav (2006) argue that British capitalist eventually favored education reforms because they were facing a shortage in skilled labor and therefore were the prime beneficiaries from higher levels of human capital.

Compared to Germany's system, the British school system did not develop as a large range of secondary schools. However, some schools that served as continuation schools existed. The 1851 census, for instance, lists almost two hundred factory schools, colliery schools, chemical work schools, and industrial and agricultural schools (Goldstrom 1972). But little is known about whether they were more effective than the more than five hundred workhouse schools that were established following the 1834 Poor Laws Amendment Act (repealed 1844).

Prussia and the German states had implemented compulsory schooling in part for the reasons of instilling moral values and social order, involvement that British liberal philosophers feared from the government. But religious divisions in Germany did not hinder the state involvement in education. In fact, Protestants pushed for compulsory schooling, so that children could study the Bible (Becker and Woessmann 2009). British nonconformists, however, were wary of state influence, as they suspected more influence of the Anglican Church. The resulting sectarian fights and liberal ideals impeded the involvement of the British state in education.

## THE MECHANICS' INSTITUTES AND HIGHER EDUCATION

In response to the lack of formal education in Great Britain, the Mechanics' Institute movement emerged. It was again a private-market solution. Coalitions of artisans and capitalists issued subscriptions to build Mechanics' Institutes aimed at teaching artisans the science underlying their trade. The institutions offered lectures and classes on various subjects. Typically, students could subscribe to individual classes. Roderick and Stephens (1978) document that by 1826 over 100 private Mechanics' Institutes were founded across Britain. In 1850, the number skyrocketed to 677 with 116,076 subscribers and more than 750,000 books in the institutes' libraries.

The conservative establishment rejected Mechanics' Institutes, as they perceived it as a threat to the social order. Capitalist, however, supported the idea, initially hoping that artisans could make additional economic contributions—for instance, by improving machinery—with scientific knowledge. Yet the share of skilled workers in the labor force declined rapidly between 1841 and 1861. Wrigley (1982) argues that this decline reduced the autonomy of skilled workers, which in turn led to diverging interests of skilled workers and capitalists, who engaged in power struggles over the curriculum. Capitalists now favored a narrower technical education, while skilled workers saw that as undercutting their skills and power on the shop floor. At the same time, the foundation of colleges, such as the Owens College in 1851, offered capitalists an alternative choice for their sons' education.[42]

By the midpoint of the century, it became clear that Mechanics' Institutes had failed to educate the working class. Beyond the political economy, the Mechanics' Institutes faced two additional major obstacles. First, lectures rarely helped illiterate workers, which forced the institutes to also offer some elementary education (Wrigley 1982). Second, in Germany, formal education could shorten the military service to one year with officer rank, and it was needed to complete the apprenticeship; no comparable incentives to attend and complete classes existed in Britain. Thus, a common complaint at British Mechanics' Institutes was infrequent attendance, and, as Sadler (1908) concludes, their effect remained small.[43]

After the decline of the Mechanics' Institutes, questions over how the British state should support continued education were raised. Sadler (1908) notes the Technical Instruction Act of 1889 gave county councils, which were established only the year before, educational powers. When the British Government Education Department started providing funds, it did so only to encourage the teaching of pure science as equally applicable to all industries. Thus, in contrast to the German state that left the allocation of funds to the local authorities from the beginning, allowing for a system tailored to local needs, the British government delegated power to the local authority late, and when it did, it prohibited the use of state funds for teaching the application of science and art to specific trades or industries (Bennett 1937).

Institutions in higher education, mainly Oxford and Cambridge, were financially independent from the state, and reformers had to rely on internal forces

42 Shapin and Barnes (1977) argue that the Mechanics' Institutes were never intended to educate the working class in the first place but rather were a tool for social control, since the middle class controlled the institutes' agendas and not the workers as originally proposed.

43 Tiffen's study of the Liverpool Mechanics' Institute highlights the problems that these institutions faced. He concludes that the classes were in demand until about 1884, when the Education Act of 1870 finally began to be felt. In addition, elementary schools started evening classes. The institute's classes in botany, mineralogy, phrenology, and naval architecture proved disappointing, as did the classes in German and Spanish. Although drawing classes were attended by joiners and mechanics, attendance was infrequent (Tiffen 1935).

to modernize the institutions. The state started to play an active role only with the founding of the University College and later University of London, which was instituted and expanded after long political fights. The first serious state financial investment started in the 1850s with the establishment of provincial colleges across the country (Vernon 2004). Over time the colleges added more science classes, as exemplified by the Imperial College of Science, Technology, and Medicine. Yet the development in Britain is in sharp contrast to the experience in the German states, which, in order to foster local economic development, were powerful allies of industrialization proponents (Wrigley 1986). The early establishment and success of technical institutions (and Gewerbeschulen) was also aided by the fact that the German states, striving to hire the best and brightest, provided incentives to complete formal education by offering high-paying positions to engineers and skilled craftsmen. The British government, however, did not (Summerfield and Evans 1990).

## APPRENTICESHIP AND SKILL CONTROL

Meisenzahl and Mokyr (2012) argue that, in the first Industrial Revolution, Britain's apprenticeship system worked exceptionally well in producing highly skilled workers. The Statue of Artificers of 1563, which regulated apprenticeship, was often ignored, and the influence of guilds, which attempted to enforce apprenticeship contracts, was limited (Humphries 2003; Wallis 2008).[44] The statue was abolished in 1814, and in 1835 the Municipal Corporations Act ended the need for town charters to exercise a trade, removing one of the remaining privileges of guilds (Deissinger 2002). In other words, the British state relied on market solutions. It did not set minimum standards or recommended test or establish a system of third-party skill certification, which made the skills more firm-specific and harder to verify.

After the decline of the Mechanics' Institutes, only a few British institutions offered additional formal education to apprentices. As a result, Smail (1914) calculates that apprentices in Germany would receive up to five times more (formal) education than the ones in Britain, which was hardly a surprise.

Vocational training took place on the shop floor. Eisenberg (1986) points out that in Britain, capitalists hired skilled workmen who then were in charge of hiring and training apprentices. Hence, skills were controlled on the shop

---

44 Mechanical occupations were not covered under the statue. Millwrights, for instance, were entirely produced through the unregulated part of apprenticeship system. The comparatively large number of high-skilled, competent craftsmen laid the foundation for the British success. Using tax data on apprenticeship contracts, van der Beek (2010) documents that from 1710 to 1772, the English system produced large numbers of apprentices in high-skilled occupations.

floor and not by firm owners. Over time, the separation of managerial control and skill control led to a "labor aristocracy" (Lazonick 1990). In this hierarchy apprentices did not only pay journeymen for teaching them new skills, but the structure also gave older workers the opportunity to condition the young generation to use old technologies. By doing so, older workers ensured that the young workers also had an incentive to resist the introduction of new technologies (Krusell and Rios-Rull 1996). In the late nineteenth century, British trade unions drew their strength, in part, from the ability to control skills. Not only did unions (successfully) attempt to limit the number of apprentices and the use of semiskilled workers, they also negotiated demarcations—that is, the exclusive right of a trade to perform specific tasks. Lorenz (1991) finds that these demarcations caused several production delays in the shipbuilding industry.

While in Britain skills were controlled on the shop floor, Prussia, and later Germany's Innungen, which preserved the guild structure, left skill control in the hands of the employers, enabling the state to delegate skill certification to the industry and to set minimum standards, which ensured the transferability of skills. When the British government considered reforms in the training of apprentices in the last quarter of the nineteenth century, it faced fractionalized employers without skill control and fractionalized unions, which controlled skills but suspected that government involvement would decrease union bargaining power.[45]

## CONCLUSIONS

How was Germany able to catch up and, in some sectors, overtake Britain in competence during the Second Industrial Revolution? Myriad educational institutions developed in the German states from the beginning of the nineteenth century onward. The complex system of continuation schools in Germany, offering classes in drawing, mechanics, sciences, accounting, and foreign languages, produced competent workers at all levels tailored to local needs. Thus, continuation schools transformed mere literacy into productivity.

Except for the elite institutions, the story is a local one. Municipalities were responsible for local schools. The federal government rarely intervened, and if it did, it left most of the responsibilities and the budget burdens to the local authorities. The large discretion at the local level in elementary and continued education may therefore explain the finding by Becker, Hornung, and

---

45 For a discussion of the evolution of British employer organizations and unions and how skill control affected union bargaining, see Meisenzahl (2009).

Woessmann (2011) that high preindustrialization literacy rates explain industrial development in Prussia. Continuation schools, whose precondition was literacy, provided the necessary theoretical background, and hence higher literacy rates facilitated faster technology adaptation. The main role of the federal government was to provide incentives to make use of the continuation schools system by requiring standardized exams and skill certification as well as reducing the military service for graduates of Gewerbeschulen. These incentives that boosted Germany's competence during the Second Industrial Revolution were absent in Britain.

Another crucial factor was skill control. In Britain, unions retained skill control on the shop floor, which led to a "labor aristocracy" and eventually hindered British development. Older workers, who had little incentive to render their skills obsolete, were in charge of hiring and teaching apprentices, who then would be locked in the old technologies themselves. In Germany, employers retained skill control through the Innungen, which preserved the guild structure. This preservation allowed the governments of the German states, which set the standards for apprenticeship, to delegate quality control and skill certification to employer organizations. Again, the setup and enforcement were left to local authorities. In addition, the German apprenticeship system used the continuation school system both to provide theoretical knowledge and to further minimize quality differences among apprentices. In other words, the institutional system provided a division of labor among the government, the local authorities, and the employers in the apprenticeship system. By contrast, the British system—with fractionalized and in-fighting employers without skill control, fractionalized and in-fighting unions with skill control, and an unpopular political class—was confronted with a more complex political environment and liberal ideal than Germany that stalled reforms. These hurdles, combined with the lack of comparable secondary and continued education, resulted in a relative decline of the British economy.

In conclusion, the British approach strived for individual excellence, which, as Smail (1914, 5) notes, "may be regarded as more philanthropic than patriotic; the ideal is admirable, but the bulk of the nation's workers are not catered for by the ideal." For the German approach of continued education, he writes that "[it] may be termed as long view which must eventually lead the German nation to and maintain in a foremost place of an industrial world power."

## AUTHOR'S NOTE

The opinions expressed in this chapter are those of the author and do not necessarily reflect the views of the Board of Governors or the staff of the Federal Reserve System.

# BIBLIOGRAPHY

Adelmann, Gerhard. 1967. *Der gewerblich-industrielle Zustand der Rheinprovinz im Jahre 1836.* Bonn: L. Rohrscheid Verlag.

Allendorf, Hugo. 1904. *Das Finanzwesen der Stadt Halle a. S. im 19. Jahrhundert.* Jena: Gustav Fischer Verlag.

Arnold, Gerhard. 1972. "Hoppe, Carl." In *Neue Deutsche Biographie 9,* 614. Berlin: Duncker & Humblot.

Auspos, Patricia. 1980. "Radicalism, Pressure Groups, and Party Politics: From the National Education League to the National Liberal Federation." *Journal of British Studies* 20: 184–204.

Barro, Robert J., and Xavier Sala-i-Martin. 1995. *Economic Growth.* New York: McGraw-Hill.

Becker, Sascha O., Erik Hornung, and Ludger Woessmann. 2011. "Education and Catch-up in the Industrial Revolution." *American Economic Journal: Macroeconomics* 3: 92–126.

Becker, Sascha O., and Ludger Woessmann. 2009. "Was Weber Wrong? A Human Capital Theory of Protestant Economic History." *Quarterly Journal of Economics* 124: 531–96.

Benhabib, Jess, and Mark M. Spiegel. 1994. "The Role of Human Capital in Economic Development: Evidence from Aggregate Cross-country Data." *Journal of Monetary Economics* 34: 143–73.

———. 2005. "Human Capital and Technology Diffusion." In *Handbook of Economic Growth,* vol. 1, edited by Philippe Aghion and Steven N. Durlauf, 935–66. Amsterdam: Elsevier/North-Holland.

Bennett, Charles A. 1937. *History of Manual and Industrial Education 1870 to 1917.* Peoria, IL: Manual Arts Press.

Beringer, Ludwig. 1906. *Die Gesetzgebung der Innungen in Deutschland und der Gewerblichen Genossenschaften in Österreich während der letzten hundert Jahre.* Mainz: Druckerei Lehrlingshaus.

Biernacki, Richard. 1995. *The Fabrication of Labor: Germany and Britain, 1640–1914.* Berkeley: University of California Press.

Brix, Adolph. 1831. *Statik fester Körper, mit besonderer Rücksicht auf technische Anwendung.* Berlin: Duncker & Humblot.

Bröcker, Marie-Louise. 1955. "Benz, Carl Friedrich." In *Neue Deutsche Biographie 2,* 57–59. Berlin: Duncker & Humblot.

Clark, Gregory. 2008. *A Farewell to Alms: A Brief Economic History of the World.* Princeton: Princeton University Press.

Deissinger, Thomas. 1994. "The Evolution of the Modern Vocational Training System in England and Germany: A Comparative View." *Compare* 24: 17–36.

———. 2002. "Apprenticeship Systems in England and Germany: Decline and Survival." In *Towards a History of Vocational Education and Training (VET) in Europe in a Comparative Perspective: Proceedings of the First Internal Conference,* edited by CEDEFOP, 28–45. Luxembourg: Office for Official Publications of the European Communities.

Diesel, Eugen. 1957. "Diesel, Rudolf Christian Karl." In *Neue Deutsche Biographie 3,* 660–62. Berlin: Duncker & Humblot.

Dintenfass, Michael. 1992. *The Decline of Industrial Britain 1870–1980.* London: Routledge.

———. 1999. "Converging Accounts, Misleading Metaphors, and Persistent Doubts: Reflections on the historiography of British Decline." In *The British Industrial Decline,* edited by Jean-Pierre Dormois and Michael Dintenfass, 7–26. London: Routledge.

Eisenberg, Christiane. 1986. *Deutsche und englische Gewerkschaften: Entstehung und Entwicklung bis 1878 im Vergleich.* Göttingen: Vandenhöck and Ruprecht.

Elbaum, Bernard. 1989. "Why Apprenticeship Persistent in Britain but Not in the United States." *Journal of Economic History* 49: 337–49.

Elbaum, Bernard, and William Lazonick. 1984. "The Decline of the British Economy: An Institutional Perspective." *Journal of Economic History* 44: 567–83.

———. 1986. "An Institutional Perspective on British Decline." In *The Decline of the British Economy*, edited by Bernard Elbaum and William Lazonick, 1–17. Oxford: Clarendon.

Friederich, Gerd. 1987. "Das niedere Schulwesen." In *Handbuch der Bildungsgeschichte Band III*, edited by Karl-Ernst Jeismann and Peter Lundgreen, 123–51. Munich: C. H. Beck Verlag.

Frommberger, Dietmar, and Holger Reinisch. 2002. "Development of Disparate Structures of Dutch and German Vocational Education." In *Towards a History of Vocational Education and Training (VET) in Europe in a Comparative Perspective: Proceedings of the First Internal Conference*, edited by CEDEFOP, 75–87. Luxembourg: Office for Official Publications of the European Communities.

Galor, Oded, and Omer Moav. 2006. "Das Human-Kapital: A Theory of the Demise of the Class Structure." *Review of Economic Studies* 73: 85–117.

Goldstrom, J. M. 1972. *Education; Elementary Education: 1780–1900*. New York: Barnes and Noble.

Harney, Klaus. 1987. "Fortbildungsschulen." In *Handbuch der Bildungsgeschichte Band III*, edited by Karl-Ernst Jeismann and Peter Lundgreen, 281–92. Munich: C. H. Beck Verlag.

Herrmann, Walther. 1972. "Horch, August." In *Neue Deutsche Biographie 9*, 622–23. Berlin: Duncker & Humblot.

Hilgert, Anton. 1910. *Das Finanzwesen der Stadt Coesfeld von 1815–1909*. Leipzig: C.L. Hirschfeld Verlag.

Howard, Earl D. 1907. *The Cause and Extent of the Recent Industrial Progress in Germany*. Boston: Houghton Mifflin.

Humphries, Jane. 2003. "English Apprenticeships: A Neglected Factor in the First Industrial Revolution." In *The Economic Future in Historical Perspective*, edited by Paul A. David and Mark Thomas, 73–102. Oxford: Oxford University Press.

Jacobi, Victor. 1842. *Nachrichten über das Gewerbeschulwesen in Preußen und Sachsen, auch Stuttgart, Nürnberg und Karlsruhe*. Leipzig: Adolph Wienbrad Verlag.

Jeismann, Karl-Ernst. 1969. *Staat und Erziehung in der Preussischen Reform 1807–1819*. Goettingen: Vandenhoeck & Ruprecht.

———. 1987. "Schulpolitik, Schulverwaltung, Schulgesetzgebung." In *Handbuch der Bildungsgeschichte Band III*, edited by Karl-Ernst Jeismann and Peter Lundgreen, 105–22. Munich: C. H. Beck Verlag.

Kaelble, Hartmut. 1972. *Berliner Unternehmer während der frühen Industrialisierung*. Berlin: Saladruck.

Kirby, M. W. 1992. "Industrial Rigidities and Economic Decline: Reflections on the British Experience." *Economic History Review* 45: 637–60.

Klauhold, Alfred. 1855. *Kurhessisches Rechtsbuch*. Kassel: Oswald Bertram Verlag.

Kleinschmidt, Christian. 2007. *Technik und Wirtschaft in 19 und 20. Jahrhundert*. Munich: Oldenbourg Wissenschaftsverlag.

König, Wolfgang. 2006. "Vom Staatsdiener zum Industrieangestellen: Die Ingenieure in Frankreich und Deutschland 1750–1945." In *Geschichte des Ingenieurs: Ein Beruf in sechs Jahrtausenden*, edited by Walter Kaiser and Wolfgang König, 179–232. Munich: Claus Hanser Verlag.

———. 2009. *Technikgeschichte*. Stuttgart: Steiner Verlag.

Königliches Statistisches Bureau. 1888. *Statistisches Handbuch für den Preußischen Staat Band 1*. Berlin: Verlag des Königlichen Statistischen Bureaus.

Kruger, Else G. 1986. "Technical Education in Great Britain." In *Education—Past, Present and Future*, edited by Elsa G. Kruger, T. C. Bischoff, S. M. Van Heerden, I. S. J. Venter, and T. L. Verster, 168–79. Pretoria: Euro Publications.

Krusell, Per, and Jose-Victor Rios-Rull. 1996. "Vested Interest in a Positive Theory of Stagnation and Growth." *Review of Economic Studies* 63: 301–29.

Landes, David. 1969. *The Unbound Prometheus: Technological Change and Industrial Development in Western Europe from 1750 to the Present*. London: Cambridge University Press.

Lazonick, William. 1990. *Competitive Advantage on the Shop Floor.* Cambridge, MA: Harvard University Press.

Lee, Simon. 1997. "Culture and Economic Decline." In *The Political Economy of Modern Britain*, edited by Andrew Cox, Simon Lee, and Michael Sanderson, 65–107. Lyme, NH: Elgar.

Lorenz, Edward H. 1991. *Economic Decline in Britain: The Shipbuilding Industry.* Oxford: Clarendon.

Lundgreen, Peter. 1987. "Fachhochschulen." In *Handbuch der Bildungsgeschichte Band III*, edited by Karl-Ernst Jeismann and Peter Lundgreen, 293–305. Munich: C. H. Beck Verlag.

Magnus, Sir Philip. 1888. *Industrial Education.* London: K. Paul, Trench.

Manegold, Karl-Heinz. 1970. *Universität, Technische Hochschule und Industrie.* Berlin: Duncker & Humblot.

Marsch, Ulrich. 2000. *Zwischen Wissenschaft and Wirtschaft: Industrieforschung in Deutschland und Großbritannien 1880–1936.* Paderborn: Friedinand Schöningh.

McCloskey, D. N. 1973. *Economic Maturity and Entrepreneurial Decline: British Iron and Steel 1870–1913.* Cambridge, MA: Harvard University Press.

McCloskey, D. N., and Lars G. Sandberg. 1971. "From Damnation to Redemption: Judgments on the Late Victorian Entrepreneur." *Explorations in Economic History* 9: 89–108.

Meisenzahl, Ralf R. 2009. "Organization Matters: Trade Union Behavior in Peace and War." Paper presented to the European Historical Economics Society meeting, Geneva, September.

Meisenzahl, Ralf R., and Joel Mokyr. 2012. "The Rate and Direction of Invention in the British Industrial Revolution: Incentives and Institutions." In *The Rate & Direction of Inventive Activity Revisited*, edited by Josh Lerner and Scott Stern, 433–79. Chicago: University of Chicago Press.

Ministerium der geistlichen, Unterrichts- und Medicinal-Angelegenheiten. 1859. *Centralblatt für die gesamte Unterrichtsverwaltung in Preußen.* Berlin: Wilhelm Hertz Verlag.

Mitch, David. 2004. "Education and Skill of the British Labour Force." In *The Cambridge Economic History of Modern Britain*, vol. 1, edited by Roderick Floud and Paul Johnson, 322–56. Cambridge: Cambridge University Press.

Mokyr, Joel. 1999. "The Second Industrial Revolution, 1870–1914." In *Storia dell'economia Mondiale*, edited by Valerio Castronovo, 219–45. Rome: Laterza.

———. 2009. *The Enlightened Economy: An Economic History of Britain 1700–1850.* New Haven, CT: Yale University Press.

Morton, Ann. 1997. *Education and the State from 1833.* Richmond, UK: PRO.

Nelson, Richard R., and Edward S. Phelps. 1966. "Investments in Humans, Technology Diffusion, and Economic Growth." *American Economic Review* 56: 69–75.

Olesko, Kathryn. 2009. "Geopolitics and Prussian Technical Education in the Late Eighteenth Century." *Actes D'Historia de la Ciencia I de la Tecnica, Nova Epoca* 2: 11–44.

Parr, Klaus. 2001. "Porsche, Ferdinand." In *Neue Deutsche Biographie 20*, 638–40. Berlin: Duncker & Humblot.

Riedel, Manfred. 1999. *Friedrich Lutzmann—Ein Pionier des Automobilbaus.* Dessau: Anhaltische Verlagsgesellschaft.

Roderick, Gordon W., and Michael D. Stephens. 1978. *Education and Industry in the Nineteenth Century: The English Disease?* London: Longman.

Sadler, Sir Michael. 1908. *Continuation Schools in England & Elsewhere.* Manchester: Manchester University Press.

Sanderson, Michael. 1999a. *Education and Economic Decline in Britain, 1870 to the 1990s.* Cambridge: Cambridge University Press.

———. 1999b. "Education and Economic Decline in Britain, 1870–1914: An Innocent Suspect." In *The British Industrial Decline*, edited by Jean-Pierre Dormois and Michael Dintenfass, 155–74. London: Routledge.

Schiersmann, Christiane. 1979. *Zur Sozialgeschichte der preussischen Provinzialgewerbeschulen im 19. Jahrhundert.* Weinheim: Beltz Verlag.

Schildberger, Friedrich. 1957. "Daimler, Gottlieb Wilhelm." In *Neue Deutsche Biographie 3*, 485–87. Berlin: Duncker & Humblot.

Schindler, Georg. 1969. "Hecker, Johann Julius." In *Neue Deutsche Biographie 8*, 182–83. Berlin: Duncker & Humblot.

Schriewer, Jürgen. 1986. "Intermediäre Instanzen, Selbstverwaltung und berufliche Ausbildungsstrukturen im historischen Vergleich." *Zeitschrift für Pädagogik 32*: 69–90.

Schubarth, Ernst L. 1835. *Elemente der technischen Chemie*. 2nd ed. Berlin: August Rücker.

Schulz, Werner. 1985. "Lilienthal, Otto." In *Neue Deutsche Biographie 14*, 560–62. Berlin: Duncker & Humblot.

Seherr-Thoß, Hans Christoph Graf von. 1979. "Komnick, Franz." In *Neue Deutsche Biographie 12*, 483–84. Berlin: Duncker & Humblot.

———. 1982. "Lang, Franz." In *Neue Deutsche Biographie 13*, 532–33. Berlin: Duncker & Humblot.

———. 1990. "Maybach, Wilhelm." In *Neue Deutsche Biographie 16*, 523–25. Berlin: Duncker & Humblot.

———. 1998. "Otto, Nicolaus August." In *Neue Deutsche Biographie 19*, 700–702. Berlin: Duncker & Humblot.

Shapin, Steven, and Barry Barnes. 1977. "Science, Nature and Control: Interpreting Mechanics' Institutes." *Social Studies of Science 7*: 31–74.

Smail, James C. 1914. *Trade and Technical Education in France and Germany*. London: King and Son.

Smiles, Samuel. 1879. *Lives of the Engineers: The Locomotive; George and Robert Stephenson*. London: John Murray.

Stone, Lawrence. 1969. "Literacy and Education in England 1640–1900." *Present and Past 42*: 69–139.

Stratmann, Karlwihlhelm. 1982. "Geschichte der Beruflichen Bildung: Ihre Theorie und Legitimation seit Beginn der Industrialisierung." In *Enzykopädie Erziehungswissenschaft Band 9.1*, edited by H. Blankertz et al., 173–202. Stuttgart: Klett-Cotta Verlag.

———. 1987. "Betriebliche Berufsausbildung." In *Handbuch der Bildungsgeschichte Band III*, edited by Karl-Ernst Jeismann and Peter Lundgreen, 269–80. Munich: C. H. Beck Verlag.

Summerfield, Penny, and Eric Evans. 1990. "Introduction: Technical Education, the State, and the Labour Market." In *Technical Education and the State Since 1850*, edited by Penny Summerfield and Eric Evans, 1–18. Manchester: Manchester University Press.

Sunder, Franz. 1904. *Das Finanzwesen der Stadt Osnabrück von 1648–1900*. Jena: Gustav Fischer Verlag.

Tenorth, Heinz-Elmar. 1987. "Lehrerberuf und Lehrerbildung." In *Handbuch der Bildungsgeschichte Band III*, edited by Karl-Ernst Jeismann and Peter Lundgreen, 250–69. Munich: C. H. Beck Verlag.

Thelen, Kathleen A. 2004. *How Institutions Evolve: The Political Economy of Skills in Germany, Britain, the United States, and Japan*. Cambridge: Cambridge University Press.

Tiffen, Herbert. 1935. *A History of the Liverpool Institute Schools, 1825 to 1935*. Liverpool: Liverpool Institute Old Boys' Association.

Vandenbussche, Jerome, Phillipe Aghion, and Costas Meghir. 2006. "Growth, Distance to Frontier and Composition of Human Capital." *Journal of Economic Growth 11*: 97–127.

van der Beek, Karine. 2010. "Technology-Skill Complementarity on the Eve of the Industrial Revolution: New Evidence from England." Paper presented to the Economic History Association meetings, Evanston, September.

Vernon, Keith. 2004. *Universities and the State in England 1850–1939*. New York: Routledge Falmer.

Wallis, Patrick. 2008. "Apprenticeship and Training in Pre-modern England." *Journal of Economic History 68*: 832–61.

West, Edwin G. 1991. "The Rise of the State in Education." Unpublished manuscript, Carleton University, Ottawa.

Wrigley, Julia. 1982. "The Division between Mental and Manual Labor: Artisan Education in Science in Nineteenth-Century Britain." *American Journal of Sociology* 88 (supplement): S31–S51.

———. 1986. "Technical Education and Industry in the Nineteenth Century." In *The Decline of the British Economy*, edited by Bernard Elbaum and William Lazonick, 163–88. Oxford: Clarendon.

Zincke, Gisela. 2001. *Joseph Vollmer—Konstrukteur und Pionier*. Wessel: Buch & Bild.

# REGULATING CHILD LABOR

The European Experience

## CAROLYN TUTTLE AND SIMONE A. WEGGE

Child labor did not begin during the Industrial Revolution of Great Britain but had existed for centuries across Europe. Children worked with their families on the farm, in their homes, and in small cottage enterprises. They worked all day almost every day of the week to help their family put food on the table. Child labor was not condoned by society, and parents did not think twice about having their sons and daughters work instead of attending school.

Children did not have full power over the decision to work or not work, making it similar in nature to other labor markets like slavery. Like children, slaves did not have the freedom to make their own individual labor market decisions or to weigh the long-term consequences of hard physical labor and their underinvestment in education. Given just the negative long-term health consequences, many child laborers and slaves were not paid their true wage. In a study of over six hundred child laborer autobiographies, Humphries (2010, 371), documents some long-term effects of working as a child, namely less time spent in school and actual physical deterioration or maldevelopment.

Attitudes toward children working all changed during the nineteenth century when child labor was identified as a social problem. The passionate pleas of humanitarians, medical officials, intellectuals (Friedrich Engels), and enlightened industrialists became louder and louder until government officials took notice.[1] Eventually various European governments ordered investigations of child labor in the industrial sector. In the case of Great Britain, the government commissioned individuals to gather data from the industries thought to have the worst abuses; these industries were part of the formal economy and were considered the leading industries of the Industrial Revolution—textile mills and mines. It is important to note that these industries, although the most visible to society, did not employ the majority of children. The laws, moreover, did not attempt to eliminate the employment of children but instead regulate

---

1 Ashley declared on the floor of Parliament, "Sir, I hardly know whether any argument is necessary to prove that the future of a country must, under God, be laid in the character and condition of its children; however right it may be to attempt, it is almost fruitless to expect, the reformation of its adults; as the sapling has been bent, so will it grow" (quoted in Best 1964, 91).

it.[2] Thus, from the outset, the child labor regulations could have only a minor impact on the employment of children within the country.

Once institutions became aware of the extent of the problem of child labor in mills, factories, and mines, they were in a position to have an impact on the number of child workers as well as their working conditions. Did the laws, once they were passed, make any difference in the employment of child labor during European industrialization? We attempt to answer this question by analyzing the impact of key child labor laws in three countries—Great Britain, Belgium, and Germany (primarily Prussia). This comparison is useful because each of these countries made extensive use of child labor during industrialization while experiencing the "takeoff" in different decades. In all three countries it was extensive in the sheer number of types of manufacturing processes that children were involved in. In Belgium and Great Britain, it was further extensive in that a large percentage of factory workers were children. We compare the evolution of labor and educational reforms across the three countries to assess how they differentially affected the decisions of industrialists to hire children and their parents to send them to work. Great Britain's legislative history with regards to child labor laws, beginning in 1802, preceded that of Belgium's and the German states and contained many laws passed across the nineteenth century; Belgium, in contrast, was slow in passing any legislation and focused its efforts on two laws; several German states passed key legislation in the middle of the nineteenth century, while the Prussian law from 1853 became the standard later for a unified Germany. By examining the timing and enforcement of and the motivation behind key laws we will show that legislation played a negligible role in the regulation of child labor. The countries had considerably different experiences with the timing and importance placed on education. Great Britain was not an education leader in preparing its citizens whereas Germany was the leader in the eighteenth century and throughout the nineteenth century with higher school attendance and literacy rates. By comparing the incidence of child labor and the rise of schooling attendance across each country we will show the relationship between schooling laws and a decline in child labor. How labor and educational reforms contributed to the decline in child labor while each nation's economy was undergoing tremendous industrial and social transitions has significant implications for child labor in developing countries today.

## THE SUCCESS OF SOCIAL REFORM LEGISLATION

Considerable debate remains as to the effectiveness of early attempts of governments to regulate child labor as industrialization pulled many children into fac-

---

2  The exception to this was the laws directed at mines where the objective was to prevent young children and women from working underground.

tories and mines. Scholars have grappled with how the motivations for reform by representatives of the government and certain groups in society determined the degree of compliance and the level of enforcement. The mere existence of regulations, moreover, did not imply that the laws changed the behavior of employers or parents. Understanding the distinction between a "law on the books" and a "law in action" is imperative in determining the impact of social reform legislation on the lives of children. There are two schools of thought on the effectiveness of the child labor laws and schooling laws on the employment of children. The traditional view claims that the child labor laws adopted and applied by governments caused an improvement in working conditions and a dramatic decline in the employment of children. They attribute the success of the laws to the tenacity of the men fighting for the legislation and the diligence of inspectors enforcing the laws (Alfred [1857] 1966; Hutchins and Harrison 1966; Marvel 1977; Peacock 1984; Thomas 1948; and Ward 1962). In his analysis of the factory movement in 1857, Alfred applauded the efforts of the self-sacrificing, strong-minded, persevering, and benevolent proponents of factory legislation (viii).[3] Despite considerable opposition by "the greatest industrialists and intellectual figures," reformers participated in every heated debate on the floor of Parliament until their bill was passed (Ward 1962, 406). Thomas viewed the inspectors quite favorably.[4] As problems arose with enforcement of age and hour restrictions, inspectors developed solutions that improved the identification of violators (Thomas 1948, 121–45). Peacock argues that attempts to enforce the Factory Acts of 1833, 1844, and 1847 were genuine and effective. Using data from the Factory Prosecution Returns over the period 1834 to 1855, he refutes the myth that the Factory Acts were not effective.[5] Marvel (1977, 384) claims that the inspectors in England, Robert Rickards and Leonard Horner, were especially diligent and successful in getting convictions for many of the charges they brought forward. Fines were substantial for some violators.[6]

Research by early economists concluded that the Factory Acts were effective in reducing the hours worked by children and adults in the factories. Chapman

3 He believed factory legislation succeeded in improving the lives of the overworked and helpless children (Alfred [1857] 1966, 289).

4 According to Thomas (1948, 114), although inspectors of the Factory Acts were given tremendous latitude in executing and enforcing laws, they were "intelligent, far-sighted men, with a tremendous appetite for work, and though they were called upon to face a bitter and sustained opposition, it was to them alone that the successful development of industrial control, with its ever-widening ramifications, was due."

5 He shows that very few cases were dismissed, fines in excess of 5 pounds were not uncommon, and the conviction rate by magistrates was in excess of 80 percent (Peacock 1984, 198–207).

6 One Halifax mill owner was fined 200 pounds (Marvel 1977, 384). Marvel shows using figures from the Factory Inspector Reports that the numbers of convictions and penalties were higher for water-powered districts. Smaller rural water-powered mills were more likely, on average, to get caught, be convicted, and pay a sizable fine for employing underage children.

used employment data from factory inspectors' reports to show that child labor in textiles declined once the law took effect. The percentage of children under thirteen dramatically decreased from 13.2 percent in 1835 to 4.7 percent in 1838 (Chapman 1904, 122). He argued that "children had been displaced by the Act of 1833; the simpler regulations of the Act of 1844 caused their recall" (93). Plener (1873) studied the response of factory owners and concluded that the effect of the Factory Acts was not only to reduce the number of hours children worked but also to cause a reduction of all labor hours in general.

The opposing view, or neoclassical view, argues that child labor laws had little impact on the employment of children. Proponents of this view believe that the decline in child labor that occurred after the passage of the British Factory and Mining Acts was attributed to reductions in the demand for child labor (due to technological change) and reductions in the supply of child labor (due to rising real income of the father). They claim that enforcement was not effective and voluntary compliance by employers was uncommon; parents found ways around the laws and public officials were ideologically opposed to the laws and usually decided in favor of employers. In his examination of British government inspections, Bartrip argues that inspectors were not effective in changing the behavior of factory owners and mine owners. He showed that the obstacles facing enforcement were insurmountable. The limited powers of the inspectors and the lack of coordination among them made it difficult to overcome the opposition of magistrates, owners, and parents to government intervention.[7] According to Nardinelli (1980, 748), in theory the Factory Act of 1833 imposed an implicit tax on owners of factories employing children. The tax, however, imposed no real burden on factory owners because conviction rates and fines were extremely low. Instead technological change and increases in family real income caused the removal of children from textile factories after 1835. Nardinelli (1990, 123) argues that "effective child labor laws were passed only after changes in the child labor market significantly reduced opposition to such laws." Kirby's research on the 1842 Mines Act comes to a similar conclusion.[8] Similarly, and in spite of their support for the overall effectiveness of the factory movement, Alfred ([1857] 1966), Henriques (1971), and Thomas (1948) admit that early attempts to restrict hours and ages of employment were impractical. Violations were widespread because no systematic registration

7  The laws appointed too few inspectors with low salaries and very small budgets to carry onsite inspections of all of the textile factories and coal mines in Britain (Bartrip 1982).

8  He claims that "the Mines Act was passed during a period of unprecedented decline in the viability of child labour" (Kirby 1999, 117). Kirby argued it was technical factors and the interests of the largest and most powerful coal owners that were responsible for removing children from working underground. The system of enforcement was flawed at the outset because only one inspector was appointed for the entire industry and he did not want to venture underground. Instead he relied on the word of watchmen and constables who were instructed to spy on the mouths of the pits (Kirby 1999, 114).

of births existed, magistrates were biased in favor of mill owners and parents lied about their children's age (Alfred [1857] 1966, 82; Henriques 1971, 12–15; Thomas 1948, 116–25). It appeared to some members of Parliament that the 1802, 1819, and 1833 Factory Laws were constructed in such a way that they were not intended to be obeyed (Alfred [1857] 1966, 82).

Scholars have found that the inability of regulations to reduce the employment of children in industry also applies to other countries during industrialization. Moehling (1999, 74) concludes in her study of child labor laws in the United States that minimum age limits for manufacturing employment had "relatively little effect in the occupation choices of children at the turn of the century" and further "that these restrictions contribute little to the long run decline of child labor." Similarly, in an extensive study of legislative reform in the United States Hindman (2009, 482) concludes that "state child labor laws are given little credit for the reduction of child labor in early twentieth-century America." His research reveals that an abundance of evidence exists that "in spite of our laws, widespread and persistent violations occur."

## CHILD LABOR LAWS AND THEIR IMPACT ON CHILD LABOR

The intention of lawmakers during the nineteenth century was to regulate not eliminate child labor. Institutions chose to control the ages and hours of child workers and thereby indirectly affect the number of children working in selected industries. Did the adoption of child labor laws make any difference in the employment of child labor during the industrialization period in Great Britain, Belgium, or Germany? The impact and effectiveness of child labor legislation on the employment of children depends on a number of social and political factors. Whether a country wanted to recognize the extensive employment of child labor as problematic, as in the case of Great Britain and Germany, or as necessary, as in the case of Belgium, affected the degree to which people obeyed the law. The motivations of the creator(s) of the bills and the reaction of those affected would indicate the degree of cooperation and extent of compliance. The timing of the laws is also important in determining whether regulations had the potential of altering the behavior of families and industrialists. Laws that preceded the increase in child labor would be the most effective, while laws passed during or after the peak of their employment were dead letters. The level and degree of enforcement of the regulations is critical in understanding both the commitment of the government to reduce the abuses of child labor and the incentives of employers to violate the laws. Finally, the incidence of child labor in the occupations covered by the regulations once enforcement was established will shed light on whether the laws resulted in a decline in child labor. An examination of these specific characteristics of child labor legislation for each country will explain their relative impact on the employment of children.

This comparison promises to show that child labor laws had a negligible effect on the number of children who worked and the nature of their employment.

## THE FACTORY QUESTION

In Great Britain the issue of legislation arose early in the industrial process because of the documented atrocities of the parish apprentices who toiled under miserable conditions in the workhouses and the chimney sweeps who climbed up the narrow chimneys of British homes.[9] Three decades later the horrible conditions in the textile factories were exposed in a letter written by Richard Oastler called "Slavery in Yorkshire." This letter, published in the local paper, *Leeds Mercury*, became famous for its condemnation of children in factories.[10] Many working men supported Oastler's letter, and a group of forty Bradford employers formed a Short Time Committee that promoted a law to limit all workers' hours to ten per day. Debates raged on the Parliament floor between the Reformers and Radicals who were appalled by this new form of child labor and capitalists and factory owners who did not believe the nature of child labor had changed from work on the farm or in the cottage. Humanitarians showed compassion for the factory children and wanted to mitigate the evils of industry. Utilitarians, many of whom were Benthamites, believed working children were denied the right to an education. Doctors who examined many of the factory children were worried about the health and development of children and the prospects for the future generation (Best 1964, 91; Hutchins 1908, 223–26). In addition to these paternalistic motives behind the legislation there were anticapitalist and anticompetitive motives.[11] Although Parliament was convinced they could help the factory children by limiting their hours without hurting the

9   The first suggestion of regulation in textile mills resulted from the recommendations of several medical officers asked to investigate the outbreak of a fever in the cotton works at Radcliffe in 1784.

10   Here is a quote from that letter: "The very streets which receive the droppings of an 'Anti-Slavery Society' are every morning wet by the tears of innocent victims at the accursed shrine of avarice, who are compelled (not by the cart-whip of the negro slave-driver) but by the dread of the equally appalling thong or strap of the over-looker, to hasten, half-dressed, but not half-fed, to those magazines of British infantile slavery- the worsted mills in the town and neighborhood of Bradford!" (Oastler, 1830).

11   Radicals disliked the "millocrats" as much as they sympathized with the mill workers (Best 1964, 81). Tory paternalists "believed factories were turning society into an individualistic, competitive, secular, urban society" (Best 1964, 84). Larger mill owners wanted to eliminate the competition by making it more difficult for small, rural mill owners to earn profits. As Marvel (1977) and Nardinelli (1980) argue, the reduction in children's hours would restrict output and raise prices, which placed heavier labor costs on small mill owners whose operations depended on water power. Marvel (1977, 397, 400, and 401) argues the data on violations and textile characteristics in Northern England support this explanation.

cotton industry, to most of the mill owners the idea of constructive legislation was foreign to their minds, as many claimed as Prime Minister Peel did, that the regulation of children's hours would reduce exports and profits (Hammond and Hammond 1923, 64). Others opposed legislation on ideological grounds that the government should not intervene in the family or economy.[12]

In an attempt to settle the debates and pass the appropriate laws, the House of Commons and the House of Lords formed commissions to study the problem of child labor and collect data. Once the data were presented before Parliament and after passionate debates and difficult compromises, a number of child labor laws were passed (see Table 13.1). Whether these laws are an example of the government acting on behalf of "public interest" or instead merely to placate the public, the laws were directed at the textile and mining industries.[13] MP Sadler wanted a bill passed to limit work hours to ten and conducted interviews for Sadler's 1832 factory report. Many considered his report biased because he interviewed only workers and "ran out of time" to interview employers. He lost his seat and Lord Ashley (previously Lord Shaftesbury) took up the cause and successfully campaigned for the Factory Act in 1833, the 1842 Mines Act, and the Ten Hour Bill in 1847.[14] The Factory Act of 1833 was the first significant regulation on child labor, and the Ten Hours Bill of 1847 was the first enforceable regulation of the factories. Lord Ashley was also instrumental in directing Parliament's attention on the women and children working underground in the coal mines.[15] A resulting inquiry led to the 1842 Mines Report that included evidence and woodcuts of women and children working underground that shocked members in the House of Commons. The Report on the Mines "took Victorian England by storm," and the 1842 Mining Act was passed quickly and almost unanimously (Hammond and Hammond 1923, 70).[16] Subsequent laws covered loopholes in previous laws, improved enforcement, expanded coverage to other industries, and raised the minimum age of employment.

12  Brougham claimed that the law was "contrary to the order of nature and the direction of Providence, who has implanted in the bosom of the mother and father a care for their offspring of which is the great object of that Providence to secure the rearing and the life" (quoted in Hutchins and Harrison 1966, 101).

13  Fraser (1973), Roberts (1960), and Webb (1966) argue that child labor laws are early examples of social legislation because once knowledge of abuses were known and the public demanded reform, Parliament responded and took action.

14  Ashley did not see the Ten Hours Bill through to the end. He introduced it two days before resigning, and John Fielden, a mill owner of Lancashire, pushed it through Parliament.

15  He persuaded the government to establish a commission to investigate the use of child labor in mining.

16  Some scholars argue that the 1842 Mines Act was passed due to concerns over girls learning how to be good housewives and mothers. Humphries (1981, 23–25) argues that instead the commissioners were worried about the morals and sexual behavior of the female miners underground.

**TABLE 13.1** Child Labor Laws in Great Britain

**First Factory Act of 1802**

Set maximum hours for children at 12 and improved conditions in cotton mills

**Cotton Factories Regulation Act of 1819 (Peel's Act)**

Set minimum working age to 9 and maximum hours at 12 in textile factories

**1825 Bill**

Prevented evasions of 1819 act

**Regulation of Child Labor Law 1833**

Set maximum hours for children at 9, prohibited night work and allowed inspections

**Mining Act of 1842**

Prohibited girls and women from working in mines

**Factory Act of 1844**

Limited hours for children in textiles to 6.5 per day

**Ten Hours Bill of 1847**

Limited hours to 10 for young persons and women

**Act of 1850**

Prevented evasions of Ten Hours Bill, set workday hours

**Act of 1853**

Included children under coverage of 1847 act, regulated their workday hours

**Factory Act Extension Act of 1867**

Extended 1847 Ten Hours Bill to all manufactories

**Act of 1874**

Raised the minimum age of employment in factories to 9 and limited hours to 10

**Consolidation Act of 1878**

Combined all previous regulations under one law

**Act of 1893**

Set minimum age for factory and workshop employment at 11

**Act of 1902**

Raised minimum age of employment to 12

*Source*: Tuttle (1999, 68–69).

The lawmakers in Belgium were not as proactive as the Whigs, Tories, and Peelites in Great Britain's Parliament because the dominant ideology of the population was bourgeois liberalism, which was very hostile to government intervention.[17] They adopted and applied "Manchesterism" from the British industrialists and believed that conditions in factories were better than those in the cottage industry and farming. If there were problems, moreover, markets and economic agents were self-correcting and did not require government intervention (Hutchins and Harrison 1966; Scholliers 2009). Facing this widely held economic doctrine, the group of enlightened officials, physicians, and philanthropists who supported child labor legislation fought an uphill battle getting the government to sympathize with the working children of the poor. The rationale for legislation was neither humanitarian nor utilitarian but instead practical. Proponents of restrictions on child labor argued that children's physical and emotional health were stunted by factory work. Overworked children would produce underdeveloped adults.[18] Child labor laws were meant to remove children from industries whose working conditions damaged their health. In a report for the National Consumers' League, McLean (1906, 113) stated, "It is perhaps well to remind ourselves that in both France and Belgium the original agitation for the abolition of child labor took the form not of making rigid and high age requirements but of barring out children from certain industries which were emphatically dangerous to their health." Factories were also thought to destroy social and moral order because they were known as places where fighting, promiscuity, and drunkenness were everyday occurrences. Reformers believed children needed to be removed from these environments to learn moral values in schools.

The first law to protect children working in manufacturing was announced by King Leopold in 1842 in the middle of the Belgian Industrial Revolution. The protection was only symbolic since the decree lacked enforcement. Needing documentation to understand the extent and potential abuses of child labor, Belgium followed a similar path to Great Britain. A special commission was appointed in 1843 to investigate the working and living conditions of the working class and the nature of child labor. The commission gathered information from 164 industrialists, fourteen chambers of commerce, eight mining engineers, and nineteen medical associates. The Report of the Ministere de

---

17  During the general assembly of Catholics in 1867, Dognee De Villers proclaimed, "We must not deprive the father of the family of his guardianship over his children. . . . This serious harm to freedom of industry and the authority of the father is likely to bring the most serious disturbances and produce greater evils than those to which we all want to remedy" (quoted in Loriaux 2000, 63).

18  A minister of justice in Belgium argued that regulating child labor was in the interests of industrialists, "preserving the worker from excessive and stressful labor, while also considering children's strength (its limits), it's creating strong and intelligent workers and increases the effectiveness of the worker in the future" (quoted in Loriaux 2000, 72).

l'Interieur in 1848 revealed that poor working conditions and unsanitary living quarters were a reality for the working class. In addition, it documented that young children were working long hours in abusive conditions in the mechanized textile industry, as well as the cottage industry and farming. They were primarily found in spinning mills, paper mills, and coal mines. In response to this, a law was proposed by the chairman of the Investigation Committee that would prohibit child labor under the age of ten and restrict the working day for ten- to fourteen-year-olds to 6.5 hours. This law was never introduced on the floor of Parliament, however, because industrialists controlled the power in Belgian politics and successfully argued that these restrictions would reduce their competitiveness with the cottage industry and other countries making similar goods. They feared it would lead to a shortage of labor and a reduction in exports. Hence, in the 1840s the Belgium government chose not to regulate industrial work, including women and child labor, despite the damning evidence and similar legislation being passed in Great Britain, Prussia, and France (Hilden 1993, 29). Politically, liberals took power in 1850 and maintained it until 1884. Two other bills were drafted, one in 1859 to restrict industrial work and one in 1872 to restrict mining work, but neither passed. Economic historians have concluded that "the period was characterized by the most purely laissez-faire system anywhere in the industrialized world" (Hilden 1993, 31). This bourgeois ruling class ignored the cries of humanitarians, prominent Catholics, and the working class.

Unlike the situation in Great Britain, in Belgium one person did not champion the cause to regulate child labor; instead a diverse group of enlightened industrialists, physicians, and philanthropists fought for the children. Their united efforts were successful in the passage of the Royal Decree of 1884, the first significant regulation on child labor (see Table 13.2). This law applied only to work in the mines, however. A severe economic recession and ensuing labor strikes in 1886 led to another investigation into working conditions. As a result, the Labor Commission was successful and the Royal Decree of 1889 became law. It established age and hours regulations for a range of industries, including mines and textile factories. It was the first enforceable law in Belgium because it appointed mining engineers and factory inspectors to levy fines on violators. According to contemporaries, the 1889 law set very low standards, contained many exceptions, and was difficult to enforce (McLean 1906; Dubois 1902). McLean argued that the statute "created a system where the administrative bodies assigned to enforce them are likely to be both strict and lenient wherever they are permitted to interpret the law" (106). The Royal Decree of 1895 attempted to rectify this problem by reorganizing the inspection system. Although there were cries for a new law "based on the progress of thought during the last decade" (McLean 1906, 106) nothing materialized. The next significant piece of legislation to affect child labor was the introduction of compulsory schooling in 1914.

**TABLE 13.2**  Child Labor Laws in Belgium

**Royal Decree of 1842**

Protected children working in manufacturing (King Leopold)

**Royal Decree of April 28, 1884**

Set minimum working age in mines at 12 for boys and 14 for girls

**Law of December 13, 1889**

Set minimum working age at 12 for any industry; set maximum hours for
boys aged 12–16 and girls aged 12–21 at 12 for no more than 6 days a week;
prohibited night work for boys under 16 and girls under 21; set minimum
age of 10 for boys working in underground coal mines and prohibited all
women from working underground in mines

**Royal Decree of December 26, 1892**

Limited working hours of children to 11.5 in textiles and 11 in wool,
organized the system of half-time for children aged 12–13 in textiles;
prohibited girls under 21 from working in underground mines

**Royal Decree of March 15, 1893**

Limited working hours in mines to 10.5 for children under 16

**Royal Decree of February 19, 1895**

Set minimum working age to 16 in 65 industries

**Royal Decree of August 5, 1895**

Regulated the employment of children in rag shops

**Royal Decree of October 22, 1895**

Appointed inspectors to enforce the laws

*Source*: Dubois (1902, 205–18).

In the early part of the nineteenth century, Prussia was the leader among
the German states and principalities in passing laws concerning the working
conditions of children. Like in Belgium, several interest groups were interested
in passing legislation to regulate child labor. The earliest efforts at regulating
child labor came out of the Rhine area, perhaps because this area of Germany
also had more than its fair share of new factories. Child labor was already of
some bureaucratic and political interest in Prussia, and more broadly gained
attention as part of the socioeconomic and political discussions on what was

appropriate for children in terms of schooling, training and military service. An important concern of the Prussian government was the long-term effect of hard labor as a child on a person's later ability in the Prussian army (Kuczynski 1958, 150). In 1815, Karl F. A. Grashoff, the director of public education in the Lower Rhine area, published a rather negative report of his travels through the region and what he found in terms of children working in factories (Adolphs 1979, 20). This report served as probably the first official document of Prussian child labor conditions.

Two years later, the Prussian prime minister, Karl A. von Hardenberg, asked his regional presidents to answer a survey about economic conditions in light of the downturn of 1816, with a brief reference to child workers.[19] Some conclusions of this report were that factories should not be prevented from expanding and advancing or hiring children, but that the schooling, military training, and overall education of the Prussian youth needed to be taken into consideration. In spite of von Hardenberg's reputation as a social reformer, Adolphs (1979, 24) argues that the "social-political and educational consequences of this survey were non-existent." Yet another report was generated in 1824 when the local governments in the industry-heavy regions of Prussia were asked by the cultural minister Altenstein to comment on the working conditions of their child workers and propose possible legal measures (Adolphs 1979, 25). In 1828, child labor again received official attention at the highest levels, when the Prussian king, Friedrich Wilhelm III, became concerned that military recruitment was inadequate, especially in the areas where child labor was prevalent. A few years later, in 1834, the same cultural minister, Altenstein, sent a school director around the Rhineland to report back on factory conditions for children; the resulting report was scathing, in terms of the few hours factory children spent in school substituted instead with a large number of hours worked in the factory, along with the overall lack of any sort of meaningful education they received (Adolphs 1979, 28–29). Still, Altenstein hesitated in establishing some sort of child labor law. This impasse was resolved only when the president of the Rhine province, worried about school absenteeism among factory children, proposed a way to ensure some minimum schooling for children working in factories. With the support of the Westphalian president and some dire news reporting by local newspapers, the provincial government initiated a petition in which they described regulations that ended up forming the law of 1839 (Adolphs 1979, 29–31).

By the mid-1840s, more Germans had become more familiar with the abuses of child labor with the publication of Friedrich Engels's series of articles in the

---

19 Child labor was briefly touched on, mostly in regard to children being locked into certain jobs for the rest of their lives, and what the consequences of child factory labor may have been for the agricultural and artisan sectors as well as for the Prussian military (Adolphs 1979, 21–22).

*Rheinische Zeitung* describing the conditions of the Manchester working class, a prelude to his 1845 book titled *The Condition of the Working Class in England* (originally published in German). This work obviously garnered much attention at the time and led Germans to question further whether conditions were as bad for German children working in factories as they were for the English youth Engels described.

Other German regions looked to Prussian legal advances as a model for reforming their own policies. Table 13.3 displays the various laws passed in the nineteenth century by Prussia before 1871 and by Germany thereafter. A few German states and principalities outside of Prussia quickly followed by passing child labor laws, including both Bavaria and Baden in 1840, and the city of Bremen in 1842. Other areas took much longer, such as Württemberg, which passed legislation only in 1862, as shown in Table 13.3.

The 1839 Prussian law made employment of children younger than the age of nine illegal in factories, mines, and other industrial establishments. It also required children to complete three years of schooling. A subsequent labor law in 1853 raised the age requirement for factory work to twelve years—along with limiting factory work hours to six a day for those between the ages of twelve and fourteen and also introduced factory inspections. By the beginning of the 1890s, children younger than thirteen could not work in factories or mines unless they had finished their schooling requirements. Prussia remained, however, the "most socially advanced region in Germany" (Kuczynski 1958, 156). Its stricter child labor laws from 1853 were adopted by the North German Confederation in 1869 and applied soon after for all of Germany upon political unification in 1871 (Friderici 1962, 228).

In all three European countries a similar theme can be found: many industrialists and politicians were concerned over the competitiveness of the country's leading industries in Europe and how any child labor laws would impact the growth of businesses and more widely, the economy. In large part, they were reluctant to adopt child labor laws. Some factory owners did favor legislation; the members of the Short Time Committee in Great Britain and the industrialists in the Ghent textile industry in Belgium imposed restrictions on themselves. Otherwise, at least in the case of British factory owners, most of them had an overall disregard for the data collected by the British government-appointed commissions except in the case of the mining industry.[20] It is thus not surprising that the laws were ignored by most of the industrialists who employed them.

20 Political parties also questioned how representative the reports were, in terms of who gathered the data and whether only the worst examples of child exploitation were included. They argued that the reports were biased against the factory owner and capitalist and exaggerated the problems with the working conditions.

**TABLE 13.3** Child Labor Laws in Germany

| Year, Region | Age of child | Work time limits | Mandated break times | Misc. |
|---|---|---|---|---|
| Before 1839 | Unlimited | Unlimited | None | No law |
| 1839, Prussia | 9–16 years | 10 hours | Two 15 minutes; one 1 hour | 3 years school |
| 1840, Bavaria | 9–12 years | 10 hours | One 1 hour; one 30 minutes | 2 hours/day school |
| 1840, Baden | 11 years + | 10 hours | One 15 minutes; one 1 hour | 2 hours/day school |
| 1842, Bremen Cigar factories | 10 years + | | | |
| 1853, Prussia | 12–14 years | 6 hours work, 3 hours school | Two 30 minutes; one 1 hour | Established inspections |
| 1853, Prussia | 14–16 years | 10 hours | Two 30 minutes; one 1 hour | |
| 1854, Bavaria | Small changes in the 1840 law | | | |
| 1861, Saxony | 10–14 years | 10 hours | One 1 hour; other breaks | School hours apply |
| 1862, Württemberg | Must fulfill school and religious training, etc. | | | |
| 1878 | Same as 1853 | Same as 1853 | Same as 1853 | Obligated factory inspections |
| 1891 | 13–14 years | 6 hours per week | Same as 1853 | Schooling must be completed |
| 1891 | 14–18 years | 10 hours per week | Same as 1853 | Same as 1853 |

*Sources*: This table was adapted from Adolphs (1979, 116). Information on Bavaria, Baden, and Württemberg is from Hoppe (1958, vol. 2).

*Note*: After 1871, the default law is that of Prussia. "Same as 1853" refers back to the Prussian law of that year.

## TOO LITTLE, TOO LATE

The timing of the enforceable laws within the period of industrialization for Great Britain and Belgium clearly demonstrates that child labor laws were passed in the later stages of industrialization (see Table 13.4). GDP per capita figures from Crafts (1984) show how Great Britain, somewhat closely followed by Belgium, both industrialized earlier than Germany. The British child labor laws of the mid-nineteenth century came at a period when Great Britain was well into its second phase of industrialization. Similarly, by 1889, with the first effectively enforced law, Belgium had already experienced multiple decades of industrialization. For Prussia, in contrast, the more effective law of 1853 came comparatively earlier in Prussia's industrialization process, but it did not stem the child labor abuses of previous decades that government officials had begun documenting in 1815. While the timing was different, in all three places the laws were reactive, not proactive, and took several, and sometimes many, years to be implemented due to the lack of consensus among government representatives. Actual enforcement thus typically came much later. As a consequence they were not a deterrent to employers hiring children as industrial workers. It took Britain until the mid-nineteenth century to establish comprehensive and enforceable child labor legislation that curtailed the employment of young children in factories and mines. The Mining Act of 1842 prohibited the employment of females and boys below the age of ten, eliminating only the youngest children from working. The Ten Hours Bill of 1847, moreover, reduced the workday to ten hours from the twelve that had been set by the 1844 Factory Act. At this point, the Industrial Revolution was nearing its later stages and child laborers had been fully employed since 1780. Employment statistics show that the largest numbers of children were employed in the 1830s, fifteen years before any significant legislation was in place.

Similarly, the government of Belgium waited until the end of the nineteenth century to pass any legislation despite awareness of the problem and reform movements in Great Britain and France. The employment of children peaked around 1860 while the first effective law was not enforced until after 1889. As contemporaries have noted, once the government did act the bar was set very low (McLean 1906). The Royal Decree of 1884 set a minimum age of twelve for boys in the mines and fourteen for girls, allowing older girls to work underground. The Royal Decree of 1889 was extremely complex and set different industry specific age and hour restrictions. In industry (textiles and mines) the minimum age was set at twelve with maximum hours "restricted to" twelve a day for a maximum of six days a week. The law also permitted night work for boys over sixteen and girls over twenty-one. Belgium's labor legislation was not effectively enforced until the late nineteenth century, permitting children to secure employment in the textiles, paper mills, metal quarries, and mines in the early stages of industrialization.

**TABLE 13.4** Timing of Child Labor and Education Laws

| Country | Type | Child labor laws | School laws | GDP per capita (1970 US $) | | |
|---|---|---|---|---|---|---|
| | | | | $400 | $550 | $900 |
| Great Britain | 1st law | 1st Factory Act of 1802 | 1880 Compulsory | 1760 | 1840 | 1870 |
| | 1st significant | Regulation of Child Labor, 1833 | 1891 Free/Compulsory | | | |
| | Mining | Mining Act of 1842 | | | | |
| | Enforcement | Ten Hours Bill of 1847/ Act of 1850 | | | | |
| Belgium | 1st law | Royal Decree of 1842 | 1914 Free/Compulsory | N/A | 1850 | 1890 |
| | 1st significant | Law of Dec. 13, 1889 | | | | |
| | Enforcement | Royal Decree of Oct. 1895 | | | | |
| Germany | 1st law | 1839 Law in Prussia | 1717, Prussia, Launch of Volksschule | 1850 | 1870 | 1910 |
| | 1st significant | 1853 Law of Prussia | 1763, Prussia: Compulsory | | | |
| | Enforcement | 1878 Law of Germany | 1794, Prussia: state-control of education | | | |
| | | 1891 Law of Germany | 1809, Prussia: von Humboldt reforms | | | |
| | | | 1810, Prussia: teacher certification | | | |

*Sources:* For GDP: Crafts (1984, 440, 446). We assumed table 1 on p. 440 is correct, given a mistake for Germany in table 6 on p. 446.

In a similar vein, Prussian politicians had had access to reports of various ministers and school officials on the status of child workers for more than twenty years, but did not pass any regulation until 1839. Historians believe that a decline in the use of child labor took place in Germany not after the law of 1839 but gradually after the Revolution of 1848 and more perceptibly so during the 1860s. Adolphs (1979, 10, 56) argues that the worst had passed in Germany by 1869, but that child labor had by no means disappeared in the last decades of the nineteenth century.

Some industrialists had decreased demands for child workers due to the improvement in machines and the more complicated fabrication processes that created a higher demand for skilled workers, as argued by several German historians (Kuczynski 1958, 165; Ludwig 1965, 72; Schulz 1996, 76). A difference in production processes that required higher-level skills and/or a higher average adult wage may have made a difference in lowering the employment of children in the first place. German industrialization happened at a later period than in Great Britain and in Belgium, and factory owners able to adopt the best-practice techniques of the time often were incorporating machines and production processes that were from a more advanced period of industrialization and that were already more automated or required more skilled (older) workers (Adolphs 1979, 77).

The incidence of child labor in Prussian factories and mines fell gradually, from approximately 9.74 percent of factory workers in 1846 to 3.27 percent (see Table 13.8, scenario 2). It is unclear, however, whether the decrease in this statistic has to do more with an actual substantial decrease in the incidence of child labor in German factories or more with factory owners' concealment of child workers. Ludwig (1965, 78), argues that the Prussian data contained problems that led to an undercounting of the number of child workers. What may be more reliable is the distribution of child workers among the different industries, so that one can observe the probable differential incidence across types of economic activities.

## OBEDIENCE AND ENFORCEMENT

Although the earliest law to protect child workers in factories in Great Britain was passed in 1802, no real effective laws were on the books until the labor laws of 1833 and 1842. The labor laws of 1844, 1847, and 1850 had more teeth in them and attempted to limit working hours and improve enforcement. The Regulation of Child Labor Law in 1833 was unique in that it contained a clause that appointed four full-time inspectors to enforce the law and established fines of one and a half pounds per offense to be levied on factory masters or parents for the first offense, to be doubled in the case of second offenses (Dunlop and Denman 1912, 288–89). The system of enforcement, however, supported an inadequate number of inspectors and lacked consistent methods of enforcement. Of the three or four inspectors hired, some did not visit all factory premises, others gave notice of their visits, and some relied upon questionnaire returns. An inspector's only power of enforcement was to levy fines, and it was not always clear who should be fined since the parents often employed the child. In addition, the age and hour limitations established in the laws were extremely difficult to enforce due to the absence of birth records and the adoption of the relay system (Kirby 2003, 107–8). Parents and sometimes doctors falsified age certificates so young children could work. This is evident in the following response of Thomas Hadfield and Robert Bottem to a factory commissioner: "'Is the present law often violated?—Yes, many parents, after passing of the last Bill, signed the names of their children that they were more than eighteen, to get them work.' 'Do they frequently sign that they are nine when they are not?—Yes; many of the parents do that.'" (British Parliamentary Papers [BPP] 1833b [519] XXI).

Many employers were noncompliant and simply ignored the regulations. They knew enforcement was minimal—inspections were rare and fines negligible when compared to the revenue generated from that worker. As Table 13.5 reveals, the number of factory inspectors remained small until 1874, decades after the extensive use of child labor in textile factories. The ratio of inspectors to the number of factories was 1:263 in 1844 and had almost doubled by 1874 when it was 1:540. Similarly, the number of inspectors assigned to enforce the laws in mines was ridiculously low with only one inspector from 1844 to 1854. There was virtually no threat of inspection; in 1854 the ratio of inspectors to mining pits was 1:384 and in 1855 was to 1:223.

The Mining Act of 1842 created an enforcement mechanism that was doomed to failure. The budget for mines inspections was very small, only 10 percent of that allocated for factory inspections. The law appointed only one full-time inspector for all of the mines and did not allow him to go underground to evaluate the working conditions (safety, temperature, air quality, etc.). Instead, the inspector was to deduce the conditions underground based on the overall health of the workers once they surfaced. As it was physically impossible to visit all of the mines each year, the inspector often asked local constables and commercial business owners to spy on the workers once they surfaced from the pits. As a result, mine owners knew, moreover, that inspections were unlikely and inconsequential. Seven years after the law passed, Tremenheere, the only mining inspector for all of Great Britain, admitted he had never been in a mine (BPP 1849 [613] VII)! Only in 1850 were inspectors given permission to go underground and the Royal School of Mines was established to train inspectors. This had little effect on the method or frequency of an inspection as inspectors were reluctant to face the dangers and hostile colliers underground. It is apparent after reading Tremenheere's biannual *Reports on the Mining Districts* that prosecutions occurred only after a mining explosion revealed young boys

**TABLE 13.5** Inspection of Factories and Mines in Great Britain

| Year | # factory inspectors | # mining inspectors | Factory budget (£) | Mining budgets (£) |
|---|---|---|---|---|
| 1834 | 11 | 0 | 5,362 | 0 |
| 1839 | 19 | 0 | 8,850 | 0 |
| 1844 | 19 | 1 | 9,700 | 900 |
| 1849 | 20 | 1 | 10,979 | 900 |
| 1854 | 18 | 7 | 10,715 | 4,400 |
| 1859 | 19 | 13 | 11,525 | 10,400 |
| 1864–65 | 22 | 13 | 13,350 | 10,000 |
| 1869–70 | 43 | 13 | 25,479 | 12,650 |
| 1874 | 54 | 26 | 28,295 | 22,303 |

*Source*: Bartrip (1982, 615, table 3).

among the dead. And even in these cases, at most two prosecutions occurred in a year and a promise that underground agents would be vigilant in preventing men from taking boys down with them was preferred to fines.[21] Almost ten years after the Mining Act was passed, Tremenheere continued to lament in his reports that because "no machinery has been provided for carrying it into effect" and despite the fact that "occasional prosecutions have had the result of causing the Act to be observed to a certain extent, it is nevertheless notorious that great numbers of boys under ten years of age are continually at work in collieries" (BPP 1851b [1406] XXIII).[22]

The first law in Belgium, the Royal Decree of 1842, was largely ignored by factory owners because no one was responsible for enforcing the law. The first effectively enforced child labor law in Belgium was not passed until 1889, nine decades after the beginning of the Belgian industrialization process with the introduction of the first steam engine in 1800 (recall Table 13.2). Herdt (1996, 37) concludes in his research that as a consequence of the fact that Belgium lagged so far behind other industrializing countries in passing restrictive legislation there was "a higher level of child labour than existed in other countries at a similar stage of economic development." Although Prime Minister Charles Rogier introduced protective legislation for women working underground in mines (not children) in 1861 and the king issued a Royal Decree

21 The section on "prosecution" in the Inspector's Reports lists only two violations of the law each year from 1852 to 1858, and a fine of five pounds plus legal costs was levied only half of the time (BPP 1857–58 [2424] XXXII).

22 The machinery that Tremenheere is referring to is an enforcement mechanism whereby certificates of age are used to verify children's ages and registers listing employees are required of each colliery.

to institute mine inspections, the "inspectors were few and careless" (Hilden 1993, 33). As in the case with Great Britain, the first significant law was rarely enforced. The law of 1889 established fines of twenty-six to one hundred francs for industry leaders upon conviction for a violation with a maximum of one thousand francs if there were many children employed illegally. A second conviction doubled the fines. Parents who allowed their children to work were to be fined between one and twenty-five francs. The enforcement was carried out by a few individuals who were already charged with other duties. Like Britain, the number of inspectors was far too small given the number of manufacturers and mines. McLean remarked in 1906 that "there have been very bitter comments on the smallness of the inspection corps and various attempts have been made to enlarge it, so far without avail" (310). Similar to the history of protection of children in Great Britain, effective legislation was not established in Belgium until enforcement was ensured by appointing more inspectors whose only duties were inspection for the Labor Bureau. The Royal Decree of 1895 appointed six federal inspectors, eight provincial inspectors, and six deputies.[23] Although an inspection system was put into place, several problems still existed with enforcement; there were still not enough inspectors, the factory and mine owners were not cooperative, and inspectors often received inadequate support from their superiors. When industries did violate the law, moreover, the courts chose the lower end of the range of fines. In 1902 a brickyard and printing press were fined merely five francs for employing children under the age of twelve (Loriaux 2000, 93). Dubois, a contemporary, found that the laws were not evenly or consistently adhered to in 1902 and concluded, "Nothing is more demoralizing, from the social point of view, than to possess laws to which officials either cannot or will not compel obedience" (220).

In Germany, as in Great Britain and in Belgium, the child labor laws were "laws on the books" rather than "laws in action." After 1839, the Prussian government made a series of orders for the collection of information on child laborer conditions; the resulting reports paved the way for a tougher law of 1853. Kuczynski claims that the child labor laws were useless, especially before the revolution of 1848, but that change came gradually thereafter, but more so in the 1860s than in the 1850s (Kuczynski 1958, 152–57). The 1853 law, however, formalized factory inspections, something left vague in the 1839 regulation. These new factory inspectors worked for the government and had the ability to administer fines to disobeying factory owners given their full authority as city police (Adolphs 1979, 34). With the new tougher law of 1853 politicians must have seen a need for greater protection of child workers along with enforcement or at least the appearance of such. How effective enforcement was must be judged by contemporaries of that time.

---

23  A number of medical inspectors were also appointed and they were specifically charged to monitor the healthfulness of the work place.

Like in Great Britain and Belgium the first attempts at inspections were completely shoddy. Even after 1853, enforcement of the child labor law seems to have been very difficult, as only three of the regional areas of Prussia instated inspectors for a grand total of three inspectors for all of Prussia. It took many years for the number of inspectors to increase: in 1875, there were fourteen inspectors for all of Germany, with ten in Prussia and four in Sachsen (Adolphs 1979, 52). Inspectors were part of the royal or federal police force but confronted many challenges at the local level, working with local police, factory owners, parents, and children, all of whom did not necessarily have the same interest in seeing the 1853 laws respected (Adolphs 1979, 40). Anton (1891) reports that at least prior to 1853 honest inspections were difficult, hampered by the fact that factory owners were usually members of the highest social standing and often had control over the salaries of the town mayor, among others. (Schwiedland 1892, 503). The effectiveness of inspections for the different German regions was mixed: by 1857, Aachen had established a serious inspection program, but Düsseldorf experienced many violations, especially the release of children from school before the age of fourteen (Adolphs 1979, 43; Schwiedland 1892, 504).

## AN INEFFECTIVE DETERRENT AS CHILD LABOR CONTINUES

The cases of Great Britain and Belgium, and to some extent Germany, lend further support to the argument made by several economic historians that social reform legislation was more of a response to social change than a stimulus of it. The political climate, timing, viability, and enforcement of the laws in Great Britain, Belgium, and Germany clearly support the argument that child labor legislation had very little impact on the decline of child labor during the period of industrialization. Although at first glance it appears that all three countries passed child labor laws in the early or relatively early stages of industrialization—1802 in Great Britain, 1842 in Belgium, and 1839 in Germany—they were mostly ignored. The laws were not effective because manufacturers and parents were not compliant and governments were not committed to enforcement. The first inspectors appointed to enforce the restrictive laws were appointed in Great Britain in 1833, in Belgium in 1895, and in Prussia in 1853. Child labor had peaked and begun to decline by the time effective laws were implemented. In Great Britain, employment statistics show that the largest numbers of children were employed in the 1830s, while the first enforceable law was passed in 1847 (the Ten Hours Bill). The labor force participation of children in textiles peaked in 1835, fell by 1838, and then fluctuated through 1850 (see Table 13.6). By 1845 the percentage of children working was roughly half what it was in 1835. Similarly, the employment of children in Belgium peaked in the late 1860s, and the first effective law was not enforced until after 1889.

**TABLE 13.6**  Incidence of Child Labor in Textiles in Great Britain

| Industry | % of labor force under 13 (males + females) | | | | | | |
|---|---|---|---|---|---|---|---|
| | 1833 | 1835 | 1838 | 1839 | 1843 | 1845 | 1850 |
| Cotton textiles | 15 | 16 | 8 | 9 | 7 | 9 | 8 |
| Wool textiles | 17 | 22 | 14 | 14 | 10 | 13 | 13 |
| Worsted | NA | 25 | 14 | 15 | 9 | 15 | 14 |
| Flax | 17 | 20 | 10 | 9 | 8 | 12 | 7 |
| Silk | 30 | 26 | 22 | 24 | 20 | 16 | 13 |

*Sources*: For 1833: BPP (1833b [519] XXI, 33–37). For 1835 and 1839: BPP (1840 [227] X, 119). For 1838, 1843, and 1845: BPP (1845 [639] XXV, 51–52). For 1850: BPP (1851a [1304] XXIII, 64).

As Table 13.7 illustrates, in 1846 children under the age of sixteen made up over 20% of factory workers. Child labor had declined significantly by 1896, especially for children under the age of twelve. Older children were still working, however, with the labor force participation declining from 20.8 percent to 11.3 percent despite the fact that the Royal Decree in 1895 had prohibited children under the age of sixteen from working.

In Germany, it is not clear when the peak in child labor incidence occurred, as usable statistics for wide regions exist first only in 1846. We know, however, that after 1846 it fell, at least for Prussia, where much of the industrial activity was taking place. German industrialization lagged behind Britain and Belgium in many sectors; the timing of the takeoff can be placed in the middle of the nineteenth century. Two different data sources show quite different pictures of the incidence of child labor in the year 1846, either 5.6 percent or 9.74 percent.[24] We are relying more on the second data source and thus on 9.74 percent for 1846.[25]

As a main early area in terms of factory employment, textiles can shed some light on trends over time. In 1846, textile workers were about 60 percent of all factory workers and still 42 percent in 1858. In textiles, children dropped perceptibly as a percentage of all textile workers during the middle half of the nineteenth century: 12.07 percent in 1846, 11.50 percent in 1849, 9.62 percent in 1852, 7.29 percent in 1855, and finally 4.99 percent in 1858. What changed

24  The first source (scenario 1 in Table 13.8, Prussia (1849)) tallies up about a half million factory workers for all of Prussia, while the second scenario (Prussia 1867) counts up about 180,000 fewer, thus making for two different denominators. By 1855 the sources both show that the incidence of child labor in factories was about five percent.

25  Here we use the second data source (Prussia 1867, Yearbook for the Official Statistics of the Prussian State), as the numbers on weaving in the first source (Prussia 1849, Communication of the Statistical Bureau of Berlin) look suspect for 1846.

**TABLE 13.7** Incidence of Child Labor in Belgium (All Industries)

| Age | 1846 | | 1896 | |
| --- | --- | --- | --- | --- |
| | Number | % | Number | % |
| Under 12 | 21,293 | 6.76 | 439 | 0.06 |
| Under 16 | 66,385 | 20.89 | 76,147 | 11.36 |
| Over 16 | 248,457 | 78.90 | 595,449 | 88.70 |

*Sources*: Recensement General (1846, vol.: Industrie, Table X); Recensement General (1896, vol.: Industrie, 203–06).

**TABLE 13.8** Incidence of Child Labor in Germany

Scenario 1: All industries, including mining

| | 1846, Prussia (%) | 1855, Prussia (%) | 1875, Germany (%) |
| --- | --- | --- | --- |
| Boys | 3.10 | 2.80 | 0.96 |
| Girls | 2.50 | 2.20 | 0.61 |
| Total | 5.60 | 5.00 | 1.57 |

Scenario 2: Factories in Prussia

| | 1846 (%) | 1849 (%) | 1852 (%) | 1855 (%) | 1858 (%) |
| --- | --- | --- | --- | --- | --- |
| Boys | 5.45 | 5.00 | 3.84 | 2.82 | 1.71 |
| Girls | 4.29 | 4.13 | 3.00 | 2.23 | 1.56 |
| Total | 9.74 | 9.13 | 6.84 | 5.05 | 3.27 |

Scenario 3: Textile factories in Prussia

| | 1846 (%) | 1849 (%) | 1852 (%) | 1855 (%) | 1858 (%) |
| --- | --- | --- | --- | --- | --- |
| Boys | 8.94 | 8.74 | 7.46 | 5.70 | 3.50 |
| Girls | 19.99 | 17.81 | 13.67 | 10.18 | 7.56 |
| Total | 12.07 | 11.50 | 9.62 | 7.29 | 4.99 |

*Sources*: For scenario 1: For 1846: Prussia (1849, 1:68–85). Numbers on weaving are suspect, as zero children and women are listed in some subcategories. For 1855: Prussia (1858, 204–53). For 1875: Germany (1879, vol. 34, pt. 2, 852–53) (businesses with five or more employees). For scenario 2: Prussia (1867, 242). For scenario 3: Prussia (1867, 244–46, 258–60).

in these years was a drastic fall in total workers in the area of weaving due to the heavier adoption of the power loom. Overall, as shown in Table 13.8, the incidence of child labor in Prussian factories fell to five percent between 1846 and 1855 (from 9.74 percent); by 1875, the incidence for all of Germany was 1.57 percent. The steep drop-off seems to have come at least after the passage of the 1853 law, which excluded children younger than twelve from working in factories and mines and limited children of twelve to fourteen years of age to six hours of work a day. Any earlier fall in the incidence of child labor is not as relevant given the low levels of industrial activity in the Prussian economy.

Thus, by the time the countries set up an enforcement system that provided the existing laws with "teeth," much employment of children had already diminished.[26] In all three countries, therefore, the laws were for a time "laws on the books" and not "laws in action." Progress was slow, as Hutchins and Harrison (1966, 21) so aptly concluded for Great Britain: "Socially and industrially the first two or three decades of the nineteenth century form a gloomy period, in which, as Spencer Walpole observes, it took twenty-five years of legislation to restrict a child of nine to a sixty-nine hours week, and only in cotton mills."

## SCHOOLING LAWS AND THEIR IMPACT ON CHILD LABOR

Children were permanently removed from the work force once they attended school full-time. Historians, economists, and officials at the International Labor Organization and UNICEF argue that the elimination of child labor occurs after mandatory schooling laws are in place. This implies that "compulsory schooling legislation is the policy instrument by which the state effectively removes children from the labor force" (Weiner 1991, 3). Several scholars argue this was the case in Great Britain during industrialization: "compulsory schooling legislation appears to have been the dominant force after 1850 that lowered children's participation in the labor force" (Mitch 1992, 190). It is therefore important to determine whether this was true historically since child labor is pervasive in most developing countries today. Did schooling laws reduce the employment of children in Great Britain, Belgium, and Germany? Were they more effective than the child labor regulations that preceded them? The emphasis of our analysis is to discern how schooling legislation impacted children employed in the formal economy. In particular, did attending school preclude children from working? A discussion of how successful the early schools were

---

26   Scholars such as De Vries (1994), Nardinelli (1990), Tilly and Scott (1978), and Tuttle (1999) have identified increases in wages or family income, changes in technology, and the changing view of childhood as the reasons for the decline in child labor in Great Britain. In Belgium it was a combination of a severe economic recession and major labor strikes that reduced child labor (Herdt 1996).

in educating children and whether or not they increased literacy are beyond the scope of this chapter and have been the focus of many scholars (Green 1990; Maynes 1985a; Mitch 1992; Vincent 1989; West 1970). Our focus in this section is on schooling, which is not synonymous with education. Education is a broader term and refers to a general process of preparation for adulthood. Schooling, the focus of this section, is a specific institutional form of education. In early modern Europe schooling was not considered a full-time endeavor for six or eight years but instead a part-time activity for a few years of a child's life. Society adopted a loose definition of schooling and viewed workhouse schools, Sunday schools, and night schools as places that sufficiently taught children the fundamentals.[27] Even less formal arrangements created makeshift schools which often existed "from the coal-hole of the engine house to the highest grade of infant education." Teachers were the engine man, the spinner, the overlooker, the bookkeeper, and even the wife next door (Hutchins and Harrison 1966, 78).

During the eighteenth and nineteenth centuries both formal and informal schooling was used to prepare children for adulthood in Great Britain, Belgium, and Germany. Formal education was only a privilege of the wealthy and landowning class of many European countries, and the poor and working class believed it had little benefit in their world. Instead they valued and relied on informal methods which varied considerably in their time away from home and connection to work. There were several options available to poor and working-class British children. Many poor and orphaned children ended up in workhouses and ragged schools where they learned to perform a simple task in the production process. Once they proved useful they worked very long hours until they could survive on their own. Others became apprentices and were removed from the home, worked full-time and typically had no time for formal schooling. The apprenticeship system was seen as a substitute for any formal schooling because it provided hands-on training in a craft or trade which would become the child's vocation in adulthood.[28] In addition, working-class children attended Sunday school where they received lessons in religion, morality, and habits of industry. Despite the fact that Sunday school was pervasive throughout Great Britain by 1833, it was not a substitute for formal education and it did not prevent children from spending the bulk of their time working during the week.

Unlike in Great Britain, Belgium's flexible schooling alternatives were set up by factory owners, not churches, to improve literacy. A proliferation of "schools

27   The fundamentals taught in "schools" changed over time. Initially only reading was thought to be necessary and writing was added later. The more modern view that schools must teach children the three Rs occurred much later.

28   Children were typically made an apprentice from the age of nine until they turned eighteen. They received room, board, and often clothing in exchange for their work time, for which they were not paid a wage. Their "master" was obligated to teach them the skills necessary for a trade. The children learned by listening, watching, and doing what their masters told them to do.

of industry" which trained children for existing occupations and taught the "habits of productive industry" occurred as Belgium industrialized (Chadwick 1865, 15). For example, the city council in Ghent in 1853 set up evening classes for adult factory workers and in 1861 opened a Sunday school for 350 students (Herdt 1996, 33). Although the Sunday school education was successful in reducing illiteracy, it did not prevent children from working in factories. Belgium had an apprenticeship system similar to Great Britain where young children served from the age of five or six until they were eighteen learning the skills of a trade. Many of the apprentices, usually girls, were organized in lace schools in Flanders or "second-chance" schools in lace and linen handwork (Herdt 1996, 33). They were established to "re-educate girls who had become unemployed due to the decline in the Flemish linen industry" (33). These "schools of industry" prepared workers for new occupations using a combination of mental and physical training. They did not, however, remove children from work but instead committed ten to twelve hours per day to industrial pursuits.

In Prussia, where a compulsory school law had existed since 1763, there were fewer alternatives to regular state-sponsored schools. Of course, "schools" had long existed to take care of orphans and very poor children. Factory schools, or *Industrieschulen*, served this same purpose and joined the practical with the usual subjects of reading, writing, and arithmetic, while deemphasizing religious instruction. They were popular toward the end of the eighteenth century and the beginning of the nineteenth century, but their numbers declined considerably thereafter (Kuczynski 1958, 34–35). Many factory schools or *Industrieschulen* consisted primarily of those which trained children in handicrafts and textiles (Kesper-Biermann 2001, 122; Kuczynski 1958). Apprenticeships were the usual training method for most artisans; depending on what age they started at, future apprentices could attend some years of school.

None of these alternative methods of schooling in Britain and Belgium and in some cases in Germany, prevented children from spending the majority of their time working in the cottage industry or industrial factories. The educational reform that spread across Europe attempted to replace these flexible schooling arrangements with a more formal educational process which required longer hours and regular attendance for at least six years. The effectiveness of mandatory schooling laws in removing children from the workplace depended on several political, social and economic factors. The decisions parents made regarding their children's allocation of time weighed these sociopolitical factors with pressing economic needs. The nature and intensity of the political (and public) debate about popular education reveals the level of commitment reformers had in educating the masses. As in the case of child labor regulations, the timing of the legislation that made attending school both mandatory and free is important in determining whether the law had the potential to decrease child labor. If legislation was passed after the industrial epoch, its impact on the child labor that accompanied industrialization is a moot point. In countries where schooling laws were in place early and a system of national education existed, the degree of enforcement is critical in discerning compliance by parents. Finally, and probably the most important factor in determining the law's impact, was the economic resources available to the family. Regardless of their preferences for educating their children or pressures from society, parents who could not survive without their children's contribution had no choice but to send their children to work instead of school.

## POLITICAL AND SOCIAL SUPPORT FOR EDUCATION

Although the poor and working classes were not very interested in education, the wealthier and more privileged members of society began to show considerable interest in the education of the masses and, more specifically, working children. Reformers in Great Britain believed children needed "proper" socialization to counter the bad influence of their parents.[29] As a consequence, educating children became paramount, and social control was the impetus behind the creation of formal schooling. At the same time there was fear that too much education might instill ambition among proletariats and upset the status quo. The people who controlled the political power of the government and the economic power of the new industries (the wealthy, industrialists, and capitalists) wanted their workers to remain passive uneducated slaves (Hammond and Hammond 1937, 39). Given the lack of consensus among the ruling classes, a decentralized, part-time educational system evolved that relied on voluntarism.

Despite local interest and support for education in Belgium, there was strong opposition by a majority of Parliament and many manufacturers to mandatory schooling requirements for the general population (Dubois 1902, 208). The opposition by lawmakers to general education stemmed from the belief that schooling requirements would infringe upon the rights of parents to rear their children as they saw fit (Pinchbeck and Hewitt 1973, 2:357–59). In addition, they believed that "social unrest and even social revolution would ensue if the lower social classes received too much education" (Herdt 1996, 35). The pleas of humanitarians that children had a right to an education were drowned out by the cries of orators in Parliament that popular education would lead to universal suffrage and eventually socialism. Manufacturers also made the case that the work children did was vital to the economy and country and passionately argued that without child labor their industries would have to close. Industrialists firmly believed the training children received by working in their factories taught them the virtues of hard work and the necessity of a trade for adulthood (Herdt 1996, 35). This strong opposition explains the early defect in the Belgian

---

29  The aristocracy believed that the working class was lazy, immoral, impulsive, and decadent (see Chadwick's speech to the president of the Department of Economy and Trade in 1864).

labor laws that contained no provisions for the education of children. A voluntary system was consciously adopted that was dominated by religious education in Catholic Sunday schools such that children could still work six days a week. The Catholic Church, moreover, was opposed to the idea of *laique* (secular) schools and would not fund them. At the time the government did not want to devote resources to education and without church funding no schools could be built. The myriad of objections to popular secular education left Belgium, for most of the nineteenth century, with no formal schooling system, not even part-time as in Great Britain.

In Germany the establishment of a universal, centralized system of education was very much based on an organizational initiative by the state. A compulsory school law preceded the first child labor law by three quarters of a century.[30] Scholars of Continental Europe believe state-provided education to be a German invention (Fyfe 2009; Green 1990; Maynes 1985a). Prussia led the way, with reforms starting already in the eighteenth century. Important dates in Prussian education history are in Table 13.4.

In the minds of many Europeans, the Prussian education system was state of the art in this period, in particular in establishing a universal, centralized, and three-tier (elementary, secondary, university) system of education. Lindert (2004, 89) describes various foreigners making investigative visits to Germany in the 1830s and thereafter in an attempt to understand better the German, especially Prussian education systems. Proponents of national education for the masses argued that it was of national interest in terms of military needs, economic development, and the education of military officers and religious and government bureaucrats (Maynes 1985b, 48). Social concerns played a role as well: for example, Education Minister von Humboldt used his ideas on *Bildung* in his reforms of 1810, changes that he thought should apply to all or most Prussian children. Other German states emulated Prussia, and most had laws on the books that made some schooling compulsory. Maynes (1985b, 50) argues that "although these laws were on the books as early as the 17th century, these were actually beginning to be enforced in the opening decades of the 19th century."

## TIMING AND ENFORCEMENT

For most parts of Germany, including Prussia and the principality of Hesse-Cassel, school attendance was mandatory for children aged six to fourteen by the end of the eighteenth century (Kesper-Biermann 2001, 73; Lamberti 1989).

---

30  Martin Luther had already advocated in the sixteenth century that it was the duty of the state to provide compulsory education, with the goal that everyone would have access to the Bible in the vernacular.

*Schulpflicht*, or literally "school-duty," required those parents of children ages six to fourteen to be responsible for the payment of money to the local school. The responsibility of providing educational opportunities and enforcing the school laws fell on local communities and their authorities. Not all towns and villages were equally prepared to make the necessary expenditures to make room for a school or pay a teacher. Some areas of Germany enjoyed state subsidization of schooling through various taxes, which allowed for lower school fees. In general, school fees were substantially lower in some German regions than in parts of France (Maynes 1985b, 26).

Even if a community did not have a school, however, it did not mean that its youth had no access to education. The smallest villages often sent their children to schools in larger nearby communities, which is clearly evident in the historical village survey of the 1850s for the principality of Hesse-Cassel.[31] Maynes (1985b, 26) describes some regional variety of school density, with the southwestern area of Germany as very densely populated with schools and villages without a school as outliers.[32] The curriculum in most places included reading, writing, arithmetic, and religious studies.

Like with child labor laws, school attendance depended on the actual enforcement of the school laws, putting local authorities in a difficult spot. Of course, parents could be fined for not following the law. School attendance varied greatly based on the types of job opportunities that children had access to and how well schools could work around the demands of different types of economic activities. Older children tended to have higher truancy rates than younger ones, related to the availability of work opportunities (Maynes 1985b, 88–90). Still, in spite of such factors that lowered attendance, both Prussian and German school enrollment statistics are some of the highest attendance rates before 1870.

Great Britain lagged behind Germany and did not establish a universal compulsory educational system until the end of the nineteenth century. In contrast to Germany, schooling laws followed child labor laws by many decades and compulsory education was not in place until 1880. This was not, however, for lack of trying. As early as 1820 Brougham's Bill proposed universal, compulsory, state-funded education, but the bill was defeated. According to historians, Lord Ashley's support of child labor regulations was to "bring the children within the reach of education" (quoted in Heeson 1981, 81). The 1833 Child

---

31  The historical village survey of the 1850s for Hesse-Cassel, contained in the Hessian State Archive's Bestand H3, provides information on the economy and society of each village. Schools and teachers are counted, and much note was made of pupils attending school in villages where they did not live, presumably because their home village did not have a school.

32  In contrast Maynes mentions a particular eastern region of Prussia named Neumark and currently part of Poland as much less oriented toward education, with only a third of its communities with schools. This was geographically very far removed from much of the economic activity considered a part of the German industrialization.

Labor Law provided funding to build new elementary schools, inspect existing schools, vest control of schools in trustees, and divide costs among the government, poor rates, and parents.[33] The law had little to no effect, however, because it did not require children to attend these schools. Consequently evasions were high, and the law was a dead letter, as the *Leeds Mercury* reported in 1834.[34] In fact, the education clause in this law lengthened the process of removing children from work because it created a "part-time" schooling system. Proponents of this clause within Parliament believed it was best to have children work and attend school, but inspectors found it impossible to enforce this clause, and it was subsequently removed in the 1844 child labor law.[35]

Parliament's unwillingness to commit to direct compulsion doomed the Committee of Council on Education, established in 1839, to failure. The first schooling law was passed in 1870 where local school boards could require attendance for children in their area. However, most of the working-class and youth did not generally attend. Only 40 percent of the English population resided in urban areas, where the law applied, and 100 percent coverage did not exist until 1881. Finally in 1881 elementary education became compulsory, and then in 1891 compulsory education became free. By this point, the industrial epoch had passed and child labor had already declined from its peak. Even if the law had been passed earlier, it would not have been an effective deterrent to parents. As in the case of child labor laws, however, noncompliance was common because fines and convictions were low. Of the 66,882 violations reported in London in 1873, fewer than 5 percent resulted in a conviction (BPP 1875 [1184] XVI). Fines on parents, moreover, rarely exceeded five shillings, which was a little more than a child's weekly earnings of four shillings and far less than a child's expected annual earnings of eight pounds (Mitch 1992, 179). Although prosecutions peaked in the mid-1880s and compliance had improved considerably, the employment of children remained largely unchanged. During this time period school officials indicated that schooling laws increased enrollment of previously unregistered children but did not increase attendance. Not surprising, in 1870 only 2 percent of fourteen-year-olds were in school full-time; in 1902 this increased only slightly, to 9 percent, and by 1938 the figure was 38 percent (Kirby 2003, 112). Lindert's figures on British school attendance rates, although not age-specific and measuring overall attendance instead, may well be higher.

In Continental Europe, Belgium was considered the slowest country to adopt mandatory schooling laws despite the examples set by Germany and

33 It also required children to have two hours of schooling per day.

34 "It is clearly proved, as we foretold, that the plan for enforcing education has failed; the object was excellent, but the means of attaining it were ill-judged" (quoted in G. Ward 1935, 115).

35 For a thorough discussion of the problems of enforcement, see Hutchins and Harrison (1966), Thomas (1948), G. Ward (1935), and J. T. Ward (1962).

France.[36] A law was passed in 1842 that required each community to support at least one primary school providing free education to poor children. Although local communities were not opposed to providing schools for the poor and working-class children, parents were not required to comply. Not only was this law ignored, but unlike every other industrializing country in Europe, education clauses were entirely absent from subsequent child labor regulations. As Dubois (1902, 208) declared, "This defect in the Belgian law is due to the opposition that compulsory education has met with and still meets [in 1902] among a notable part of the population and among the majority of Parliament." By the time the first child labor law was passed in 1889 in Belgium, English, German, and French child labor laws contained provisions for the education of children (Dubois 1902, 208). It wasn't until 1914, over fifty years after the industrial epoch, that Belgium made education compulsory.

## PARENTAL SUPPORT

Parental attitudes and preferences of the working class toward education cannot be discerned from their children's attendance at school. Even for parents who valued education, sending their child to a full-time school was usually not an option. Most families were so poor they had no choice but to send their children to work. In other words, the overall costs of schooling far outweighed the benefits for working-class families. Even if school fees were small, the opportunity cost of time spent at work (foregone wages) was large. The benefits, moreover, were unclear and uncertain. During industrialization many of the occupations employing children did not require the skills of reading or writing. In Mitch's (1992, 213, 214) classification of common occupations during the British Industrial Revolution, operators in the textile manufacturing sector and laborers in the mining sector were "unlikely to use literacy." In addition, a wage premium was associated with age and experience and not with schooling.

The consequences of the limited economic resources of poor and working-class families on child labor were similar in Great Britain, Belgium, and Germany. Full-time schooling was incompatible with the early industrial family economy. In Great Britain the combined costs of school fees, tuition, and lost wages outweighed the potential benefits of higher adult wages, improved marriage prospects and better reading and writing skills (Mitch 1982; Kirby 2003). Parental school fees were the major source of funding for common day schools and ranged from three pence to one shilling six pence (four pence for Dame schools) during the 1830s and 1840s (West 1970, 84). Children employed in mills, factories, and mines made substantial contributions to family income,

36 For information about the educational system in France, see Chartier, Julia, and Compère (1976).

and their wages often made the difference between starvation and survival (Humphries 1981, 13–14). In factories and mines, children's wages were as much as a third of adult male wages and increased with age (Anderson 1971; Humphries 2010; Tuttle 1999). Many working-class parents, moreover, felt the curriculum taught in the elementary schools was irrelevant to their children's lives and work because it emphasized religious and moral instruction (Mitch 1992; Vincent 1989). Similarly, in Germany many parents were reluctant to send their children to school because they felt that school would not be useful in daily life and was thus a waste of time, especially in some rural areas and for young girls.[37] School enrollment statistics show that older children in Germany had lower attendance rates than younger children, reflecting that parents may well have supported school attendance until paid employment became available (Maynes 1985b, 89). Borscheid's study of the textile industry in the Württemberg region of Germany suggests similarly that parents had very practical reasons to put their children to work. In various Württemberg towns, average family wealth for the families involved in textile work was substantially higher for those with one to three children than for those with no children at all (Borscheid 1978, 407). School fees may not have been as onerous in parts of Germany: Maynes (1985b, 27) argues that at least in southwestern Germany, school fees were low enough not to be a "deterrent." As in the case with Germany and Great Britain, poor Belgian families could not afford to send their children to school either, even if it was free, because their earnings were crucial for family survival. In Ghent, the most important textile center in Belgium, children contributed between 9 and 20 percent of the family income (Van den Eeckhout 1993, 91). Across Belgium, children's contributions to family budgets were substantially higher, at 33 percent (Scholliers 1995, 159–61).

## ENROLLMENT AND ATTENDANCE

Literacy and literacy rates are important indicators of the success of schools in teaching children how to read and write. They are not necessarily indicators of children's presence in school since the Catholic and Anglican churches often taught these skills in Sunday school. Instead, enrollment rates and attendance rates indicate better whether attending school by compulsion (as in the case of Germany) or voluntarily (as in Great Britain and Belgium) led to a decline in child labor. If an increasing proportion of children were attending formal schools that required a full-time, daily commitment, it would be nearly impossible for them to work.

The early compulsory education laws in Germany appeared to have removed many children from the workplace. In the decades before the 1870s,

---

37  This was the case for the principality of Hesse-Cassel (Kesper-Biermann 2001, 77).

Prussia had the highest reported rates of average public school enrollment of all European countries: 68.7 percent in 1830, 73.6 percent in 1840, 72.2 percent in 1850, and 69.8 percent in 1860 (Lindert 2004, 91). Thereafter, according to Lindert's sources, public school attendance wavered between 70 percent and 80 percent for all of Germany between 1860 and 1900. Only scant evidence for other countries on school enrollment before 1860 exists: France had a 51.1 percent and Belgium a 54.9 percent rate in 1850 for public and private schooling. No other European nations, besides Prussia and Norway, surpassed 60 percent at this time (Lindert 2004, 91); within some nations, in particular Scotland, enrollment rates were greater than 60 percent.

Even with compulsory school laws, not everyone attended school, as evident from the historical enrollment rates that were still quite a ways off from 100 percent (see Table 13.9). Among those who attended, not every child attended consistently. In the German principality of Hesse-Cassel, for instance, many parents skirted the law by keeping children at home once they had completed their first communion, effectively shaving up to two years off the mandatory schooling time (Kesper-Biermann 2001, 74). Reports out of Prussia show that in the early 1800s, half of the children of the city of Aachen and a third of the children in the city of Iserlohn did not attend school (Herzig 1983, 335).[38]

Given the similar educational policies, enrollment rates may have been at comparable levels in the German regions outside of Prussia. Kesper-Biermann (2001, 84) argues that attendance levels steadily increased over the nineteenth century across the various regions of Germany and were close to the 100 percent mark toward the end of the century. Germany may represent a special case where early education laws helped reduce child labor, at least in keeping the incidence of child labor lower in the early stages of its industrialization process. The government built schools and trained teachers, and parents felt compelled to comply with the law and send their children to school. Enrollment and attendance rates were higher and the incidence of child labor was lower than in Great Britain and Belgium. The composition of the German macroeconomy was also distinct: the German agricultural sector remained much larger than those of Great Britain and Belgium well into the latter part of the nineteenth century (Crafts 1984). Less manufacturing and more agriculture meant more support of regular school attendance, especially since most school calendars were set to accommodate harvest schedules.

In sharp contrast, in Great Britain children who were not employed usually stayed at home rather than attend school (Mitch 1982, 318). Few working-class parents voluntarily sent their children to school, and parents were frequently willing to risk conviction to secure their children's earnings (Mitch 1992, 179). According to research by Mitch, enrollment rates were extremely low during the period of industrialization and did not become significant until the turn

---

38  These are attendance rates for individual cities and thus may differ from Lindert's evidence.

**TABLE 13.9** Students Enrolled in Primary Schools, per 1,000 Children of Ages 5–14

| Country and area | Type | 1830 | 1840 | 1850 | 1860 | 1870 | 1880 | 1890 | 1900 | 1910 |
|---|---|---|---|---|---|---|---|---|---|---|
| Belgium: All | Pub. + prv. | 346 | 526 | 549 | 557 | 582 | 522 | 434 | 592 | 618 |
| Belgium: All | Pub. only | | | | | 427 | 371 | 312 | 358 | 339 |
| Germany: All | Pub. only | | | | 719 | | 711 | 742 | 732 | 720 |
| Germany: Prussia | Pub. only | 687 | 736 | 722 | 698 | 717 | 741 | 747 | 763 | 757 |
| Germany: Prussia | Pub. + prv. | 695 | 714 | 730 | 719 | 732 | 749 | 755 | 768 | 764 |
| U.K.: All | Mostly pub. | | | | 521 | 559 | 549 | 646 | 720 | 729 |
| U.K.: England–Wales | Pub. + prv. | 274 | 351 | 498 | 588 | 609 | 555 | 657 | 742 | 748 |
| U.K.: Scotland | Pub. + prv. | | | 592 | 643 | 697 | 776 | 802 | 765 | 729 |
| U.K.: Scotland | Pub. only | | | 572 | 620 | 673 | 749 | 774 | 748 | 724 |
| U.K.: Ireland | Pub. + prv. | | | | 294 | 384 | 443 | 508 | 525 | 574 |
| U.K.: Ireland | Pub. only | | | | 218 | 285 | 379 | 462 | 525 | 574 |

*Source:* All data are from Lindert (2004, 91–93, table 5.1).

*Note:* Statistics for Northern Ireland are not available in these years.

of the century. The increase in enrollment during the ten years after education became compulsory in 1881 was negligible, rising only 3 percent (Mitch 1982, 10). Although Belgium took the longest to make education mandatory, more parents voluntarily sent their children to school. In Belgium enrollment and attendance increased during the first half of the century despite the absence of compulsory schooling laws. Attendance increased between 1830 and 1850, although it varied widely by province (Loriaux 2000, 84). Enrollment also increased from 48 percent of children aged five to fourteen in 1846 to 60 percent in 1865 and then remained stagnant until 1914 (Herdt 1996, 35). It is unclear, however, if parents kept children in these schools full-time or "voluntarily" withdrew them during periods of harvest and economic hardship.

The case of compulsory schooling legislation was considerably different than child labor legislation. Except for Germany, the timing of the first schooling laws was relatively late in the industrialization process compared to child labor laws. In Great Britain, the first mandatory schooling requirement was passed in 1870, twenty years after the Industrial Revolution. Similarly, the first schooling law appeared in Belgium in 1914, more than fifty years after the period of industrialization. Prussia, on the other hand, had its first compulsory law in place in 1763, many decades before the initial period of industrial growth. The timing of the legislation indirectly reveals how important the education of the youth was to society and the government. In Great Britain, education was not a priority, partially because there was no economic return seen in the form of job opportunities or wages. In Belgium, however, teaching literacy was deemed to be quite important. The government focused on educating adults, and factory owners tried to set up schools for children. Despite the differences in social priorities, the results were the same for the poor and working class. Whether or not a family could send their child to school depended on the economic status of the household and whether the benefits outweighed the costs. In Great Britain, Belgium, and Germany, poor households could not afford to give up the wages of their working children to send them to school.

## CONCLUSION

It does not appear that early adoption of child labor laws made much difference in the employment of child labor during the industrialization period. Whether a country wanted to recognize the extensive employment of child labor as problematic, as in the case of Great Britain and Germany, or as necessary, as in the case of Belgium, child labor laws were usually ignored by those employing the children. Employers found loopholes in the laws and took advantage of the fact that governments did not have the infrastructure to enforce the laws or were reluctant to enforce laws for ideological reasons; when laws were enforced, fines were negligible. In all cases it took time for the incidence of child labor to decrease. What served as some measure of success is that the new labor laws probably took many of the youngest out of the factories and mines.

The impact of mandatory schooling laws met a similar fate in Great Britain and in Belgium. Before schooling laws were in place the existing alternatives or flexible arrangements did not prevent children from working. It was presumed by parents, industrialists and society that children's role during industrialization was to work. Apprenticeships, factory schools, "schools of industry," and *Industrieschulen* were places of on-the-job training in an industry or trade, not schools. The excessively long hours of these work arrangements made it impossible to receive any type of schooling. Attending Sunday school or night school did not interfere with working ten to twelve hours a day in a mill, factory, or mine. The part-time system of education reinforced the desires of industrialists while placating humanitarians and philanthropists. As full-time formal schooling was introduced voluntarily, it was immediately clear that schooling and industrial work were incompatible. Few working-class parents could afford to send their children to school, with the costs outweighing the benefits. As a consequence, the extensive use of child labor in industry persisted. By the time the nineteenth century ended and compulsory schooling laws were in place in all three countries, child labor had already declined significantly.

Germany, and in particular Prussia, was a leader in education from the early nineteenth century, thus before its rise in manufacturing activity. Prussian education policy was more centralized such that there was more control over education policy at the highest government levels. Two factors at least kept the overall percentage of all Prussian children in factories low: (1) mandatory schooling laws played a role in keeping children out of the factories in the first place as Prussia exhibited the highest school enrollment statistics of mid-nineteenth-century Europe, and (2) the manufacturing sector was very small before 1860, while the agricultural sector remained a substantial part of the economy until well toward the end of the nineteenth century.[39] In terms of the Prussian factories children could be found in, such as the textile factories, the rate of child labor incidence was also lower than in the textile factories of Great Britain and Belgium. Still, even with the lower incidence of child labor in Prussia, it took many years after the first child labor law of 1839 for the incidence of child labor to fall.

Finally, the issues raised in this chapter are highly relevant to contemporary discussions of economic growth and transition. Modern economic growth theory claims that education is an important variable influencing long-term economic growth. Today, many businesses in developing nations compete by employing and exploiting child workers, which effectively serves as a solution to their respective society's income maximization problem in the short run. In the long run, societies must concern themselves with increasing their eco-

39   Great Britain's agricultural sector was miniscule in comparison (Crafts 1984).

nomic growth rates; this requires more productive and more skilled workers and can come about only with a reduction in child exploitation combined with a greater investment in education. Last, all developing nations can boast of legal codes that prohibit the use of children for factory work. As contemporary academics and journalists can attest, these institutional setups are irrelevant, given the high incidence of child labor. As we know from the example of nineteenth-century Europe, the transition toward a modern economy is more complicated and requires multiple factors to create incentives that discourage and eventually eliminate child labor.

## BIBLIOGRAPHY

Adolphs, Lotte. 1979. *Kinderarbeit im 19. Jahrhundert; Lehrerverhalten im 19. Jahrhundert; Schulrevision im 19. Jahrhundert*. Duisburg: W. Braun.

Alfred [Samuel Kydd]. (1857) 1966. *The History of the Factory Movement*. London: Simpkin, Marshall, and Co.

Anderson, Michael. 1971. *Family Structure in Nineteenth Century Lancashire*. Cambridge: Cambridge University Press.

Anton, Günther K. 1891. *Geschichte der preußischen Fabrikgesetzgebung. Staats- und sozialwissenschaftliche Forschungen*. Leipzig: Gustav Schmoller.

Bartrip, P. W. J. 1982. "British Government Inspection, 1832–1875: Some Observations." *Historical Journal* 25 (3): 605–26.

Becker, Gary. 1965. "A Theory of the Allocation of Time." *Economic Journal*. 75 (299): 493–517.

———. 1973. "A Theory of Marriage: Part I." *Journal of Political Economy* 81: 813–46.

———. 1981. *A Treatise on the Family*. Cambridge, MA: Harvard University Press.

Berg, Maxine, ed. 1991. *Markets and Manufacture in Early Industrial Europe*. London: Routledge.

Best, G. F. A. 1964. *Shaftesbury*. New York: Arco.

Bolin-Hort, Per. 1989. *Work, Family and the State: Child Labor and the Organization of Production in the British Cotton Industry*. Lund: Lund University Press.

Borscheid, Peter. 1978. *Textilarbeiterschaft in der Industrialisierung: Soziale Lage und Mobilitat in Württemberg (19. Jahrhundert)*. Stuttgart: Klett-Cotta.

British Parliamentary Papers. 1831/2. Children, Mills and Factories Bill. Sel. Cttee. Rep., Mins. of ev. (T. Sadler). H.C. [706], vol. XV.

———. 1833a. Factories, Employment of Children. R. Com. 1st rep. Mins. of ev. (Lord Ashley). H.C. [450], vol. XX.

———. 1833b. Factories, Employment of Children. R. Com. 2nd rep. (Thomas Took and Edwin Chadwick). H.C. [519], vol. XXI.

———. 1834. Factories, Employment of Children. Supplementary rep. (Thomas Took and Edwin Chadwick). H.C. [167], vol. XIX.

———. 1840. First Report from the Select Committee on the Act for the Regulation of the Mills and Factories. H.C. [227], vol. X.

———. 1842a. Children's Employment (mines) App. to 1st rep. pt. II Sub-Commissioners rep. and evidence. H.C. [382], vol. XVII.

———. 1842b. Children's Employment (mines) R. Com 1st rep. (Thomas Took and T. Southwood Smith). H.C. [380], vol. XV.

———. 1843a. Children's Employment (Trades and Manufactures) App. to 2nd rep. pt. II Sub-commissioners reps. and evidence. H.C. [432], vol. XV.

————. 1843b. Children's Employment (Trades and Manufactures) R. com. 2nd rep. (Thomas Took and Southwood Smith). H.C. [430], vol. XIII.

————. 1843c. Mines and Collieries. Midland Mining Commission 1st rep. (Thomas Tancred). H.C. [508], vol. XIII.

————. 1845. Factory Inspector Reports. H.C. [639], vol. XXV.

————. 1849. Coal Mines, Accidents in Mines. Sel. Cttee. HL Rep., mins. of ev. (Lord Wharncliffe). H.C. [613], vol. VII.

————. 1851a. Factory Inspector Reports. H.C. [1304], vol. XXIII.

————. 1851b. Mining Districts Commissioner's rep. (Tremenheere). H.C.[1406], vol. XXIII.

————. 1857–58. Mines and Minerals. Commissioner's rep. (Tremenheere). [2424], vol. XXXII.

————. 1865. Children's Employment (trade and manufactures). R. com. 4th rep. (Tremenheere). H.C. [3548], vol. XX.

————. 1875. Factory Inspectors Report. H.C. (1184), vol. XVI.

Brown, John. 1990. "The Condition of England and the Standard of Living: Cotton Textiles in the Northwest, 1806–1850." *Journal of Economic History* 50 (3): 591–615.

Chadwick, Edwin. 1865. "Opening Address of the President of the Department of Economy and Trade, at the Meeting of the National Association for the Promotion of Social Science, held at York in September 1864." *Journal of the Statistical Society of London* 28 (1): 1–33.

Chapman, S. J. 1904. *The Lancashire Cotton Industry.* Manchester: Manchester University Publications.

Chartier, Roger, Dominique Julia, and Marie-Madeleine Compère. 1976. *L'education en France du XVI au XVIII siècle.* Paris: Société d'édition d'enseignement supérieur (SEDES).

Collier, Francis. 1964. *The Family Economy of the Working Classes in the Cotton Industry 1784–1833.* Edited by R. S. Fitton. Manchester: Manchester University Press.

Colon, A. R., and P. A. Colon. 2001. *A History of Children: A Socio-cultural Survey across Millennia.* Westport, CT: Greenwood.

Crafts, N. F. R. 1984. "Patterns of Development in Nineteenth Century Europe." *Oxford Economic Papers* 36: 438–58.

Crump, W. B., ed. 1931. *The Leeds Woollen Industry, 1780–1820.* Leeds: Thoresby Society.

Cunningham, Hugh. 1990. "The Employment and Unemployment of Children in England c. 1680–1851." *Past and Present* 126: 115–50.

Davin, Anna. 1982. "Child Labour, The Working-Class Family, and Domestic Ideology in 19th Century Britain." *Development and Change* 13: 633–52.

De Vries, Jan. 1994. "The Industrial Revolution and the Industrious Revolution." *Journal of Economic History* 54 (2): 249–70.

Dubois, E. 1902. "Child Labor in Belgium." In *Social Legislation and Social Activity,* edited by the American Academy of Political Sciences of Philadelphia, 201–20. New York: McClure, Phillips.

Dunlop, Jocelyn, and R. D. Denman. 1912. *English Apprenticeship and Child Labour.* New York: Macmillan.

Engels, Frederick. (1845) 1969. *The Condition of the Working Class in England.* Translated by the Institute of Marxism-Leninism, Moscow. Edited by E. J. Hobsbaum. Chicago: Academy Chicago Publishers.

Engelsing, Rolf. 1973. *Analphabetentum und Lektüre; zur Sozialgeschichte des Lesens in Deutschland zwischen feudaler und industrieller Gesellschaft.* Stuttgart: J. B. Metzler.

Field, Alexander. 1979. "Occupational Structure, Dissent, and Educational Commitment: Lancashire, 1844." *Research in Economic History* 4: 235–87.

Fraser, Derek. 1973. *The Evolution of the British Welfare State: A History of Social Policy since the Industrial Revolution.* London: Macmillan.

Friderici, Robert. 1962. "Kinderarbeit in kurhessischen Farbiken und Bergbaubetrieben." *Hessiches Jahrbuch fur Landesgeschichte* 12: 211–29.

Fyfe, A. 2009. "Worst Forms of Child Labor: Agriculture." In *The World of Child Labor: An Historical and Regional Survey,* edited by Hugh Hindman, 82–85. London: M.E. Sharpe.

Germany. 1879. *Hauptwiederholung der Betriebs- und Personalverhältnisse, Statistik des Deutschen Reichs* [German census of 1875]. Vol. 34, pt. 2. Berlin: kaiserlichen Statistischen Amt.

Green, Andy. 1990. *Education and State Formation: The Rise of Education Systems in England, France and the U.S.A.* Basingstoke: Macmillan.

Gronau, R. 1977. "Leisure, Home Production, and Work—The Theory of the Allocation of Time Revisited." *Journal of Political Economy* 85: 1099–1123.

Hammond, J. L., and Barbara Hammond. 1920. *The Skilled Labourer, 1760–1832*. London: Longmans, Green.

———. 1923. *Lord Shaftesbury*. London: Constable & Co.

———. 1937. *The Town Labourer*. New York: Doubleday.

Heeson, Alan. 1981. "The Coal Mines Act of 1842, Social Reform and Social Control." *Historical Journal* 24 (1): 69–88.

Henriques, Ursula. 1971. *The Early Factory Acts and Their Enforcement*. London: London Historical Association.

Herdt, Rene De. 1996. "Child Labour in Belgium: 1800–1914." In *Child Labour in Historical Perspective 1800–1985: Case Studies from Europe, Japan and Colombia*, edited by Hugh Cunningham and Pier Paolo Viazzo, 23–39. Florence: UNICEF.

Herzig, Arno. 1983. "Kinderarbeit in Deutschland in Manufaktur und Protofabrik 1750–1850." *Archiv für Sozialgeschichte* 23: 311–75.

Hesse-Cassel. Hessian State Archives, Marburg. Bestand (Collection) H3, Vols. 1–80 (Village survey).

Hilden, Patricia. 1993. *Women, Work, and Politics: Belgium 1830–1914*. Oxford: Clarendon.

Hindman, Hugh D. 2002. *Child Labor: An American History*. Armonk, NY: M.E. Sharpe.

———. 2009. "Evolution of U.S. Child Labor Policy." In *The World of Child Labor: An Historical and Regional Survey*, edited by Hugh Hindman, 482–86. London: M.E. Sharpe.

Hopkins, Eric. 1994. *Childhood Transformed: Working Class Children in Nineteenth-Century England*. Manchester: Manchester University Press.

Hoppe, Ruth. 1958. *Geschichte der Kinderarbeit in Deutschland 1750–1939*. Vol. 2. Berlin: Verlag Neues Leben.

Horan, Patrick, and Peggy Hargis. 1991. "Children's Work and Schooling in the Late Nineteenth-Century Family Economy." *American Sociological Review* 56 (5): 583–96.

Horrell, Sara, and Jane Humphries. 1992. "Old Questions, New Data, and Alternative Perspectives: Families' Living Standards in the Industrial Revolution." *Journal of Economic History* 52 (4): 849–80.

———. 1995. "The Exploitation of Little Children: Child Labor and the Family Economy in the Industrial Revolution." *Explorations in Economic History* 32 (4): 485–516.

Howard, Earl Dean. 1907. *The Cause and Extent of the Recent Industrial Progress of Germany*. Boston: Houghton Mifflin.

Humphries, Jane. 1981. "Protective Legislation, the Capitalist State and Working-Class Men: The Case of the 1842 Mines Regulation Act." *Feminist Review* 7: 1–33.

———. 2003. "Child Labour in the Industrial Revolution." Working paper presented at the 2003 Economic History Society meetings, Trevelyan College, University of Durham.

———. 2010. *Childhood and Child Labour in the British Industrial Revolution*. Cambridge: Cambridge University Press.

Hutchins, B. L. 1908. "Gaps in Our Factory Legislation." *Economic Journal* 18 (70): 221–30.

Hutchins, B. L., and A. Harrison. (1903) 1966. *A History of Factory Legislation*. New York: A. M. Kelley.

Johnson, Richard. 1970. "Educational Policy and Social Control in Victorian Britain." *Past and Present* 49: 96–110.

Kesper-Biermann, Sylvia. 2001. *Staat und Schule in Kurhessen 1813–1866*. Göttingen: Vandehoeck & Ruprecht.

Kirby, P. 1999. "The Historic Viability of Child Labour and the Mines Act of 1842." In *A Thing of the Past? Child Labour in Britain in the 19th and 20th Centuries*, edited by Michael Lavalette, 101–17. New York: St. Martin's.

———. 2003. *Child Labour in Britain, 1750–1870*. Hampshire, England: Palgrave Macmillan.

Kuczynski, Jurgen. 1958. *Geschichte der Kinderarbeit in Deutschland 1750–1939*. Vol. 1. Berlin: Verlag Neues Leben.

Lamberti, Marjorie. 1989. *State, Society, and the Elementary School in Imperial Germany*. New York: Oxford University Press.

Landes, W., and L. C. Solomon. 1972. "Compulsory Schooling Legislation: An Economic Analysis of Law and Social Change in the Nineteenth Century." *Journal of Economic History* 22 (1): 54–91.

Levine, David. 1985. "Industrialization and the Proletarian Family in England." *Past and Present* 107: 168–203.

Lindert, Peter. 2004. *Growing Public. Social Spending and Economic Growth since the Eighteenth Century*. Vol. 1. New York: Cambridge University Press.

Lindert, Peter, and Jeffrey Williamson. 1983. "English Workers' Living Standards during the Industrial Revolution: A New Look." *Economic History Review* 36 (1): 1–25.

Litchfield, Burr. 1978. "The Family and the Mill: Cotton Mill Work, Family Work Patterns and Fertility in Mid-Victorian Stockport." In *The Victorian Family*, edited by Anthony Wohl, 180–96. London: Croom Helm.

Loriaux, Florence. 2000. *Les Enfants-machines: Historie de travail des enfants en Belgique aux XIX et XX siècles*. Brussels: CARHOP.

Ludwig, Karl-Heinz. 1965. "Die Fabrikarbeit von Kindern im 19. Jahrhundert. Ein Problem der Technikgeschichte." *Vierteljahrschrift für Sozial- und Wirtschaftsgeschichte* 52: 63–85.

Lundberg, Shelly, and Robert Pollak. 1994. "Noncooperative Bargaining Models of Marriage." *American Economic Review* 84 (2): 132–37.

Marvel, Howard. 1977. "Factory Regulation: A Reinterpretation of Early English Experience." *Journal of Law and Economics* 20 (2): 379–402.

Marx, Karl. (1906, 1909) 1912. *Capital*. Chicago: Charles H. Kerr.

Maynes, Mary Jo. 1985a. *Schooling for the People: Comparative Local Studies of Schooling History in France and Germany, 1750–1850*. New York: Holmes & Meier.

———. 1985b. *Schooling in Western Europe: A Social History*. Albany: State University of New York Press.

McLean, Francis. 1906. "Child Labor in Belgium." *Annals of the American Academy of Political and Social Science* 28: 105–13.

Mitch, David. 1982. "The Spread of Literacy in Nineteenth Century England." PhD dissertation, University of Chicago.

———. 1984. "Underinvestment in Literacy? The Potential Contribution of Government Involvement in Elementary Education to Economic Growth in Nineteenth-Century England." *Journal of Economic History* 44 (2): 557–66.

———. 1992. *The Rise of Popular Literacy in Victorian England: The Influence of Private Choice and Public Policy*. Philadelphia: University of Pennsylvania Press.

———. 1993. "The Role of Human Capital in the First Industrial Revolution." In *The British Industrial Revolution*, edited by Joel Mokyr, 267–307. Oxford: Westview.

Mitchell, B. R., and P. Deane. 1962. *Abstract of British Historical Statistics*. Cambridge: Cambridge University Press.

Moehling, Carolyn. 1999. "State Child Labor Laws and the Decline of Child Labor." *Explorations in Economic History* 36 (1): 72–106.

Mokyr, Joel. 1976. *Industrialization in the Low Countries, 1795–1850*. New Haven, CT: Yale University Press.

———. 1993. *The British Industrial Revolution: An Economic Perspective*. Boulder, CO: Westview.

———. 2002. *The Gifts of Athena: Historical Origins of the Knowledge Economy*. Princeton: Princeton University Press.

Nardinelli, Clark. 1980. "Child Labor and the Factory Acts." *Journal of Economic History* 40 (4): 739–55.

———. 1982. "Corporal Punishment and Children's Wages in Nineteenth Century Britain." *Explorations in Economic History* 19 (3): 238–95.

———. 1988. "Were Children Exploited during the Industrial Revolution." *Research in Economic History* 2: 243–76.

———. 1990. *Child Labor and the Industrial Revolution.* Bloomington: Indiana University Press.

Oastler, Richard (1830). "Editorial letter" in *Leeds Mercury*, October 16, 1830.

Ogg, Frederic Austin. 1917. *Economic Development of Modern Europe.* New York: Macmillan.

Parsons, Donald, and Claudia Goldin. 1989. "Parental Altruism and Self-Interest: Child Labor among Late Nineteenth-Century American Families." *Economic Inquiry* 27 (4): 637–60.

Peacock, A. E. 1984. "The Successful Prosecution of the Factory Acts, 1833–55." *Economic History Review* 37 (2): 197–210.

Pinchbeck, Ivy. 1930. *Women Workers and the Industrial Revolution, 1750–1800.* London: Routledge.

Pinchbeck, Ivy, and Margaret Hewitt. 1973. *Children in English Society.* Vols. 1–2. London: Routledge and Kegan Paul.

Plener, Ernst Elder Von. 1873. *English Factory Legislation.* London: Chapman and Hall.

Pollard, Sidney. 1965. *The Genesis of Modern Management.* Cambridge, MA: Harvard University Press.

———. 1980. "A New Estimate of British Coal Production, 1750–1850." *Economic History Review* 33 (2): 212–32.

Prussia. 1849. *Mittheilungen des statistischen Bureau's in Berlin* [Prussian factory census for 1846]. Vol. 1. Berlin: E. S. Mittler und Sohn.

———. 1858. *Tabellen und amtliche Nachrichten über den Preussischen Staat für das Jahr 1855.* Berlin: A. W. Hayn.

———. 1867. *Jahrbuch für die Amtliche Statistik des Preussischen Staats. II Jahrgang.* Vol. 2. Berlin: Koeniglichen Statistischen Bureau.

Recensement General. 1846. *Statisque de la Belgique. Volume: Industrie.* Brussels: Ministere de l'Interieur.

———. 1896. *Statisque de la Belgique. Volume: Industrie.* Brussels: Ministere de l'Interieur.

Redford, Arthur. 1926. *Labour Migration in England 1800–1850.* Manchester: Manchester University Press.

Roberts, David. 1960. *Victorian Origins of the British Welfare State.* New Haven, CT: Yale University Press.

Sanderson, Allen. 1974. "Child-Labor Legislation and the Labor Force Participation of Children." *Past and Present* 56: 75–104.

Scholliers, Peter. 1995. "Grown-ups, Boys and Girls in the Ghent Cotton Industry: The Voortman Mills, 1835–1914." *Social History* 20: 201–18.

———. 2009. "Child Labor in Belgium." In *The World of Child Labor: An Historical and Regional Survey*, edited by Hugh Hindman, 602–5. London: M.E. Sharpe.

Schulz, Günther. 1996. "Schulpflicht, Kinderschutz, technischer Fortschritt und öffentliche Meinung." In *Von der Landwirtschaft zur Industrie. Wirtschaftlicher und gesellschaftlicher Wandel im 19. und 20. Jahrhundert*, edited by G. Schulz, 61–76. Paderborn, Germany: Ferdinand Schöningh.

Schwiedland, Eugen. 1892. "Review of Gunther Anton's 'Geschichte der preussischen Fabrikgesetzgebung bis zu ihrer Aufnahme durch die Reichsgewerbeordnung.' Leipzig, 1891." *Zeitschrift für Volkswirtschaft und Sozialpolitik und Verwaltung* 1: 502–5.

Stone, Lawrence. 1977. *The Family, Sex and Marriage in England 1500–1800.* London: Weidenfeld and Nicolson.

Thomas, Maurice. 1948. *The Early Factory Legislation: A Study in Legislative and Administrative Evolution.* Leigh-on-Sea: Thames Bank.

Tilly, L. A., and J. W. Scott. 1978. *Women, Work and Family.* New York: Holt, Rinehart and Winston.

Tuttle, Carolyn. 1999. *Hard at Work in Factories and Mines: The Economics of Child Labor during the British Industrial Revolution*. Boulder, CO: Westview.

Ure, Andrew. (1835) 1861. *The Philosophy of Manufactures*. London: Frank Cass.

Van den Eeckhout, P. 1993. "Family Income of Ghent Working-Class Families ca. 1900." *Journal of Family History* 18: 87–110.

Vincent, David. 1989. *Literacy and Popular Culture in England 1750–1914*. Cambridge: Cambridge University Press.

Wadsworth, A. P., and J. de L. Mann. (1931) 1965. *The Cotton Trade and Industrial Lancashire, 1600–1870*. Manchester: Manchester University Press.

Ward, G. 1935. "The Education of Factory Child Workers, 1833–1850." *Economic Journal (Economic History Supplement)* 3: 110–24.

Ward, J. T. 1962. *The Factory Movement, 1830–1855*. London: Macmillan.

Webb, Sidney. 1966. "Introduction." In Hutchins and Harrison, *A History of Factory Legislation*. New York: A. M. Kelley.

Webb, S., and B. Webb. 1898. *Problems of Modern Industry*. London: Longmans, Green.

Weiner, M. 1991. *The Child and the State in India: Child Labour and Education Policy in Comparative Perspective*. Delhi: Oxford University Press.

Weisbrot, Mark, Robert Naiman, and Natalia Rudiak. 2002. "Can Developing Countries Afford to Ban or Regulate Child Labor?" www.umass.edu/peri/pdfs/child.PDF.

West, E. G. 1970. "Allocation and Growth in the Early Nineteenth-Century British Education." *Economic History Review*, new series 23 (1): 68–95.

Williamson, Jeffrey. 1985. *Did British Capitalism Breed Inequality?* Boston: Allen & Unwin.

Wrigley, E. A., and R. S. Schofield. 1981. *The Population History of England 1541–1871: A Reconstitution*. Cambridge, MA: Harvard University Press.

# DECOMPOSING THE WAGE GAP

Within- and Between-Occupation Gender Wage Gaps at
a Nineteenth-Century Textile Firm

## JOYCE BURNETTE

Women are paid lower wages than men, and they tend to work in different occupations. This is true now, and it was true in the nineteenth century. Women's lower wages may be due to the fact that they receive lower pay for the same jobs, or to the fact that women are concentrated in lower-paying occupations. Theoretically it is possible to have equal pay for equal work within jobs, but still have a large gender wage gap if women are concentrated in low-paid work. Conversely, it is possible to have a wage gap without occupational segregation if women are paid less than men for doing the same job. This chapter explores the relative importance of these two causes of the gender wage gap.

In 1922 Edgeworth suggested that "the crowding of women into a comparatively few occupations . . . is universally recognized as a main factor in the depression of their wages" (439). Bergmann (1974) developed a model of occupational crowding in which men and women working in the same occupation earn the same wage, but women's earnings are low because they are crowded into a limited number of occupations. Empirical evidence suggests that the majority of the wage gap is due to occupational sorting rather than gender wage differences within occupation, but the size of the within-occupation wage gap depends on how narrowly occupation is defined. Groshen (1991) examined small job cells for five U.S. industries; on average only about ten workers share the same job cell. Given the narrow definition of a job, female and male wages differed by only 1 percent within job cell. Milgrom, Petersen, and Snartland (2001) also find small gender gaps within four-digit occupations in Sweden. The overall gender wage gap was 13 percent for blue-collar workers and 27 percent for white-collar workers, but within occupation-establishment pairs the gender wage gap was only 1.4 percent for blue-collar workers and 5.0 percent for white-collar workers. If occupations are defined more broadly there are larger gender gaps within occupation. Zveglich and Rodgers (2004) use two-digit occupations and find that, for Taiwan in 2000, 97 percent of the wage gap is the result of within-occupation wage differences. Thus, while broader occupational definitions can alter the conclusion, when occupations are defined specifically within-occupation wage gaps are quite small. This suggests that the gender gap is largely due to the concentration of women in lower-wage occupations. Jacobsen (1994, 241) provides evidence of this, noting a negative correlation between the percentage of workers in the occupation who are female and median weekly earnings.

Occupational differences were also important in the nineteenth century. Occupational differences explained the racial wage gap. Higgs (1977) notes that blacks and whites earned the same wages when they did the same work; the racial wage gap was mainly due to occupational segregation. Hareven (1982, 262) concludes that occupational segregation was the main reason for the gender wage gap at the Amoskeag mill in the early twentieth century: "Occupational opportunities for men and women differed because certain higher-paying jobs were closed to women. The jobs of card tender, framefixer, and loomfixer were restricted to men; others, such as burling, were explicitly limited to women. In jobs held by both men and women, such as spinning, drawing in, and weaving, there was no wage differentiation along sex lines. The average wages of women, in fact, in one Amoskeag weave room in 1928 were at times higher than those of men." Minoletti (2011) finds that occupational segregation was an important cause of gender wage differences in British textile manufacturing. He suggests that an important source of gender discrimination was the failure to hire women as overseers. Overseers earned substantially higher wages than other workers, and were overwhelmingly male. Minoletti concludes that, since strength was not required and women who worked in the factories should have acquired the necessary skills, the absence of women overseers was due to gender ideology.

This chapter examines what portion of the gender wage gap at a nineteenth-century textile firm was due to occupational sorting, and what portion was due to within-occupation wage differences. I decompose the wage gap into two portions, the within-occupation gap and the across-occupation gap. Using this decomposition and detailed employment records for a single firm, I test the hypothesis that the wage gap was mainly due to occupational segregation. I find that the portion of the wage gap due to within-occupational wage differences declined between 1856 and 1883, but in both cases was higher than within-occupation gender gaps found in the labor market today. I argue that, at least for weavers, these within-occupation wage differences reflect differences in output. I also examine Minoletti's hypothesis that the absence of women overseers made a significant contribution to the wage gap, and find that occupational segregation between overseers and other production workers accounts for a substantial portion of the wage gap. However, examining the extent of sorting does not tell us whether this occupational segregation is due to sorting in efficient labor markets or to gender discrimination.

## DATA

This chapter examines workers at a large textile firm, the Pepperell Manufac-turing Company of Biddeford, Maine.[1] I examined the payroll records of this firm in October 1856 and March 1883. Wages were paid for a four-week period, and in each case I have the complete payrolls for the firm.[2] The firm was an integrated cotton textile manufacturer. At both dates the firm operated three different mills, each with separate rooms for carding, spinning, dressing, and weaving. The workforce was divided among three mills and a "mixed payroll" that covered the nonproduction workers. The "mixed payroll" included repair-men, night watchmen, cloth inspectors, and accountants. Within each room workers were often given occupational designations that varied somewhat in specificity. For each date I know earnings and number of days worked for each worker, and the units of output and piece rate for each piece-rate worker.

The scope of work done at Pepperell was similar in 1856 and 1883; in both years the mill was integrated, processing cotton from raw fiber to finished cloth. First the raw cotton was cleaned by pickers, and then it was carded by rotating cylinders with fine wire teeth. Drawing created combed cotton slivers which were then combined into loose ropes of cotton called rovings on a fly frame. Rovings were then spun into yarn. Mules were used in both periods, though their relative importance declined over time. Mule spinners were always men, though women were used for spinning on other machines. In 1883 the alterna-tive to mule spinning was ring spinning, and 71 percent of ring spinners were female. In 1856 the alternative form of spinning was not specified, but was most likely the throstle. These nonmule spinners were 57 percent female. The intro-duction of rings seems to be associated with a decline in the relative number of spinners (from 20 percent to 9 percent of total employment), and an increase in the relative number of fly frame workers. Spun yarn was used either for warp, the threads running the length of the cloth, or for weft, the threads running the width of the cloth. Warp yarn was dressed with paste to make it stronger and wound around a beam. To prepare the warp for the loom the yarn had to be threaded into the harness that raised and lowered the threads, a process called drawing-in. Weaving was by far the largest occupation, and remained a con-stant percentage of the labor force (38 percent in 1856 and 39 percent in 1883). After the cloth was woven it had to be inspected and folded.

Table 14.1 shows the number of workers of each sex in the largest 10 occu-pations in 1883. (Mule spinners do not make the list because there were only 24

---

1 Account books used in this study are at Harvard's Baker Library.

2 For 1856, the workers were not all paid on the same date. About half the workers were paid on October 25 and about half on November 8. The four-week pay periods overlap, but are not exactly the same.

**TABLE 14.1** Employment by Gender in the Ten Largest Occupations, 1883

| | M | F | A | Total | Percentage F | M wage | F wage |
|---|---|---|---|---|---|---|---|
| Weavers, piece rate | 136 | 487 | 32 | 655 | 78.2 | 1.06 | 1.01 |
| Ring spinners | 36 | 90 | 3 | 129 | 71.4 | 0.61 | 0.67 |
| Spoolers | 2 | 100 | 2 | 104 | 98.0 | 0.97 | 0.93 |
| Unspecified, general staff | 57 | 1 | 7 | 65 | 0.2 | 1.00 | 1.00 |
| Web drawing, piece rate | 0 | 62 | 0 | 62 | 100.0 | | 0.98 |
| Fly frame piece-rate workers | 1 | 52 | 1 | 54 | 98.1 | 1.07 | 1.04 |
| Unspecified, in weaving rooms | 46 | 3 | 2 | 51 | 6.1 | 1.01 | 0.71 |
| Strippers (in carding rooms) | 45 | 0 | 1 | 46 | 0.0 | 0.99 | |
| Section hands | 40 | 1 | 3 | 44 | 2.4 | 1.59 | 1.60 |
| Back boys, mule-spinning rooms | 40 | 0 | 0 | 40 | 0.0 | 0.46 | |

*Note:* Workers whose gender could not be determined are counted as "ambiguous" and listed under the "A" column.

**TABLE 14.2** Employment and Wages at Pepperell Manufacturing Company

|  | 1856 | 1883 |
|---|---|---|
| Number of employees |  |  |
| Male | 573 | 844 |
| Female | 912 | 1005 |
| Ambiguous | 54 | 108 |
| Total | 1,539 | 1,957 |
| Imputed male | 606 | 915 |
| Imputed female | 933 | 1,042 |
| Percentage female | 60.6 | 53.3 |
| Percentage of employees |  |  |
| Percentage of males in all-male occupations | 37.3 | 44.8 |
| Percentage of females in all-female occupations | 20.8 | 11.1 |
| Percentage of workers in single-sex occupations | 27.3 | 26.9 |
| Wages |  |  |
| Average male wage ($/day) | 0.89 | 1.15 |
| Average female wage ($/day) | 0.61 | 0.92 |
| Wage ratio | 0.68 | 0.80 |
| Weighted average of wage ratios in mixed occupations | 0.73 | 0.96 |
| Average wage in all-male occupations | 1.13 | 1.12 |
| Average male wage in mixed occupations | 0.74 | 1.03 |
| Average female wage in mixed occupations | 0.61 | 0.93 |
| Average wage in all-female occupations | 0.60 | 0.98 |

of them; all mule spinners were male.) The sex of an individual worker could usually be determined by the worker's first name. In cases where only an initial was given, or where the first name was not clearly gendered, I categorized the worker's gender as "ambiguous." Ambiguous workers were assigned a gender based on the gender of other workers in their occupation. For example, there were thirty-two weavers of ambiguous gender. Since weavers were 78 percent female, I assumed that 78 percent of the thirty-two, or twenty-five workers, were female, and that the remaining seven workers were male. (Fractional workers were allowed.)

Pepperell employed 1,539 workers in October 1856 and 1,957 workers in March 1883. Table 14.2 shows employment and wages by sex. Over the twenty-seven years between the two observations, male employment grew faster than female employment, so that the percentage of the labor force that was female declined from 61 percent to 53 percent. This decline is consistent with the historical narrative emphasizing the entry of male immigrants into textile factory work in the middle of the century (Layer 1952, 171; Gitelman 1967; Dublin 1979, 138–39).

Men were more likely than women to work in single-sex occupations. In 1856, 38 percent of men, rising to 45 percent in 1883, worked in all-male occupations. By contrast, the percentage of women working in all-female occupations was lower and declined to only 11 percent in 1883. Overall about 27 percent of workers worked in single-sex occupations. Unfortunately I do not know anything about workers' ages, so I do not know if males in predominantly female occupations were younger than other males. The Pepperell labor force was fairly integrated by gender. In contrast, Groshen (1991) examined five industries and found that the percentage of workers in single-sex job cells ranged from 37.4 percent in computer and data processing, to 69.9 percent in nonelectrical machinery.

The female-male wage ratio rose substantially between 1856 and 1883, from 0.68 to 0.80. In both cases the wage ratio is higher if we look only at mixed-gender occupations. If we look at the employment-weighted average of the wage ratio within mixed-gender occupations, we find a wage ratio of 73 percent in 1856 and 96 percent in 1883. All-male occupations paid relatively high wages, higher even than the average earnings of men in mixed occupations. Relative wage levels are consistent with younger men working in mixed occupations and older, more skilled men working in single-sex occupations. Women were clearly sorted into low-wage occupations. Jacobsen (1994, 241) finds, for the United States in 1992, a negative correlation between the percentage of workers in an occupation who are female and the average wage in that occupation (−.57). The same was true at Pepperell; in 1856 the correlation was −.56, and in 1883 the correlation was −.43. This means that women were concentrated in low-wage occupations.

## DECOMPOSITION OF THE WAGE GAP

To quantify more specifically the importance of occupational sorting, I decompose the difference in wages into the portion caused by within-occupation wage differences and the portion caused by occupational sorting. Noting that the average wage for each gender can be seen as a weighted average of the wages in each occupation, we can write the difference in average wages as

$$\bar{w}_m - \bar{w}_f = \sum_j \frac{M_j}{M} w_{mj} - \sum_j \frac{F_j}{F} w_{fj}$$

where $M$ is the total number of men, $M_j$ is the number of men in occupation $j$, and $w_{mj}$ is the average wage of men in occupation $j$. Adding and subtracting the same term gives

$$= \sum \frac{M_j}{M} w_{mj} - \sum \frac{F_j}{F} w_{fj} - \sum \frac{F_j}{F} w_{mj} + \sum \frac{F_j}{F} w_{mj}$$

$$= \sum \left( \frac{M_j}{M} - \frac{F_j}{F} \right) w_{mj} + \sum \frac{F_j}{F} (w_{mj} - w_{fj})$$

The first term measures the portion of the wage difference due to occupational segregation, and the second portion measures the difference due to wage differences within occupations. Zveglich and Rodgers (2004) used this technique to examine the gender gap in Taiwan.

A practical problem with this calculation is that we cannot observe the wage if no workers of a particular sex are hired. For occupations held only by men, this is not a problem because the second term is zero due to the fact that $F_j$ is zero. However, for occupations hiring no men, we must make an assumption about the average male wage in that occupation. For occupations where no men are hired, I estimate the male wage from the female wage in three different ways. First, I assume that the female-male wage ratio within the occupation is equal to the average female wage for the whole labor force, divided by the average male wage for the whole labor force. Second, I assume that the female-male wage ratio within the occupation is equal to a weighted average of the within-occupation wage ratios, where each occupation is weighted by its total employment. Third, I assume that missing male wages were equal to female wages in that occupation (i.e., that the female-male wage ratio within the occupation is one). Comparing the results of these assumptions gives us some idea of how sensitive the results are to the assumptions made.

As with the Oaxaca decomposition, there is another similar way to decompose the wage gap. Adding an subtracting a different term gives

$$= \sum \frac{M_j}{M} w_{mj} - \sum \frac{F_j}{F} w_{fj} - \sum \frac{M_j}{M} w_{fj} + \sum \frac{M_j}{M} w_{fj}$$

$$= \sum \frac{M_j}{M} (w_{mj} - w_{fj}) + \sum \left( \frac{M_j}{M} - \frac{F_j}{F} \right) w_{fj}$$

While the first decomposition weights the occupational differences by the male wage, the second decomposition weights the occupational differences by the female wage. In general the two decompositions will give different answers, though neither one is incorrect. The main drawback of the second method is that there are more occupations missing female wages, so more wages would have to be estimated. For this reason I do not use the second decomposition.

Table 14.3 shows the results of this decomposition for 1856 and 1883. For each year three different decompositions are shown, each using a different wage ratio to estimate missing wages. The method used to assign male wages makes a difference, and it makes more of a difference in 1856, when there were more all-female occupations, but no matter what assumption is used the percentage of the wage gap due to within-occupation wage differences shrinks substantially between the two time periods. In 1856 within-occupation wage differences account for at least 62 percent of the wage gap, while in 1883 they account for at most 26 percent. This change is consistent with the observation above that the weighted average of within-occupation wage ratios rose substantially, from 73 percent to 96 percent.

The decomposition used here is sensitive to the number of occupational categories. In the extreme, we could assign each worker a unique job title, and the entire wage gap would be between occupations. Because the firm was less thorough in recording job titles in 1856, there are fewer occupational categories in that year (forty-nine rather than seventy-four). To check whether the number of occupations is driving the result, I combine some of the occupations in 1883, and recalculate the decomposition using only thirty-one job titles. The results are given in Table 14.4. If the change over time is driven by the number of occupational categories, then the restricted 1883 data should look like 1856 data. Instead, I find that the results look quite similar to the results in Table 14.3, suggesting that the change over time represents a real change, and is not just an artifact of the number of job titles recorded.

**TABLE 14.3**  Decompositions of the Wage Gap

|  | 1856 | 1856 | 1856 | 1883 | 1883 | 1883 |
|---|---|---|---|---|---|---|
| Wage ratio used to estimate missing male wage | 0.683 | 0.731 | 1.000 | 0.800 | 0.961 | 1.000 |
| Gender difference in daily wage ($/day) | | | | | | |
| Total | 0.281 | 0.281 | 0.281 | 0.230 | 0.230 | 0.230 |
| Within | 0.232 | 0.220 | 0.175 | 0.059 | 0.042 | 0.035 |
| Between | 0.049 | 0.061 | 0.106 | 0.170 | 0.188 | 0.195 |
| Percentages | | | | | | |
| Percentage within | 82.6 | 78.4 | 62.1 | 25.8 | 18.3 | 15.1 |
| Percentage between | 17.4 | 21.6 | 37.9 | 74.2 | 81.7 | 84.9 |

**TABLE 14.4**  Decompositions of the Wage Gap in 1883, with Fewer Job Titles

|  | 1883 | 1883 | 1883 |
|---|---|---|---|
| Wage ratio used to estimate missing male wages | 0.808 | 0.965 | 1.000 |
| **Gender differences in daily wage ($/day)** | | | |
| Total | 0.219 | 0.219 | 0.219 |
| Within | 0.064 | 0.052 | 0.050 |
| Between | 0.155 | 0.167 | 0.169 |
| **Percentages** | | | |
| Percentage within | 29.3 | 23.9 | 22.9 |
| Percentage between | 70.7 | 76.1 | 77.1 |

## OVERSEERS

Paul Minoletti (2011) notes that there were few female overseers in British textile firms, and suggests that this occupational segregation was the result of discrimination. Female overseers were not absolutely unknown, but they were extremely rare. Minoletti rejects both strength and experience as potential reasons for the lack of female overseers, and concludes that gender ideology must be the explanation. In this section I will not discuss the reasons why overseers were men, but will simply ask how important this segregation was to the overall wage gap. Overseers were the highest-paid production workers in the mills, and only a few nonproduction workers earned more, so the absence of women from this occupation should have contributed to the wage gap.

The 1883 wage books clearly identify individuals as "Overseers," "Second Hands," and "Section Hands." We can either define overseers narrowly, as those with the title "Overseer" or "Second Hand," or more broadly, including section hands. The 1856 wage books do not identify overseers, but I am fairly confident that the highest-paid employee in each production room was the overseer. The 1856 accounts clearly label the room each individual worked in (as, for example, "Weaving Room 1"), so I identify the highest-paid employee in each room as the overseer. I also identify the second-highest-paid employee as the assistant overseer and include this person in the broad definition of overseer. In my data the highest level at which a woman was employed is as a "Section Hand," so if the narrow definition of overseers is used, no women were overseers. If the broader definition is used, women were present but rare. The situation at Pepperell thus seems to match the situation in British textiles that Minoletti discusses.

**TABLE 14.5**  The Importance of Overseers, 1856

|  | Narrow definition | | Broad definition | |
|  | Number | Wage | Number | Wage |
|---|---|---|---|---|
| **Overseers** | | | | |
| M | 17 | 2.37 | 29 | 1.94 |
| F | 0 | | 0 | |
| **Other production workers** | | | | |
| M | 466 | 0.76 | 454 | 0.75 |
| F | 923 | 0.61 | 923 | 0.61 |
| **Mixed roll/nonproduction** | | | | |
| M | 123 | 1.14 | 123 | 1.14 |
| F | 10 | 0.65 | 10 | 0.65 |
| **Decomposition** | | | | |
| **All three categories** | | | | |
| Total wage gap | | 0.28 | | 0.28 |
| Within | | 0.16 | | 0.15 |
| Between | | 0.12 | | 0.13 |
| Percentage within | | 58 | | 53 |
| Percentage between | | 42 | | 47 |
| **Production workers only** | | | | |
| Total wage gap | | 0.22 | | 0.22 |
| Within | | 0.16 | | 0.14 |
| Between | | 0.06 | | 0.07 |
| Percentage within | | 74 | | 67 |
| Percentage between | | 26 | | 33 |

Tables 14.5 and 14.6 examine the labor force divided into three catego-ries: overseers, other production workers, and "Mixed Roll" nonproduction workers. I apply the decomposition discussed above to a labor force divided into only these three groups. I define overseers either narrowly (only overseers and second hands) or broadly (including also section hands). In 1856 there were no women overseers. Occupational segregation between the three main

**TABLE 14.6**  The Importance of Overseers, 1883

|  | Narrow definition | | Broad definition | |
|---|---|---|---|---|
|  | Number | Wage | Number | Wage |
| **Overseers** | | | | |
| M | 31 | 2.30 | 74 | 1.89 |
| F | 0 | | 1 | 1.6 |
| **Other production workers** | | | | |
| M | 636 | 1.01 | 593 | 0.96 |
| F | 999 | 0.93 | 998 | 0.93 |
| **Mixed roll/nonproduction** | | | | |
| M | 248 | 1.36 | 248 | 1.36 |
| F | 43 | 0.63 | 43 | 0.63 |
| **Decomposition** | | | | |
| **All three categories** | | | | |
| Total wage gap | | 0.23 | | 0.23 |
| Within | | 0.10 | | 0.06 |
| Between | | 0.12 | | 0.16 |
| Percentage within | | 45 | | 28 |
| Percentage between | | 55 | | 72 |
| **Production workers only** | | | | |
| Total wage gap | | 0.14 | | 0.14 |
| Within | | 0.08 | | 0.03 |
| Between | | 0.06 | | 0.10 |
| Percentage within | | 56 | | 26 |
| Percentage between | | 44 | | 75 |

categories of workers, overseers, nonproduction, and other workers, explained nearly half of the wage gap.[3] If we ignore nonproduction workers, occupational segregation between overseers and other workers accounted for a quarter to a third of the wage gap. In 1883 there was one woman section hand, who counts

3  With so few occupations, there are no all-female occupations, and thus there is no need to estimate a male wage for those occupations.

as an overseer under the broader definition. In spite of this, occupational segregation between overseers and other workers accounts for a larger portion of the wage gap than in 1856 (perhaps because the wage gap among production workers was smaller). Looking at only production workers, occupational segregation between overseers and other workers accounts for between 44 and 75 percent of the wage gap. If we examine the whole labor force, occupational segregation that limited women's participation as overseers and nonproduction workers accounted for between one-half and three-fourths of the wage gap. Thus the fact that women were not overseers had an important impact on their wages.

## THE RELATIONSHIP BETWEEN SORTING AND DISCRIMINATION

So far this chapter has provided a quantitative measure of the contribution of occupational sorting to the wage gap. Occupational segregation was an important and growing cause of the gender wage gap. However, these results cannot tell us the extent of gender discrimination in this labor market because both within-occupation differences in wages and sorting across occupations can be explained by either productivity or discrimination.

Within an occupation, men and women may be paid different wages because of wage discrimination, or because of differences in productivity. Becker's (1957) model of wage discrimination suggests that employers may have a taste for discrimination, which means they incur a utility cost from hiring females. If this is true, an employer is only willing to hire females if

$$w_f + d_i \leq MP_f$$

where $w_f$ is the wage paid to females, $MP_f$ is the marginal product of a female worker, and $d_i$ is the utility cost of hiring women. If there are enough discriminating employers in the market, women can only be hired at a wage below their marginal product. The wage gap could result from discrimination against women.

Alternatively, within-occupation wage differences may be the result of gender differences in productivity. Even with mechanization, some jobs required strength. Mule spinning required strength, while ring spinning did not. Dublin (1979, 65) notes that carding and picking "demanded considerable strength and endurance." Nineteenth-century factories also employed some workers to move raw materials and products within the factory. Productivity also required familiarity with machines, and if women had shorter tenures than men they would have acquired less human capital. Reliability and effort also affected productivity. Given the many different factors affecting productivity, there is no a priori reason to expect that men and women should have equal wages.

Similarly, occupational segregation could have resulted from differences in productivity as well as from discrimination. Sorting is usually interpreted as evidence of labor market discrimination, and in Bergmann's crowding model differences in productivity are the result of occupational barriers confining women to certain occupations. But it is also possible for sorting to be the result of gender differences in productivity. To see how productivity differences would lead to occupational segregation, assume that there is some individual level of productivity (call it p) that is not equally distributed between the sexes. This productivity factor could be, for example, human capital, strength, reliability, effort, or some combination of these factors. A worker's output may depend on p, and occupations may differ in the sensitivity of output to p. To take a concrete example, suppose that there are three occupations. In occupation A productivity is not sensitive to p, but is always equal to 4. In occupation B productivity is moderately sensitive to p, and output is equal to $10p + 2$. Output is very sensitive to p in occupation C, where output is equal to $20p - 4$. Figure 14.1 graphs the relationship between p and output in all three occupations. Given this situation, individuals with $p < 0.2$ will choose occupation A, individuals with $0.2 < p < 0.6$ will choose occupation B, and individuals with $p > 0.6$ will choose occupation C. If we also assume that more women than men have $p < 0.2$, then women will be concentrated in occupation A. If more men than women have $p > 0.6$, then workers in occupation C will be mainly men. Even if workers choose their own occupations to maximize their earnings, men would be concentrated in higher-wage occupations because of their higher levels of p. Moving a woman with $p = 0.3$ from occupation B to occupation C will not help her; in occupation C she could earn only 2. In this case occupational segregation leads to a lower gender wage gap than if workers were equally distributed among occupations.

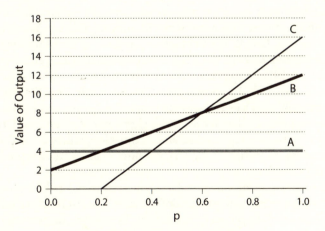

**14.1** Value of output as a function of the individual characteristic.

Gender differences in productivity, whatever their cause, would cause both within-occupation wage differences and occupational sorting. While the data presented here suggest that occupational segregation was an important cause of the gender wage gap, it cannot tell us whether there was discrimination against women.

## GENDER DIFFERENCES IN PRODUCTIVITY

While it is easy to measure gender differences in wages and occupations, it is more difficult to determine whether those differences resulted from productivity differences. Productivity is difficult to measure, but it is worth looking at the measures that are available to see if gender differences are plausible. This section argues that there were within-occupation differences in productivity, and that these differences declined over time.

One measure that should be correlated with productivity is the number of days worked per month. While the mill operated six days per week, many workers did not work every day that the mill was open. There were two main reasons that an individual would miss days. One reason is that the worker started or ended employment during the pay period. If turnover was low there should be few such people, but if turnover was high there may be many workers starting or ending their term of employment. A second reason a worker might work fewer days is irregular attendance. Nineteenth-century workers generally did not show up every day, and were not fired for missing a day of work. Absenteeism was a general problem in nineteenth-century factories (Greenlees 2007, 125–29). Spare hands, who were new workers learning the job, would sometimes substitute for workers who were absent (Dublin 1979, 71).

Evidence from other factories suggests that men had lower turnover than women. Gitelman (1967, 251) finds that, of workers present in 1855, 10 percent of men and 7 percent of women were still working five years later. At Hamilton Company in Lowell, Massachusetts, 17 percent of males working in 1836 were still working fourteen years later, compared to only 2.5 percent of females (Dublin 1979, 187). In 1860 men had an average of 5 years of experience at the firm, and women only 3.2 (Dublin 1979, 189). McHugh (1984, 37) finds that, at a southern mill, men had average experience of 8.2 years, and women 7 years. There is also evidence that women had higher levels of absenteeism than men. Greenlees (2007, 103) reports that, among throstle spinners at the Columbian Manufacturing Company in New Hampshire, males worked more days per month than females.

Both high turnover and irregular attendance would reduce productivity. If there were a systematic gender difference in days worked per pay period this may signal differences in productivity by gender. To examine whether the gender wage gap at Pepperell may be due to differences in turnover and absenteeism, I calculate the average number of days that males and females worked in each of the pay periods. The October 1856 pay period covered four weeks, which meant 24 potential working days. On average the males worked 19.1 days out of the 24 (80 percent) and the females worked 15.4 days (64 percent). This means that women were less regular than men; on average they worked 20 percent fewer days in a given pay period. By 1883, however, the gender gap had almost disappeared. The March 1883 pay period covered five weeks (30 days) and male workers averaged 22.6 days of work, while female workers averaged 22.4 days of work. Absences were still common, since on average workers worked only 75 percent of the potential days. However, the difference between the genders was negligible. Convergence between the genders in regularity of employment may explain some of the convergence in wages. What these numbers do not tell us is whether the low number of days worked per month is the result of turnover or absenteeism.

Piece-rate work offers an opportunity to examine the physical output of male and female workers. Workers can be paid piece rates only if their individual output can be effectively measured. Because piece-rate workers were paid per unit of output, each worker's total output was recorded in the wage book. The wage accounts of the Pepperell company are particularly valuable because they record not only the output and earnings of workers on piece rates, but also the number of days worked. This allows me to calculate output per day for piece-rate workers. Due to incomplete information I cannot calculate the daily output of cloth for every worker. In some cases the number of days worked is not recorded, and in many cases weavers produced different types of cloth but their only aggregate days of work are given. These workers had to be excluded from the analysis because the total number of days worked could not be allocated to the different types of cloth.

Many different types of cloth were produced, so different weavers worked at different piece rates. Table 14.7 divides weavers into groups according to the piece rate at which they worked. The piece rate is in cents per "cut," where the "cut" was the unit in which the firm measures output of woven cloth. I present data only for piece rates at which there are at least two workers of each sex. Because there were fewer male weavers in 1856, and because more weavers worked at multiple piece rates, there are fewer comparisons for 1856. Table 14.7 reveals that female weavers generally produced fewer "cuts" of cloth per day than male weavers. In only one cloth type, that paid fifty-five cents in 1883, did females earn more than males. The lowest productivity ratio was 0.60 in 1856 and 0.70 in 1883. These data suggest that differences in output across the genders may explain why women earned less than men when working in the same occupation.

Even if men and women were paid the same piece rates, discrimination could still occur if women were assigned to less remunerative tasks than men (Van Nederveen Meerkerk 2010, 181). Greenlees (2007, 91) suggests that, for

**TABLE 14.7** Output of Piece-Rate Weavers

| Rate | Number | | | Daily earnings | | Output per day | | |
|---|---|---|---|---|---|---|---|---|
| | M | F | % F | M | F | M | F | Ratio |
| 1856 | | | | | | | | |
| 28 | 3 | 28 | 0.10 | 1.12 | 0.69 | 5.33 | 3.22 | 0.60 |
| 51 | 3 | 7 | 0.30 | 0.87 | 0.77 | 1.71 | 1.50 | 0.88 |
| 1883 | | | | | | | | |
| 36 | 33 | 140 | 0.81 | 1.15 | 1.03 | 3.21 | 2.86 | 0.89 |
| 39 | 3 | 5 | 0.63 | 1.34 | 0.94 | 3.43 | 2.41 | 0.70 |
| 43 | 3 | 4 | 0.80 | 1.09 | 0.76 | 2.53 | 1.77 | 0.70 |
| 45 | 2 | 4 | 0.67 | 1.29 | 0.95 | 2.87 | 2.10 | 0.73 |
| 46 | 3 | 8 | 0.73 | 1.01 | 0.91 | 2.19 | 1.99 | 0.91 |
| 48 | 3 | 2 | 0.40 | 1.18 | 0.95 | 2.47 | 1.98 | 0.80 |
| 50 | 8 | 95 | 0.92 | 1.08 | 1.02 | 2.15 | 2.04 | 0.95 |
| 55 | 6 | 24 | 0.80 | 0.93 | 1.04 | 1.70 | 1.89 | 1.11 |
| 58 | 10 | 3 | 0.23 | 1.16 | 1.15 | 2.01 | 1.99 | 0.99 |
| 60 | 33 | 39 | 0.54 | 1.05 | 0.93 | 1.75 | 1.54 | 0.88 |
| 70 | 2 | 3 | 0.60 | 1.24 | 0.98 | 1.77 | 1.41 | 0.80 |

*Note*: Workers with ambiguous names, workers for whom days of work were not recorded, and workers who worked at multiple piece rates are not included in this analysis. This table excludes piece rates with fewer than two workers of either sex.

weavers at the British firm Grimshaws and Barcewell, "the greatest influence on the difference between wage rates at this firm was probably gender discrimination in the assignment of weaving order." There is, in fact, a negative correlation between the average daily wage for a particular type of cloth and the percentage of the weavers who were female.[4] However, sorting across types of cloth is not the main cause of the wage gap for weavers. Using the decomposition described above to divide the wage gap among the weavers in Table 14.7 into within-cloth-type and across-cloth-type components, I find that 96 percent of the gender wage gap for these weavers is due to within-cloth-type differences,

---

4 The correlation between percentage female and the female average daily wage is –.35 for the 1883 cloth types recorded in Table 14.7, and –.32 if we also include types of cloth with one or zero male weavers.

and only 4 percent of wage gap is due to sorting across types of cloth. If we add in the five types of cloth that have one or zero male weavers, segregation across types of cloth explains 22 percent of the wage gap, and wage differences within cloth types 78 percent.[5] While sorting across types of cloth is not irrelevant, it is not the main cause of the gender wage gap in weaving.

## CONCLUSION

This chapter has examined gender differences in wages and occupations at one firm, the cotton textile firm Pepperell Manufacturing Company. Over the period 1856 to 1883 within-occupation wage differences became less important, as the within-occupation wage gap fell. Occupational segregation was an important contributor to the wage gap. In both periods the lack of female overseers contributed to the gender wage gap. Unfortunately, identifying the portion of the wage gap that resulted from occupational segregation does not tell us whether the wage gap was due to productivity differences or discrimination. The gender gap within occupations may have been due to wage discrimination, or to gender differences in productivity. Occupation segregation may have been due to a glass ceiling preventing women from entering high-paid occupations, or to sorting according to individual skill. While I cannot determine what portion of the wage gap was due to discrimination, I do demonstrate the existence of gender differences in productivity. Among piece-rate weavers, where output can be measured, females produced less output than men, explaining their lower earnings. If there were gender differences in productivity for weavers, it is plausible that there were productivity differences in other occupations as well. I also present evidence of gender differences in days worked per month. In 1856 women workers averaged fewer days worked per month than men, which may have led to gender differences in productivity. By 1883 the gender gap in days worked per month had disappeared, and the within-occupation gender wage gap was much smaller.

## BIBLIOGRAPHY

Becker, Gary. 1957. *The Economics of Discrimination*. Chicago: University of Chicago Press.
Bergmann, Barbara. 1974. "Occupational Segregation, Wages and Profits When Employers Discriminate by Race or Sex." *Eastern Economic Journal* 1: 103–10.
Dublin, Thomas. 1979. *Women at Work: The Transformation of Work and Community in Lowell, Massachusetts, 1826–1860*. New York: Columbia University Press.

5  Where the male wage was missing I assumed it was equal to the female wage. This should give me an upper-bound estimate on the percentage of the wage gap due to occupational segregation.

Edgeworth, F. Y. 1922. "Equal Pay to Men and Women for Equal Work." *Economic Journal* 32: 431–57.

Gitelman, H. M. 1967. "The Waltham System and the Coming of the Irish." *Labor History* 8: 227–53.

Greenlees, Janet. 2007. *Female Labour Power: Women Workers' Influence on Business Practices in the British and American Cotton Industries, 1780–1860.* Burlington, VT: Ashgate.

Groshen, Erica. 1991. "The Structure of the Female/Male Wage Differential: Is It Who You Are, What You Do, or Where You Work?" *Journal of Human Resources* 26: 457–72.

Hareven, Tamara K. 1982. *Family Time and Industrial Time: The Relationship between the Family and Work in a New England Industrial Community.* Cambridge: Cambridge University Press.

Higgs, Robert. 1977. *Competition and Coercion: Blacks in the American Economic, 1865–1914.* Cambridge: Cambridge University Press.

Jacobsen, Joyce. 1994. *The Economics of Gender.* Cambridge, MA: Blackwell.

Layer, Robert George. 1952. "Wages, Earnings, and Output in Four Cotton Textile Companies in New England, 1825–1860." PhD dissertation, Harvard University.

McHugh, Cathy. 1984. "Earnings in the Post-bellum Southern Cotton Textile Industry: A Case Study." *Explorations in Economic History* 21: 28–39.

Milgrom, Eva, Trond Petersen, and Vemund Snartland. 2001. "Equal Pay for Equal Work? Evidence from Sweden in a Comparison with Norway and the U.S." *Scandinavian Journal of Economics* 103: 559–83.

Minoletti, Paul. 2011. "The Importance of Ideology: The Shift to Factory Production and Its Effect on Women's Employment Opportunities in the English Textile Industries." University of Oxford Discussion Papers in Economic and Social History.

Robinson, Harriet. 1976. *Loom and Spindle or Life among the Early Mill Girls.* Kailua, HI: Press Pacifica.

Van Nederveen Meerkerk, Elise. 2010. "Market Wage of Discrimination? The Remuneration of Male and Female Wool Spinners on the Seventeenth-Century Dutch Republic." *Economic History Review* 63: 165–86.

Zveglich, Joseph, and Yana van der Meulen Rodgers. 2004. "Occupational Segregation and the Gender Wage Gap in a Dynamic East Asian Economy." *Southern Economic Journal* 70: 850–75.

# 15

# THE CONTEXT OF ENGLISH INDUSTRIALIZATION

## ERIC JONES

The questions I have in mind are very broad indeed but do intersect. They are, first, what was the seedbed of industrialization in England? This is a topic to which Joel Mokyr has made such stellar contributions. Second, is it reasonable to assert, as Greg Clark does, that industrialization was long delayed? And third, how far were institutions a source either of delay or (as is more widely believed) the essential means of bringing about growth?

## DELAYED INDUSTRIALIZATION

The English economy came back into life in the 1650s and 1660s; investment began to rise again, even in long-gestation projects like communications. The recovery looks positively Mokyrian—a continuation of Elizabethan commercial expansion carried forward by political stability, a dash of science, and a prefiguring of Enlightenment optimism. Expansion long predated coal, steam, and spinning machinery, and it is possible to suspect that industrialization proper did suffer a "delay" (Clark 2007, 208). This may be so if "delay" means that plausible industrial investments were being canvassed decades before the funds were committed—a more extreme interpretation would underestimate the difficulties.[1] May we therefore take Clark's position to be merely that the Industrial Revolution did not arrive ex nihilo but had a prolonged lead-in or learning period?

## THE RIGHTS HYPOTHESIS

The political system became stable after 1688 and incorporated more interests than it had under the Tudors and Stuarts (Plumb 1969). This was so despite upsets as late as the Forty-five. Institutionists are very taken with the consequences of 1688, believing that it crucially bolstered property rights, which thereafter were better specified and more defensible. Their hypothesis is that

---

1 The extent to which economic historians have assumed away difficulties associated with new technologies is criticized by Dutton and Jones (1983).

poorly specified rights would have caused uncertainty and dissuaded investors from hazarding their capital, especially on long-gestation projects such as improved communications.

North and his collaborators think an "open access" economy was constructed (see Jones 2008, 122). Under such a regime, political, legal and economic access is open to all. Having witnessed more than enough inconclusive conflict during the Civil Wars, the elite now "agree" to compete in the marketplace—they fight by shuffling papers and dare not carry their swords. Not everyone, though, need subscribe to this informal pact; 33 percent of the population is sufficient for an economy to qualify. It is a nice idea, though where the 33 percent threshold comes from is unclear. Whether the thesis really does much more than restate the fact that gentler conditions had emerged is obscure, as is the whole issue of just how far we should try to simplify the record of economic behavior by means of abstractions. D. C. Coleman long ago warned economic historians not to overgeneralize and ignore "hampering history" (D. C. Coleman, in Fisher 1961, 229).

Max Weber's "England Problem" centered on the observation that, despite England being the country where industrialization and the enclosure movement actually occurred, rights there were poorly specified. Although he equated rationality with rule systems, he did not insist that growth absolutely required a formal, legal foundation; he seems to have thought that England was the exception proving the rule. It was Talcott Parsons who contended that "common law, with its well-developed property and contract rights, procedural propriety and consistency, adaptive efficiency, and guarantee of judicial independence, had been 'a fundamental prerequisite' of the industrial revolution" (Heller 2009, 19, 103). Views of this type are intuitively attractive and very influential but may be too distant from the complexities of the historical record.

## INSTITUTIONS AND THE LAW

The number of institutional arrangements affecting the economy involves us in a considerable and contradictory litany. It was not all plain sailing. Corruption remained high. Parliament diverted public money into the pockets of its friends and created distortions from which rents could be extracted. As early as the reign of William and Mary, Glorious Revolution or not, Parliament moved to protect trade at the very moment a free trade literature began to appear. Rent seeking may have decreased once the Stuart proclivity for bestowing monopolies was over, but it was not until the second quarter of the nineteenth century that the Old Corruption, as Cobbett called it, finally succumbed to a combination of clean-up measures. Nor was taxation tender to the poor. It became regressive, thereby cramping the mass market.

Consider the Parsonian "fundamental prerequisite" argument as it relates to the law. On the positive side, Getzler has argued the following: common law precedents were more flexible than the legal rationalism of Continental Europe; after 1688 taxation became stable and hence property was secure; Parliament solved remaining inflexibilities, for example, by Enclosure Acts (a matter to which we will come); the law was internally reformed during the late eighteenth and nineteenth centuries; and the judges shared the developmental ideology of the entrepreneurial class (Getzler 1996, 646). Yet rather than automatically supporting free markets, the judiciary was conservative when it so desired, for example, regulating the grain trade to preserve social order. The judges were insistent on their autonomy, which they secured after 1688. For this and other reasons, Getzler himself admits that legal institutions and forms of property do not neatly track social and economic change (Getzler 1996, 665–66).

The legal profession had been expanding well before this period. Statutes were enacted under Henry IV, Henry VI, and Elizabeth to restrict the number of lawyers, who were thought of as meddlesome rent seekers (Moody 1851, 208). A statute of Henry VI (1454) declared that until lately there had been only six or eight attorneys in Norfolk and Suffolk and the recent increase to twenty-four had been "to the vexation and prejudice of the counties." Numbers subsequently increased, rising 40 percent in England and Wales between the 1590s and 1630s.[2] By 1689 there were about three thousand barristers and over six thousand attorneys, and since 1660 they had been earning fees for legal services rather than merely jockeying for favors.

In an economy still based on land holding, it is nevertheless unclear how fruitful many of these services actually were; they may have involved little more than imposing strict settlements on estates. It is not even certain how soon the number of lawyers grew after 1660 or 1688. In Cheshire many transactions and disputes—over township boundaries, enclosures, fishing rights, and so on—continued to be settled satisfactorily by independent lay assessors.[3] In 1722 there were no attorneys at all in Preston, Lancashire, though by 1742 there were seventeen (Borsay 1990, 165). The initial post-Restoration economic expansion in the provinces may have taken place with limited formal legal help.

A case may be made that Parliament did favor an integrated national market in which any producer might compete with another. It rejected a petition from counties close to London, fearful of import competition, to prevent the extension of turnpikes to distant areas (Jones 2010, 185). It blocked more than one effort by grazers in the north and in the Vale of Aylesbury to ban the sowing of clover and other crops, for fear they would produce enough fodder on light

2  See Anonymous, "Lawyers in England and Wales," www.findmypast.co.uk.
3  Ex inform. Charles Foster. See also Foster (2002, 219).

land in the south to outcompete the established pastoral regions (Jones 1970, 60, 74).

## TOWNS

The situation was less unequivocally progressive in the towns. Much business was kept within coteries; tradesmen might accept cash from any customer who could pay but when it came to contracts still favor members of their own church or chapel. Certainly the Quakers, much praised for their honesty, kept capital within the Society of Friends. Moreover, firms were typically tiny and although much is made of English experience with complex organizations like the East India Company, industrial enterprises tended to grow—to be self-organized—from very small beginnings.

Much is also made of economic freedom in towns without charters. There were only six chartered towns in Lancashire and Cheshire, the heartland of early industrialization, and regulation tended to be weak wherever industries grew in the Highland Zone (Jones 2010, esp. 249). Even the conservative corporation of Preston was too feeble to prevent the rise of a linen industry there. In the West Midlands many inhibitions on change were already disappearing during the 1690s. But restrictions were also weak or disappearing in southern towns that, unlike the North and Midlands, did not retain their industries. Small towns often lacked the resources to defend their tradespeople in the courts. There was not much sign anywhere of determination like that of the German cities that kept out the Dutch loom for one hundred or one hundred fifty years; Manchester adopted it in the 1650s, afraid of losing market share to Leiden if it did not keep up with technological change (Wadsworth and Mann 1968, 285ff.).

The regulations in many boroughs were, like guild regulations, nevertheless often designed to protect existing producers. They were also much concerned with amenities and aimed at enforcing the safety and cleanliness of the streets and physical fabric. Activities were minutely regulated, with the same presentments and fines reappearing year after year; it was all very conservative, and a significant fraction of the small towns stagnated or declined. By 1770 there had been a "shake-out" of as many as one-third of the market towns of Tudor and early Stuart England (cited in Borsay 1990, 5). Yet the population of other centers grew quite fast and industries continued to concentrate. The record suggests a regulatory drag on change in some places but not others. Surprisingly little is known about all-round competition among towns and the "real business" of the industries they contained. As N. S. B. Gras commented as early as 1939, the guilds have been studied "almost to the neglect of the real business of the men who established them" (quoted approvingly in Veale 1966, vii).

## INDUSTRY AND COMMUNICATIONS

To cite a few examples from industry, it was realized in northwestern England from the 1580s or 1590s that salt springs outside the traditional (and highly regulated) "wich" settlements might be commercially exploited.[4] The use of iron pans and coal had however to be learned. A start was made about 1600, but supplies of coal were expensive to fetch; the mines soon filled with water; the quality of the salt was poor. Amassing capital took until 1650, and the market for salt was soon saturated, until expanded after a reduction of taxes in 1694. Development would have been quicker had a canal been built in Cheshire, but the gentry MPs opposed this and declined to put up the money, thinking there might not be sufficient demand for salt. Local businessmen had to save up the necessary capital; they secured gentry consent to a canal only in 1720 and obtained an Act in 1721.

Notwithstanding the fact that the technology was already known, canals were not built the moment they were envisaged. A scheme for a canal that might have sustained the long-standing Droitwich salt industry was suffocated by a maze of legal rights. Landowners' concern for privacy and amenity also impeded development; for example, costs were driven up on the Basingstoke canal in Hampshire because a local landowner insisted it be kept out of sight of his house. This motive also continually led to the distortion of the routes of roads, the "fossilized" twists and turns of which remain patent at the present day. Amenity considerations are much underplayed in the literature. Szostak has urged that the grant of the right of eminent domain overcame landowner resistance to building communications but the potential costs of pursuing recalcitrant landowners through the courts still seems to have held schemes back.[5]

The greatest delay seems to have been holding back on developing and introducing machinery to spin cotton. Most authorities promote the eventual importance of inventions in cotton spinning. Yet while these were stunning in their effects, and with hindsight may seem to have come into existence abruptly, it seems a case where the purely technical difficulties have been exaggerated. The greater hurdles were social and legal. Putting large numbers of spinners out of work seemed undesirable, even dangerous (Foster and Jones 2013). A large-scale uptake of cotton cloth derived from the attractiveness of Indian-style print dyeing, which became available in England during the second half of the seventeenth century. Vested interests protected themselves against this, creating problems over legality and taxation so that the industry did not get going before 1736. The mechanizing of spinning came later still. It was preceded by

4  Ex inform. Charles Foster. See also Foster and Jones (2013).
5  Willan (1964, 41–51) gives many instances of resistance and delays to canalization.

the prolonged development in south Lancashire of clock and watchmaking, a little studied industry where the technical problems were much harder than for spinning—yet were solved first. The machinery makers eventually borrowed the skills of artisans from these trades, and it does seem reasonable to think that, absent social objections, the problems with spinning might have been solved earlier than they actually were.

## THE LAND AND AGRICULTURE

A stimulating series of papers by Bogart and Richardson is rather enthusiastic about Parliament's concern to get the economy moving.[6] First, they claim that preindustrial rights blocked the exploitation of land and resources, although it was not until about 1671 that Sir Orlando Bridgman devised the particular restriction with which they are concerned: strict settlement. This was introduced because families understandably wished to curb profligate heirs like Sir Edward Hungerford, the most notorious member of the Hungerfords, who had been the largest flock-masters in Wiltshire. Sir Edward gambled away manor after manor at the Restoration court and was not nicknamed the Spendthrift for nothing. Strict settlement was meant to prevent men like him from dissipating the capital value of their estates, as opposed to being able to spend only the current rental income. But Bogart and Richardson claim Estates Acts counteracted settlements and made it possible for inheritors to put land and resources on the market, thus opening them to mortgage and risking them going out of the family. Some families did embrace these new instruments though others did not.

Did Estates Acts really expunge strict settlements for good, or were new go-to-jail cards drawn up to confine later heirs? At the peak, so Bogart and Richardson report, between 25 percent and 75 percent of England was under strict settlement. This extraordinarily wide bracket may suggest a churning from generation to generation, with settlements being reset to cover new heirs. May one not court a false positive by studying de-restrictions as if they were never reimposed?

Estates Acts did not sweep resources once and for all into the laps of entrepreneurs. Bogart and Richardson go to lengths to explain the periodicity of Estates Acts but do not detail when productive investment actually followed. They point out that by 1826 interpreting settlements meant delving into 674 volumes of law, which does not suggest the lock on the land had been conclusively unpicked. In reality, strict settlement persisted even beyond the Settled Estates Act of 1856. Only in 1882 did Parliament permit current life beneficiaries to sell heirlooms and the underlying land, and even then with restrictions (Johnson 2009, 1222). The barrister J. H. Baker states in his *Intro-*

---

6 From their long series of papers I take as representative Bogart and Richardson (2009).

*duction to English Legal History* that "the economic undesirability of keeping so much land out of circulation was keenly felt *in the nineteenth century*" and that strict settlement "shackled much of the land in England to the same families *until Victorian times and after*" (Baker 1971, 160, emphasis added).

Before 1640, lawyers had made their fortunes by interpreting customary rights and Cromwell himself described land law as "an ungodly jumble." Much later than that, archaisms persisted and fresh complications continued to arise.[7] As late as the 1870s C. Wren Hoskyns wrote that "it would be incredible, if it were not true, that at a time when personal property changes hands at the Banker's clearing-house in London at the rate of four Billions sterling in the twelvemonth, the title to land . . . is locked up in private boxes and stowed away in uninsured offices, to be doubtfully educed from the perishable evidence of MS. Deeds, written (in the fifth century since the invention of printing) in language requiring sometimes the translation, sometimes the deciphering, but always the interpretation of an expert" (Wren Hoskyns 1876, 97).

In this regard, Getzler has pointed out that transaction costs for transferring land were high from the seventeenth century right to the time of Bentham, Brougham, and after, and that among the reasons were the monopoly charges imposed by lawyers who alone could define and convey estates (Getzler 1996, 643–44). Estates Acts were private Acts, not the result of public demand. There was no guarantee that those who most wished to escape strict settlement were the ones who owned land suitable for development or actually followed through by exploiting their resources, as opposed to reallocating them within the family. Presumably individual landowners did seize their opportunities, but where are the estate records to demonstrate this case by case?

As wealth was created in the English economy, it was often used to buy landed estates. Between 1760 and 1820 the number of parks in the Home Counties doubled, signaling once more the intense interest in amenity (Prince 1967, 7–9). Country houses became numerous, as may be gauged from the fact that in 1955 one was being demolished every two and a half days. The purposes for which estates had been acquired were aesthetic, dynastic, social, and political; they were not expected to produce high rates of return. If they served a useful function, it was in Malthus's sense that during times of "great glut" (insufficient demand) the improvement of estates and employment of menial staff were preferable to spending out on productive labor.[8] Without infinite exaggeration, estates came close to satisfying Keynes's injunction to dig holes in the road and fill them in again.

Development was at odds with the social purposes of owning land. Assets were often brought to market reluctantly. It was customary to hold standing timber as a sort of bank deposit, to be drawn on during emergencies such as

---

7   Foster (2002, 227–28) provides examples of the lack of clarity.
8   Kates (2010), drawing on the Malthus-Ricardo correspondence.

high gambling debts (Jones 2010, 77). Even so, selling the trees was not always straightforward. The indebted grandson of the second Marquess of Ailesbury determined to break the entail in 1886 and sell the big sticks of timber in Savernake Forest—"I'll make those damned squirrels jump further," he said. Yet an uncle was able to prevent this by entangling the would-be buyer in legal challenges (Winter 1999).

The conventional story is that England escaped revolution because, unlike the Continent, its society was permeable. There are indeed tales of upward mobility converting workers into industrialists into landowners. New landowners were however quick to imitate the ways of the gentry, live high, and pauperize the rustics. It was surely despite, not because, of the perpetual re-creation of the institutions of landed society that revolution did not occur and industrialization was not stifled. The economy offset the depressing vogue for landed estates by creating enough (though only just enough) urban and overseas outlets for farm workers (see Jones 2010, chap. 10).

Second, Bogart and Richardson observe that Parliament created statutory authorities that built infrastructure and obtained rights to collect tolls to pay for it. Improvement Acts were certainly passed and by 1800 over one hundred separate bodies of improvement commissioners had been established in towns in England and Wales. The investment that followed did not fluctuate with passing downturns in economic activity. But if what is in mind is industrialization the results may not be quite what they seem (Jones and Falkus 1979). Improvement Acts have been described as the provincial towns' exit from medievalism. This may have been so but as much in the sense of producing smarter-looking townscapes as in providing fresh commercial facilities.

Besides improving roadways and other business-related features, the Acts increased the provision of civic amenities (Jones and Falkus 1979, 221). It might be possible to argue that appearance and commerce coevolved. The towns involved were predominantly southern market towns: between 1736 and 1799 there were 110 Acts in market towns and nonindustrial ports but only 15 in industrial areas (Jones and Falkus 1979, 220, table 3). This reflects an agrarian economy where traders and professional men organized the provisioning of London and as a result lived ever more elegantly in its wide surrounding arc of market towns. It is consistent with agrarian expansion rather than industrial growth.

The third claim by Bogart and Richardson is that Enclosure Acts exposed land and resources to market forces, the implicit assumption being that this must have raised productivity. It does not necessarily follow. Acquiring more land at the expense of commoners who had no legally enforceable rights, but continuing to farm it with existing methods, would have been a gain in itself: after all, those promoting enclosure would have secured a bigger acreage. But if the gain were readily within the grasp of the greedy we may ask why the enclosure movement was so very long drawn out.

An Enclosure Act, Bogart and Richardson say, began with a series of public meetings where residents of the village debated the issue, after which (they observe) "four-fifths" could sign that they wanted an enclosure. This was, they declare, an accessible, affordable, and predictable system. It was not. The four-fifths mentioned refers to acreage owned, not votes among the inhabitants. It was property, not people, that counted.

Petitions were almost always drafted with the support of the lord of the manor, and in the rare cases where this was not forthcoming, seldom succeeded (Tate 1967).[9] Enclosure Acts were private Acts and the Members of Parliament promoting them were mostly friends and relations of the petitioners. In very few cases did dissentient smallholders avail themselves of the costly luxury of briefing counsel. They could neither have afforded nor dared to do so. Wealth, status, and power were grotesquely unequal, and deference was required if one wanted to keep one's job or hoped to get work on the new ring-fenced farms. The predictable result was that the majority whose rights were merely customary lost out.

Almost as predictable was the fact that the larger owners sometimes struggled to agree among themselves. This may be a central reason why the enclosure movement was so long drawn out. Delays were caused less through protests by village communities than by dissension among the elite over how to apportion the costs and benefits of enclosure. The appropriate theory is Michael Heller's tragedy of the anti-commons, or group exclusion, whereby a small number of owners could block change if they held a large enough share of the acreage (Heller 2008, esp. 16–22). One owner could do so if he or she predominated, as we know did happen. To cite a single example, at Church Oakley, Hampshire, enclosure was delayed from 1742 to 1773 because at the first date "all consent to enclose, except one person who in crossness sticks out" (quoted in Jones 2010, 234n16).[10]

The idea that enclosure procedures were consensual overlooks all record of disputes, however futile most objections by the poor turned out to be. It ignores evidence that blatant rent seekers and asset strippers were prowling around (Jones 2010, 225). One cannot tell the level of resistance simply by looking at those Acts that were actually passed, which would risk another false positive.[11] "The real property laws of this country, from the period immediately succeeding the Conquest down to the present time, presents a history consistent with itself in one particular, that of a perpetual struggle of rival interests" (Wren

9   An example was East Leake, Notts., where a petition of 1784 had failed but one with the lord of the manor's support passed in 1798 (Tate 1967, 96n8).

10   Robert Tennyson (2009, 23, 28) refers to the difficulty of securing enclosure and the further difficulty of enforcement where there were recalcitrant individuals.

11   Maurice Beresford (1961) cites many examples of resistance to enclosing and converting land to pasture, though in the context of an increasing acceptance of rearranging the countryside along lines of comparative advantage.

Hoskyns 1876, 23). That was Wren Hoskyns's view in the 1870s; in the 1960s I failed to persuade a Newbury solicitor to deposit in an archive documents dating as far back as the sixteenth century. He thought they might still come in useful.

Bogart and Richardson quote Oliver Williamson to the effect that institutions to solve disputes underpin modern capitalist economies. They come dangerously close to implying that eighteenth-century parliamentarians anticipated Ronald Coase. But Williamson and Coase offer no evidence of how modern economies came into existence; they mainly reassert the rights hypothesis. In truth, in the words of the great historian of enclosure, W. E. Tate, for over a century after the 1660s governments "took not the least notice of the agrarian revolution then in progress" (Tate 1967, 128–29). Only in 1774 were general principles formulated concerning the terms on which enclosure might take place. The standing orders for that year reveal how gross the abuses were: some proprietors not informed, no notice given, extortion by the commissioners, draft bills containing neither the commissioners' names nor details of the compensation proposed to be allotted to the lord of the manor and the owner of the tithes.

Enclosure was an ambiguous procedure because it may have led to agricultural improvement, the transfer of land into private hands, or both. The assumption of contract theory, that privatization allocates resources to the people best able to use them, is at variance with the evidence of the social loss from innumerable measures to extend private benefits. The most famous paper on the "tragedy of the commons" (over three hundred thousand mentions on Google) was developed by Garret Hardin from the somewhat cursory lectures of the Oxford economist William Forster Lloyd (Jones 2010, 218–19). Gains to enclosure are implied because communal husbandry is assumed to have meant overuse, which privatization "must" have curbed. But neither Hardin nor Forster Lloyd cited examples. In reality village communities had been able to protect themselves against overuse of the commons, century after century. What they could seldom do was protect themselves against parliamentary enclosure. Nor could they prevent the frequent diversion of routes to secure privacy and improve amenities for landowners—road capture—obliging people at large to travel out of their way. This was a common, yet overlooked, feature of the rural economy, individually small in scale but not inconsiderable in aggregate. It demonstrates the sweep of landowner greed and power: road capture did not conduce to productive advance.

## CONCLUSION

That eighteenth-century Parliaments thought ahead to growth in the whole economy, much less industrialization, is highly unlikely. As late as 1776, Adam

Smith had almost no inkling of what the future might hold. Legislation reflected current interests, pressure groups, and solicitations by individuals; many of the bills brought before the House, perhaps most of them, received only cursory consideration. Parliament was not staffed with expert policy makers: the Spendthrift, who patently could not manage his own affairs, sat in the House for thirty-three years supervising the business of the nation (Burke [1860] 2005)!

Institutions did not operate smoothly, much less fairly or optimally, and should be thought of as a curate's egg. The record is too mixed for superior property rights and a growth-promoting Parliament to account for economic growth or industrialization. There was too much defensiveness about initial positions and too much concern to spend profits on pleasure. Serious reform of Chancery, the division of the legal system that dealt with wills, did not start until the second quarter of the nineteenth century. Charles Dickens made it plain in *Bleak House* that root-and-branch reform was needed to avoid the problems of "dilatory and costly procedures, of wasted lives and of legal obstructionists."[12] Among the notorious examples from which he drew his inspiration, the Jennings case was spun out for eighty years from 1798 to 1878, with costs of £250,000. Even worse institutional arrangements may conceivably have been blocking growth in foreign countries. But the imperfections of English institutions are just as likely to have been responsible for what Clark calls the "great and enduring puzzle" of sluggish industrialization as they were to have gone far toward promoting growth.[13]

Nevertheless a delay is not the same as a stop. As has been said of the law, there were offsetting expedients and "something in the mix did the trick" (Harris 2004, 236). Institutional inadequacies were overcome by the vigor of market competition possible within the existing legal framework; the vigor was amplified by different regional endowments and small, cumulative improvements in transport. These obscure local developments are where we should look. Competition was the key, acting as it did in conditions of unprecedented political stability and, as Joel Mokyr has forcefully emphasized, against a background of Enlightenment optimism.

## ACKNOWLEDGMENTS

I am grateful to John Anderson for commenting on a draft of this chapter.

---

12 Quoted by Doreen Roberts in an introduction to the historical context of Charles Dickens's (1993, xxiii–xxiv) *Bleak House*. *Bleak House* was published in 1852–53.

13 This is not to dismiss purely technical difficulties. On industry, see Dutton and Jones (1983). On agriculture, Robert Allen (2008) has observed that biological constraints greatly slowed change.

## BIBLIOGRAPHY

Allen, Robert. 2008. "The Nitrogen Hypothesis and the English Agricultural Revolution: A Biological Analysis." *Journal of Economic History* 68: 182–210.

Baker, J. H. 1971. *An Introduction to English Legal History*. London: Butterworth.

Beresford, Maurice. 1961. "Habitation versus Improvement: The Debate on Enclosure by Agreement." In *Essays in the Economic and Social History of Tudor and Stuart England*, edited by F. J. Fisher, 40–69. Cambridge: Cambridge University Press.

Bogart, Dan, and Gary Richardson. 2009. "Property Rights and Parliament in Industrializing Britain." www.socsci.uci.edu/~dbogartparliamentacts11aug2009.pdf.

Borsay, Peter, ed. 1990. *The Eighteenth Century Town*. London: Longman.

Burke, Bernard. (1860) 2005. *Vicissitudes of Families*. books.google.com/books/about/Vicissitudes_of_families.html?id.

Clark, Greg. 2007. *A Farewell to Alms*. Princeton: Princeton University Press.

Dickens, Charles. (1852–53) 1993. *Bleak House*. London: Wordsworth.

Dutton, H. I., and S. R. H. Jones. 1983. "Invention and Innovation in the British Pin Industry, 1790–1850." *Business History Review* 57: 175–93.

Fisher, F. J., ed. 1961. *Essays in the Economic and Social History of Tudor and Stuart England*. Cambridge: Cambridge University Press.

Foster, Charles F. 2002. *Seven Households: Life in Cheshire and Lancashire 1582 to 1774*. Northwich: Arley Hall Press.

Foster, Charles F., and Eric L. Jones. 2013. *The Fabric of Society and How It Creates Wealth*. Northwich: Arley Hall Press.

Getzler, Joshua. 1996. "Theories of Property and Economic Development." *Journal of Interdisciplinary History* 26 (4): 639–69.

Harris, R. 2004. "Government and the Economy, 1688–1850." In *The Cambridge Economic History of Modern Britain*, vol. 1, edited by R. Floud and P. Johnson, 204–37. Cambridge: Cambridge University Press.

Heller, Michael. 2008. *The Gridlock Economy*. New York: Basic Books.

Heller, Michael G. 2009. *Capitalism, Institutions, and Economic Development*. London: Routledge.

Johnson, Calvin H. 2009. "Fixing Capital Gains at the Core." *Tax Notes*, December 14, 1222.

Jones, E. L. 1970. "English and European Agricultural Development 1650–1750." In *The Industrial Revolution*, edited by R. M. Hartwell, 42–76. Oxford: Basil Blackwell.

Jones, E. L., and M. E. Falkus. 1979. "Urban Improvement and the English Economy in the Seventeenth and Eighteenth Centuries." *Research in Economic History* 4: 219–23.

Jones, Eric. 2008. "Missing Out on Industrial Revolution." *World Economics* 9: 101–28.

———. 2010. *Locating the Industrial Revolution: Inducement and Response*. Singapore: World Scientific.

Kates, Steven. 2010. "Influencing Keynes: The Intellectual Origins of the General Theory." *History of Economic Ideas* 18 (3): 1–34.

Moody, Henry. 1851. *Notes and Essays . . . Hants and Wilts*. Winchester.

Plumb, J. H. 1969. *The Growth of Political Stability in England 1675–1725*. Harmondsworth: Penguin.

Prince, H. C. 1967. *Parks in England*. Shalfleet: Pinhorns.

Tate, W. E. 1967. *The Village Community and the Enclosure Movements*. London: Victor Gollancz.

Tennyson, Robert. 2009. "A Cheap Bill for Deviant Enclosures: Legal Change and the Eighteenth-Century Enclosure Movement." http://works.bepress.com/robert_tennyson/4.

Veale, Elspeth M. 1966. *The English Fur Trade in the Later Middle Ages*. Oxford: Clarendon.

Wadsworth, A. P., and J. De Lacy Mann. 1968. *The Cotton Trade and Industrial Lancashire*. New York: Augustus M. Kelley.

Willan, T. S. 1964. *River Navigation in England 1600–1750*. London: Frank Cass.

Winter, James. 1999. *Secure from Rash Assault: Sustaining the Victorian Environment*. Berkeley: University of California Press.

Wren Hoskyns, C. 1876. "The Land-Laws of England." In *Systems of Land Tenure in Various Countries*, edited by J. W. Probyn, 81–124. London: Cassell Petter & Galpin.

# CONTRIBUTORS

## EDITORS

**AVNER GREIF** is professor of economics, the Bowman Family Endowed Professor in Humanities and Sciences at Stanford University, a senior fellow at the Freeman Spogli Institute for International Studies (Stanford), and a fellow in the Canadian Institute for Advanced Research (CIFAR). His research interests include the historical development of economic institutions, their interrelations with political, social, and cultural factors, and their impact on economic growth. Among his publications are *Institutions and the Path to the Modern Economy: Lessons from Medieval Trade* (Cambridge University Press, 2006) and *Analytic Narratives* (coauthored, Oxford University Press, 1998).

**LYNNE KIESLING** is an associate professor of instruction in the Department of Economics at Northwestern University. At Northwestern she is also a faculty member in the Northwestern Institute on Complex Systems (NICO) and a faculty affiliate in the Center for the Study of Industrial Organization (CSIO). Her specialization is industrial organization, regulatory policy, and market design in the electricity industry. In particular, she examines the interaction of market design and innovation in the development of retail markets, products, and services and the economics of "smart grid" technologies.

**JOHN V. C. NYE** holds the Frederic Bastiat Chair in Political Economy at the Mercatus Center and is professor of economics at George Mason University. He also serves as a research director at the Higher School of Economics in Moscow. He has pursued research on economic history, development, and the new institutional economics. His book *War, Wine, and Taxes: The Political Economy of Anglo-French Trade 1689–1900* appeared in 2007 from Princeton University Press.

## CHAPTER CONTRIBUTORS

**GERGELY BAICS**, an assistant professor of history and urban studies at Barnard College–Columbia University, is an urban social and economic historian. He is completing a book on the economic, social, and geographic history of food provisioning and access in New York City, 1790 to 1860, on which he has also written articles for the *Journal of Urban History* and *Urban History*.

**HOYT BLEAKLEY** is an associate professor of economics at the University of Michigan. He is also a member of the National Bureau for Economic Research. When the chapter was written, he was a Senior Investigator for the Center for Population Economics at the University of Chicago.

**FABIO BRAGGION** is an associate professor of finance at Tilburg University and a research fellow of the European Banking Center (EBC) specializing in financial history, corporate finance, and banking. One strand of his research studies the working of financial markets and companies in the United Kingdom at the turn of the twentieth century. In particular, he focuses on the role of social networks as a tool to provide companies with external finance and on the working of dividend policies in an unregulated environment. A second area of his research studies banking in a long-run setting and banks' mergers and acquisitions during the late nineteenth century: a period when banking and antitrust regulations were absent. He has also studied the role of monetary policy in alleviating credit crunches in small open economies. His work has been published in *Review of Financial Studies, Journal of Monetary Economics, Journal of the European Economic Association, Journal of Economic History*, and *Business History*. He received his PhD in economics from Northwestern University and his BA from Bocconi University.

**JOYCE BURNETTE** is professor of economics at Wabash College. An economic historian focusing on women's participation in the labor market, she has worked extensively with British agricultural workers. Her book *Gender, Work and Wages in Industrial Revolution Britain* (2008) examines the role of market forces in determining women's wages and occupations.

**LOUIS CAIN** is professor emeritus of economics at Loyola University Chicago and an adjunct professor of economics at Northwestern University. He is affiliated with the Center for Population Economics at the University of Chicago and with the National Bureau for Economic Research. He is the coauthor of *The Children of Eve* (2012) and *American Economic History* (2011).

**MAURICIO DRELICHMAN** is an associate professor in the Vancouver School of Economics at the University of British Columbia, and a fellow in the Institutions, Organizations, and Growth program of the Canadian Institute for Advanced Research. He has published widely on the economic, institutional, and legal history of early modern Spain. His recent book, *Lending to the Borrower from Hell* (with Hans-Joachim Voth, Princeton University Press, 2014), is an in-depth study on sixteenth-century sovereign debt markets.

**NARLY R. D. DWARKASING** is an assistant professor of finance at the University of Bonn, Germany. She has a PhD and a Master of Science in financial management and investment analysis from Tilburg University. Her research focuses on corporate finance, banking, economic history, and financial intermediaries.

**JOSEPH FERRIE** is a professor of economics at Northwestern University. He is also affiliated with the Center for Population Economics at the University of Chicago and with the National Bureau for Economic Research.

**NOEL D. JOHNSON**, an associate professor of economics at George Mason University, a research fellow at the Mercatus Center, and a faculty member at the Center for Study of Public Choice, is an economic historian who studies the relationship between state capacity and the origins of tolerance in the West. He has recently published articles on this topic in *Explorations in Economic History, Journal of Comparative Economics*, and *Journal of Law & Economics*. He received his PhD from Washington University in St. Louis and his BA from Kenyon College.

**ERIC JONES** is an emeritus professor, La Trobe University, and former professorial fellow, Melbourne Business School, University of Melbourne. His most recent books are *Locating the Industrial Revolution: Inducement and Response* (2010), *The Fabric of Society and How It Creates Wealth* (with Charles F. Foster, 2013), and *Revealed Biodiversity: An Economic History of the Human Impact* (2014).

**MARK KOYAMA** is a professor in economics at George Mason University and a senior scholar at the Mercatus Institute. He obtained his DPhil in economics from the University of Oxford in 2010 and he was previously a lecturer in economics at the University of York and a postdoc at Brown University. His wide-ranging research interests focus on the institutional foundations of modern economic growth. Recently he has begun working on the emergence of religious and political liberty in Western Europe.

**RALF R. MEISENZAHL** is an economist in the Systemic Financial Institutions & Markets section (Division of Research and Statistics) at the Board of Governors of the Federal Reserve System. His research focuses on finance, institutions, and growth.

**PETER B. MEYER** was a software engineer and is now a research economist in the U.S. government. He has a PhD in economics from Northwestern University. He does research on open scientific and technological processes such as those that led to the inventions of the airplane and the personal computer, and the development of open-source software.

**JOEL MOKYR** is the Robert H. Strotz Professor of Arts and Sciences and professor of economics and history at Northwestern University and Sackler Professor (by special appointment) at the Eitan Berglas School of Economics at the University of Tel Aviv. He specializes in economic history and the economics of technological change and population change. He is the author of *Why Ireland Starved: An Analytical and Quantitative Study of the Irish Economy*, *The Lever of Riches: Technological Creativity and Economic Progress*, *The British Industrial Revolution: An Economic Perspective*, and *The Gifts of Athena: Historical Origins of the Knowledge Economy*. His most recent book is *The Enlightened Economy*, published by Yale University Press and Penguin in 2009. He has authored over eighty articles and books in his field. He served as the senior editor of the *Journal of Economic History* from 1994 to 1998, was editor in chief of the *Oxford Encyclopedia of Economic History* (published in July 2003), and still serves as editor in chief of the Princeton University Press Economic History of the Western World. He served as president of the Economic History Association in 2003–4 and president of the Midwest Economics Association in 2007–8, and is a director of the National Bureau of Economic Research. He serves as chair of the advisory committee of the Institutions, Organizations, and Growth program of the Canadian Institute of Advanced Research. He served as chair of the Economics Department at Northwestern University between 1998 and 2001 and was a fellow at the Center for Advanced Studies in the Behavioral Sciences at Stanford between September 2001 and June 2002. He has an undergraduate degree from the Hebrew University of Jerusalem and a PhD from Yale University. He has taught at Northwestern since 1974, and has been a visiting professor at Harvard, the University of Chicago, Stanford, the Hebrew University of Jerusalem, the University of Tel Aviv, University College of Dublin, and the University of Manchester. He is a fellow of the American Academy of Arts and Sciences, a foreign fellow of the Royal Dutch Academy of Sciences, the Accademia Nazionale dei Lincei, and a Fellow of the Econometric Society and the Cliometric Society. His books have won a number of important prizes including the Joseph Schumpeter memorial prize (1990), the Ranki prize for the best book in European economic history, and more recently the Donald Price Prize of the American Political Science Association. In 2006 he was awarded the biennial Heineken Prize by the Royal Dutch Academy of Sciences for lifetime achievement in historical science. He is currently working on the intellectual and institutional origins of modern economic growth and the way they interacted with technological elements. His current other research is an attempt to apply insights from evolutionary theory to long-run changes in technological knowledge and economic history.

**LYNDON MOORE** is a senior lecturer in the Department of Finance at the University of Melbourne. His research interests include financial history, derivatives pricing, and asset pricing more generally. His research has been published in *Journal of Finance*, *Review of Financial Studies*, *Journal of Economic History*,

*Explorations in Economic History, Journal of Futures Markets,* and *Business History.* He received his PhD in economics from Northwestern University and also holds a BEc(Hons) from the University of Tasmania.

**CORMAC Ó GRÁDA** is professor emeritus, University College Dublin. His most recent books include *Famine: A Short History* (Princeton University Press, 2009) and *Jewish Ireland in the Age of Joyce: A Socioeconomic History* (Princeton University Press, 2006).

**RICK SZOSTAK** is professor of economics at the University of Alberta and president of the Association for Interdisciplinary Studies. His research spans the fields of economic history, methodology, interdisciplinary theory and practice, and information science. He has authored a dozen books including *The Role of Transportation in the Industrial Revolution* (1991), *Technological Innovation and the Great Depression* (1995), *Technology and American Society: A History* (with Gary Cross, 2nd ed., 2004), and *The Causes of Economic Growth: Interdisciplinary Perspectives* (2009).

**CAROLYN TUTTLE** is Betty Jane Schultz Hollender Professor of Economics at Lake Forest College, where she has taught for thirty years. She is a macroeconomist and economic historian. She has two books and several articles on the role of women and children in industrialization. Her first book, *Hard at Work in Factories and Mines: The Economics of Child Labor during the British Industrial Revolution* (1999), focused on child labor during the British Industrial Revolution, while her second book, *Mexican Women in American Factories: Free Trade and Exploitation on the Border* (2012), examines the work of Mexican women in the maquiladoras operating in the free trade zones.

**KARINE VAN DER BEEK**, assistant professor in the Economics Department at Ben-Gurion University of the Negev, is an economic historian whose interests concentrate on premodern European growth. Her publications include *The Effects of Political Fragmentation on Investments: A Case Study of Watermill Construction in Medieval Ponthieu, France* (2010) and *Political Fragmentation, Competition and Investment Decisions: The Medieval Grinding Industry in Ponthieu, France: 1150–1250* (2010).

**HANS-JOACHIM VOTH** is professor of economics at the University of Zurich. A native of the old Hanseatic city of Lübeck, he studied in Bonn, Freiburg, Florence, and Oxford. He holds a doctorate from Nuffield College, Oxford. He was a professor at UPF, Barcelona, from 1998 to 2013 and has held visiting appointments at MIT, Stanford, Princeton, and NYU–Stern. His latest book is *Lending to the Borrower from Hell* (with Mauricio Drelichman, Princeton University Press, 2014).

**SIMONE A. WEGGE** is an economic historian at the City University of New York (CUNY). Her primary area of research focuses on historical migration processes. Other areas of research include European child labor, transoceanic passenger rates, immigrant letters, and the savings of immigrants in New York City. Her work has appeared in various journals, including *Journal of Economic History*, *European Review of Economic History*, *Explorations in Economic History*, *History of the Family*, and *Journal of American Ethnic History*. Her work has been supported by the German Marshall Fund of the United States, the German Academic Exchange (DAAD), the National Endowment of Humanities (NEH), and CUNY. She serves as a deputy chair in the Department of Economics at both the College of Staten Island–CUNY and at the Graduate Center–CUNY.

# INDEX

Page numbers in *italics* refer to figures and tables.